0-7876-2068-8

Notable
Hispanic American
Women
BOOK II

Joseph M. Palmisano, Editor

Foreword by Elisa Maria Sánchez,
President of MANA, A National Latina Organization

GALE

DETROIT · LONDON

Notable
Hispanic American
Women
BOOK
II

STAFF

Joseph M. Palmisano, *Editor*

Allison McClintic Marion, David G. Oblender, Rebecca Parks, *Associate Editors*
Elizabeth Shaw, *Assistant Editor*
Sharon Malinowski, *Contributing Editor*
Linda S. Hubbard, *Managing Editor,* Multicultural Team

James A. Edwards, Mark F. Mikula, *Technical Training Specialists*

Victoria B. Cariappa, *Research Manager*
Barbara McNeil, Andrew Guy Malonis, *Research Specialists*
Tracie A. Richardson, Cheryl L. Warnock, *Research Associates*
Patricia Tsune Ballard, Jeffrey D. Daniels, Wendy K. Festerling, *Research Assistants*

Susan Trosky, *Permissions Manager*
Margaret A. Chamberlain, *Permissions Specialist*
Shalice Shah, *Permissions Associate*
Keasha Jack-Lyles, *Permissions Assistant*

Mary Beth Trimper, *Production Director*
Evi Seoud, *Assistant Production Manager*
Debbie Milliken, *Production Assistant*

Cynthia Baldwin, *Product Design Manager*
Eric Johnson, *Art Director*

Barbara J. Yarrow, *Graphic Services Manager*
Randy Bassett, *Image Database Supervisor*
Michael Logusz, *Imaging Specialist*
Pamela A. Reed, *Photography Coordinator*

Eleanor Allison, *Manager, Data Entry Services*
Beverly Jendrowski, *Data Entry Coordinator*
Timothy Alexander, *Data Entry Associate*

Contents

Foreword

Recently I was asked to share my thoughts on the "lessons of the twentieth century" at an annual conference of a sister Latina organization. The invitation immediately piqued my interest because everyone seems to be focused on the future, and few are reflecting on the past and how we can learn from it.

The invitation was especially important because it was an opportunity to express what I believe to be one of the greatest lessons of the twentieth century—the persistent denial of the development and equality of women. In the Latino community, the tenacious insistence that Latinas are one dimensional—mothers and wives—contributes to a lack of commitment to the development and full inclusion of Latinas at all levels. The result is that the progress of the entire community suffers.

By and large, Latinas remain underdeveloped, their skills and potential untapped. Unfortunately, the schools that they attend as children, the families that they belong to as daughters, sisters, mothers, and wives, and the communities that they take care of and love, all disregard Latina potential.

All signs tell Latinas that the more successful they become in terms of the American mainstream culture, the less successful they are as Latinas. Studying, pursuing careers, and trying to succeed may look, at best, like a mixed blessing. Independent and assertive Latinas, who are not married, are often seen as rejecting Latino culture. Frequently, they are overtly seen as unaccomplished because they are not married and raising children. Occasionally, they may even get the message, "good for you," from other women who have experienced limitations in their lives. Oftentimes, Latinas feel vulnerable and apprehensive about losing the affection and esteem of loved ones, because they anchor so much of their self-identity there. Thus, for Latinas striving for and achieving a successful career, these aspirations jeopardize their ability to fit into a culture predominantly defined by family-oriented goals.

In schools, by and large, Latinas are tracked—as is true for most Latinos—into vocational rather than academic curricula. Therefore, they are effectively being prepared for lower paying careers and less-enriched lives. The experience recounted by former MANA president Rita Jaramillo, now chief of staff for Congressman Ruben Hinojosa, is not uncommon:

> When I got to high school, my world was turned upside down. . . . I didn't know what tracking was then, but I knew I didn't want to be what someone else thought I should be. I was in Future Business Leaders [of America]. I was thinking business administration and business owner. My teachers . . . were thinking secretary. Anglo students went to college, and Chicanas went to secretarial school. . . . I had always been a good student, but I went into a slump and my grades dropped.

The irony is that despite these difficult situations, Latinas have not become embittered. They are responding assertively by breaking barriers, challenging the status quo, and creating opportunities for themselves, their families, and their communities. The exceptional women in *Notable Hispanic American Women, Book II,* to whom you will be introduced, prove that fact.

One example of this situation is the tremendous success of Latinas in business. Latina-owned businesses have made impressive strides in the following areas:

- From 1987 to 1992, Latina-owned business grew by nearly 17 percent. (In comparison, the number of all minority women-owned businesses increased by 13 percent.) In actual numbers, this represented an increase of 131,000 new businesses! In addition, *Hispanic* magazine estimated the number of Latina-owned businesses to have increased to 453,000 by 1996.
- In terms of revenue, Latina-owned businesses have also made impressive accomplishments. Overall, they increased their revenue by 32 percent, from $4.33 million in 1987 to $17 million in 1992.
- According to the National Foundation of Women Business Owners, the number of employees at Latina-owned businesses grew from 54,000 in 1987 to 200,000 in 1992.

In addition to business, Latinas in the 1990s have excelled in many other fields, including literature, science, public service, sports, and entertainment. Though these are impressive achievements, we must, however, recognize that there is still much to be done.

For MANA, the development of Latinas has always been coupled with the development of the Latino community. It is part and parcel of who we are. The equality of Latinas in their community and also the broader society has always been our goal. With the community facing formidable societal challenges that are influencing family, language, and culture, it cannot afford to be divided: it must pull together for the betterment of all. Latinos cannot achieve their own greatness at the expense of Latina development and equality.

The challenges that Latinas have and continue to face stem from the perception that they are needy and a liability to this country. This is a perception that, to a large extent, I believe all Latinas have internalized. That must change. Latinas must begin to recognize that, similar to the listees in *Notable Hispanic American Women, Book II,* they have skills, talents, and qualities that are important and valuable. They must become aware that within them lies the ability to make a difference. They must realize that they truly are assets to their families, community, and country. But having the ability and putting it to work are two different things. . . .*entre el dicho y el hecho hay un trecho!*

Latinas must tap into that sense of self-determination that has been so much a part of their culture and use it in new and innovative ways. Latinas must support each other in a real *hermandad:* To mentor young women in an ongoing basis; to encourage and nurture activism in their families and communities; to build true communities across families; and to follow the examples of successful Latinas and become the architects of their future.

The Latino community is like a bird: It needs two strong wings to fly, to survive, and to fulfill its promise. If only one wing is encouraged, nurtured, and developed, and the other wing is ignored and prevented from attaining its highest potential, the bird will be unstable and paralytic. It will be unable to take flight and never achieve the greatness that is possible. At the very least, it will fly in circles, very low circles. If, however, the other wing—Latinas—is equally encouraged, nurtured, and developed in order to reach its highest potential, then a Latino community that is more compassionate and more powerful will result.

Elisa Maria Sánchez, President
MANA, A National Latina Organization

Introduction

Notable Hispanic American Women, Book II offers 200 biographical profiles of historical and contemporary women who have achieved local, national, or international prominence in a broad range of professions, including:

- Activism
- Art
- Business
- Education
- Film, radio, and television
- Government
- Humanities
- Science and medicine
- Sports
- and more.

The entries in *Notable Hispanic American Women, Book II* range from approximately 500 to 3,000 words in length and cover the noteworthy personal, education, and career details that helped shape and define each woman's life. For literary figures, film and television personalities, and musical entertainers, a selected list of works has also been included. In addition, full bibliographic citations are listed in the majority of the entries. Finally, more than 100 of the entries are accompanied by a personal photograph.

Advisory Board Selected Entrants

To determine the "notables" among Hispanic American women, an advisory board of distinguished Hispanic American women (see p. xxiii) was assembled in order to recommend and evaluate names. In general, the advisory board and the editor focused on women whose contributions on the local, national, or international level have positively impacted their respective fields of endeavor or society at large. Though every attempt was made to include key figures, we make no claim to have isolated the "most notable" Hispanic American women—an impossible goal. We are pleased that most of the biographies that we wanted to feature are included; however, time constraints and research and interview availability prevented us from listing some women deserving of inclusion. Our hope is that in presenting these entries, we are providing a basis for future research on an important segment of the American fabric: Hispanic American women.

We followed the U.S. Census Bureau's criteria in defining "Hispanic" women as those who identify their origin or descent as being from Mexico, Puerto Rico, Cuba, Spain, or any of the Spanish-speaking countries of Central and South America. In considering the term "American," we included not only U.S. citizens but also those individuals who live and work in the United States and who have made contributions to U.S. culture. In the case of historical figures, we extended this definition to include those territories that are now part of the United States.

Personal Interviews Ensure Timeliness and Accuracy

Many of the biographical profiles in *Notable Hispanic American Women, Book II* draw upon books, critical essays, articles from such periodicals as *Hispanic, Hispanic Business, Latina, Moderna,* and *Temas,* various prominent newspapers, as well as Internet sites. However, the scarcity of in-depth published sources on Hispanic American women became evident during the compilation of this volume. For most of the entries that comprise this book, therefore, telephone interviews were conducted to secure current information; in a number of cases, these interviews provided the only source of information. Consequently, this book contains a good deal of material that cannot be found anywhere else.

Numerous Points of Access

Entries in *Notable Hispanic American Women, Book II* are arranged alphabetically by surname. In cases involving compound surnames, entries are alphabetized under the first or second surname based on the presence or absence of a hyphen. For example, Linda Chavez-Thompson is listed under "C", while Margarite Fernández Olmos is listed under "O". To facilitate access, cross-references have been provided in the list of entrants and in the main text for locating names involving compound surnames, hyphenated names, pseudonyms, and name variations. In addition to the alphabetical list of entrants (see p. xi), there are listings of entrants by occupation (see p. 353) and by ethnicity (see p. 359) at the back of the book to assist those seeking names from a given profession or heritage. There is also an extensive subject index (see p. 363) containing names, book titles, and general subjects, such as "Acting, film," "Chicano literature," "Information science," "Presidential appointments," "Salsa music," and many others. Finally, entries that appeared in *Notable Hispanic American Women, Book I* are listed in the frontmatter (see p. xix), as well as the subject index with page references to the first volume.

Special Thanks

The editor wishes to thank the board of advisors for its invaluable assistance in assembling the final list of profiled individuals. Further appreciation is due the contributors and Gale staff members who assisted in the compilation of *Notable Hispanic American Women, Book II.* Finally, the editor extends heartfelt gratitude to Gloria DeLeon for the support shown throughout the production of this reference work.

Comments Welcomed

Although considerable lengths were taken to ensure the accuracy of the information presented in this volume, the editor is aware that mistakes and/or omissions are inevitable. Therefore, all feedback related to the content of this second volume of *Notable Hispanic American Women, Book II* is welcomed, and all comments and suggestions will be kept on file. The editor also welcomes your recommendations of other names worthy of inclusion in future volumes.

Please send comments and suggestions to:

> The Editor
> *Notable Hispanic American Women, Book II*
> Gale Research Inc.
> 835 Penobscot Bldg.
> Detroit, MI 48226

Entrants

Individuals Profiled in
Notable Hispanic American Women

These profiles appear in *Notable Hispanic American Women,* published by Gale Research in 1992. For those individuals who have died since the initial release, birth and death dates have been provided.

Marie Acosta-Colón
Marjorie Agosín
Marilyn Aguirre-Molina
Alicia Alonso
Maria Conchita Alonso
Linda Alvarado
Yolanda H. Alvarado
Linda Alvarez
Hortensia Maria Alvirez
Consuelo González Amezcua
Lupe Anguiano
Miriam Angulo
Mari Carmen Aponte
Concha Maria de Concepción Arguello
Lucie Arnaz
Dolores S. Atencio
Paulette Atencio
Yamila Azize
Maria Teresa Babín
Judith F. Baca
Polly Baca
Joan Baez
Lourdes G. Baird
Laura Balverde-Sanchez
Romana Acosta Bañuelos
Maria Gertrudes Barcelo
Santa Barraza
Petra Barreras del Rio
Graciela Beecher
Maria Antonietta Berriozabal
Gloria Bonilla-Santiago
Lucrezia Bori
María Brito
Silvia Brito
Georgia L. Brown
Cheryl Brownstein-Santiago
Angelina Cabrera
Lydia Cabrera
Olivia Cadaval
Judy Canales
Cordelia Candelaria
Luisa Capetillo
Alice Cardona

Vikki Carr
Ruth Carranza
Lynda Carter
Lourdes Casal
Rosemary Casals
Elena Castedo
Sylvia L. Castillo
Lillian Castillo-Speed
Lorna Dee Cervantes
Maggie Cervantes
Linda Chavez
Linda Christian
Marlene Cintron de Frias
Evelyn Cisneros
Imogene Coca
Margarita H. Colmenares
Miriam Colon
Victoria Corderi
Elaine Coronado
Lucha Corpi
Oralia Lillie Corrales
Martha P. Cotera
Celia Cruz
Alicia Cuaron
Graciela Daniele
Angela de Hoyos
Debora de Hoyos
Adelaida Del Castillo
Jane L. Delgado
Dolores Del Rio
Patricia Diaz Dennis
Rosana De Soto
Remedios Diaz-Oliver
Rita DiMartino
María Elena Durazo
Mary Salinas Dúron
Sheila E.
Rita Elizondo
Marisol Escobar
Margarita Esquiroz
Rita Esquivel
Clarissa Pinkola Estés
Sandra María Esteves

Susan Elizabeth Ramirez
Tina Ramirez
Diana Ramírez de Arellano
Tey Diana Rebolledo
Susanna Redondo de Feldman
Shirley Rodríguez Remeneski
Hermelinda Renteria
Rita Ricardo-Campbell
Chita Rivera
Mireya Robles
Belgica Rodriguez
Gloria Rodriguez
Helen Rodriguez
Lina S. Rodriguez
Patricia Rodriguez
Rita M. Rodriguez
Linda Ronstandt
Margarita Roque
Ileana Ros-Lehtinen
Lucille Roybal-Allard
Martha Saenz
Carol A. Sanchez
Dolores Sanchez
María E. Sánchez
Milcha Sanchez-Scott
Alicia Sandoval
Irma Vidal Santaella
Fabiola Santiago
Isaura Santiago
Saundra Santiago
Miriam Santos
Cristina Saralegui
Hope Mendoza Schechter

Isabel Schon
Norma Brito Selvera
Lupe Serrano
Faustina Solís
Adaljiza Sosa-Riddell
Shirlene Ann Soto
Marta Sotomayor
Beatriz Olvera Stotzer
Carmen Tafolla
Tessa Martínez Tagle
Grace Martinez Tatum
Emma Tenayuca
Isabel Toledo
Maria Elena Toraño
Celia G. Torres
Maria de los Angeles Torres
Estela Portillo Trambley
Teresa Urrea
Nydia Margarita Velázquez
Lisa Velez
Evangelina Vigil-Piñon
Alma Luz Villanueva
Nelly Vuksic
Raquel Welch
Mary Rose Wilcox
Judith Zaffirini
Bernice Zamora
Carmen Zapata
Iris M. Zavala
Patricia Zavella
Maxine Baca Zinn
Teresa A. Zubizarreta

Advisory Board

Graciela Beecher
President, Cuban-American Legal Defense and Education Fund
Chairperson, National League of Cuban American Community Based Centers
Past President, National Association of Cuban-American Women of the U.S.A.

Lillian Castillo-Speed
Head Librarian, Ethnic Studies Library, University of California at Berkeley

Margarita Ortiz
Librarian, Bowen Branch, Detroit Public Library

Tey Diana Rebolledo
Professor of Spanish, Latin American Literature, and Chicana Literature, University of New Mexico
Past Coordinator, National Association for Chicana/o Studies

Contributors

Donald F. Amerman, Jr., Saylorsburg, Pennsylvania
Joan Axelrod-Contrada, Florence, Massachusetts
Gerri Azzata, Medford, Massachusetts
Beth A. Baker, Royal Oak, Michigan
Kari Bethel, Rocheport, Missouri
Rose Blue, Brooklyn, New York
Barbara Boughton, El Cerrito, California
Carol Brennan, Grosse Pointe Park, Michigan
Lynne M. Cohn, Ferndale, Michigan
Nancy J. Condry, New York, New York
Amy Cooper, Ann Arbor, Michigan
Denise Crittendon, Detroit, Michigan
Howard Distelzweig, Ann Arbor, Michigan
Grant Eldridge, Pontiac, Michigan
Kimberly Burton Faulkner, Ann Arbor, Michigan
Joel Golden, Royal Oak, Michigan
Mary A. Hess, Geneseo, New York
Jason R. Hirsch, Southfield, Michigan
Jean Irvin-Stanley, Detroit, Michigan
Mary C. Kalfatovic, Arlington, Virginia
Brenda Kubiac, Chesterfield, Michigan
Sarah Madsen-Hardy, Jamaica Plain, Massachusetts
Bernadette A. Meier, Warren, Michigan
Jackie Mitchell, Detroit, Michigan
Ted Morgan, Saylorsburg, Pennsylvania
Sally A. Myers, Defiance, Ohio
Corinne Naden, Dobbs Ferry, New York
J. Robert Parks, Chicago, Illinois
Maria L. Sheler-Edwards, Ypsilanti, Michigan
Kenneth R. Shepherd, Wyandotte, Michigan
Jane Spear, Canton, Ohio
Ginger Strand, New York, New York
Märie Thompson, Ben Avon, Pennsylvania
Sheila Velazquez, Knoxville, Tennessee
Denise Worhach, Austin, Texas
Nancy Hatch Woodward, Chattanooga, Tennessee

Photo Credits

Photographs appearing in *Notable Hispanic American Women, Book II* were received from the following sources:

Courtesy of Raydean M. Acevedo: p. 1; Courtesy of Alma Flor Ada: p. 3; Michael Bergman Photography, courtesy of Deborah Aguiar-Vélez: p. 4; Courtesy of Camila A. Alire: p. 9; Archive Photos, Inc.: pp. 13, 33, 52, 157; Courtesy of Melba Alvarado: p. 15; Courtesy of Aida Alvarez: p. 17; Courtesy of Doris Alvarez: p. 19; Photograph by Sara Eichner, reproduced by permission of William Eichner: p. 21; Courtesy of Frances R. Aparicio: p. 26; AP/Wide World Photos, Inc.: pp. 30, 49, 65, 123, 146, 266, 297, 308, 324, 334; Courtesy of María Celeste Arrarás: p. 31; Courtesy of Patricia Mares Asip: p. 36; Courtesy of Alicia Borinsky: p. 41; Courtesy of Norma V. Cantú: p. 44; Photograph by Eduardo Fuss: p. 54; Courtesy of Linda Chavez-Thompson: p. 63; Arte Público Press Archives, University of Houston: pp. 70, 84, 179, 222, 342, 346, 349; Courtesy of Maria Antonieta Collins: p. 71; Santa Barbara News-Press: p. 73; Courtesy of Gilda Cruz-Romo: p. 76; Courtesy of Blanquita Cullum: p. 79; Carolyn Curiel: p. 81; Photograph by Alberto Alejandrino, courtesy of Lolita de la Vega: p. 87; Courtesy of Rima de Vallbona: p. 91; Courtesy of Cari M. Dominguez: p. 95; Courtesy of Maria Echaveste: p. 98; Courtesy of Martha M. Escutia: p. 100; Courtesy of Zulima V. Farber: p. 105; Courtesy of National Women's Political Caucus: p. 107; Courtesy of Grace Flores-Hughes: p. 117; Corbis: pp. 119, 177; Courtesy of Tina Guerrero Fuentes: p. 121; Photograph by Linda Sue Scott: p. 127; Courtesy of Stephanie Gonzales: p. 130; WTVJ, Miami-Fort Lauderdale: p. 131; Courtesy of Sandra Guzmán: p. 142; Photograph by Renee Moreno: p. 148; Courtesy of María Herrera-Sobek: p. 151; Courtesy of Susana Jaime-Mena: p. 156; Courtesy of Eugenia Kalnay: p. 159; Courtesy of Susan Leal: p. 164; Courtesy of Nancy León: p. 166; Kaylor Management, Inc.: p. 168; Courtesy of Sheila Lichacz: p. 171; Photograph by Chuck Solomon: p. 176; Courtesy of Christine Marín: p. 190; Courtesy of Leticia Márquez-Magaña: p. 192; Courtesy of Patricia Preciado Martin: p. 194; Courtesy of Julie A. Martines: p. 195; Courtesy of Milagros Mateu: p. 201; Courtesy of Conchita Maria Mendoza: p. 204; Courtesy of Theresa Annette Mendoza: p. 206; Courtesy of Natacha Seijas Millán: p. 208; Courtesy of Maria Robledo Montecel: p. 210; UPI/Bettmann: pp. 211, 233; Photograph by Catherine Martinez, courtesy of Linda L. Montoya: p. 213; Courtesy of Velma Montoya: p. 215; Courtesy of Cecilia Muñoz: p. 223; Courtesy of Sonia M. Nieto: p. 228; Courtesy of Ana Nogales: p. 231; Courtesy of U. S. National Aeronautics and Space Administration (NASA): p. 235; Courtesy of Margarite Fernández Olmos: p. 237; Courtesy of Ana Maria Perera: p. 245; Courtesy of Edith A. Perez: p. 249; Courtesy of Minerva Peréz: p. 251; Courtesy of Guadalupe C. Quintanilla: p. 253; Courtesy of Irma Rangel: p. 260; Courtesy of Thelma T. Reyna: p. 264; Photograph by Latino Institute: p. 270; Eliana Suarez Rivero: p. 271; Courtesy of Belen B. Robles: p. 275; Courtesy of Teresa Rodriguez: p. 279; Photograph by Michael Schwibs: p. 286; Courtesy of Loretta Sanchez: p. 291; Photograph by Luis Castaneda: p. 295; Courtesy of Liz Torres: p. 311; Courtesy of Gloria Tristani: p. 313; Photograph by Gabriel Moulin Studios: p. 315; Courtesy of María-Luisa Urdaneta: p. 318; Photograph by Vern Evans: p. 320; Courtesy of Diana L. Vargas: p. 322; Courtesy of Norma Varisco de García: p. 326; Courtesy of Enriqueta Longeaux Vásquez: p. 329; Courtesy of Lydia Villa-Komaroff: p. 338; Courtesy of Cathi Villalpando: p. 340; Courtesy of Carmen Delgado Votaw: p. 343.

A

Raydean M. Acevedo
(1951–)
Business executive, entrepreneur

Raydean Marie Acevedo started her own business when it became obvious that the corporate environment was not offering her the respect, opportunity, or income enjoyed by her male counterparts. In 1987 she incorporated Research Management Consultants, Inc. (RMCI) in Golden, CO, an environmental engineering and telecommunications firm. At $20 million in corporate resources, RMCI is among the fastest growing Hispanic-owned firms in the nation. In 1995, *Washington Technology* ranked it among the "Fast 50"—the fastest growing high technology firms in the United States. Acevedo, named by *Hispanic Business* in

Raydean M. Acevedo

1997 as among the "100 Most Influential Hispanics in the United States," is founder, president, CEO, and sole owner of this dynamic enterprise.

In a telephone interview Acevedo shared the secret to her success. "You must always remain true to your values. Stay committed, make sure you're bringing someone else along with you. Your success is hollow without reaching back and joining hands with others to help them experience a similar success. This is more important than anything in the world. This is not a solo act. We must make certain we are responsible to others who may not have had similar opportunities."

Appreciates the Foundation of Family

Acevedo was born at Queen of Los Angeles Hospital in Los Angeles. Of the hospital name, she laughed and said, "It was a good start!" Both her parents were born in California where her father, a widower, still resides. His ancestors are Mexican, her mother's are English and German. "I am truly an example of the proverbial melting pot," Acevedo said with humor. Acevedo, who has two "magnificent" sisters, said she is ". . . very, very blessed with a close family. Our parents took incredibly good care of us. They provided an exceptional example and were a source of strength—during good times and also when I needed someone to pick me up off the floor. I believe children have a responsibility to give back to their parents. As our parents live longer and we can celebrate their lives, we have an opportunity to give back to the people who helped us become who we are." When she brings her father to visit, which is often, he stays in a special room in her home, which she calls "Pa's Room."

Encounters Discrimination in the Corporate World

Acevedo received her bachelor of arts in sociology; a master's in research methodology and bilingual and bicultural education, sociology of medicine; and completed doctoral course work in sociology at the University of California, Santa Barbara. She worked for several different firms before being recruited to National Computer Systems in 1981 as federal program manager, selling and marketing optical mark reader systems and services. In a book entitled *America's Competitive Secret, Utilizing Women as a Management Strategy*, author Judy B. Rosener profiles Acevedo's response to the discrimination she encountered in the corporate world. "She was an immediate success. . . and yet she always felt like an outsider because she was a woman. Acevedo was not included in the "old boys' network," even though her male colleagues clearly respected her performance. She knew she was viewed as different. She became a workaholic in an effort to win acceptance." So successful was she that when a competitor wanted to hire her and she declined, the competitor acquired her division just so they could have her on their staff. Still, she felt like an outsider and was even paid a lower base salary than her male counterparts, including one she hired. When a customer suggested she start her own business, she did her homework, and took the plunge.

Creates an Environment of Celebration

Acevedo started Research Management Consultants, Inc. (RMCI), an environmental engineering and telecommunications firm. She deliberately created an environment in which her employees could realize their full potential. "I wanted to make a difference—to the world outside and to those people who devote themselves to our business," she said. "I wanted to create something that would celebrate its employees and provide the highest standard of customer service. I wanted to create a model of what happens when you treat people with respect and kindness, then use that model as a catalyst outside the walls of the business. I believe we can do that by showing and setting the example of the potential of human beings. If people experience that within the business realm, I believe they in turn take it outside into families and communities—that love and respect experienced in one environment is transferred to another." Acevedo has been presented with a multitude of awards from around the nation, evidence that her success philosophies are appreciated.

Gives Back to the Community

Acevedo is grateful to have had a variety of people to encourage her in her various careers, and she is now very active in community programs, volunteering her time and addressing audiences across the nation. She was on the advisory board of the Arthur Flemming Fellowship Leadership Institute, a national leadership development program for up-and-coming political representatives making major contributions to the community. She was also an advisor for the W.K. Kellogg Foundation National Fellowship Program, which mentors future leaders in academia and the private sector in areas, such as medicine, agriculture, and education. As advisor, she conducted two classes over a six-year period, each class spanning three years. In that role, she counseled participants and helped them create individual learning plans, plan seminars, and develop other leadership skills.

Acevedo is likewise passionate about issues that affect women. She said, "Women need to realize they hold inside themselves tremendous strength and power, and they need to use that to make a difference in this world, regardless of the path they choose—be it business, education, or anything else. We only get one chance to do it, and we need to take that responsibility very seriously and use it in every single thing we undertake."

Current Address: Research Management Consultants, Inc., 1746 Cole Blvd., Bldg. 21, Ste. 300, Golden, CO 80401.

Sources:

Rosener, Judy B. *America's Competitive Secret: Utilizing Women as a Management Strategy.* New York: Oxford University Press, 1995.

Thompson, Märie L. Biographical material from and a telephone conversation with Raydean M. Acevedo, April 27, 1998.

Alma Flor Ada
(1938–)
Author, professor

Selected writings:

El enanito de la bared y otras historias. Arica, 1974.
La gallinita costurera y otras historias. Arica, 1974.
Las pintas de las mariquitas. Arica, 1974.
Saltarín y sus dos amigos y otras historias. Arica, 1974.
Various titles in the *Hagamos Caminos Series.* Addison-Wesley, 1985.
Various titles in the *Rimas Y Risas Greer Series.* Hampton-Brown, 1988.
Amigos (Friends). Santillana, 1989.
Various titles in the *Cuento Mas Series.* Hampton-Brown, 1989.
Various titles in the *Libros para Contar Series.* Santillana, 1989.
La hamaca de la vaca (In the Cow's Backyard). Santillana, 1991.
La moneda oro (The Gold Coin). Simon & Schuster, 1991.
Various titles in the *Early Learning Pack Series.* Hampton-Brown, 1991.
El papalote (The Kite). Santillana, 1992.
Olmo y la mariposa azul. Laredo, 1992.
Various titles in the *Dias y Dias de Poesia Series.* Hampton-Brown, 1992.
Various titles in the *Chorus of Cultures Series.* Hampton-Brown, 1993.
Various titles in the *Cuentos con Alma Series.* Laredo, 1993.
El unicornio del oeste (The Unicorn of the West). Atheneum, 1994.
Me llamo María Isabel (My Name is María Isabel). Atheneum, 1994.
Querido Pedrin (Dear Peter Rabbit). Atheneum, 1994.
Where the Flame Trees Bloom. Atheneum, 1994.
Como nacio el arco Iris. Santillana, 1995.
Mediopollito/Half-Chicken. New York: Doubleday, 1995.
Jordi's Star. New York: G.P. Putnam's Sons, 1996.
El arbol de navidad (The Christmas Tree). Hyperion, 1997.

Gathering the Sun: An Alphabet in Spanish and English.
   Shepard Books, 1997.
The Lizard and the Sun. New York: Doubleday, 1997.
I Love Saturdays. . . y domingos! Simon & Schuster, 1998.
The Malachite Palace. Simon & Schuster, 1998.
Yours Truly Goldilocks. Simon & Schuster, 1998.

Overview

Alma Flor Ada is a professor of education at the University of San Francisco and a writer of numerous children's books. She has received the Marta Salotti God Medal Award (Argentina) and the Christopher Award (United States). Her books have been published in Argentina, Colombia, Mexico, Peru, Spain, and the United States. Many of her books have appeared in both English and Spanish versions or with both languages paralleled under the same cover. She has been well recognized as a major contributor to children's literature for telling stories in a way that crosses cultural barriers and promotes cultural understanding.

Childhood Influences Career Decisions

Ada was born in Camaguery, Cuba, on January 3, 1938, to Modesto Ada, a professor, and Alma (Lafuente) Ada, a teacher. Ada's childhood experiences influenced her decision to become an educator and a writer. Before she was three years old, her grandmother taught her to read by writing the names of plants and flowers on the ground with

Alma Flor Ada

a stick. Her grandmother also taught her to love nature, which is often reflected in her stories. Her grandmother was just one of many people who shaped Ada's love for books and stories. Ada stated in an interview with WB39 WDZL-TV in Miami, Florida, "My grandmother and one of my uncles were great storytellers. And every night, at bedtime, my father told me stories he invented to explain to me all that he knew about the history of the world. With all these storytellers around me, it's not a surprise that I like to tell stories."

Also, as a child, Ada was displeased with the boring classroom textbooks at school, especially when she had wonderful storybooks she loved waiting for her at home. Because of her desire for stories and the influence of those surrounding her, Ada committed herself at a young age to a vocation as a writer who would write exciting stories and make schoolbooks fun.

Completes Her Studies

Ada studied in Spain, Peru, and the United States. She received her undergraduate degree from the Universidad Central de Madrid in 1959. She earned a master's degree in 1963 and a doctorate degree in 1965 from Pontificia Universidad Catolica del Peru. She completed her studies at Harvard University, where she pursued post-doctorate studies from 1965 to 1967. In 1961, Ada married Armando Zubizarreta and has four children (Rosalma, Alfonso, Miguel, and Gabriel) from this marriage. Ada and Zubizarreta divorced in 1971. Ada married again in 1984, to Jorgen Voss.

Ada began her career as an educator during her doctoral studies. She was an instructor and head of the Spanish department at the Colegio Alexander von Humboldt in Lima, Peru, from 1963 to 1965. After completing her post-doctorate work at Harvard, she returned to this position from 1967 to 1969. Her next post brought her to the United States, where she has lived ever since. From 1970 to 1972, she was an associate professor of Romance languages at Emory University in Atlanta, Georgia. She spent another two years as a professor of language and codirector of the Institute for Bilingual Bicultural Services at Mercy College in Detroit, Michigan. In 1979 Ada found her academic home as a professor of education at the University of San Francisco, where she has remained for almost 20 years.

Writes Early Stories in Spanish

Ada's first stories were written in Spanish and were published in Lima, Peru in 1974. These stories included *El enanito de la bared y otras historias, La gallinita costurera y otras historias, Las pintas de las mariquitas,* and *Saltarín y sus dos amigos y otras historias.* Since that time, she has written many more children's stories. Throughout her writing career, Ada has used her skill as a bilingual writer to reach both English-speaking and Spanish-speaking children with stories of culture, pride, courage, determination, and understanding.

Many of Ada's stories develop out of her own life experiences. In *Me llamo María Isabel (My Name is María Isabel)*, Ada deals with the feelings of a child when a teacher will not call her by her real name, something Ada dealt with herself as a child. *El unicornio del oeste (The Unicorn of the West)* developed from bedtime stories Ada made up for her nieces. In addition, many of the stories in *Where the Flame Tree Blooms* were first told to her by her grandmother or other relatives in Cuba. According to a review by the National Council of Teachers of English, "Whatever the source, each [story] clearly comes from the heart and gives readers the opportunity to meet the people of Cuba from an earlier era." Ada models her own grandchildren's life in the story *I Love Saturdays . . . y domingos!* The story is about a young girl with two sets of grandparents who are very different.

Retells the Old Tales

Ada has also made major contributions to children's literature by translating popular children's tales from Spanish to English. She retells the traditional Spanish folktale *Mediopollito* in the English version *Half-Chicken*. She also wrote *Blancaflor* so that children in the United States could learn a beloved Spanish children's story. Even her own writings often take on the flavor of a folktale, using a moral as a theme. Setting the story *La moneda oro (The Gold Coin)* in South America, Ada tells of a hardened thief who goes to extreme lengths to rob a woman of a gold coin, only to find himself transformed by her kindness in the process.

The many books written by Ada all reflect her love for a well-told story. She has made an impact in children's literature, not only for her variety of stories, but also for her ability to make those stories available to children from different cultures.

During the 1990s, Ada has written numerous children's titles, many of which have received very favorable reviews from literary critics and librarians. Commenting on her ability to write bilingual books, Ada said, "Knowing two languages has made the world richer for me." Undoubtedly, through her gift of writing, Alma Flor Ada continues to enrich the lives of all children.

Current Address: Dept. of Education, Univ. of San Francisco, San Francisco, CA 94117.

Sources:

Battle, Jennifer. "Me llamo María Isabel." *Language Arts,* March 1996.
Corsaro, Julie. "The Lizard and the Sun." *Booklist,* December 15, 1997, p. 698.
"Dear Peter Rabbit." *Booklist,* May 1, 1994, p. 1606.
Houghton Mifflin Education Place. Available at http://www.eduplace.com.
Martinez, Miriam and Marcia F. Nash. "Where the Flame Trees Bloom." *Language Arts,* November 1995.
"My Name is María Isabel." *Booklist,* June 1, 1993.
Putnam Berkley Online. Available at http://www.mca.com/putnam.
Schon, Isabel. "Gathering the Sun: An Alphabet in English and Spanish." *Booklist,* November 15, 1997.
WB39 WDZL-TV Home Page. Available at http://www.wb39.com.

Deborah Aguiar-Vélez

Information technology executive, entrepreneur, professor

Deborah Aguiar-Vélez is one of her state's most respected small-business leaders. The one-time chemical engineer is the founder and president of two companies that provide an array of information-technology services to clients, both corporate and individual. She is active in New Jersey's Hispanic American business community and has even served as head of the state's Division of Small Businesses.

Deborah Aguiar-Vélez

Puerto Rican Roots

Aguiar-Vélez earned a degree in chemical engineering from the University of Puerto Rico in 1977, but was already one of a small number of young people interested in the burgeoning field of computer science. After graduation, she spent another year at the university as an instructor in computer languages. In 1978 she was hired by the petrochemical giant Exxon as a senior analyst, and she moved to New Jersey to take the job. At the company's Florham Park offices, she developed computer applications in its global refinery operations. She also created computer training programs for other Exxon personnel and traveled to Exxon facilities in South America and Europe to give instruction.

Founds Sistemas

Aguiar-Vélez left Exxon in 1983 to strike out on her own, and her former employer became one of the first major clients of her newly-launched Sistemas Corporation. Sistemas is a highly specialized computer consulting firm for Fortune 500 companies that have extremely complex information-systems needs. Aguiar-Vélez and her staff plan and carry out computer network installations, provide programming and applications software, and offer customized database design. Sistemas's client base includes AT&T, BASF, Colgate-Palmolive, and Xerox, as well as Exxon. Aguiar-Vélez's husband, German Vélez, is a vice-president of the company and one of its senior consultants.

The success of Sistemas within the information-technology industry—a sector known for its paucity of minority entrepreneurs—brought Aguiar-Vélez to the attention of New Jersey Governor Tom Kean in 1988. He named Aguiar-Vélez as director of the state's Small Business Division and Women and Minority Businesses, a post she held for the next two years. The state agency, part of the New Jersey Department of Commerce and Economic Development, had a budget of $2.5 million. Aguiar-Vélez supervised a staff of 33 employees who worked to improve the state's small-business climate; during her tenure as director she introduced a partnership agreement between private and public businesses, developed a plan to create a $10 million fund for new enterprises, and launched New Jersey's first conference on small businesses, a two-day workshop that attracted 1,700 attendees.

Downshifts to the PC Field

Aguiar-Vélez began her career in the computer science field at the uppermost level, the creation and use of complex programming languages for scientific applications. Unlike the career trajectories of many in her field— yet quite similar to the computer industry itself—Aguiar-Vélez has gradually become involved in more and more accessible applications of information technology. She began teaching at the college level again in the 1990s when she became an instructor at Mercer County College in West Windsor, New Jersey.

That new direction was also manifested in her founding of an offshoot of Sistemas, Sistemática, Inc., in 1996. Through Sistemática, Aguiar-Vélez provides computer training and bilingual professional services for a variety of corporate clients, small businesses, and individuals. Though one of its first training sites was next door to her home in Kendall Park, New Jersey—allowing her to spend more time with her children and be there after school for homework assistance—Sistemática also opened a 4,000-square-foot site in downtown Trenton. Statistically, the New Jersey state capital has been called the state's second most-distressed city, with a corresponding number of underemployed citizens with few or no computer skills.

Revitalizes Urban Area

Sistemática aimed to provide a solution to this problem. Its offices are in the middle of Trenton's city center, near the maze of state and city government buildings, but are also centrally located to make it easy for city residents to reach them. Thus low-income families, as well as a large number of government employees in the area, have access to its services, which are obtainable at a reasonable fee because of its location in an urban enterprise zone. This gives Sistemática tax breaks, which in turn it can pass on to private citizens or other small businesses in the enterprise zone. Sistemática, a fully bilingual company, also brings its courses to the work site and teaches Adobe PageMaker, MS Office, JAVA, and HTML, among other software packages and programming languages.

Aguiar-Vélez is extremely committed to bringing minorities into the twenty-first century through her companies and community involvement. Studies show that the computer-literacy skills of minorities are below the national average, and Sistemática provides a remedy for that condition. "We're here to assist corporations and governmental agencies, as well as small businesses, individuals and families," Aguiar-Vélez told Jim Fitzsimmons in the *Trentonian*. "We want them to be active computer and Internet players in the next millennium instead of spectators watching from the sidelines or stands while others actively reshape the world in their image."

Looks to the Far East

Aguiar-Vélez belongs to Trenton's Latino Chamber of Commerce, and in 1997 this group's accomplishments helped earn Trenton the number two spot on *Hispanic Business* magazine's list of the best cities in the United States for Hispanic entrepreneurs—after Miami, Florida. She has also been involved in the Leadership New Jersey and Leadership America programs that select outstanding community and corporate achievers for a year-long program. Aguiar-Vélez finds time to lend her insights through participation in a series of conferences called China 2010;

for this she travels to Washington, DC, regularly to take part in joint American/Pan-Asian conferences that bring together women business leaders to help formulate international trade policy.

Aguiar-Vélez sits on the boards of the Franklin Institute, Thomas Edison State College Foundation, the Center for Private Enterprise, and CoreStates New Jersey National Bank. Among her other honors, she has received the 1993 Humanitarian Award from the National Conference of Christians and Jews and was twice cited by the Society of Hispanic Professional Engineers for an Engineer of the Year Award—in 1989, for Outstanding Achievement on Affirmative Action, and in 1991 in the Entrepreneurship category. She lives in Kendall Park, New Jersey, with her husband and two daughters. Computer literacy runs in the family. "My 12-year-old can disassemble a computer in 45 minutes," Aguiar-Vélez told *Trenton Times* reporter Kelly Beamon. "Everyone in our family knows how to put in a hard drive."

Current Address: Sistemas Corp., 80 Henderson Rd., Kendall Park, NJ 08824-1509.

Sources:

Beamon, Kelly. "City Rated 2nd in Cultivating Hispanic Trade." *Trenton Times,* September 24, 1997, p. A12.
Beamon, Kelly. "Cover Story Unfolds." *Trenton Times,* August 27, 1997.
Fitzsimmons, Jim. "Computer Whiz Takes a Byte Out of Trenton." *Trentonian,* May 1, 1997, p. 27.
"Sistemática Brings Internet Training to Trenton."*Trentonian,* August 17, 1997.
Additional information for this profile was provided by Sistemas Corporation, March 1998.

Aguirre, Hilda Perera
See **Perera, Hilda**

Pamela A. Aguirre
(1958–)
Manufacturing executive

Pamela Aguirre leads a flourishing Michigan company that manufactures parts used in automotive interiors. Her company, Mexican Industries, was founded by her father in 1979 and has since become the largest minority-owned automotive supplier in the United States, posting 1996 sales of $158 million. The Aguirres are also one of the most financially successful Hispanic families in the United States and, as the torchbearer at Mexican Industries since her father's death in 1994, Pamela Aguirre has carried on his legacy in building strong ties with the surrounding community. At its main facility in southwest Detroit—the center of the city's Hispanic American community—Mexican Industries provides hundreds of nearby jobs to local residents. The company also displays its gratitude to a loyal workforce by investing profits into an array of educational, health-related, and social initiatives to improve the quality of life in southwest Detroit.

"Baseball Brat"

Aguirre's father was Hank Aguirre, a former professional pitcher for the Detroit Tigers, and she was born in 1958, the year he began his ten seasons there. After 1968, Hank Aguirre spent a season each with the Los Angeles Dodgers and the Chicago Cubs. The family of four lived in suburban Chicago but still kept a residence in Detroit, which her father had grown to like. Aguirre remembers fondly her early life as the offspring of a professional baseball player, recalling that most players on the team lived near one another and brought their kids along to the ball field for home games. During spring training in Florida, Aguirre and other players' children attended on-site classes they used to call "baseball brat" school.

When her father retired from baseball after the end of the 1970 season, Aguirre and her family moved to California for a time while Hank Aguirre managed a Triple A team, but they then returned to Michigan permanently. After graduating from an all-girls' Catholic high school in suburban Detroit in 1977, Aguirre considered a career in interior design, but instead attended cosmetology school for a year. In 1979 Hank Aguirre, who for the last several years had worked as an advertising executive, founded Mexican Industries, and Pamela—along with sisters Jill and Robin and brother Rance—were recruited to help out. In fact, they were among the first employees at the southwest Detroit facility, cleaning the secondhand industrial building and then learning how to run the manufacturing equipment as it arrived.

Helps to Launch Business

Over the next few years, Aguirre acquired experience at nearly every workstation at the company. She inspected parts, worked in the glue booth, and like her siblings, did anything that needed to be done. "[The jobs] were all different, and they were all difficult to start because we didn't know," Aguirre recalled about these early days in a telephone interview. "We knew what we were doing, but every one of them we had to learn from the bottom up. . . .There's not an employee that was hired that did a job that we hadn't done first."

Mexican Industries soon grew into Michigan's third largest Hispanic company. It assembled wheel covers, leather steering wheels, air bags, head rests, arm consoles, and other interior details. As the company won bigger contracts during the 1980s, Aguirre moved into the operations end of the company, eventually becoming a purchasing officer. Although their workforce of nearly 1000 employees—about 85 percent of whom were of Hispanic heritage—was spread over seven facilities in southwest Detroit, some nearby suburbs, and Tempe, Arizona, company offices and their biggest facility remained in southwest Detroit.

Tragedy Strikes

When Hank Aguirre was diagnosed with cancer in 1993, the company he had founded was a thriving entity with sales exceeding $100 million annually. He owned 100 percent of it and hesitated to make arrangements for the future, thinking he would successfully combat his disease. But as his health worsened in the summer of 1994, he called a meeting and made each of his four children members of the company's board. Upon his death that September, direct ownership was transferred to the family. Three months later Pamela Aguirre and her older brother Rance were named executive vice-presidents, and within a year she had become the company's chief executive officer and chair of the board. Robin Aguirre-Krych, personnel director of Mexican Industries' plant in Tempe, Arizona, also became an executive vice-president; only Jill Aguirre is not involved directly in the company.

Rebuffs UAW

Aguirre has displayed an aptitude for not just maintaining control over the company her father founded but also successfully expanding it. By 1997, Mexican Industries had grown from seven plants to nine, with a 50 percent increase in the workforce. Nearly all of those 1,500 employees are minority—about 86 percent Hispanic and the rest African-American—and 75 percent are women. In 1995, that workforce profile caused the United Auto Workers union to allege that the company paid below-average wages to workers who did not have either the language skills or the transportation to find similar, but better-paying work outside of southwest Detroit. The company mounted a campaign, centered around the slogan "Let's Keep Mexican Industries Family"—and its employees eventually voted against the union. "Detroit is a union town, and Mexican Industries employs a lot of people, so we continue to be of interest to the UAW, and probably always will," Aguirre said in 1998. "We're not anti-union per se—the unions have done a lot of good in America, in places where they're really needed, but we continue to believe strongly that a union would not be in the best interests of our employees. . . Our culture is such that it's just not needed."

Ironically, the company could profit by relocating part of its manufacturing operations to Mexico, as many automobile manufacturers or suppliers with UAW ties have done in recent years. In Mexico, unions have little power, and wages are accordingly lower. For years Hank Aguirre was courted by investors from south of the border, but he declined; his heirs maintain that policy, looking to expand in other ways. In 1997 Mexican Industries announced a joint venture with Manchester Plastics to build instrument panels for General Motors. The new corporate entity would be named Aguirre and Manchester Plastics, with expected sales of $66 million per year.

A Community Force

As a thriving company, Mexican Industries is able to offer an array of services to employees, including high school equivalency diploma classes, English and Spanish language courses, college tuition reimbursement, low-interest loans, an annual bonus program, a scholarship program to a renowned Catholic school in southwest Detroit for children of employees, and a spirited, community-oriented workplace. Both Hispanic and African-American holidays are celebrated; on Cinco de Mayo, employees dress up, bring food, and decorate Cinco de Mayo trees.

Carries on a Legacy

Aguirre, moreover, continues to carry on the legacy of community activism that her father began. "We believe it's most important for us to be the leaders in the effort to better the community," she said in 1998. ". . . I don't think there's anything that goes on in this community that we aren't involved in." The company provides funding for several noteworthy programs that serve the nearby community, including a Head Start preschool facility, youth recreation groups, and numerous other ventures affiliated with local groups such as Latino Family Services and the Southwest Detroit Business Association. The company is involved in the Detroit Lions Courage House for families with children undergoing medical treatment at an area hospital, and, since Hank Aguirre's death, has launched a health-awareness project for employees. Working in conjunction with a local hospital, the Hank Aguirre Cancer Awareness Foundation offers free cancer screening to all Mexican Industries employees as well as a training program that will eventually offer the same to the southwest Detroit community with bilingual medical personnel.

"We're always willing to listen to new projects, and especially those that directly impact southwest Detroit," Aguirre said in 1998. She herself is active in Latin Americans for Social and Economic Development (LASED) of Detroit, but finds little time for hobbies between running a company and running a household. She and her three children live just eight miles from her office, and for recreation she professes to enjoy reading and jet-skiing. She cites her offspring as her own personal role models and is well aware of the unintended burden they carry. Aguirre recalled that when she and her siblings were coming of age and their father was busy with his company, "[A]s his biological children, we had to learn that he had this huge other family that he was responsible for. . . and my kids are learning that too. They're all straight-A kids, and how they handle me being here, especially the last three or four years, is just amazing."

Aguirre looks to the baseball wives of her mother's day—when families were large and athletes' salaries were small—as role models for her as well. She also finds inspiration among her own employees: "I watch them, and their determination and their pride, and their work ethic—that's a huge role model for me." Her one regret is being less than bilingual; she can understand Spanish, but has a hard time speaking it. "My dad used to speak Spanish to us when we were little, and we laughed at him. . . .Now we wish we had listened a little more."

Current Address: Mexican Industries, Aguirre Plaza, 1801 Howard St., Detroit, MI 48216.

Sources:

Autoparts Report, October 1, 1997.

Brennan, Carol. Information obtained from Mexican Industries public relations materials and a telephone interview with Pamela Aguirre, March 16, 1998.

Corcoran, Megan E. "Woman to Woman: Five Women Share How They Climbed the Ladder of Success." *Detroit News,* October 20, 1997, p. S1.

Neely, Anthony. "Aguirre's Son Hopes to Be Named." *Detroit Free Press,* September 8, 1994, p. 2E.

Neely, Anthony. "Aguirres Get New Duties on Board." *Detroit Free Press,* November 2, 1994, p. 2E.

Neely, Anthony. "Determination Is Aguirre's Legacy." *Detroit Free Press,* September 7, 1994, p. 5C.

"Pamela Aguirre: A Daughter Leads Company Synonymous with Her Father into Its Own." *Detroit News,* October 20, 1997, p. S6.

Sherefkin, Robert. "Mexican Industries Fights UAW Campaign." *Crain's Detroit Business,* May 8, 1995, sec. 1, p. 1.

Sherefkin, Robert. "Who Will Be Chairman? Mexican Ind. Board Ponders Aguirre Successor." *Crain's Detroit Business,* September 12, 1994, sec. 1, p. 27.

Norma Alarcón

(1943–)

Professor, entrepreneur, publisher, writer, editor, lecturer

Selected writings:

Bibliography of Hispanic Women Writers. Chicano-Riqueno Studies, 1980.

The Sexuality of Latinas. Third Woman Press, 1993.

Chicana Critical Issues. Third Woman Press, 1994.

Writing Self, Writing Nation. Edited with Elaine H. Kim. Third Woman Press, 1994.

T(r)opographies of Hunger: Conjugating Subjects in a Transnational Frame. Duke University Press, 1998.

Overview

From her birth in a small Mexican community, Norma Alarcón has moved into the upper levels of academia. A respected educator, scholar, author, and editor, she is well-known for her championing of feminist Chicana causes.

Alarcón was born in Monelova, Coahuila, in northeastern Mexico, on November 30, 1943. The family, which included her parents, Manuel and Elidia, and a younger brother, was poor. Looking for a better life, the Alarcóns migrated to the United States in 1955. At first, Norma's father worked in a gas station in San Antonio, Texas. From there the family moved to Chicago; Newark, Ohio; and finally to Indiana, where the elder Alarcón found work in Indianapolis, followed by the steel mills and railroad yards of Gary and Bloomington.

Alarcón remembers that her mother once worked in a candy kitchen. This was especially attractive because, as Alarcón stated during a telephone interview, "She brought home discount chocolates, nuts, and damaged Easter eggs."

Norma Alarcón credits her hardworking family and her simple beginnings with giving her the values that aided her climb up the career ladder. Eventually, she would become known as a scholar and respected educator. She also credits her love of reading. "I just like to know things," she said.

Choosing a Career

Armed with her love of books and a history of good grades, Alarcón entered Indiana University. She graduated Phi Beta Kappa in 1970 with a A.B. in Spanish, earned an M.A. in 1972, and a Ph.D. in 1983, also from Indiana.

She began her professional career in 1983 as an assistant professor at Purdue University in Lafayette, Indiana. Her next stop was the University of California, Berkeley, where in 1987 she became an assistant professor, later in 1991 an associate professor, and since 1996 has served as a full professor in both the Ethnic Studies (Chicano Studies Program) and Women's Studies Departments. In addition, she received a fellowship from the prestigious Chancellor's Ethnic Minority Postdoctoral Fellowship Program. Such fellowships, which pay the recipient several thousand dollars yearly, are set up to encourage minority students in the United States to pursue teaching and research at the university level. She also worked on her study of Hispanic

American women writers, entitled "Colonialism, Nationalism and Feminism: The Poetics and Politics of Identity."

Alarcón has explained the aim of Chicano studies in this manner: "To understand historical and cultural ways in which we [Chicanos] have influenced the course of life in this country. How we have shaped the new environment. The degree of how much people from other places absorb the new culture and keep the roots and traditions of the old varies with the individual."

Emerges as Editor, Writer, and Lecturer

In 1981, Alarcón, with the aid of a publication grant, founded Third Woman Press. As an international literature and arts publishing house, Third Woman Press has shown a special interest in an array of Chicana topics.

In addition to teaching and her work with Third Woman Press, Alarcón has been a contributing editor, since 1975, to *The Americas Review* and finds time to write. Some of her books and articles include: *T(r)opographies of Hunger: Conjugating Subjects in a Transnational Frame* (Duke University Press, 1998); *Chicana Critical Issues* (Third Woman Press, 1994); "Cognitive Desires: An Allegory of/for Chicana Critics," in *Listening to the Silences: New Essays in Feminist Criticism* (Oxford University Press, 1994); *The Sexuality of Latinas* (Third Woman Press, 1993); "Chicana Feminism: In the Tracks of the Native Woman" in *Cultural Studies*, 1990; "Making Familia From Scratch" in *Americas Review*, 1987; and "What Kind of Lover Have You Made Me, Mother?: Towards a Theory of Chicanas' Feminism and Cultural Identity Through Poetry," in *Women of Color* (Indiana University Press, 1985).

Well-known for her scholarly interests in Chicano matters, Alarcón is a sought-after speaker on the lecture circuit. Her lecture and seminar subjects include: U.S./Third World women's literature and theory; Mexican consciousness in the twentieth century; and transnational subjects of feminism. In addition to being fluent in both Spanish and English, she has a reading knowledge of French and Portuguese.

Through her scholarly work, Alarcón has gained educational funding from several impressive sources. These include: a fellowship for study in Madrid, Spain, from Indiana University; a Ford Foundation Grant; a curriculum development grant; and various publication grants for Third Woman Press.

As a working single mother—her son, Joseph McKesson, was born in 1964—Alarcón has advice for young people, especially children of immigrant families, who dream of achieving their career goals: "Explore your environment. Ask questions, including: What is this new place in which I find myself? What is my relationship is to this place? Walk through the streets."

Current Address: Chicano Studies Program, Ethnic Studies Dept., 506 Varrows Hall, Univ. of California, Berkeley, Berkeley, CA 94720.

Sources:

Blue, Rose. Telephone conversation with Norma Alarcón, March 12, 1998.
Blue, Rose. Telephone conversation with University Communications, Univ. of California, Berkeley, March 12, 1998.

Camila A. Alire
Educational administrator, writer, community activist

Selected writings:

Serving Latino Communities: A How-to-Do-It Manual for School and Public Librarians. Neal-Schumann Publishers, 1998.

Camila A. Alire

Overview

The year 1997 was memorable for Dr. Camila A. Alire. She was appointed dean of the Colorado State University Libraries, thus becoming the first Hispanic to head a U.S. Association of Research Libraries facility. She received the Elizabeth Futas Catalyst for Change National Award. She was named Librarian of the Year by REFORMA, the Hispanic American affiliate of the American Librarian Association. In addition, she was chosen among the 100 most influential Hispanic professionals in the United States by *Hispanic Business.* The magazine conducted a survey to find those individuals who made a difference in improving the quality of life for Hispanics in urban and inner-city communities.

Spends Formative Years in Colorado

The daughter of Joe and Mary Alire, Camila Alire was born in Monte Vista, in the San Luis Valley. She traces her drive to achieve to her parents, who were both active in community and minority causes in their small town. However, she finds it amusing that in high school she was talkative enough to be "kicked out of the library nearly every day" for that offense. Today, as she said in an interview, "I get paid to be in the library all day and talk!"

From high school, Alire went to Adams State College in Alamosa, Colorado. She graduated with B.A. degrees in history and secondary education in 1970. From there, she earned an M.L.S. at the University of Denver in 1974, and then an Ed.D. in higher education administration from the University of Northern Colorado at Greeley in 1984.

When asked why library service became her career choice, Dr. Alire credits her own undergraduate experience while working in the library at Adams State College. "Much to my surprise," she said, "I found myself becoming a valuable resource for my friends in the residence hall because of my knowledge about the library." Now, as a professional, she is sharing that knowledge with as many young people as possible.

Early Career Moves

Alire's first job after college took her out of her home state to Nebraska. She became the library director at McCook College in 1974. Four years later, however, she returned to Colorado as a librarian/information specialist for Mathematical Policy Research in Denver. The next stop on her academic career was Colorado Springs, where she became the director of the Learning Research Center at Pikes Peak Community College. By 1989, Alire was back in Denver, this time at the University of Colorado. She was the assistant director of instruction and research services at Auraria Library and eventually became dean/director.

Disaster Hits CSU Library

In 1997, Alire left Denver to become dean of libraries at Colorado State University in Fort Collins. She said when she accepted the position that "I want to be part of the progressive and creative activities CSU Libraries is known for and work with this group of staff as we enter one of the most opportunity-filled times for providing library services. This is an excting time to step up to the leadership position in an [Association of Research Libraries] library."

The excitement at Colorado State, however, was a little more than Alire and the university had bargained. By July 28, 1997, she was just settling into her new position, getting acquainted with her staff and the newly renovated Morgan Library, which was now under her control. Then, disaster struck: a flash flood hit Fort Collins, sending a ten-foot wall of water sweeping through the university grounds. In just a few hours, seven inches of water were dumped onto the city, causing five deaths. Fortunately, there were no fatalities on the university campus, but flood waters poured into the library and reached to the ceiling. Nearly half a million books and bound journals were submerged. Rarely, if ever, had there been such devastation to a U.S. library. Experts were called in to begin the process of restoring the library materials. The books and journals were freeze-dried and then inspected one by one before they could be returned to the shelves.

After the flood, Alire said, "Looking at the damage, I felt nothing but disbelief at first. But then the adrenaline starting pumping . . . . The restoration undertaking was enormous, involving a crew of 100 to 170 workers who had to examine each book, enter it into the database, and then decide whether it could be returned to the shelves, looked at by a library specialist, or tossed out as beyond hope." By late fall, Alire was proud to report that "the library is back - not totally and completely, but back and in working order for the new semester."

Understands Importance of Her Role

Alire takes her position in the library administration field and role as an Hispanic professional very seriously. "I realize I'm a groundbreaker as far as being an administrator, a woman, and a member of a minority population," she said, "but I really don't dwell on that. At the same time, I know I have a tremendous responsibility as a role model."

Alire believes that she has both a professional and a moral obligation to see that those who follow her have the chance to be successful in whatever their career field. To that end, she has become involved with mentoring programs. In addition, she is the author of such publications as *Library Services to Latino Populations,* written with her colleague, Orlando Archibeque (Neal-Schumann, 1998); "Recruitment and Retention of Librarians of Color" in *Creat-*

ing Our Future: Essays on Librarianship (McFarland, 1996); and "Minorities and the Symbolic Potential of the Academic Library" in *College and Research Libraries* (1995).

When Alire was nominated for the first Elizabeth Futas Catalyst for Change Award in 1997, she was not certain just what she had done to affect change. Then, she looked around and found that, as she said, "I had quite a history."

One of the changes included the fact that while at the University of Denver library school, more students of color enrolled than before any other time. Her tenure on the Committee on Library Services to Ethnic Minority Populations developed a statewide model for library services to that community. With her assistance, a scholarship for M.L.S. students who serve minority populations was established as well as a statewide mentoring program. In addition, Orlando Archibeque and Alire have, through the years, presented workshops all over the United States concerning library services to Hispanic readers. This is part of her commitment to aiding future minority generations. As a result, the library association in her home state recognized that commitment by honoring her as the first recipient of the CLA (Colorado Library Association) Exemplary Library Services to Ethnic Populations Award (1995).

Maintains Active Community Role

Community service is another of Alire's commitments to her home state and minority populations. She has been involved with the Anti-Defamation League, the Colorado Endowment for the Humanities Board, and the Colorado Library Education Fund Board. Finally, Alire is an active and long-standing member of such groups as the American Library Association (ALA), REFORMA (National Association to Promote Library Services of the Spanish-Speaking), and the Association for College and Research Libraries (ACRL).

If Alire has any spare time at all, she says she likes to spend it waiting for the "leaves to change to gold, red, and yellow on scrub oaks at home. The colors are spectacular." She lives with her husband, Alan Radcliffe, a systems analyst, and two dogs and two cats in Sedalia, Colorado.

Current Address: University Libraries, Colorado State University, Fort Collins, CO 80523-1019.

Sources:

Blue, Rose. Telephone conversation with and Colorado State University publications from Camila Alire, February 23, 1998.
Foster, Jim. "Hispanic publication honors dean of libraries." *The Coloradoan*, November 11, 1997.

Zate, Maria. "100 Most Influential Hispanics. *Hispanic Business,* October 1997, pp. 38-42, 48.

Adela A. Allen
(1928–)
Educational administrator, author, organization executive, chairperson, consultant

Selected writings:

Library Services for Hispanic Children. Oryx Press, 1985.

Overview

Adela Allen is associate vice president of Inter-American Relations and associate dean of the Graduate College at the University of Arizona. She has taught at the University of Arizona since 1975 and is known for her support of international and minority students and her research contributions to the fields of bilingual education, language development, and multicultural children's literature.

Born in New York City

Adela Artola Allen was born to Perry Allen and Adelaida Artola Arias de Allen on July 26, 1928, in New York City. She received her bachelor of arts degree in philosophy in 1954 from the University of the Americas. Her education continued in the South, when she earned a master of arts degree in Spanish from the University of Houston in 1963. She worked as a teaching assistant in the Department of Modern Languages at the University of Houston while completing her master's degree and then was hired as an instructor in that department from 1963 to 1967. She also served as a teaching assistant and as a research associate at the next university she attended, the University of Arizona. It was here that she earned her doctorate in Spanish, in 1974. Before earning her Ph.D., however, Allen gained experience as a training coordinator for the Title VII Bilingual Bicultural Socialization Project and as a junior high and high school teacher.

Starts Career at University of Arizona

Allen began at the University of Arizona as an instructor in 1975 and, a year later, was hired as an assistant professor of reading in the College of Education. She was tenured and promoted to associate professor in 1981. In 1984 Allen was appointed head of the department and, in 1986, she became division head of Language, Reading, and Culture and director of Bilingual Education Graduate Programs. In 1988 she became associate dean of the Graduate College. In this role, Allen is responsible for monitoring all new graduate courses submitted for approval, supervising the Graduate Office of Degree Certification and the teaching assistants' orientation, and advising and directing international graduate students. During her years at Arizona, Allen has taught courses in bilingual reading, Spanish reading and instruction, language and culture, and reading comprehension. She also directed the Diagnostic and Instructional Reading/Writing Clinics in the College of Education for two years.

Putting It in Writing

As editor of *Library Services for Hispanic Children* and author of various articles about library services and literature for young Hispanics, Allen has displayed her strong interest in the education of young minorities. In an article written for *Library Trends,* Allen presented results of research regarding study access to children's literature in several urban areas with high Hispanic populations. Her conclusions were that most school librarians had limited knowledge of the Spanish language and that few books in Spanish were available. Allen said in this article, "It is generally accepted that the responsibility of the school library is to provide books for all children—for information and pleasure reading. If libraries are not providing students with books they can read for information and pleasure, we need to reconsider the mission statement of the school library media center." According to Allen, "By the year 2000, one out of every four American public schoolchildren will come from a minority ethnic group. This multicultural student body, reflecting the country's pluralistic society, dictates immediate attention in terms of available resources."

Other articles written by Allen include "Vocabulary Instruction and Reading Comprehension with Bilingual Learning Disabled Students" (with C.S. Bos and D. J. Scanlon, 1989); "The Language of Literature" (1985); and "Holiday Mood Books: Views and Reviews" (1985). In 1984 Allen was involved in the production of a videotape instructional module entitled *A Contrastive Analysis of English-Spanish Phonemes.* In addition to her published research, Allen has written a story titled "Relajo en la Cocina," which will appear in a forthcoming Spanish literature textbook published by Harcourt Brace Jovanovich.

Initiates Programs for Minorities

In 1988 Allen was responsible for the initiation of minority programs at the University of Arizona, which resulted in a significant increase in recruitment and retention of minority students. She was also able to increase financial support for minority students through Graduate College fellowships that totaled $520,000 a year. In addition, she has been awarded federal grants for minority students totaling approximately $750,000. Allen attributes the high recruitment and retention rates partly to her "open door" policy, which means students can come by her office once a week to discuss problems or concerns and work on solutions.

Plays Role in National and International Advocacy

In addition to her work as division head, professor, and scholar, Allen has served as associate vice-president for Inter-American Relations since 1995. Part of her responsibility in this position is to represent the president and vice-president for research at national and international events whenever they cannot attend. She also advises and facilitates the matriculation process for international students from Mexico and South and Central America; arranges international academic events; collaborates with other organizations regarding international and minority education; and organizes research symposia that result from collaborative efforts between the University of Arizona and researchers from Mexican universities.

Allen also works with other universities in the United States, Mexico, and Canada as director of a Fund for the Improvement of Post Secondary Education (FIPSE) grant for North American Mobility. In addition, she has been a member of the Arizona Mexico Commission since 1972 and has served on the advisory board since 1992. As chair of this organization's Education Committee, she assists in the direction of a summer exchange program. She co-directs a cadre of researchers at the University of Arizona and the University of Sonora and supervises a faculty development program in which faculty from the University of Sonora receive a leave of absence in order to pursue a doctoral degree. Yet another project of Allen's is supervising a master's degree in architecture in conjunction with a program at the University of the Americas in Puebla. She has also been a member of the Consortium of North American Higher Education Consortium, a U.S.-Mexico border consortium that promotes international education between the two countries. In addition to the numerous grants Allen has been awarded, she has received the Antonio Certossimo Award, which is an award given by the governor of Arizona to the one person who has contributed the most to international relations every two years between the United States and Mexico.

Current Address: Graduate College Administration, Graduate College, Univ. of Arizona, Tucson, AZ 85721.

Sources:

Bethel, Kari. Telephone conversation with Adela Allen, May 1998.
Library Trends, Winter 1993.
University of Arizona Home Page. Available at: http://arizona.edu.

Isabel Allende
(1942–)
Author

Selected writings:

Civilice a su troglodita: Los impertinentes de Isabel Allende.
Lord Cochran, 1974.

La casa de los espiritus.: Plaza y Janes, 1982; translated by
Magda Bogin and published as *The House of the Spirits.*
Knopf, 1985.

La gorda de porcelana. Alfaguara, 1984.

De amor y de sombra. Plaza y Janes, 1984; translated by
Margaret Sayers Peden and published as *Of Love and
Shadows.* Knopf, 1987.

Eva Luna. Plaza y Janes, 1987; translated by Margaret
Sayers Peden and published as *Eva Luna.* Knopf, 1988.

Cuentos de Eva Luna. Plaza y Janes, translated by Margaret
Sayers Peden and published as *The Stories of Eva Luna.*
Atheneum, 1991.

El plan infinito. Plaza y Janes, translated by Margaret Sayers Peden and published as *The Infinite Plan.*
HarperCollins, 1993.

Paula, translated by Margaret Sayers Peden.
HarperCollins, 1995.

Afrodita: Cuentos, Recetas y Otros Afrodisiacos. Harpercollins,
1997; translated by Margaret Sayers Peden as *Aphrodite:
A Memoir of the Senses.* Harpercollins, 1998.

Overview

The author of several novels and a short fiction
collection, as well as plays and stories for children, Isabel
Allende has received international acclaim for her writing.
She earned the Quality Paperback Book Club New Voice
Award nomination for her debut novel, *La casa de los
espiritus* (1982; *The House of the Spirits*), which became a best
seller in Spain and West Germany in the 1980s and a 1994
movie, and the *Los Angeles Times* Book Prize nomination
for *De amor y de sombra* (1984; *Of Love and Shadows*). In 1988
Allende's third novel, *Eva Luna,* was voted One of the
Year's Best Books by *Library Journal.* At a nationally televised
ceremony at the John F. Kennedy Center for the Performing
Arts on September 23, 1996, Allende was one of the six
recipients of the Hispanic Heritage Awards, one of the
most prestigious awards in the Hispanic American community.
In addition to her writings, Allende has led the "Read
About Me" campaign to fund multicultural book collections
and promote multicultural authors.

Expresses Feminine Perspective, Drama, Magic
Realism

Many of Allende's books are noted for their feminine
perspective, dramatic qualities of romance and struggle,

Isabel Allende

and the magic realism genre often found in Latin American literature. Her female characters survive hardships—
imprisonment, starvation, the loss of loved ones—but
never lose their spirit or ability to love others. Of Allende's
House of Spirits, which has been compared to that of the
Nobel prize-winning author Gabriel Garcia Marquez's *One
Hundred Years of Solitude,* Lori Carlson observed in *Review:*
"There is a lot of love in *The House of the Spirits.* The love-
making of powerful men and naive women, worn-out
married couples and anxious rebels might even conjure up
the reader's personal experience. But there is another kind
of love in this book with which the reader cannot identify.
It is a kind that requires forgiving the person whose
torturous hand has shoved your face into a bucket of
excrement. A spiritual force that can overcome a world
sutured with evil, to beget art. Isabel Allende . . . tells in
this, her first novel, a vibrant story of struggle and survival
dedicated to her mother, grandmother, and 'other extraordinary' women in a country unnamed. Given the descriptions of events and people in the book . . . Chile quickly
comes to mind."

Spends Youth in South America

Allende was born on August 2, 1942, in Lima, Peru. Her
parents, Tomas, a Chilean diplomat, and Francisca (Llona
Barros) Allende divorced when she was three, and she
traveled with her mother to Santiago, Chile, where she was
raised in her grandparents' home. Allende graduated from
a private high school at the age of 16; three years later in

1962, she married her first husband, Miguel Frias, an engineer. Allende also went to work for the United Nations Food and Agricultural Organization in Santiago, where she was a secretary for several years. Later, she became a journalist, editor, and advice columnist. In addition, she worked as a television interviewer and on movie newsreels.

Flees Chile

When her uncle, Chilean president Salvador Allende, was assassinated in 1973 as part of a right-wing military coup against his socialist government, Allende's life changed profoundly. Initially, she did not think that the new regime would endure, but later she came to realize that it was too dangerous to stay in Chile. As a result, Allende, her husband, and their two children fled to Venezuela. Although she had established a successful career as a journalist in Chile, Allende nevertheless had a difficult time finding work in journalism in Venezuela. During her life in exile, Allende was inspired to write *The House of the Spirits*. The novel was adapted for the screen by the Danish writer and director Bille August and released in the United States in 1994. Translated into nearly 30 languages, *The House of the Spirits* is based on Allende's memories of her family and the political upheaval in her native country, the book chronicles the personal and political conflicts in the lives of successive generations of a family in an anonymous Latin American country. These events are principally communicated through the memories of the novel's three central characters: Esteban and Clara, the patriarch and matriarch of the Trueba family, and Alba, their leftist granddaughter who falls into the hands of torturers during a military coup.

Publishes *Of Love and Shadows*

The House of Spirits was followed by *Of Love and Shadows*, which concerns the switching at birth of two infant girls. One of the babies grows up to become the focus of a journalist's investigation, and the revelation of her assassination compels the reporter and photographer to go into exile. The *Detroit Free Press* described *Of Love and Shadows* as "a frightening, powerful work," in which Allende "proves her continued capacity for generating excellent fiction," while the *Toronto Globe and Mail* commented that "Allende has some difficulty in getting her novel started because she has to weave two stories separately, and seems to be relying initially too much on her skills as a journalist."

On a lecture tour to San Jose, California, to promote the publication of *Of Love and Shadows* in the United States, Allende met William Gordon, a lawyer, who was an admirer of her work and with whom she fell in love. Having been divorced from her first husband for about a year, she married Gordon in 1988, and has lived with him in their suburban home in Marin, California, ever since.

Becomes Powerful Storyteller

Allende's next book, *Eva Luna*, focuses on the relationship between Eva (an illegitimate scriptwriter and storyteller) and Rolfe Carle (an Austrian emigre filmmaker haunted by his father's Nazi past). The novel received positive reviews; for example, Abigail E. Lee in the *Times Literary Supplement* wrote, "Fears that Isabel Allende might be a 'one-book' writer . . . ought to be quashed by Eva Luna. . . . Allende moves between the personal and the political, between realism and fantasy, weaving two exotic coming-of-age stories—Eva Luna's and Rolfe Carle's—into the turbulent coming of age of her unnamed South American country." Further, Alan Ryan of the *Washington Post Book World* asserted that Eva Luna is "a remarkable novel, one in which a cascade of stories tumbles out before the reader, stories vivid and passionate and human enough to engage, in their own right, all the reader's attention and sympathy."

Allende followed up this novel with *Cuentos de Eva Luna* (1991; *The Stories of Eva Luna*), in which the heroine of Eva Luna relates several stories to her lover Carle. According to Alan Ryan in *USA Today,* "These stories transport us to a complex world of sensual pleasures, vivid dreams and breathless longings. It is a world in which passions are fierce, motives are profound and deeds have inexorable consequences." Anne Whitehouse of the *Baltimore Sun* noted that "Ms. Allende possesses the ability to penetrate the hearts of Eva's characters in a few brief sentences. . . . These are profound, transcendent stories, which hold the mirror up to nature and in their strangeness reveal us to ourselves."

Exhibits Stylistic Departure

The Eva Luna stories were followed by *El plan infinito* (1993; The Infinite Plan) which, in a stylistic departure for Allende, features a male hero in a North American setting. Gregory Reeves is the son of a traveling preacher and prophet who settles in the Hispanic barrio of Los Angeles after becoming ill. As the only Anglo boy in the district, Reeves is tormented by local gang members. Eventually, he finds his way out of the barrio, does a tour of duty in Vietnam, and goes on to study law at Berkeley. *The Infinite Plan* received less praise than Allende's previous books, Michiko Kakutani of the *New York Times* described the novel as a "Bildungsroman-cum-family saga that owes more to Judith Krantz than to Gabriel Garcia Marquez," concluding that it is "disappointing and mechanical." Still, as novelist Jane Smiley pointed out in her *Boston Globe* review, "Not many [emigre authors] have even attempted writing a novel from the point of view of a native of the new country."

Allende's 1995 work, *Paula,* was a heartrending, autobiographical account of the circumstances surrounding the lengthy illness and death of her daughter in 1991. It was written to relieve the emotional pain during the many hours that Allende spent in hospitals while her daughter lay in a year-long coma caused by prophyria. Commenting on the deeply emotive effect of *Paula*, the reviewer for *Publishers Weekly* declared that "[only] a writer of Allende's passion and skill could share her tragedy with her readers and leave them exhilarated and grateful."

Writes on Food, Eroticism

In 1998, Allende turned to the subject of food and eroticism in *Afrodita: Cuentos, Recetas y Otros Afrodisiacos*, translated in 1998 by Margaret Sayers Peden as *Aphrodite: A Memoir of the Senses*. A *Booklist* contributor remarked that Allende wanders delectably through the ways food arouses the senses, citing tales and truths, folklore and science. Although the book offers recipes, Allende's focus is on the link between food and eroticism. According to *Kirkus Reviews*, "Her tact amplifies the eros that pornography kills."

Sources:

"Aphrodite: A Memoir of the Senses." *Kirkus Reviews,* February 1, 1998.

Baltimore Sun, March 3, 1991.

Booklist, February 1, 1998.

Boston Globe, May 16, 1993, pp. B39, B42.

Chicago Tribune Book World, May 19, 1995, pp. 37-38.

Christian Science Monitor, June 7, 1985; May 27, 1987.

Cosmopolitan, January 1991.

Dallas Morning News, February 1991, pp. 6J, 8J.

Detroit Free Press, June 7, 1987.

Detroit News, June 14, 1987.

Globe and Mail (Toronto), June 24, 1985; June 27, 1987.

Hart, Patricia. *Narrative Magic in the Fiction of Isabel Allende.* Rutherford, NJ: Fairleigh Dickinson University Press, 1989.

London Review of Books, August 1, 1985, pp. 26-27.

Los Angeles Times Book Review, June 16, 1985; May 31, 1987; February 10, 1988; December 28, 1990, p. E5.

Mother Jones, December 1988, pp. 42-46.

Nation, July 20/27, 1985, pp. 52-54; March 11, 1991, pp. 314-16.

New Statesman, July 5, 1985, p. 29.

Newsweek, May 13, 1985, p. 82.

New York, April 11, 1994, p. 56+.

New York Newsday, July 23, 1993.

New York Review of Books, July 18, 1985, pp. 20-21.

New York Times, May 2, 1985; May 9, 1985, p. 23; May 20, 1987; February 4, 1988; June 25, 1993.

New York Times Book Review, May 12, 1985, pp. 1; May 22-23; July 12, 1987; October 23, 1988; January 20, 1991.

Observer, June 7, 1985, p. 21.

People, June 10, 1985, p. 145; June 1, 1987.

Philadelphia Inquirer, March 3, 1991.

La Prensa de San Antonio, June 16, 1996, p. 2B.

Publishers Weekly, March 1, 1985, p. 70; May 17, 1985; March 20, 1995.

Review, January-June, 1985, pp. 77-78.

Spectator, August 3, 1985.

Time, May 20, 1985, p. 79.

Times (London), July 4, 1985; July 9, 1987; March 22, 1989; March 23, 1989.

Times Literary Supplement, July 5, 1985; July 10, 1987; April 7-13, 1989.

Tribune Books (Chicago), October 9, 1988.

U.S. News and World Report, November 21, 1988.

USA Today, June 7, 1985, p. 4D; March 1, 1991.

Village Voice, June 4, 1985, p. 51; June 7, 1985.

Voice Literary Supplement, December, 1988.

Washington Post Book World, May 12, 1985, pp. 3-4; May 24, 1987; October 9, 1988.

Melba Alvarado
(1919–)
Organization executive, community activist

On the second Sunday of each October in New York City, the normal, slower pace of the weekend is changed by the bright colors and joyous sounds of the United Hispanic American Parade. One of the founders of this spectacular event is Melba Alvarado, a Cuban-born community activist who has spent many years of her life bringing this celebra-

Melba Alvarado

tion to fruition. Her efforts to display the beauty and diversity of Hispanic American culture have resulted in this annual festival that has become a much-anticipated community event.

Melba Alvarado was born on August 5, 1919, in Mayari, Cuba. The Alvarado family—parents Luis and Mariana, Melba, and her seven younger siblings—came to the United States when she was 15 years of age. They settled in New York City where she attended Harlem Evening High School. "I had to work and then go to school at night," Alvarado said in a telephone interview. "I was the oldest of eight children, and I had to help contribute to the family's livelihood." The elder Alvarado had been a tailor in his homeland, and he opened his own dry cleaning and tailor shop in Manhattan. Mariana Alvardo worked with him and also helped to support the family with her sewing.

Juggles School, Career, and Civic Duty

Even as a teenager, Alvarado showed signs of civic interest. While in high school, she founded an American Culture Club for Spanish-speaking students. After graduation, she attended City College of New York (CCNY), part of the City University of New York system. She finished two years of college before the demands of work became too much, and she was forced to drop out.

For the next thirty years, Alvarado worked for Faye Knit Wear in New York City. She began as a floor girl doing piecework and worked her way up to manager and then supervisor. "I was one of the family," Alvarado said of her years at Faye Knit Wear, which closed its doors in 1966. Her next job was with Travelers Premium doing public relations and promotion. When that firm closed in the 1980s, she worked for DFJ Tours for eight more years and then retired.

Brings the Parade to Life

"My life is divided into three parts," Alvarado said. "Family, work, and civic activism. I never mingled my work with civic activities. My work was my work." When Alvarado began her working career, she was already forming the organization that would become the United Hispanic American Parade, or Desfile de la Hispanidad, of which she is a cofounder. She has also served as the parade's president, vice president, and financial secretary through the years. Each year, this celebration unites the people of all Hispanic countries in the Americas. The parade route in New York City is from 44th Street straight up 5th Avenue to 79th Street. As Alvarado explains, "Each nation sends two delegates to the parade committee. The entire purpose of the parade is to maintain and show the culture of different Hispanic nations and exhibit their special qualities. Each nation is diverse and has its own culture and music."

For her work in bringing this joyous celebration to fruition, Alvarado was named Woman of the Month in October of 1997 by *Temas* magazine, a Hispanic publication. Alvardo says that she is not a political person and will not join any political organization. "I go for culture," she says. "Bringing people together, getting cultures together. Humanity, not politics. I always believe we must never forget our roots and we must know American culture as well and integrate." Alvarado has received praise from the king of Spain, among others, and medals from such organizations as the Federation of Hispanic Societies, the American Legion, and Club Cubano, an inter-American organization that helps immigrants find work and learn English. Alvarado is a member and she says that Club Cubano has been doing civic and cultural work for more than half a century. "It's the oldest Cuban club in the East," she says with pride.

For Alvarado, one of the many positive aspects of the parade is its celebration of the marriage between Hispanic culture and U.S. mainstream culture, a marriage she has seen at work in her own life. "I've learned to balance two cultures," said Alvarado. "As a child we kept our Hispanic culture at home. I also love American life, art, and the theater. There have always been two cultures in my life and I always enjoyed them both." Thanks to Alvarado, many other can now celebrate the two cultures.

Sources:

Blue, Rose. Telephone interview with Melba Alvarado, March 3, 1998.

Aida Alvarez

Federal government agency director

Aida Alvarez is the first Hispanic woman to head the U.S. Small Business Administration (SBA) and the first person of Puerto Rican descent to hold a Cabinet-level post in the U.S. government. As such, she is part of the economic policy-making team in the Clinton White House, responsible for ensuring that small businesses in the United States receive the federal support needed to be successful. She has helped minorities and women break into the business world by making it easier for them to qualify for loans.

Born in Aguadilla, a seaport in northwestern Puerto Rico, Alvarez grew up in New York City. She graduated cum laude from Harvard and holds honorary law degrees from Iona College in New York, Bethany College in Kansas, and Inter-American University in Puerto Rico.

Aida Alvarez

Maintains Varied Interests

Alvarez brings a rich and varied career background to her position as administrator of SBA. Before becoming involved in banking and business, she spent eleven years as a newspaper and television journalist in New York City. She won a Front Page Award and an Associated Press Award for her reporting at the *New York Post*. As a reporter for Metromedia Television (Channel 5), she received an Associated Press Award for Excellence, and as a reporter/ anchor for the *Ten O'Clock News,* Alvarez won an Emmy nomination for her work.

Her tenure in New York City was not devoted entirely to journalism. She found time for public service as well, serving as vice president of public affairs and special projects for the New York City Health and Hospitals Corporation. For that work, she was cited for distinguished service to the people of New York by the New York State Hispanic Chamber of Commerce. She was a member of both the governor's State Judicial Screening Committee and the mayor's Committee on Appointments. In addition, she was a commissioner on the New York City Charter Revision Commission, which restructured the city government.

Leaving the journalism field, Alvarez entered the world of investment banking. She worked in public finance for seven years, first in New York City and then in San Francisco, for Bear Stearns and First Boston Corporation, where she led teams of bankers in marketing tax-exempt bond issues. While in California, she was a member of the United Way's San Francisco County Leadership Board, the Rebuild L.A. Finance Task Force, and the California Council for Environmental and Economic Balance.

Enters Government Finance

In March of 1993, President Bill Clinton chose Alvarez to become the first director of the Office of Federal Housing Enterprise Oversight (OFHEO). This appointment meant a move to Washington, DC, for Alvarez, her husband, Dr. Raymond J. Baxter, and daughter, Aurora Alvarez-Baxter. OFHEO, pronounced "o-free-o" in government lingo, was set up to oversee the soundness and safety of the Federal National Mortgage Association (Fannie Mae) and the Federal Home Loan Mortgage Corporation (Freddie Mac). As director of this small but powerful government regulatory agency, Alvarez established the structure for oversight of Fannie Mae and Freddie Mac, the nation's two largest housing finance companies. They constitute the basis of the trillion-dollar secondary mortgage market. After accepting the job at OFHEO, Alvarez remarked to *American Banker,* "I remember all the warnings that I had gotten when I first came on board—about how the job was too big, too difficult, undoable, whatever. I didn't really believe it then, and I know I was right. . . ."

New to Washington, DC, Alvarez witnessed the irony of being empowered with building up a new agency in a city where the focus in the late twentieth century is consolidating or scaling down. Although she initially went to a local office supply store for basic office items—and paid for them out of her own pocket—she quickly learned the ways of Washington, DC. By the time she left OFHEO, the staff had climbed to 45 people, and Congress had appropriated a budget of several million dollars.

At OFHEO, Alvarez established herself as a hands-on manager, conceding in an interview with *Savings & Community Banker* that this was not a nine-to-five job with "people in defined boxes." However, she tried to set an example by "coming in first and leaving last." In fact, the quality of her staff was given the most credit for the success of the office during her tenure at OFHEO. "I think that the people you hire make a significant difference," Alvarez said. "Everybody was really enthusiastic about the challenge."

Seeks Greater Challenges

A new and even greater challenge was in store for Aida Alvarez in 1997 when, on March 7, she was sworn in as the twentieth administrator of the U.S. Small Business Administration. This position elevated her to Cabinet-level rank in the Clinton Administration, the first Puerto Rican and the first Hispanic woman to be so honored. The SBA, founded in 1953, delivers comprehensive financial and business development programs for entrepreneurs. It is the nation's largest single financial backer of small business, with direct and guaranteed business and disaster loans worth more than $45 billion. The agency's primary functions are to guarantee small business loans made by banks, to advocate the awarding of federal government contracts to small firms owned by "socially and economically disadvantaged" persons, and to make long- and short-term loans to businesses that experience loss or damage, due to natural disasters.

Although Alvarez went to the SBA without a background in small business, her investment banking and finance company experience served her well as head of an administration that was on somewhat shaky ground. In an era of budget cuts and increasing need for access to capital by small business entrepreneurs, the resources of the SBA were strained. Some minority business leaders criticized the agency for lack of responsiveness to their concerns.

Addresses SBA Budgetary Crisis

Almost immediately, Alvarez was faced with a crisis. Funding was stretched to the limit, making the shutdown of the SBA's largest loan program that is depended upon by some 8,000 lenders, a real possibility. Some tight recalculating of the agency's costs saved the program at the last minute. But the SBA still faces trials. As reported by *American Banker,* Paul Leliakov, president of commercial lending for the MoneyStore, acknowledged that Alvarez has "inherited a fairly difficult set of circumstances." Anthony J. Feraro was quoted in the same source as saying, ". . . [H]er number one job is to figure out the problem with the continued shortfall (in SBA lending authority) and how to fix it long-term."

Once on the job, Alvarez quickly aligned herself with minority businesses. In a speech shortly after she was sworn in by Vice President Al Gore, she said, "[b]ecause of the dynamic growth in the number of women- and minority-owned businesses, the SBA needs to find ways to help create access to credit and capital, to procurement opportunities, and to information, counseling, and business development training." Because she believes that the demographics of the United States are changing, Alvarez wants to strongly focus the SBA on lending billions of dollars to those small businesses owned by women, African Americans, native Alaskans, and Native Americans. In late 1997, she told the *Chicago Tribune* that the SBA must "increase the number of loan guarantees to these groups, just as the agency has toward Hispanic-owned businesses." It is her intention that by the year 2000, Hispanic-owned businesses will have received a total of $2.5 billion in guaranteed loans.

Creates More Hispanic Business Opportunities

In January 1998 the SBA and the Texas Association of Mexican American Chambers of Commerce (TAMACC) signed the Memorandum of Understanding agreement designed to create additional business opportunities for Hispanic American entrepreneurs in Texas. According to Alvarez, "This historic partnership means that many more Hispanic-owned businesses will be able to learn about and take advantage of SBA's programs, services, and financial assistance." Additionally, the SBA and TAMACC will jointly conduct workshops for Hispanic American women entrepreneurs to provide training on access to capital entrepreneurial skills and the basics of forming a business. It is hoped that the agreement will serve as a model for agreements in the future and will build more effective working relationships between the SBA and business organizations throughout the United States.

Strengthens Loan Program for Women, Minorities

The new director's answer to lack of access to capital by small business owners is to strengthen her agency's prequalification loan program. Minority and women business owners have historically had trouble qualifying for business loans. Alvarez has started to change that situation. According to the current program, companies owned by women and minorities can prequalify through the SBA for loans of $250,000 or less. Those businesses can qualify for up to $25,000 in short-term, smaller loans provided by nonprofit groups, which are approved by the SBA. Alvarez believes in her work. "It is critical," she told *Hispanic,* "to the economy of our nation that the small business community continues to flourish. Together with our private sector partners, our mission at the SBA is to provide entrepreneurs with access to capital and credit, business education and training opportunities, and to serve as an advocate for small business. We acknowledge with pride and gratitude the contributions made by the small business community to the nation's economic growth and quality of life."

Current Address: Small Business Administration, 409 3rd St., SW, Washington, DC 20416.

Sources:

Buck, Genevieve. "Official Pledges to Focus Billions on Minority Firms." *Chicago Tribune,* October 14, 1997, sec. 3, p. 3.

Nixon, Brian. "Inventing government: a profile of Aida Alvarez." *Savings & Community Banker,* April, 1994, pp. 27-33.

Prakash, Snigdha. "Keeping tabs on risk as Fannie and Freddie evolve." *American Banker,* October 11, 1996, p. 9.

Riley, Jennifer. "Small Business Advocate: Hispanics hope the SBA will be responsive under Aida Alvarez." *Hispanic,* September 30, 1997, p. 34.

Villa, Diana. "Hispanic Entrepreneur: SBA Offers More to Texas Entrepreneurs." *Hispanic,* May 1998, p. 64.

Who's Who in America, 51st edition. New Providence, NJ: Marquis Who's Who, 1996.

Doris Alvarez

Principal, writer, lecturer

Doris Alvarez is a revolutionary within the school system, fervently working to ensure that high schools provide quality education for all students, regardless of race, social, or economic background. Through her tireless efforts, she improves the educational opportunities available to immigrant, minority, and economically disadvantaged secondary school students by redefining the role and function of the high school. Evidence of her success can be seen in Hoover High School in San Diego, CA. Since she was appointed principal of that school in 1987, Hoover's dropout rate has declined significantly from 13 percent to 2.3 percent, and the percentage of its students gaining acceptance to college has risen to 50 percent.

Making A Difference

Alvarez was profoundly influenced in her youth by her mother, a hard-working woman who stressed to her children the need to show commitment to a vocation and trustworthiness to others. She also learned valuable lessons from her philosophy teacher while attending the American High School in Mexico City. His course, which made use of

Doris Alvarez

project-based and inquiry-oriented teaching, forced students to demonstrate their understanding of the material through self-expression rather than multiple choice examination. Alvarez found the experience exhilarating, and has applied similar methods in her own teaching.

After graduating from high school, Alvarez continued her training. She received an B.A. in social science and English and an M.S. in counseling from San Diego State University, and a Ph.D. from the joint doctorate program of Claremont Graduate School and San Diego State University. She also received credentials in administrative services and pupil personnel services from San Diego State University.

Choosing A Career Path

Alvarez obtained her first teaching position at a junior high school in 1962. Her supervisor took an active role in her professional development, often visiting Alvarez's classes and offering constructive criticism regarding her performance. By the end of her first year, Alvarez was selected to attend a Good Teachers Conference in Los Angeles. Alvarez accepted a teaching position at Anaheim High School in 1964, remaining there for only one year before joining an adult education program in Claremont, CA.

Alvarez embarked on a career change in 1972, becoming a junior high school counselor. She left that position after one year, altogether abandoning the field of education for several years to pursue professional development and other personal goals. Fortunately, Alvarez's career path led her back to the field of education. In 1977, she signed on as an educational consultant with a private-sector company, but only worked there for one year. While there, she also published her first works, "Be a Winner" and "With a Little Luck," written in conjunction with R. Busby, in *Student Resource Publications* issued by the San Diego Unified School District. The experience was enough renew her interest in education and, in 1978, Alvarez returned to the school system as district head counselor for the San Diego Unified Guidance Department. She remained in this position for three years before entering educational administration as vice principal of Correia Junior High in San Diego, CA in 1981.

Innovative Educator

San Diego's education system was not without challenges, thus demanding a new way of thinking to tackle these obstacles. At Correia Junior High Alvarez began to develop her own approach to the education of an ethnically, socially, and economically-diverse urban student body. In 1986, five years after she was named vice principal of Correia, Alvarez landed the same post at San Diego's Hoover High School. This school is composed of many of the diverse ethnic groups scattered across the United States, including several recent immigrant groups. More than 30 different native languages are spoken here; more than half of the student body is Hispanic American; roughly 20 percent is Asian American, and another 20 percent is African American. Most of the students are from impoverished homes. At the time Alvarez came on board, the dropout rate was 13 percent, and many who managed to graduate did not pursue higher learning.

The statistics looked bleak but Alvarez remained undaunted. In 1987 she was named principal of Hoover, a position she continues to hold today. As the school's leader, Alvarez seeks to adjust academic programs to meet the needs of students instead of making students conform to traditional curricula and schedules. Alvarez recognized that social and economic obstacles were educational barriers for many of her students, and she sought to remove those hurdles. She established night and weekend classes for working students. For students distracted by health problems but lacking access to decent health care, Alvarez set up a health clinic within the school. The Catholic Diocese of San Diego opposed the clinic, citing its intention to distribute contraceptives and birth control information and provide abortion referrals. Alvarez refused to give up and sought common ground between supporters and opponents of the clinic. Eventually a compromise was reached: all of the clinic's reproductive health services would be located off-campus. The clinic was then able to open.

As Alvarez continued to revolutionize her school and the performance of Hoover students began to improve, she received increasing recognition of her achievements from local, state, and national education organizations. Her services to education in the San Diego area were officially recognized for the first time in 1987, when Alvarez received a PTA Honorary Service Award. She was named by the Apple Computer Company as a "Person Who Has the Power to Be Her Best" in 1989, and received designation as the "California Principal of the Year" by Metlife and the National Association of Secondary School Principals (NASSP) in 1996. National recognition came from Phi Delta Kappa, which bestowed upon Alvarez its Service Award for 1994-95, and the NASSP, which named her "National Principal of the Year" in 1997. She also had the honor of delivering the graduation address for the College of Education at San Diego State University the same year.

Alvarez is in demand as a writer and speaker in the fields of counseling and education. She regularly publishes articles, including "Professional Growth Seminars Encourage Shared Decision Making, Collaboration" in *NASSP Bulletin* in January of 1992 and "Prevention in Practice" in *Medlink* in June of 1989; and has addressed national bodies, including the National Reading Conference and the American Education Research Association.

Practicing lessons she learned from her mother as a child allows Alvarez to increase educational opportunities for all Hoover High students. She encourages hard work, commitment, loyalty, and collective responsibility among both her students and her staff. She also follows the examples of her own mentors by providing constant, constructive feedback to her teachers and encouraging the use of project-based and inquiry-oriented teaching and learning methods. The success of her efforts is shown by her school's declining dropout rate and phenomenal 98 percent graduation rate. Under Alvarez's direction Hoover has been recognized by the U.S. Department of Education as one of five urban high schools on the cutting edge of educational reform.

Despite her many successes in Hoover, Alvarez's enthusiasm and commitment to the school has intensified, as she continues to introduce innovative solutions to seemingly formidable situations. The most recent evidence of Alvarez's commitment to her students is shown by her unselfish pledge to use the NASSP National Principal of the Year Award's $10,000 grant to establish a fund to help Hoover students create their own businesses.

Current Address: Herbert Hoover High School, San Diego City Schools, 4474 El Cajon Blvd., San Diego, CA 92115-4397.

Sources:

Eldridge, Grant. Curriculum vitae and other materials provided by Doris Alvarez, 1998.
Henry, Tamara. "Principal Honored for Thinking Small and Creating Big Change." *USA Today,* February 6, 1997, p. D11.
"100 Most Influential Hispanics." *Hispanic Business,* October, 1997, p. 50.
"San Diego High School Principle Honored." *Los Angeles Times,* February 7, 1997, p. B10.

Julia Alvarez
Author, poet

Selected writings:

Homecoming. New York: Grove Press, 1984.
How the Garcia Girls Lost Their Accents. New York: Plume, 1991.
In the Time of Butterflies. New York: Penguin USA, 1995.
The Other Side/El Otro Lado. New York: New American Library, 1996.
Yo! New York: Algonquin, 1997.

Overview

In her poetry and prose, Julia Alvarez has expressed her feelings about her immigration to the United States. Although she was born in New York City, she spent her early

Julia Alvarez

years in the Dominican Republic. After her family's immigration to America, she and her sisters struggled to find a place for themselves in their new world. Alvarez has used her dual experience as a starting point for the exploration of culture through writing. Alvarez's work voices many of the concerns of Hispanic women and has received critical acclaim.

Life in the Dominican Republic

Reminiscing on her youth in an article in *American Scholar,* Alvarez wrote, "Although I was raised in the Dominican Republic by Dominican parents in an extended Dominican family, mine was an American childhood." As she described her family background, her father's once-wealthy family had supported the wrong side during the revolution while her mother's parents benefitted from their support of the people in power. They lived on her mother's family property. Life in the compound was somewhat communal; Alvarez and her sisters were brought up along with their cousins and supervised by her mother, maids, and many aunts.

Although her own family was not as well off as their relatives, Alvarez did not feel inferior. None of the cousins were allowed to forget that she was born in America. Her father, a doctor who ran the nearby hospital, had met her mother while she was attending school in America. While such extravagances as shopping trips to America were beyond their financial means, Alvarez's family was highly

influenced by American attitudes and goods. If her mother could not buy her daughters American clothing, she made sure that Alvarez and her sisters were as fashionable as their cousins. The children ate American food, attended the American school, and for a special treat, ate ice cream from the American ice cream parlor. American cars were bought at the American dealership, shopping was done at the American's store, and American appliances were flaunted in the compound. The entire extended family was obsessed with America; to the children, it was a fantasy land.

As Alvarez acknowledges in her article in *American Scholar,* her family's association with the United States may have saved her father's life. The members of her mother's family were respected because of their ties with America. Alvarez's uncles had attended Ivy League colleges, and her grandfather was a cultural attaché to the United Nations. The dictator of the Dominican Republic, Rafael Leonidas Trujillo Molina, could not victimize a family with such strong American ties. He would not destroy them for their money, and he hesitated to struggle with them for political reasons. When Alvarez's father secretly joined the forces attempting to oust Trujillo, the police set up surveillance of the compound. It was rumored that, respected family or not, her father was soon to be apprehended. Just before the police were to capture her father in 1960, a U.S. agent, known to Alvarez as Tio Vic, warned him; he ushered the family into an airplane and out of the country. Describing the scene as their plane landed in America in *American Scholar,* Alvarez wrote, "All my childhood I had dressed like an American, eaten American foods, and befriended American children. I had gone to an American school and spent most of the day speaking and reading English. At night, my prayers were full of blond hair and blue eyes and snow. . . . All my childhood I had longed for this moment of arrival. And here I was, an American girl, coming home at last."

Experiences Acculturation Problems in the United States

Alvarez's homecoming was not what she had expected it to be. Although she was thrilled to be back in America, she would soon face homesickness, alienation, and prejudice. She missed her cousins, her family's large home in the compound, and the respect her family name demanded. Alvarez, her parents, and her sisters squeezed themselves and their possessions into a tiny apartment. As she related to *Brújula <> Compass,* the experience was like a crash: "The feeling of loss caused a radical change in me. It made me an introverted little girl." Alvarez became an avid reader, immersing herself in books and, eventually, writing.

Alvarez went on to college. She earned undergraduate and graduate degrees in literature and writing and became an English professor at Middlebury College in Vermont. She received grants from the National Endowment for the Arts and The Ingram Merrill Foundation in addition to a PEN Oakland/Josephine Miles Award for excellence in multicultural literature. She published several collections of poetry including *Homecoming*, which appeared in 1984, and by 1987 she was working on a collection of stories. When Alvarez published *How the Garcia Girls Lost Their Accents* in 1991, the 290-page novel received considerable attention. The past decade had seen a surge of ethnic novels, and *Garcia Girls* came to be known as a notable example of the genre.

How the Garcia Girls Lost Their Accents

Rather than a straight narrative, *How the Garcia Girls Lost Their Accents* is a reverse-chronological order series of 15 interwoven stories chronicling four sisters and their parents. A comparison with Alvarez's article in *American Scholar* suggests that these stories are autobiographical; like her family, the Garcia family is Dominican and displaced in America. Like Alvarez and her sisters, the Garcia girls struggle to adapt to their new environment and assimilate themselves into American culture.

The first group of stories is dated "1989-1972." Thus, the novel's first story seems to be its ending. Entitled, "Antojos," which is Spanish for "cravings," this story is a memory of one of the sisters, Yolanda, and her return to the Dominican Republic as an adult. Yolanda (whose story ends the novel and acts as Alvarez's alter ego) has secretly decided to make her home here, having found life in the United States unfulfilling. When she ignores the warnings of her wealthy relatives and drives into the country for the guava fruit she has been craving, she faces disappointment. She is regarded as an American despite her native roots, and although she finds her guavas, her romantic journey is marred by her feelings as an outsider. Alvarez ends this story ambiguously—similar to the rest of the stories. The attempts of Yolanda and her sisters to lead successful lives in the United States are presented more as memory fragments than stories with definite beginnings and endings.

The next story focuses on Sofia, the youngest of the girls. At this point, however, the four girls are women, with husbands and careers. The details of Sofia's break with her father over her decision to take a lover before marriage are presented, and the events at a birthday party she prepared for her father are recounted. Sofia cannot be totally forgiven, nor can she ever return to the Dominican Republic; in the process of becoming an American girl of the 1960s, she has gone beyond the moral limits imposed by her father, who personifies life in the old world.

The third story relates some background information as it reveals a mother's perceptions of her four girls. During a family gathering, Mamita tells her favorite story about each of the girls, and the reader learns that Sandi spent time in a mental institution after almost starving herself to death. The fourth story about Yolanda reveals that she too had a mental breakdown of her own after a failed relationship, and in the next story she becomes the narrator. In "The Rudy Elmenhurst Story," Yolanda's tale of her reluctance

to sleep with the dashing young man she loved because of his casual approach to the matter explains her ensuing trouble with men as well as her problems assimilating into American youth culture: "Catholic or not, I still thought it a sin for a guy to just barge in five years later with a bottle of expensive wine and assume you'd drink out of his hand. A guy who had ditched me, who had haunted my sexual awakening with a nightmare of self-doubt. For a moment as I watched him get in his car and drive away, I felt a flash of that old self-doubt."

The memories in the second section of the novel recall the years from 1960 to 1970. The girls are younger, and they are experiencing their first years as immigrants. Attempts they made to reconcile themselves to their new culture are challenged by their parents, who want their children to "mix with the 'right kind' of Americans," and the girls are threatened with having to spend time on the Island, which they have come to dread. In this section, the girls save their sister from a macho cousin's imposition, a pervert exposes himself to Carla, and Yolanda sees snow for the first time and thinks it is fall-out from a nuclear bomb.

The final story in this section, "Floor Show," focuses on Sandi's perception of events as the family spends a scandalous evening with an American doctor and his drunkenly indiscreet wife in a Spanish restaurant. Sandi is shocked and upset when this woman kisses her father and later dances with the flamenco dancers that the young girl so admires. Cautioned by her mother to behave at the important dinner, Sandi does as she is told and stays quiet until she is offered a flamenco doll by the American woman, who seems to understand her desire for it. "Sandi was not going to miss her chance. This woman had kissed her father. This woman had ruined the act of the beautiful dancers. The way Sandi saw it, this woman owed her something." The woman gave Sandi something more than the doll; her smile "intimated the things Sandi was just beginning to learn, things that the dancers knew all about, which was why they danced with such vehemence, such passion."

In the third and final section, "1960-1956," America is still a dream—the family is still on the island. The first story is divided into two parts and recalls the family's traumatic encounter with the guardia, or secret police, and their subsequent flight from their home. From that moment on, the tales regress to the girls' early memories of life in the huge de la Torre compound. Yolanda tells of the presents her grandmother brought the children from America and an ensuing encounter with her cousin, Sandi recalls her art lessons and the fright she had at the instructor's home, Carla remembers the mechanical bank her father brought her from F.A.O. Schwartz in New York and the maid who desperately wanted it.

Finally, Yolanda concludes the novel with one of her earliest memories—she stole a kitten (which she named

Schwartz, after the famous toy store) from its mother and then abandoned it, even though she had been warned by a strange hunter: "To take it away would be a violation of its natural right to live." The mother cat haunted the girl until she left the island, and, as Yolanda confides in her narration, "There are still times I wake up at three o'clock in the morning and peer into the darkness. At that hour and in that loneliness, I hear her, a black furred thing lurking in the corners of my life, her magenta mouth opening, wailing over some violation that lies at the center of my art."

The praise Alvarez received for her first novel outweighed the criticism that a new novelist often encounters. *The New York Times Book Review* found that Alvarez "beautifully captured the threshold experience of the new immigrant, where the past is not yet a memory and the future remains an anxious dream." *Hispanic*'s critic wrote, "Well-crafted, although at times overly sentimental, these stories provide a glimpse into the making of another American family with a Hispanic surname." And the *Library Journal* reported, "Alvarez is a gifted, evocative storyteller of promise."

Recent Work Receives Praise

Alvarez followed up the success of her first novel with *In the Time of Butterflies* in 1995. The story follows the lives of the four Mirabel sisters during the time of the Trujillo regime in the Dominican Republic. Alvarez fictionalized the lives of these real-life revolutionaries—three of whom were murdered for their resistance to regime—to form this compelling novel. The following year, Alvarez published a second collection of poetry titled *The Other Side*, which was also released in Spanish under the title *El Otro Lado*.

Alvarez revisits the Garcia characters in her 1997 novel, *Yo!*, which is constructed via a series of monologues about the character Yolanda as told by those around her. Besides providing a profound character study of Yolanda, the book is a meditation on the writing life and continues to explore the theme of cultural duality introduced in Alvarez's earlier works. The myriad of voices and stories create a multifaceted novel that spotlights the Hispanic experience.

Alvarez told *Brújula <> Compass* that while she had a few ideas for her next work and thought she may write another novel, she was not certain what she would write. "That is the most passionate part of the process of writing. It is only possible to discover it as it is done; upon writing the ideas . . . a direction is found. A voice is discovered, the rhythm, the characters, but one cannot know beforehand." Her work is praised for its significance to Hispanic culture and to Hispanic women in particular. In the words of a critic for *Más*, Alvarez brings "a bilingual and bicultural vision" that highlights women's experiences.

Current Address: Algonquin Books of Chapel Hill, PO Box 2225, Chapel Hill, NC 27515.

Sources:

Alvarez, Julia. "An American Childhood in the Dominican Republic." *American Scholar,* Winter 1987, pp. 71-85.
Book Review. *Atlanta Journal and Atlanta Constitution,* August 11, 1991, p. A13.
Book Review. *Publisher's Weekly,* April 5, 1991, p. 133.
Brújula <> Compass, January-February 1992, p. 16.
Estrada, Mary Batts. "Four Sisters and a World of Difference." *Washington Post,* June 20, 1991, p. D11.
Fisher, Ann H. Book Review. *Library Journal,* May 1, 1991, p. 102.
Freeman, Judith. "A Powerful Move Back to Ethnic Roots." *Los Angeles Times,* June 7, 1991, p. E4.
Heller, Amanda. Book Review. *Boston Globe,* May 26, 1991, p. A13.
Hispanic, June 1991, p. 55.
Más, November-December 1991, p. 100.
Nuestro, November 1984, pp. 34+; March 1985, pp. 52+; January-February 1986, pp. 32+.
Rifkind, Donna. "Speaking American." *The New York Times Book Review,* October 6, 1991, p. 14.
School Library Journal, September 1991, p. 292.

Angeles Alvariño
(1916–)
Marine scientist

Selected writings:

Atlantic Chaetognatha, Distribution and Essential Notes of Systematics. Travaux Spanish Institute of Oceanography, 1969.
Siphonophores of the Pacific, with a Revision of the World Distribution. Bulletin Scripps Institution of Oceanography, University of California Press, 1971.

Overview

Angeles Alvariño de Leira, known professionally as Dr. Angeles Alvariño, is a fishery research biologist and marine scientist. For more than four decades, she has made an immense contribution to knowledge about marine zooplankton and its ecology and geographic distribution. During the course of her work, she has discovered 22 new ocean species.

Born in Spain

Alvariño was born on October 3, 1916, in El Ferrol, Spain, to Antonio Alvariño Grimaldos and Maria del Carmen Gonzales Diaz-Saavedra de Alvariño. An intelligent, curious child, Alvariño often enjoyed her physician-father's library, including his volumes on natural history. She aspired to become a physician herself, but her father discouraged such a choice. He did not want her to experience, as he had, the pain associated with patients whose suffering could not be alleviated. Alvariño studied a wide range of courses in physical and natural sciences, social science, and humanities during her undergraduate years from 1930 to 1933 at the Lycee. After passing final examinations and completing two dissertations for baccalaureate degrees in both science and letters, she graduated summa cum laude in 1933 from the University of Santiago de Compostela, Spain. During the next year, Alvariño's desire to study medicine persisted, but her father's viewpoint remained unchanged. Therefore, she entered the University of Madrid in 1934 to study natural sciences. Her studies were interrupted when the university was closed during the Spanish Civil War (1936-39). It was not until 1951 that she earned her master's degree.

An institute appointment in 1952 as a marine biologist-oceanographer resulted from Alvariño's success in a competitive examination. In 1953 a British Council Fellowship enabled her to work on zooplankton at the Marine Biological Laboratory in Plymouth, England. At the Plymouth lab, she met Dr. F. S. Russell, who directed her attention to chaetognaths, siphonophores, and hydromedusae, in which she has never lost interest. In order to do active research, Alvariño left teaching in 1948 to become a research biologist with the Spanish Department of Sea Fisheries in Madrid. That same year, despite a ban against women, she began to conduct research and study oceanography at the Spanish Institute of Oceanography in Madrid. The quality of her work persuaded officials to admit her as a student researcher in 1950. During those same years, academic work at the University of Madrid led in 1951 to a doctoral certificate, for which she wrote three separate theses, in experimental psychology, chemistry, and plant ecology. In 1940 Alvariño married Sir Eugenio Leira Manso, Captain of the Spanish Royal Navy and Knight of the Royal and Military Order of Saint Hermenegild. Alvariño continued her studies at the University of Madrid and in 1941 was awarded a master's degree in natural sciences. From 1941 to 1948, she taught biology, zoology, botany, and geology at various colleges in El Ferrol.

Gains New Opportunities in the United States

A Fulbright fellowship in 1956 enabled Alvariño to conduct research in Massachusetts at the Woods Hole Oceanographic Institute. Impressed by her work, Mary Sears, president of the first U.S. Oceanographic Congress, recommended Alvariño to Dr. Roger Revelle, the director of the Scripps Institute of Oceanography at La Jolla, California. He offered Alvariño a position as a biologist, and she accepted. Alvariño's years of research at Scripps produced a significant body of knowledge about chaetognaths, siphonophores, and hydromedusae. Her Scripps research also contributed toward completion of work toward a doctoral degree at the University of Madrid, which award-

ed her a doctor of sciences degree in 1967, summa cum laude.

To expand her research opportunities further, Alvariño accepted a position as a fisheries biologist in 1970 with the Southwest Fisheries Science Center (SWFSC) in La Jolla, a division of the newly formed National Marine Fisheries Service. There, she continued research on predatory chaetognaths, siphonophores, and hydromedusae and their relationship to larval fish survival.

Continues Studies into Retirement

Although she officially retired in 1987, Alvariño continues her work, adding to the body of knowledge about zooplankton she has already compiled. She has shed light on how zooplankton relate to the dynamics of the oceanic environment and about which ones are "indicator species," those species associated with specific currents or concentrations of other aquatic life, including spawning fish and their eggs and larvae. On July 23, 1993, Alvariño was awarded the Great Silver Medal of Galicia by King Juan Carlos I and Queen Sophia of Spain. She participated in numerous expeditions aboard research vessels of several countries and was the first woman to serve as a scientist aboard a British research vessel. Alvariño and her husband live in La Jolla. Their only child, Angeles Leira-Alvariño, is an architect and city planner. In addition to her first love, marine science, Alvariño enjoys classical music, literature, and art. She believes visual art and music in their clarity are "the best expression of the human being."

Sources:

Smith, Susan and Connie Blair. Interviews with Dr. Angeles Alvariño.

Gloria E. Anzaldúa
(1942–)
Author, editor, women's rights activist

Selected writings:

This Bridge Called My Back: Writings by Radical Women of Color. Edited with Cherríe Moraga. Persephone Press, 1981. Also published under the title *Esta puente, mi espalda: Voces de mujeres tercermundistas en los Estados Unidos.* Spanish translation by Ana Castillo and Norma Alarcón. ISM Press, 1988.
Borderlands/La Frontera: The New Mestiza. Spinsters/Aunt Lute Press, 1987.
Making Face/Making Soul: Creative and Critical Perspectives by Women of Color. Spinsters/Aunt Lute Press, 1990.

Friends from the Other Side. Children's Book Press, 1993.
Prietita and the Ghost Woman. Children's Book Press, 1995.

Overview

An outspoken feminist, lesbian, writer, and activist, Gloria Anzaldúa refuses to be labeled and defies those who expect political correctness from her. As co-editor, with Cherríe Moraga, of *This Bridge Called My Back: Writings by Radical Women of Color,* she contends that oppressed people "of all stripes"—Third World women, lesbians, feminists, and feminist-oriented men—must band together in order to create a truly broad-based political movement for change. Anzaldúa's writings on personal identity as well as feminist and lesbian issues have drawn considerable critical attention.

Grows Up Poor

Born in south Texas on September 26, 1942, Anzaldúa is the daughter of Hispanic migrant workers. Both parents labored in the fields of a settlement ranch called Jesus Maria of the Valley, making barely enough money to support the family. Despite their own lack of opportunities, they encouraged their children to seek a better life through education. When Anzaldúa was 15 years old, her father died, leaving the family more destitute than ever. There was little choice but for mother and children to continue to work the fields, traveling back and forth between Texas and Arkansas to find work. Anzaldúa's mother, who was only 16 years old when Gloria was born, kept alive the dream of education. Her dream was focused, however, on her sons. She dreamed of the day they would finish high school. Yet, it was her daughter, Gloria, who would not only complete high school, but college as well.

By continuing to work the fields each weekend and during the summer months, Anzaldúa was able to attend Pan American University in Edinburg, Texas. She graduated with a B.A. in English, secondary education, and art in 1969.

Starts Her Career

While studying for her master's degree in English and education at the University of Texas in Austin, Anzaldúa began to teach in the area. She taught preschool, special education classes, and high school English. In addition, she began to instruct teachers and administrators in ways to educate the largely illiterate migrant worker population. By 1972, she had earned her master's degree and began concentrating on Chicano studies.

Moves to California

When her dissertation graduate work was rejected by the University of Texas, Anzaldúa transferred to the University of California at Santa Cruz, where she now lives. With the publication of *This Bridge Called My Back* in 1982, she became a popular public speaker on both feminist and lesbian issues. This anthology of writings against racism by women of color, co-edited with Cherríe Moraga, won the American Book Award from the Before Columbus Foundation and still enjoys widespread recognition. "We want to express to all women," wrote Anzaldúa and Moraga, "the experiences which divide us as feminists . . . . We want to create a definition that expands what 'feminist' means to us."

Since that first publication, Anzaldúa has authored other, often controversial works. In *Borderlands* (1987), she creates a new language, mixing text and poetry in a combination of Chicano Spanish, Tex-Mex, and other speech patterns. The book is a collection of works on Anzaldúa's family history, lesbian feminism, the Aztec and Catholic religions, problems of migrant workers, and the pain involved in writing. It is a work that Anzaldúa considers to be her masterpiece. Largely autobiographical, *Borderlands* explores what it means to live on borders, both literally and figuratively. Reviewers praised the book for its innovative style and energetic voice. The book was selected as among the 38 best books of 1987 by the *Library Journal.*

With Annie Cheatham and Mary Claire Powell, she published *This Way Daybreak Comes* (1986). She has also authored two books for children, *Friends From the Other Side* (1993) and *Prietita and the Ghost Woman* (1995). Among awards she has received for her work are a McDowell Artists Colony Fellowship in 1982 and a National Endowment of the Arts award for fiction in 1991.

In 1990, Anzaldúa edited a collection called *Making Face/Making Soul: Creative and Critical Perspectives by Women of Color.* It focuses on the differences among women of color and the difficulties they encounter with self-identification. This very precise focus on ethnic complexity sets Anzaldúa apart from other feminist/lesbian writers and also tends to draw some sharp criticism from them. But Anzaldúa goes her own way, refusing labels, refusing to be identified, refusing to place the fact of her lesbianism above or below her other identities. She often writes of conflicting cultural traditions and how spiritual and physical boundaries have defined her life.

In her work, Anzaldúa reminds readers of the oppression that she and other minority peoples have endured and that the oppression can become a source of strength and unity. Some critics say she places her lesbianism on a "political pedestal," but others, notably critic Shelley Fishkin, believe that she represents those who "had the wrong race, class, gender, ethnicity, or sexual preference" and so were devalued or dismissed. If Anzaldúa is bothered by the criticism of her peers, she does not show it. She refuses any attempts to label her or her writings. "What am I?" she asks in an essay called "La Prieta" in *The Bridge.* She answers, "A third-world lesbian feminist with Marxist and mystic leanings."

Anzaldúa maintains a busy lecture schedule at literary criticism and women's studies conferences and at universities. She also works closely with the feminist publication, *Sinister Wisdom,* to which she has been a contributing editor since 1984. She will certainly continue to command the attention of literary critics and readers alike with her forceful narrative voice and the power of her ideas.

Sources:

Blue, Rose. Telephone interview with Gloria Anzaldúa, March 6, 1998.

Tyrkus, Michael J. *Gay & Lesbian Biography.* Detroit: St. James Press, 1997.

Frances R. Aparicio

Frances R. Aparicio
(1955–)
Professor, author, editor, filmmaker, community activist

Selected writings:

Canto de la locura y otros poemas/Song of Madness and Other Poems. With Francisco Matos Paoli, Pittsburgh Latin American Literary Review Press, 1985.

Versiones, interpretaciones, creaciones: instancias de la traducción literaria en Hispanoamérica en el siglo vente. Edited with Susana Chavez Silverman, Editorial Hispamérica, 1991.

Writers of America: Latino Voices. Millbrook Press, 1994.

Listening to Salsa: Gender, Latin Popular Music, and Puerto Rican Cultures. University Press of New England, 1997.

Tropicalizations: Transcultural Representations of Latinidad. Edited with Suzanne Chávez Silverman, University Press of New England, Re-Encountering Colonialisms Series, 1997.

Overview

Frances R. Aparicio has devoted her professional and academic life to the study and understanding of Hispanic culture in all its diversity. A recipient of numerous academic awards and grants, she uses her academic pursuits and life experiences to improve understanding of Hispanic culture among both the non-Spanish and Spanish-speaking segments of the population. Aparicio is also committed to preparing Hispanic youth to participate more fully in American social, economic, and political life.

Music and a New Direction

After graduating from high school, Aparicio enrolled in the Conservatorio de Música de Puerto Rico, with the intent of pursuing a career in music. She transferred to the Indiana University School of Music to continue her studies, but eventually changed her focus and graduated with a double major in comparative literature and Spanish in 1978. She received the Outstanding Graduate Award from Indiana University in the year of her graduation. Aparicio continued her academic career at Harvard, receiving her M.A. in 1980 and a Ph.D. in Romance languages and literature in 1983.

At Harvard, Aparicio had the opportunity to develop the university's first course in Spanish for native speakers. Given the innovative nature of this undertaking, Aparicio was able to create her own pedagogical materials and to identify the benefits of Spanish-language training for Hispanic students attending institutions of higher learning in the United States.

Career and Family

Upon completion of her doctorate, Aparicio accepted a position as lecturer in Spanish at Stanford University. In this capacity she developed the course "Spanish for Bilinguals," and, in collaboration with Professor Tomas Ybarra-Frausto, created a comparative Latino language and culture course entitled "Chicano-Riquena Literatures and Cultures." The research done to establish these courses further fueled Aparicio's interest in the diversity of Hispanic culture and language, as well as the benefits of linguistic and cultural education for Latino students. She soon focused her studies on the politics of languages among Hispanics in the United States. With her career path becoming established, Aparicio gave birth to her daughter, Gabriela, in 1984 and faced the difficult life of a single mother with an increasingly demanding professional career.

In 1985 Aparicio was recruited by the University of Arizona to create and implement curricula and programs in Spanish for bilinguals. She also translated *Canto de la locura y otras poemas*, a book of poetry by Francisco Matos Paoli, the same year. Aparicio remained at the University of Arizona for two years and expanded her studies to examine the relations between popular music and fiction in contemporary Puerto Rico. During this time Aparicio met Eliano Rivero and Elizabeth Davis, who became her friends and assisted her with child care and her studies.

Upon receiving a Ford Foundation postdoctoral grant in 1987, she moved to the University of California at Berkeley and began to study Latin American musicology and ethnomusicology, as well as popular Puerto Rican music and literature. Her rising status within her field was recognized with her appointment as chairperson of the Committee on the Literatures and Languages of America of the Modern Language Association for 1989-90.

Aparicio accepted a tenured position as Arthur F. Thurnau professor with the Department of Romance Languages at the University of Michigan in 1990, where she continues to teach in both the Spanish and Latino Studies Programs. Her role as a leader in the study of Hispanic culture was further cemented by her appointment as a member of the Executive Committee of the Puerto Rican Studies Association in 1992.

She married Chicano cultural activist Julio Cesar Guerrero on September 29, 1990, and her second daughter, Camila Guerrero, was born in 1991.

Into the Future

Aparicio remains active in organizations representing Latinas and women of color at the University of Michigan. She has also edited several literary books and published her own two works: *Versiones, interpretaciones, creaciones: instancias de la traducción literaria en Hispanoamérica en el siglo vente* compiled in conjunction with Susana Chavez Silverman, a friend from graduate school, in 1991; and *Listening to Salsa: Gender, Latin Popular Music, and Puerto Rican Cultures* in 1997. The latter work, which focuses on gender roles and politics as they are articulated in salsa and other traditional Latin popular music, reflects Aparicio's increasing concern over the role of Hispanic women in public life. She is currently producing a video documentary on women of color at the University of Michigan titled *Through My Lens* and is working on a number of books that examine Latin music. Aparicio is also serving as a member of the Research Committee of the Latin Popular Music Project being conducted by the Smithsonian Institution

and the National Museum of American History. Her services as a contributor to scholarly journals, translator of Spanish literature and poetry, and speaker on Latino, multicultural education, and feminist issues are much in demand.

As she looks to the future, Aparicio believes that programs centering on the cultural and educational development of youth are essential to the continued growth of Hispanic communities and cultures in the United States. Along with Latina community activist Christina Jose Kampfner, Aparicio has implemented tutorial programs for Latino youth, which foster appreciation for each student's own cultural heritage and for not only diverse Hispanic cultures, but also for the entire spectrum of cultural diversity in present-day North America.

Her interest in music has led Aparicio to study gender roles as portrayed in salsa and other traditional Latin music, as well as the reaction of contemporary female singers to these roles. She is active in opposing initiatives to make English the official language of the United States, supporting instead the maintenance of bilingual and multicultural curricula in U.S. schools.

Current Address: Program in American Culture, Dept. of Romance Language and Literatures, 410 Mason Hall, Univ. of Michigan, Ann Arbor, MI 48109-1029.

Sources:

Eldridge, Grant. Curriculum vitae and other materials provided by Frances R. Aparicio, February 1998.

Ross, James E. "Book Review—Listening to Salsa: Gender, Latin Popular Music, and Puerto Rican Cultures." *Library Journal*, November 15, 1997, p. 59.

Who's Who in the Midwest. New Providence, NJ: A. N. Marquis, 1996.

Anna Maria Arias
(1960–)
Publisher, entrepreneur

In 1994, Anna Maria Arias launched *LATINA Style,* the first magazine for the professional Hispanic American woman. It is the first and only magazine owned solely by Hispanics, giving it a credibility that no other Hispanic publication can offer. At a time when news stories about Hispanic Americans focused mainly on negative stereotypes and realities such as teen pregnancies, drug abuse, the high drop-out rate, and gangs, Arias' mission is to be the positive voice of the Hispanic American female professional, focusing on all of the Hispanic American accomplishments that were never published. As such, *LATINA Style* accesses the heretofore untapped professional Hispanic American market segment of more than two million potential readers.

Family Acts as Major Influence in Career Choice

Arias is the oldest of three children and the only daughter of Jesse Arias Jr. and Rita Arias whose maiden name is Contreras. Her two younger brothers are Marco and Steven. The family home is in San Bernadino, a southern California city. On her father's side she is a third-generation Mexican American. Jesse Arias, Sr., her grandfather, came from Chihuahua, Mexico. The senior Jesse Arias emphasized the importance and power of education. Influenced by this philosophy, the younger Jesse Arias attended and graduated from law school at the University of California in Los Angeles, becoming a lawyer whose main interest was helping those in the community. In fact, Arias says that some of her earliest and fondest memories involve going to peoples' homes with her father to offer help.

At first, Arias, Jr., entered private practice, and while he had many clients, most were very poor. Many could not pay at all, while others bartered for legal services with butchered pigs. After some time, Arias, Jr., realized that, while he was literally bringing home the bacon, he still needed to pay the mortgage and utility bills.

This economic need led Jesse Arias, Jr., to work for the Los Angeles Public Defender's Office. He started legal aid evenings in San Bernadino, where he and other lawyers would spend an evening answering legal questions from those who had no other legal recourse. Also, in the 1960s, he was the first Hispanic city councilman in San Bernadino, where he served for two terms. He died of a cerebral aneurysm in 1994.

Arias's mother, Rita, began working at her husband's law firm, then went to work as an officer for the San Bernadino County Equal Employment Department. In the late 1990s, Mrs. Arias ran for, and served on, the same city council district as her late husband.

Learns Perseverance from Mother's Positive Attitude

Rita Arias' positive attitude towards life had a profound impact on her daughter. Rita Arias encountered a subtle form of prejudice during her husband's bid for city council. There were very few, if any, Hispanics at political affairs, and no one would talk to her. Because of the snubs, she began to dread the parties and receptions, but although she was lonely, she was never bitter. Anna Maria Arias recalled in a phone interview, advice her mother gave her, gleaned from this difficult period of discrimination:

"If you worked really hard, you could accomplish what you want, that there was more than one way to skin a cat. In other words, if you couldn't accomplish something one way you tried a different way. Always have a plan 'B' and always have a plan 'C'." Arias emphasized that, "This has always helped me in my life, to never take 'no' for an answer. Just re-negotiate, re-think about it, get creative and find another way to do it." Arias points to her parents as excellent role models and as her career motivators.

Decides on Career in Journalism

While thinking of a career choice as a teenager, Anna Maria Arias was very interested in pursuing a career in law, since she was attracted to the way her father had used law to help others. However, the lessons she had learned from her parents over the years also pointed her in the direction of journalism. "My mother and father raised my brothers and me to not just accept what was on the surface," Arias said. "Things may not always be as they appear on the surface. . . Don't just ingest what you see on the surface, but dig a little deeper. I think that had a big influence on where I am today." One of her motivations for entering journalism was her attraction to the exciting, glamorous portrayal of journalists on television. She was also intrigued by the people that one might possibly meet as a journalist. In the case of Arias, her interviewing credits have included George and Barbara Bush, Rita Moreno, and a number of influential Hispanic political figures and business people.

After high school, Arias first attended San Diego State University and then Hawaii Pacific University where she completed her communications degree. While in school, she focused on broadcast journalism, taking broadcast news internships at a Hawaii NBC affiliate. However, when she graduated, Arias found that there were not any available jobs that paid decently in journalism, so she applied for a fellowship program with the Congressional Hispanic Caucus Institute. Subsequently she was chosen among 11 fellows to go to Washington where the institute paid her a salary for a limited time and helped her find a job.

Search for Media Experience Leads to Magazines

When she arrived in Washington, Arias determined that her goal was to get some national campaign media experience. She called Beverly Ellerman, then the executive director of the Congressional Hispanic Caucus Institute, and shared this desire, explaining that nobody at the Democratic National Committee (DNC) would, "give me the time of day." Ellerman, a Hispanic woman, called a professional contact, Polly Bacca, one of the vice chairpersons of the DNC. It was Bacca who arranged Arias's interview, eventually getting her the job working media for women's issues and Hispanic issues at the DNC on the 1988 Dukakis/

Benson campaign. However, the campaign ended when Dukakis lost, and Arias found herself unemployed once again.

After she left the DNC, Arias landed a job as a temporary employee at the *L.A. Times* Washington bureau. While there, Arias met Maria Elena Sharpe, then managing editor of *Hispanic* magazine. While Arias was focused on broadcast journalism at the time, Sharpe emphasized some advantages of print, especially magazines. As Arias said: "She reminded me that in magazines you can go more in-depth. You can do more research. When you're on radio and TV, everything is quick deadlines and you really can't do in-depth journalism. At that time I thought I wanted to develop a reputation as a sound journalist, so I thought maybe I should try print. So I did and I just fell in love with it."

When Arias informed the *L.A. Times* bureau chief that she was quitting to join *Hispanic,* he promptly offered her a research assistant position. Arias was tempted, but chose to join the magazine staff because she wanted to write and the position allowed her to remain in Washington, DC.

Joins Staff of *Hispanic*

Once at *Hispanic* Arias started as the assistant to the publisher. Her job description was: Do whatever needs doing. She wrote stories, worked in circulation, and did everything except advertising. The experience gave her the chance to learn about all aspects of the publishing business. Soon after Arias moved to editorial, a couple managing editors came and went. Then, after a year with the magazine, she became managing editor, a position she stayed in for four years, and where she might have remained had the publisher, Alfredo Estrada, not decided to move *Hispanic* to Austin, TX. Arias liked Washington, DC, too much to consider leaving, and began to think of other employment opportunities.

Begins *LATINA Style*

While still at *Hispanic,* Arias began interviewing for a position as press secretary for Vice President Al Gore. Arias was a strong contender for the position and had been interviewed at least three times, but she could not silence the inner voice that was telling her to start her own magazine. With some trepidation, she called the vice president's office and asked to be removed from the list of applicants. From that moment she never looked back.

There were a number of factors that led Arias to start her own business, but one of the most influential factors was another magazine aimed at a minority demographic: *Essence.* The *Essence* audience consists of professional African American women. It had just celebrated its 25th anniversa-ry in 1994, and Arias was struck by the fact that there was no equivalent for Hispanic American women who numbered approximately three million at the time.

On July 1, 1994, Arias started working on *LATINA Style.* For the first four months, she ran the magazine out of her condo because she could not afford office space. Raising the initial capital was difficult, and she finally had to turn to family for a good portion of her start-up money. However, companies like Nissan, Nordstrom, and Coca-Cola also thought that Arias had targeted an untapped market, and they soon signed up to advertise in the premiere issue. If these corporate giants had known the truth of what was happening behind the scenes though, there might never have been a *LATINA Style.*

At this time, Arias was extremely busy, traveling around the country, going to an endless series of meetings, doing all of the things one needs to do when launching a major commercial effort. Arias said that everybody she knew told her to slow down, that she was going to have a heart attack. The prototype of *LATINA Style* came out in October of 1994. On February 23, 1995, Arias' heart began racing. She was taken to the emergency room and remained hospitalized with aplastic anemia. From her hospital bed she launched the magazine nationally. Because she did not want her advertisers to be concerned, she kept it a secret that while she was holding the telephone in one hand, she was getting blood transfusions in the other arm. Arias credits her two assistants, Theresa Trujillo and Eileen Torres, for helping her keep the secret and going to bat for *LATINA Style.* Arias said, "They are awesome women. Without them, there would be no *LATINA Style.*"

Establishes Clear Goals for Magazine

Since its launch in 1994, Arias has had a clear vision of her magazine's goals: "We try to profile the Hispanic American professional working woman in a positive light. We try to entertain and educate this woman with the stories that we write. We're also a very issues-oriented magazine. We are and can be an advocate type of magazine." For Hispanic American women, Arias and her magazine provide help when there is no one else. She encourages women to call her when she goes to public speaking events. She said that her goal is to help empower Hispanic American women. "We will go to the mat for Hispanic women," Arias said.

Current Address: *LATINA Style,* 1730 Rhode Island Ave., NW, Ste. 805, Washington, DC 20036.

Sources:

Golden, Joel. Telephone interview with Anna Maria Arias, March 1998.

Armida

(1913–)

Actress, dancer, comedienne

Selected filmography:

Show of Shows. Warner Bros., 1929.
On The Border. Warner Bros., 1930.
General Crack. Warner Bros., 1930.
Wings of Adventure. Tiffany, 1930.
Under a Texas Moon. Warner Bros., 1930.
Border Romance. Warner Bros., 1930.
Under the Pampas Moon. Fox, 1935.
Rootin' Tootin' Rhythm. Republic, 1937.
Border Cafe. RKO, 1937.
La Conga Nights. Universal, 1940.
Always in My Heart. Warner Bros., 1941.
Fiesta. United Artists, 1941.
South of Tahiti. Universal, 1941.
Gaity. Hal Roach, 1943.
Melody Parade. Monogram, 1943.
Here Comes Kelly. Monogram, 1943.
The Girl From Monterey. PRC, 1943.
Machine Gun Mama. Universal, PRC, 1943.
Bad Men of the Border. Universal, 1945.
Congo Bill. Columbia, 1948.
Jungle Goddess. Screen Guild, 1948.
The Gay Amigo. United Artists, 1949.
Rhythm Inn. Monogram, 1951.

Overview

Born Armida Vendrell in Sonora, Mexico, this diminutive actress was merely known as "Armida" onscreen. She starred in numerous B-grade Westerns during the 1930s and 1940s, creating a sparkling screen personae. Armida was not only a gifted actress, but a talented dancer and comedienne as well, having appeared in vaudeville sketches before her motion picture career. In Hollywood, she worked with stars like Gene Autry in 1937's *Rootin' Tootin' Rhythm*, Walter Huston in 1941's *Always in My Heart*, Myrna Loy in 1930's *Under a Texas Moon*, and even animal star Rin-Tin-Tin in *On the Border*, also in 1930. Armida faded from public view after her last screen appearance in 1951's *Rhythm Inn*.

Early Life and Career

Standing only 4'11" and weighing less than 100 pounds, Armida packed a great deal of talent into her small frame. Her family moved to the United States from Mexico in 1915 when she was only two-years old, and she spent all of her early years among the Spanish and Mexican communities of the Southwest. She had little contact with English-speaking society until her late teens. The family lived in

Armida

Douglas, Arizona, a town near the Mexican border, for a short time, then moved to Phoenix. There, Armida's father, a renowned stage actor originally from Barcelona, Spain, performed in Spanish vaudeville theaters. Armida came from a large, gifted family. Her father, Joaquin Vendrell, fostered Armida's talents, and encouraged Armida and her five sisters and two brothers to pursue stage careers. The family performed song and dance acts together.

When Armida was only seven, she visited friends in San Diego. There she made her stage debut singing, dancing, and acting in Spanish theater. This early stint in theater did not last long, but Armida returned to the stage for good at age 13 when she began to appear on stage at the Hidalgo Theatre in Los Angeles. She dropped her last name, and her sisters acted in supporting roles as Armida took center stage in various tear-filled melodramas. She was a big hit, the show became popular with the Spanish community, and the sisters were booked in Los Angeles, where the family finally settled. Along with her last name, Armida tried desperately to rid herself of her Spanish accent. Ironically, though, it was her accent that would become a large part of her stage charm and became one of her distinctive stage characteristics.

Word of her successful Spanish-language productions spread. Her shows soon drew the attention of the English-speaking community. Reporters from English-language papers visited the Spanish quarter of Los Angeles. One of these was Fanchon Royer. Royer was so impressed with

Armida's stage presence that she informed vaudeville producer Gus Edwards. Edwards then saw Armida in a dance act with her siblings. He, too, was impressed, and the producer left the theater with a signed contract to bring Armida to New York. This contract ended the family's act together. Armida came to New York and starred with Ray Bolger (the scarecrow in *The Wizard of Oz*) in a vaudeville sketch called "Ritz Carlton." On the vaudeville stage, Armida displayed her comedic and dance talents. She became the show's biggest hit, and appeared there for over a year.

Film Career

After appearing in various vaudeville productions, Armida returned to Los Angeles with Edwards to make motion pictures. She made several short films for MGM beginning in 1929. Armida came to the attention of Hollywood star John Barrymore, who cast her as the female lead in 1930's *General Crack*.

Her popularity with audiences continued to grow. Armida regularly appeared in B-westerns throughout the 1930s and 1940s. She became well-known for her Spanish dancing and a boisterous screen personae. Her most memorable starring performances include 1930's *On the Border* with Rin-Tin-Tin and *Border Romance* in the same year, 1943's *The Girl From Monterey* with Jack LaRue, and 1944's *Machine Gun Mama*, also with LaRue. She also worked with Academy Award-winning director Michael Curtiz (*Casablanca*) in 1930's *Under A Texas Moon*. Armida delivered many strong supporting roles as well, and worked with many of the biggest screen stars of her era, like Gene Autry and Myrna Loy.

In addition to her film career, Armida appeared on stage, most notably in a play titled *Nina Rose*, where she delighted Broadway audiences. She also appeared on radio with stars such as Rudy Vallee and eventually had her own radio program.

Armida's film career faded when the short, light-hearted westerns that had been so popular in the 1940s began to lose favor with audiences. She had been stereotyped as a Mexican dancer, which limited her film roles and her opportunities to show the full range of her talent. However, Armida made the best of her many supporting roles, always bringing spark and flair. She raised the level of the B-pictures in which she appeared and developed a loyal following of fans.

Sources:

The Internet Movie Database. Available at http://us.imdb.com/Bio?Armida.

"Lines for Scrapbooks; Mr. Donlin and Two Actresses, Who Seem to Be Helen Mehrmann and Armida." *The New York Times,* November 2, 1930.

Rainey, Buck. *Sweethearts of the Sage: Biographies and Filmographies of 258 Actresses Appearing in Western Movies.* Jefferson, North Carolina: McFarland & Company, Inc., 1992.

María Celeste Arrarás
(1960–)
Television host, journalist, author

Selected writings:

Selena's Secret: The Revealing Story Behind Her Tragic Death. Simon & Schuster, 1997.

Overview

María Celeste Arrarás is not only one of the most well-liked news personalities worldwide, she is also an accomplished broadcast journalist. Those unfamiliar with her news magazine show *Primer Impacto* might know her best as the journalist who won an exclusive interview with Yolanda Saldivar, the murderer of Tejano singing sensation Selena Quintanilla, and who wrote a best-selling book about the

María Celeste Arrarás

tragic case in 1997. To many of the 45 million U.S., Latin American, and European viewers of the Spanish-language network Univision, Arrarás is familiar as the trusted and beloved host of a top-rated daily television news magazine. Few public figures are as versatile as Arrarás, whose accomplishments range from being the first Hispanic to win the prestigious Genesis Award, bestowed by the National Ark Trust Fund, to being chosen as one of *People* magazine's "Most Intriguing People of 1997."

Arrarás received a bachelor of arts and sciences degree from Loyola University of New Orleans in 1982. She majored in communications and graduated with honors. Her first big career break came in 1986 when she became the top anchor/reporter for a San Juan, Puerto Rico, station with an all-news format similar to CNN. In the early 1990s she held a series of positions at Univision affiliates. Arrarás was key news anchor at WXTV-Channel 41 in New York, then substitute anchor and the network's bureau chief in Los Angeles. She also worked as substitute anchor and correspondent for *Portada,* a news magazine similar to *60 Minutes* that is broadcast in the United States and 18 Latin American countries.

Finds Niche at Univision

Apparently it was the experience working in the news magazine format at *Portada* that allowed both Arrarás and Univision executives to realize that she had found her niche. Her next position at Univision was anchor of *Primer Impacto,* another news magazine with a lighter approach to reporting, sometimes categorized as "info-tainment." In her capacity as anchor, Arrarás saw the show's popularity skyrocket. A nighttime special edition of *Primer Impacto* hosted by Arrarás attained the second highest rating ever reached in the Nielsen Hispanic Index. Overall, Nielsen rates *Primer Impacto* as one of the top three shows in Hispanic television. The show is broadcast throughout the United States, 15 Latin American countries, and Europe via Univision's affiliate Galavision. Arrarás has been the subject of numerous magazine cover stories and featured in newspapers, including *USA Today* and the *New York Times.* She is recognized by people all over the world.

During her years at Univision, Arrarás covered a broad range of stories and won an Emmy for her reporting. She covered special news assignments in the former Soviet Union, Europe, Korea, the Philippines, the Virgin Islands, and the Marshall Islands, as well as many locations in Latin America and the United States. Her most notable stories included live coverage of U.S. presidential conventions, the Olympics, and state elections in California, Florida, and New York. Using her international news savvy, Arrarás coordinated and hosted the first live satellite transmission between the former Soviet Union and the Caribbean. She also conducted one-on-one interviews with U.S. presidential candidates, Latin American presidents, and movie stars.

Gains Selena Scoop

After 23-year old Hispanic American star Selena was murdered in a Corpus Christi, TX, motel room, Arrarás won the trust of her grieving family, as well as her accused killer, Yolanda Saldivar. Both parties granted her a series of exclusive interviews. Selena was a commercially successful, Grammy-winning Tejano singer who had a huge following among both Hispanic and non-Hispanic music fans in the United States and Mexico. Salvidar was not only a friend and business associate of Selena's, but was also the founder of the Selena fan club. The dramatic story of the young singer's murder made a huge impact on *Primer Impacto's* audience, and Arrarás's access to those involved enhanced her status as a news personality. The most significant interview Arrarás conducted on this assignment was with Saldivar from prison just after she had been found guilty and sentenced to life in prison. During the interview, Salvidar implied that there was an undisclosed "secret" that had not been brought out in the trial, which would explain the series of incidents leading up to the killing.

Saldivar's provocative implication whetted the public's appetite for more information even though the trial was over. Given her inside sources, Arrarás was in the perfect position to further investigate the story. In 1997 she published a book on the case in both Spanish and English, *Selena's Secret: The Revealing Story Behind Her Tragic Death.* In *Publisher's Weekly* a reviewer states that Arrarás promises to reveal the secret between the lines of her book but never offers any real answers, saying "the promised revelation is much ado about nothing." While the review is negative, *Publisher's Weekly* did not fail to note that the book was also "Simon and Schuster's most successful frontlist title." It was an instant bestseller, further bolstering Arrarás's visibility.

Achieves Greater Popularity

After the success surrounding the Selena case, Arrarás reached new heights of popularity. She became an even stronger presence in U.S. popular culture, recognized increasingly by the non-Spanish-speaking public, while maintaining the loyal affection of her Univision fans. In 1997 she was chosen as one of the "Most Intriguing People of 1997" in *People* magazine's annual special issue. She also made a cameo appearance in a major motion picture, *Contact,* starring Jodie Foster. When she returned to *Primer Impacto* in February of 1998, after a three-month maternity leave, the show reached its highest rating, a 19.8 national average, very high for the show's late afternoon time slot. Only a month earlier MCI/Telecom Plus research found Arrarás "the most likeable and credible talent in commercial television." Arrarás is notable for combining professionalism and charisma and for succeeding in an increasingly multicultural media environment.

Current Address: Primer Impacto-Univision, 9405 NW 41st St., Miami, FL 33178.

Sources:

Madsen Hardy, Sarah. Letter from María Celeste Arrarás, March 20, 1998.
Publisher's Weekly, January 27, 1997, pp. 90-91.

Martina Arroyo
(1936–)
Singer, professor

Harlem-born soprano Martina Arroyo once belonged to an emerging vanguard of opera performers who broke through invisible color barriers in the 1950s and 1960s. Following such stellar predecessors as Marian Anderson and Leontyne Price onto the stage of New York's Metropolitan Opera House, Arroyo's 1965 debut there was part of a new era in the rarefied, often European-focused world of opera. Of Puerto Rican and African American heritage, Arroyo's confidence in herself, in part inherited from her solid, achievement-oriented family, as well as a down-to-earth sense of humor, provided ballast during the more

Martina Arroyo

difficult early years of her career. "If you take yourself too seriously in a profession like this, you're in trouble," Arroyo told Rosalyn M. Story in *Opera News.*

Arroyo was born in 1936 and grew up in Harlem near 111th Street and St. Nicholas Avenue. The family, though far from rich, enjoyed a comfortable lifestyle in an lively neighborhood. Her father, Demetrio Arroyo, had emigrated from Puerto Rico and married Lucille Washington, formerly of Charleston, South Carolina. The couple had one son, 16 years older than Martina, who would become a minister. The senior Arroyo was a mechanical engineer, and his salary from his Brooklyn Navy Yard job meant that Arroyo's mother was able to stay at home, unlike many other women in their neighborhood. The income also allowed the family to occasionally venture from Harlem to experience more of Manhattan's rich cultural offerings.

Imagines Herself Onstage

By her own admission Arroyo led a relatively sheltered childhood and seemed to have little in common with her schoolmates. She was taught piano by her mother, took ballet classes, and sang in her Baptist church choir. But it was the 1940s era musicals she saw at the movies that ignited her passion for the stage. "I had a lot of dreams when I was a kid, and my mother humored them," Arroyo told Alan Levy in the *New York Times Magazine.* "She said she'd help me be a singer or dancer or a pianist or whatever. . . *provided* I had another profession to fall back on." At the time, there were very few minorities in the classical performing arts such as opera; as a backup plan, Arroyo knew she would have to decide upon a profession that would provide a steady income, so she opted for a teaching career.

An above average student, Arroyo attended the elite Hunter High School, part of Hunter College. Because of her interest in music, she gained special admittance to a graduate-level opera workshop at the College. "One day I got up nerve and said I'd like to sing," Arroyo recalled in a 1968 interview with Thomas Cole of the *New York Times.* "When I was through with Gounod's 'Jewel Song' from *Faust,* they said that was fine, but what language was I singing?" Her French, it turned out, was nearly unrecognizable; she had learned it only phonetically from singing along with her opera records.

This shortcoming was remedied with a degree in Romance languages from Hunter College, which Arroyo earned in 1956. By then, the determination she had displayed to the opera workshop instructor, Joseph Turnau, impressed him. Turnau arranged for her to audition for a well-known voice teacher in New York City, Marinka Gurewich, who immediately took her on as a pupil. Arroyo also found a loyal concert manager in Thea Dispeker, who approached her after a recital and offered her services at no charge until her career took off. Both remained with

Arroyo for much of her career; she worked with Gurewich until the teacher's passing in 1990.

Has Few Role Models

Despite her early achievements, Arroyo faced challenges on many fronts in the 1950s. From her peers in Harlem she suffered ostracism—not because she attended a private high school, but because she dreamed of becoming an opera singer. During her college years, she was sometimes sidetracked by extracurricular pursuits and did not always take her training seriously. Gurewich finally threatened to sever their ties, which Arroyo termed "a turning point for me. Up to then, I must have been, in my mind, treating singing as a hobby, a lark—something I loved that I was dabbling in," Arroyo confessed to Levy in the *New York Times Magazine* interview. "Opera wasn't a real possibility." Part of Arroyo's lack of focus stemmed from the fact that she had so few role models. Only in 1955 did an African American, Marian Anderson, sing solo on the stage of New York's Metropolitan Opera Theater; Price debuted there six years later.

Arroyo followed her mother's advice and became a teacher after earning her degree in comparative literature. Yet she found that combining her duties at a Bronx high school with continued training under Gurewich's tutelage quite taxing, and so she took a job as a welfare caseworker for New York City instead. For two years at the East End Welfare Center, she managed a case load of over 100 welfare recipients needing assistance, but found this work extremely satisfying. "My life had been centered on music for so long, and suddenly there I was, deeply involved in other people's problems," Arroyo said of this time in a 1967 interview in the *New Yorker*. She recalled one challenge to cut through bureaucratic obstacles and procure a simple ironing board and iron for one family with a young daughter too embarrassed to go to school in her unpressed dresses. "I'm as proud of having succeeded in that as of anything I've ever done," Arroyo said.

In 1957, Arroyo auditioned for the Metropolitan Opera and was turned away and told to try again next year. In 1958, she entered the Met's national "Auditions of the Air" competition. She chose a particularly difficult piece from *Aida* to sing and earned one thousand dollars and a scholarship to the company's Kathryn Long School for it. There she studied German, English diction, drama, and fencing. Her debut as a professional came in the fall of 1958 and happened at Carnegie Hall by sheer chance. She had been scheduled to perform in *Assassinio nella cattedrale* (Murder in the Cathedral), an opera by Ildebrando Pizzetti, at a festival in upstate New York. At the last minute, the tent that was to house the stage was felled by bad weather, and the entire production was rescheduled for Carnegie Hall. Her first critical mention in the *New York Times*, according to Levy's profile, noted that Arroyo displayed "a voice of amplitude and lovely color" as well as "remarkable potential."

Finds Success Abroad

Arroyo soon gave up her welfare department job to begin performing overseas, where an abundance of European opera companies offered up-and-coming singers many opportunities to train and perfect their voices. There she found much steady work, but struggled to win the larger, name-making roles. She once performed in 45 cities in 48 days and became known as a reliable interpreter of difficult roles in minor or avant-garde operas. It was while performing in Italy in 1959 that Arroyo met her future husband, professional violist Emilio Poggioni.

By 1965 Arroyo was a permanent member of the Zurich Opera Company. She was in New York visiting her family when a call came that would propel her career to the next level. At her New York City apartment that day, Arroyo received a telephone call from someone saying he was Rudolf Bing, the Met's famed general manager. Arroyo loved a good joke as much as her friends and tried to go along with what she assumed was a crank call asking her to temporarily fill in for star soprano Birgit Nilsson as the lead in *Aida*. When she told the caller that she usually went to the movie matinee that day with her mother, and thought she could make it in time for the evening's performance, the reaction from the other end of the line alerted her to the authenticity of the call.

Arroyo debuted at the Met on February 4, 1965. Prior to the curtain's rise, she listened to "the chilled moan," as Levy described it, from the audience when it was announced that a replacement would perform in Nilsson's stead that night. In the end, *Aida*'s audience gave Arroyo a standing ovation for her Met debut as an Ethiopian princess. Bing immediately offered her a first-level contract with the opera company, and over the next few years Arroyo's star rose dramatically. She won rave reviews for her interpretations of roles created by Giuseppe Verdi—the foremost of Italian opera composers—as well as for her adroitness in performing the spirited German *lieders* of Richard Strauss and Wolfgang Amadeus Mozart. One music insider of the day, quoted in the *New York Times Magazine* by Levy, praised Arroyo as "a dramatic soprano with a voice capable of expanding to slingshot power and of diminishing to kittenish pathos"; another called hers "one of the most gorgeous voices before the public today."

Becomes an International Star

Arroyo made her debut at London's Covent Garden in 1968 as Valentine in *Les Huguenots*; that year also marked a more political milestone in the world of opera when she became the first singer of color to appear onstage in the very Germanic role of Elsa in *Lohengrin*, an opera from nineteenth-century German composer Richard Wagner. During the early 1970s, Arroyo led a jet-set life, appearing in some of the foremost opera productions on both sides of the Atlantic. She sang in Covent Garden with Placido Domingo, then a rising star, opened both the 1970 and

1971 season at the Met, and played Lady Macbeth in Verdi's version of the Shakespeare tragedy in early 1973. She won praise for her roles as Elvira in *Ermani,* Elizabeth in *Don Carlo,* Amelia in *The Masked Ball,* and the notoriously difficult Santuzza in *Cavaleria Rusticana.* She became one of Leonard Bernstein's favorite singers, and the eminent American conductor requested that Arroyo perform at a concert honoring his 1,000th performance with the New York Philharmonic.

Arroyo was also becoming a well-known name outside of the cultish world of opera. She appeared on *The Tonight Show* as well as the 1970s television sitcom *The Odd Couple,* alongside Jack Klugman and Tony Randall. Yet this success often spelled hardship for her marriage to Poggioni: with his performance schedule confining him to Europe and hers taking her there and elsewhere, they spent little time together. Once, both decided to surprise the other by boarding trans-Atlantic flights—unbeknownst to one another—on the same night. Each arrived on another continent to find the other gone. Arroyo told the *New York Times*'s Cole that their interracial marriage presented no dilemma; instead Cole remarked that according to her, Poggioni "is somewhat of a specialist in contemporary music [and] is a rough critic." There were times in Arroyo's career, however, when she did encounter difficulties because of her skin color. In a restaurant in Germany, a man once made a snide remark about her African heritage using the German word for "cannibal." She recounted this incident in the *New York Times* article, telling Cole that she "shot him a look and said, 'Yeah but we only use a little pot; you use ovens.'"

At the peak of her career, Arroyo made several recordings with eminent orchestras. These range from Mozart's *Don Giovanni* and Verdi's *La Forza del Destino* to *Judas Maccabeus* from Handel and Beethoven's *Ninth Symphony.* In 1989 she announced her official retirement, but returned to the stage two years later to appear in *Blake,* a new opera by Leslie Adams based on an 1857 novel about a slave family. "I had Miss Arroyo in mind even as I was writing the role of Miranda," its composer told *Opera News.* "I was attracted to her soaring quality, especially on the high notes, and her beautiful richness of tone that seems to come from around her rather than directly from her."

Gives Generously of Her Time

By then Arroyo maintained homes in both New York City, near Lincoln Center, and in St. Croix, the Virgin Islands. She had married a second time, to banker Michel Maurel, and sat on the board of trustees at her alma mater, Hunter College. She was also an honorary member of the Carnegie Hall board. Her eminence has led to invitations from numerous U.S. universities as a distinguished visiting professor. These include the University of California at Los Angeles, Louisiana State University, University of Delaware, Wilberforce University, and Indiana University, as well as the International Sommerakademie-Mozarteum in

Salzburg, Austria. She stressed, in the 1991 interview with *Opera News,* the need to extend a helping hand to a new generation of opera hopefuls. "Whatever positive influence we have been for whatever person, or whomever we may use as a role model, what's important is that it's a positive force," Arroyo declared. She also confessed to occasionally checking in on her former Harlem neighborhood by bribing a taxi driver to take her to 111th Street. "My parents taught me to be proud of our neighborhood," Arroyo told *Opera News.* "I go there. . . not to forget."

Current Address: School of Music, Indiana University, Bloomington, IN 47405.

Sources:

Cole, Thomas. "'Martina, You Watch What You Say, Hear?'"*New York Times,* April 28, 1968, section I, p. 21.
Current Biography Yearbook. New York: H. W. Wilson Co., 1971.
Levy, Alan. "Life at the Opera With Madame 'Butterball'." *New York Times Magazine,* May 14, 1972, pp. 20, 26-31, 38.
"No Nerves."*New Yorker,* April 8, 1967, pp. 33-35.
Sadie, Stanley, ed. *The New Grove Dictionary of Opera.* Grove's Dictionaries of Music, 1992.
Story, Rosalyn M. "Positively Martina." *Opera News,* September 1991, pp. 26-28.

Patricia Mares Asip

Business executive, entrepreneur, consultant

Patricia Mares Asip is best known for her innovative work with JCPenney Company, Inc., where she served as manager of multicultural affairs. After 24 years with the company, Asip left to form her own corporation, believing that there was much more she could do in the area of multicultural affairs.

Early Years in Argentina

Asip was born in Prague, Czechoslovakia, to Francisco Mares and Maria Sonnek. While an infant, her family moved to Argentina where her father became one of the first cotton producers in North Argentina. Asip studied political science at the University of La Plata and business administration at the University of Buenos Aires. In 1952, she went to work for L. Lovreiro Ron as a corporate lawyer and foreign investor liaison.

Patricia Mares Asip

Comes to the United States

In 1955, while working for L. Lovreiro Ron, Asip became a partner and convinced the law firm to send her to the United States as their representative. She impressed the company by bringing back accounts that included the brand names Muzak and Lovable Brassieres; in 1956 she established the company's New York branch office, RonPat International. While manager of RonPat, she soon found herself offering legal and tax counsel for businesses in the United States that were interested in engaging in ventures with South American companies. During this time, she also worked for both Metropolitan Life and the Nicaraguan consulate on a part-time basis and translated a book for a psychiatrist. In 1963 Asip joined MacGraw Hill as a senior editor, where she remained for the next seven years. Also in 1963, she married Thomas Patrick Asip. The couple has one daughter, Helena.

Multicultural Awareness at JCPenney

In 1973, Asip began her employment with JCPenney, first as a catalog editor. While working for the retailer, Asip found that many Spanish-speaking people liked the company's merchandise, but were unable, because of the language barrier, to place an order through their catalog. In 1978 Asip designed a Spanish-language shopping guide. "I did my own research in Queens," Asip was quoted as saying in an article in *Minority Business News DFW*. "I did a mock magazine in Spanish giving assistance in how to

shop, and people really liked the idea. I went with the guide to talk with store managers to see how they felt, and they were very enthusiastic. So I made the presentation to the managers, and they bought the idea." The catalog was well-received by the Spanish community, and the following year JCPenney produced and distributed *GuiaPractica. . . Para El Uso De Nuestros Católogos* to the general public. The free catalog was the first such publication in Spanish and was considered a major merchandising breakthrough in boosting the company's catalog sales. Estimates have credited the catalog with generating nearly a half million dollars in publicity revenue alone.

The Hispanic market is estimated to be worth over $170 billion a year, and Asip and JCPenney knew that reaching out to the Hispanic and minority communities made good business sense. JCPenney promoted Asip to the position of national manager of multicultural affairs, a position she held for her remaining years with the company. As manager, she developed Penney's marketing approach to minorities. Asip also said in the *Minority Business News DFW*, article that "The reason I have stayed so long is because the promise for this type of awareness takes a long time to realize. It has to start; it has to prove itself; it has to have the support of top management, which has always been the case here."

Her marketing strategy included advertising, public relations, government relations, and special events for JCPenney's minority markets, helping to establish the company as a welcoming force in the minority communities. "We give support," said Asip, in *Minority Business News USA*. "We demonstrate in many different areas that the company is committed to not only building community relations, but also to understanding issues of these communities." One event that met with success was the Hispanic Designer Model Search, which offered college scholarships and modeling opportunities to one male and one female model annually in the United States. Asip felt that this event helped the company tap into the youth market and helped the young models by opening doors for them and providing money for college. The first model search, held in 1989, attracted approximately 500-600 women and men in each of the 11 districts where the competition was being held. Over the years, some of the finalists have landed lucrative modeling deals, including the 1989 winner, Isbelia Quijada, who was offered several national contracts for modeling jobs.

Working for Rights in the Greater Community

In addition to her corporate duties, Asip has been involved with several other organizations that strive to incorporate multicultural values into society. In 1992 President Bush named Asip to the Glass Ceiling Commission. The six-member commission, chaired by Lynn Martin, then U.S. Department of Labor Secretary, was designated to study opportunities for and artificial barriers to the advancement of women and minorities in the corporate world. According to a press release from the Associate Information Programs, the group was designed to "... develop strategies to help eliminate these artificial barriers and... recognize employees who excel at developing diverse management staffs." Asip served on the commission until 1995.

Nationally, Asip has also been a member and served on the board of the National Council of La Raza (1988-1996), the National Hispanic Leadership Agenda, the United States Committee for UNICEF, and the League of United Latin American Citizens (LULAC). She was also a member of the U.S. Hispanic Chamber of Commerce, the Small Business Advisory Committee for the Federal Communications Commission (1985-1991), and the American Heart Association's National Communications Committee. In addition, Casper Weinberger appointed her to the Defense Advisory Committee on Women in the Services; and she served as a member of the Advisory Committee to the U.S. Senate Republican Conference Task Force on Hispanic Affairs.

In 1996, as chair of the board of directors of the Hispanic Policy Development Project (HPDP), Asip worked with then president, Siobhan Nicolau, to make HPDP into a "Can we help you?" organization that provided resources, networking, and training for members of both the Hispanic and Anglo communities. Asip had been a member of the organization for 16 years and has supported the group's goal of analyzing policies that affect Hispanics in the United States.

Other civic and community affiliations include membership on the boards of the Dallas Women's Foundation, the Hispanic 50, Goodwill Industries of Dallas, Inc., SER, Jobs for Progress, Inc., American Management Association, and Private Industry Council of New York City.

Mares Inter-Americas Corporation

In 1997 Asip made the decision to leave JCPenney and start her own company, Mares Inter-Americas Corporation. She believed this step was inevitable as she realized that even though her work at JCPenney was not finished,

there was much more that she could accomplish on her own. In a news release issued by Asip's new company, she said, "My work with JCPenney has given me many opportunities to affect change in the national arena. Now it's my turn as an individual to forge new frontiers toward the 21st century that will favorably impact Hispanics in the United States and the Americas."

Mares Inter-Americas is an international affairs and business development company that targets the U.S. Hispanic market and provides liaisons for trade and commercial import and export opportunities with emerging Latin markets. Asip also provides counseling on glass ceiling and diversity issues for businesses and organizations. Through this organization, Asip hopes to continue her work, encouraging multicultural respect and opportunities.

Current Address: Mares Inter-Americas Corp., 4816 Bear Run Dr., Plano, TX 75093.

Sources:

Associate Information Programs Communication Department press release, September 15-17, 1992.
Dimeo, Jean. "Penny a Model for Hispanic Market." *Dallas Times Herald,* June 6, 1990, p. B1.
Luhrs, Joyce. "ORGANIZATIONS: Policy Project Has a Will and Always Finds a Way." *Hispanic Outlook in Higher Education,* December 6, 1996, p. 7
Sorter, Amy. "Working with Ethnic Groups is Fast Becoming a Part of Strategic Marketing." *Minority Business News, USA,* January 15 - February 15, 1997, p.30.
Sorter, Dave. "JCPenney Expands Multi-Cultural Communications Focus Encouraged by Patricia Asip's Great Ideas." *Minority Business News DFW,* July, 1995.
Woodward, Nancy Hatch. Telephone interviews with Patricia Mares Asip. March 12 and 19, 1998.

Avila, Inés Hernández
See **Hernández-Avila, Inés**

B

Barrios Robinson, Emyré
See Robinson, Emyré Barrios

Sandra Benítez
(1941–)
Author

Selected writings:

A Place Where The Sea Remembers. Coffee House Press, 1993. *Bitter Grounds.* Hyperion, 1997.

Overview

Sandra Benítez remembers the sea, or at least, she remembers what it is to have borders that eventually merge into a smattering of cultures. Benítez has spent 18 years of her life transcribing on paper what has always been in her mind. In that time span, Benítez has penned two and a half novels, a handful of short stories, and countless essays. The first novel is hidden under her bed—"a book too dreadful to submit, but a book that taught me the discipline needed to rise and face the page each day," Benítez expressed in a 1994 feature article that appeared in *The Writer.* "That first book taught me that writing is an act of faith: We must keep faith each day with our writing if we want to call ourselves writers."

Sandra Benítez was born March 26, 1941, in Washington, DC, the daughter of James Q. Ables and Marta A. Benítez Ables. Her father's profession as a diplomat resulted in the family moving several times during Benítez's childhood, and she spent a significant amount of time in Mexico, El Salvador, and Missouri. She graduated with a B.S. from Northeast Missouri State University in 1962 and taught ninth-grade Spanish and English in Affton, MO, until 1968. She returned to Northeast Missouri State University and earned her M.A. in 1974. Her career took a few turns in the latter half of the seventies as she worked as a freelance Spanish-English translator and acted as the marketing liaison in the International Division of the Wilson Learning Corporation.

Career Takes Off

In 1980, Benítez found her niche both personally and professionally. She married James F. Kondrick, a writer and game inventor, and she began teaching creative writing at the University of Minnesota in Duluth with the Split Rock Arts Program. Though Benítez had a long-time love of literature, she did not truly embrace her own writing until the 1980s. "I came to writing late," Benítez told *Contemporary Authors.* "I was 39 before I gathered enough courage to begin. When I hear other writers talk about writing, or what they have to say about their art, I am amazed by those who say they always knew they had to write. When I was a girl, I never wished to do it. Being a writer was something magical I never dreamed I could attain. When I was young, it was a doctor I planned to be. Becoming a doctor seemed much more possible than being a writer. But while growing up, I frequently had a book in my lap, and so I was linked, even then, to writing and to the spell that stories cast."

Writes *A Place Where the Sea Remembers*

The quality of Benítez's work did not achieve national recognition until the publication of her first novel, *A Place Where the Sea Remembers,* in 1993. The novel discusses the aspirations and disillusionments of the residents of a Mexican village as they relate to a quarrel between two sisters. The work was praised for the strength of its characters and the complexity of the narrative style. The critical acclaim was followed by several prestigious awards, including the Barnes and Noble Discover Great New Writers Award in 1993 and the Minnesota Book Award for Fiction in 1994. The novel was also selected as a finalist in the *Los Angeles Times* Book Award. The success of *A Place Where the Sea Remembers* led to Benítez's selection as a participant in the National Writers' Voice Project.

Publishes *Bitter Grounds*

Benítez followed up the success of her first novel with a powerful second offering, *Bitter Grounds,* in 1997. The story recalls Benítez's life as the daughter of a foreign diplomat in El Salvador, one of Latin America's most politically and economically polarized nations. The multigenerational saga spans the lives of three generations of mothers and daughters caught in the violence of recent Salvadoran history. The novel was acclaimed for its poetry, historical detail, and rich narrative style.

In 1997, Benítez became the Edelstein-Keller distinguished writer in residence for the winter quarter at the University of Minnesota. Her writing continues to draw on her Hispanic heritage that includes Puerto Rican, Mexican and Salvadoran influences. Benítez told *Contemporary Authors*, "In my heart are stored the Latino stories of my Puerto Rican heritage and of a childhood lived in Mexico and El Salvador. When I write, I have to suppress the knowledge that mainstream America often ignores the stories of 'the other America.'" Through the beauty of her writing, Benítez can finally voice those stories.

Sources:

Baxter, Kevin. "Rediscovering Roots Through Her Writing." *Los Angeles Times,* October 28, 1997, p. 3.

Benítez, Sandra et al. "Writing a First Novel." *The Writer,* June 1994, pp. 21-24.

"Sandra Benítez." *Contemporary Authors,* Detroit: Gale Research, 1994.

Star-Tribune Home Page. Available at http://www.startribune.com/bookmark/authors/Benítez.html.

University of Minnesota English Department Home Page. Available at http://www-engl.cla.umn.edu/Visitng/SandraBenítez.

Minerva Bernardino
(1907–)
Ambassador, women's rights activist, author

Selected writings:

Minerva Bernardino, su lucha por los derechos de la mujer. Amigo del Hogar, 1976.

Lucha, agonia y esperanza: trayectoria triunfal de mi vida. Editora Corripio, 1993.

Champions Women's Rights

Minerva Bernardino's impact on the condition of women in the world is tremendous. As secretary for the women's rights organizations Acción Feminista in the Dominican Republic, her efforts were critical in the battle to win suffrage for Dominican women. But not content to improve the lot of her countrywomen, Bernardino worked to improve the lives of women globally. She contributed to the formation of the United Nations, and then used her influence to win important concessions for women in the founding documents of the organization.

Minerva Bernardino, the eldest child in a family of four girls and three boys, was born in 1907 in the tiny village of Seibo in the Dominican Republic. Both her parents, Alvaro and Altagracia, were decidedly more liberal than most of their neighbors in their views on child-rearing. They encouraged Minerva and her siblings to get out and embrace life, disregarding the widely observed prohibition against the appearance in public of unattended young girls.

Bernardino recalled in an interview with Ann Foster in the *Christian Science Monitor,* "My mother was very progressive, and I was reared in an atmosphere that was, at that time, most unusual in my country." The grandchildren of a provincial governor, Bernardino and her siblings were orphaned when she was 15, leaving Minerva and her oldest brother to support the family. The liberal upbringing of their parents was by that time deeply ingrained. Bernardino said in the Foster interview that she and her brother, now suddenly responsible for providing for their younger siblings, "both believed in equality from the beginning and were determined that he should go in for law, that my sister should do as she also wished, and become a doctor, and that I should enter public life."

Bernardino first entered into civil service in 1926, heading the file office of the Dominican Republic's Department of Development and Communications. Two years later, she took over the supervision of a division of the Department of Agriculture. While holding down these civil service jobs, she was pursuing her higher education, eventually winning a bachelor of science degree. After three years in the Agriculture Department, she took over as chief of the statistics division of the Department of Education, where she served from 1931 through 1933.

Begins Feminist Work

Early in her career, Bernardino became a passionate advocate for women's rights, taking on the post of secretary of the women's rights organization Acción Feminista Dominicana in 1933. This group was later credited with improving the lot of Dominican women, including winning the franchise for them, under the amended constitution adopted in 1942. In addition to her responsibilities with the rights group, Bernardino served for a year, starting in 1933, as supervisor of vocational schools in the capital district of Santo Domingo. It was also in 1933 that Bernardino was named the Dominican delegate to the Inter-American Commission of Women, an organization that had been established in 1928 under the umbrella of the Organization of American States. The commission's mission was "to work for the extension of civil, political, economic, and social rights" of women in the Americas and to study problems unique to women, searching for possible solutions. The organization submitted reports on the status of women to the International Conference of American States, which was held every five years. In 1933, the year she joined the commission, Bernardino attended the conference, held in Montevideo, Uruguay. Five years later, she attended the next conference in Lima, Peru, delivering a report at the meeting.

Bernardino assumed the newly created post of vice-chairperson of the women's commission in 1939. At the same time, Ana Rosa de Martínez Guerrero was elected chairperson of the group. Three years later, Bernardino led the opposition to a move to relocate the commission's headquarters to Buenos Aires. Just a few months later, she called on Chilean and Argentinian women to pressure their governments to break diplomatic relations with the Axis powers of Germany, Italy, and Japan. When Martínez Guerrero fell out of favor with her government, a new Argentinian delegate to the commission was named to replace her. The departure of Martínez Guerrero necessitated an election to select a new chairperson. In November of 1943, her fellow commission members elected Bernardino to assume the post at the beginning of 1944.

Bernardino represented her country as its delegate to the Inter-American Conference on Problems of War and Peace, held in Chapultepec, Mexico, in 1945. She was one of four women seated at the conference but the only one with the power to vote. The conference produced the Act of Chapultepec, which pledged all American republics to oppose aggression against any one of them.

Helps Set Up United Nations

Later in 1945, Bernardino was a full delegate from the Dominican Republic to the San Francisco conference at which the framework for the United Nations was established. In January of 1946, she was a delegate to the first meeting of the United Nations General Assembly held in London. One of only four women to sign the United Nations charter, Bernardino became a member of the UN Economic and Social Council's Commission on the Status of Women in March of 1946, moving into the commission's vice-chairmanship a month later. In May of 1946, after a whirlwind series of open and closed meetings, the commission produced a report calling for universal suffrage for women, as well as equal civil rights, equal education, and full equality on the labor market. Later that year, when the General Assembly convened in New York City, Bernardino strongly endorsed a resolution from the Danish delegate that "the Assembly recommend that all members not already having done so grant the same political rights to women and to men."

Bernardino was honored in 1948 as "Woman of the Americas" for her campaign to increase the rights of women, receiving both the Bolívar and San Martín medals of the Pan American Union. As chairperson of the Inter-American Commission of Women at its August 1949 conference in Buenos Aires, Bernardino clashed with honorary chair Evita Perón over whom should be allowed to address the conference. Shortly after that meeting, Bernardino resigned from the chairmanship of the commission.

In January of 1950 Bernardino assumed the post of Dominican Minister Plenipotentiary to the United Nations. During her years at the United Nations, Bernardino was an active participant in and supporter of the organization's Children's Fund. She played an important role in having references to "free men" in the UN's Covenant of Human Rights changed to "free human beings."

Looks Back on Accomplishments

In June of 1995, as world leaders from Bill Clinton to South African Archbishop Desmond Tutu gathered in San Francisco to observe the fiftieth anniversary of the founding of the United Nations, Bernardino, in attendance, recalled her struggle to get women's rights recognized. Only through sheer persistence, she remembered, was she able to include a mention of women's rights in the organization's charter. She suggested that the organization needed to do more for women.

Looking back on the 1945 San Francisco meeting that hammered together the United Nations charter, Bernardino recalled in an interview that on the eve of a speech she was to deliver to the conference, she broke her ankle at the Sir Francis Drake Hotel. "They told me I needed a cast to my knee. I said no. They said I would lose my foot. I said, 'I have to make a speech tomorrow and prefer to lose my foot.'"

Her tireless efforts on behalf of equal rights for women have earned Bernardino a number of honors, including New York City's Silver Big Apple Award and the honorary title of "Ambassador Extraordinaire" from her native country. In 1995, at the age of 88, she accepted the Hispanic Heritage Award for Excellence in Education "on behalf of the women in my native country and all women and children throughout the world, and the elderly, like me." In March of 1997, United Nations Secretary-General Kofi Annan, marking the fiftieth anniversary of the United Nation's Commission on the Status of Women, saluted the contribution of Bernardino, saying the commission was largely her creation. She was present for the anniversary celebration.

Sources:

Contin, Margarita. "A Proud Past, Present, and Future." *Latina Style*, December 6, 1995.

Pike, Rayner. "Ambassador Minerva Bernardino: Hispanic Champion of Women's Rights." *New York Beacon*, September 21, 1995.

Rothe, Anna, ed. "Bernardino, Minerva." *Current Biography.* New York: H.W. Wilson Co., 1951, pp. 41-42.

Walsh, James. "United Nations: The U.N. at 50: Who Needs It?" *Time*, October 30, 1995, p. 72.

Alicia Borinsky

Professor, author, poet, critic

Selected writings:

Mina Cruel. Corregidor, 1989.
Theoretical Fables: The Pedagogical Dream in Contemporary Latin American Fiction. University of Pennsylvania Press, 1993.
Mean Woman. University of Nebraska Press, 1993.
La pareja desmontable. Corregidor, 1994.
Sueños del seductor abandonado. Corregidor, 1995.
Madres Alquiladas. Corregidor, 1996.
Cine Continuado. Corregidor, 1997.
Dreams of the Abandoned Seducer. University of Nebraska Press, 1998.

Overview

Alicia Borinsky's exile to the United States, prompted by the military dictatorship in her home country of Argentina, may have very well been a key element in her maturation as an award-winning writer. She received advanced degrees in Hispanic literature after her arrival in the United States and is presently professor of Latin American and comparative literature and director of Latin

Alicia Borinsky

American Studies at Boston University. This accomplished author, winner of the 1996 Latino Literature Award, has published 11 books.

Speaks of Writing Influences

"I started writing when I was very young," Borinsky said in a telephone interview. "I grew up in a house in which there was a grandfather who had great confidence in my being a writer, so I don't remember making a conscious decision to start writing. But I remember being encouraged ever since I started being able to read." In childhood, Borinsky's writing focused on the beautiful elements of everyday life—"the childhood moment in which one is always zapped by beauty," she recalled. "When I was little, I wrote poetry about the sea, landscapes, and so on." The serious work began in adolescence. "I was very taken with issues of marginal characters who were particularly interesting to me, either because they were poor, or because they led alternate lifestyles," she said.

Writes as an Exile

Borinsky's own writing stems from her experience of travel and displacement. "I would say that I was being shaped as a writer by the very experience of exile. My writing is quite marked by that special kind of attachment to a culture other than the one received at birth, the kind of attachment one develops when one goes away from home at an early age and is able to consider the new place as a homeland as well," said the professor and author who writes as fluently in English as in Spanish.

Creates Writing in the Americas Program

Recently Borinsky created the Writing in the Americas Program, a one-of-a-kind project consisting of seminars, public conferences and summer institutes. It is supported by a six-year grant from The Andrew W. Mellon Foundation and is destined to shape a new generation of Latin Americans by bringing together writers and literary scholars of North and South America.

Borinsky is a member of the Boston University-Chelsea Management Team, but is, first and foremost, a literary scholar, fiction writer, and poet. Her work has been published extensively in the United States, Latin America, and Europe in both Spanish and English. Before accepting a position at Boston University, Borinsky has taught at the Johns Hopkins University. She also served as a visting professor at Washington University in St. Louis and Harvard University. Borinsky is the recipient of the Metcalf Award for Excellence in Teaching at Boston University. She earned a M.A. and a Ph.D. from the University of Pittsburgh, the latter in 1971. Her creative work has been translated and included in anthologies, as well as published in *The Massachusetts Review, Confluencia, The American Voice,*

Under the Pomegranate Tree, New American Writing, Tameme, and *Beacons.*

Writes Philosophy

"Writing for me is very much a part of my everyday life," Borinsky said. "I am not the kind of person who thinks of writing as occurring part of the day. Through my daily experiences I have, shall we say, a third eye, that is looking and hearing everything that happens and thinks of recasting it in print." Borinsky identifies strongly with the Hispanic American community. "I hope that the kind of humor and the kinds of situations that exist in my fiction and the poetry and the essays have some impact on the life of the community," she said. Married to writer Jeffrey Mehlman, Borinsky lives in Boston with her husband. They have two children.

Current Address: Modern Foreign Languages and Literatures, Boston Univ., 718 Commonwealth Ave., Boston, MA 02215.

Sources:

Boston University Home Page. Available at http://web.bu.edu/UNI/Faculty/borinsky.html
Cohn, Lynne. Telephone interview with Alicia Borinsky, March, 1998.
"100 Most Influential Hispanics." *Hispanic Business,* October 1997, p. 58.

Brixey, Loretta
  See **Sanchez, Loretta**

Burgos, Julia de
  See **de Burgos, Julia**

C

Caballero, Linda Belle
See **La India**

Norma E. Cantú
(1947–)
Professor, author

Selected writings:

Canícula: Snapshots of a Girlhood en la frontera. University of New Mexico Press, 1995.
Soldiers of the Cross: Los matachines de la Santa Cruz. Texas A & M Press, 1998.

Overview

Norma Elia Cantú speaks with a voice that echoes from the United States' borderlands with Mexico. As a writer and teacher, she appreciates the impact of literature on civilization. As a Chicana writer and a teacher of Chicana/Chicano literature, Cantú has worked diligently to offer a view into her culture that can bridge many cultures. Her community activities demonstrate her commitment to the arts, social services, and education. Cantú's work with Amnesty International and Network Educators for the Americas and as a literacy volunteer only begin to tell her story and her contribution to her "borderlands" culture.

Crosses the Bridge

Norma Elia Cantú was born in Nuevo Laredo, Tamaulipas, Mexico, on January 3, 1947. She immigrated to the United States the next year with her parents, Florentino and Virginia Ramon Cantú. Her childhood in Laredo, Texas, was an ethnic childhood in a border town. Life there meant crossing over into Nuevo Laredo, across the International

Bridge into Mexico, for their special needs of daily life. Cantú believes that growing up as such an integral part of two cultures makes her experience different from other Hispanic American women. She sees it as an "... often non-immigrant experience of this country." In 1968, she became a naturalized citizen of the United States.

In 1973, Cantú graduated cum laude from Texas A & M International University in Laredo. She received a bachelor of science degree with a major in education, English, and political science. She obtained her masters of science degree in 1976 from Texas A & M International University in Kingsville with an honors major in English and a minor in political science. Cantú left Texas in order to pursue a doctorate degree at the University of Nebraska in Lincoln. She was granted her Ph.D. in 1982.

Heads Home to Laredo

Upon obtaining her Ph.D., Cantú returned to Texas A & M International University in Laredo, where she has been on the faculty since 1980. As an English professor, Cantú has taught upper level and graduate courses in world and U.S. literature, writing, and criticism. Other duties at Texas A & M International University have included a term as interim dean of the School of Education and Arts & Sciences in 1991-1992; and chairperson of the Division of Arts & Sciences from 1987 through 1991. In the 1994-1995 academic year, Cantú was a visiting professor at Georgetown University. Her expertise and enjoyment of folklore led her to work with the National Endowment for the Arts as a senior arts specialist from 1993-1995, and as a liaison for NEA with the Task Force on Folk Arts in the Schools.

Cantú has received numerous awards and honors. In 1997, she received the Outstanding Alumni Award from the University of Nebraska's College of Arts and Sciences. She was selected to be the commencement speaker at Texas A & M International University in 1996. She also received a research grant from the Guadalupe Cultural Arts Center/Rockefeller Gateways Program to research Quinceanera traditions in Laredo in 1996. In 1995, Cantú was elected to the Laredo Women's Hall of Fame.

Writes with Reverence for Chicano Heritage

In 1993, Cantú began work on her book *Canícula: Snapshots of a Girlhood en la Frontera.* In a 1995 interview with

Tapestry, a publication of the Vidal M. Trevino School of Communications and Fine Arts, Cantú talks further about *Canicula: Snapshots of a Girlhood en la Frontera,* ". . . I can't really tell you what insights it offers about the Mexican American culture of Laredo because those insights will differ from reader to reader—it's a matter of how a text works for a reader. For someone who grew up in Laredo at the same historical time, the events in the stories, such as the 1954 flooding of the river that washed away the international bridge, will exist in their memory. Then again, for those who share some of the same experiences of living in the borderlands, say someone from Nogales, Arizona, the insights gleaned may have more to do with similarities and differences about life in a border town. . . " Cantú says she initially thought of this work as "fictional autobiography," but a friend suggested that the tales are really "ethnographic," revealing a people's entire way of life.

In that same interview, Cantú addressed the emergence of Chicana literature into the mainstream of publishing. She remarked, "I feel that the mainstream success of writers like Cisneros, Viramontes, Castillo, Chavez, Anaya, and Gilb among others is fantastic. About time, is what I say. I feel that as a professor of English in the United States in the 1980-90s it would have been irresponsible not to promote their work. I began teaching Chicana/Chicano literature in the 1970s in Nebraska when getting the books was only one of the obstacles. Although we now have more access, there are still gaps—recently my students at Georgetown had trouble finding Judith Ortiz Cofer's *Silent Dancing* because it's published by a small press. . . "

Cantú's contributions to her students, her readers, and the world community she serves can be easily summarized. They are born of no less than the pride she carries from her own Chicano heritage. Cantú achieves a quiet glory, especially inside of her classroom, as she explores those things that will bring all cultures to a greater understanding of each other. In 1998, Cantú published a new book entitled *Soldiers of the Cross: Los matachines de la Santa Cruz.*

Current Address: Dept. of English, Spanish, and Fine Arts, Texas A&M International Univ., 5201 University Blvd., Laredo, TX 78041–1990.

Sources:

Cantú, Norma Elia. *Canícula: Snapshots of a Girlhood en la frontera.* Albuquerque: University of New Mexico Press, 1995.
Norma Elia Cantú Home Page. Available at http://www.tamiu.edu.cantu.
Rooney, Terrie M. and Gariepy, Jennifer, Ed. *Contemporary Authors,* Volume 152. Detroit: Gale Research, 1997.
Tapestry "An Interview with Norma Cantú." Laredo: Vidal M. Trevino School of Communications and Fine Arts, 1995.
Vita. Available at http://www.tamiu.edu.vita.htm.cantu.

Norma V. Cantú
(1954–)
Federal government official

Norma V. Cantú is the assistant education secretary for civil rights at the U.S. Department of Education. Her hard-driving approach to her work has served her well in an office that maintains vigilance against civil rights infractions in publicly-funded educational institutions. "I believe a future with equal opportunity is inevitable, and my job is to make the inevitable happen faster," she told *NEA Today.*

Norma Cantú was born on November 2, 1954, in the Rio Grande Valley border community of Brownsville, TX. The oldest of six siblings, Cantú was influenced by parents who emphasized the importance of education. Her mother attended night school while raising the children and holding a full-time position. Her father did not complete high school so he could serve in the military, but he later completed his GED and passed the civil service exam to work as a postal carrier. In an interview with *USA Today,* Cantú recalls "us all sitting around the table, my mom studying for college, my father for the civil service exam and us children doing our homework. We all knew we had

Norma V. Cantú

to do the best we could." A high achiever, Cantú received her high school diploma in 1971 after just three years (with honors), then graduated summa cum laude in two and a half years from Pan American University (now the University of Texas-Pan American) with a double major—English and education—in 1973, at the age of 19.

Cantú taught English during the 1974 school year in Brownsville, and again in 1979 in San Antonio, TX. Proud of her teaching background, Cantú views it positively in light of her present position in the Office of Civil Rights. She told *USA Today,* "I was a teacher before I went to law school. . . . Mostly what I bring to the job is commitment to being an advocate for children." Cantú continued her academic studies at Harvard University, where she received her law degree in 1977 at the age of 22. Hired by the Texas Attorney General's office the same year, Cantú spent two years as a member of the Nursing Home Task Force of the Texas attorney general. Her work focused on investigations into corruption and fraud inside nursing homes.

Mexican American Legal Defense and Education Fund

Beginning in 1979, Cantú gained valuable experience as an attorney for the Mexican American Legal Defense and Education Fund (MALDEF). MALDEF was formed in 1968 to guard against civil rights violations of Hispanic Americans in the United States and to promote Hispanic interests. Working within the legal system, MALDEF has been instrumental in using litigation as a means of leveling the educational field for all Hispanic Americans.

Cantú pursued increased spending for colleges and school districts that educated Hispanic Americans and initiated lawsuits to achieve mandatory busing. She also worked as an attorney on *Gomez v. the State Board of Education of Illinois,* where the state failed to administer and regulate the quality of English proficiency programs, and *LULAC v. Richards,* a case filed on behalf of a 1.5 million Mexican Americans over funding discrepancies at state universities.

Providing access to quality education has always been a key concern of Cantú's. As a lawyer striving to improve Texas colleges, she fought against such educational imbalances as deficient curricula, the absence of computers, and a library that served not only the student body, but the community at large. She took the state of Texas to court over inequitable resources allocated to its institutions of higher education in the southern part of the state, where over 90 percent of the population was Hispanic. This was a special time for Cantú, as she was working in her home state, and out of her parents' home in Brownsville. "It was the first time my parents saw firsthand what I did," she told *The New York Times.* In preparing for the trial, she made use

of her parents' dining-room table and of her father himself: he drove witnesses to the courthouse. "That was a pretty close time for all of us," remembers Cantú. From 1983 to 1992, Cantú was the national director for the Education Litigation and Advocacy Project for MALDEF and also served as regional counsel for MALDEF from 1985 to 1993.

Joins the Office of Civil Rights (OCR)

On May 24, 1993, Cantú was unanimously confirmed by the U.S. Senate and sworn in as the assistant secretary for civil rights at the U.S. Department of Education after being nominated by President Bill Clinton on March 5. Cantú listed her office's core issues as: race-based scholarships; increased opportunities for female athletes; quality English proficiency programs for immigrant children; the termination of sexual and racial harassment in education; and equality in higher education regardless of race or disability.

Cantú faced obstacles upon her appointment. Her predecessor, Michael L. Williams, a George Bush appointee, had drawn attention to the issue of race-based scholarships when he had questioned their legality. He claimed that they created a civil rights problem for white students and that statistics showed only a small number of minorities receiving these scholarships. Cantú disputed this claim in an interview with *NEA Today* by responding, "a government study found that race-targeted scholarships helped increase educational opportunities."

It has been a hard fight. In the case of *Podberesky v. Kirwan* (1995), the court concluded that race-based scholarships offered at the University of Maryland-College Park were unconstitutional. The decision was a disappointment for Cantú. "In an age of fierce global economic competition in which 89 percent of new jobs require some form of postsecondary education, our nation cannot afford to retreat from its commitment to maximize every student's potential regardless of national origin or race," she told *Ethnic NewsWatch.* "It remains our job at the Department of Education to work with colleges to provide access to education using every available tool."

Cantú initiated several changes in the Office of Civil Rights (OCR) by increasing the number of complaints they investigate, hiring additional bilingual staffers, and issuing numerous regulations on race and sexual harassment in education. As she stated to *NEA Today,* "In earlier administrations, very few investigations were initiated by the government. The public perception was that the office was toothless, that it wasn't serious about enforcing the civil rights of students. At one point, several civil rights groups convinced a federal judge that OCR wasn't doing the job Congress mandated. As a result, we have quite a shameful history that we've been working to overcome."

Supports Affirmative Action

Cantú supports affirmative action policies, a position that has drawn criticism. Challenges to the legality of affirmative action admissions policies at some educational institutions have been recognized as unconstitutional by the legal system. In one case, the Fifth U.S. Circuit Court of Appeals ruled that even though the University of Texas Law School attempted to increase minority enrollment through its affirmative action policies, the policies actually introduced reverse discrimination against whites. The school was ordered to create race-neutral policies. Even though Cantú firmly believes in the positive results of affirmative action policies, as a government official she was compelled to support the court and its ruling. Thus, in April of 1997, she issued a statement from the Department of Education that stated that educational institutions in Louisiana, Texas, or Mississippi would not be compelled to offer affirmative action programs if they contradicted the Fifth U.S. Circuit Court of Appeals ruling.

Takes Proactive Approach

Cantú feels that the OCR can be effective in resolving civil rights issues by taking a proactive stance, and she believes that an open government approach to civil rights issues will help educators find solutions before it reaches a legal battle ground in the courts. "Before officials launch investigations, they are first going to pick up the phone and talk to someone on the campus to see if the matter can be resolved," Cantú told *Ethnic NewsWatch*. Her hope is that two-way communication between the educators and the OCR will help resolve conflicts. According to Cantú, her office has been "successful in resolving complaints in a timely fashion and opening up the dialogue between the government and university officials." But, despite OCR's responsibility, it is her strong opinion that "true equality and social progress rest within the community."

The OCR published guidelines for defining and dealing with racial harassment in colleges and universities. The guidelines clearly indicated how the OCR would investigate racial harassment incidents and share these responsibilities with educational institutions to ensure a non-hostile environment for students. Due to the increase in racial harassment complaints filed with the OCR in 1993, the guidelines were a welcome tool in the fight against racial harassment. Cantú and the OCR also fight for the rights of disabled students. "The disabled child," Cantú told *NEA Today,* "can't be placed in a mainstream classroom without the support that provides equal educational opportunity." In addition, school districts that identify students with limited English proficiency—"but then don't serve them"—is a real problem. Cantú expresses disappointment with school programs that give students only a half-hour of language instruction each week. "That's an inadequate response that produces watered-down education and denies equal opportunity."

Remains Active in Hispanic Community

Cantú maintains strong ties with the Hispanic community. In 1995, she spoke to the East Coast Chicano Student Forum on the issue of Hispanic students' struggle to succeed in higher education and the need for the Hispanic community as a whole to show them support. As the keynote speaker at a meeting of the Chicano Bar Association in 1997, Cantú addressed affirmative action and the continued need for these policies to ensure educational opportunities. "We need to recognize there is a continuum of activities ranging from the wholly acceptable promotion of minority recruitment to the illegal pursuit of racial quotas. It is far too easy to confuse what we are debating under the general heading of affirmative action. In the long run, we seek to retain a system which allows us to promote scholarship, achieve diversity, and remedy past discrimination."

Cantú has been involved with various Hispanic organizations, such as: Center for Hispanic Health Policy Development; Texas Human Rights Commission; City of San Antonio Health Facilities Commission; Leadership San Antonio; Mexican American Bar Association of San Antonio; YWCA of San Antonio, Pro Bono Legal Counsel; City of San Antonio Committee on Drafting Regulations; Committee on Minority Concerns, State Bar of Texas; and the Advance Parent Child Training Program.

Cantú has received numerous awards from such groups as: Mexican American Democrats, San Antonio Neighborhood Youth Organization, National League of United Latin American Citizens, State League of United Latin American Citizens, and Texas Association of Chicanos in Higher Education. She also won the Appreciation Award from the Texas Senate, the Reynaldo G. Garza Award from the Hispanic Issues section of the State Bar of Texas, and the Public Policy Award in San Antonio.

Cantú is an active crusader for social equality, especially educational equality. "People who know me know how much I love my work as an advocate for children and education," Cantú told *The New York Times*. It is the drive to achieve equal opportunity for all U.S. students that motivates Cantú. In the same interview, she revealed that her biggest frustration is "having to accept that a lot of folks aren't even aware that there is discrimination." Still, "I don't feel like I'm on a mission impossible. Every time I hear of a new instance of discrimination, I also hear of a new instance where people are treated more equitably. That's what keeps me going."

Current Address: Office of the Asst. Secretary for Civil Rights, U.S. Dept. of Education, 400 Maryland Ave., SW, Washington, DC 20202.

Sources:

Adam, Michelle. "Giving Back after Graduation." *Hispanic Outlook in Higher Education,* October 1, 1995, p. 6.

Cantú, Norma V. Biographical sketch. *United States Department of Education,* 1993.

"Cantú, Norma V." *Federal Staff Directory,* 1997.

Celis, William. "An Impatient Advocate Stirs Up the Education Department's Rights Office." *The New York Times,* August 3, 1994, p. B6.

"Conferences: Giving Back after Graduation." *Ethnic NewsWatch,* August 1, 1995, p. 6.

Galloway, B. T. "Bar Association Marks 20th Year." *La Voz de Colorado,* February 19, 1997, p. 7.

Hawkins, B. Denise. "Angst, Confusion Over Race-Based Scholarships Unfounded: A Controversial Legacy Lives On." *Black Issues In Higher Education,* February 23, 1995, p. 16.

Henry, Tamara. "Civil Rights Crusader Begins New Mission." *USA Today,* June 17, 1993, p. 4D.

Kossak, Jennifer. "Latino Leaders." *Hispanic Outlook in Higher Education,* September 15, 1995, p. 6.

"Norma Cantú: She's the Enforcer." *NEA Today,* December 1994, p. 7.

Pinto Alicea, Ines. "Outlook on Washington: Guidelines on Campus Racial Harassment." *Hispanic Outlook in Higher Education,* September 1, 1994, p. 6.

Salas, Abel. "In the Trenches of MALDEF." *Hispanic,* October 1997, p. 32.

Stern, Gary M. "Leaders: Prominent Hispanics on Education." *Hispanic Outlook in Higher Education,* September 1, 1994, p. 9.

Wright, Scott. "New Community College Affirmative Action Policies Announced: California Keeps Some Elements of Old Hiring Programs." *Black Issues In Higher Education,* May 30, 1996, p. 7.

Irene Cara
(1959–)
Actress, singer, dancer

Selected discography:

Anyone Can See. Epic, 1982.
What a Feelin'. Geffen, 1983.
Carasmatic. Elektra, 1987.

Selected filmography:

The Electric Company (TV series), 1971.
Aaron Loves Angela, 1975.
Sparkle, 1976.
Roots: The Next Generations (TV miniseries), 1977.
Fame, 1980.
Guyana Tragedy: The Story of Jim Jones (TV miniseries), 1980.
Sister, Sister (TV movie), NBC, 1982.
For Us, The Living (TV special), 1983.
D.C. Cab, 1984.
City Heat, 1984.
Killing 'Em Softly, 1985.
Certain Fury, 1985.
Busted Up, 1986.
Caged in Paradiso, 1989.
Gabriel's Fire (TV series), 1990.
The Magic Voyage, 1993.
Happily Ever After, 1993.

Overview

As a singer, Irene Cara achieved acclaim in the early 1980s for her stirring movie themes, especially the theme songs from and *Fame* and *Flashdance.* Her powerful vocals earned her an Oscar and a Grammy Award. In addition to her singing talent, Cara has demonstrated an ability to act in a wide range of projects for film, theater, and television, having proven her versatility in a career that spans three decades.

This native New Yorker was born Irene Escalera in the Bronx on March 18, 1959. It seemed inevitable that she would become part of the entertainment world. Her father and brother are both musicians, and Irene herself was on the Broadway stage at the age of seven. At ten-years old, she performed at Madison Square Garden in a tribute to Duke Ellington.

Demonstrates Broad Range of Acting Experience

Cara got her start in the spotlight in 1971 at the age of 12 with a role in the children's television series *The Electric Company.* In the late 1970s, she tried her hand at acting on the stage in the original production of *Ain't Misbehavin',* following up that experience with a role as part of the touring company of *The Wiz.* Her first movie, *Aaron Loves Angela* (1975), cast her opposite Kevin Hooks in a Romeo and Juliet love story set in New York City. With music scored by Jose Feliciano, it told the story of a romance between a Puerto Rican girl and an African American boy in Harlem. In 1976 she played the title role in the movie *Sparkle,* a movie about three sisters from Harlem who aspire to singing careers. The following year Cara appeared in the critically-acclaimed television mini-series, *Roots.* After the success of that mini-series, Cara appeared in another mini-series, *Guyana Tragedy: The Story of Jim Jones,* in 1980. The movie was based on the true story of Jim Jones, a self-proclaimed prophet who convinced 1,000 of his followers to commit suicide.

Receives Accolades for *Fame*

However, it was for her work in another 1980 film, *Fame,* that Cara's career really achieved star status. Cara acted in the hit movie in addition to singing several songs on the movie's soundtrack. Her performance of the title song, "Fame," earned her *Billboard Magazine*'s accolades as "Top New Single Artist," and *Cashbox Magazine* named her as "Top Female Vocalist" of 1980. "Fame" also won an Oscar for Best Song in a Motion Picture.

Concentrates on Singing Career

Cara continued to ride the crest of critical acclaim when she earned an Image Award for her role in the 1982 NBC television movie, *Sister, Sister.* However, Cara devoted more time to her singing career in the early 1980s. She released an album in 1982 titled, *Anyone Can See.* The following year she released her most popular album, *What a Feelin',* which was propelled to the top of the charts when the title song became the signature tune of the hit movie, *Flashdance.* *Cashbox Magazine* proclaimed Cara to be the Top Female Vocalist of 1983, and *Bravo Magazine* gave her an Otto Award for Most Popular Female Singer that same year. Cara's powerful vocals on "What a Feelin'," earned her an American Music Award for both Best R&B Female Artist and Best Pop Single of the Year in 1983, as well as a Grammy Award for Best Pop Vocal Performance in 1984.

Returns to Acting

Cara followed up her singing success by playing Myrlie Evers in the television special, *For Us, The Living,* starring Howard E. Rollins, Jr. and Roscoe Lee Browne. The film depicts the life of slain civil rights leader Medgar Evers and is based on the book by the same title written by his wife and former NAACP chair, Myrlie Evers-Williams. In 1984, Cara returned to film with a pair of comedies, *D.C. Cab* and *City Heat. D.C. Cab* follows the lives of a rag-tag group of cabbies in Washington D.C., and *City Heat* starred Clint Eastwood and Burt Reynolds as a hard-boiled cop and a private detective fighting the Mafia. Her next effort in 1985 was the film, *Killing 'em Softly* in which she played the girlfriend of a man accused of murder who must clear his name. That same year she starred in the film, *Certain Fury,* in which she played one of two women running from the law after they are mistaken for prostitutes who had opened fire in a courtroom.

In April of 1985, Cara made a different sort of headline by filing a multimillion-dollar lawsuit against her former manager, whom she charged with breach of contract among other violations. The singer/actress claimed that the manager was witholding royalties from her. The suit was later settled in her favor. After releasing the film, *Busted Up,* in 1986, Cara took time out from her career to marry stuntman Conrad Palmisano. The following year she released a third album, *Carasmatic,* which did not achieve the fame of her prior musical offerings. Another movie, *Caged in Paradiso,* failed to draw an audience to the theaters in 1989.

Enters New Career Phase

In 1990, Cara entered a new phase of her career in the television series *Gabriel's Fire,* in which she played the daughter of a neighborhood hero and single father, starring James Earl Jones. In recent years Cara has turned her vocal talents to the world of animation, supplying her voice to characters in the movies *The Magic Voyage* and *Happily Ever After.*

Sources:

Blue, Rose. Telephone interview with member of Irene Cara's staff, March 9, 1998.
The Penguin Encyclopedia of Popular Music. New York: Viking Penguin, 1989.
Videohound's Golden Movie Retriever. Detroit: Visible Ink Press, 1996.

Mariah Carey
(1970–)
Singer

Selected discography:

Mariah Carey. Columbia, 1990.
Emotions. Columbia, 1991.
Mariah Carey: MTV Unplugged. Columbia, 1992.
Music Box. Columbia, 1993.
Dreamlover. Columbia, 1993.
Merry Christmas. Sony, 1994.
Daydream. Columbia, 1995.
Butterfly. Sony, 1997.

Selected filmography:

Maria Carey: MTV Unplugged. MTV, 1992.
Mariah Carey: Daydream from New York to Tokyo. TV special, 1995.
Divas Live. VH-1, 1998.

Overview

Pop diva Mariah Carey sold more than 80 million albums between 1990 and 1997 by fusing her soaring, gospel-style vocals with melodious pop, rock, rhythm & blues, and soulful hip-hop music. Her vocal range is remarkably diverse, ranging between five and seven octaves, and she has been compared to Whitney Houston and other lauded female vocalists from the gospel-influenced tradition. Her early music was characterized by lyrics that champion optimism, unwavering devotion, undying love, and a follow-your-dreams chirpiness. Carey branched out in the musical

Mariah Carey

realm of rap and hip-hop in 1997 with her fifth album, *Butterfly,* hoping to create a rougher, more urban sound and to appeal to a more youthful, cutting-edge audience. *Butterfly* features collaboration with many of rap and hip-hop's prominent artists, and signals a fresh, new direction for Carey.

Carey was born on March 27, 1970, and raised in the Long Island section of New York. Her childhood, in sharp contrast to her young adult years, was marked by harsh poverty. Her Irish mother, Patricia, was an opera singer and vocal coach, and her African-Venezualan father, Alfred Roy Carey, was an aeronautical engineer. After years of staving off bigotry and weathering such incidents as having their dogs poisoned and a car destroyed by a bomb, the couple parted due to the stress. Mariah, then three-years old, lived with her mother; her sister lived with her father, and her older brother soon went off to college. Carey's mother was left to make ends meet on her own, and the struggle was so difficult that Carey and her mother sometimes lived with family friends for months.

Carey demonstrated a clear aptitude for music at an early age. She could sing on perfect pitch as a young child, exactly duplicating a given sound. Carey performed in talent shows as a girl, sang for friends, and performed at local folk-music festivals. By the time Carey was 13-years old, she was writing her own songs. In high school she commuted to Manhattan to study music with music professionals, and after she graduated from high school in 1987, she moved to Manhattan to seek her fame and fortune as a singer.

A Cinderella Story Marriage

Carey worked as a waitress, coat check girl, beauty salon janitor, and part-time backup singer to pay the rent on her apartment in New York City in 1988. While she was working as a backup singer for rhythm-and-blues singer Brenda K. Starr, she attended a music industry party with her demo tape in hand. Sony Music Entertainment President and C.O.O. Tommy Mottola was at the party too and ended up taking the tape home with him. According to *Entertainment Weekly*'s Degen Pener, music industry folk-lore has it that Mottola fortuitously took the tape away from another guest at the party. Mottola, 20 years older than Carey, signed Carey to his label within days of meeting her and hearing her demo tape. Carey left a boyfriend for Mottola, Mottola left his wife for Carey, love blossomed into marriage, and Carey's luminous career was launched.

In 1990 Carey released *Mariah Carey;* her strong debut album sold over six million copies and forced many to take notice of an astounding new talent. Carey received Grammys in 1990 for Best New Artist and Best Female Pop Vocalist for the song "Vision of Love." The vocals on "Vision of Love" were so impassioned and strong that they sounded almost airborne. Carey's debut album immediately solidified her career and popularity, and prompted comparisons with Whitney Houston, whose vocal style is similarly strident.

Reaping Copious Rewards

Carey released *Emotions* in 1991, which was nominated for two Grammys: Best Female Pop Vocalist and, with Walter Afanasieff, Best Producer. *Emotions* served to complement Carey's debut album, underscoring her stature as the leading female vocalist of the vocals-driven pop domain. The songs on *Emotions* focus on love: the love-struck and the lovelorn. Then, after a successful live appearance on MTV's "Unplugged" series, Carey released her third album, *Mariah Carey: MTV Unplugged* in 1992.

Carey yielded a record-breaking four consecutive #1 hit singles from her debut album in 1990 on Billboard's Top Pop Singles Chart for "Vision of Love," "Love Takes Time," "Someday," and "I Don't Wanna Cry." *Emotions* generated her fifth consecutive #1 hit single, rendering Carey as one of the top ten artists with the most consecutive #1 hits. In February of 1997, Sony's Columbia Records rewarded Carey with her own label, Crave Records.Carey generates up to $200 million in annual revenues for Sony-owned Columbia Records.

The number and diversity of musical awards that Carey has received is mind-boggling. In addition to her two Grammy Awards, she has garnered Soul Train Awards for Best New Artist, Best Album (*Mariah Carey*), and Best Single, Female ("Vision of Love," 1990), Billboard Awards for Top Adult Contemporary Artist, Top Pop Artist, Top Album Artist, Top Pop Album Artist, Top Pop Singles Artist, and Top Pop Singles Artist, Female (1991), and Hot 100 Singles Artist of the Year and Special Hot 100 Singles Award for "One Sweet Day" (1996).

Carey has also received American Music Awards for Favorite Female Artist/R&B (1992), Favorite Female Artist, Pop/Rock, and Favorite Album, Adult Contemporary (1993), Favorite Female Artist, Pop/Rock (1995), and Favorite Female Artist, Pop/Rock, Favorite Female Artist, Soul/R&B (1996), and Best Female Soul/Rhythm and Blues Artist (1998). Her World Music Awards include World's Best-Selling Pop Artist and World's Best American Recording Artist, and World's Overall Best Performing Artist (1995), World's Best-Selling Overall Recording Female Artist of the Year, World's Best-Selling Pop Artist of the Year, World's Best-Selling American Female Artist of the Year, and World's Best-Selling Overall Recording Female Artist of the Year (1996). Finally, her Blockbuster Awards include Favorite Single ("Fantasy") and, with Boyz II Men, Favorite Adult Contemporary Single ("One Sweet Day") in 1996.

Reaching Out to the Rap Realm

Carey and Mottola married with much pomp and circumstance in 1993, pouring a half a million dollars into their highly-publicized, fairy-tale style nuptials, and inviting celebrities such as Barbra Streisand and Robert De Niro. The couple then moved into a $10 million estate in the Westchester, NY, community of Bedford. Carey became firmly ensconced in marriage at the youthful age of 23. Mottola was both husband and boss, which sometimes presented a unique dilemma for the couple.

Carey released *Music Box* in 1993, which has sold over 23 million copies, and *Merry Christmas* in 1994; *Merry Christmas* sold over eight million copies shortly after its release. *Daydream* was released to critical acclaim in 1995. The multi-platinum *Daydream* album earned six Grammy nominations and edged her career sales close to the 80 million mark. *Daydream* also marked the first vocal departure from Carey's tried-and-true range; she presented a softer version of her usual style, allowing the music to occasionally overpower or match her vocals. Critics who deemed her earlier style too overwhelming lavished praise on *Daydream*'s softer sound.

Butterfly, released in 1997, ushered in a new era for the 27-year old musical megastar. On May 30th in 1997, Mottola and Carey announced that they intended to divorce. Carey highlighted her newfound independence from Mottola by releasing an album with rap and hip-hop undertones—in spite of the fact that Mottola would remain her boss at Sony. *Butterfly* was precisely the type of album Carey had wanted to release earlier in her career, but Mottola and her label's executives reportedly wanted Carey to stay true to the formula that worked for her from the

onset of her career: sweet ballads, soaring vocals, and a wholesome, girl-next-door image.

Carey's aptly-titled *Butterfly* album included collaboration with a roster of rap and hip-hop artists that included Sean "Puffy" Combs, The Ummah, Stevie J., Poke and Tone, Mace & The Lox, and Krayzie Bone and Wish Bone from Bone-Thugs-N-Harmony. Her video for the album's single, "Honey," was racier than her established fan base would have expected. In the video, she assumes the role of a James Bond-type, clad in a nearly strapless black dress, who escapes from her captors only to be chased over land and sea.

Business with A Twist

It was inevitable, considering Carey's recent divorce, that the media would draw parallels between the video for "Honey" and her marriage to Mottola, but in all interviews she denied any deeper, symbolic meaning beyond the video's entertainment value. Carey's divorce from Mottola did not affect her artistic license or hamper their professional relationship. In addition, the critical acclaim of *Butterfly* reassured those at her label who worried that Carey's established fan base might not accept Carey's new musical direction.

With the release of *Butterfly* in 1997, it is clear that Carey will be exploring new musical terrain and presenting her own, updated musical vision. On April 14, 1998, Carey joined other female vocalist legends such as Aretha Franklin and Gloria Estefan in a VH-1 televised concert titled *Divas Live*. The concert raised money to fund music education in elementary schools. *Entertainment Weekly*'s Pener reported that Carey would like to pursue an acting career as well. She co-writes almost all of her songs, and with over 20 prestigious music awards under her belt at the age of 27, she has a bright musical future and follows an impressive muse.

Current Address: Columbia/Sony Records, 51 West 52nd St., New York, NY 10019.

Sources:

Celebsite Home Page. Available at http://www.celebsite.com/people/mariahcarey/content/biocontent.html.

E! Home Page. Available at http://www.eonline.com/Reviews/Music/Leaves/0,6,523,00.html.

Farley, Christopher John. "Pop's Princess Grows Up." *Time*, September 25, 1995, p. 75.

iMusic Home Page. Available at http://imusic.com/showcase/contemporary/maria.html.

Mr. Showbiz Home Page. Available at http://mrshowbiz.com/news/todays-stories/970829/8-29-974carey.html.

New York Post, September 19, 1997.

Pareles, Jon. "A New Gentleness from a Pop Diva." *New York Times*, September 21, 1997, p. 25.

Pener, Degen. "Butterflies Aren't Free." *Entertainment Weekly,* September 26, 1997, pp. 24-32.

Sony Music Home Page. Available at http://www.music.sony.com/Music/ArtistInfo/MariahCarey/newsflat.html.

Wall of Sound Home Page. Available at http://www.wallofsound.com/reviews/stories/3088-51.html.

Barbara Carrasco
(1955–)
Muralist

A recognized Chicana artist best known for her public murals in Los Angeles, Barbara Carrasco uses her art to battle against all types of discrimination, especially those that concern women of color in the Western world. Carrasco has been accused of having a stormy temperament and a stubborn will, but she remains true to her political beliefs. One of her latest artworks, produced for an exhibition of Chicana art called "Image & Identity," symbolizes the issue of skin color and its effect on the Chicano community—a matter close to Carrasco's personal experiences. She believes that this particular issue often determines the roles that people assume in their families, neighborhoods, and in society as a whole.

Carrasco's spirit of independence, which is evident in her art, developed at a very early age. She had to repeat the first grade because she would not stop drawing on her desk. Although she left the Catholic religion at the end of the eighth grade, she was confirmed in the religion. When asked to select a confirmation name, Carrasco shocked the nuns by choosing Joan of Arc. She explained that her initial choice was Saint Bernadette, who symbolized martyrdom and suffering, but Joan of Arc represented strength and fighting for one's beliefs.

Carrasco was raised in a working-class neighborhood in Culver City, CA, populated predominantly by African Americans and people of Hispanic descent. She never forgot being taunted by her classmates for looking "too white," or that the nuns in her Roman Catholic grade school seemed to give preferential treatment to white students. A third-generation Mexican American, Carrasco has roots in El Paso, TX, and Durango, Mexico. Carrasco's devout Catholic parents expected her to be a model of purity and femininity. Yet, to the horror of her mother, Carrasco developed a "tough girl" attitude in order to survive in her neighborhood. She created a new, independent image by wearing army surplus boots and jackets.

Develops Her Art

According to Carrasco, although neither of her parents had a developed sense of art, both were very talented artists. She credits them with fostering her interest in becoming an artist. Her father died when she was 12-years old, but she always remembered his admonition that anyone could be a bus driver, as he was, but that few could become an artist. Carrasco attended high school in Venice, CA, where she was encouraged by an art teacher to work with a ball-point pen—first developing the use of sharp lines still prominent in much of her work. At UCLA, Carrasco studied sculpture, painting, and graphic art, graduating with both a bachelor's degree and a master's of fine art. After graduation, she created artwork for the fight for Mexican American rights known as El Movimiento (The Movement). The Times Square billboard in New York City soon displayed Carrasco's view of the way farm workers are harmed by pesticides.

Ever concerned with issues of sexism and racism, Carrasco's childhood experiences were never far from her work. An exhibit entitled "The 13 Stations of the Double Cross" featured in a Los Angeles museum in the 1980s, recalls her experiences in the indoctrination of a Catholic education. She ran into controversy in 1983 when a Los Angeles city agency commissioned her to paint a mural for the 1984 Olympic Games. When the work was completed, the agency objected to the series of 51 scenes in a mural called "LA History - A Mexican Perspective." The scenes, woven into the hair of the Queen of the Angels, showed violent racism, lynchings, and discrimination against various peoples— such as the internment of Japanese Americans in camps during World War II. The agency claimed that Japanese visitors to the Olympics would be offended by the mural, and insisted that she redo it. Carrasco refused, but did not win her fight against the city. Instead, she gave the moveable wooden mural to the United Farm Workers Union, then led by César Chávez, where it remains today.

Carrasco's art can be seen around the world. During the 1980s, she traveled to the former Soviet Union to paint murals for a children's museum, and to Central America to paint art for a Nicaraguan organization. Today, the drawings of Carrasco continue to show a desire to explore art forms as they relate to one's own existence.

Sources:

Shorris, Earl. *Latinos: A Biography of the People.* New York: Avon, 1992.

Barbara Carrera
(1945–)
Actress, ambassador

Selected filmography:

Puzzle of A Downfall Child. Universal, 1970.
The Master Gunfighter. Taylor-Laughlin Productions, 1975.
Embryo. Cine Artists, 1976.
The Island of Dr. Moreau. American International Pictures, 1977.
Centenial. 1978.
When Time Ran Out. International Cinema Corporation, 1980.
Masada. NBC-TV, 1981.
Condorman. Walt Disney Productions, 1981.
I, The Jury. American Cinema Productions, 1982.
Lone Wolf McQuade. Orion Pictures, 1983.
Never Say Never Again. Warner Bros., 1983.
Wild Geese II. Thorn EMI Screen Entertainment, 1985.
Dallas. CBS-TV, 1985-1986.
Love At Stake. Nelson Entertainment, 1987.
The Underacheivers. 1987.
Loverboy. 1989.
The Wicked Stepmother. MGM, 1989.
Point Of Impact. 1993.

Overview

Born New Year's Eve, 1945 in Nicaragua, actress and model Barbara Carrera became a screen icon in the 1980s, successfully making the transition from supermodel to actress. Leaving a prosperous modeling career, Carrera moved on to Hollywood. There she worked with some of the biggest names in entertainment, including Burt Lancaster in 1977's *The Island of Dr. Moreau* and Sean Connery in 1983's *Never Say Never Again*. Carrera then moved to the small screen, starring in several miniseries and playing the role of Angelica Nero on the popular night time soap opera *Dallas*. She continued to appear in less-known films throughout the 1990s. In 1997, she was named ambassador at large for her native Nicaragua.

Early Life and Career

Barbara Carrera was born in Managua, Nicaragua to a Nicaraguan mother and an American father. Her father was a courier in the U.S. embassy in Managua, and Carrera spent most of her early years there. When she was 10, her parents separated, and Carrera spent her formative years being raised by nuns at various convent schools, including one in Memphis.

Carrera claims to have been an ugly child, having said "the only thing that paid any attention to me was the stray

Barbara Carrera

dog." She said she longed to be a "blue-eyed blonde," and thought her "eyes were too far apart, [her] lips were too large, [her] cheekbones and chin too prominent, [her] eyes and hair too dark." These impressions changed when Carrera was recruited by modeling matriarch Eileen Ford when she was just seventeen. When she became a model, Carrera said all the things she hated "were accentuated and made to work for [her]." Pleased with her looks now, Carrera has said she would not want to look like anyone else.

With her exotic looks and 5'9" frame, she quickly became a popular cover girl, gracing the pages of such fashion magazines as *Vogue* and *Bazaar*. She appeared on the cover of *Playboy* in 1977, when the magazine's editors purchased some revealing pictures from a fashion photographer. Carrera longed to be more than just a pretty face and feared her Playboy appearance would ruin her career. Ex-boyfriend Robert Evans describes her as "a playgirl who wanted to be taken seriously." With this in mind, and despite her modeling successes, Carrera became bored with modeling, saying she was "tired of being a high-priced hanger."

Carrera appeared in a Chiquita banana commercial and in the obscure 1970 film *Puzzle Of A Downfall Child*. In 1975 she enrolled at the Sorbonne to pursue another passion, painting. Carrera, however, never attended. Actor Tom Laughlin, star of *Billy Jack*, invited her to Hollywood to screen test after seeing her photo in a fashion magazine. From there, Carrera says, she "never looked back."

Film and Television Work

She starred with Laughlin in the 1975 western *The Master Gunfighter*. The next year, she starred with Rock Hudson in the horror film *Embryo*, playing a Frankenstein-like creature grown by a mad scientist. She then co-starred with Burt Lancaster and Michael York in the 1977 film of H. G. Well's *The Island of Dr. Moreau*. In 1983, Carrera gave her most memorable screen performance, as the villainess Fatima Blush. Playing opposite Sean Connery's James Bond, Carrera made a memorably campy impression as a vixen who killed with a poisonous snake.

Despite positive reviews of that performance, the pickings were slim after her Bond girl role. The unique appearance that served her so well in modeling became a hindrance in Hollywood. Carrera's mysterious accent (she speaks French, Spanish, Italian, and German, as well as English) made casting in Hollywood difficult, limiting her to foreign roles. Carrera laments this stereotypical notion of the All-American girl. Carrera said, "This country is a conglomerate of all types of women, all colors and shapes and sizes. But for some reason they are trying to convince us that the typical young American female is blonde or red-haired, blue-eyed and freckle faced and a distinctive voice. This apple pie portrait is wrong. The All-American girl is a minority."

After appearing in 1985's *Wild Geese II*, Carrera turned to the small screen, appearing on the CBS series *Dallas* as mystery woman Angelica Nero, a character whom she described as "explosive, unpredictable, outrageous." Carrera's various other television appearances include miniseries like 1978's *Centennial* and 1981's *Masada*, and the 1982-85 detective series *Matt Houston*. Other notable film appearances include 1989's *Loverboy* with Kirstie Alley and *The Wicked Stepmother* with Bette Davis in the same year.

Personal Life

Carrera's personal life has been as varied as her on-screen characters. She has been married and divorced four times, first to German baron Otto K. von Hofman, then Uva Harden, a German model. Her third marriage was to Nicholas Mavroleon, a Greek businessman, and her fourth to journalist Cameron Docherty. Carrera has also had a host of celebrity boyfriends, including actor Richard Gere, ballet star Alexander Godunov, and famed Hollywood producer Robert Evans. Carrera was also romantically linked to the Duke of Northumberland, but Carrera insists they were merely good friends. Mavroleon said Carrera "maintains a tremendous moral fiber," and Evans remembers her fondly.

Carrera enjoys traveling and has been all over the world, collecting outfits from India, the Far East, and Middle East. She has said she enjoys being pampered and indulges

herself with facials and massages. She also loves the classical music of Mozart, Rachmaninoff, and Bach, and the work of Mexican artist Frida Kahlo.

In 1991, Carrera put her lavish Bel-Air home on the market, with plans to move to Europe and focus on her painting. In 1996, Carrera returned to her native Nicaragua to support presidential candidate Arnoldo Aleman. In 1997, she was named ambassador at large for Nicaragua.

Carrera made the most of her talent and beauty. She created a look of her own, expanding traditional notions of beauty in both the fashion industry and Hollywood. When asked if she had any regrets, Carrera responded categorically, "none at all."

Sources:

Crowe, Jerry. "Arts and Entertainment Reports from the Times, National and International News Services and the Nation's Press." *Los Angeles Times,* November 11, 1997, p. F2.

Green, Michelle. "From the Jet Set To Your TV Set, Dallas' Barbara Carrera Knows Her Role — Lady of Mystery." *People,* November 18, 1985, p.173.

Monaco, James, ed. *Baseline's Encyclopedia of Film,* Perigee, 1991.

Reuters North American Wire, October 7, 1996.

Ryon, Ruth. "Hot Property: Actress Paints Moving Picture." *Los Angeles Times,* September 22, 1991, p.K1.

Scott, Vernon. "Scott's World: Carrera: No All-American Girl." *United Press International,* February 9, 1981.

Taylor, Christopher. "I wanted to be a blue-eyed blonde." *London Daily Mail,* April 27, 1995, p.50.

Casárez Vásquez, Enedina
See **Vásquez, Enedina Casárez**

Marie Romero Cash
(1942–)
Painter, sculptor, author, santera

Selected writings:

Santos, a Coloring Book for Children. Rubble Press, 1990.

Built of Earth and Song: Churches of Northern New Mexico. Red Crane Books, 1993.

Altares de la Gente: Devotional Spaces in Northern New Mexican Homes. Museum of New Mexico Press, forthcoming.

Santos: Enduring Images of Northern New Mexican Villages. University of Colorado Press, forthcoming.

Overview

Marie Romero Cash is a native Sante Fe folk artist known as a santera. She creates artwork depicting the religious figures popular in the spiritual life of many Hispanic Americans living in New Mexico and the Southwest. Using simple lines and bright colors, she brings her own whimsical accent to traditional carved and painted folk art.

Cash was born in 1942 into a family of well-known artists. Her parents, Emilio and Senaida Romero, are famous tinsmiths. She was educated in Santa Fe schools where she learned several types of art such as stained glass, mosaic tile, copper enameling, and sketching. She is pursuing her bachelor's and master's degrees in cross-cultural studies through Lesley College in Cambridge, MA.

Cash's sister Anita, also a santera, first encouraged Marie to try the art of painting *retablos,* or pictures of saints, in the early 1970s. She began with simple retablos of San Francisco, San Pascual, and other popular saints that she placed into tin frames and sold at the Santa Fe Spanish Market. She received a grant from the National Endowment of the Arts to learn the art of tinwork from her parents, and added it to her many artistic skills.

Marie Romero Cash

Wood Carvings Are Her Forte

In 1976, Cash tried her hand at carving large wooden figures of saints called *bultos,* which she then decorated with color. Her carving instructor was a fellow Santa Fe artist, Malcolm Withers, who also taught Cash the art of mixing colors and dry gesso. Cash found she had a natural talent for woodworking and decided that, in order to compete in the folk art market, she would focus on creating large, high-quality, colorful *bultos* for collectors. Her first piece was a hollow-frame statue of the Virgin Mary whose skirt she painted with a colcha embroidery stitch motif. It was purchased for a show at the Albuquerque Museum.

The *bultos* Cash creates are often based on Old Testament characters, such as Jonah and the Whale. She has a series called *Tales from the Old Testament* that depicts 15 separate stories from the Bible. Her work entitled "Heaven and Hell" consists of 50 small carved devils, angels, and saints enclosed in a three-tiered wooden case.

Cash is renowned for her carving of distinctive chess sets. The first, in which the chess pieces are figures of saints, is now in a museum's permanent collection. Her second was recently designed for Lesley College and reflects her skill at combining traditional southwest Hispanic American style and an imaginative modern flair.

Designs *Reredos* for Churches

In 1982, Cash's art found new expression when she was commissioned by the pastor of San Juan Nepomuceno Church in El Rito, NM, to create a *reredos,* or an altar screen, to commemorate the 150th anniversary of the church's founding. The completed work consisted of nine panels, each with a patron saint from the nearby missions, and the entire piece is topped with a lighted crown. Following this success, she designed unique altar screens for several New Mexico and Colorado churches. In 1997, Cash created and installed the entire Stations of the Cross for St. Francis Cathedral in Sante Fe. In an interview with Don Toomey for *Tradición Revista,* she recalled how moved she was by the emotional content of this work, and came to the realization that "these works are me!" and they were "going to reflect everything I am and have experienced in my life, and they were going to be forever." A testament to her calling as santera, this work has brought her great joy and lasting inner peace.

In 1987, Cash became project director for a survey funded by the National Endowment of the Arts and the New Mexico Arts Division to document the eighteenth and nineteenth century tinwork, furniture, and other cultural artifacts in New Mexico's churches. The result is a book entitled *Built of Earth and Song: Churches of Northern New Mexico,* published by Red Crane Books in 1993. Cash's personal observations and the accompanying pictures by

Santa Fe photographer Jack Parsons capture the beauty and scope of New Mexico's colonial folk art and people. She lectures widely at museums and galleries, and she is a private consultant for many collectors of Spanish colonial art.

Traditional Art; Contemporary Vision

Marie Romero Cash is a santera who skillfully combines the Hispanic American culture of centuries-old religious folk art with a contemporary vision of spiritual awareness. Her carved and painted work *Cristo and Mourning Figures* in mixed media greets visitors to Albuquerque as they enter the airport. She told Toomey for the *Tradicion Revista* article that she views her art as "an extension of those early santeros' works. . . one tiny step forward in the perpetuation of an age-old spiritual craft." She wants to inspire children and beginning woodworkers to use their imaginations and create art using those unique ideas hidden in each of us. She brings the secular world and the spiritual realms closer together in a celebratory way. Romero Cash published *Santos, a Coloring Book for Children* from Rubble Press, Santa Fe, in 1990. Forthcoming books include *Santos: Enduring Images of Northern New Mexican Villages* from the University of Colorado at Boulder, and *Altares de la Gente: Devotional Spaces in Northern New Mexican Homes* from the Museum of New Mexico Press in Santa Fe.

Current Address: 295 Lomita, Santa Fe, NM 87501.

Sources:

Lesley College Home Page. Available at http://www.lesley.edu/ news/publications/lesley_news/96_10/art.html.
Toomey, Don. "Folk Art of Marie Romero Cash." *Tradición Revista,* Summer 1997, pp. 31-36.

Carmela R. Castellano

Organization executive, community activist

As chief executive officer of the California Primary Care Association, Carmela Castellano champions the rights of all people seeking medical assistance and actively promotes equal access to health care. Throughout her career, Castellano has worked to increase the health care opportunities available to the economically disadvantaged and all minority groups. Castellano's efforts as an advocate of public health care have earned her recognition as one of the most influential Hispanic Americans in public health law.

Lays Groundwork for Advocacy Career

Early on, Castellano laid the groundwork for a career as an advocate of human rights. In 1986, she received a B.A. in political science, with highest honors, from the University of California at Berkeley. Following graduation, she served as a fundraising and community outreach program administrator for San Jose City College from January to August of 1987. Castellano was then named a Rotary Foundation international scholar and spent the next year attending La Universidad Central de Venezuela in Caracas. She served as a summer intern in 1989 with the law firms of Pillsbury, Madison & Sutro in San Jose, CA, and in 1990 with Morrison & Foerster of San Francisco. That same year, Castellano entered Yale Law School.

At Yale, Castellano sharpened her skills as a lawyer. She received an appointment as a research assistant, joined the Latino Law Students' Association, and served as the notes topics editor for the *Yale Law Journal.* She was also awarded a Coker Fellow/Federal Civil Procedure teaching assistantship. In addition, Castellano was named chairperson of the Professor Catherine MacKinnon Yale Legal Services Prison Clinic. She graduated from Yale Law School in May of 1991.

Becomes Involved in Law, Public Health, and Activism

Shortly after receiving her law degree, she accepted in September of 1991 a position as staff attorney with Public Advocates, Inc., a San Francisco law firm. Her responsibilities with this firm allowed her to develop her interest in improving the social and political position of minorities and the economically disadvantaged. Castellano's most notable cases included representing minority law enforcement officers to insure enforcement of a previous consent decree by the San Francisco Police Department, as well as representing minority, low-income, and non-English-speaking communities that had been unfairly charged higher rates by insurance companies. Her efforts did not go unnoticed, and in October of 1996, Castellano was named a managing attorney with the San Francisco firm.

Even though Castellano's schedule was full, her concern about the barriers blocking impoverished minorities from the public health care system never wavered. Her concerns led Castellano to establish in August of 1992 the Latino Coalition for a Healthy California (LCHC), which promotes equal access to quality health care for Californians of Hispanic descent. As founder of the LCHC, Castellano's responsibilities were vast, including health policy analysis and advocacy, fundraising, budget development and oversight, media relations, community outreach, and staff supervision. Under Castellano's direction, the LCHC became a statewide network of health advocates and service providers working to bring together public and private sector organizations to formulate and implement projects. The projects included enforcement of cultural and linguistic competency standards within state-managed care provider organizations. Castellano's work had far-reaching impact and soon caught national attention. Localized debates about obstacles in the public health care system became a national focus, largely because of Castellano's persistent efforts in California on this subject. She first addressed public health and civil rights organizations on the national level in October of 1992, when she appeared at a conference entitled "An African-American Health Care Agenda," held in Baltimore, MD. She frequently speaks before the U.S. Surgeon General's workshops, American Public Health Association conferences, and national and state public health and civil rights organizations.

Castellano's services as an administrator are widely sought after on the local, state, and national level. In 1993, she was named a member of the board of the California Cultural Competency Project and the California Adolescent Nutrition and Fitness Program, as well as a member of the San Francisco Community Hospital advisory council and the California State Department of Health Services' cultural and linguistic subgroup. She became a member of the steering committee of the Women's Health Leadership Program and a member of the board of directors of the Mission Neighborhood Health Center in San Francisco in 1994. She served as a member of the Health Care Options Working Group in 1997. Castellano has served as co-chairperson of the California Pan-Ethnic Health Network since 1992, as a member of the board of directors of the Chicana/Latina Foundation since 1993, as the chairperson of the Cultural and Linguistic Standards Task Force since 1996, and as a member of the national advisory council of the National Health Service Corporation. Castellano's efforts have also brought her recognition as a national leader in public health activism. In 1996 and 1997 she received numerous local, state, and national awards, including being named among the "100 Most Influential Hispanics in the United States" by *Hispanic Business* and a member of the "Top 20: Who's Who of Latino Medicine" by the *Medical Herald*.

Remains Tireless Civil Rights Advocate

Castellano left her position as managing attorney with Public Advocates to accept the position of chief executive officer with the California Primary Care Association (CPCA) in November of 1997. The CPCA represents a network of 270 nonprofit, community-based primary care health clinics and promotes equal access to health care for all individuals. The CPCA concentrates on advancing multicultural health policy initiatives, emphasizing reform of state-run managed care programs to make them more responsive to the needs of minority and non-English-speaking populations. In this capacity, Castellano is responsible for the financial direction of the CPCA, serving as its liaison with government agencies and state organizations. She is also a spokesperson for the organization at state, national, and international professional conferences. Castellano also provides consultant services to municipalities seeking to develop voluntary affirmative action programs. She remains a tireless civil rights advocate for minorities and the economically disadvantaged, working to ensure that they receive employment opportunities and access to health care.

Current Address: California Primary Care Assn., 1201 K St., Ste. 1010, Sacramento, CA 95814.

Sources:

Eldridge, Grant. Curriculum vitae and other materials provided by Carmela R. Castellano, March, 1998.

Olivia Castellano
(1944–)
Poet, author, playwright

Selected writings:

Blue Mandolin, Yellow Field. Tonatiuh-Quinto Sol International, 1980.
Blue Horse of Madness. Crystal Clear, 1983.
Spaces That Time Missed. Crystal Clear, 1986.

Overview

Olivia Castellano was born into a life of subsistence in Del Rio, Texas, on July 25, 1944. She was the second of five children born to Secundino Peña Castellano, a Southern Pacific Railroad worker with a fifth-grade education, and Cruz Guerrero Castellano, who had left school in the second grade to help raise ten siblings. In "Canto, Locura y Poesía" (1990) Castellano recalls that in 1958 her father, "tired of seeing his days fade into each other without promise," moved his family to California where they became farmworkers. She then became serious about education, convinced that only through books and songs would she "be free to structure some kind of future" for herself.

Childhood Memories Serve as Source of Creative Energy

The memories of her early Texas childhood are her source of creative energy; her work emerges from the Texas landscape. Her mythology is composed of horses, blue sky, yellow earth, and feelings of anger for her childhood artistic pursuits having been suppressed by her family and formal educators. The colors blue and yellow represent her strongest ties to south Texas: the vast blue sky above the landscape and *la tierra* (the land), vividly yellow due to its lack of mineral content. During her high school years in California, Castellano found encouragement to pursue her education, having discovered a love for French while learning it through songs and stories. This new language freed her to express herself artistically, eventually in English as well as French. Although Castellano felt her native Spanish connected her to her family and culture, she did not see it as a language of the learned. It was not until later in her writing career that she found artistic inspiration in being able to write from a cultural voice.

Castellano's artistic education was gained at home in the evenings where she voraciously read those authors whom she admired: the Marquis de Sade, Arthur Rimbaud, Honoré de Balzac, Comte de Lautréamont, and other French writers in translation, as well as Fyodor Mikhaylovich Dostoyevski, Walt Whitman, and Karl Marx. Despite her record as a straight-A student, Castellano felt anxiety in the classroom. At home she felt very isolated in her academic and artistic pursuits as a result of her family's insensitivity. In "Canto, Locura y Poesía," Castellano recalled family members saying, "Te vas a volver loca con esos libros. Esta nunca se va a casar" (You'll go nuts with those books. She'll never get married). In her junior year of high school she composed a poem in imitation of John Keats's "La Belle Dame Sans Merci" for her advanced composition course and was told by her teacher, "Stick to essay writing; never try to write a poem again because a poet you are not!" Reflecting on these painful comments, the poet wrote, "This was the tenor of my adolescent years. When nothing on either side of the two cultures, Mexican or Anglo-American, affirms your existence, that is how rage is shaped."

University Program Changes Life, Career Direction

Beginning in 1962, Castellano's primary goal was to achieve a bachelor's degree in English at Sacramento State College (later called California State University, Sacramento) to further her skills as a writer, but, because of her strong feelings of alienation from traditional English departments, she settled on pursuing a degree in French with a minor in English. She graduated with a BA in June of 1966, and after two years of teaching French and English in high school, she returned to the university in 1968 for a master's degree through a program called the Mexican-American Experienced Teachers' Fellowship. In "Canto, Locura y Poesía," Castellano described the program that changed her life and the course of her career: "I was allowed to express my rage and to examine it in the company of peers who had a similar anger. Most of the instructors, moreover, were Chicano or white professors sensitive to Chicanos. For the first time, at 25, I had found my role models. I vowed to do for other students what these people had done for me." Castellano's vast reading experience and her formal education have greatly shaped her poetic voice. Her master's thesis, devoted to the study of contemporary Mexican dramaturgy, concludes by offering these partial solutions: "Become aware that drama has a history of being a mirror of society and that it can be used to reflect as well as to prefigure the course of events in a

social movement. . . by doing this—and so much more—we Chicanos can create for ourselves a prouder self-image."

Soon after filing her thesis, she suffered a serious depression which led to a nervous breakdown. Though traumatic, the breakdown in terms of her writing was "the best thing that ever happened to me. It made me more sensitive to myself as a writer and how close the powers of creativity always are to the brink of insanity." In the fall of 1971 Castellano, fully recovered, went back to California State University, Sacramento—this time to teach part-time. She accepted a full-time lecturer position in 1972. In the classroom Castellano uses Chicano literature to promote literary and racial awareness. She created her department's first course in the genre. By teaching Chicano literature, by bringing Chicano poets and writers to the university, and by sharing her works with students and fellow Chicano poets, Castellano provides what she did not have as a young writer: the nurturing atmosphere necessary for the creation of Chicano literature.

Poetry Uses Imagery and Bicultural Archetypes

Throughout Castellano's poetry, she skillfully integrates English and Spanish, leaving a truly bilingual, Chicano mark on the language. However, the mainstay of her work as a poet is the remarkable use of imagery from her personal mythology that transcends language and includes archetypes from both English and Spanish cultures. Her first published poems appeared in *Grito del Sol* (1977). They are a sample of her larger body of poems published in 1980 under the title *Blue Mandolin, Yellow Field*. The title of this book brings together the image of the earth and sky of her childhood memories. The book is broken into seven sections, but the many sections do not thematically connect. The themes seem to separate, rather than incorporate, in the tight form of textual structure that Castellano has chosen to shape her first book of poems. In choosing the title, Castellano wanted to give the impression of a small child standing between a bright blue sky and a vibrant yellow, Texas earth. Castellano's personal concerns in the creation of *Blue Mandolin, Yellow Field* were to be a disciplined poet conscious of poetics and to experiment with how far she could linguistically push herself.

Castellano's second book of poetry, *Blue Horse of Madness,* reads like a collection of *cuentos* (stories) in poetic prose told by a poet-persona more confident than the younger voice in *Blue Mandolin, Yellow Field.* The individual poems are much freer than the tight, compact, imagistic pieces of the earlier collection. Although divided into eight sections of various themes, *Blue Horse of Madness* is tied together by a single narrative voice. The narrator is fully immersed in the memories being written about, drawing the readers into the poet's world. Castellano paints a vivid portrait, creating an imaginary place rooted in childhood where all can visit. Written in an adolescent voice, as demonstrated by "Learning to Play," Castellano conveys the serenity of growing up in Comstock, Texas, dwelling on the many voices and images that reside there. In *Blue Horse of Madness,* one begins to understand the experiences which are her source of mythology. Whenever the young Castellano looked up from playing, there seemed to be a horse looming above her as ranchers rode through Comstock. She always felt inches away from being trampled. The images of blue horses in her poetry come from Texas horses that once stood over her; but in her writing she has given them wings, symbolizing the flight of the imagination.

The image of the blue horse reappears in her next book, *Spaces That Time Missed* (1986), a work that reflects a sense of balance and a maturity of voice acquired through the writing experience. *Spaces That Time Missed* is divided into four sections that examine childhood, poetry, perception, and current events. This was Castellano's last collection of poetry before she decided to concentrate fully on writing fiction. The poems are more meditative and mature than in her two previous books. They are written by an adult voice involved in the pure enjoyment of the writing process. The themes presented are thought-provoking and the characters interesting, and as a result, the reader yearns to learn more about the world of south Texas. In this way, *Spaces That Time Missed* serves as a springboard into fiction.

Self-Publishes Books of Poetry

Castellano published her last two books of poetry herself, a method she prefers over solicitation, for she finds that in this way she "creates art for art's sake" rather than for profit or fame. By being a self-published writer, she keeps the writing in her own hands. Because her books are not readily available through bookstores or published by large publishing houses, few articles have been written about them. Sandra Cisneros's review of *Blue Mandolin, Yellow Field* in *Third Woman* magazine (1984) is one of the few critical pieces available on Castellano's work. Cisneros writes, "Though her literary influences are diverse, Castellano assembles a voice that is intimately hers with a sparseness and depth. . . ." Tey Diana Rebolledo, in an article on the inspirations of Chicana poetry, says of Castellano, "the writing of poems, even in the face of despair[,] creates a sense of connectedness and functions as solace for the poet."

Continues Exploring New Genres

Castellano continues to explore new genres. Her projects include: *The Comstock Journals,* a novel or collection of short stories about a young Chicana growing up in a Texas-Mexico border town; *The Jimmy Blues,* a serious drama about destructive behaviors in a Chicano family; and *Fantasies in a Blue Garden,* a musical comedy celebrating a Chicano barrio through music, dance, and song. She is also working on her fourth book of poetry, tentatively named *For Women: Thank God the Moon is Forgiving.*

Castellano's recent work exudes the relaxed sense of an artist comfortable with the craft of writing, a more mature voice that is no longer trying to prove what metaphor and rhyme are. The stories and songs from her culturally rich childhood in south Texas are rooted to that land, and as a poet, storyteller, novelist, and playwright, she will continue to write of the spaces that time missed in her remembrances of things past.

In addition to her writings, Castellano recently began a peer mentor pilot program in the Department of English at California State University, Sacramento. As she explained in an interview, the program makes promising minority students apprentices to professors. The purpose of the peer mentoring program is two-fold: It provides students with another channel of communication to professors, and it allows professors to redirect their energies, which are demanded by so many students, in a more effective manner.

Sources:

Cárdenas, Roberto, ed. *The Life and Poetry of Olivia Castellano* [videotape] Sacramento: California State University, Film Archives, Communication Studies Department, 1989.

"Peer Mentoring: An Interview with Professor Olivia Castellano." *The Teaching Newsletter,* California State University, Sacramento. Available at http://www.csus.edu/ctl/mentorin. html.

Rebolledo, Tey Diana. "Soothing Restless Serpents: The Dreaded Creation and Other Inspirations in Chicana Poetry," *Third Woman,* 2, no. 1 (1984): 83-102.

Rocard, Marcienne. "The Remembering Voice in Chicana Literature," *Americas Review,* 14 (Fall-Winter 1986): 150-159.

Ana Castillo
(1953–)
Poet, author, women's rights activist

Selected writings:

Otro Canto, 1977.
The Invitation, 1979.
Clark Street Counts, (play)1983.
Pajaros enganosos. Cross Cultural Communications, 1983
Women Are Not Roses. Arte Publico Press, 1984.
The Mixquiahuala Letters. Bilingual Review Press, 1986.
My Father Was a Toltec. West End Press, 1988.
So Far From God. Norton, 1993.
The Sexuality of Latinas. Edited with Norma Alarcón and Cherríe Moraga. Third Woman Press, 1993.

Massacre of the Dreamers: Reflections on Mexican-Indian Women in the United States 500 Years After the Conquest. Plume, 1995.

Loverboys. W.W. Norton, 1996.

La Diosa de las Americas/Goddess of the Americas. Riverhead Books, 1996.

Overview

Initially known for her elegant feminist poetry, Ana Castillo is one of a group of distinguished Chicana writers from the Chicago area. Over the years, Castillo has broadened her artistic contribution to include musical performance and prose. Her feminist message can be found in such diverse media as high school textbooks and musical theater pieces.

Born in Chicago

Ana Castillo was born in Chicago on June 15, 1953, to Mexican American parents who had migrated from the Southwest. Her interest in different aspects of creative experience prompted her to major in art and minor in secondary education at Northeastern Illinois University, where she received her B.A. in 1975. Following graduation, Castillo taught ethnic studies at Santa Rosa Junior College in Sonoma County, California, for one year. The heady artistic, activist, and intellectual climate of the 1970s fostered her interest in writing and performing her poetry. She was an early contributor to *Revista Chicano-Riquena* (now *The Americas Review*), a literary magazine edited by Nicolás Kanellos, which captured the artistic ferment of Midwest Hispanics. Her first collection of poems, *Otro Canto,* was published as a chapbook in 1977 with a grant from the Illinois Art Council, where she served as a writer in residence from 1977 to 1979. Two years later, coinciding with her graduation from the University of Chicago with a M.A. in Latin American and Caribbean studies, she published a second collection of poems, *The Invitation,* with a grant from the Playboy Foundation. In 1991 she earned a Ph.D. in American studies from the University of Bremen in Germany.

In the early 1980s, Castillo's work took on musical tones. Her interest in flamenco dancing led her to create and manage the Al-Andalus flamenco performance group from 1981 to 1982. She adapted her collection of poems in *The Invitation* for music, and they were performed at the 1982 Soho Art Festival in New York City. Castillo also wrote the play *Clark Street Counts,* performed by the Chicano Raza Group in June of 1983.

Castillo has received attention for her elegant style and feminist themes. As a result, her work has appeared in a variety of anthologies including *Women Poets of the World,* published by McMillan in 1982, *The Third Women: Minority*

Women Writers of the U.S., published by Houghton-Mifflin in 1979, and a high school text, *Zero Makes Me Hungry* published by Scott, Foresman in 1975. Her next two poetry collections were *Pajaros enganosos,* published by Cross Cultural Communications in 1983, and *Women Are Not Roses,* published by Arte Publico Press in 1984.

Expands Her Literary Horizons

In later years, Castillo has developed into a prolific writer of poetry and prose fiction. Her first novel, *The Mixquihuala Letters,* was published by Bilingual Press in 1986. This novel, written in epistolary form, was widely acclaimed for its treatment of women. It received the Before Columbus Foundation Book Award in 1987 and earned an award from The Women's Foundation of San Francisco, California in 1988. Castillo's poetry collection *My Father Was a Toltec,* published by Bilingual Press, was released in 1988. This collection, like her earlier collection *Women Are Not Roses,* "explores the life of Latinas and comments on gender roles in the Hispanic community," according to Achy Obejas in the *Chicago Tribune.* In 1993 she published the novel, *So Far From God,* which dealt with the issue of environmental racism. This novel earned Castillo the 1993 Carl Sandburg Literary Award in Fiction and the Mountains and Plains Bookseller Award of 1994. In 1995, she published *Massacre of the Dreamers: Reflections on Mexican-Indian Women in the United States 500 Years After the Conquest,* a non-fiction work. Castillo published a collection of short stories entitled *Loverboys* in 1996. As the title implies, *Loverboys* is a collection of short stories about the experiences of love, including the wonderful and painful. That same year, she edited *La Diosa de las Americas/ Goddess of the Americas,* an anthology of writings about the Virgin of Guadalupe.

In addition to writing, Castillo has actively participated in public speaking engagements and served as a contributing editor for *Humanizarte* and *Third Woman* magazines. She also founded the Premio Ana Castillo, a literary prize for aspiring poets. Castillo currently resides in Gainesville, Florida, with her son, Marcel Ramon Herrera, and husband, George R. Esenwein, an associate professor of history at the University of Florida.

Sources:

Archives, Arte Publico Press, Houston, Texas.

Guide to the Ana Castillo Papers. Available at http://www.library.ucsb.edu/speccoll/castillo.html.

Obejas, Achy. "Novelist Ana Castillo Brings Southwest to Homecoming." *Chicago Tribune,* May 16, 1993.

Valiente, Victoria I. "Way Past Cool: Ana Castillo Talks About Her Work, Her Life, and the True Test of Fame." Available at http://www.minorities-jb.com/hispanic/castillo.html

Rosemary Catacalos
(1944–)
Poet, journalist

Selected writings:

As Long as It Takes. Iguana, 1984.
Again for the First Time. Tooth of Time, 1984.

Overview

Rosemary Catacalos writes works that combine Greek mythology and Mexican-American folklore. Her poetry, a paean to her ancestry, was published as the book, *Again for the First Time,* a collection she wrote over a ten-year span. (All the poems in *As Long as It Takes,* a chapbook also published in 1984, are included in *Again for the First Time.*) Catacalos incorporates themes, styles of language, and types of lyricism that bring to mind works by the Mexican writer Rosario Castellanos and the Argentine Alfonsina Storni. She has earned an international reputation, yet her poetry is not as well known as that of some other Hispanic women writers. Much of this lack of attention is due to Catacalos's resistance to being part of the "poetry scene" and her commitment to letting her work speak for itself. However, she has gradually begun to read her work in public more often and to become more involved in literary circles. Catacalos has received several prizes and awards, among these the 1985 Texas Institute of Letters poetry prize for the best collection of poetry published by a Texas-connected writer and, in 1986, the Dobie Paisano Fellowship, a writing grant awarded jointly by the University of Texas at Austin and the Texas Institute of Letters.

Experiences Greek-Mexican Childhood

Born on March 18, 1944, to Greek-Mexican parents (Demetres and Beatrice Catacalos) in San Antonio, TX, Catacalos attended local schools in the area. Because both her parents worked in their small commercial-sign shop, Catacalos was raised by both sets of grandparents, although for a time she lived only with her paternal grandparents. She spent a great deal of time with her paternal Greek grandfather and her maternal grandmother, who was from Mérida, Yucatán, in Mexico. Baptized in the Greek Orthodox church, Catacalos was as strongly grounded in the Greek community as in the Mexican. Her extended family, which included both sets of grandparents and one sister, Linda, interacted on a daily basis. Most families in the San Antonio barrio were poor, as was her family. Her parents eventually built their sign business into a statewide endeavor. The young Catacalos worked in their shop, cleaning brushes and handing her father tools and paints. This sense of family and community is a recurring theme in her work, as is her rich bicultural heritage. Greek and Mexican myths, names, and cities are characteristics of Catacalos's work.

A bookish child and an excellent student, Catacalos spent a lot of time alone, talking to herself. From about the age of five, she "talked" on paper but believes she was about twelve when she consciously began to write poetry. None of her childhood poems exist; however, a love of words, images, and the stories told by her grandparents remained and later surfaced as poems. Catacalos cites the nightly family story sessions as a time of learning and great happiness. Much of this feeling was based on the stimulation given her by her grandparents, the languages spoken at home, and the richness of the ethnically mixed barrio. The stories and songs that were part of her daily life were the stimuli that fed her imagination. Her bedtime stories were from Greek mythology.

Works to Benefit the Arts

Catacalos has worked as copywriter, arts publicist, and newspaper reporter. From 1974 to 1985 she conducted bilingual poetry workshops in Arizona, Arkansas, and Texas, at the elementary and secondary-school level, and edited over 30 student anthologies. As a producer of cable-television programs on the arts, Catacalos also worked with the San Antonio Arts Council. In 1985 she co-chaired the City of San Antonio's first fine arts and cultural advisory committee and helped to develop the city's arts-funding process. She has also co-chaired the Texas and Arizona Arts Commissions and served as a National Endowment for the Arts literature panelist. In 1986 she was elected to the Texas Institute of Letters and the year before was the recipient of a National Endowment of the Arts creative writing fellowship.

From 1986 to 1989 Catacalos served as director for the literature program at the Guadalupe Cultural Arts Center, a multidisciplinary Hispanic arts group in San Antonio. In 1987 she initiated and organized the first San Antonio Inter-American Bookfair, which has attracted national and international attention due to a cultural exchange program that has included writers such as Isabel Allende, Alice Walker, and Carlos Fuentes. Catacalos has taught poetry in San Antonio schools, and in 1986 she held an appointment as visiting scholar at the University of Texas at Austin. She held the prestigious Wallace Stegner Fellowship at Stanford University from 1989 to 1991, and she is completing a new poetry collection. She is now the director of the Poetry Center at San Francisco State University.

Interweaves Greek and Mexican Influences

As many Hispanic women poets do, Catacalos utilizes some Spanish in her work, embellishing verses with the lyricism inherent in the language. She also uses some Greek, but she remains essentially a writer of English, the language in which she is most comfortable. Her bilingual poems, unlike those written only in English, are infused with the sounds of the San Antonio barrio, as in "From Home": "Desde tu tierra te dicen [News from home]/ The chicharras [cicadas] are beginning to die again/ and it is the end of summer fruit./ The mornings become brittle and cool/ without their sound. Camarada [comrade]/ the moon is on the rise,/ dogs howl through the night,/ and it is September." The cicadas, the summer insects that each summer invade sections of the Southwest, are a metaphor for Mexican migrants who each summer cross the U.S. border to work. Indeed, Catacalos's poetics are based in the community and express the human condition of Mexicans and Hispanics living a marginal existence.

In *Again for the First Time* Catacalos explores Greek-Mexican duality. The retelling of old stories throughout her early years familiarized Catacalos with Greek characters such as Penelope and Theseus, and also with Mexican folk legends, including that of La Llorona, the wailing woman who searches for the children she killed—a legend learned from her Mexican maternal grandparents, in particular her grandfather who taught her to speak Spanish and about Mexican folklore. In "A Vision of La Llorona," Catacalos departs from the usual portrayal: "I see your mother every week/ now that you're gone./ Sometimes she knows me/ and remembers to be polite. . . ."

Catacalos's work is not an attempt at neoclassicism but the merging of classical myths and the present: the Chicano barrio of San Antonio and everyday people the writer has known, yet who may exist in any Southwest barrio. In "One Man's Family" she depicts Dog Man, a transient from the neighborhood who "carries his mother's wedding dress around in that filthy sack."

Her paternal Greek grandfather, who fled the Turkish army and at 16 landed on Ellis Island, lived for a time in Seattle, where he worked as a carpenter. He later earned a living selling popcorn and ice cream from a wagon on San Antonio's West Side. A strong man with a soft heart, he is immortalized in the poem, "Katacalos" (the old spelling of the name, no longer used by the family): "The Old Man, we always called him./ We said it with respect./ Even when he embarrassed us/ by wearing his plaid flannel work shirt/ to church under the fine blue suit/ He had come off a hard island birthplace,/ a rock long ago deserted by the gods. . . ."

"Rosemary Catacalos is a poet who can see beyond the simple event," critic Dave Oliphant wrote in 1985. She "comes into her own as a spokeswoman for the 'daily returns' of a life that through her writing offers in itself mythic relations to worlds past, present, and future. Woven into the sixty-eight pages of *Again for the First Time* is a series of poems wherein Catacalos takes on the character of different women, from Penelope to La Llorona." Oliphant claims that whether writing of her Mexican or Greek side, Catacalos is concerned throughout her book with "old ties."

Indeed the ties between writer and community are most evident in the first part of the book, which reflects *chicanismo* (an orientation toward Chicano cultural values), the Mexican side of Catacalos, while the second alludes to her Greek ancestry and Greek gods and goddesses. In "Ariadne to Dionysios," Catacalos melds myth to reality: "We have hiked hours to get to this place./ Nothing stands between us now. Now we know/ what it is to be on an island. Nothing stands/ between us and the *sea,*/ Dionysios./ Even before, when you lay in all the red and purple/ beds of Asia, did you think about my breasts?/ That they are the fruit of the sacred wine?/ The way I would delight again in twining/ around your famous staff if you could only/ get me into the sun long enough?"

Sexuality, in the work of Catacalos, while subtle and sensuous, is often related to unrequited love, to women who wait for a lover. Another recurring theme is that of the sea as sexual, pulsating with salty waters, spray, foam, and life. In this same poem she writes, "you ride me like a dolphin, half in, half out / of the water / Your teeth, ancient shells, imprinting my skin. . . ."

Acts as the Solitary Muse

For most writers, personal space and the insulation it provides are crucial to their work. It is not surprising that much of Catacalos's work relates to loneliness and pain. Catacalos remembers that because she studied and worked most of the time, she was a "solitary child, with few playmates, who spent her free time in the company of adults." In "(There Has To Be) Something More Than Everything" the voice of the solitary muse is heard: "But there are things that have been torn away./ From all of us. And we need to collect the shadows,/ the pain as it ghosts along the soul in faded fragments./ We need to put as many old pieces as we can together/ to make something else entirely./ As many times as we have to and as long as it takes."

A politically astute Catacalos evokes the works of Carolyn Forché, author of *The Country Between Us* (1981), whose works remark on human suffering and are highly political. Catacalos's "Learning Endurance From Lupe at the A & J Ice-house" is about the plight of Salvadoran refugees such as Lupe, who, after witnessing the cold-blooded killing of his wife and family, has escaped to the United States. Lupe spends his days in a stupor, as he sweeps ice at a local icehouse in return for the free beer that will dull his pain.

Works to Bring Poetry to the Community

In addition to being a fine poet, Catacalos is committed to working with the Hispanic community of her hometown, particularly with literacy programs. She has served the San Antonio community both as an administrator and as a teacher of poetry. This love for community is evident in her writing; for example, the *chicharras* in some of her poems make sounds like the voices of the talkative women of the barrio—women Catacalos portrays with love and kindness.

A primary goal for Catacalos has been to bring poetry to the schools and Hispanic communities of Texas. In 1985, in the aftermath of a large Mexican earthquake, she designed and produced mailers featuring student poetry and drawings as gifts for the children of that country, a work that later was exhibited at the United Nations offices in Mexico City and featured in the 1986 San Antonio Festival. At the international level, Catacalos took part in the Tercer Encuentro de Poetas del Mundo Latino (Third Conference of Poets of the Latin World), held in 1988 in Mexico City, and sponsored by the Mexican Secretariat of Foreign Relations, the National Fine Arts Institute, and the National Autonomous University of Mexico.

Rosemary Catacalos resides in the California Bay Area, where she is working on a new collection of poetry and a personal memoir. She is also working on a series of interviews with Mexican women immigrants which will be accompanied by her own essays. Her poems are published widely in national journals, college textbooks, and anthologies, including *Best American Poetry 1996*. She is currently an affiliated scholar with the Stanford University Institute for Research on Women and Gender.

Sources:

Kellman, Steven G. "State Without Words as Writers Convene." *San Antonio Light,* April 15, 1985, p. 8.

McDermott, Marise. "It took Houston to find Catacalos." *San Antonio Light,* March 11, 1988, p. 11.

Oliphant, Dave. "Three San Antonio Poets." *Cedar Rock,* Winter 1985, pp. 6-8.

Stanford University Home Page. Available at http://www-leland.stanford.edu/group/IRWG/Institute/Affiliated/.

Whitaker, James. "Tangled Lines." *Texas Monthly,* September 1984, pp. 184-188.

Denise Chávez
(1948–)
Playwright, author, professor

Selected writings:

Life Is a Two-Way Street, 1980.
The Last of the Menu Girls. Arte Publico Press, 1986.
The Woman Who Knew the Language of the Animals. Houghton Mifflin, 1992.
Face of an Angel. Farrar, Straus, and Giroux, 1994.

Overview

"You don't have to go anywhere. Not down the street. Not even out of this house. There's stories, plenty of them all around." With these words the mother of a character in the title story of Denise Chávez's short story collection, *The Last of the Menu Girls,* gives advice on writing to her daughter. Chávez might have been writing these words to herself, for her short stories and plays are characterized by their focus on characters and scenes from everyday life. She explains that the presence of the ordinary in her work springs from her belief that as a Chicano writer she needs to speak for those who have no voice. "My work as a playwright is to capture as best as I can the small gestures of the forgotten people, the old men sitting on park benches, the lonely spinsters inside their corner store," Chávez told *Contemporary Authors.*

Denise Chávez was born on August 15, 1948, in Las Cruces, New Mexico, the daughter of Ernesto E. Chávez, an attorney, and Delfina Rede Favor Chávez, a teacher. Her interest in theater blossomed during her years at Madonna High School in Mesilla, New Mexico, and she was awarded a scholarship in drama to New Mexico State University. In 1971, she earned a B.A. in theatre from New Mexico State University and in 1974 received a M.A. in fine arts from Trinity University in San Antonio, Texas. In 1982, she obtained a M.A. in arts from the University of New Mexico. Although Chávez considers herself a full-time playwright, she has also spent several years as a teacher. From 1977 to 1980, Chávez taught English and theatre at Northern New Mexico Community College in Española. She has also taught at the American School in Paris, and she has served as a professor of theater at the University of Houston in Texas from 1988 until 1991.

Early Writings Earn Critical Acclaim

In 1970, Chávez's writing talents received early recognition. In that year she won the New Mexico State University Best Play Award for her work, *The Wait.* During the remainder of the decade, she wrote nearly a dozen plays and saw most of these produced in Taos, Santa Fe, or Albuquerque, New Mexico. In addition to her plays, Chávez published a poetry anthology, *Life Is a Two-Way Street,* in 1980, and a collection of short stories, *The Last of the Menu Girls,* in 1986. The stories in the *The Last of the Menu Girls* revolve around the life of Rocio Esquibel, a 17-year-old girl whose job involves delivering menus to hospital patients. Writing in *New York Times Book Review,* Beverly Lyon Clark noted that many of the stories revealed "Chávez's strengths in dialogue and in juxtaposing evocative scenes." *The Last of the Menu Girls* received New Mexico State University's Steele Jones Fiction Award and the Puerto del Sol Fiction Award. Chávez has also written and performed two one-woman shows *Novena Narrativas,* and *Women in the State of Grace,* as well as a one-act adaptation of *The Last of the Menu Girls.* Her work has been selected for publication in several collections, including *An Anthology of Southwestern Litera-*

ture, *An Anthology: The Indian Rio Grande,* and *Voces: An Anthology of Nuevo Mexicano Writers.*

In 1992, Chávez wrote a children's fable entitled *The Woman Who Knew the Language of the Animals.* She published her first novel, *Face of an Angel,* in 1994. The novel enjoyed wide critical acclaim and earned Chávez the 1995 American Book Award. In addition, *Face of an Angel* won the 1995 Premio Aztlán, which is awarded to an outstanding novel written by a Chicano/Chicana writer. In 1996, Chávez's story "La Macha Grande" appeared in *Latina Magazine* and her essay "Crossing Bitter Creek: Meditations on the Colorado River" was included in a collection of essays about rafting the Colorado River, *Writing Down the River,* in 1998.

Winner of Numerous Awards

Chávez's work has earned her many personal awards. She has received grants from the New Mexico Arts Division, the National Endowment for the Arts, and the Rockefeller Foundation. In 1982, she received a creative writing fellowship from the University of New Mexico and, in 1990, a creative artist fellowship from the Cultural Arts Council of Houston, Texas. In 1995, Chávez received the Mesilla Valley Writer of the Year Award and was inducted into the honorary literary society, Writers of the Pass. She was presented with the Luminaria Award by the New Mexico Community Foundation of Santa Fe, as well as the Soroptimist International of the Americas Club's Woman of Distinction Award in 1996. In 1998, Chávez earned the Papen Family Arts Award, which is presented to the individual who has proven invaluable to the arts in Las Cruces, New Mexico, and the surrounding area.

Married to photographer and sculptor Daniel Zolinsky, Chávez currently resides in Las Cruces, New Mexico. She is the assistant professor of creative writing, playwrighting, and Chicano literature at New Mexico State University and has served as the artistic director of The Border Book Festival since 1994. Throughout her career, Chávez has demonstrated a social consciousness that has led her to serve as a teacher at Radium Springs Center for Women, a medium-security prison, and as co-director of a senior citizen workshop in creative writing and puppetry at Community Action Agency in Las Cruces, New Mexico. This social consciousness is also present in her written work as a continuing theme of love, a theme that Chávez finds in the landscape of the American Southwest. She explained this concept in *Contemporary Authors:* "I write about the neighborhood handymen, the waitresses, the bag ladies, the elevator operators. They all have something in common: they know what it is to love and to be merciful. . . . My work is rooted in the Southwest, in heat and dust, and reflects a world where love is as real as the land. In this dry and seemingly harsh and empty world there is much beauty to be found. That hope of the heart is what feeds me, my characters."

Current Address: 480 La Colonia, Las Cruces, NM 88005.

Sources:

"The Last of the Menu Girls." *New York Times Book Review,* October 12, 1986, p. 28.
Trosky, Susan M., ed. *Contemporary Authors New Revision Series,* Volume 131, Gale, 1991.

Linda Chavez-Thompson
(1944–)
Organization executive, labor activist

Emerges on Labor Front

From her early jobs of cleaning houses and picking cotton, Linda Chavez-Thompson has emerged as the leading woman in the national labor movement. She is the executive vice president of the AFL-CIO, the first person of color to serve on the executive council. In this capacity, she acts as a bridge between the labor movement and minorities, which traditionally have had a hostile relationship.

Linda Chavez-Thompson

Demonstrates Early Negotiating Skills

Chavez-Thompson, a second generation Mexican American, was born in Lubbock, TX, on August 1, 1944. She was one of eight children of sharecropper parents. At the age of ten, she started working in the west Texas cotton fields in the summer, and it was then that the seeds of her future career were planted. While her entire family toiled all day in the hot Texas sun for thirty cents per hour, Chavez-Thompson convinced her father that it would be better for the family if her mother stayed home and took care of the house rather than working in the cotton fields during the day. Thus began her "negotiating" career. While her parents were going through an especially difficult period, Chavez-Thompson dropped out of high school in the ninth grade to help support her family. She married her first husband at 19 years of age and went to work cleaning houses.

Climbs Ladder of Labor Union

In 1967 Chavez–Thompson began her trade union career when she joined the Laborers' International Union, a labor group of which her father was also a member. Chavez-Thompson served as the secretary for the union's Lubbock local, where she began to learn the workings of the labor movement. Since she was the only Spanish-speaking official, she also served as a union representative for the Hispanic American members.

From 1971 to 1973 she served in San Antonio, TX, as an international representative for the American Federation of State, County and Municipal Employees (AFSCME), AFL-CIO. This arm of the AFL-CIO represented members in Arizona, Colorado, Nevada, New Mexico, Oklahoma, Texas, and Utah, a region that generally was opposed to labor organizing. She became assistant business manager for AFSCME Local 2399 in San Antonio in 1973 and later rose to business manager. Eventually she was named executive director of the local and served in this capacity from 1977 through February of 1995. Meanwhile, in 1986 the Labor Council for Latin American Advancement, AFL-CIO, chose Chavez-Thompson to be its national vice president, a position which she still holds.

In 1988 Chavez-Thompson was elected AFSCME vice president and pursued organizing efforts in the seven-state region. Of that time, she said, "Trying to defend the rights of government workers in Texas was a difficult proposition, because Texas law didn't allow for unions of government workers to be recognized as such. You had to maneuver and 'persuade' state officials. . . ." Her efforts yielded significant results, however. The New Mexico legislature passed a law for bargaining by public employees, and several states sharply increased their membership in the union.

Expanding on her long career with the AFSCME, Chavez-Thompson was elected executive director of Texas Council 42, AFSCME, on February 4, 1995, and continues to serve in this capacity. The council comprises about 17 locals with a total membership of ten thousand. Chavez-Thompson is undertaking legislative and education programs to help the rank and file in its fight against downsizing, budget cuts, and companies that contract out to nonunion sources.

Elected to AFL-CIO

Facing formidable opposition, Chavez-Thompson was elected in 1995 as executive vice president of the AFL-CIO, largely due to the efforts of the federation's president, John Sweeney. He pushed for increasing the number of council members and for including a woman. Chavez-Thompson's election was hailed by AFSCME International Vice President Gerald W. McEntee as the "boldest step that the AFL-CIO has ever taken to reflect the nation's diverse work force in labor's highest council." Chavez-Thompson campaigned for the post by calling for a reorganization of the labor federation. She said after the election: "The face of labor is changing, and you can tell this by the mere fact that I am a woman, and a woman of color." In her capacity as vice president and third ranking leader of the AFL-CIO, she is working to forge closer ties between the union and women and other minorities.

Chavez-Thompson also is aiming to build up the union's general membership, which in recent years has been shrinking. Union membership is now only about 15 or 16 percent of the total work force, compared with 34 percent back in the 1950s. Part of the new strategy to increase the union's numbers will focus on organizing workers in the service sector. Another major focus will be on the community. Chavez-Thompson claims that too often the unions have become isolated from the communities. Invited to address a workshop held in 1996 by the Women in Municipal Government on the challenges facing women leaders in local government, the new AFL-CIO vice president told her audience: "We in city government and the labor movement have the same goals, the same visions. I propose that we work together, talk together, and maybe even dream together as we never have before."

Serves as Bridge Between Cultures

Chavez-Thompson had to work hard to gain the respect of her colleagues. Even so, there were whispers after the election from the opposition that she was a "token" and lacked the experience necessary for such a post. Despite these charges, she has drawn wide praise from leaders in the labor movement and other sectors of society. Many supporters see her as a bridge between the cultures. "She is a master at interweaving the Latino culture with the majority culture," said Arturo Rodriguez, president of the United Farm Workers.

In looking back at some of her earlier accomplishments as AFL-CIO vice president, Chavez-Thompson is especially proud of the "Union Summer" movement. "It has injected powerful new energy into all aspects of labor's struggles and at the same time given new hope to young people across the country," she said in an interview. She added that the ideas from that project will feed the labor movement for years to come. She is particularly gratified by the warm reception she gets from Hispanic Americans. "During the campaign, I was approached repeatedly by Latinos who said they were so proud. 'You talk like us. You look like us. We know we're headed in a good direction.'"

Chavez-Thompson has become active on many fronts since her election to the AFL-CIO council. She is on the board of governors of the United Way and a vice chairperson of the Democratic National Committee. She is also on the executive committee of the Congressional Hispanic Caucus Institute and the board of trustees for the Labor Heritage Foundation. Chavez-Thompson is also furthering her causes and increasing her visibility nationally through her participation on President Clinton's Race Advisory Board. As the only Hispanic American on the board, she is bringing the problems of minorities to the attention of the board in an open and frank manner.

Sources:

AFL-CIO Home Page. Available at http://www.aflcio.org./chavez.htm.
Amerman, Don. Letter to Linda Chavez-Thompson, February 24, 1998.
Bernstein, Harry. "Is Revitalizing America's Labor Movement a Sisyphean Task?" *Los Angeles Times,* February 4, 1996, p. 3.
Silverstein, Stuart. "Working Within Two Cultures: Many See Linda Chavez-Thompson's Election to No. 3 Post at AFL-CIO as Inspired Choice." *Los Angeles Times,* October 27, 1995, p. 1.
Sun Herald Online Home Page. Available at http://sunherald.com/whmod/whmod3a.htm.

Sandra Cisneros
(1954–)
Author, poet

Selected writings:

Bad Boys. Mango Publications, 1980.
The House on Mango Street. Arte Publico, 1983.
The Rodrigo Poems. Berkeley, CA: Third Woman Press, 1985.
My Wicked, Wicked Ways. Berkeley, CA: Third Woman Press, 1987.
Woman Hollering Creek and Other Stories. New York: Random House, 1991.
Hairs: Pelitos. New York: Knopf, 1994.

Loose Woman. New York: Knopf, 1994.

Overview

Drawing heavily upon her childhood experiences and ethnic heritage writer Sandra Cisneros creates characters who are distinctly Hispanic and often isolated from mainstream American culture by emphasizing dialogue and sensory imagery over traditional narrative structures. Her powerful, sensual work has been influential in ushering in a cadre of minority writers into the mainstream publishing world. Both a poet and a short story writer, Cisneros has garnered awards and honors for both mediums to emerge as one of the leading fiction writers of today.

Experiences Rootless Childhood

Sandra Cisneros was born December 20, 1954, in Chicago. Her father migrated from Mexico leaving a family of some privilege and means; her mother's family, also of Mexican descent but working class, had been in the United States for several generations. The married couple and their seven children travelled constantly between Chicago and Mexico, having to find new living quarters after each trip. Cisneros' childhood was spent in a variety of rundown Hispanic neighborhoods which offered experiences that have found their way into her writing. Constant moves, and changes of schools made Cisneros an introspective child who retreated to books and the writing of poetry. Her love of books came from her mother, who saw to it that the

Sandra Cisneros

young poet had her first library card before she even knew how to read. It took her years to realize that some people actually purchased their books instead of borrowing them from the library. As a child she escaped into her readings and even viewed her life as a story in which she was the main character manipulated by a romantic narrator. In 1966, her parents purchased their first home, a small two-story bungalow, painted red, in a Puerto Rican neighborhood. Experiences in this north side of Chicago served as inspiration for many of the tales in her first book, *The House on Mango Street.*

Decides to be a Writer

As Cisneros wrote her first poems, modeling them on the rhythmic texts in her primary readers, she had no notion of formal structure, but her ear guided her in matters of rhyme and rhythm. After the sixth grade, however, Cisneros stopped writing for a while. In her junior year in high school she was exposed to works by the finest of British and American writers and by Latin American poets who impressed her deeply. Finally, in her junior year at Loyola University, she was introduced to writers such as Donald Justice, James Wright, and Mark Strand, poets who had influenced a whole generation of Spanish writers, thus bringing Cisneros into touch with her cultural roots. She was also introduced to the Chicago poetry scene, where there was great interest in her work. She was encouraged to study in a creative-writing program and was admitted to the Iowa Writer's Workshop; she had hoped to study with Justice but discovered that he and Marvin Bell were on sabbatical leaves that academic year.

Cisneros looks back on those years and admits she did not know she was a Chicana writer at the time, and if someone had labeled her thus, she would have denied it. She did not see herself as different from the rest of the dominant culture. Her identity was Mexican, or perhaps Puerto Rican, because of the neighborhood she grew up in, but she mostly felt American; all her reading was from mainstream literature, and she always wrote in English. Spanish was the private language of home, and she spoke it only with her father. Cisneros knew no Hispanic writers in Chicago, and although she was the only Hispanic majoring in English at Loyola, she was unaware of being different—in spite of her appearance, which was considered exotic by her female classmates.

Discovers Narrative Voice Through Being Different

When Cisneros entered the University of Iowa's Writer's Workshop, she became very aware of how different she was from her elite and priveleged classmates. The styles, structures, and themes which the workshop encouraged, just did not fit her; she felt like a weed amidst a collection of cultivated hot-house blooms. The poet struggled in these years with finding a voice for her writings. She imitated her teachers, her classmates, and what she calls the "terrible East-coast pretentiousness" that permeated the workshop,

without finding satisfaction. An important friend at this time was Joy Harjo, a Native American from Oklahoma, who was well centered in her southwestern heritage and identity, and who also felt lonely and displaced in the Iowa workshop. This friendship offered Cisneros the assurance that she had something to write about that would distinguish her from her classmates. By probing into her past inner-city life and those experiences she had always been embarrassed about, she found within, the child-voice that emerged in the short tales from *Mango Street.* That side of her life inspired many poems, as well.

Begins Writing Poetry

The bulk of Cisneros's early writing emerged in 1977 and 1978. She began writing a series of autobiographical sketches influenced by Vladimir Nabokov's memoirs. She purposely delighted in being iconoclastic, in adopting themes, styles, and verbal patterns directly opposed to those used by her classmates.

The poem "Roosevelt Road," written in the summer of 1977, is most important to Cisneros because it forced her to confront the poverty and embarrassment she had lived with all her previous years, and to admit the distinctiveness of this background as a positive resource that could nourish her writing. In this poem the language is completely straightforward and descriptive of the tenement housing where the poet lived as a child. Lines run into one another, so that the reader is compelled to follow the inherent rhythm, while working on the sense of the message: "We lived on the third floor always/ because noise travelled down/ The milkman climbed up tired everyday/ with milk and eggs/ and sometimes sour cream./ Mama said don't play in alleys/ because that's where dogs get rabies and/ bad girls babies/ Drunks carried knives/ but if you asked/ they'd give you money./ How one time we found that dollar/ and a dead mouse in the stone wall/ where the morning glories climbed. . . ."

Once the journals *Nuestro* and *Revista Chicano-Riquena* accepted her first poems, Cisneros gained enough confidence to submit her work to other publications. These early texts were more concerned with sound and timing, more with the *how* than with the *what* of what she was saying. A case in point is "South Sangamon," in *My Wicked Wicked Ways* (1987), a poem which, when read aloud, corroborates the fact: "His drunk cussing,/ her name all over the hallway/ and my name mixed in./ He yelling from the other side open/ and she yelling from this side no./ A long time of this/ and we say nothing/ just hoping he'd get tired and go."

Cisneros's master's thesis, titled *My Wicked, Wicked Ways,* is full of such poems on a diversity of topics—daily events, self-identity, amorous experiences, and encounters with friends. Her penchant for sound is obvious, as is her representation of a world that is neither bourgeois nor mainstream. Revised and enlarged, the thesis was published as a book in 1987.

While Cisneros taught at Latino Youth Alternative High School in Chicago (July 1978-December 1980), she spent time on writing but never finished projects fully as collections. Her involvement with many aspects of student life was too draining and consumed her creative energy. However, one poem she wrote was selected to be posted on the Chicago area public buses, thus giving her much-needed exposure and publicity. Cisneros was also seduced by the adulation and applause awarded to writers who read their material at public performances. After a period of "too much performing" (in her words) in coffee-houses and school auditoriums, she gave up the lecture circuit to spend more time on her writing.

Another Chicano poet, Gary Soto, was instrumental in helping publish Cisneros's chapbook *Bad Boys* in 1980. The seven poems depict childhood scenes and experiences in the Mexican ghetto of Chicago. One poem, "The Blue Dress," is Cisneros's effort to paint a scene full of visual imagery that depicts a pregnant woman as seen through the eyes of the expectant father. The language of these poems has a musical ring, with short, run-on lines and compact statements.

Writes *The House on Mango Street*

Shortly after participating in the Iowa Workshop, Cisneros decided to write about conflicts directly related to her upbringing, including divided cultural loyalties, feelings of alienation, and degradation associated with poverty. Incorporating these concerns into *The House on Mango Street,* a work that took nearly five years to complete, Cisneros created the character Esperanza, a poor, Hispanic adolescent who longs for a room of her own and a house of which she can be proud. It is dedicated to "the women" and, in forty-four short narratives, ponders the disadvantages of choosing marriage over education, the importance of writing as an emotional release, and the sense of confusion associated with growing up. The short tales recounted by Esperanza reflect the incisive musings of this young person as she observes other women around her, and then matches their existential situation with what may possibly await Esperanza herself in the future.

The reader sees many portraits of colorful neighbors—Puerto Rican youths, fat ladies who do not speak English, childhood playmates—until finally Esperanza sees herself and her surrounding experiences with greater maturity. Thus the reader sees her at her first dance in the tale "Chanclas," where attention is first focused on the bulky, awkward saddle oxfords of a school-girl, then the vision is directed upward as Esperanza blossoms into a graceful and poised dancer, who draws everyone's glances. Esperanza retells humorous experiences about her first job and her eighth-grade girlfriend who marries; then Esperanza reveals more of her intimate self in the last two tales. In "A

House of My Own" and "Mango Says Goodbye Sometimes," it is revealed that the adolescent has been nurturing a desire to flee the sordid, tragicomic environment where she has grown up. The image of the house is also useful to reveal the need for the narrator to find a self-identity. Esperanza yearns for "a house all my own. . . . Only a house quiet as snow, a space for myself to go, clean as paper before the poem." Cisneros's speaker feels the need to tell the world the stories about the girl who did not want to belong to that ugly house on Mango Street. Esperanza admits, at the conclusion of her stories, she is already too strong to be tied down by the house; she will leave and go far, only to come back some day for those stories and people that could not get away. The conclusion is that, in essence, Cisneros takes within her the memories from the house as she also carries her mementos from Mango Street, her bag of books and possessions. These are her roots, her inspirations, and the kernels of what Cisneros sensed, years ago in Iowa, that distinguished her from other American writers. While humorous in many ways, each story offers a brief portrait of young women in Esperanza's immediate neighborhood, most of whom have less than ideal lives. Thus, the *persona* observes adolescent girls who are rushing into adult experiences, others who already face the dilemmas of a domineering husband or father, the raising of children, being trapped in a life situation that offers little hope for improvement or growth. In essence, the tongue-in cheek-humor of each story also reveals a tragic side.

An important contribution by Cisneros to Hispanic letters is that this book about growing up offers a feminine view of the process, in contrast to that exemplified by leading works by men. As critics Erlinda Gonzales-Berry and Tey Diana Rebolledo have aptly pointed out, young Esperanza is a courageous character who must combat the socialization process imposed on females; the character breaks from the tradition of the usual protagonist of the female bildungsroman by consistently rejecting the models presented to her and seeking another way to be Chicana: "I have begun my own kind of war. Simple. Sure. I am one who leaves the table like a man, without putting back the chair or picking up the plate." Esperanza's experiences parallel those depicted by other Chicana writers. This book earned Cisneros the 1985 Before Columbus Book Award, as well as important recognition as an author. Written in what Penelope Mesic called "a loose and deliberately simple style, halfway between a prose poem and the awkwardness of semiliteracy," the pieces in *The House on Mango Street* won praise for their lyrical narratives, vivid dialogue, and powerful descriptions.

Matures as a Poet

Cisneros turned back to poetry, following the success of *Mango Street. The Rodrigo Poems* is a collection that reflects a more mature poet, many texts inspired during Cisneros' travels in Europe. Gone are the child's voice and humorous observations. Instead, one reads about amorous encounters with roguish European men, all of whom can be identified by the name "Rodrigo." In this collection, Cisneros uses much of the style, imagery, and technique that characterizes her most recent work. She uses words as a painter would use brief strokes of a brush; each word, its sound, its shape and placement on the paper, serve to produce a sensation for the reader. Her style could be called minimalist, for its compactness, whether the text take the shape of a poem or of prose; in the balance, Cisneros is essentially a poet. The poem "No Mercy" presents a theme common to Cisneros, that of the unfaithful man who hurts women, who in turn must somehow vindicate themselves. In this text two previous wives have abandoned a pitiful man, plucking from the kitchen sink their long hair, their rings and domestic comb. "You must've said something cruel / you must've done something mean / for women to gather / all of their things."

The Rodrigo poems were included in *My Wicked, Wicked Ways,* when it was published in 1987. Only a few of these texts are voiced by the small child who observes people and events in her neighborhood. In her third volume of verse, Cisneros writes about her native Chicago, her travels in Europe, and, as reflected in the title, sexual guilt resulting from her strict Catholic upbringing. A collection of 60 poems, each of which resemble a short story, this work further evidences Cisneros's penchant for merging various genres. Reviewer Gary Soto explained in *Bloomsbury Review*: "Cisneros's poems are intrinsically narrative, but not large, meandering paragraphs. She writes deftly with skill and idea, in the 'show-me-don't-tell-me' vein, and her points leave valuable impressions." In her poetry, as in all her works, Cisneros incorporates Hispanic dialect, impressionistic metaphors, and social commentary in ways that reveal the fears and doubts unique to Hispanic women. She stated in an article for *The Americas Review*: "If I were asked what it is I write about, I would have to say I write about those ghosts inside that haunt me, that will not let me sleep, of that which even memory does not like to mention. . . . Perhaps later there will be a time to write by inspiration. In the meantime, in my writing as well as in that of other Chicanas and other women, there is the necessary phase of dealing with those ghosts and voices most urgently haunting us, day by day."

Portrays Women Characters

Cisneros's next published work, *Woman Hollering Creek and Other Stories* is a very rich album of female portraits. It is a collection of 22 narratives revolving around numerous Mexican-American characters living near San Antonio, TX. Ranging from a few paragraphs to several pages, the stories in this volume contain the interior monologues of individuals who have been assimilated into American culture despite their sense of loyalty to Mexico. In "Never Marry a Mexican," for example, a young Hispanic woman begins to feel contempt for her white lover because of her emerging feelings of inadequacy and cultural guilt resulting from her inability to speak Spanish. Although Cisneros

addresses important contemporary issues associated with minority status throughout *Woman Hollering Creek and Other Stories,* critics have described her characters as idiosyncratic, accessible individuals capable of generating compassion on a universal level. The dedication reads: "for my mama. . . .y para mi papa. . . ." signalling both the bicultural and bilingual nature of this work. Although written totally in Cisneros's polished inimitable style of English, there appear enough Spanish references or words to root the stories in a long tradition of Mexican-American culture. The tales show a progression in narrative voice and in the fictional world depicted. They begin with the voice of the adolescent narrator, found in early poems, and in *Mango.* "Mericans" is a very representative story recounting the dilemma faced by Chicano authors in life and in their art. The protagonists are children born and raised in the United States, who travel to visit grandmother in Mexico. While one of them recounts her observations of religious rituals and superstitious beliefs practiced by the older generation, they are addressed in broken Spanish by an American tourist who offers them chewing gum in exchange for taking a snapshot of lovely "native" children. The tourist is perplexed when she hears the children dialogue amongst themselves in perfect English; of course, they admit they are "mericans," a curious neologism signifying a mixture of Mexican and American.

The outstanding fact about all of the stories is that they focus on the conditions of women, are narrated from a woman's vantage point, and describe how women adjust, submit, rebel, or perhaps work through the dynamics of the interrelationship of the sexes. The lead story, which gives the book its title, tells about a young Mexican woman who marries a Mexican American. Her life goes from poor to wretched, yet towards the end, it is a female network that saves her and shows her there are other ways to exit from her life situation. The beauty and richness in this book is that Cisneros has intricately woven together a myriad of cultural details, popular sayings, folk traditions, and legends, in a way not seen before.

Woman Hollering Creek and Other Stories is a rare example of a work by a Hispanic woman being published by a mainstream press. Writer Ann Beattie has said of this collection: "My prediction is that Sandra Cisneros will stride right into the spotlight—though an aura already surrounds her. These stories about how and why we mythologize love are revelations about the constant, small sadnesses that erode our facades, as well as those unpredictably epiphanic moments that lift our hearts from despair. A truly wonderful book."

In 1994, Cisneros broke into a new genre with the publication of her children's book, *Hairs: Pelitos.* The bilingual book draws children into a rhyme about all the different kinds of hair that exist, as a way to celebrate diversity. The importance of family ties is also a major theme that is presented.

That same year, Cisneros published another collection of poems titled, *Loose Woman.* The underlying emotion of the majority of the poems is joy; the dominant poetic voice is that of an exuberant, liberated female persona who basks in her womanhood. The work is a reaffirmation of the self, and continues to follow the short-lined, biting style of her other works.

Wins Honors for Writing

Although Sandra Cisneros considers herself a poet and a short-story writer, she has also authored articles, interviews, and book reviews concerning Hispanic writers. She has taught creative writing at all levels and has experience in educational and arts administration. Her creative work, though not copious, has already been the subject of scholarly papers in the areas of Hispanic and women's studies. She has read her poetry at the Colegio de Mexico in Mexico City; at a symposium on Chicano literature at the Amerikanistik Universitat in Erlangen, Germany; and over Swedish Educational Radio. Some of her poetry is included in a collection of younger Hispanic poets published in Calcutta, India.

Cisneros has earned several grants that have permitted her to devote herself full-time to her writing. In the spring of 1983 she was artist-in-residence at the Fondation Michael Karolyi in Vence, France. Earlier, in 1982, she received a National Endowment for the Arts grant, which she used to travel through Europe. In the late 1980s Cisneros completed a Paisano Dobie Fellowship in Austin, TX, and then spent additional time in Texas. She also won first and third prizes for her short stories in the Segundo Concurso Nacional del Cuento Chicano, sponsored by the University of Arizona. Cisneros as a writer is growing rapidly. She feels that writers like herself, Soto, Lorna Dee Cervantes, and Alberto Rios belong to a new school of technicians, new voices in Chicano poetry. Cisneros wants to maintain her distinctiveness and her dual inheritance and legacy, and not fuse into the American mainstream. She cannot tell in which direction her poetry will lead her, but she hopes that years from now she will still be worthy of the title "poet."

Sources:

Benson, Sheila. "From the Barrio to the Brownstone." *Los Angeles Times,* May 7, 1991, p. F1.

Chicano-Riquena, Fall-Winter, 1985, pp. 109-19.

Cisneros, Sandra. "Ghosts and Voices: Writing from Obsession." *Americas Review,* Spring, 1987, pp. 69-76.

Cisneros, Sandra. "Only Daughter." *Glamour,* November, 1990, pp. 256-57.

Kingsolver, Barbara. "Poetic Fiction with a Tex-Mex Tilt." *Los Angeles Times Book Review,* April 28, 1991, p. 3.

Nino, Raul. Review of *Loose Woman. Booklist,* May 1, 1994, p. 1576.

Pulido, Rachel. "Sandra Cisneros: The Foremost Mexican-American Woman Writer Dishes Up a Particularly Spicy Brand of Tex-Mex." *Mirabella,* April, 1991, p. 46.

Soto, Gary. Review of *My Wicked Wicked Ways. Bloomsbury Review,* July-August, 1988, p. 21.

Judith Ortiz Cofer
(1952–)
Poet, author, professor

Selected writings:

Peregrina. Riverstone Press, 1986.
Terms of Survival: Poems. Arte Publico Press, 1987.
Reaching for the Mainland. Bilingual Review Press, 1987.
The Line of the Sun. University of Georgia Press, 1989.
Silent Dancing: A Partial Remembrance of a Puerto Rican Childhood. Arte Publico Press, 1990.
The Latin Deli: Prose and Poetry. University of Georgia Press, 1993.
An Island Like You: Stories of the Barrio. Orchard Books, 1995.
Bailando en Silencio: Escenas de Una Ninez Puertorriquena. Pinata Books, 1997.

Overview

"**W**e lived in Puerto Rico until my brother was born in 1954," wrote poet, essayist, and fiction writer Judith Ortiz Cofer. "Soon after, because of economic pressures on our growing family, my father joined the United States Navy. He was assigned to duty on a ship in Brooklyn Yard. . . that was to be his home base in the States until his retirement more than twenty years later." In these brief sentences from an essay published in *Georgia Review* and included as part of her *Silent Dancing: A Partial Remembrance of a Puerto Rican Childhood,* the reader is introduced to the dual reality that makes up Cofer's literary universe. Her work focuses on the effect on Puerto Rican Americans of living in a world split between the island culture of their homeland and the teeming tenement life of the United States.

Although Cofer was born on February 24, 1952, in Hormigueros, Puerto Rico, the daughter of J. M. and Fanny Morot Cofer, she was brought to the United States when quite young. The family's official residence was in Paterson, New Jersey, but whenever her father's Navy job took him to sea, Cofer and her mother and brother stayed in Puerto Rico with her maternal family. As a child Cofer spoke only Spanish at first and, later, was introduced to the English language, a process she found difficult, but rewarding.

Judith Ortiz Cofer

Begins Career as English Teacher

She eventually earned a bachelor of arts degree in English from Augusta College in 1973 and a master of arts degree in English from Florida Atlantic University in 1977. Since receiving her advanced degree, Cofer has served as an English instructor at several institutions, including the University of Miami, the University of Georgia, and the Georgia Center for Continuing Education. "It was a challenge, not only to learn English," she notes in *Contemporary Authors*, "but to master it enough to teach it and—the ultimate goal—to write poetry in it."

Cofer's first books of poetry were three chapbooks—*Latin Women Pray*, *The Native Dancer*, and *Among the Ancestors*—published in the early 1980s. Three more volumes of poetry followed in the same decade: *Perregrina* in 1986 and *Terms of Survival* and *Reaching for the Mainland* in 1987. Branching out from poetry by the end of the decade, Cofer saw the release of her novel, *The Line of the Sun*, in 1989, and a volume of poetry and personal essays, *Silent Dancing*, in 1990. Among the honors she has received for her work are a 1989 National Endowment for the Arts fellowship in poetry and the 1990 Pushcart Prize for Nonfiction.

Cofer's first novel, *The Line of the Sun*, was lauded by various critics for its people qualities. In the *New York Times Book Review*, for example, Roberto Márquez described

Cofer as "a prose writer of evocatively lyrical authority." In the *Los Angeles Times Book Review* Sonja Bolle also referred to the beauty of many of the novel's passages. The book is narrated by Marisol Santa Luz Vivente who tells the story of three generations of her family. The first part of the book describes the origins of the Vivente clan in the Puerto Rican village of Salud and introduces the reader to the culture and landscape of the island. The second part of the novel is set in Paterson, New Jersey, where Marisol strives to find an equilibrium between the clashing values of her Puerto Rican ancestors and those of her new U.S. mainland home.

Work Delves into Dual Culturalism

The same conflict appears in the autobiographical essays and poems that make up Cofer's *Silent Dancing*. The title is derived from the author's memories of a silent home movie filmed at a New Year's Eve party when her parents were young, which ends with a silent conga line of revelers. As each of the dancers comes into view, she comments on how each has responded to the cultural differences in their lives. She writes of her fascination with the short clip in the book's title essay: "The five-minute movie ends with people dancing in a circle—the creative filmmaker must have set it up, so that all of them could file past him. It is both comical and sad to watch silent dancing."

In *Contemporary Authors* Cofer explained her use of autobiographical elements in her poetry. Her words seem equally applicable to her more recent works of fiction and autobiography. "My family is one of the main topics of my poetry," she notes. "In tracing their lives, I discover more about mine. The place of birth itself becomes a metaphor for the things we all must leave behind; the assimilation of a new culture is the coming into maturity by accepting the terms necessary for survival. My poetry is a study of this process of change, cultural assimilation, and transformation."

In 1993, Cofer published a collection of poems, stories, and essays entitled *The Latin Deli*. *The Latin Deli* was highly acclaimed by reviewers and critics and earned Cofer the Anisfield-Wolf Book Award. She published another book of poems, *An Island Like You: Stories of the Barrio*, in 1995. In 1997, Cofer released a work in Spanish entitled *Bailando en Silencio: Escenas de Una Ninez Puertorriquena*

Sources:

Contemporary Authors New Revision Series, Volume 32, Gale, 1991.
Georgia Review, spring/summer, 1990, pp. 51-59.
Los Angeles Times Book Review, August 6, 1989, p. 6.
New York Times Book Review, September 24, 1989, pp. 46-47.
Women's Review of Books, December, 1990, p. 9.

Maria Antonieta Collins

Television anchor, news correspondent

Born and raised in Mexico, but living in the United States since the 1970s, Maria Antonieta Collins uses her knowledge of both countries in her role as news correspondent and TV anchor for *Noticiero Univision* in Miami. She is part of a national and international nightly newscast aired in the United States and 13 Latin American countries. In addition to her work as a journalist, she is often invited to speak at lectures and conferences.

Collins is the oldest of five children; her father was an agricultural engineer, her mother, a U.S.-born housewife. She attended high school in Veracruz, Mexico, and graduated from Veracruz University Law School in 1973. Her first job was as a general assignment reporter for Televisa in Mexico City. While there, she also served as an investigative reporter and researcher for the popular U.S. television program, *60 Minutes.* "I was very lucky," Collins commented in a telephone interview. "Mexican TV was just beginning in 1974."

In 1980, Collins became Televisa's first correspondent in California. By 1985, she was a news editor and anchor,

Maria Antonieta Collins

broadcasting the first Spanish-language newscast for the San Diego area. She became a traveling correspondent, covering Mexican major league baseball players, international news in Mexico, and issues related to undocumented Mexicans living in the United States. At the same time, she wrote articles for *Siempre,* a Mexican political magazine, and for the Mexican newspaper *Novedades.* In 1988, Collins joined Televisa's 24-hour-a-day international Spanish network as an anchor, producer, and writer. Since 1995, she has been the prime-time weekend anchor for *Noticiero Univision* in Miami, acting as the late edition anchor throughout the week.

Throughout her career, Collins has been on the site of many prominent news stories, including the election of Pope John Paul I, the 1984 Olympic Games in Los Angeles, three papal trips, four Mexican presidential elections, two World Cup soccer matches, and four World Series. She has also witnessed earthquakes, explosions, and prison riots.

Collins' investigative and television work has not gone unnoticed. In 1990, she was voted best anchor in Mexico. In 1993, Coatzacoalcos, Veracruz, Mexico, voted her Woman of the Year. She won an Emmy in 1992 for her breaking news story on a Guadalajara explosion and another Emmy in 1994 for her investigative report on Cardinal Posada's assassination. An industry association named her best female correspondent of 1996 and best national anchor of 1997.

Identifies with the American Dream

"The American dream is myself," Collins remarked in the telephone interview. She said that she left her native Mexico in hopes of a better future for her family. "I'm like a thousand immigrants that come to the United States, with a bag filled with dreams. I'm very proud of my origins. I came from a family that worked a lot and, like many Mexican immigrants, we were poor, but just poor for money, not for dreams." When asked what advice she had for young people of Mexican heritage, she returned to the dream theme: "I always knew I could rise high if I would think, work hard, and dream. . . . I teach my daughters that dreams really can come true." Yet she cautioned, "Never forget your roots. I keep picturing my home in Mexico. It will always be my home because my heritage will always be with me."

Current Address: Univision, 9405 NW 41st St., Miami, FL 33178.

Sources:

Blue, Rose. Telephone conversation with Maria Antonieta Collins, April 8, 1998.
Noticiero Univision press release, 1998.

Maria Contreras-Sweet

Organization executive, business executive, entrepreneur, women's rights activist

Maria Contreras-Sweet knows what it is like to rise from utter poverty to corporate success. Born in Mexico, she spent her childhood in California, where her mother cleaned houses. She was moved from relative to relative, since no home had enough room to keep all of her brothers and sisters together. From this difficult beginning, Contreras-Sweet nevertheless went on to become vice-president of the Southern California operations of Seven-Up/Royal Crown Bottling Companies, and a major community activist. As founding president of Hispanas Organized for Political Equality (HOPE) and as the owner of Contreras-Sweet Communications, she works to further the education and participation of women, particularly Latinas, in the political process. She also has served on the boards of numerous community organizations in California.

Spends Early Childhood in Poverty

Maria Contreras-Sweet was born in Guadalajara, Mexico, to Guadalupe and Rafael Contreras. Her father owned several pharmacies in Mexico. Soon after she was born, her parents divorced, and her mother brought Maria and her siblings to California. Because their mother worked long hours cleaning houses, the children had to be separated and sent in turn to different relatives' homes. When Contreras-Sweet was six, this harsh life changed for the better. Through a colleague at work her mother met and married Hoyt Ramsey, who was able to move the family to a house in the southern California town of Baldwin Park—a tiny house, but one where they could all be together.

Contreras-Sweet learned English in this new setting and became an avid reader of literary classics such as *Little Women*. She still remembers how her third grade teacher did not believe that she had read all of the books that she had discussed and made her write a report to prove it. She went on to become a high school class legislator and homecoming queen. But she definitely feels that she was alone in pursuing any ambitions. As she said many years later in a *Los Angeles Times* article, "No counselor gave me a sense of direction. . . . I don't remember anyone saying, 'Maria, you're going on to college.'"

While in high school, she also met her future husband, Ray Sweet, who was visiting there to discuss teaching a marriage counseling class to students. They literally ran into each other in a hallway, as she was carrying a box of candied apples for a fundraising event. Sweet definitely made an impression by buying all of the apples. After graduating, she attended Mt. San Antonio College (Walnut, California), but admitted later to the *Los Angeles Times* that she had hated her studies there to become a secretary.

Interest in Politics Is Born

With these studies behind her, Contreras-Sweet took a job with the speaker of the California Assembly at the time, Leo McCarthy. Part of her job involved coordinating the work of graduate student interns, which helped inspire her to attend the University of California at Santa Barbara. However, she admits that she left that school quickly, finding the students too liberal for her to be comfortable. She then went to work for another Assembly member, Joseph Montoya, volunteered with the Jimmy Carter presidential campaign in 1976, and attended political science classes. Contreras-Sweet made her first speeches before the City Council while working with Montoya and realized that she loved politics. Because she was becoming more interested in Sweet, she did not pursue a political career herself. Instead, she took a job overseeing the U.S. Census for part of Los Angeles.

Becomes Corporate Executive and Activist

By 1980 Contreras-Sweet had married Ray Sweet, who had become an executive search consultant. She also had taken a position as a marketing trainee at the Seven-Up/Royal Crown Bottling Companies (Seven-Up). She became a great success in the corporate world, largely due to her ability to get people from different viewpoints to reach a common solution. In 1986, she was instrumental in devising an anti-litter law that involved deposits on beverage containers, after bottling companies and environmentalists had argued about this issue for 20 years.

By the mid-1990s, Contreras-Sweet had risen to the position of vice-president for public affairs at Seven-Up. Along with her growing corporate responsibilities, Contreras-Sweet became increasingly concerned about the Hispanic American community and the position of women in the workplace. She was aware of how she had to crack a corporate "glass ceiling" at age 30 to become an executive, and she became involved in a number of community activities and advisory groups on both a local and national level.

Contreras-Sweet built a reputation as a skillful negotiator and soon was serving in such diverse organizations as Loyola Marymount University (chosen as a regent even though she did not graduate from college herself), the executive committee of Blue Cross of California, and the board of RLA (formerly Rebuild L.A.). She also has acted as chairperson of the Mexican-American Opportunity Foundation, advisor to the Hispanic Women's Council, Inc., president of the California-Nevada Soft Drink Association Board, board of the California Endowment (a private foundation that works on improving access to health care), and board of governors of the Town Hall of California.

In 1991 Contreras-Sweet was selected as a member of the Federal Glass Ceiling Commission, which examines the position of minorities and women in U.S. business and makes recommendations on how to improve the situation. She became concerned that the only commission representative of the chief power figures in corporate America—white males—was the chair, Robert Reich (then U.S. Secretary of Labor). So, in her usual style, she organized a group of discussions to address this issue.

Works to Advance Hispanic Political Involvement

In 1989, Contreras-Sweet joined a group of influential Hispanic American women who wanted to establish an organization in California to further the education and participation of women, particularly Latinas, in the political process. The result was Hispanas Organized for Political Equality (HOPE), for which Contreras-Sweet was chosen as the founding president (a position she still held in 1998). One of HOPE's earliest activities was an annual symposium begun in 1991, which included both issues forums and a theatrical presentation. In 1995, HOPE held its first annual Latina Action Day, an opportunity for participants to meet state and federal policymakers. A separate organization, HOPE-PAC, was established in 1993 to conduct political advocacy work. HOPE also set up an Education and Leadership Fund that now produces the annual symposium and conducts educational forums. As an adjunct to her work in HOPE, Contreras-Sweet is president of Contreras-Sweet Communications, a business consulting service specializing in diversity issues.

Contreras-Sweet continues to divide her attention among her greatest interests: her community work and her family. Based on her work in the community, she has received several awards. These include being selected as Woman of the Year by the National Hispanic Women's Conference, and Humanitarian of the Year by the Rossi Youth Foundation. Contreras-Sweet and her family (husband Ray and children Rafael, Francesca Maria, and Antonio) live in Rowland Heights, California.

Current Address: Hispanas Organized for Political Equality (HOPE), 634 S. Spring St., Ste. 1007, Los Angeles, CA 90014.

Sources:

HOPE (Hispanas Organized for Political Equality) Home Page. Available at http://www.latinas.org.

Michaelson, Judith. "Front and Center: She Cracked the Glass Ceiling at 30." *Los Angeles Times,* July 16, 1995, p. E1.

"100 Influentials Directory." *Hispanic Business,* October 1996. Available at http://www.hispanstar.com.

France Anne Córdova
(1947–)
Astrophysicist, educational administrator, editor

Selected writings:

Multiwavelength Astrophysics. Cambridge University Press, 1988.

Overview

It does not take a rocket scientist to figure out that there are no limits to what France Anne Córdova can do. After winning early success as a novelist, cookbook author, and guest editor for *Mademoiselle* magazine, Córdova went back to school to study physics. She has since established herself as a preeminent physicist. In 1984, *Science Digest* named this

France Anne Córdova

rising young star among "America's 100 Brightest Scientists Under 40" for her attempts to unlock the secrets of the universe. From 1993 to 1996, Córdova worked as the chief scientist at the National Aeronautics and Space Administration (NASA), the youngest person ever to hold that post. She now serves as the vice chancellor for research at the University of California at Santa Barbara (UCSB).

Inspires Many Others

A 1997 article in *Woman,* a supplement to the *Santa Barbara New-Press* asked a colleague to describe Córdova. "I find her to be one of the most inspiring persons on campus right now," says Victoria Vesna, an art studies professor at UCSB. "She truly has a vision and it is broad and expansive. Her vision is beyond her own ego: It allows her to be free and take risks."

Córdova was born August 5, 1947, in Paris. While there her father, a Mexican American and West Point graduate named Frederick Córdova, oversaw the Cooperative for American Remittances Everywhere (CARE), a nonprofit organization set up after World War II to distribute food and clothing overseas. As *Woman* recounts: Frederick Córdova expected his firstborn to be a boy and planned to name the child Frederick III. The mother even embroidered a little "F" on all the baby's clothes. When the baby turned out to be a girl, she was baptized Françoise in the Notre Dame Cathedral. (Córdova later Americanized the name to France.)

Córdova grew up in California as the big sister who helped care for 11 siblings. Her after-school chores included babysitting, folding diapers, and ironing school uniforms. Despite the ever-present demands at home, Córdova managed to study hard and received top grades at school. As a senior in high school, she earned a spot among California's "Ten Outstanding Youth."

As an undergraduate at Stanford University, Córdova majored in English. But while on an anthropology tangent as a junior, she spent a summer at an archaeological dig near a Zapotec Indian pueblo in Oaxaca, Mexico. This foray into her Mexican heritage prompted her to write a short novel, called *The Women of Santo Domingo,* based on her experiences. In 1969, the year she graduated, her book was declared one of the ten best entries in the guest editorship contest held by *Mademoiselle* in New York City. As part of her contest entry, Córdova also compiled a collection of Zapotec recipes and turned them into a cookbook.

Changes Career Direction

In the summer of 1969, news coverage of the U.S. Apollo 11 spaceflight held the attention of the budding writer,

along with the rest of the nation. Córdova sat transfixed by the televised landing of men on the moon, as they touched down July 20. Now hooked on space exploration, Córdova later saw a television show on the origins of the universe and decided to change her own direction in life. Subsequently, Córdova told *Woman*: "What's fascinating about science is all the mystery. Who are we? Where did we come from? We are not all there is."

But even while pursuing a doctorate in physics, Córdova wrote and edited many newspaper articles as a staff member of the *Los Angeles Times* news service. Nonetheless, Córdova earned a Ph.D. in physics from the California Institute of Technology in 1979. She was one of only two women in a class of eighteen.

After graduation she went to work as a scientist at the Los Alamos National Laboratory in New Mexico. According to *Woman*: "As a young astronomer, Córdova pioneered a new approach to studying the stars. She helped mobilize hundreds of her colleagues around the world, amateurs and professionals alike, to simultaneously point their telescopes at the same fleeting events in space; the stars that pulse, flare, and explode." She was one of the first astrophysicists "to measure the X-Ray radiation emanating from white dwarfs, old stars with intense gravitational fields and pulsars, stars that flash rhythmically like fast-spinning lighthouses in space."

From 1980 through 1986, she also served as project leader for a project called Astrophysical Processes in Strong Gravitational Fields. Her primary duty was to direct a research group whose interests included pulsars, X-Ray binaries, cataclysmic variable stars and the dust shells of novae. In the middle of this project, she fell in love. While rock climbing in 1983, Córdova met Christian Foster, a high school science teacher. They married and in June of 1986, at the age of 38, Córdova gave birth to a daughter named Anne-Catherine, followed by a son named Stephen in November of 1987.

Publishes *Multiwavelength Astrophysics*

Although she had taken on the rewarding job of mother, Córdova did not abandon her professional goals. She produced another book in 1988 as the editor of *Multiwavelength Astrophysics,* a collection of selected review papers representing all aspects of the field including scientific application, data analysis, and instrumentation. In 1989, Córdova was promoted to deputy group leader of the space astronomy and astrophysics group at Los Alamos. She was also put in charge of the Optical Monitor Digital Processing Unit on the European Space Agency's X-Ray Multi-Mirror Mission, with $6 million in dedicated funding by NASA from 1989 through launch in 1999. As the U.S. principal investigator, Córdova agreed to direct research scientists, graduate students, and support staff at UCSB, plus direct the efforts of teams of scientists and engineers at Sandia and Los Alamos national labs. That same year, Pennsylvania State University tapped Córdova to take a professorship and head its astronomy and astrophysics department. By 1993, she was elected to a three-year term as a vice president at Penn State. Later in the year, NASA appointed her chief scientist; she became the second woman to hold that title. She was stationed at the Langley Research Center, just outside Washington, DC.

By 1995, according to *Woman*: "Córdova was put to the test." In an era of finding more efficient and quicker ways to do the job at a lower cost, NASA officials recommended reducing its nine research centers to two. Córdova was not giving up without a fight. She argued that severe cuts would hamper their research and virtually render their efforts ineffective. Thanks to her efforts not one of the centers was shut down, and she was able to save some of the most critical programs needed to move the research forward and even created a new institute for the study of space biomedical sciences. Her valiant efforts won her praise from NASA comptroller Malcolm Peterson. He was quoted in *Woman* as saying: "None of the other chief scientists brought to the job the energy and inquisitiveness and the understanding of the challenges before us: not enough money and too many great ideas." Córdova hopes that contracting to private organizations could save money, protect expertise, and help preserve the agency's science programs. "The main challenge is to make sure we have a viable science effort at the end of the day," she said in an article for *Science*.

Offers Advice to Hispanic American Youth

As a high-profile science administrator, Córdova has had to overcome personal and professional criticism. In a 1996 article in *The Hispanic Outlook in Higher Education*, she relayed her personal coping tactics and gave advice to Hispanic American youths during a question-and-answer session: "I'm by nature optimistic. Reaching goals isn't for pessimistic people. At all steps of my career, there was someone saying, 'I wouldn't do that. You're too old, too young, too inexperienced.' There are always naysayers. Ask yourself: What is important to me? What is my vision?" She challenged students to look beyond the present into the future to determine what they want to accomplish in life. She also encouraged them to ask if they would have the conviction and vision to stand by their dreams in the face of adversity.

Public Broadcasting Service put the spotlight on Córdova in April of 1996. PBS produced a television miniseries that profiled the careers of 20 Native American, African American, and Hispanic American scientists and engineers. The six-hour series, billed as a celebration of science, conveys their enthusiasm for their chosen disciplines and encourages minorities to pursue careers in math and science.

Accepts Administrative Position at UCSB

In July of 1996, Córdova left NASA with high marks and high honors to accept one of the top administrative posts at UCSB. At that time, she had more than 100 scientific papers to her credit. As vice chancellor of research, Córdova pledged to get the entire campus more involved with research in space. She also championed the integration of the arts and sciences. In her first year at UCSB, she wrung $550,000 out of the campus budget for three years of research on topics that would bring together artists and engineers, sociologists and oceanographers, and musicians and computer engineers.

In 1997, Córdova proudly accepted an honorary doctorate from Loyola-Marymount University in Los Angeles. However, that accolade could not compare to another she received later that year: As a way of recognizing Córdova's contribution to the Mars Pathfinder Space Program, NASA put her name inside a spacecraft that landed on Mars in 1997. When the Pathfinder landed July 4 on Mars, it was carrying a CD-ROM with a dedication to Córdova.

Sources:

American Men & Women of Science, 19th edition. New Providence, NJ: R. R. Bowker, 1996.

Bourne, Kay. "Documentary Examines Roles of Minorities in the Sciences." *Bay State Banner,* April 18, 1996, p. 15.

Breakthrough: The Changing Face of Science in America Home Page. Available at http://breakthrough.blackside.com/bios/cordovabio.htm.

Burns, Melinda, "Head in the Stars, Feet on the Ground." *Woman, Santa Barbara News-Press Magazine,* Summer 1997, pp. 16-20.

"The Changing Face of Science in America." *Hispanic Times,* April 30, 1996, p. 18.

Goodwin, Irwin. "NASA Gets New Chief Scientist; DOE Loses a Nuclear Veteran." *Physics Today,* October 1993, pp. 111-112.

Goodwin, Irwin. "Zare Takes Helm of Science Board; U of California Chooses Córdova." *Physics Today,* July 1996, pp. 51-52.

Hispanic Business Home Page. Available at http://www.HispanStar.com.

Lawler, Andrew. "NASA Plans Major Science Overhaul." *Science,* May 26, 1995, pp. 1122-1123.

Lawler, Andrew. "Pace of NASA Change Worries Advisers." *Science,* March 17, 1995, p. 1589.

Stern, Gary M. "Hispanics in Science; What Does it Take to Succeed?" *Hispanic Outlook in Higher Education,* October 11, 1996, p. 11.

Worhach, Denise. Curriculum vitae from France Anne Córdova, April, 1998.

Gilda Cruz-Romo
(1940–)
Singer, professor

Gilda Cruz-Romo is an internationally acclaimed soprano who has performed with some of the finest opera companies in the world. She traveled across Europe, appearing with Italy's La Scala in Milan, and Teatro Comunale in Florence, the Teatro dell' Opera in Rome, the Vienna Staatsoper, the London Royal Opera, the Paris Opera, Spain's Teatro Liceo of Barcelona, and Moscow's Bolshoi Opera. In the United States, Cruz-Romo performed with the Metropolitan Opera (Met) in New York City and the Lyric Opera in Chicago. Although retired from the stage, she remains active in music, serving as an assistant professor of voice at the University of Texas at Austin.

Beginnings

Cruz-Romo's roots can be traced to Guadalajara, Jalisco, Mexico, where she was born. She studied to become an accountant, graduating with a degree in accounting from the Colegio Nueva Galicia, Guadalajara, in 1958, and landing a job as a bookkeeper. Cruz-Romo found the job stifling and disappointing, and she decided to pursue a

Gilda Cruz-Romo

more creative career. She studied voice and performed locally to support her studies. Composer and conductor Carlos Chávez heard one of her performances and encouraged her to compete for a scholarship to attend the National Conservatory of Music in Mexico City. The one-time bookkeeper won the scholarship and studied with Angel Esquivel at the Conservatory from 1962-64. While at the conservatory, she made her operatic debut with the Mexico City International Opera (MCIO) in 1962, singing the part of Ortlinde in *Die Walküre*.

Becomes Rising Star

Cruz-Romo soon became a regular lead singer with both the MCIO and the National Opera of Mexico (NOM), performing in *Tosca, Nedda,* and as Elisabeth in *Tannhäuser*. She was invited to join the Dallas Civic Opera (DCO) in 1966, and over the next two years she performed leading roles in *Tosca* and *Anna Bolena*. During that time, Cruz-Romo married Texan Bob Romo, a bass-baritone with the Dallas Chorus, on June 10, 1967. She then moved to the United States and relinquished her positions with the MCIO and NOM. Cruz-Romo, however, continued to sing, touring Australia, New Zealand, and South America with the DCO before entering the Met's National Audition competition in 1969. Upon winning the southwest regional category of the competition, Cruz-Romo was offered a contract by the New York City Opera (NYCO) and gave up her position with the DCO. She spent three years with the NYCO, appearing in numerous productions, including *Mifistofele*. Cruz-Romo's career soared to international prominence in 1970 when she won the Metropolitan Opera's National Audition and was named a leading soprano with the company. She placed second as the U.S. representative to the International Madama Butterfly Competition in Japan the same year. Her first performance with the Met occurred on December 18, 1970, when she played the title role in *Madame Butterfly*.

Attains International Diva Status

Cruz-Romo's international star continued to rise during the early seventies. Her increasingly busy schedule forced her to leave the NYCO in 1972, and Cruz-Romo played Covent Garden in London for the first time that same year. She received the Union Mexicana de Cronistas de Teatro y Musica Critics Award in 1973 and also made her debut at La Scala. Admiration for Cruz-Romo extends beyond her voice. Her outgoing personality and idiosyncratic habits, which include eating pasta immediately before going onstage—a direct contravention of the standard operatic practice of fasting prior to a performance—has attracted as much attention as her memorable voice.

However, it is Cruz-Romo's powerful voice that made her one of the most sought after operatic stars. In 1974, she toured Moscow with the La Scala company and made her first recorded performance. Two years later, she made her first film appearance in 1976, playing the title role in *Aida* at the Orange Festival in France. Cruz-Romo was named Best Singer for 1976-77 and received the Cronistas de Santiago de Chile in 1976.

Cruz-Romo joined the Lyric Opera of Chicago (LOC) in 1975 and maintained an extremely active performance schedule well into the 1980s. She made her most notable television appearance in 1979, performing in *Otello* with the Met. She performed the title role of *Medea* in Bridgeport, CT, in 1987 and sang the part of Matilde in the first U.S. performance of Mascagni's *Silvano* at Englewood, NJ, in 1989. Cruz- Romo also developed a second career as a concert vocal soloist during the 1970s and 1980s.

Receives Prestigious Mexican Awards

Cruz-Romo has received high marks for her dramatic efforts. In the early 1980s, she received numerous awards, including the Premio Jalisco, the Testimonio de Honeor, Excuela Music Universidad Guadalajara, and the Merito Cultural of the Instituto Cultural Mexicano- Norte Americano. Cruz-Romo also received the Minorca al Rate, Mexico, and Ninerva al Arte, Mexico, awards in 1991.

Begins Teaching Career

In the early 1990s, Cruz-Romo was ready to contribute to the development of aspiring singers. She accepted positions as voice teacher, assistant professor, and coach at the University of Texas at Austin in 1990 and continues to serve in those positions. Although she now devotes most of her time to teaching, Cruz-Romo is still listed as a leading soprano by both the Met and the LOC.

Current Address: School of Music, Univ. of Texas at Austin, Austin, TX 78712.

Sources:

Baker, Theodore, ed. *Baker's Biographical Dictionary of Musicians.* New York: Schimmler Books, 1992.

Cattell, Jacques, ed. *Who's Who in American Music: Classical.* New York: R. R. Bowker, 1983.

Cummings, David M. and Dennis K. McIntyre, eds. *International Who's Who in Music and Musician's Directory.* Cambridge, England: Melrose Press, 1990.

Eldridge, Grant. Curriculum vitae and other materials provided by Gilda Cruz-Romo, March, 1998.

Hamilton, David, ed. *Metropolitan Opera Encyclopedia.* London: Thames and Hudson, 1987.

Rich, Maria F., ed. *Who's Who in Opera.* New York: Arno Press, 1976.

Tiger, Harriet L., ed. *Who's Who in America.* New Providence, NJ: Reed Reference Publishing, 1997.

Who's Who of American Women. New Providence, NJ: Reed Reference Publishing, 1997.

Zachary, Ralph. "Latin Expression." *Opera News,* December 19, 1970.

Linda Garcia Cubero
(1958–)
Business manager, military officer

Linda Garcia Cubero grew up in a military family; both of her parents served in the Air Force, and she and her two sisters joined the military as well. In 1976 Garcia Cubero was among the first group of women to attend and graduate from the three U.S. service academies (West Point, Annapolis, and the Air Force Academy). She also was the first Hispanic American woman to graduate from any U.S. service academy. After serving in the Air Force for several years following her graduation, Garcia Cubero decided to leave the Air Force and became a systems engineer and then a corporate manager. While in the Air Force and afterward, Garcia Cubero received many awards, both for her professional work and for being an outstanding role model for Hispanic American women.

Spends Childhood Travelling with Military Family

Linda Garcia Cubero was born in Shreveport, Louisiana, to Juan Garcia, a second-generation Mexican American, and Sally Garcia, a Puerto Rican. Her parents, both from poor families, had met in the Air Force, where her mother was an airman second class and her father was a pilot. Garcia Cubero, her two brothers, and her two sisters spent their childhood traveling from base to base, as their father continued to serve as a pilot. The siblings became close, which helped them adjust to the constant moves. But Garcia Cubero remembers how lonely that rootless life was, with her father often absent and her mother left to raise the five children. She later wrote in a poem (quoted in the *New York Times Magazine*) about her mother's life: "She did it all with love and joy and never showed the pain."

Nevertheless, she and her father were also close, and he advised her on several occasions during the hardest parts of her time at the Air Force Academy and in the Air Force. Of the five children, all three sisters (but not her brothers, Juan Jr. and Luis) decided to go into the military. Her older sister Amanda went into the Air Force through a university ROTC program, Garcia Cubero chose the Air Force Academy, and later her younger sister Mara also graduated from the Air Force Academy.

Becomes First Hispanic Woman to Graduate from Service Academy

The first women who entered U.S. service academies in the fall of 1976 did not receive an overwhelming welcome, and they were closely observed by the media. Garcia Cubero was among 157 women who entered the Air Force Academy. At the three academies (West Point, Annapolis and the Air Force Academy), women students made up only 357 out of the 4,376 total student body. She recalled for the *New York Times Magazine* how her male classmates would taunt the women students: "Every time we turned around a corner, some upperclassman would be telling us to get out." But, like most of her woman classmates at the three academies, Garcia Cubero remained for the entire four years and graduated in 1980. She also had the distinction of being the first Hispanic American female graduate of the three academies. The Mexican American Opportunity Foundation honored her achievement by naming her its Woman of the Year for 1980 and, the following year, the National Conference of Puerto Rican Women named her its Woman of the Year.

Following her graduation, Garcia Cubero joined the Air Force and was committed to at least five years of military service. She was assigned to Washington, DC, where she held several intelligence positions. Her assignments were at a very high level for such a young officer, and included briefing the U.S. Secretary of Defense and the Joint Chiefs of Staff. But Garcia Cubero was worried; having such a noteworthy beginning sometimes made her feel that she had nowhere to go but down. She also began to wonder how the rootless military life would affect the family that she hoped to start some day.

Leaves Air Force and Enters Civilian Life

By the time she had completed her required service, Capt. Garcia Cubero was undecided about whether to remain in the Air Force. She began to receive job offers from numerous companies and, at the same time, she was encouraged by people in the Air Force who thought she could become a general. She was awarded the Joint Service Commendation Medal (JSCM), the JSCM with Oak Leaf Cluster, and the Joint Service Achievement Medal.

Garcia Cubero maintained close ties to the Air Force Academy, even while deciding whether to resign from the Air Force, which certainly made the decision more difficult. As she had told the *New York Times Magazine* while deciding whether to resign or stay in the Air Force, she would not hesitate at all to go through the same experience at the academy. During the entire seven years that she spent in the Air Force, she served as an Academy admissions liaison officer. She also was a member of Senator John Warner's Academies Review Board from 1983 to 1987.

In 1987 Garcia Cubero, after much thought, decided to leave the Air Force. Given that she had led a military lifestyle all of her life (along with most of her family), the decision to leave was both difficult and courageous. Garcia Cubero's first civilian position was as a senior systems engineer with GE Aerospace from 1987 to 1991. She was a manager at GE Aerospace/Martin Marietta Corporation's Systems Engineering Programs from 1992 to 1993, during which time she also attended Virginia Polytechnic Institute and State University, earning an M.S. degree in systems engineering in 1992. In 1994 she became a manager in Martin Marietta Corporation's Mergers and Acquisitions Division. While starting this new life she also began the family she had wanted prior to leaving the Air Force; she married and had a daughter, Jennifer Ashley. By the late 1990s, all three Garcia sisters had left the Air Force and, along with their brothers, had established successful civilian careers.

Achieves Successful Business Career

Garcia Cubero was as successful in business as she had been in the military, receiving the Hispanic Engineer National Achievement Awards Committee's Pioneer Award (1991), GE Aerospace's Data Systems Programs Communicator of the Year Award (1992), and the Hispanic Aerospace Workers' Consortium of Rockwell International Achievement Award (1994). She also was highlighted as a Hispanic American role model in two national television programs in the 1991-1992 series, "Success Through Education; A Salute to Hispanic Excellence." In civilian life, Garcia Cubero became active in community organizations. She joined the board of the Washington, DC, chapter of the Hispanic Chamber of Commerce, was a founder and member of the executive board of the Washington Area Diversity Council of the Martin Marietta Corporation, served as a mentor for the National Council of Hispanic Women, and was appointed to the selection committee within the Hispanic Engineer National Achievement Awards Committee.

Current Address: Group Development, Mergers and Acquisition Div., Martin Marietta Corp., 6801 Rockledge Dr., Bethesda, MD 20817.

Sources:

Adde, Nick. "'Long Overdue' Tribute Celebrates Contribution Women Made to Freedom (includes Personal: Sally Garcia)." *Army Times Online,* October 14, 1997. Available at http://www.armytimes.com/wommem4.html.

Fein, Esther B. "The Choice: Women Officers Decide to Stay In or Leave." *New York Times Magazine,* May 5, 1985, p. 32.

LULAC Editorial Staff. "Linda Garcia: Making Hispanic and American History." *League of United Latin American Citizens,* November-December 1979, p. 8.

Blanquita Cullum

Radio host, television host, entrepreneur, organization executive

Conservative talk show host Blanquita Cullum was named among the top 100 broadcasters of 1996, 1997, and 1998 by *Talkers,* the trade journal of the industry. She broadcasts from Washington, DC, on weekdays with *The BQ View* and in the evenings with *Live From the Capitol.* She believes that the biggest problem facing Americans is their dependency on the federal government. "We are now a society that is more enslaved than ever before," she said in an interview with *Insight on the News,* "because we are working for the masters of the federal plantation, and we are willing servants and we comply with everything. It's a sad fact, but I'm still optimistic."

Raised in Multicultural Household

Cullum was born in Ventura, CA, to Henry Willson Walsh and Blanca Tona Walsh. Her father's heritage is English, and her mother is a Mexican national. "I grew up with enchiladas and scones," she said. Cullum's parents taught her to take pride in her Mexican heritage, which included a grandfather who served as a powerful political figure in Sonora, Mexico, and who was close personal friends with the revolutionary Pancho Villa. They also stressed the importance of her English heritage and ensured that their children could speak both English and Spanish with fluency. Family life in the Walsh household was formal, especially at dinnertime. "We had to be home for dinner at a certain time," Cullum said. "My father would engage us in conversation around the table. It would be about current events, and we had to participate." After spending much of her youth in La Jolla, CA, Cullum and her family moved to Brownsville, TX.

When it was time for college, Cullum majored in art at the University of Texas, but her education was cut short by the death of her father, and she returned home to be with her mother. When Cullum could not find a job in her chosen field, her mother suggested that she apply for a job at a radio station in San Antonio. By claiming that she could type and also write commercials, she got her first job in radio at a country-western station. Cullum took a typing class and circumvented the fact that the station did not allow women on air by writing herself into the commercials she wrote. Eventually, Cullum did get on the air for a radio show in San Antonio, TX. However, she had to use the name "Toni" because the station did not think the listening audience would be able to remember the name "Blanquita." The *Tom and Toni* program aired for approximately three years and became the top program in the city.

Finds Work in Television and Radio

In 1974, the radio star met nightclub owner and jazz musician James Albert Cullum when, as a publicity stunt, he and his band pretended to kidnap her. Three months later they were married. When Blanquita Cullum became pregnant two years later, her radio station management fired her because they did not want a pregnant woman on the air. Cullum refused to let this be the end of her career.

She returned to broadcasting three years later on the CBS television affiliate in San Antonio, KENS-TV—this time using her real name on the air. She anchored *Good Day USA,* conducted in-depth interviews on news programs, and hosted a daily game show. She also started the Crime Stoppers Program in the city and produced the televised segments. She later became a consultant to the San Antonio Police Department for several years and received the prestigious Gold Badge Award for her efforts.

In 1981, Cullum delivered her second child. She left KENS-TV and began co-hosting the *Bruce and Blanquita Show* on KTSA radio. She also served as mistress of ceremonies for the "Fiesta Noche del Rio on the San Antonio Riverwalk" and hosted and produced the controversial television talk show, *Texas Showdown.* Later she changed stations and hosted the morning drive radio program on KSJL radio. During this period, Cullum created and emceed the first "Christmas Riverwalk Parade" on the San Antonio Riverwalk. She was also introduced to politics for

Blanquita Cullum

the first time when she covered the 1984 Democratic Convention in San Francisco.

In 1984, Cullum formed San Antonio Broadcasting, Inc., along with three other women in order to pursue the license to own and operate a cable television station. This venture provided Cullum with her first visit to Washington, DC, where she and other groups testified before the Federal Communications Commission. Cullum was appointed by the Bexar County commissioners to serve on the VIA Metropolitan Transit Authority, where she was elected as secretary of the board of directors.

Divorced after ten years of marriage, Cullum committed herself to serving as a positive role model for her children, Blanquita Etelvina and James Willson. "When I began there were no Latina role models, I had to cut through the obstacles with a machete on my own," Cullum said in a telephone interview. "When my daughter told me that she wanted to go into the field of theater, she felt it might be difficult. Then she said, 'I'm getting my courage from you.' I was so touched that she noticed."

Strong Ties to Hispanic Community Leads to Jobs

Cullum was eventually hired by Coors Brewing Company as a marketing director because of her strong ties to the Hispanic community of San Antonio. She became close friends with Ambassador to the Americas Holland Coors who invited her to be a representative af the first International Conference for Women in Guatemala. Attended by female heads of state and business leaders from the Western Hemisphere, it was where Women of Our Hemisphere was formed. This organization has provided aid and goodwill to countries through the efforts of women leaders.

Believing that she had accomplished all that she wanted to do in San Antonio, Cullum began looking for a change. The opportunity presented itself when she was invited by the Republican party to host an inaugural gala for George Bush. She was so successful in the event that the party offered her a job in Washington, DC. The cross-country move was a big risk for a single mother with not much money, but Cullum took the plunge and became a Hispanic marketing director for the Census Bureau.

Cullum hoped to get a job working with President Bush, but was told that there was no chance for her to attain such a position without a political background. However, a White House contact who had worked with her on the inaugural gala recommended her as a White House liaison at the Federal Emergency Management Agency. She got the job. Her position allowed her to have top-security clearance, and Cullum learned about the inner workings of Washington, DC.

Takes to the Capitol Airwaves

After Bush lost the presidential election in 1992, Cullum decided to go back to radio and created a syndicated show based out of Richmond, VA. After meeting with more success, she next moved to Washington, DC, and formed a partnership with Radio America. She currently hosts a television show, *Morning View,* that reaches 16–18 million viewers a day. The show is a two-hour news block, immediately followed by another Cullum show, *American Family.* Besides being president of the National Association of Radio Talk Show Hosts—the first Hispanic to be so honored—her company, Cullum Communications, owns two radio talk shows, *Live from the Capitol* and *The BQ View.*

Live from the Capitol is a conservative talk show syndicated on 50 radio stations. It is the only radio show to be broadcast from the Capitol building. This one-hour program airs Monday through Thursday from 7 to 8 pm EST. Produced in the context of a nightly town hall meeting, Cullum is host and interviewer to various members of Congress. Although she is conservative, she told *Hispanic Magazine,* "I am balanced and honest . . . I represent a show that is extremely fair on the issues."

Earns Praise for Radio Show

The BQ View has been called provocative and dynamic, and Cullum, or "BQ," as she is known to her thousands of listeners, earns high praise for this nationally syndicated program. It airs on weekdays from 12 noon to 3 pm EST. Fast-paced and entertaining, it attracts liberals and conservatives who call with their views and disagreements. The show originates just blocks from the White House, and Cullum likes to keep things controversial as she schedules top figures from the political and entertainment fields.

"*The BQ View* has been featured in such publications as the *New York Times, Washington Post, National Review,* and *Hispanic Business,* among others, and was even the subject of a Doonesbury cartoon. Cullum herself is a frequent panelist and guest on NBC *Nightly News, Good Morning America,* and many other television and radio broadcasts.

Holds Views on Success

In business, Cullum sets a standard for her crew, and the people who work for her must meet it. "It's important to find meaningful work," she said in a telephone interview, "and I'm not jealous of my peers because I don't run anyone else's race." To stay on top and keep her shows lively and timely, Cullum reads several newspapers each day and tries to keep abreast of everything happening in the communications field. "If you want something, put your foot in the water and go for it. Always say yes to offers. If you say no, there's no option." She credits a good deal of her radio success to the fact that she respects her audience. "I won't insult them or their intelligence, and I want them to participate."

Her busy broadcasting schedule leaves her little time for outside interests other than her family. However, she feel strongly that people with influence have an obligation to build a base in the community. She has served on the Virginia Commission for the Arts and was awarded the 1996 Corporate Achievement Award by *Vista* magazine for helping Hispanic Americans enter the broadcasting field.

Sees Bright Future for Hispanic Growth

Cullum has commented on the growth of Hispanic Americans as entrepreneurs. "The numbers show that we are more than the busboys and maids in this country. We are proving that as one of the youngest groups of immigrants, we are contributors. We are now proving that we are the employers as well as the employees, and that makes a difference." Cullum made those remarks after publication of a *Washington Post* article on a 1996 survey of minority-owned businesses in the Washington, DC, area. It showed that the number of Hispanic-owned businesses—from conglomerates to mom-and-pop stores—came in at six times the growth rate of all U.S. firms between 1987 and 1992. In the Washington geographical area, Hispanic-owned business firms increased 160 percent. The increase was attributed to both an increase in the Hispanic population in the area and to an expansion of strong entrepreneurial spirit. According to Cullum, being employers instead of employees makes for "economic power."

Blanquita Cullum believes that in order to be successful, you must decide whether you want a career or just a job. If a career is your choice, then you must take the time to pursue it, she says. Cullum knows about making the decision between a career and a job. When her radio show first went on the air, it was said that no one could hear her out of the parking lot! Now that she is well-known in the industry, most think the sky is the limit. Stated Cullum of her success, "I represent all the mom and pop'ers in the world who say you don't need all the big guns. If you have the resolve, you can do it yourself. Doing it on my own has given me a sense of presence and power in the industry." Cullum also believes that young Hispanic Americans sometimes have a hard time being successful because the standards set for them are too low. "It's a subtle form of racism," she said. "They're confined to a socioeconomic status and not pushed up. So, kids must push themselves. I tell them, 'Push harder. Be the best. Don't settle for second best. Never!'"

Current Address: Cullum Communications, 1030 15th St., NW, Ste. 700, Washington, DC 20005.

Sources:

Blue, Rose. Telephone interview with Blanquita Cullum, March 4, 1998.

Goode, Stephen. "Talk queen Blanquita Cullum speaking from Capitol Hill. "*Insight on the News,* December 9, 1996, pp. 18-20.

Hispanic Magazine Home Page. Available at http://www.hisp.com/nov96/blanquitacullum.html.

Carolyn Curiel
(1954–)
Ambassador

In an era when public servants are often regarded with disdain and mistrust, the Honorable Carolyn Curiel is one "American who is proud to be in public service." Curiel made that declaration during her confirmation hearing before the Senate Foreign Relations Committee on October 24, 1997, about two months after President Clinton nominated her to post of U.S. Ambassador to Belize. In her positions as a newspaper reporter, special assistant to the President and senior presidential speechwriter specializing in domestic issues, and now as an U.S. ambassador, Curiel continues on a path of success.

Carolyn Curiel

Faces Early Cultural Challenges

Curiel was born on June 9, 1954, in Hammond, IN, to Mexican immigrants Alex, a steelworker, and Angie, a housewife. Curiel was six years old when her parents, two sisters, and four brothers moved out of the barrio into a blue-collar neighborhood, where her parents still live. She described her childhood environment, saying, "we were the only brown faces in town. Inside our walls, little changed from our old life. The traditional life went on. The pictures of John F. Kennedy and the Pope had their places of honor, next to my aunt the nun, and my cousin, the priest. . . Outside was another story. I felt I had to become another person when I went outside. . . " That is the picture she painted in a keynote presentation she gave May of 1997 called "Overcoming Latino Humility" before the National Association of Hispanic Journalists' annual convention in El Paso, TX. Yet as different as Curiel felt, she found a place in journalism. While at Morton High School in Hammond, she was editor of the school newspaper. Following graduation in 1972, she attended Purdue University in West Lafayette, IN. At Purdue she discovered a penchant for sports reporting. "For a person who always felt out of place, it was perfect," she once said. "I was a woman reporting college football and basketball in the 1970s—I was supposed to look out of place."

Begins Journalistic Career

Curiel earned a B.A. from Purdue and went directly to work as a communications consultant for Illinois Bell in Chicago in 1976 and, a year later, she was assigned the additional task of account executive. She left that job in 1978 for an assignment with *United Press International,* in Chicago, where she reported on international events, Midwest affairs, and sports. In 1984, she moved to Washington, DC, to serve as editor of the foreign desk of *UPI,* but quickly moved on to oversee Caribbean affairs in San Juan, Puerto Rico. While there, she was named minority fellow by the American Newspapers Association.

Curiel returned to Washington in 1985, and for a year she worked as a freelance writer for *ABC News.* She returned to newspaper writing in 1986 as an editor at the *Washington Post,* working on the national copy desk. In 1987, Curiel accepted a similar position at the *New York Times,*eventually serving as an editor on the foreign copy desk and the "Week in Review" section. While at the foreign desk at the *New York Times,* Curiel handled everything from the story on the demonstrations and tragedy at Tiananmen Square to the dismantling of the historic Berlin Wall to the tumultuous Gulf War. Curiel's hard work earned her the *New York Times* Publisher's Award, the newspaper's in-house recognition for journalistic excellence. In 1992, Ted Koppel of *Nightline,* a production of *ABC News,* hired Curiel as his writer and producer. She would have little time to leave a lasting mark in that position because in less than a year, the White House

sought out Curiel to work as a presidential speechwriter. Without hesitation, she accepted the prestigious position.

Her distinguished journalistic career has earned Curiel the honor of being singled out as one of the nation's most influential Hispanic Americans, a recognition given by the *Hispanic Business* magazine in 1995. A year later, she received the 1996 Las Primeras Award from MANA, A National Latina Organization.

Fulfills Childhood Dream

Curiel was candid about her early goals. In the speech before the Hispanic Journalists Convention, she explained: "It may sound contrived, but the truth is, I dreamed as a child of working for an American president. I just never told anybody until I was an adult. I was embarrassed to. It seemed too grand, too out of reach, and I must have felt unworthy." Her first encounter with Bill Clinton occurred when he was governor of Arkansas and she was at the *New York Times.* Clinton had just declared his candidacy and was at the office to meet the *Times* editors. Curiel's boss suggested she attend. "When I walked into the room, a line of *Times* editors was standing along one long side of a conference table. The governor was opposite them. I walked in, immediately adding diversity to the room I should add, but I must have looked uncomfortable. Without missing a beat, the governor looked at me and said: 'Come sit by me. Nobody is sitting by me.' And he pulled up a chair," Curiel has said in describing her first meeting with Clinton.

While she was working on the late-night copy desk—a tough assignment by her accounts—Curiel let a friend and co-worker know that she was interested in being a speechwriter for a president, "if only a Democrat could get elected." When Clinton took office, Curiel had little knowledge of just how close she was to realizing her dream. The person to whom she confided her dream of becoming a presidential speechwriter relayed this information to the talent scout for the Clinton White House. She was later hired to the position.

Curiel is not only the first person of color, but the first Hispanic American woman to serve as a speechwriter to a U.S. President. President Clinton gave Curiel special recognition following his speech on affirmative action at the National Archives and Records Administration on July 19, 1995. He acknowledged that she had personally helped him to craft the speech that may well go down in history as one of his best speeches.

Becomes U.S. Ambassador to Belize

As influential and successful as Curiel was with speechwriting, there were still other areas needing her expertise. After realizing her dream to be a speechwriter, Curiel soon rose to even greater heights. Three months after Clinton nominated her ambassador to the Central

American nation of Belize, the Senate confirmed her nomination on November 10, 1997. The event took place in Purdue University's Clumet Alumni Hall amongst family, friends, and local Hammond officials. True to her roots, Curiel noted in a prepared statement that, "it's a great honor to have a swearing-in ceremony at home. Having this take place in my hometown before family and friends—the people who have helped shape my life—holds symbolic importance to me." Her home in Indiana remains as important to Curiel as the home she has made for several years in Washington, DC. When she speaks to young adults, Curiel reminds them that they must never forget their roots and must use those roots as the groundwork for their future good and for the good of others.

On January 19, 1998, Curiel officially presented her credentials to Governor General Sir Colville Young at Belmopan, Belize. She pledged to continue the close partnership of the two nations, particularly in meeting the challenge of combatting drug trafficking. In her closing remarks, the new U.S. ambassador offered this promise: "During my tenure I will look for the answers in partnership with our friends in Belize, and I will work in the common interest of both of our nations."

Takes Pride in Her Heritage

Even though she expressed childhood feelings of inadequacy in facing the other culture "outside her door," Curiel draws upon her Hispanic heritage to fortify her in her pursuit of service to others and to her country. Curiel challenges other Hispanic Americans to carry the banner with her. She encourages them to be the role models for the next generation. It is this younger generation that must know that pride and hard work can make a difference, as it has made for her. "The younger generation needs role models," Curiel told the National Hispanic Journalist Association. "Seek out these kids before they reach junior high; tell them that staying in school is worth it. Teach them the savvyness you wish you had as a child. They will look up to you; you will be everyday heroes." In this way, too, Curiel is a hero for all searching their place in an ethnically diverse country.

Sources:

Curiel, Carolyn. "Overcoming Latino Humility." Address to the National Association of Hispanic American Journalists, May, 1997.
———. Remarks on the Presentation of Her Credentials, January 19, 1998.
———. Senate Foreign Relations Committee Hearing statement, October 24, 1997.
———. U.S. State Department information sheet, 1998.
———. U.S. State Department, curriculumn vitae, 1998.
Yovich, Daniel J. "Hammond Woman to Become Ambassador today." *Times,* January 1998.

D

de Alba, Alicia Gaspar
See Gaspar de Alba, Alicia

Julia de Burgos
(1914–1953)
Poet, nationalist

Selected writings:

Poemas exactos a mi misma. privately printed, 1937.
Poema en veinte surcos. San Juan, PR: Imprenta Venezuela, 1938.
Canción de la verdad sencilla. San Juan, PR: Baldrich, 1938.
El mar y tú y otros poemas. San Juan, PR: Printing and Publishing Co., 1954.
The Complete Poems of Julia de Burgos, Obra Completa Poetica, translated by Jack Agueros, Willimantic, CT: Curbstone, 1997.

Julia de Burgos

Overview

Julia de Burgos was one of the foremost poets to come out of Puerto Rico in the first half of the twentieth century. Her poverty-stricken background and African heritage were factors in the evolution of the revolutionary politics de Burgos espoused as part of the independence movement in Puerto Rico. She also attracted attention for her unconventional lifestyle: she divorced her first husband and lived openly with her lover at a time when such behavior was virtually unthinkable for most Puerto Rican women. "A woman of great sensibility, rebellious spirit, and exceptional intelligence, Julia de Burgos no doubt felt imprisoned by circumstances," explained *Notable American Women* contributor Carmen Delgado Votaw. "Her discomfort with social ills, her love for Puerto Rico, and her preoccupation with justice and death, all come out in the torrents of her poetry with its richly emotional metaphors."

Poverty and Education

De Burgos was the oldest of 13 children born to Paula García de Burgos and Francisco Burgos Hans. Although her father worked for the National Guard and farmed near the town of Carolina, Puerto Rico, when she was born, the family later removed to the barrio of Santa Cruz. De Burgos grew up on the banks of a major branch of the Rio Grande de Loiza and attended the University of Puerto Rico High School thanks to donations from local townspeople. After graduation in 1931, she entered the University of Puerto Rico in San Juan and obtained her certification as a teacher two years later. She began her teaching career working at the Barrio Cerdo Arriba in Naranjito, a provincial town some distance from the capital.

In Naranjito, de Burgos became reacquainted with the social problems and poverty that had haunted her own childhood. "From early on. . ." after her high school career, related Votaw, ". . . she was committed both to learning and to social change." In 1934, however, she married Ruben Rodrigues Beauchamp, a match that essentially ended her teaching career. During the three years of her marriage, de Burgos sharpened her social conscience by working at a publicly-run day-care center managed by the Puerto Rico Emergency Reconstruction Administration. At the same time she honed her writing skills by writing educational plays and songs for radio broadcast by the Puerto Rico Department of Education's *Escuela del Aire*. In 1937, the same year her marriage to Beauchamp ended in divorce, de Burgos saw her first volume of poetry, *Poemas exactos a mi misma*, privately published.

De Burgos published two more volumes of poetry, *Poema en veinte surcos* (1938) and *Canción de la verdad sencilla* (1939), which won a prize from the Institute of Puerto Rican Literature, before she left Puerto Rico in 1940. She spent part of that year in New York City working as a journalist. Late in the year, however, de Burgos fled the city with her new love, Dr. Juan Isidro Jimenes Grullón, for Cuba, where she began writing for newspapers. For the next two years she lived in Cuba, writing and enrolling as a graduate student in literature and philosophy at the University of Havana. In 1942 she went back to New York, where she found support for her poetry from the Circle of Ibero-American Writers and Poets. She also married again, choosing for her second husband a fellow poet, Armando Marín. Most of the work she published during this period was journalism, especially editorials and interviews. In 1946 the Institute of Puerto Rican Literature awarded her another prize for "Ser o no ser la divisa," an editorial she wrote for the journal *Semanario Hispano*.

Lyrical Poetry

Modern critics believe that de Burgos's poetry anticipated the work of feminist writers and poets as well as that of other Hispanic authors. "Writing in the 1930s through the 1950s," declared a reviewer for *Publishers Weekly*, "de Burgos was ahead of her time in grasping connections between history, the body, politics, love, self-negation and feminism that would later prove to be the foundations for writers like [Adrienne] Rich and [Sylvia] Plath." "Her poems," stated Votaw, "reveal her gift for lyricism, while their erotic content and their cosmic symbolism provide autobiographical glimpses into a troubled and pagan soul which often felt itself lost and abandoned."

De Burgos combined these themes with a use of her native language that critics compare to that of Carlos Fuentes or Jorge Luis Borges. Colleen Kattau in *Symposium*, noted de Burgos's use of ambivalent language to describe a 'Julia de Burgos' that was in some ways like the writer and in others very different. In one of de Burgos's best-known poems, "A Julia de Burgos" (originally published in *Poema en veinte surcos*), the poet depicted ". . . a feminine subject who transgresses the borders of predetermined standards of behavior." "While 'Julia de Burgos' is severely criticized for conforming and thus leading an existence devoid of meaning," Kattau continued, "the other . . . 'I' of the poem advances a totality of existence and meaning" that places it outside normal standards of behavior. "In 'A Julia de Burgos,'" stated Votaw, "and in

'Yo misma fuí mi ruta,' de Burgos calls attention sharply to the restrictions imposed on women by a society that forces them to live by laws and by social and ethical patterns not of their making."

This concern with proper standards of behavior reflected elements in de Burgos's own life. In the 1930s she joined other Caribbean writers in a literary protest against European colonialism and its denigration of African culture. *Négritude,* as the movement was called, promoted the idea that artists of African descent must look to their African heritage for inspiration rather than relying on Western traditions and aesthetics. The Négritude movement was not as big in New York as it was in Paris, but it gave de Burgos a cause to identify with and injustices to speak out against. "Because she was dedicated to the cause of social change," wrote Votaw, "de Burgos may often have felt that what she had to say was more important than how she said it; literary craftsmanship thus gave way at times to her impulse to speak out."

De Burgos's poetry also used images of love, sex, and death in a way similar to that of other Latin American poets, including Pablo Neruda. However, she mixed these images with the pain that her own life and upbringing brought her. In "Río Grande de Loíza," one of her most anthologized works, for example, she begs the river to absorb her, both body and soul: "Muy señor río mío. Río hombre. Unico hombre / que ha besado en mi alma al besar en mi cuerpo." In her last years, which were marked by depression, alcoholism, and despair, the poet revealed an ever darker concept of life. She wrote in "Farewell from Welfare Island," one of her last poems, "The past is only a shadow emerging from / nowhere. / Life was somewhere forgotten / and sought refuge in depths of tears / and sorrows; / over this vast empire of solitude and darkness. / Where is the voice of freedom, / freedom to laugh, / to move / without the heavy phantom of despair?"

Decline and Death

The mid- to late 1940s marked an important period in de Burgos's life. In 1940 and 1941 her poetry was performed in New York City and had been honored by several organizations, including the Asociación de Periodistas y Escritores Puertorriqueños. In 1942, however, the relationship between de Burgos and her lover, Dr. Juan Isidrio Jimenes Grullón, fractured and she returned to New York. The breakup of her relationship greatly depressed de Burgos and she neglected her writing in an attempt to find work. She found temporary employment working for an optician and as a secretary before meeting and marrying Armando Marín, her second husband, in 1943. During the last years of World War II, she lived and worked with her husband in Washington, DC, serving in the office of the Coordinator of Interamerican Affairs. In 1946, de Burgos was diagnosed with cirrhosis of the liver, the result of years of alcoholism. She also developed a papilloma on her vocal cords and had to seek treatment in a variety of hospitals.

De Burgos's mental and physical health continued to degrade and made her almost a recluse during the late 1940s. She continued to be hospitalized for treatment of her alcoholism and her liver problems. Even the acceptance for publication of a new collection of poetry, *El mar y tú y otros poemas*, failed to raise her spirits. The papilloma in her throat was removed in December of 1952, but her health was so poor that she had to stay in Goldwater Memorial Hospital in New York City through the first months of 1953. Letters that she wrote to her relatives in Puerto Rico during this period show that de Burgos was obsessed with death and dying. Her poem "Farewell from Welfare Island," written in English in February of 1953, indicates that she was deeply depressed and possibly suicidal: "It has to be from here, / forgotten but unshaken, / among comrades of silence / deep into Welfare Island / my farewell to the world."

Toward the beginning of May, 1953, de Burgos was finally released from the hospital and went to live with friends in Harlem. The last letter her family received from her was dated June 28, 1953. In July, she disappeared. Later it was revealed that she had been discovered unconscious on the street and taken to the Harlem Hospital where she died. The coroner's certificate indicated that the cause of death was a pulmonary condition. Because de Burgos had no identification on her when she died, her body was buried in a public cemetery. A month after her death, the coroner's photograph of her body finally led to her identification.

Posthumous Recognition

De Burgos's husband and her friends from the Circle of Ibero-American Writers and Poets immediately launched an effort to have her body moved back to Puerto Rico for burial. Many important Puerto Rican officials, including Margot Arce Vázquez and Juan Avilés, formed a committee to expedite the process. De Burgos's body finally returned to the island of her birth on September 6, 1953. She received last honors from the Sociedad de Periodistas and was given a Christian burial in the municipal cemetery at Carolina.

Public praise for de Burgos and her work began almost immediately after her funeral. In November of 1953, the journal *Artes y Letras* produced a special issue entitled *Homenaje a Julia de Burgos: su vida y su obra*. The issue featured articles and literary criticism by many prominent Hispanic writers, who honored de Burgos for her poetry, and political figures, who honored her for her social activism. They included Antonio J. Colorado, Margot Arce de Vázquez, Nilita Vientos Gastón, Angel M. Arroyo, César Calvo Araujo, Samuel R. Quiñones, Juan Avilés, Emilio Pagán Garcia, Juan B. Pagán, Adela Alvelo, Violeta López Suria, and Armando Rivera. Her final original collection of poems, *El mar y tú y otros poemas*, was published in 1954.

Since de Burgos's death several collections of her work have been published. An anthology entitled *Obra Poética* appeared in an edition published by the Instituto de Cultura Puertorriqueña in 1961. Another collection, entitled *Antología poética*, was published in 1967 by the Puerto Rican publishing house Editorial Coqui. That same year Editorial Coqui brought out the first major full-length study of de Burgos's work, *Julia de Burgos: vida y poesía*, by Ivette Jiménez Báez. In 1987 the University of Puerto Rico awarded de Burgos the posthumous degree of Doctor Honoris Causa in recognition of her contribution to the island's literary culture. The poet's devotion to social causes was recognized in the 1980s when Public School 9 was renamed the Julia de Burgos School and an experimental bilingual Spanish-English curriculum was introduced.

Sources:

Buck, Claire, ed. *The Bloomsbury Guide to Women's Literature.* New York: Prentice Hall, 1992.

"Cronologia De Julia de Burgos." Available at http://uprhmate01.upr.clu.edu/espanol/JuliaDeBurgos/.

Hurd Green, Carol, and Mary Grimley Mason, eds. *American Women Writers: A Critical Reference Guide from Colonial Times to the Present.* New York: Continuum Publishing, 1994.

Kattau, Colleen. "The Plural and the Nuclear in 'A Julia de Burgos'." *Symposium,* Winter, 1995, pp. 285-93.

Sicherman, Barbar, Carol Hurd Green, et al, eds. *Notable American Women: The Modern Period, A Biographical Dictionary.* Cambridge, MA: Belknap Press, 1980.

"Song of the Simple Truth: The Complete Poems of Julia de Burgos, Obra Completa Poetica." *Publishers Weekly,* February 24, 1998, p. 85.

de García, Norma Varisco
See **Varisco de García, Norma**

de Gautier, Felisa Rincón
See **Rincón de Gautier, Felisa**

de Kleven, Concha Ortiz y Pino
See **Ortiz y Pino de Kleven, Concha**

Lolita de la Vega

Publisher, entrepreneur

A refugee from the ravages of the Spanish Civil War, Lolita de la Vega has gone on to become the first lady of Spanish-language publications in the United States, having founded *Temas* magazine with her husband José in 1950. *Temas* is widely recognized today as the oldest Spanish-language magazine in the United States. Her commitment to the marriage of quality journalism with Hispanic culture has been recognized all over the world.

Experiences Life as a Refugee

A native of Spain, de la Vega was a teenager when her country was torn apart by the outbreak of a bloody civil war. In 1936, forces within the military, supported by conservative elements in the country, launched a coup against Spain's Republican government. The coup failed to win control of the entire country, thus setting the stage for full-blown fighting across the country between the Nationalists, as the rebel forces were known, and the Republicans. De la Vega's father, a major in the military loyal to the Republican government, was taken prisoner by Nationalist forces and shot.

Lolita de la Vega

With her mother and four brothers and sisters in tow, de la Vega and her husband crossed the Pyrenees Mountains on foot into France in January of 1939. The youngest of her siblings was barely three-years old. Once over the border into France, de la Vega and her husband lingered there for awhile. Both longed to come to the United States, but they lacked sufficient funds to make the trip to the United States together. José came first, leaving Lolita behind until enough money could be put aside to pay for her passage from Europe. Finally, on December 5, 1939, she arrived in New York, after taking passage on a ship from the Netherlands. José was waiting for her at dockside.

Recalls Acculturation Challenges in the United States

Neither Lolita nor José spoke English. Since they had no friends or money, their early years in the United States were very difficult indeed. De la Vega recalled in a letter to the author, "The first three years were tough. I gave piano lessons to Spanish-speaking children for a dollar an hour. I would go to their homes to conduct the lessons, paying for my own transportation costs out of the little I was paid for the lessons." She also went door-to-door in Harlem selling perfumes and books. After the United States was drawn into World War II, José went to work for the Office of War Information. Shortly after that, both the de la Vegas launched a Spanish-language radio program, serving the growing Hispanic population in the metropolitan New York City area.

Launches *Temas*

In November of 1950, the de la Vegas launched *Temas,* fulfilling a longtime dream of establishing a Spanish-language publication that could be used to inform and bring culture and entertainment to the large Spanish-speaking audience throughout the United States. For more than 40 years, until his death in 1994, José de la Vega directed the operations of the magazine as its publisher. Upon his death, Lolita assumed the position of publisher, taking on full responsibility for directing and editing the magazine, tasks for which she and the magazine have received consistent praise. Family-oriented in its content, *Temas* enjoys a circulation of about 110,000 and features articles on culture, current events, fashion, and home decoration. Each issue features interviews with people prominent in the arts and humanities. Evidence of the high quality of the magazine's content and the esteem in which it is held is reflected in the many articles reprinted in reading packages at high schools and colleges throughout the United States.

Is Honored by Adopted City

In November of 1995, New York City Mayor Rudolph Giuliani proclaimed the 30th of that month *Temas* Magazine 45th Anniversary Day in recognition of the publication's many contributions to the city, and particularly to New York's huge Hispanic population. At a ceremony in the Blue Room at City Hall, Giuliani said, "For the past 45 years, *Temas* has been a valuable source of information, education, and entertainment. The dedicated staff behind the success of this magazine deserves our recognition." The city's proclamation recognized that "members of New York City's large Spanish-speaking community come from many countries, each with its own distinctive history and cultural heritage. *Temas* magazine carries information for people of all ages and with many interests." Accepting the mayor's congratulations and a copy of the proclamation and speaking on behalf of those who have made the magazine what it is today, de la Vega said, "This acknowledgement on our landmark anniversary is a source of great pride to all of us. It gives us renewed energy to continue our work."

Gains Wide Recognition for Accomplishments

Through the years, de la Vega has been honored by a number of U.S. and foreign organizations for her accomplishments as founder and publisher of *Temas*. One of the first honors she and her husband received came in 1951, when the two were named honorary citizens of Ambato, Ecuador. The following year de la Vega received a high honor from her native country, when she was named a member of Royal Academy of Sciences and Noble Arts of Cordoba, Spain. In 1960, New York City Mayor Robert F. Wagner honored de la Vega for the contributions she had made to her adopted city.

In 1967, the Puerto Rican cities of San Juan and Ponce conferred honorary citizenship on de la Vega. San Juan even presented her with the keys to the city. In 1979, she won a prize from the Institute of Puerto Rico for her journalistic achievements and was made an honorary citizen of Quito, Ecuador. In 1994, de la Vega was honored with a bronze plaque presented by the National Association of Cuban-American Women. The following year she received a public service award from the U.S. Social Security Administration. In 1996, the publisher of *Temas* was honored by the cities of Miami, and Union City, NJ, and the states of New York and New Jersey. In a proclamation recognizing *Temas* and its publisher, a representative of the city of Miami said that "a news sense is really a sense of what is important, what is vital, what has color and life—what people are interested in. That's journalism. . . . Through the years, *Temas* has maintained the highest standard of professionalism carrying information for people of all ages and different idiosyncrasies, while emphasizing the rich cultural heritage of the Spanish-speaking people of the Western Hemisphere."

The College of Cuban Journalists in Exile honored de la Vega in 1997, as did the Autonomous Council of Hispanic American Workers and the Bergen County (New Jersey) Hispanic Republican Organization. In March of 1998, the New Jersey Association of Women Business Owners, in its "Salute to Women Leaders" honored de la Vega, saying she had been "instrumental in giving prestige to the Hispanic community by showcasing culture and entertain-

ment in her informative publication." Lolita de la Vega was the only Hispanic American, among the several women recognized by the women's organization.

Current Address: Temas Magazine, 300 W. 55th St., 14–P, New York, NY 10019.

Sources:

Amerman, Donald. Letter to Anna Maria Pereira, April 8, 1998.
Amerman, Donald. Letter to Lolita de la Vega, April 15, 1998.
Proclamation (in honor of *Temas*), City of Miami, FL, 1996.
Proclamation (in honor of *Temas* Magazine 45th Anniversary Day), New York City, November 1995.
"A Salute to Women Leaders." New Jersey Association of Women Business Owners, March 1998.

de Leira, Angeles Alvariño
See **Alvariño, Angeles**

Delgado Votaw, Carmen
See **Votaw, Carmen Delgado**

Nancy A. de los Santos
Producer, director, screenwriter

Selected filmography:

Mi Familia (associate producer), 1995.
Selena (associate producer), 1997.

Overview

Nancy de los Santos is one of Hollywood's most active writer-producers. As an associate producer for *Mi Familia* (1995) and *Selena* (1997), she played a pivotal role in assuring the success of both films. An award recipient for her own works, de los Santos has also directed teleplays based on her scripts. *Hispanic* magazine named her among the "Top Ten to Watch" in Hollywood. Working behind the scenes of the entertainment industry for nearly two decades, de los Santos's career started in radio and television. Her first major break came as a producer for the Chicago-based television series *At the Movies,* hosted by famed movie critics Gene Siskel and Roger Ebert. Later moving to Hollywood, she added to her resumé a variety of work on several feature films, including *The Abyss* (1989), *Alien Nation* (1988), and *A Time for Destiny* (1988).

Breaks Ground in Filmmaking

De los Santos has been in the industry since Hispanic American filmmakers first started breaking ground in Hollywood in the 1980s. With many studios fearful that Hispanic-themed films will not attract a large commercial audience, Hispanic films have struggled to gain a place in the U.S. film industry. Filmmakers such as de los Santos are bringing Hispanic American productions to the box office to let audiences judge for themselves.

In 1981, show producer de los Santos anxiously prepared a taping of *At the Movies* in which *Zoot Suit*, the first Chicano movie to undergo national distribution, was to be reviewed by influential film critics Gene Siskel and Roger Ebert. De los Santos knew that a favorable review of the film would contribute to a successful release; and a successful release could pave the road for other Hispanic American movies. She was ultimately disappointed, however, because the critics gave Luis Valdez's filmed stage play "two thumbs down." "The reason they gave *Zoot Suit* the thumbs down is they said it was not a real film, that it was just a filmed play," she told Alex Avila in *Hispanic*. "But Valdez was only given a $2 million budget to do the film. He needed to film it as a play just to get it done. It was a conscious decision made during *Zoot Suit*'s production. So they slammed the film for being what it set out to be."

De los Santos eventually went to Hollywood to be a film producer and was able to take an active role in boosting the success of Hispanic American motion pictures. In 1995 she served as an associate producer for Gregory Nava's *Mi Familia* (also known as *My Family*), a story about a Mexican American family. De los Santos was credited as a key player in the film's keen marketing strategy. The cleverly targeted marketing approach included creating support prior to the general release through screenings held for Hispanic leaders and opinion-makers; holding grassroots screenings to allow Hispanic community organizations to use the film for fundraising efforts; and premiering the film in cities with strong Hispanic populations. For a film that was rejected by mainstream Hollywood studios, the movie was highly acclaimed. Much to the credit of its production team, in its opening weekend *Mi Familia* reportedly performed better in the box office than did *The Perez Family*, another Hispanic-themed movie released in 1995, but with a director, writer, and big-name stars who were not Hispanic.

De los Santos was also integral to the production of *Selena*, a 1997 movie based on the life of the slain Tejano music star. In an article she wrote for *Hispanic*, de los Santos said she and her co-associate producer had the best job on the movie. She freely admitted that what she enjoyed most about her work on the film was meeting so many of Selena's fans. One of de los Santos' primary jobs was the monumental task of conducting a national open casting call for the role of Selena at ages 10 and 22. Before the final selections were made, de los Santos helped screen more than 22,000 Latinas. Among her many accomplishments in assisting with the film's production was organizing more than 32,800 dedicated Selena fans in a San Antonio stadium for the re-creation of a concert scene. It was an emotional filming, during which a tearful de los Santos told reporters for *People* magazine, "We shouldn't be making a movie about Selena. We should be making one with her."

Produces Further Accomplishments

Involved in the production of several documentaries, de los Santos keeps adding to her credits. She helped produce the award-winning *Port Of Entry*, which details a Mexican family's journey to Chicago, and *Twenty Years. . . Y Que?*, an examination of the twentieth anniversary of the 1972 Chicano Moratorium Against the Vietnam War. More recently, she directed a short film, *Breaking Pan With Sol*, from her own script for the Universal Television Film Project. It received the Best Short Film award from the Chicago International Latino Film Festival. She co-produced *The Bronze Screen: The History of Latinos in Hollywood* and developed a teleplay, *Mothers Against Gangs*, with Olmos Productions. The Hispanic American community and Hollywood will undoubtedly continue to see more quality work from de los Santos.

Sources:

de la Torre, Chito. "Selena Movie Flickers On." *La Prensa de San Antonio*, May 26, 1996, p. 1B.

De Los Santos, Nancy. "Working with Fans Behind the Scenes." *Hispanic*, March 1997, p. 34.

Llano, Todd. "How Hispanic Films Make It to the Big Screen. *Hispanic*, July 31, 1995, p. 22.

"Viva Selena." *People*, March 24, 1997, pp. 160-161.

de Mireles, Jovita González
See González de Mireles, Jovita

Mirta de Perales
Entrepreneur, business executive

"**I** believe you can't be beautiful outside if you are not beautiful inside," said Mirta de Perales in a *Miami Herald* article entitled "Mirta de Perales' Gospel of Beauty." De

Perales, president and CEO of Mirta de Perales, Inc., a five million dollar hair-care and beauty products business based in Florida, rose from a life of poverty in her native Cuba to become a millionaire and philanthropist. Today, de Perales owns a famous hair salon, an entire line of hair and beauty products, and a television station.

Necessity Sparks Success

De Perales was born in Santa Clara, Cuba. When she was seven, surgery left her with a bald spot on her scalp. Tormented by her playmates, she continually tried techniques to encourage hair growth and styles to conceal the spot. She loved working with hair, was good at it, and often did her neighbors' hair for free. Tragedy struck de Perales at age eight when her father was disabled in a serious car accident. Her family was destitute and her mother moved to Havana to earn money as a housekeeper. De Perales was left to raise her three siblings. It became apparent that the fifteen dollars a month her mother sent home could not provide for them so de Perales took matters into her own hands and determined to earn money by charging five cents per hair cut. Armed with comb, scissors, and stool, she took her new business door-to-door. When she earned one and a half dollars her first day, de Perales eagerly wrote to her mother, instructing her to come home and enjoy their wealth.

Soon, de Perales was travelling to other villages to style hair. At age 15, in the mid-1940s, she moved to Havana, stayed with a cousin, and advertised in a newspaper that catered to the wealthy as a way of building a clientele. Many of her first-time customers allowed her to style their hair out of pity because she was so young and small. They quickly discovered, however, that a style by de Perales was not charity work, and de Perales' list of elite customers rapidly grew. She soon had enough money to open a tiny salon. Within a year, she had moved her entire family to Havana.

At 17, de Perales fell in love with a pharmacist, a widower with two children. He asked her to marry him but requested that she give up her business as a condition of the marriage. As the sole supporter of her family, de Perales worried that a divorce would leave them all destitute once again, so she temporarily declined his offer. Two-and-a-half years later, after establishing her family and turning her business over to her sister, de Perales married him. For two years she threw herself into her new situation. However, de Perales yearned to return to the business world and became anxious and ill. A doctor who was a family friend told her husband he must let her go back to work or he would lose her. De Perales plunged into her career. Within a year of her return, her salon, now in a stylish part of town, employed 12 personally trained beauticians. By 1956, that number had grown to 36, replete with de Perales' own line of 115 products, and a television show. Four years later, she was running a two million dollar business.

Loses Business During Cuban Revolution

In 1961 de Perales' world changed overnight. Fidel Castro's revolutionaries walked into her salon, took her prisoner, and kept her for nine days. She was traumatized by the experience, yet, when her family arrived to take her home, they found de Perales focusing on the needs of others. To their surprise, she was entertaining other prisoners and giving them beauty tips to bolster their spirits.

De Perales returned to freedom to find everything she owned had been confiscated. She had two children to support without the help of her husband, from whom she was now divorced. Fleeing the country with her children became her first priority. A friend with an airline company helped them escape to Miami. She had five dollars in her purse when she arrived. Safe but virtually penniless, she was taken in by an elderly couple, the family of one of her employees in Havana. Her ex-husband loaned her four hundred dollars, and she began rebuilding her life. She said in the *Miami Herald,* "I told myself, 'I have folded a page of my book. Mirta de Perales was born the day she set foot in this country.'" She began working as a stylist out of her home, and within six months, she brought her mother, two siblings, and their families to Miami. Two years later she opened her first salon in Coral Gables.

De Perales worked long, hard hours in that salon. In 1964, she launched her own line of hair-care and cosmetic products entitled "Mirtha's" in Miami and Puerto Rico. Today, they can be found in stores in New York, New Jersey, Puerto Rico, Miami, Chicago, and California. She runs her business from her beach front condominium in Key Biscayne. From her television station in her home, she produces *Five Minutes with Mirta de Perales,* appearing several times a week, promoting her products and sharing her philosophies. She told *Latina* magazine, "Your failures, you should never even tell people about, because that means you've allowed yourself to think about them all over again. You can't allow a bad thought to stay in your mind. Now, your successes you should trumpet to everybody you see. And you should always believe that, no matter how impossible, you can have whatever you want. People who try to convince you otherwise, just move them out of your way. And remember to pray, pray every day."

Donates Money to Charities

De Perales has earned more love and respect than perhaps even she could have imagined. The philanthropic entrepreneur donates money to charities that assist children, as well as other social causes. She has received many prestigious awards, among them an invitation in 1987 to the White House for an event honoring 180 successful minorities. President Reagan singled her out, briefly recounted her story, asked her to stand, and said to the audience, "That's the American Dream."

Vivacious, flamboyant, and generous, de Perales attributes her success to her faith in God, whom she sees as a guiding light in every aspect of her life. From this faith springs an optimism that is undaunted by circumstances. Eternally positive, she said in an interview with the *Miami Herald*, "I go on a trip, and 40 things may go wrong, but I never come back to tell them. I tell only the good. By repeating the bad, you simply swallow bitter every time." Her generosity is as unbounded as her enthusiasm for life, and she gives away a significant portion of her income. When someone suggested she would be a multimillionaire had she not given so much away, she answered, "If I don't give anything, perhaps I will have nothing. When I was a little kid, I went barefoot. Now I run an empire."

Current Address: Mirta de Perales, Inc., 214–16 Andalusia Ave., Coral Gables, FL 33134.

Sources:

Acosta de Villalta, Loló. "Han Triunfado!" *Vanidades,* August, 1989.

Chardy, Alfonso. "Nickle-and-Dime Roots Grew into Tale of Riches." *The Miami Herald,* May 11, 1992.

Martín, Lydia. "Cinco Minutos con Mirta de Perales." *Latina Magazine,* April-May, 1997, pp. 70-73.

Reagan, Ronald. Remarks at minority groups business briefing. Press release, The White House, Office of the Press Secretary.

Veciana-Suarez, Ana. "Mirta de Perales' Gospel of Beauty." *The Miami Herald,* July 19, 1988, p. C1.

Wetzstein, Cheryl. "A Cuban Refugee Snips Her Way to Millionaire Status." *The Washington Times,* September 24, 1987, p. E2.

de Tío, Lola Rodríguez

See **Rodríguez de Tío, Lola**

Rima de Vallbona
(1931–)
Author, professor, critic

Selected writings:

Noche en Vela. Editorial Costa Rica, 1968.
Yolanda Oreamuno. Editorial del Ministerio de Cultura de Costa Rica, 1971.

Polvo del Camino. Editorial Escritores Unidos de Costa Rica, 1973.
La Salamandra Rosada. Editorial Geminis, 1979.
La Obra en Prosa de Eunice Odio. Editorial Costa Rica, 1981.
Mujeres y Agonías. Arte Publico, 1982.
Las Sombras Que Perseguimos. Editorial Costa Rica, 1983.
Baraja de Soledades. Ediciones Rondas, 1983.
Cosecha de Pecadores. Editorial Costa Rica, 1988.
El Arcangel del Perdon. Editorial Palacios, 1990.
Mundo, Demonio y Mujer. Arte Publico, 1991.
Vida i Sucesos de la Monja Alférez. Arizona State University Press, 1992.
Los Infiernos de la Mujer y Algo Mas. Ediciones Torremozas, 1992. Translated as *Flowering Inferno: Tales of Sinking Hearts*. Latin American Review Press, 1993.

Overview

Rima de Vallbona, born Rima Gretel Rothe in Costa Rica, is the author of numerous short stories, novels, and volumes of literary criticism, mostly available only in Spanish. After her marriage to a young Spanish physician, Carlos Vallbona, she moved permanently to the United States. De Vallbona's work focuses chiefly on the lives of Latin American women and children and draws strongly on her Costa Rican heritage. She taught for over 30 years at the University of St. Thomas (Houston, TX), and now is an emeritus professor there. Her writing has received many literary awards, and she remains active in organizations that advance Hispanic culture and literature.

Rima de Vallbona

Escapes Painful Childhood Through Writing

Rima de Vallbona was born in Costa Rica to German immigrant Ferdinand Rothe and his wife Emilia Strassburger Rothe. She was named after the character in the novel *Green Mansions.* Although her family was well off financially, de Vallbona was sent to a public school where most of the children were very poor. She was uncomfortable at being so conspicuously different and was known for being incredibly shy as well. Her father influenced her later career by encouraging her early interest in literature and art. Ferdinand Rothe's early death when de Vallbona was only nine also had an impact on her later work. Because of Rothe's German heritage, he was placed in a Costa Rican detention camp when World War II began and either died or was murdered there. While one of her brothers became an outspoken critic of religion after their father's death, de Vallbona became a devout Catholic.

Although Ferdinand Rothe had left funds behind to support his wife and children, Emilia was so worried that she refused to make any expenditures that she considered unnecessary, including education for her daughter, and insisted that de Vallbona leave high school and become a secretary. De Vallbona, who had begun to write stories even before her father's death, managed to find a job that allowed her to pay for classes. She finally was able to escape this stifling life when she won a scholarship to the Sorbonne in Paris.

Marries and Comes to the United States

In Paris, de Vallbona earned a diploma in French and so could make a living teaching. She also met a young Spanish medical student, Carlos Vallbona. They agreed to marry, but had to wait until he had finished his residency in Texas. In the interim, de Vallbona returned to Costa Rica and taught while also attending the University of Costa Rica. In December of 1956, she moved to Houston, not knowing the language and without any friends there. She and Carlos married the day after Christmas; his friends had made all of the wedding arrangements for the couple, since they had no family in their new country.

De Vallbona had three children early in her marriage, which delayed her plans to study at a local university. At home with her children, she decided to secretly continue work on a novel that she had begun while studying in Paris. Her husband discovered the manuscript and encouraged her to publish it. This first novel, *Noche en Vela* (published in 1968), dealt with the adolescence of a Costa Rican girl, Luisa. De Vallbona's fourth child, Maria Luisa (Marisa) was named after this character.

Turns to Short Stories and Teaching

While working on her first novel, de Vallbona completed a master's thesis at the University of Costa Rica. She accepted a temporary offer to teach Spanish at a small Houston Catholic school, the University of St. Thomas. De Vallbona remained a professor at this school, eventually becoming a specialist in Latin American literature, until her retirement in 1995.

Because of the conflicting demands on her time, de Vallbona began to write short stories and literary criticism as well as novels. By the late 1990s, she had completed a solid body of published work in all of these fields. As described by Lee H. Dowling in *Biographical Dictionary of Hispanic Literature in the United States*, de Vallbona's writing revolves around five themes: "the questioning of established roles and norms, women's demand for freedom in the modern world, the world as seen through the eyes of children and adolescents, the search for religious faith, and the question of the line separating fantasy from reality." Dowling also notes that de Vallbona's language is always "richly expressive."

De Vallbona's second published work, *La Salamandra Rosada,* was an unusual collection of stories, personal vignettes, and poems, based on events in the lives of her own children. Another notable work is *Polvo del Camino,* a volume of short stories in which de Vallbona questions accepted social practices and which have a decidedly feminist tone. Many of the characters become the objects of social scorn and discrimination through events not in their control. The short stories in *Mujeres y Agonías,* while exploring the situation of women, also deal with the themes of war, insanity, and protest.

Las Sombras Que Perseguimos, a novel, employs a Costa Rican dialect. Its three key characters—a peasant, a writer, and an abused wife—each explore their differing views of reality. The story of the death of de Vallbona's own father in a World War II detention camp is told in this novel. *Los Infiernos de la Mujer y Algo Mas* (translated into English as *Flowering Inferno: Tales of Sinking Hearts*) is another short story collection. It was described by a *Los Angeles Times* book critic as the "intriguing, if uneven" depiction of "a world of magical realism in which reality grows tenuous."

Retires from Academia But Continues to Work

In 1995 de Vallbona became professor emeritus at the University of St. Thomas. However, she remains very active professionally. She is a member of many national and local organizations centered on literature, teaching, and Hispanic culture. These include: the Asociación de Literatura Femenina Hispanica; the Latin American Writers Institute; the Houston Hispanic Women in Leadership Organization; the Institute of Hispanic Culture of Houston; and the American Association of Teachers of Spanish and Portuguese.

De Vallbona also has received numerous literary prizes around the world in recognition of her work: the National Novel Prize (Costa Rica, 1968); the Jorge Luis Borges Short Story Prize (Argentina, 1977); the Agripina Montes del

Valle Latin American Novel Prize (Colombia, 1978); the Prof. Lilia Ramos Children's Poetry Prize (Uruguay, 1978); the SCOLAS (Southwest Conference of Latin American Studies) Literary Prize (United States, 1982); and the Ancora Award for the best fiction book of the year (Costa Rica, 1984). She is also proud of the many awards she has received for her cultural work, such as: the Medal of Civil Service for her cultural work in the Hispanic world (presented by King Carlos of Spain, 1989); the Willie Velázquez-Channel 48 Excellence Award for Outstanding Services to the Hispanic Community (Houston, TX, 1991); and the Hispanic Women Hall Award from the Houston Hispanic Women in Leadership Organization (1993). In 1997 de Vallbona was inducted into the Houston Hispanic Forum's Hall of Fame, and the Instituto Literario y Cultural Hispánico gave her a plaque in acknowledgement of her "valuable contribution to Spanish American literature."

In her retirement, de Vallbona continues to write, her most recently completed work being a children's story, *Tormy, La Gata Prodigioso de Donaldito.* Some of her existing body of work has been translated from Spanish into English, French, German, and Portuguese. *Protestas, Interrogantes y Agonías en la Obra de Rima De Vallbona* is a collection of scholarly criticism of her work through 1997.

Current Address: Modern Languages Dept., Univ. of St. Thomas, 3800 Montrose Blvd., Houston, TX 77006.

Sources:

Arancibia, Juana Alcira, and Luis A. Jiménez, eds. *Protestas, Interrogantes y Agonías en la Obra de Rima De Vallbona.* Westminster, CA: Instituto Literario y Cultural Hispánico, 1997.

Kanellos, Nicolás, ed. *Biographical Dictionary of Hispanic Literature in the United States.* Westport, CT: Greenwood Press, 1989.

Marting, Diane E., ed. *Women Writers of Spanish America.* Westport, CT: Greenwood Press, 1987.

Solomon, Charles. Book review of *Flowering Inferno. Los Angeles Times,* March 27, 1994, p. 9.

Urbano, Victoria, ed. *Five Women Writers of Costa Rica.* Beaumont, TX: Asociación de Literatura Femenina Hispanica, 1978.

Cameron Diaz
(1973–)
Actress

Selected filmography:

The Mask, 1994.

The Last Supper, 1995.
She's the One, 1996.
Feeling Minnesota, 1996.
Head Above Water, 1996.
My Best Friend's Wedding, 1997.
A Life Less Ordinary, 1997.
Very Bad Things, 1998.
Fear and Loathing in Las Vegas, 1998.

Overview

With her classic Hollywood good looks, Cameron Diaz experienced the fast and easy rise to stardom that many young women dream, but few get the chance to experience. After a successful modeling career, she landed her first movie role, opposite the rising superstar Jim Carrey in *The Mask.* Carrey's subsequent mega-stardom provided visibility for the film that assured Diaz not only more film work, but the chance to pick and choose among roles. It almost seemed an understatement when she told the Los Angeles newspaper, *Newsday,* "I'm so fortunate. . . . You don't even know."

California Dreamin'

Born in 1973, Diaz was raised in Long Beach, CA, the second of two daughters. Her father is a foreman for Union of California Oil and a second generation Cuban American. Her mother is an exporting agent whose background is German, English, and Native American. Diaz has a warm and supportive family with whom she remains very close. As children, Diaz and her sister were taken everywhere with their parents and treated as adults. As a teenager, her parents allowed her a great deal of freedom and responsibility, trusting her to make the right choices.

Long Beach was one of the sources of a vibrant, new multicultural urban aesthetic. Diaz attended Long Beach Polytechnic, the same high school attended by gangster rapper Snoop Doggy Dogg. As a teenager, Diaz wore a feathered haircut and was an avid attendee at heavy metal concerts by groups such as Van Halen, Ozzy Osborne, and Metallica. Even this interest was supported by her parents, who sometimes took her to concerts and let her use their Volkswagon minibus when she could drive so she could take her friends.

Modeling Beckons

The model-turned-actress claims that she never aspired either to modeling or acting. Rather, her first interest was zoology. But at the age of 16, Diaz attended a Hollywood party where a photographer handed her his card and asked her to have her parents call him. Zoology was quickly forgotten when, less than a week later, she was offered a contract by the prestigious Elite modeling agency.

Before long, Diaz was on her way to Japan, in the company of a 15-year old friend who acted as her "chaperone." Her parents not only agreed, but they were supportive. Their only demand was that she finish high school when she returned. The girls were set up in a two-bedroom apartment and lived the stereotypical model's life of parties and clubs. "Believe me, you can get into a lot of trouble being 16 years old in a foreign country with no adult telling you when to come home," Diaz later told Oliver. "The difference is knowing what is right and what is wrong. And people who want to get you to believe what's wrong is right can. They know how. I don't care how smart a kid you are. The only way you learn what's not right is from experience."

Diaz learned at least part of that lesson the hard way. Modeling took her to Australia, Morocco, Paris, and Mexico. While in Australia, she nearly killed herself with alcohol poisoning. For a year, she says, she was unstable and unhappy because of the importance placed on appearance and the continual rounds of rejection that are part of a model's life. In addition, erotic photos taken of her when she was 17 returned to haunt her after her stardom when they appeared in *Celebrity Sleuth* magazine.

While on a shoot for L.A. Gear in the United States, Diaz met video producer Carlos de La Torre. The two began dating and moved in together shortly after Diaz graduated from high school. Their relationship lasted five years, until Diaz's big break propelled her to stardom.

Reaches Overnight Film Success

Diaz never became a "supermodel," but earned a good living doing print and television ads. She was not looking for a career change, but one day while at the office of the agent who placed her in TV commercials, Diaz noticed a movie script on the agent's desk. She told *Rolling Stone* when she asked what it was, her agent replied, "It's a movie script. Do you think you can handle it?" Diaz claims that she was joking when she answered, "Sure, no problem." But when they asked her to read for the part in *The Mask,* she began to take it seriously. Expected to read for the role of seductress in the film, her instructions were to dress for the role. Doubting she could land the lead female role though, Diaz dressed more conservatively and asked to instead read for the part of the journalist. Over one month later, she had landed the role of the seductress.

Even while working on the film, Diaz suggests she had little idea she was taking part in what would turn out to be a megahit. She admitted her naivete in *Rolling Stone,* "Halfway through the filming I was like 'Is there any place my friends and family can see this movie?' I was so ignorant." That ignorance disappeared, however, as *The Mask* became a hit, and Diaz was widely praised for her performance. Although her role did not provide much of an opportunity to showcase acting talent, critics felt that Diaz added as much wit to the role. In an interview for the Associated Press, Diaz attributes her own success largely to Carrey's. "I came from out of nowhere with *The Mask,*" she says. "But if it hadn't been for Jim's success with *Ace Ventura,* who

knows what would have happened to *The Mask?* Really, I only benefited because of Jim's success." Diaz also attributes her success to the fact that she was never a very famous model. People did not see her as a model-turned-actress, a category that inevitably breeds skepticism about an actress's ability to act.

Contends with Stereotype

Following up on such a meteoric rise was not easy. "I'm always going to be the babe from *The Mask,* which is fine with me," Diaz told *Sassy* magazine. "But it's my responsibility to figure out what I want to do. I don't want to play a babe in every movie."

Diaz's success in doing so has been mixed. After *The Mask,* she took the role of a plain woman in the independent dark comedy *The Last Supper.* Her character helps her graduate student friends murder a right-wing dinner guest. In spite of the recent trendiness of independent films, *The Last Supper* was largely ignored. The next few films Diaz made were disliked by critics, although the actress was praised for her efforts. In the 1996 *Feeling Minnesota,* she played opposite Keanu Reeves. The first feature by director Steven Baigelman tells the story about an unlucky prostitute who is forced to marry by a drug dealer. She promptly falls in love with her new husband's brother, an ex-felon, and runs away with him right after the wedding. The film unfolds as the two evade their pursuers. *Rolling Stone's* critic called *Feeling Minnesota* "a terrible film that should carry a straight-to-video warning." In the same year, Diaz starred with Jennifer Aniston in *She's the One,* playing an ex-prostitute. While not disliked as much as *Feeling Minnesota, She's the One,* directed by Edward Burns, was considered not much more than a sitcom. Again, Diaz was praised for her beauty and her ability to pull off light comedy.

In 1997, Diaz appeared in *Head Above Water,* in which she played a housewife who is pursued by killers. Starring Harvey Keitel, the film was also disliked and largely ignored. Diaz, however, was honored with ShoWest's coveted Female Star of Tomorrow Award, following in the footsteps of Winona Ryder, Nicole Kidman, and Juliette Lewis.

Makes Big Breakthrough

Diaz clearly tried to choose her projects carefully. However, finding good roles in good films turned out to be difficult. The actress was blunt about that fact when she was interviewed for a *Newsday* article: "A girlfriend of mine, who's this amazing actress—we're both kind of fed up with not finding anything interesting. She's like, 'I want the guy roles!' I said 'Well, just rewrite them!' . . . That's what we should do: Start demanding that the good roles get rewritten for females!"

It is a sign of how few good roles there are for actresses that Diaz made her big breakthrough playing the cute, prim, debutante Kimmy in the blockbuster Julia Roberts' vehicle *My Best Friend's Wedding.* For Diaz, the role was a relief.

Diaz's work in *My Best Friend's Wedding* made her truly famous. Critics responded well to the film's frothy comic touch and admired Diaz in her supporting role. The unexpected friendship between her character and Roberts' emerged as one of the surprising treats of the film, and Roberts was praised for risking being upstaged by the beautiful Diaz.

Searches for Quality Roles

In 1997, Diaz starred in *A Life Less Ordinary,* the third feature by trendy director Danny Boyle of *Trainspotting.* Playing opposite Ewan McGregor, she portrayed a spoiled rich girl who actually helps a disgruntled employee kidnap her and quickly falls in love with her captor. The film was not well received; the *Chicago Tribune* called it "a poor try at screwball comedy." Like most critics, the *Washington Post's* reviewer praised Diaz while disliking the film, calling it a "Diaz-zling Failure." The *Los Angeles Times* praised Diaz's gift for romantic comedy and declared that the film "should place her in the next 'Julia Roberts—new Sandra Bullock' slot Hollywood is always eager to fill."

Diaz is not demanding top billing for all future projects. After *A Life Less Ordinary* she accepted a supporting role in a dark comedy with Christian Slater called *Very Bad Things.* Starring in a movie, she told *Newsday* is ". . . a lot of responsibility."

Diaz may still get her wish and find some exciting, well-written roles to play. Meanwhile, she continues to call her mother every day and maintains close, supportive relationships with her father and sister as well. In 1996 she began dating former teen-idol Matt Dillon, but she does not attempt to run in Hollywood's fast lane. "I'm pretty confined to my group of friends," she told *Interview* magazine. "Knowing you have a support system—family, whatever—really helps. Then you don't need other people's acceptance."

Sources:

Cohen, Debbi. "Lights, Cameron, Action!"*Sassy,* August 1996, p. 42.

Dunn, Janice. "Diaz." *Rolling Stone,* August 22, 1996, pp. 50, 112.

Gliatto, Tom. "Unmasked." *People Weekly,* August 22, 1994, pp. 51-52.

Hunter, Stephen. "'A Life Less Ordinary': A Diaz-zling Failure." *Washington Post,* October 24, 1997, p. D7.

Kilian, Michael. "Seldom Seen." *Chicago Tribune,* September 15, 1996, p. 12.

Mathews, Jack. "This 'Water' is No Day at the Beach." *Los Angeles Times,* June 25, 1997, p. F4.

Oliver, Lauren. "Lights, Cameron, Action!" *Interview,* August 1994, p. 74.

Rowe, Douglas J. "For Cameron Diaz 'Fate is Sort of in Control.' *Associated Press,* October 27, 1997.

Smith, Steven. "Model Career" *Los Angeles Newsday,* October 26, 1997, p. D13.

Cari M. Dominguez
(1949–)
Consultant

Overview

Cari M. Dominguez is in the midst of a battle. Her target is shattering the glass ceiling—a very real but invisible shield keeping women and minorities from climbing to corporate America's upper echelon and establishing a presence in white male-dominated fields. She first took up the cause while serving as assistant secretary for Employment Standards Administration, the U.S. Department of Labor's largest agency. Whether as director of the Office of Federal Contract Compliance Programs at the Department of Labor or in executive offices in the private sector,

Cari M. Dominguez

she served as a vocal proponent, calling for an end to racial and gender discrimination in the workplace. Dominguez, now a partner with Heidrick & Struggles, one of the world's leading executive search firms, has met personal success in her own climb. She is on the firm's board and financial services practices committee.

Flees Cuba

Dominguez was born in Cuba in 1949 during tumultuous times. Her family was close but the political upheavals of that era put a strain on the family. Her father, fearing for their safety, sent his family to the United States in 1961. The family went directly to Oxon Hill, MD, a suburb of Washington, DC, to the home of her mother's sister. The move was not an easy transition, as this was the first time the family had been separate from the father. But Dominguez's father, like so many others, hoped that the upheaval resulting from the Revolution would eventually calm, and that life in Cuba would return to what he had known. Sensing that his hope may well be a child's fancy, her father, after a six-year separation, left Cuba for the United States.

Rough transitions and uncertainties in her family life did not discourage Dominguez from pursuing her education. She graduated from Montgomery-Blair High School in Maryland in 1967, the same year her father joined them in the United States. She chose to enroll in The American University School of International Service, in Washington, DC, where she pursued both her B.A. and M.A. in international affairs. Dominguez looked forward to a career as a foreign service officer. Fate had other plans and, through an interesting turn of events, Dominguez was hired by the U.S. Government's Internal Revenue Service. From there she went to the Veterans' Administration, where she was employed at the end of the Vietnam War. Dominguez recounts her experience with the administration as one of great honor. But she soon left there for the Department of Labor, where she worked for a total of nine years.

Challenges of Corporate America

Dominguez was not one to shy away from challenges, so when the offer came to leave the walls of government to explore the private sector, she took it without hesitation. She left D.C. in 1983 and headed to San Francisco, the headquarters for Bank of America. Her extensive career in the U.S. government made her curious about life in corporate America. While at the Bank of America she held various human resources positions, including that of vice-president. As director of executive programs, Dominguez worked diligently to place more women into the top-level positions. In a mere two and a half years, her program, "Upward Mobility," helped more women and minorities reach the upper ranks. It was the fastest rate of growth compared with any other time in the company's long history.

Targets The Glass Ceiling

Upon President Bush's election in 1988, Dominguez was asked to return to the Department of Labor, this time as director of the Office of Federal Contract Compliance Programs. Dominguez led the charge to uncover the obstacles blocking passage to the upper limits of corporate America. Many barriers were discovered, some to a greater degree than initially suspected, when Secretary of Labor Lynn Martin issued the findings of Dominguez's study in August of 1991. In the midst of that debate, Dominguez launched the Labor Department's *Glass Ceiling Initiative.* As Dominguez outlined the problem in an article published in the November of 1991 issue of *The Labor law Journal,* entitled, "The Glass Ceiling and Workforce 2000," she wrote: ". . . there is a ceiling, a glass ceiling that minorities and women can see through but cannot get through. . . the invisible barriers, real or perceived, which appear to stymie advancement opportunities for minorities and women." The initiative set forth first with a pilot study investigating how positions of upper-and mid-level management in corporate America were filled, as Dominguez went on to explain in her article. This was to be an examination of the most basic components of career advancement. "Specifically," she says, "we looked at developmental programs, training, rotational assignments, and reward structures, all of which serve as indicators of upward mobility in corporate America."

Indeed, Dominguez led the effort to seek compliance in alleviating this situation. In an article in *ENR* in January of 1991, Helen Bradford wrote of Dominguez, "Since starting in 1989, financial settlements wrested from employers have doubled under her tenure, in part because of increased productivity leading to investigation of more cases." There, too, the author noted that, "Dominguez feels that demographics are on her side." She quotes Dominguez as saying that workplace discrimination is ". . . no longer a moral or legal issue. It is an economic issue." Dominguez was aligned with President Bush in his lack of confidence in a "quota" system for hiring. She believed there were more constructive ways of dealing with opportunities in equal employment. With its Mega Construction Project Initiative, Dominguez led the OFCCP in a new approach. Such projects as monumental as the building of the new Denver Airport, and Boston's Central Artery/Inner Harbor Tunnel served as the testing ground for how the office would reach compliance. Under the program, these agreements with contractors and agencies were resolved before hiring began. Bradford also mentions in her article that this was an example of what Dominguez considered, "the most exciting" of the programs.

Returns to the Private Sector

A shift in the White House in 1992, from Republican President Bush to Democrat President Clinton, forced Dominguez to leave the government. She opted to return to San Francisco to join the executive search firm of

SpencerStuart. She soon left there to return home and joined the executive search firm of Heidrick & Struggles in their Washington, DC office. Her close ties to her family, still living in the nation's capital, greatly influenced her decision as well as the excitement of another professional challenge.

In her new position, Dominguez serves as a consultant to businesses across the country, specializing in diversity issues. She is a fellow of the Advanced Study Program in Public Management of the Massachusetts Institute of Technology in Cambridge, MA. Her recognized skill earned Dominguez extensive senior management assignments from business and industry throughout the world.

Dominguez does not limit her energy to work with Heidrick & Struggles. She serves on many nonprofit boards, including the Human Resources Planning Society and the Leadership Foundation. She continues as an advisor member of the Corporate Governance Registry for the State of California, and as a member of the Senate Commission on Corporate Governance, Shareholders Rights and Securities Transactions under the Senate Rules Committee of the California Legislature.

While she has enjoyed celebrity status in recent years, Dominguez says that it is only an honor to be able to serve her country along with the people who struggle to make it work. What is more important is that she has accomplished the myriad of goals she has set for herself and for her country. For this reason, she has been widely recognized for her achievements. The magazine *Hispanic Business* has recognized Dominguez as among the "100 Most Influential Hispanics in the United States." The American Biographical Institute has listed her as among the *2,000 Notable American Women.*

Dominguez concluded her 1991 article in *The Labor Law Journal*, with "... working together to dismantle glass ceilings, wherever they exist, will get us closer to living our lives to the farthest reaches of our human potential." Now, in the world of business, Dominguez has a chance to more aggressively work toward that goal. She searches the most qualified talent pool in America to fill the top positions in the corporate business world. In doing this, Dominguez hopes to contribute to the assembling of a workforce that is truly representative of the multicultural heritage in which America shares.

Current Address: Heidrick & Struggles, 1301 K St., NW, Ste. 500 East , Washington, DC 20005.

Sources:

Bradford, Hazel. "Agency Head Returns to Her Roots." *ENR*, January 21, 1991.
Dominguez, Cari M. "The Glass Ceiling and Workforce 2000." *Labor Law Journal*, November 1991.
Spear, Jane. Telephone conversation with and biographical material from Cari M. Dominguez, March 19, 1998.

Dominguez Weir, Diana
See **Weir, Diana Dominguez**

E

Maria Echaveste
(1954–)
Federal government official

How does the daughter of itinerant immigrant farm workers leave the fields to become the highest-ranking Hispanic American in the White House? Maria Echaveste, who did just that, started with books. Appointed by President Clinton as director for public liaison early in 1997, Echaveste said that at a very young age she discovered, through reading books, a world far beyond her experience. She wanted to experience that world and saw education as the vehicle to take her there. "I knew my world was not *all* of the world," Echaveste said in an telephone interview. "People in those books went to college, had interesting

Maria Echaveste

jobs, travelled to interesting places. I wanted that, too." Today, Echaveste—a graduate of Stanford University with a B.A. in anthropology and a law degree from the University of California at Berkeley—is the president's chief representative in the nation's business community, promoting his policies to the public and advising him of public opinion. Commenting on her new role, Echaveste said in an interview with the *Seattle Times*, "The office of public liaison is precisely about ensuring that all the different voices, all the different views on the whole gamut of issues, are heard when the president and his senior policy advisers are considering courses of action."

Turns to Law and Government

So why did an anthropology major turn to law and government? Echaveste, who said she still loves anthropology and often reads books on the subject, said in a telephone interview, "I felt that a good-paying job in anthropology would be difficult to find. As the oldest child from a poor background, it was very important for me to have a stable, lucrative livelihood. Actually, I love practicing law. It's a real challenge." Echaveste, who seems to thrive on challenge, said "I also feel very grateful to have the tremendous good fortune to work in government—to try to make a difference. Government is by no means the total solution, but it can help people to maximize their potential. I feel honored to be part of that process." She added, "Ambition for ambition's sake is not something I subscribe to, however. Jobs like the one I'm in will eventually be gone. There is great value in never forgetting where you came from. . . remembering what's really important, like trying to be a good person and do the right things."

Determination Pays Off

The road to the White House was not easy for Echaveste, whose parents left their small village in Mexico in the early 1950s. Born in Texas on May 21, 1954, the first of seven children, she began working in the fields about the time other children were entering kindergarten. She and her siblings all attended school, however, and by second grade, Echaveste was a prolific reader. When she was 12 years old, the family moved to California. As the oldest girl in the family, she was expected to contribute significantly to household duties and the care of her siblings. "At a very young age, I was much too responsible," she said in an interview with *The Seattle Times*.

Yet, Echaveste still took responsibility for her own future. "I had it in my head that I wanted go to college. I worked hard in high school. I was a good student, and I got a great scholarship," she said. Her father was adamantly opposed to her attending university. In the Mexican tradition, a young woman's role was to marry and have children. "It's pretty hard when you're 18 to defy your father. However, he was grateful down the road because it set a standard for my siblings, all of whom graduated from college."

While working on her degree in anthropology, Echaveste interned with the National Council of La Raza, a nonprofit organization which serves as a parent organization to more than 170 community-based Hispanic American groups nationwide. Upon graduating in 1976, she moved to Washington, DC to work with the U.S. Commission on Civil Rights. After returning to the West Coast and earning her law degree, she spent three years as an attorney in Los Angeles. She also joined the Mexican American Bar Association and volunteered with the Mexican American Legal Defense and Education Fund (MALDEF) as a mentor to minority students in their efforts to pass the California Bar examinations.

Accepts White House Position

Even after accepting a position with a New York law firm and attaining the rank of special council in bankruptcy law in 1990, Echaveste made time to contribute her talents to organizations like the New World Foundation, where she became a board member. Her association with political personnel in New York opened a new door, and she stepped into her political career in 1992 when the future President Clinton invited her to become deputy director of personnel, assistant secretary of the Department of Labor, and administrator of that department's Wage and Hour Division. In so doing, Echaveste not only became an important liaison between Clinton and the Hispanic American population, she played an enormous role in bringing illegal and abusive labor practices in the garment manufacturing industry to the attention of both the government and the public. "Apparel is still a major American industry employing close to a million people, and a vast number work in conditions that are both dangerous and exploitive," said Echaveste in a *New York Newsday* article. In California's "sweat shops," workers—primarily immigrant women and, in many cases, children—work behind locked doors often up to twelve hours a day, six or seven days a week for less than minimum wage and no overtime pay or benefits. Perhaps because she grew up in a migrant worker family and experienced welfare and streets rife with crime, Echaveste readily identified with the garment workers' plight.

Echaveste emphasizes her success story is not about Maria Echaveste, but about how anyone can succeed. "*Every* child has the potential to be a productive member of society," she said. "But, for some reason, there are so many young people who are unable to find that certain set of factors or circumstances to help them reach their potential. Perhaps it's hope—or strength of believing. I don't think that strength comes from family encouragement alone, because my mother's greatest vision for me was that I just not have to work in the fields."

Stresses Education and Family

When asked what she saw as the driving force behind overcoming the adversities of her childhood, Echaveste said, "I suppose it was a series of factors, one of the most important being reading. I want to stress to young people the value of education. It gives you a certain power and freedom that cannot be minimized. No one can ever take it away from you. But perhaps the most important factor was that I had very strong family ties. We sat around the dinner table together every night. Now, that can be very suffocating and difficult at times, but at the same time it is an anchor—a foundation for the rest of your life."

Current Address: Office of Public Liaison, The White House, 1600 Pennsylvania Ave., NW, Washington, DC 20500.

Sources:

Crowe, Kenneth C. "The Return of the Sweatshop: Garment Industry Still Plagued by Conditions." *New York Newsday,* March 20, 1994, p. 1.

Galvin, Kevin. "After a Rags-to-Riches Struggle, a White House Post." *The Seattle Times,* May 2, 1997.

Silverstein, Stuart. "Survey of garment industry finds rampant labor abuse." *Los Angeles Times,* April 15, 1994, p. D1.

Thompson, Märie L. Telephone conversation with and biographical information from Maria Echaveste, March, 1998.

Zoroya, Gregg. "The Great Persuader: As the Top Liaison Between the Public and President, Maria Echaveste Uses the Tenacity and Energy that Got Her Out of the Strawberry Fields." *Los Angeles Times,* April 27, 1997, p. E1.

Escalera, Irene
See Cara, Irene

Beatriz Escalona
(1903–1980)
Actress

Sources:

Hispanic-American Almanac. Detroit: Gale Research, 1993.
Kanellos, Nicolás. *A History of Hispanic Theater in the United States.* Austin, TX: University of Texas Press, 1990.

Beatriz Escalona is noted as the first U.S.-born Hispanic to become an outstanding theatrical performer and vaudeville personality. Her stage name was La Chata Noloesca, a rearrangement of the letters in her last name. Throughout a long career that began in 1920, she continued to perform publicly until her death in 1980.

Emerges as Vaudeville Star

Escalona was born in San Antonio, TX, on August 20, 1903. As a teenager, she had a job at the Teatro Nacional as an usher and cashier. It was at this theater that Escalona began to associate with the Areu Brothers, a Spanish-Cuban performing troupe. She joined their act, married José Areu, and made her vaudeville debut in El Paso, TX, in 1920. By the time Escalona became a star, vaudeville entertainment was well established in the United States, its heyday lasting from the mid-1890s through the early 1930s. Vaudeville performances usually consisted of ten to fifteen individual acts, featuring comedians, jugglers, trained animals, magicians, acrobats, singers, and dancers. Escalona's performances varied from melodrama to comedy. She eventually became known for her comic personality as a *peladita,* or streetwise maid, a sort of underdog character with a spicy way of talking.

Goes Solo

In 1930, now known on the stage as La Chata Noloesca, Escalona left the Areus troupe to strike out on her own. She toured the southwestern United States and northern Mexico with her own company, Atracciones Noloesca, made up mostly of other Mexican American women from San Antonio. Six years later, back in San Antonio, she reformed the company into Compañía Mexicana and, in the midst of the Great Depression, performed in Chicago, New York City, and Tampa, FL, as well as Puerto Rico and Cuba. Escalona became renowned for presenting Mexican folklore, humor, and music to her audiences.

The advent of talking pictures, the Depression, and the beginning of World War II brought an end to the vaudeville era. Still, in 1941, just before the U.S. entry into WWII, Escalona settled in New York City to perform for a nine-year period as the mainstay on the Hispanic vaudeville circuit, including the Teatro Hispano, Teatro Puerto Rico, Teatro Triboro, and the 53rd Street Theater. When Escalona finally left vaudeville, she retired to her native San Antonio. She periodically performed at special community events in the area until her death in 1980.

Martha M. Escutia
(1957–)
State representative, professor

Martha Escutia has a vision to empower the Hispanic American community. Elected in November of 1992 to the California State Assembly, Escutia represents the 50th assembly district, an area populated primarily by Hispanic Americans. Seen as a rising star in California politics, her peers elected her to chair the Freshman Democratic Caucus, and she also chairs the Assembly Judiciary Committee, the first woman ever to do so. During Escutia's extensive experience in public service, she was legislative director for the National Council of La Raza, a nonprofit organization which serves as a parent organization to more than 170

Martha M. Escutia

community-based Hispanic American groups nationwide. An honors graduate from the University of Southern California in public administration, she also holds a law degree from Georgetown University and certificates in advanced international legal studies of trade and tariffs from the World Court in The Hague, Holland, and in foreign investments from the National Autonomous University in Mexico City. "Education is the key to our success," said Escutia in a telephone interview. "Latino children have not attained as much education as they could. I am here to encourage young people. I want them to know that higher education is *not* out of reach, no matter what they might think. If you work hard, you can accomplish anything. But you must have a will to succeed and be prepared to defer the fun and games for the future while you are laying your foundation," she said. "I came from very humble beginnings, but I just stuck it out and worked hard."

Overcomes Obstacles

Escutia was born in Los Angeles on January 16, 1957, the first of four children. Her parents, Martha Sandoval and Paul Escutia, were born in Mexico but met in Chicago. Escutia faced her first obstacle as a young child starting school. She and her family spoke only Spanish and her grade school was an English-only school. Escutia learned English quickly, but her parents became concerned because her Spanish was deteriorating. In second grade, they sent her to school in Mexico City where, for two years, she learned Spanish and lost her English. At the age of ten, she went to an all-English school in East Los Angeles, which was a traumatic experience. "I remember very clearly sitting in classes not knowing a single word that was being said. It was an awful, awful feeling," she said in a 1997 *Los Angeles Times* interview. "I went through a lot of suffering." Escutia credits her recovery of the English language to a "dedicated teacher" who took time after class to help her translate Spanish into English. "She unlocked my English," she said. "I picked it up so well that I even skipped a grade."

Although this determined woman now speaks English, Spanish, Japanese, and French, she remains sensitive to the plight of today's young children facing the language barrier. Along with several other Hispanic American legislators with similar "language lockout" experiences, she opposed a political measure in 1997 to eliminate bilingual programs from California's schools. In the *Los Angeles Times* article, she said, "I did well picking up language, but for every one of me, there must be ten who don't."

Places Importance on Education and Mentoring

In her continuing effort to educate, encourage, and empower the next generation of Hispanic Americans, Escutia teaches and mentors students in her political science classes at Huntington Park Community College where she sponsored an intensive eight-week, eight-hours-a-day program called Fast Track L.A. This program is designed to develop the basic skills of participants in preparation for entering the work force or higher education. Escutia said she was mentored in her political career by California Sen. Richard Polanco, who recruited her to run for the California State Assembly while she was still vice president of government affairs for United Way of Los Angeles. Already actively volunteering in political campaigns, Escutia accepted the challenge. She said of Sen. Polanco, "He encouraged me, taught me how to campaign and raise money, and was just a wonderful supporter." Escutia credits her accessibility to the public to her political victory. "I walked the precincts daily going door-to-door," she said. "Even though my opponents had name recognition and political experience, I felt I had far more relevant hands-on experience than they did."

Personal drive and determination, coupled with the guidance and counsel of a trusted mentor, has been a powerful combination for Escutia. As assemblywoman, some of her many achievements include chair of the Assembly Ways and Means Subcommittee on Transportation, vice chair of the Assembly Standing Committee of Transportation, and chair of the Select Committee on the Alameda Corridor Project—a $1.8 billion project to consolidate train traffic between ports in Long Beach and downtown Los Angeles. She serves on the Joint Committee on Oversight of the State Library, the Select Committees on California-Africa Affairs, California-Mexico Affairs, Restructuring Government, and Statewide Immigration Impact. Her legislative successes include a statewide comprehensive service center for women with HIV and several environmental protection bills, some of which specifically address concerns for children and the elderly. She has numerous awards and honors to her credit and is profiled in *Who's Who in American Politics* and *Who's Who Among Hispanic Americans*.

Focuses on the Future

Escutia's example paves the way for future Hispanic American leaders. "Apart from my son and my husband, empowering the Latino community is my passion, my vocation, my hobby," she said. "I give money to Latino candidates, work on their campaigns, encourage them to run for office, work with PTA groups and similar organizations to encourage and prepare their members to lobby politically—to stand up for their rights; to become citizens with a civic consciousness. This type of commitment is sorely lacking in the Latino community and, as a result, we are so subject to political abuse. We need to become educated and self-sufficient. Empowerment will lead to that. I envision our community as a diaspora, similar to the Jewish community." As a symbol of her conviction, Escutia resigned in anger from the Assembly Labor and Employment Committee in June of 1997 following what she called in a *Los Angeles Times* article "a racist comment" directed to her and another Hispanic American assemblywoman by the committee chairman.

Along with her vision for the future of her people, Escutia has a vision for her own future. "I see myself running for state senate," she said, "and I *will* get in. I see myself there for eight years and then, well, maybe I will make a bid for state-wide office. . . the state of California, of course. I was born here. I'm Californian by state, and Californian by heart."

Current Address: California State Capitol, P.O. Box 942849, Sacramento, CA 94249-0001.

Sources:

Ingram, Carl. "Legislator Accused of Racism Over Remark."*Los Angeles Times,* June 26, 1997, p. A25.

Mitchell-Bray, Marsha. "New Program Helps Young People Get on the Fast Track." *Los Angeles Sentinel,* June 7, 1995, p. B6.

Skelton, George. "A Lawmaker's Firsthand View of the Bilingual Issue." *Los Angeles Times,* October 23, 1997, p. A3.

Thompson, Märie L. Telephone conversation with and biographical information from Martha M. Escutia, March, 1998.

Gloria Estefan
(1958–)
Singer, songwriter

Selected discography:

Otra Vez. Sony.
Rio, Sony, 1978.
Eyes of Innocence. Epic, 1984.
A Toda Maquina. Sony, 1986.
Primitive Love. Epic, 1986.
Anything For You. Epic, 1988.
Let It Loose. Epic, 1988.
Cuts Booth Ways. Epic, 1989.
Into the Light. Epic, 1991.
Greatest Hits. Epic, 1992.
Mi Tierra. Sony, 1993.
Hold Me Thrill Me Kiss Me. Epic, 1994.
Christmas Through Your Eyes. Epic, 1995.
Abriendo Puertas. Epic, 1995.
Destiny. Epic, 1996.
gloria! Epic, 1998.

Selected filmography:

Homecoming Concert. CBS, 1989.
Evolution. CBS, 1990.
Coming Out of the Dark. CBS, 1991.
Into the Light World Tour. Sony Music Video, 1992.

Everlasting Gloria. Sony, 1995.
Divas Live. VH-1, 1998.

Overview

From Hispanic roots to the pop music mainstream, Gloria Estefan and the Miami Sound Machine are the embodiment of the American dream come true. The Miami Sound Machine was originally a Cuban American quartet that performed popular music with decidedly Latin influences. The band grew from being a sensation in Spanish-speaking countries to international best-seller status, due to the talent and hard work of Gloria Estefan and the sound business sense of her husband, Emilio, a onetime member of the band and later its manager.

Estefan was born Gloria Fajardo in Cuba in 1958; as a toddler she fled Cuba with her family when Communist dictator Fidel Castro rose to power. Her father, José Manuel Fajardo, had been a Cuban soldier and bodyguard of President Fulgencio Batista. After coming to the United States, Fajardo was recruited into the 2506 Brigade, a Central Intelligence Agency-funded band of Cuban refugees that was involved in the unsuccessful 1961 Bay of Pigs invasion. After President John F. Kennedy negotiated the release of the captured soldiers, Fajardo rejoined his family. He eventually joined the U.S. Army and served for two years in Vietnam.

As a child Estefan liked to write poetry, and though she took classical guitar lessons, she found them tedious. She had no inkling that she would some day become a popular music star, but music played a very important role for her as a teenager. After her father's return from Vietnam, he was diagnosed as having multiple sclerosis, possibly as a result of having been exposed to the herbicide Agent Orange while serving in the army. Estefan's mother, who had been a teacher in Cuba, worked to support the family during the day and attended school at night. Young Gloria was left to take care of her father and younger sister. She had little social life, and because she felt the weight of such responsibilities she turned to music as a release. "When my father was ill, music was my escape," Estefan told Washington Post reporter Richard Harrington. "I would lock myself up in my room for hours and just sing. I wouldn't cry—I refused to cry. . . . Music was the only way I had to just let go, so I sang for fun and for emotional catharsis."

Joins Future Husband's Band

In 1975 Gloria met keyboardist Emilio Estefan, a sales manager for the rum dealer Bacardi who also led a band called the Miami Latin Boys. The band played popular Latin music, but because there was no lead singer, the quartet members took turns singing. A mutual friend asked Emilio to advise Gloria and some friends about organizing a band for a special event. Emilio heard Gloria sing, and when he met her again at a wedding at which the Miami Latin Boys were entertaining, he asked her to sit in with the band. A few weeks later Emilio asked Gloria to perform as lead singer with the band, and she accepted. At first Gloria sang only on weekends, because she was still attending the University of Miami. A year and a half after Gloria joined the group, by then renamed the Miami Sound Machine, the band recorded its first album for a local label. *Renacer* was a collection of disco pop and original ballads sung in Spanish.

Although Estefan was somewhat plump and very shy when she joined the band, she slimmed down with a rigorous exercise program and worked to overcome her natural reticence. After several months on a professional level, Emilio and Gloria's professional relationship turned personal, and on September 1, 1978, they were married. Their son Nayib was born two years later, about the time that Emilio quit his job at Bacardi to work full-time with the band, then made up of bassist Marcos Avila, drummer Kiki Garcia, keyboardist, arranger, and saxophonist Raul Murciano, keyboardist Emilio, and soprano Gloria.

By 1980 the group had signed a contract with Discos CBS International, the Miami-based Hispanic division of CBS Records. Between 1981 and 1983 the Miami Sound Machine recorded four Spanish-language albums made up of ballads, disco, pop, and sambas. The Miami Sound Machine first met with success in Spanish-speaking countries. The group had dozens of hit songs around the world--particularly in Venezuela, Peru, Panama, and Honduras—but enjoyed little recognition in the United States.

Finds Success in North America with First English Songs

The Miami Sound Machine's first North American hit was from the band's first English album, *Eyes of Innocence.* The disco single "Dr. Beat" went to the top of the European dance charts. The song's popularity prompted CBS to move the group to Epic, a parent label, and inspired group members to write songs in English, first with a couple of numbers on the otherwise Spanish-language record *Conga.* The rousing dance number "Conga" itself became the first single to crack Billboard's pop, dance, black, and Latin charts simultaneously. Estefan reminisced to Jesse Nash of the *New York Tribune,* "I'll never forget when we first did 'Conga.' A producer told us that the song was too Latin for the Americans and too American for the Latins. 'Well, thank you,' I said, 'because that's exactly what we are!'" Estefan and the group, the membership of which has changed over the years, pride themselves on the combination of Latin rhythms, rhythm and blues, and mainstream pop that makes up their hybrid sound.

In 1986 the album *Primitive Love,* the band's first recording entirely in English, set off a string of hit singles. "Bad Boys" and "Words Get in the Way" made their way onto Billboard's Top 10 pop chart. Behind the scenes was the work of the trio known as the "Three Jerks"—producer-drummer Joe Galdo and his partners Rafael Vigil and Lawrence Dermer—who wrote, arranged, and performed the majority of the music on *Primitive Love* and the follow-up album, *Let It Loose.* As a band, the Miami Sound Machine developed a split personality. In the studio the "Three Jerks" and session players made records, and for concerts the road band, which included Garcia and Avila, performed. Estefan was the common denominator. Extensive tours, concerts in 40,000-seat stadiums, and music videos on MTV and VH-1 made the Miami Sound Machine a leading U.S. band. Estefan gradually became the star attraction, and the act came to be billed as Gloria Estefan and the Miami Sound Machine or sometimes simply Gloria Estefan. Some commentators on the popular music scene called Estefan a demure, Hispanic version of Madonna.

After the *Let It Loose* album, Galdo and friends quit working with the Miami Sound Machine, so the band was on its own creatively. Early in its evolution, the band's biggest hits were rousing dance numbers, but by the end of the 1980s it was Estefan's ballads that engendered its success. "Ballads are basically what I'm about," Estefan confessed to Dean Johnson of the *Boston Herald.* "I just feel you can express yourself more completely and eloquently in a ballad. It's easier to identify with someone else and form a closer bond with the audience." From the *Let It Loose* album the singles "Rhythm Is Gonna Get You," "Betcha Say That," and "1-2-3" made it to Billboard's Top 10 list, but it was the ballad "Anything For You" that topped the charts.

Despite the group's popularity with English-speaking listeners, the Estefans have not forgotten their roots. There are always Spanish-language projects in the works, and the title of their 1989 album *Cuts Both Ways* attests to their intention to live up to their international reputation. Estefan contributed to *Cuts Both Ways* in more capacities than as just the lead singer. She was involved in its planning and production, composed some of the music, and wrote lyrics to most of the songs. The rollicking salsa finale "Oye Mi Canto" ("Hear My Song") rivaled "Conga" for its appeal.

Fractures Spine in Traffic Accident

Emilio Estefan relinquished his position as keyboardist with the Miami Sound Machine after the birth of son, Nayib. He then devoted his considerable energy and managerial talent to promoting the band and the other enterprises that were to eventually make the Estefans producers of their own and others' records. While Estefan toured with the band, her husband ensured that Nayib would have at least one parent at home. A close family, the Estefans would arrange to meet as often as possible during tours. While traveling together on March 20, 1990, the band's bus was involved in an accident with a tractor trailer on snowy Interstate 380 near the Pocono Mountains of Pennsylvania. While Nayib suffered a fractured shoulder and Emilio received minor head and hand injuries, Gloria suffered a broken vertebra in her back. In a four-hour operation several days later, surgeons realigned Estefan's spine and implanted steel rods to buttress the fracture. With a prognosis for complete recovery doubtful, Estefan retired to her home on Star Island, near Miami, to begin her long recovery.

Makes Miraculous Comeback

Thanks to extensive physical therapy, intense determination, and the support of her family and fans, Gloria Estefan made what many consider a miraculous comeback. She marked her return to performing with an appearance on television's American Music Awards in January of 1991, and beginning in March, she launched a year-long tour to tout her comeback album *Into the Light*. According to *People*, her "long, sometimes uncertain recovery" gave the singer-songwriter "a renewed feeling about life," as she told writer Steve Dougherty. "It's very hard to stress me out now. It's hard to get me in an uproar about anything because most things have little significance compared with what I almost lost." She added that "so many people got behind me and gave me a reason to want to come back fast and made me feel strong. Knowing how caring people can be, how much they gave me—that has changed me forever."

During the next four years Gloria released four albums and embarked on a world tour. The albums alternated in style from Latin to pop. After recording the platinum album *Destiny* in 1996, Gloria began a high-tech world tour called Evolution. Each show commenced with a suspended globe moving above the audience from which Gloria emerged. The $14 million in receipts from the North American leg placed it as the 24th highest grossing tour of 1996.

Affirms Position in Music Industry

In 1998 Gloria continued to combine pop, dance and Latin rhythms in her 12th album, *gloria!*. She also performed on the VH-1 concert special, *Divas Live* along with Celine Dion, Aretha Franklin, Shania Twain, and others. The concert raised money to fund music education in elementary schools. Inclusion in this event affirmed her position among the top female singers in the music industry.

Current Address: Epic Records, 51 W. 52nd St., New York, NY 10019.

Sources:

Boston Herald, March 7, 1990; March 14, 1990.
Detroit Free Press, August 1, 1988.
Hispanstar Home Page. Available at http://histanstar.com/crnt-t+/rlist.html.
Los Angeles Daily News, September 12, 1989.
Los Angeles Herald Examiner, January 29, 1989.
Miami Herald, September 30, 1988; May 7, 1989; July 9, 1989; May 27, 1990.
New York Post, July 25, 1988; February 28, 1990; March 21, 1990; March 22, 1990; March 23, 1990.
New York Tribune, September 14, 1988; December 13, 1989.
People, October 27, 1986; February 18, 1991.
Rolling Stone, June 14, 1990.
Washington Post, July 17, 1988.

Estela Bolado Castilla y O'Donnell, Marie Marguerita Guadalupe Teresa
See Margo

F

Zulima V. Farber
Lawyer

After arriving in the United States as a teenage refuge from Fidel Castro's Cuba, Zulima Farber earned several degrees, became partner at a prestigious law firm, and went on to be the first Hispanic American woman appointed to serve in a New Jersey cabinet post. In 1992 Governor Jim Florio named Farber as New Jersey's Public Advocate and Public Defender at a time when the office was facing severe budget cuts. "I don't think one draws back when the going gets tough. You simply go do it," Farber stated to Donna Leusner when she was nominated to serve as the voice for New Jersey's homeless, indigent, mentally ill, disabled, and otherwise voiceless citizens. In her varied and

Zulima V. Farber

successful professional life, Farber often confronted such difficult challenges, but her early experiences as a political refuge taught her to face adversity head on.

Flees from Cuba

Farber, born Zulima Victoria Feraud, lived in Santiago, Cuba until she was 16 years old. In 1961 her younger brother was caught carrying anti-Castro literature and was jailed. In fear for the rest of the family's safety, Farber's parents arranged for Zulima and her sister to go to Jamaica, where they stayed until they were able to obtain visas to the United States. Farber arrived at the West New York, New Jersey, home of her aunt, Millie Rodriguez, carrying only one suitcase of her possessions. She believed that she would be able to return to her home in Cuba, but the political repression continued and soon Farber's parents also fled from Cuba and joined their daughters in the United States. With the aid of the International Rescue Committee, the younger brother was eventually released and immigrated to the United States as well.

The family faced hard times starting off in a new country. Farber's father had been a physician and a city councilman in Cuba, but the family fled with only what they could carry and struggled economically as new immigrants. Farber graduated from high school and accepted a secretarial position in a law office in order to save money for college. This was her first experience with the legal profession. With the help of her mother's earnings as a factory worker and a small scholarship, Farber was eventually able to continue her education at Montclair State College.

Finds Vocation in Law

After the family's sacrifices to send her to college, Farber was highly motivated to achieve. At first she set out to become a Spanish teacher and scholar. Farber earned a bachelor's degree in Spanish and a master's degree in Spanish literature, both from Montclair State. She continued to pursue her goal by enrolling in a doctoral program in Spanish literature at the City University of New York, where she studied for one year. However, at this time, her husband, law student Eugene Farber, ignited her interest in the field of law. She left the doctoral program and, with his encouragement, she enrolled in law school at Rutgers University.

It was clear that Farber found her vocation in the profession of law. She received her law degree in 1974 and accepted a job as a legal specialist with the Newark Department of Health and Human Welfare. She followed up this position with a job as assistant prosecutor for Bergen County, New Jersey, where she was involved in a number of major trials. Three years later she was recruited to work as assistant counsel to Governor Brendan Byrne. In this role Farber was responsible for criminal legislation and also legislation dealing with the Department of the Public Advocate, gaining skills and contacts that would aid her later in her career.

Farber moved to the private sector in 1981, joining the large and prestigious law firm of Lowenstein, Sandler, Kohl, Fisher & Boylan where she specialized in administrative and health care law. She made partner in 1986, reaching the landmark of being the first female partner at the firm. At Lowenstein Sandler she served on the executive committee and had responsibilities that touched on all areas of criminal and civil litigation.

Accepts Challenge of Public Advocate

In 1992 New Jersey Public Advocate Wilfredo Caraballo stepped down from office in opposition to severe budget cuts. Caraballo, who is also Hispanic American, alleged that the $5.5 million Republican budget cuts were a response to the office's outspoken positions on racially charged matters such as school desegregation. Governor Jim Florio nominated Farber to fill the post based on her excellent credentials and her past work with the office as assistant counsel to Governor Byrne. Farber took over the politically-charged position at a time when the office's power was under threat and was asked to fulfill its mission with significantly reduced resources. As the State of New Jersey's public advocate and public defender, Farber administered a staff of about 1,000, including 430 attorneys, charged with advocating for the interests of the public in a range of policy issues ranging from the regulation of utility rates to the protection of the disabled, mentally ill, and abused children. The office was also responsible for providing legal representation for indigent criminal defendants in New Jersey courts. Though she had the reputation of being a tough and skilled litigator, she took the position that the office should resort to litigation only when all other negotiating measures had failed. She was the first woman to serve at this post and the first Hispanic American woman ever appointed to a New Jersey cabinet. Two

years later Farber returned to her position at Lowenstein Sandler.

Active in Professional and Civic Organizations

Farber's activism and accomplishment in the legal field is evidenced by her membership in large number of professional and civic organizations and committees, including the Hispanic National Bar Association (of which she served as president), the National Abortion Rights Action League (of which she served on the board of directors), and the Black Women Lawyers Association of New Jersey. She has also been distinguished as the recipient of many honors and awards, including the United Way of Hudson County's Congresswoman Mary T. Norton Award, the Women's Political Caucus of New Jersey's Woman of Achievement Award, and the Christopher Columbus Award for Outstanding Contributions to Civic and Community Affairs.

Current Address: Lowenstein Sandler PC, 65 Livingston Ave., Roseland, NJ 07068–1791.

Sources:

Gannon, Bill. "Hispanic Lawyer in Line as Public Advocate," *Star Ledger,* July 23, 1992.

Gray, Jerry. "Vowing a Fight, Florio Names an Advocate," *New York Times,* July 24, 1992.

Leusner, Donna. "Nominee for Public Advocate Vows to Fight Department Cuts," *Star Ledger,* July 24, 1992.

Madsen Hardy, Sarah. Letter to Zulima V. Farber, April 2, 1998.

Anita Perez Ferguson
(1949–)
Organization president, radio commentator

Overview

The time she spent serving as political aide to a California assemblyman helped fuel Anita Perez Ferguson's interest in politics. After several years of involvement within the Santa Barbara, California, political community and a three-

Anita Perez Ferguson

year apprenticeship in the office of California Assemblyman Gary Hart, she decided to have a run at office herself. A Mexican American, Perez Ferguson has twice been the recipient of the Democratic nomination for Santa Barbara's 19th congressional district, in both the 1990 and 1992 elections. Now, as the first Hispanic American to head the National Women's Political Caucus (NWPC), Perez Ferguson lobbies for such important issues as reproductive freedom, health care reform, and equality in the workplace on behalf of all women.

Educational Background

Born in 1949, Perez Ferguson attended Westmont College, where she obtained a B.A. in communications studies in 1971. After completing a M.A. in counseling psychology at the University of Santa Clara four years later, she began working as a counselor and instructor for the California Community College System, moving to her alma mater, Westmont College, to head their admissions department in 1977. Perez Ferguson served as Westmont's director of admissions for four years, spending her evening hours at the University of Redlands, accumulating academic credit towards a second M.A.—this time in management—which she obtained in 1982.

In 1981 Perez Ferguson left Westmont College; in fact, she left the continent and spent the following year in Kenya as volunteer registrar and director of curriculum development for Daystar International Institute's Nairobi campus.

Back in the United States by 1983, she joined the staff of Gordon College, where she worked as a development officer for two years.

Changes Career Fields

In 1986 Perez Ferguson made a jump from the hallowed halls of academia onto the fast-moving political field, joining both the National Women's Political Caucus and the staff of California Assemblyman Gary Hart as a field representative based out of Santa Barbara. Two years later she joined Hart and other fellow democrats as a delegate to the 1988 National Democratic Convention. While the excitement of the convention was contagious, Perez Ferguson decided to leave Hart's camp a year later to pursue her involvement in politics a little closer to home: at the community level. Active in Santa Barbara's Chamber of Commerce Hispanic Business Committee and Earth Day Committee, she had already been appointed commissioner of Santa Barbara County's Department of Affirmative Action in 1986 and served on the Labor Council for Latin American Advancement; she left both those positions in 1989 in order to focus her energies and talent in other political arenas.

In 1990 Perez Ferguson took on the high-profile position of community consultant for Citizen 2000, a forward-looking organization dedicated to improving life in the Santa Barbara community for all its citizens during the coming years. Her soon-to-be-announced nomination as a candidate for the U.S House of Representatives drew the optimistic and energetic Hispanic American woman even further into the political limelight.

Enters Political Race

In 1990 Perez Ferguson campaigned as the Democratic nominee for Santa Barbara's 19th congressional district. This marked the first time that a Hispanic American woman ran for the U.S. House of Representatives from the state of California. Running on a platform that included a plan to re-distribute monies allocated for defense into health care, housing, education, and research and development, she also campaigned on her promise to battle the legislation that allowed the number of oil rigs dotting the Santa Barbara coastline to proliferate over the previous two decades. In addition, she ran pro-choice: "I believe that choice is every woman's, every family's right," Perez Ferguson later told the *Los Angeles Times.* "I talked about choice at every meeting and in every interview. Our analysis shows, and intuitively I know, that Republicans came over to vote for me on that issue alone." With a swelling of volunteer support—Los Angeles City councilwoman Gloria Molina and state representatives Ed Roybal and Esteban Torres each added their efforts to her bid for office—and $200,000 in campaign funds, she was able to make a strong showing against eight-term Republican incumbent Bob Lagomarsino, despite the fact that the district contains only 60,000 registered Hispanic American voters—enough to be a deciding factor but, at twenty percent of the electorate, not enough to carry an election.

While Perez Ferguson lost both bids for office, she was not discouraged by the experience. "We had 500 volunteers in a congressional race. That's fantastic," she told the *Los Angeles Times* in 1990. "We had more Hispanics involved than ever had been before in Santa Barbara or Ventura. We came from nowhere and closed to within eight percentage points of the incumbent winner. We didn't run as an Hispanic candidate, or a woman candidate; we ran as a candidate who cared about human issues, family issues."

Continues to Serve Community

Perez Ferguson continued to serve her community. In 1991, in addition to teaching at the Ventura campus of California State University—Northridge, she served as the Santa Barbara planning commissioner. Her other public service positions later included Santa Barbara affirmative action commissioner and chair of the Ethnic Advisory Board for Education in California. Since pursuing the second leg of her failed bid for political office, Perez Ferguson served as White House liaison to the U.S. Department of Transportation and the national director of education and training for the Democratic National Committee.

Heads NWPC

In 1995, Perez Ferguson became president of the National Women's Political Caucus (NWPC) and the first Hispanic American to head the organization. Founded in 1971, the mission of the NWPC is to identify, recruit, train, and support women that are seeking elected and appointed office. The national office initiates programs from Washington, DC, while several hundred state and local chapters host training seminars and support women for public office. Perez Ferguson's extensive leadership experience and political skills has served her well in her current NWPC role. Perez Ferguson was re-elected to a second term in 1997. In addition to her executive position with the NWPC, Perez Ferguson serves as a weekly commentator on National Public Radio (NPR).

Receives Noteworthy Acknowledgements

Perez Ferguson's efforts on behalf of others have been rewarded by numerous organizations: She was awarded special recognition for her efforts on behalf of United Way in 1984; in 1991, she received both the Woman of Distinction Award from the Soroptomist Club and the Santa Barbara County Commission for Women's Outstanding Woman Award; in 1996, she was one of ten women honored for her accomplishments by the National Action Agenda for the Advancement of Women and Girls, named one of the "rising stars of politics" by the *Campaigns & Elections* magazine, and cited in *Hispanic Business*'s "100 Most Influential Hispanics in the United States" directory;

and in 1997, she was named to *Roll Call Newspaper*'s "Politics Fabulous 50" and *Hispanic* 's "25 Most Powerful Hispanics in Washington, DC" lists.

Current Address: National Women's Political Caucus, 1211 Connecticut Ave., NW, Ste. 425, Washington, DC 20036.

Sources:

Arias, Anna Maria and Beatriz Johnston-Hernandez. "Issues, Elections, Representation: Hispanic political candidates." *Hispanic,* October 1990, pp. 26-30.

Perez Ferguson, Anita and Ward Connerly. "Q: Are Ethic and Gender-based Special-Interest Groups Good for America?" *Insight on the News,* July 7, 1997, p.24-28.

Information provided by the National Women's Political Caucus staff, April, 1998.

Mo, Jordan. "Where's the Next Gloria Molina?: Is Anyone Checking Santa Barbara?" *Los Angeles Times,* March 10, 1991, p. 6.

"100 Most Influential Hispanics in the United States." *Hispanic Business,* October, 1996. Available at http://www.hispanstar.com.

"25 Most Powerful Hispanics in Washington, DC." *Hispanic,* November, 1997. Available at http://www.hisp.com/nov97/13perez.html.

Giselle Fernandez
(1961–)
Television host

Giselle Fernandez advanced quickly through the ranks of television journalism to become a top anchor on some of the most prestigious news shows on television. But even as she reached the upper echelons of her profession, Fernandez continued to stretch herself in new directions, leaving the world of news reporting in order to embrace her role as host of the entertainment news show, *Access Today.* Now as host of her own talk show, *Café Olé with Giselle Fernandez,* on the Spanish-language cable station, Galavision, Fernandez is still pushing her boundaries.

Spends Summers in Mexico Doing Research

Fernandez was born on May 15, 1961, in Mexico City, Mexico. At the age of four, her family relocated in East Los Angeles. Her father worked as a flamenco dancer and her mother was a folklorist and professor at the University of California, Los Angeles (UCLA). In a telephone interview with Sally Foster, Fernandez recalled spending summers with her mother doing research in isolated Mexican villages. In her studies of mystical and mythological traditions and stories of Mexican traditions, Fernandez's mother interviewed hundreds of villagers. Fernandez attributes her ambition to "get the story from the people" to her experiences with her mother in Mexico.

At the age of 15, Fernandez moved to West Lake Village, CA, where she attended and graduated from the public schools. When selecting a college, she was attracted to Goucher College in Baltimore, Maryland, because of its reputation as a women's college and the recommendation of a number of friends. She entered college in the hopes of becoming an ambassador to some exotic country and embarked on an internship in Washington, D.C. Her disillusionment with the sexism and 'pack-mentality' of political life she encountered in this experience caused her to decide against a career in politics. However, her exposure to the news media piqued her interest in that field. Fernandez returned to California and transferred to the strong journalism program at Sacramento State University in California. There she participated in many internships in radio news. She also tried her hand at print journalism by working as a reporter for the school newspaper, completing a brief stint with *Executive Place Magazine*. In 1983, she was awarded her bachelor of arts degree in journalism with a minor in international relations.

Breaks into Broadcast Journalism

Hoping to break into the field of broadcast journalism, Fernandez made a rudimentary demo tape and sent it to one hundred stations across the country. Of those one hundred, only one responded with an offer. She became a reporter at KRDO, an ABC affiliate located in Pueblo, CO. The blue-collar town was home to many Hispanic families who worked in the local steel mill. As parts of the mill closed, Fernandez had the opportunity to become involved with many human-interest stories. Offered advancement at KEYT in Santa Barbara, she was promoted to reporter and weekend anchor. In 1986, Fernandez had the opportunity to move to a larger media market in Los Angeles. KTLA, the largest independent broadcaster in Los Angeles, hired her as a reporter and weekend anchor.

In the early stages of her career, Fernandez was fortunate to have sidestepped the job discrimination that faces so many Hispanics attempting to break into traditionally Anglo fields. She was quoted in *Contemporary American Success Stories: Famous People of Hispanic Heritage* as saying, "[My ethnicity] got me in all the doors in this business. It helped me get my jobs. It always put me ahead of the pack." This initial advantage came with a disadvantage for the young reporter, when Fernandez found that her abilities were called into question. "I was always battling the fact that I was being hired because I was pretty and Hispanic. When you're young and still learning your craft, you have to work three times as hard to prove yourself." Fernandez found this to be painfully true when she moved to Chicago in 1988 to work as a weekend anchor and reporter at a CBS

affiliate. She fell in love with the man who hired her, Ron Kershaw, and their relationship sparked rumors that Fernandez was using him to advance her career.

The following year, Kershaw died of pancreatic and liver cancer at the age of 43, and the death of Fernandez's father from Alzheimer's disease the following month devastated her. Hoping a change of environment would comfort her, Fernandez took the position of weeknight anchor with a Miami station. In Miami, Fernandez was exposed to a wide range of stories that further broadened her experience as a reporter.

Becomes News Anchor

In October of 1991, Fernandez was hired by CBS News as a correspondent and substitute anchor. In this position, she had access to several high-profile anchor spots as she substituted for Paula Zahn on *CBS This Morning*, Dan Rather on *CBS Evening News*, and Connie Chung on *CBS Weekend News*. Just a few months later she became a regular contributor to the *Eye in America* series in addition to reporting on stories for *CBS Sunday Morning*, *Face the Nation*, and *48 Hours*. When her contract with CBS ended, Fernandez chose to leave her position as a correspondent in order to become weekend host of the NBC *Today* show and anchor of the Sunday edition of *NBC Nightly News*.

Several of the stories Fernandez covered highlight her skills as a journalist. While serving as local news anchor in Miami, her coverage of the role of Israel in the Gulf War was of particular importance to the large Jewish community in the Miami area. The ability to furnish timely coverage on a major world event with a significant local perspective was very rewarding to both Fernandez and the viewing audience. Her live coverage of a Scud missile attack during the war earned her an Emmy Award—just one of five Emmy awards to her credit. In 1994, she was the first reporter in more than two decades to interview Fidel Castro in English. With such an impressive list of credits to her name, it looked as though Fernandez was securely in place as one of the top anchors in the broadcast news business.

Exchanges News for Entertainment

In a surprising move, however, Fernandez left the world of hard-hitting news coverage in order to become host of a new daily entertainment news magazine show, *Access Hollywood*. In that capacity, she has conducted interviews with some of Hollywood's biggest names, including Tom Cruise, Harrison Ford, and Michelle Pfeiffer. Regarding her decision, Fernandez told Leila Cobo-Hanlon in *Latina Publications*, "I love being a reporter and covering hard news, but I needed to break away from strict news. I have a creative spirit that wants to explore new possibilities." Fernandez continued to keep her career in motion by becoming the host of a weekly half-hour talk show called *Café Olé with Giselle Fernandez*. The show, which was launched in November of 1997, features interviews with Hispanic celebrities from the world of music, film, and television. The show appears on the Spanish-language cable station Galavision, although it is done mostly in English. On December 13, 1997, Fernandez hosted the Latino Laughs Festival, a pay-per-view special, with Cheech Marin. In addition to these projects, she hopes to launch her own production company and make movies and documentaries that will have an impact on both the Hispanic and English marketplace.

Current Address: Galavision, 605 3rd Ave., 12th Fl., New York, NY 10158–0180.

Sources:

Cobo-Hanlon, Leila. "Giselle Fernandez has a New Attitude." *Latina Publications,* November 1997.

Foster, Sally. Telephone interview with Giselle Fernandez, September 14, 1992.

Galavision Home Page. Available at http://www.galavision.com/si-tv/cafe/fernandez/index.html.

Mavis, Barbara J. "Giselle Fernandez—Reporter, Broadcast Journalist." *Contemporary American Success Stories: Famous People of Hispanic Heritage.* Childs, MD: Mitchell Lane Publishers, 1996.

NBC Television Home Page. Available at http://www.nbc.com/tvcentral/shows/accesshollywood/biofernandez.html.

Lisa Fernandez
(1971–)
Softball player, coach

Prepares for Glory

Lisa Fernandez was born February 22, 1971, to a Puerto Rican-born mother and a Cuban-immigrant father. She comes by her love of sports naturally, both of her parents having participated in amateur athletics when they were younger. Her mother, Emilia, was Lisa's first coach in children's softball, while her father, Antonio, who had played semi-pro baseball in Cuba, has been a practice buddy throughout her life. It came as little surprise when young Lisa felt irresistibly drawn to the ballfield at a relatively early age. Her interest in the sport eventually blossomed into a knockout softball career as she pitched countless college and national teams to victories in the United States and around the world.

Fernandez began pitching when she was seven-years old. A coach spotted her on the field and invited her to try out

for his team. Although Fernandez made it on the team, it was clear that she had a lot of room for improvement; the first game she pitched ended in a 25-0 loss for her team. That very first game, however dismal her performance, taught Fernandez a very valuable lesson. With encouragement from her mother, Emilia, Fernandez determined that every time she got on the mound, she would improve a little bit more. She realized that there might be days when her performance would be disappointing and that she might backslide a bit from time to time but vowed that, come what might, she was going to be the best she could be.

That determination to always strive to improve her performance has served Fernandez well over the years—that and her refusal to let anything discourage her. She recalled a coach who told her when she was 12 that she would never be a champion pitcher because her arms were too short. History has proved him wrong. Fernandez's pitching powered her high school and college softball teams to multiple championships, and her pitching for the U.S. women's softball team won gold at the 1996 Olympic Games in Atlanta.

Reaps Honors for Schools

Growing up in Long Beach, CA, Fernandez attended St. Joseph's High School, where she pitched nearly 70 shut-out games for the girls' softball team. Her college career was even more impressive. Attending UCLA, she pitched her school to two NCAA Women's College World Series championships, compiling an astounding 93-7 record. The statistics from her college softball career are staggering. Her batting average for her entire college career was .382. She holds career records for singles (225), runs scored (142), walks (65), hits (287), pitching wins (93), and no-hitters (11). Her career winning percentage of .930 broke the existing NCAA record. She received the Honda Award for athletic achievements in 1991, 1992, and 1993. Fernandez became involved in Amateur Softball Association competition, winning the Bertha Tickey and Most Valuable Player awards in the 1991 and 1992 ASA Women's Major Fast Pitch National Championship, a feat she repeated in 1997. She was named ASA's Sportswoman of the Year in both 1991 and 1992 and took home a gold medal from the U.S. Olympic Festival held in Los Angeles in 1991.

Gains Recognition Worldwide

Fernandez made a name for herself in international softball competition in the early 1990s, playing with the gold medal-winning U.S. women's softball teams in the 1990 ISF Women's World Championship in Normal, IL, and the 1991 Pan American Games. For the next four years, she was a player on Softball USA teams that took home gold medals in international competition, winning in 1992 at the Women's World Challenger Cup games in Beijing, China, and the following year at the Intercontinental Cup games in the Netherlands. In 1994, she played for the U.S. team that won the gold medal at the ISF Women's World Championship in St. John's, Newfoundland, and also took gold in the South Pacific Classic in Sydney, Australia. In 1995, the year before the Olympics, Fernandez pitched a perfect game, a no-hitter with an earned run average of 0.00, and batted .511 to help USA Softball win the gold medal at the Pan American Qualifier in Guatemala. The U.S. team also won gold that year at the 1995 Superball Classic in Columbus, GA.

In national competition, Fernandez played in the 1994 U.S. Olympic Festival in St. Louis, MO, and was a member of the gold medal-winning North team at the U.S. Olympic Festival the following year in Denver. In 1995, she played for the California Commotion, the second-place finisher at the ASA Women's Major Fast Pitch National Championship. The Commotion, based in Woodland Hills, CA, struck gold at the ASA Fast Pitch Championship in 1996 and 1997. Fernandez also led the East squad to gold at the 1997 USA Softball National Team Festival in Midland, MI. In that series, she led all pitchers with a 3-0 record and a festival-high 37 strikeouts. She came in second in hitting, with a batting average of .381, one home run, and two RBIs.

Takes Gold at the Olympics

One of the crowning achievements of young Fernandez's softball playing career came in the 1996 Olympic Games, when she helped lead her team to gold. Batting .348, she racked up eight hits, five runs batted in, and one home run. On the pitcher's mound, she had a 1-1 record with a 0.33 ERA and a team-leading 31 strikeouts. In a real heartbreaker, Fernandez pitched a near-perfect game against Australia, only to give up a solo home run in the bottom of the 10th inning for a 2–1 loss. In the semi-final Olympics game against China, she posted a win, as the U.S. team bested China 1-0. Fernandez was also credited with a save in the gold medal game against China.

Continues Winning Ways

In 1997, Fernandez played on the Softball USA team that won silver at the Super Classic in Columbus, GA, posting a 2-0 pitching record with an ERA of 0.00 and a team-leading 26 strikeouts. In the 1996 American Challenge Series versus Olympic silver medalist China and bronze medalist Australia, she led the U.S. team to a perfect 10-0 record. Her personal pitching record was 3-0 with an ERA of 0.32 and 43 strikeouts.

An assistant coach at her alma mater, UCLA, Fernandez was honored in 1996 by MANA, a National Latina Organization, for her contributions in the field of sports. Accepting MANA's Las Primeras award at a luncheon in Washington, DC, Fernandez told the predominantly Hispanic audience, "I won this for you. I'm very grateful and humbled by this honor." She said she was pleased if she could serve as a role model for younger Latinas and encouraged young girls to carve out their destiny by aggressively pursuing their goals. She expressed deep appreciation to her parents for "believing in me and my talents" and for spending countless hours helping her practice.

Fernandez has spoken often of the huge contribution her parents have made toward her success as an athlete. Because of her parents' background in sports, she practically grew up on a baseball diamond. In an interview in *Hispanic* magazine, she said, "I was lucky not to be raised with the traditional expectations of many Latinas, to become a wife and mother. If it wasn't for the support and sacrifice from my parents, who left the East Coast and moved to California to provide opportunities for their kids, I wouldn't be here."

Sources:

Hispanstar Home Page. Available at http://www.hispanstar.com/hb/jindex.html.

MANA Home Page. Available at http://www.hermana.com/primeras.htm.

Menard, Valerie. "Out of the Loop." *Hispanic,* July 31, 1996, p. 18.

Weissbard, Lisa, ed. "Fernandez, Lisa." *Who's Who of American Women.* New Providence, N.J.: Marquis Who's Who, 1996, p. 326.

Fernández Olmos, Margarite
See Olmos, Margarite Fernández

Rosario Ferré
(1942–)
Author, publisher, women's rights activist, nationalist

Selected writings:

Papeles de Pandora. Mexico City: Joaquín Mortiz, 1976, translated by Ferré as *The Youngest Doll,* Lincoln: University of Nebraska Press, 1991.

El medio pollito: Siete cuentos infántiles. Río Piedras, P.R.: Huracán, 1976.

La caja de cristal. Mexico City: La Máquina de Escribir, 1978.

Los cuentos de Juan Bobo. Río Piedras, P.R.: Huracán, 1980.

La muñeca menor / The Youngest Doll. Río Piedras, P.R.: Huracán, 1980.

Sitio a Eros: Trece ensayos literarios. Mexico City: Joaquín Mortiz, 1980); "La cocina de la escritura" translated by Ferré and Diana L. Vélez as "The Writer's Kitchen" in *Lives on the Line: The Testimony of Contemporary Latin American Authors,* edited by Doris Meyer, Berkeley: University of California Press, 1988.

La mona que le pisaron la cola. Río Piedras, P.R.: Huracán, 1981.

Fábulas de la garza desangrada. Mexico City: Joaquín Mortiz, 1982.

"El acomodador": Una lectura fantástica de Felisberto Hernández. Mexico City: Fondo de Cultura Económica, 1986.

Maldito amor. Mexico City: Joaquín Mortiz, 1986; translated by Ferré as *Sweet Diamond Dust,* New York: Ballantine, 1988.

El árbol y sus sombras. Mexico City: Fondo de Cultura Económica, 1989.

Sonatinas. Río Piedras, P.R.: Huracán, 1989.

El coloquio de las perras, San Juan: Cultural, 1990; "Ofelia a la deriva en las aguas de la memoria" translated by Ferré as "On Destiny, Language, and Translation; or, Ophelia Adrift in the C. & O. Canal" in *The Youngest Doll,* Lincoln: University of Nebraska Press, 1991);

La cucarachita Martina. Río Piedras, P.R.: Huracán, 1990.

Cortázar. Washington, DC: Literal / Río Piedras, P.R.: Cultural, 1991.

Las dos Venecias. Mexico City: Joaquín Mortiz, 1992.

Memorias de Ponce: Autobiografía de Luis A. Ferré. Bogotá: Norma, 1992).

Overview

Rosario Ferré said *Dictionary of Literary Biography* contributor Carmen S. Rivera, "has become the 'translator' of the reality of Puerto Rican women, opening the doors for the feminist movement on the island." In her works, Ferré combines traditional island stories, classical mythology, and a modern feminist viewpoint to create "a more active and satisfying myth of Puerto Rican women," Rivera declared. Her writings reflect the dichotomy of an island society and economy divided between a traditional, rural elite and a new, burgeoning, industrial class, and the ambiguous place women hold in modern Puerto Rico.

Early Years

Ferré was born into this dichotomy in 1942, in the town of Ponce in the southern part of Puerto Rico. Her mother, Lorenza Ramírez Ferré, came from a family with long roots in sugarcane planting. Her father, Luis A. Ferré, made his money through his connections to American corporations, through banking, and in industry. He also served as governor of the island from 1968 to 1972, maintaining close relations with the United States. Ferré was largely educated in Catholic girls' schools on the island, where she learned the traditional roles of island women: they "should be virtuous and silent," explained Rivera. However, she also attended a Jesuit-run boys' school with her brothers for her early primary education. "During these years she was introduced to the fantastic world of fairy tales by the Brothers Grim, Hans Christian Andersen, and E. T. A. Hoffmann, and to the exotic world of Scheherazade in *A Thousand and One Nights,*" stated Rivera. "She also listened intently to the stories told by Gela, her black nanny." The stories she learned from Gela, Rivera concluded, eventually made their way into Ferré's later collections of short stories.

Continues Studies in the United States

Ferré continued her post-high school education in the United States, studying English literature at Manhattanville College. "During the 1960s she married and had three children," stated Rivera. "The early 1970s, however, proved to be a turning point in her life. Her mother died while her father was still serving as governor, an event that forced her to perform as official hostess of La Fortaleza, the governor's residence." It was at this time also that Rosario Ferré began to exhibit both her political and literary independence. She split with her father over the issue of Puerto Rican independence. She also became an important figure in the literary life of the island through the magazine she founded, *Zona de Carga y Descarga.* The publication offered relatively unknown Puerto Rican artists a venue for their works to see print, but it also provided a forum for political reformers to air their views without being associated with a particular political party or agenda. Although the magazine only lasted for about six years (1970-1976), it created a significant stir in the island's political scene, being challenged from both right- and left-wing politicians.

Women As Playthings and Other Metaphors

"La muñeca menor" was one of the stories included in Ferré's first collection, *Papeles de Pandora,* which "immediately established Ferré as an influential Puerto Rican feminist writer," stated Rivera. The other stories and poems in the collection continue to develop the image of the limited roles women play. "Dolls are a constant motif in this book," Rivera declared. "In 'Amalia' the child Amalia is confused with the doll named after her. In 'Marina y el león' (Marina and the Lion) the protagonist decides to give a costume party and disguises herself as a doll wrapped in a box. It becomes impossible to distinguish between a living woman and an artificial doll. Women's roles in such a society are decorative rather than functional.

Characters also mix and fuse, underlining Ferré's point that the subjugation of women happens to all, whatever their social or economic position. In "Cuando las mujeres quieren a los hombres," the white wife of a dead man envies the lush sensuality of his black mistress, while at the same time the mistress envies the social position of the wife. Ferré mingles their thoughts and desires in a stream-of-consciousness narrative that emphasizes the way their plight relates to that of all women. "At the end," Rivera explained, "the two women have the final laugh when they become partners and decide to make the house into a bordello and become rich at his expense." Ferré also breaks with Puerto Rican literary tradition by having the black mistress, Isabel la Negra, speak in the common manner of the island. "Language is used both to de-mystify and to attack the social and political structures that oppress women," said Rivera. "Isabel la Negra's popular speech is not only a realistic feature but a weapon masterfully articulated to avenge her."

By the time *Papeles de Pandora* was published in 1976, Ferré had left her native Puerto Rico for Mexico. She later moved to the United States, completing her doctorate (on the relationship between the stories of Julio Cortázar and the works of the Romantics) at the University of Maryland, teaching in Washington, DC, at Georgetown University, and traveling across the country lecturing. She also married the Mexican writer Jorge Aguilar Mora, and in 1990 moved with him back to Puerto Rico.

Feminist Critiques of Puerto Rican Society

In the early 1980s, Ferré had established her reputation as Puerto Rico's premiere proponent of feminism. Two of her works, *Sitio a Eros: Trece ensayos literarios* (Eros Besieged) and *Fábulas de la garza desangrada* (Fables of a Bleeding Crane), combined with *Papeles de Pandora,* "opened the literary world to a new scope of themes, myths, and language." The two more recent books (respectively a collection of essays and poems, and a collection of poetry) all look at problems confronting people—especially women— who, because they are excluded or limited by society, are unable to create their own true identity. The essays of *Sitio a Eros* present "a sociohistorical retrospective of women artists who left a profound imprint on the spirit of the Puerto Rican writer," declared Rivera. Ferré captures the struggle that each of these artists endures against their positions in time as well as in space. "Suicide, chosen by several of these women," the critic stated, "is perceived then not as a defeat but as a final attempt to liberate themselves from social oppression and win supremacy over their bodies and spirits."

The poems of *Fábulas de la garza desangrada* take the stories of a number of famous female literary figures and change them so that the characters take charge of their own lives. "Here Ariadne aborts the Minotaur, Daphne's lover runs away from her, Mary Magdalene seductively anoints the body of Christ, and Desdemona poisons Othello," explained Rivera. In other variations, the young Medusa refuses to allow herself to become a mother, and Helen of Troy kills herself rather than remain a symbolic plaything in the struggle between her husband Menelaus and her kidnapper Paris. The key that ties the work together, according to Rivera, is the symbol of the bleeding crane of the title, who tries to escape death by flying. Women, says Ferré, are like the crane: they are caught by the obligations imposed on them by society. "The flowing blood no longer feeds the placenta carrying a baby," stated Rivera, "but becomes the ink with which her poems are written."

Fábulas de la garza desangrada is linked thematically to Ferré's 1986 novel *Maldito amor*. Both works challenge traditional views of women, according to Marie Murphy in her *Hispanic Review* critique of the two books, by inverting female roles and recreating characters that defy and challenge male authority. *Maldito amor,* translated into English by Ferré and published as *Sweet Diamond Dust,* is a parody of both the romance novel and stories about the land, a genre that was popular in island literature between 1900 and 1950. It is divided into four separate stories that span Puerto Rican history during the twentieth century. Each of them looks at behaviors that island society regards as deviant—the independence of women and homosexuality, for instance—and shows how these forms of oppression hurt the oppressors as well as their victims. "Maldito amor," the first story of the novel, reinterprets the roles that the traditional island aristocracy and the new industrialism, represented by North American corporations, played in island history. "El regalo" shows how a mulatto girl is abused by the nuns in whose care she is placed when she chooses not to conform to their standards of modesty and morality.

Politics in Ferré's Later Works

Ferré's choices in translating *Maldito amor* into English may reflect some changes in her political stance. Although she had been an enthusiastic supporter of Puerto Rican independence during her father's term as governor, the English edition of the work refers to the United States and its role in the island's history in a more subdued and conciliatory way. Janice A. Jaffe, writing in the *Latin American Literary Review,* saw these alterations as a serious flaw in Ferré's work, and she accused the author of abusing her talents by lessening the subversive content of the original story. In doing so, Jaffe declared, Ferré reduced the work's anticolonial position.

Ferré continues her fables of persecution and liberation in her works that have been published for children, including *El medio pollito, Los cuentos de Juan Bobo,* and *La mona que le pisaron la cola.* In each of these books, said Rivera, Ferré confronts and ridicules corrupt social institutions and the inadequate social order. The half-chicken of *El medio pollito* overthrows the greedy, stupid king that oppresses the poor peasants. The title character of *Los cuentos de Juan Bobo* demonstrates through his naivety the victory of simplicity over political corruption. "Sexual symbolism is developed throughout the stories of *La mona que le pisaron la cola,*" stated Rivera. "Also predominant in the collection are children's rhymes that Ferré effectively incorporates while subverting their traditional meanings."

The House on the Lagoon, Ferré's most recent book to be translated into English, continues the author's struggle against traditional and repressive social institutions. A family saga, the work traces the conflicts and relationships of a family of European immigrants and their mulatto servants. The focus of the story is on the ties between Quintin Mendizabal, an importer of Spanish descent, and his wife, the writer Isabel Monfort. Their relationship comes to a head when Isabel begins a novel that tells the history of their two families. "Most of the novel is [composed] of this semi-fictionalized family history," stated a *Publishers Weekly* contributor, "but Ferré . . . breaks it up with third-person accounts of Quintin's reactions to his wife s manuscript and, later, with his acid commentaries on it. Ferré dramatizes the issue of who gets to write history, gracefully incorporating it into a compelling panorama of Puerto Rican experience that is rich in history, drama and memorable characters."

Sources:

Gazarian Gautier, Marie-Lise. *Interviews with Latin American Writers.* Elmwood Park, IL: Dalkey Archive Press, 1989.

Heller, Ben A. Landscape, Femininity, and Caribbean Discourse. *MLN,* March 1996, pp. 391- 416.

Jaffe, Janice A. Translation and Prostitution: Rosario Ferré's *Maldito amor* and *Sweet Diamond Dust. Latin American Literary Review,* July-December 1995, pp. 66- 82.

Murphy, Marie. Rosario Ferré en el espejo: Defiance and Inversions. *Hispanic Review,* Spring 1997, pp. 145-57.

Review of *The House on the Lagoon. Publishers Weekly,* July 3, 1995, p. 47.

Rivera, Carmen S. Rosario Ferré, *Dictionary of Literary Biography,* Volume 145: *Modern Latin American Fiction Writers.* Detroit: Gale Research, 1994.

Ruta, Suzanne. Blood of the Conquistadors. *New York Times Book Review,* September 17, 1995, sec. 7, p. 28.

Delia Fiallo

Screenwriter

Television writer Delia Fiallo is known as the queen of Spanish-language soap operas. With about 40 soaps, called *telenovelas,* to her credit, Fiallo's influence on the industry is extraordinary. As many as 80 to 100 million viewers in the United States, Europe, and Latin America watch a Fiallo soap every day.

Fiallo was born in Cuba, the only daughter of a country doctor and a housewife. Her father's career kept the family moving from town to town. Educated mainly in one-room rural schoolhouses, Fiallo became a passionate reader, especially of history and geography. At the University of Havana, where she majored in philosophy, Fiallo won the coveted Hernandez Cata Prize in 1948 for a short story. After graduation that same year, she worked for Havana's WRHC radio, writing short novels and *cuentos campesinos,* or tales from the countryside. She also worked as a public relations representative. Fiallo switched to television writing in the 1950s and produced her first telenovela, *Soraya,* in 1958. In the meantime, Fiallo married actor and producer Bernardo Pascual and had five children. The family fled the revolution on their native island in 1966 and emigrated to Miami, Florida.

It took about a year for Fiallo to restart her career from the United States. She sold a remake of one of her old soaps to a producer in Caracas, Venezuela. The producers wanted the background changed to Venezuela, a country of which she knew little. Fiallo read all the books she could find about Venezuela and even consulted with Venezuelan exchange students living in Miami. Her hard work paid off: her story was accepted and her new American-based career began. Today, Fiallo writes about 34 pages daily in a studio apartment behind the family home. She researches her subjects thoroughly, developing a plot line around a young woman, who is usually beautiful, ambitious, and searching for love. The recipe works; a Miami producer referred to her as the "premier novela writer."

Unlike English-language soap operas, which often go on for years in the same vein, *telenovelas* end after about 200 episodes. In a 1998 article featured in *Variety,* Fiallo discussed her work: "The essential theme of a novela is the story of a love that is obstructed. A couple meet, fall in love, suffer obstacles in being able to fulfill that love, and at the end reach happiness. The novela is basically about sentiment. If you don't make the public cry, you won't achieve anything." Because the romantically-linked couples at the center of Fiallo's stories experience difficulty in obtaining their happiness, there must generally be some kind of social difference between the heroine and the man she loves. In most of the *telenovelas,* the heroine comes from a more humble background than her lover who must leave his friends and/or family opposed to the match.

Unlike most Spanish-language soaps, where the locale is generally unclear, Fiallo's works are set in a particular place, for which she does a great deal of research. She commented that she almost had to graduate from law school to write the legal-themed *Leonela.* Some of her other soaps have taken place in a hospital (*Rafaela*) and a circus (*Kassandra*). In fact, her stories are so well-researched that Miami's Mount Sinai Hospital has used scenes from them to teach patients about illnesses such as cancer. In addition to the central plot, Fiallo's soaps have distinctive subplots that she thinks are sometimes more interesting than the principal stories because she has more freedom to expand them.

Hits the Top in the Soap Circuit

Fiallo is one of about a dozen well-known and respected writers of Spanish-language soaps. The influence of writers such as Fiallo can be more easily understood when one realizes that these soaps make up more than 50 percent of a Spanish-language station's air time. Salaries vary, but are generally about $70,000 for 200 episodes. In 1997, however, Fiallo signed a 10-year contract with Televisa, which draws talent from all over Latin America, to exclusively supply scripts for a sum estimated to be in the millions. As social-minded as she likes to be in her work, Fiallo becomes very upset if producers try to deviate from the standards that she sets. Her soap operas must deal with family unity and the quest to better oneself. She believes there is far too much sex and violence on most television programs.

Fiallo admits that her viewers are quite passionate about the characters in her *telenovelas* and often telephone her to discuss some aspect of a soap that is being aired. One viewer called to say that she did not have long to live and wanted to know the end of a particular soap that was currently running. Sometimes fans have enough influence to change a story. Fiallo once got so many calls about a beloved dying character that she changed her mind and let the character live.

Fiallo and her husband live comfortably with their pet Doberman in an antique-filled Miami home. Fiallo loves to talk about her children, grandchildren, and her elderly mother—her "biggest fan." When Fiallo finally retires, she plans to publish a book and catch up on her stamp-collecting hobby. Her devoted fans hope that her retirement is a long way down the road.

Sources:

Paxman, Andrew. "Delia Fiallo: doyenne of expat scribes from Cuba." *Variety,* October 7, 1996, p. 66.
Veciana-Suarez, Ana. "The Spanish Soaps Queen." *Miami Herald,* April 10, 1987, p. B1.

Rosie Flores
(1955–)
Singer, songwriter, instrumental musician

Selected discography:

Rosie Flores, Warner Bros., 1987.

After the Farm, Hightone, 1992.
Once More With Feeling, Hightone, 1993.
Rockabilly Filly, Hightone, 1995.
Honky Tonk Reprise, Rounder, 1996.
A Little Bit of Heartache, (with Ray Campi), Watermelon, 1997.
Dance Hall Dreams, Rounder, 1998.

Overview

Reviewing a Rosie Flores concert, Neil Strauss of the *New York Times* referred to her as "a spinning wheel of American roots music." While Flores has amassed her fan base outside of the country music mainstream, she has demonstrated consistent growth and increasing ambition as a guitarist, singer, and writer. After a disappointing experience with a major label, she signed on with the "indie" label Hightone and recorded a series of well-regarded albums that fused the song smarts of the Austin, Texas, scene with the rambunctious energy of early rock and roll.

Flores was born in San Antonio, Texas; early rock icon Elvis Presley and pop crooner Brenda Lee fueled her interest in music. Her father was able to record Rosie and her siblings singing together when she was seven-years old, and a snippet of one such session was included on her 1995 album *Rockabilly Filly*. When she was twelve-years old, her family moved to San Diego, California, where a variety of burgeoning pop forms influenced her tastes as well as her decision to form Penelope's Children, an all-female band, at age sixteen. In a *Guitar Player* profile, Flores recalled a left-handed compliment she received for her fretwork: a male audience member said "You're pretty good for a girl." Far from rearing up in feminist outrage, Flores noted, "I remember thinking, 'Yeah, I am pretty good for a girl, aren't I?' because back then very few girls were playing lead guitar. I felt like I was breaking new ground. But whenever some guy said that, he'd always follow by saying, 'No, I mean, you're pretty good for a guy too—I mean, you're just pretty good—period.'"

Discovers 'Wow, Girls Can Do It Too'

It was partly the work of trailblazing singer Wanda Jackson that nudged Flores in this direction. "I had heard Elvis and [1950s hitmaker and rock pioneer] Buddy Holly," she told the *Boston Globe*. "But I kinda didn't think of it as something a woman could perform until I heard her records, and then I went, 'Wow, girls can do it too.'" Flores later formed the band Rosie and the Re-boppin' Screamers and in 1984 joined the country-punk outfit Screamin' Sirens; according to *Nashville Scene* "she was the only musically adept member" of that group.

She earned a record deal with Warner Bros. as a solo artist in 1986, releasing her debut album the following year. Unfortunately, opined Kevin Ransom of *Guitar Player*, "she was pigeonholed as a C&W chick singer by Nashville types who didn't care much about her genre-bending guitar playing," which draws on hard blues and riff rock as well as the twang of country. *Musician* noted that while her Warner bow "did a nice job of showcasing Flores' smoky, out-of-breath delivery and her knack for milking the dickens out of a country lyric, she seemed somewhat boxed in by Dwight Yoakam producer Pete Anderson's heavy-handed direction."

Flores later acknowledged the contradictions of her major-label experience. "This friend of mine helped me make some demos that we sent to Warners in Nashville," she told *Request* writer Susan Hamre. "I was really surprised that the demos we made caught the attention of the A&R [talent scout] people over there. It was an even bigger surprise when they dropped me two years later because I had been told that they didn't want to change me. But my uniqueness had them a little mind-boggled, so they said go find a label that understands you."

Enjoys Artistic Control, Critical Praise

She continued to soldier on, however, moving to Austin, TX, in 1988. That town's alternative-country scene relied on folk-influenced songcraft and was in general more tolerant of stylistic eccentricity than Nashville. Flores played on the well-regarded television series *Austin City Limits* and rapidly earned cult status as a performer and songwriter. In 1989 she had a chance to sing backup with Wanda Jackson; the two became fast friends and would later collaborate in the studio. Ultimately Flores found a label that understood her, the California indie company Hightone, which she described to Hamre as "the easiest place to go to be able to do my music creatively the way that I'd like to do it." Unburdened by the conservative nature of corporate country music, which tends to distrust women who seem unusual or too eclectic, Flores could indulge her wide-ranging musical passions completely. Even if the label was not wild about every song she wrote, "they don't stop me from putting them on, and that's the freedom of artistic control."

In 1992 Flores released *After the Farm*, which she recorded with her band The Bad Boys. On this album, *Musician* reviewer Peter Cronin noted, "Flores is playing more guitar and writing better songs" than on her ill-fated Warner Bros. debut. "Most importantly, the singer sounds like she's having a blast." Ransom of *Guitar Player* called the record "a tough-minded three-guitar country-rock showcase that uses [1960s country-influenced rockers] The Byrds and The Buffalo Springfield as musical touchstones." With the aid of Wayne "DJ" Jarvis on electric and slide guitars and the versatile Greg Leisz on pedal steel, lap steel, dobro, and other guitars—along with a solid rhythm section—Flores finally had a band that could showcase the range of her talents. At the same time, her talented sidemen scarcely overshadowed her own playing. "Rosie's

solos flow instinctively from her melodies and rhythms," wrote Ransom, "while her lines weave in and out of the tough-but-tasteful textures laid down by Jarvis and Leisz." The album made the year-end Top 10 lists of several magazines, including *Pulse!* and *Request*.

More praise came with her 1993 set *Once More With Feeling*. In a *Musician* review, Chris Willman managed to compare Flores to a number of her primary influences in one fell swoop: "Imagine the pre-adolescent Brenda Lee grown up and matured without losing any of her spunk and pluck, and you've got a good idea of Flores' appeal—though her assured songwriting and aggressively rocky lead guitar bring to mind less demure forerunners like Wanda Jackson and Bonnie Raitt." John Morthland of *Country Music*, meanwhile, heard "this unique, and endlessly effective, breathy 'pull' in her voice that is reminiscent of the smoky Mountain sound of early Dolly Parton;" while complaining about some aspects of the production, Morthland felt she had great potential. The album's single "Honky Tonk Moon" received a fair amount of attention, thanks to a frequently played clip on the video stations CMT and VH-1.

"Robo Rosie" Recovers

During a 1994 world tour, Flores suffered a major setback. Running down a wet London street with her laundry, she slipped and landed on her right hand. She performed that night with her arm in a cast, leaving the guitar playing to others, and the show went well. Back in the United States, however, increased pain sent her to a specialist who warned that she might need surgery. She cancelled her tour and headed for her parents' home in San Diego. "I couldn't cook, I couldn't write, I couldn't hardly do anything," she recalled to *Pulse!* Since it was necessary for her arm to heal correctly, she had the surgery, which involved fusing the bones with metal screws. Her arm was also placed in an external device to keep it from moving the wrong way. "For eight weeks, I was Robo Rosie," she quipped to *Nashville Scene*. "It was so painful, I kept telling them, 'If I'm having to put up with this much pain, this is going to have to work.' But we didn't know how it was going to affect my guitar playing. The screws were right where I use my wrist the most. The only way I could get through it was to stay positive. I put every bit of mental positive framework into it I could. I thought, 'This is going to heal. It's going to.'"

Her positive thinking paid off. After some physical therapy, she was able to perform, and even appeared on a TNN country music special, *Live at the Ryman Auditorium*, with Jackson, alternative-country singer Iris DeMent, and country superstar Pam Tillis. Performing behind Jackson on the song "Let's Have a Party" was a particular thrill for Flores. During her guitar solo, she told *Nashville Scene*, she heard Jackson let out "this wild rockabilly scream. She said, 'Oh yeah! WOOOOOO!' It was an incredible thing." The charge of this experience, as well as some gigs on the re-emerging Nashville and Los Angeles rockabilly scenes, influenced her decision to undertake the project that would become *Rockabilly Filly.*

Reinvigorates Rockabilly

Released in 1995 and featuring guest vocals by Jackson and veteran wailer Janis Martin, *Rockabilly Filly* allowed Flores to expand her instrumental range. "My approach was more low-down and dirty," she explained to the *Boston Globe.* "Now I'm learning how to play more jazzy and that's so much a part of rockabilly," she added, noting that exploring these stylistic tributaries was "what I'm working on now, trying to make myself grow and incorporate that into my playing." The album earned a number of glowing reviews. According to Eric Levin of *People,* Flores "reinvigorates rockabilly, mixing in dabs of country steel guitar, doo-wop, boogie-woogie and swinging blues. It's all breathless fun, and the slow tunes are sexy enough to alarm a chaperone." *New Country* critic Geoffrey Himes enthused that after three albums that failed to capture the electricity of her live shows, Flores had at last "figured out how to bottle that lightning on a recording," adding that she "has come up with a handful of new rockabilly songs as exciting as anything Jackson or Martin ever recorded."

It seemed that with her travels into pure rockabilly, Flores had found a way to communicate her musical essence. And though it was clear she had always been better than just "pretty good for a girl," she commented to the *Boston Globe* about the importance of being an influence herself. "A lot of women have come up to me, and their eyes are on fire and they say 'You've really inspired me,'" she noted. "You know there's not very many of us out there playing lead. Bonnie Raitt's a role model for me, and if I can be that by playing rockabilly, I think it's neat. I inspire more girls to get out and play."

In 1996, Flores reissued her debut album *Rosie Flores* under the title *Honky Tonk Reprise.* This reissue included four additional songs. She also collaborated with rockabilly legend Ray Campi on the album *A Little Bit of Heartache,* which was released in 1997. In 1998, Flores released the album *Dance Hall Dreams,* which contained several tracks that were recorded live at a concert in San Antonio, Texas.

Current Address: Hightone Records, 220 4th St., #101, Oakland, CA 94607.

Sources:

Boston Globe, December 8, 1995.
Color Red, November 1995.
Country Music, November 1993.
Guitar Player, September 1992.
Musician, July 1992; February 1994; February 1996.

Nashville Scene, December 7, 1995.
New Country, December 1995.
New York Times, July 26, 1995.
People, December 11, 1995.
Pulse! December 1995.
Request, November 1993.
Rolling Stone, October 29, 1992.
This is Rosie Flores. Available at http://lonestar.texas.net/~dqkidd/story.html.

Flores Gonzales, Irma
   See **Gonzales, Irma Flores**

Grace Flores-Hughes
(1946–)
Entrepreneur, consultant, author

Grace Flores-Hughes is a partner of TFS & Associates, Inc., a multi-service human rights consulting firm in

Grace Flores-Hughes

Alexandria, VA. Named after the partners—Tucker, Flores-Hughes, and Spearman—the firm advises on equal employment opportunity and diversification in the work place. "Ours is a Hispanic/African American-owned firm, one of few in the country, and two partners were with the Equal Opportunity Commission. Clients are excited about our background," Flores-Hughes said in a telephone interview. Their expertise is sought by both government and private industry, including many Fortune 500 firms.

Reagan Appoints Flores-Hughes to Federal Position

Before embarking on this entrepreneurial venture in 1992, Flores-Hughes was director of community relations service with the Department of Justice from 1988 to 1992. Appointed by President Reagan and confirmed by the U.S. Senate, she was the first woman to hold that position. Named by *Hispanic Magazine* among the 100 most influential Hispanics in the United States, Flores-Hughes said, "Nobody I knew would have ever thought I would accomplish those things. Where I grew up, women were married by 13, by 20 they had five or six children, and by 25 they had serious problems."

Flores-Hughes had a different vision for her life. Rising from a junior secretary at Kelly Air Force Base to one of the highest-ranking Hispanic Americans in federal government, she is listed in *Who's Who among Hispanic Americans, Who's Who in America, Who's Who in American Law,* and *Who's Who of American Women.* She said, "I went from this little barrio to the Rose Garden at the White House, and I know of only two others who went from the very bottom levels of government to the very top."

Advances at Department of Health, Education, and Welfare

Flores-Hughes was born and raised in Taft, TX. Her mother, Catalina San Miguel, was born in Mexico; her father, Adan Flores, whom she barely knew, was born in Texas. Raised primarily by her maternal grandparents while her mother worked as a short order cook, Flores-Hughes completed high school and began her governmental career as a secretary at Kelly Air Force Base in 1966. By 1972 she had worked her way into upper management with the Department of Health, Education, and Welfare (DHEW) in Washington, D.C. Receiving her bachelor of arts from the University of the District of Columbia in 1977 and a master's in public administration from Harvard University in 1980, she was acting director of the Office of Hispanic Americans when she resigned from the DHEW in 1981. After marrying Harvey A. Hughes, now a retired lieutenant general with the United States Air Force, she was visiting professor at Nebraska Wesleyan University and the University of Nebraska from 1982 to 1984. In 1984, she was special assistant in the Reagan/Bush presidential campaign and special assistant to the 50th presidential inaugu-

ral committee. She then became associate administrator with Minority Small Business and Capital Ownership Development, and was special assistant at the Small Business Administration until her presidential appointment in 1988. She has received numerous awards, including the 1990 Outstanding Public Service Award from the National Capital Area Chapter of the American Society for Public Administration, and belongs to several organizations, including the Commonwealth Republican Women's Club, of which she is a board member. She also chairs the Harvard Journal of Hispanic Policy Executive Board. Two of her most recent articles published in *Hispanic Magazine* are "Diversity in the Work Force" and "Why the Term Hispanic?"

Influenced by Maternal Grandparents

Flores-Hughes believes her grandparents were a major influence in her life. "My grandmother was a very strong, independent woman who didn't follow the norms of the Catholic religion, which was traditionally one of the most influential factors in our village," she said. "She didn't let that decide her fate. She was very unconventional, and I think I got my independent and assertive nature from her." Her grandfather, whose family name was San Miguel, was an aristocrat whose family left Spain for Mexico and disowned him when he fell in love with, and married, their servant. "That was just unacceptable," she said. "He was a man of ideals, a very well-read, intellectual, revolutionary man who came from a wealthy family."

Flores-Hughes learned much about her true heritage from her grandfather. "Where I went to school, we weren't taught about our cultural history. We read about the heroes of the Alamo, who were American. Then we read about the horrible people, who were Mexican. Although we were Americans, we really weren't accepted. And because we were Mexican, we were horrible. It was very confusing to us. There was no mention of our rich heritage. Christopher Columbus discovered America, but our history books never linked him to Isabella, the queen of Spain, or to Hernando Cortez, the Spanish explorer who was also within the world of Spanish royalty. We were part of that blood line but we were never taught to be proud of those lineages." Flores-Hughes believes she inherited her sense of courage and adventure from her ancestors. "Our Spanish ancestors were conquistadors, fearless adventurers, travelling all over the world. Not that I agree with everything they did. But I wanted adventure—to travel, to see other parts of the world. Staying in the same house until I died was not for me."

Uses Past as Window to Future

Flores-Hughes is currently writing her memoirs entitled *The North and South of Me,* which are being considered by a major publishing company. "My story is small but I think it is a beginning to helping our population to understand and feel proud of our heritage. This is one window into the kind of community we are. I think I captured my grandfather's ideals and revolutionary thoughts," she said. "He taught me never to take things as they appear and to fight for what you believe in."

Current Address: 5208 Bedlington Terrace, Alexandria, VA 22304.

Sources:

Thompson, Märie L. Biographical material from and telephone conversation with Grace Flores-Hughes, April 16, 1998.

Daisy Fuentes
(1966–)
Television host, actress, model

Selected filmography:

Loving. ABC-TV, 1991.

Daisy Fuentes

Ghostwriter. PBS, 1993.

Overview

"**C**haucito, baby." That's the way MTV-host Daisy Fuentes signed off on each segment of her popular *MTV Internacional* show, internationally syndicated via Telemundo. From the time she first stepped in front of the camera in her first job as a Manhattan TV weather-girl, Fuentes has successfully marketed her beauty and effervescent personality before an ever-increasing Hispanic American audience.

Fuentes was born November 17, 1966, in Havana, Cuba. One of two daughters of Maria and Amado Fuentes, she and her family left Cuba in 1969 and lived in Madrid, Spain, for several years before immigrating to the United States in 1973. The family—Daisy's mother is a painter and her father a grocer and real estate investor—eventually made their home in Harrison, New Jersey, where Fuentes and her younger sister, Rosanna, learned to adapt to living in a primarily Anglo community. After some initial shyness, Fuentes became increasingly popular with her schoolmates and was elected as her high school's first Hispanic American homecoming queen. With career aspirations that included, as Fuentes told *Vogue,* "open[ing] up my own beauty shop because I was always doing my friends' hair and makeup," she graduated from high school in 1984.

Pursues Communications Career

It was while working as a runway model for an Italian couturier named Dimitri to put herself through college that Fuentes was encouraged to pursue a career in communications. An encounter with the Ecuadorian wife of an executive at a Spanish-language television station in New York led to her first job in journalism; after graduating from Bergen Community College in 1986, Fuentes applied and was hired by WXTV, where she served as a news reporter and weather anchorperson. In 1987 she moved to WNJU, Telemundo's New York base, where she kept Spanish-speaking New Yorkers informed of changes in the city climate until 1990.

Meanwhile, Fuentes, who found working the weather beat unexciting, decided to investigate other avenues in her chosen field of journalism and sent an audition tape to MTV in 1987. By the following year, Fuentes had become a VJ—short for video jockey—on MTV's Latin American programs. As the host of the Spanish-language *MTV Internacional,* Fuentes travelled to many of the 17 Latin American countries in which the popular music show is syndicated, including Costa Rica, Ecuador, Mexico, Paraguay, and Venezuela. The year 1993 found Fuentes busy, both soaking up the sun while hosting the U.S.-televised summertime show *Beach MTV,* as well as *Rock N' Jock.* She also used her bilingual skills on *MTV Latino,* a 24-hour-a-day Spanish-language show that premiered on the popular cable music-video network the following October. In the winter of 1995, a new show called *Mt. MTV* kept Fuentes busy during the winter months as well, as she hosted music video-based entertainment from an Aspen, Colorado, ski resort. In 1997 she hosted the weekly MTV program *House of Style.*

Life beyond MTV

But chatting between music video segments was not the only thing to occupy Fuentes's time. In 1991 the versatile Hispanic American woman was cast in a recurring role as the character "Tess" on ABC Television's popular daytime drama called *Loving.* In 1993, she also appeared in the pilot for PBS's *Ghostwriter* series. In an effort to boost sagging ratings, CBS brought in Fuentes to host *America's Funniest Home Videos* in 1997.

In addition to her work in front of a television camera, her face graced the cover of *Spanish Bazaar* and *Cosmopolitan* in 1990; the following year found her on the cover of both *Vanity Fair* and *Vanidades,* as well as *People* magazine's best-dressed list. By 1995 Fuentes's hosting duties had extended to the Miss USA, Miss Universe pageants, and, most recently, with Jimmy Smits at the 1998 ALMA Awards, a televised ceremony that honors Hispanic Americans involved in the fields of film, televison, and music.

With Fuentes' repeated appearances before the camera it was inevitable that she attracted the attention of the modeling world. In 1993 the photogenic Hispanic American woman signed a multiyear contract with cosmetics giant Revlon to appear in an international ad campaign entitled "Unforgettable Women." Along with such supermodels as Claudia Schiffer and fellow MTV host Cindy Crawford, Fuentes has appeared in both magazine and television ads around the world, extolling the virtues of Revlon products. But such success has not made her forget her Hispanic American roots. "I'm well known in the Spanish market and that's something I don't want to leave," Fuentes stated in the *New York Times.* I don't want all of a sudden to become this Anglo superstar and forget where I started." However, Fuentes also maintained that her varied cultural allegiances were precisely the reason she was so ideal for Revlon. "It's very difficult to find a young person in the country who doesn't sound like where they're from, which is not really great when you're aiming to all of Latin America," she explained. "I pull off a very neutral Spanish accent. People come up to me and ask me all the time where I'm from."

Fuentes still considers Secaucus, New Jersey, as her home, even though her parents left New Jersey for Miami in the early 1990s. But neither distance nor fame has changed the actress's close relationship with her parents. "Latin families never let go of their kids," Fuentes explained to interviewer Susan Wloszczyna in *USA Today.* "I have a lot of American friends, and for them, it's like, when you turn 18, you're on your own, kid. I think I could be 50 and [my parents] would still be telling me what to do, what to eat and drink your milk."

Broadens the Exposure of Hispanics

In addition to her career as a journalist, model, and budding actress, Fuentes has also tried her hand at business as co-owner of a small, trendy restaurant called Dish, located on New York City's Upper East Side and patronized by many of her friends. Even with such varied successes, Fuentes continues to expand her opportunities and her influence: she has studied acting at the American Academy of Dramatic Arts with the goal of one day starring in a television comedy sitcom. "Do you know any Hispanics who are on sitcoms, in the movies, on soaps?," she asked an interviewer for *Hispanic.* "Maybe a tiny handful. That's not enough."

Receives Media Honor

Fuentes was honored as an outstanding woman in media by the Latin Coalition for Fair Media in 1992. Accepting that honor was one of the many things that have made Fuentes fully aware of the responsibilities that go along with being an Hispanic celebrity. "At first I thought, I don't need this," she told the New York Times. "I don't want to be good for the rest of my life, but I'm trying to do the right thing, and if I screw up, I hope people will realize I'm human." And her role as a media figure has made her keenly aware of the strides still ahead for Hispanic American women. As she told for *Hispanic:* "[Revlon's] openness to me was groundbreaking. Their open-mindedness toward me as a Latina gave me hope to get out there into the mainstream and break barriers. I wish more companies would hire us. It would mean so much to us as Hispanics."

Sources:

Anders, Gigi. "What Drives Miss Daisy?" *Hispanic,* August 1993, pp. 14-15.
"Coming Up Daisy." *USA Today,* January 13, 1995, p. D1.
Kendt, Rob. "Everything's Coming Up Daisy." *Los Angeles Times,* August 17, 1993, p. F1.
Silver, Vernon. "Fast Forward." *New York Times,* April 25, 1993, p. 8; October 10, 1993, section 9, p. 3.
Van Meter, Jonathan. "MTV's Female Hosts Make Up Its Hottest Girl Group." *Vogue,* August 1991, pp. 110-116.

Tina Guerrero Fuentes
(1949–)
Painter, professor, lecturer

Christina Guerrero Fuentes is a painter, educator, and lecturer who was born in San Angelo, TX, on January 18,

Tina Guerrero Fuentes

1949. The daughter of Maria and Salvador Guerrero, she grew up in Odessa, TX, and has spent her career and artistic life in Texas and New Mexico. Fuentes received both her bachelor and master of fine arts degrees at North Texas State University in 1973 and 1975, where she trained in painting, drawing, and printmaking.

Fuentes began her career teaching art in the Texas public schools and at the Waco Art Center. She was an instructor at the University of Albuquerque from 1980 to 1985. From there, she became visiting lecturer at the University of New Mexico from 1985 to 1986. She has been an associate professor of drawing and design at Texas Tech University since 1986. Fuentes' art has been shown nationwide in galleries and exhibits for over 20 years, and she has participated in group showings and mounted one-woman shows.

Creates Large-Scale Art

Tina Fuentes is a frequent lecturer, exhibition juror, and supporter of arts education programs throughout the Southwest. She told Laura Tetreault of the *Lubbock Avalanche Journal,* "My imagery does reflect my culture, but I don't exemplify what people call Mexican art." Fuentes has always worked more in the abstract style than the figurative or pictorial forms more customary to Hispanic American art. As a tribute to her grandmother who encouraged her to hold onto her Hispanic heritage, Fuentes titles her work only in Spanish.

Fuentes' work is art on a large scale, literally as well as emotionally. She begins a project by making several small drawings of a proposed subject. As the idea grows and takes shape, she expands the size of the drawings. The final work usually increases to a canvas several feet tall and wide. Her inspiration for a piece is drawn from within. She explained her creative process to John Chinn of the *Caprock Sun,* "I let the idea emerge from me. I don't sit down and think it out. I let it evolve." Perhaps it is the personal interaction with the art during its creation that cannot help but affect the viewer. In another interview for *Artlines,* she said, "A lot of emotions go into my work. Fear, love, hate, the unknown. . . . I talk to my paintings. I express everything to them. . . . I feel I can tell them anything and everything. . . . When I am deeply lost in the work, I'll feel suddenly ecstatic or enlightened—at a brush stroke, perhaps. A figure will actually emerge from that surface. It's so exciting." Critics unanimously cite her work as beautiful and emotionally compelling.

Transforms the Human Form

Fuentes' paintings done in the 1980s favored abstract expressionism, with her use of simple but massive blocks and shapes of thick, vibrant color. Large canvasses of black, grey, beige, cream, and red masses exude emotion and a subtle subtext because the human form is all but invisible. Surface texture is as integral to the painting as the form. Paint is applied thickly and then scratched off, rubbed with sand from local areas, and built into layers with cut paper and canvas. A work from 1986, *Dame Vida,* is a *triptych,* or three-panel work, of paper, acrylic, and latex on birch wood, showing her focus on texture. It is this method of mixed-media composition that unifies and increases the impact of Fuentes' work.

In the late 1980s, Fuentes' dark human figure became more prominent. A major series of the time featured male and female figures in couples and all of the possible relationships between them. In a statement about her work, Fuentes said that she "consistently used the human form," although they "have gone through several transformations. They have been literally stated, they have been hidden in shadows. At times, they have been defined by delicate, sensuous, linear qualities that intrigue the viewer. At other times, the figures have taken on more ominous qualities, becoming dark, foreboding, mysterious forms. Within the last few years, another transformation has occurred. . . . My exploration has turned to an examination of the female form in connection to the symbol of the cross."

Couples the Feminine and the Cross

In 1990, Fuentes started combining the female figure with cruciforms. Her figures are not crucified, but relate to the cross with humility, strength, protection or pain. She said that at that time, she was re-evaluating her religion. She elaborated in an interview for *Pasatiempo,* "For me (the cross) is just a symbol. . . of strength and power. I've been dealing with the female form for so long, it seemed natural to connect them." She uses them as a metaphor for feminine strength and power. In her work *Pecho,* a red female figure arches back, pinned from behind by stakes and crosses. Taylor Bloom of the *Caprock Sun,* quoted Fuentes as saying, "Maybe it's symbolic of the crosses that we bear ourselves as individuals, or the crossroads that we come to in life. *You* decide what these two symbols mean to *you.*" Ellen Berkovitch in the *Journal North* mused in a review of Fuentes' 1996 work, "It reinforces that powerful art should magnify inner conditions and speak to larger worlds thereby."

Magnifies Inner Conditions

Fuentes' re-interpretation of the cross was enriched by her 1997 visit to the highlands of Chiapas, in southern Mexico, to view fields of immense Mayan Indian crosses, up to thirty feet tall, which rise above the graveyard in the village of San Cristobal de las Casas. To the Maya, the crosses are manifestations of both God and the creator ancestors. At times they embody either or both genders. She told a reporter for *Pasatiempo,* "(The cross) represents the grounding—being in the ground—and the tree of life. The main trunk and roots reach down into Mother Earth, and the horizontal part is branches to Father Sky." Fuentes intends to pursue her exploration and understanding of ". . . the fusion of ancestor, god, man, and woman that these crosses represent to the Maya. . . . I will continue to work on the cross image with what I believe will be an even fuller sense of its potential meaning."

Tina Fuentes admits that the balance between her studio, the classroom, and community service is a delicate one. She told Bloom, "teaching sometimes means that my studio work may go more slowly, but that's fine because I'm happy with teaching." Inevitably, Fuentes takes her artistic struggle into the classroom to inspire her students. She shared her advice to men and women with Rick Huff in an article for *Artlines:* "Be true to yourself, first of all. In the long run, you have no one to answer to but you. Do what is artistically important to you."

Sources:

Beaudin, Victoria. "Vive la difference: Three distinct artists in Marilyn Butler show all merit attention." *Scottsdale (Ariz.) Progress—Weekend,* July 1986, p. 15.

Bell, David. "Exhibition Is Paean to Power of Artists." *Journal North, August 1, 1986.*

Bell, David. "Gallery Exhibitions Have Power, Familiarity." *Journal North,* August 11, 1987, p. 4.

Berkovitch, Ellen. "Hispanic Artists Bring Passion, Vision to Show." *Journal North,* October 10, 1996, p. 4.

Bloom, Taylor. "Tina Fuentes: Charting New Ground." *Caprock Sun,* December 1997, pp. 10-11.

Chinn, John. "Tina Fuentes: Artist of the Month." *Caprock Sun,* July 1994, p. 7.

DeLeon, Nephtali. "Tina Fuentes—Maestra de lo inesperado." *Pachanga,* September/October 1994, p. 22.

Fauntleroy, Gussie. "Tina Fuentes ponders symbolism in her art." *Pasatiempo,* October 4-10, 1996, pp. 6, 61.

Huff, Rick. "Tina Fuentes: '. . . rapier-like swaths. . .'" *Artlines,* July/August 1987, p. 11.

Tetreault, Laura. "Gallery to showcase work of Hispanic artists." *Lubbock Avalanche Journal,* September 16, 1987, p. D-1.

Villani, John. "New doors opening for Hispanic artists." *Albuquerque Journal,* September 29, 1996, p. D-5.

G

Cristina Garcia
(1958–)
Author

Selected writings:

Dreaming in Cuban. Knopf, 1992.
Cars of Cuba. H.N. Abrams, 1995.
The Aguero Sisters. Knopf, 1997.

Overview

Cristina Garcia climbed the ranks at *Time* magazine before she decided to change career paths and write her

Cristina Garcia

first novel, *Dreaming in Cuban,* which was nominated for a National Book Award. Her characters delve into issues her parents faced during the Cuban Revolution of the 1950s. Garcia, who tells the story of three women who have very different perspectives of the revolution, was favorably received by critics. "Her special feat is to tell it in a style as warm and gentle as the 'sustaining aromas of vanilla and almond,' as rhythmic as the music of Beny More," maintained a *Time* reviewer.

Garcia was born July 4, 1958, in Havana, Cuba, to Frank M. Garcia and Hope Lois Garcia. Her family fled to the United States when she was two years old, and she grew up with English as her primary language. Garcia earned a bachelor's of arts degree in political science from Barnard College in 1979, and went on to graduate from Johns Hopkins University School of Advanced International Studies in Latin American studies in 1981. She married Scott Brown on December 8, 1990. As a youth, Garcia wanted to join the foreign service; her life took a different path, however, and the written word became her vehicle.

Garcia's first career move was to land a job at *Time* magazine in 1983 as a reporter and researcher. During the next seven years she held various positions at *Time,* including bureau chief and correspondent. In 1990, she decided to change direction again. Instead of reporting facts, Garcia wanted to bring the images in her imagination to life with her words in *Dreaming in Cuban.* In an *Ann Arbor News* story, Garcia said she remembered growing tired of "telling the truth." One day, she wrote a poem about three crazy women who kill themselves, and soon she was at work on her novel. She took a leave of absence from *Time,* returned three months later, and endured another six months before she finally quit. Garcia related that she was "frustrated with the constraints of journalism and the journalism of *Time.*" She was living in Miami, immersed in Cuban culture and meeting Cubans. "All the issues of my childhood came bubbling up," she remarked.

Dealing with these issues was a means for Garcia to understand her ancestors and their special struggles. Like many of those who left the country, Garcia's parents were vilified by Cuban president Fidel Castro in a harsh exile. "First generation Americans, they live cut-off from a homeland their parents cannot forgive and their new country forbids them to visit," a *Time* reporter noted in a review of Garcia's book. "In her impressive first novel, *Dreaming in Cuban,* Garcia takes back her island.

Explores Cuban Revolution in Novel

Garcia's story concerns three generations of Cuban women and their different reactions to the revolution. The book takes the reader to 1972 on the beach in Cuba. Celia del Pino, a staunch believer in communism, volunteers for stints in the sugarcane and as the local civilian judge. Meanwhile, her daughter, Lourdes Puente, owns a bakery in Brooklyn and is dependent on capitalism to make her business survive. Celia's other daughter, Felicia, is delusional and spouts politics for santeria, a religion that uses voodoo and Christian symbolism

Garcia explained in an *Ann Arbor News* story that as a child she heard many anti-Castro sentiments. "When I was growing up, I was in a virulently anti-Castro home, so Cuba was painted for me as a very monstrous place, an island prison. . . .Writing this helped me to understand my parents and their generation a little better." Her book also shed new light on Latin Americans for her readers. A reviewer in *Publishers Weekly* praised Garcia's characters. "Embracing fantasy and reality with equal fervor, Garcia's vivid, indelible characters offer an entirely new view of a particular Latin American sensibility."

Publishes Second Novel, *The Aguero Sisters*

In 1995, Garcia wrote a nonfiction work about Cuban automobiles entitled *Cars of Cuba.* Her second novel, *The Aguero Sisters,* was published in 1997. Similar to *Dreaming in Cuban,* this novel describes a family divided by geography and years of political and personal passion and folly. In a mixed book review, Michiko Kakutani wrote, "Although *The Aguero Sisters* lacks the compelling organic unity of Ms. Garcia's remarkable debut novel. . . it should ratify Ms. Garcia's reputation as a highly original, highly gifted writer. It also attests, like that earlier book, to Ms. Garcia's intuitive understanding of families and the fierce, enduring connections that bind one generation to another."

Sources:

Ann Arbor News, April 23, 1992.
Kakutani, Michiko. "Letting Fantastic Events Echo Life's Uncertainty." *The New York Times,* May 27, 1997, sec. C, p. 16.
King, Nina. "The Crook, the Thief, the Wife and the Lover." *The Washington Post,* July 13, 1997, sec. WBK, p. 1.
Publishers Weekly, January 13, 1992.
Time, March 23, 1992.

Garcia, Maria Cristina Estella Marcela Jurado
See Jurado, Katy

Garcia Cubero, Linda
See Cubero, Linda Garcia

Lorraine Garcia-Nakata
(1950–)
Artist, executive director

California-born Lorraine Garcia-Nakata, a practicing artist, was named managing director of The Mexican Museum in San Francisco in July of 1997. The museum opened its doors in 1975 under the direction of founder Peter Rodriguez and is dedicated to generating new perspectives on U.S. culture through Hispanic artistic expression. With her appointment, Garcia-Nakata returned to the museum after a ten-year absence. She served as its development director for three years in the 1980s and has a long-standing commitment to both the museum and to the Hispanic American community.

Garcia-Nakata was born in Yuba City, CA, on November 14, 1950. One of eight children, she grew up in the rural Central Valley area. Her father, John Garcia, was a construction worker, and her mother, Juanita, was a licensed vocational nurse. Her father returned to Mexico when Garcia-Nakata was five-years old, and she never saw him again. Garcia-Nakata attended Yuba College, California State University, and the University of Washington School of Art in Seattle. For ten years she lived in an unincorporated town in rural Wauconda County, WA, with a population of three. In a telephone interview, Garcia-Nakata confided, "It was an incredibly important learning experience to my future."

Emerges as Artist and Administrator

Garcia-Nakata began her career as an art professor at Big Bend Community College in Moses Lake, WA, in 1977. Later, she served as a consultant at the Sacramento Metropolitan Arts Commission & Ethnic Studies, an independent visual artist at the California State Summer School for the Arts, and a program officer for the Marin Community Foundation, Arts & Humanities. As program officer for the California Arts Council, she supervised and administered distribution of funds on a statewide basis for community arts organizations. As director of education and community programs at the Center for the Arts, Yerba Buena Gardens, she implemented a comprehensive education and community program. In addition to her administrative work, Garcia-Nakata has had a number of her original artworks featured in solo exhibitions and group exhibitions, both nationally and internationally. Her art won her a California Arts Council Artist-in-Residence in 1980 and 1993.

Becomes Museum Director

Garcia-Nakata's background brings a wealth of experience to The Mexican Museum, where she oversees the daily operations of the facility, including programs, finance, strategic planning, artistic future plans, and supervision and management of all personnel. She is especially pleased with the museum's commitment to the community. She wrote in a museum brochure: "The museum is poised to realize a long-awaited dream to become an institution which generates new perspectives on American culture through the lens of Latino/Mexicano/Chicano artistic expression."

The Mexican Museum in San Francisco is part of an arts organization collaborate known as Culture Core. It is designed to link cultural activities to those communities that do not have ready access to arts education. Garcia-Nakata hopes to reach young people with just this sort of effort. When asked in a telephone interview what special advice she might give to youngsters of Hispanic American descent, she replied, "When you are thinking in terms of a career, don't base your choice on what seems to be practical now, at the moment. Remember that the world changes. Just base your career choices on what you really aspire to do. Do what you truly choose to do. Follow your gifts."

Sources:

Blue, Rose. Telephone interview with Lorraine Garcia-Nakata, April 15, 1998.
Unterburger, Amy L., ed. *Who's Who Among Hispanic Americans* 1994-95. Detroit: Gale Research, 1995.

Alicia Gaspar de Alba
(1958–)
Professor, poet, author, women's rights activist

Selected writings:

Beggar on the Córdoba Bridge. Bilingual Press, 1989.
The Mystery of Survival and Other Stories. Bilingual Press, 1993.

Chicano Art Inside/Outside the Master's House: Cultural Politics and the CARA Exhibit University of Texas Press, 1998.

Overview

Alicia Gaspar de Alba is a professor, poet, and award-winning novelist. She has served as assistant professor of the César E. Chávez Center for Interdisciplinary Instruction in Chicana and Chicano Studies at the University of California, Los Angeles, since 1994.

Teaches English to Maquiladora Executives

Gaspar de Alba was born in El Paso, Texas, on July 29, 1958. Her professional experience began in 1979 when she taught English as a second language to Mexican executives and other staff members of the General Motors maquiladoras at the Instituto Interlingua in Juarez, Chihuahua. Her outstanding academic performance led to a Ford Foundation fellowship for minorities offered by the National Research Council (NRC) in Washington, DC in 1979. While focusing on the lack of representation of minorities at college facilities, the NRC also initiated the foundation's predoctoral and dissertation fellowships programs, which have been in place since 1986. By 1981, Gaspar de Alba was working as a teaching assistant for the English department at the University of Texas and then as a part-time lecturer in English and linguistics. In 1985, she enrolled at the University of Iowa and worked as a teaching assistant for the English department. Her other employment consisted of lecturing part-time at the University of Texas in 1986, and serving as a computer braillist for the National Braille Press in Boston, Massachusetts, in 1987.

Referring to the lack of representation of minorities at college facilities, Gaspar de Alba acknowledged in an interview with Margaret Wise Petrochenkov, a Ford Foundation employee, that "when [I] was first enrolled in the University of Iowa's American Studies program, there was not a single Chicana faculty member on campus." She added that "after a year of culture shock, [I] dropped out of the program." Four years later, she entered graduate school at the University of New Mexico, in Albuquerque. She earned a PhD with distinction in 1994 from the University of New Mexico in Albuquerque, where she studied Chicano/a art, popular culture, literature, and writing. Her dissertation, entitled "Mi Casa [No] Es Su Casa: The Cultural Politics of the Chicano Art: Resistance and Affirmation Exhibit," received the Ralph Henry Gabriel Prize for the best dissertation in American studies in 1994, and the University of Texas Press consequently published a book based on her dissertation in January 1998. More recently, several publishers are considering her book entitled *Tenth Muse: A Novel* on Sor Juana Ines de la Cruz, for publication. Gaspar de Alba received the Premio Aztlán Award for her book *The Mystery of Survival and Other Stories* in 1994. Regarding Gaspar de Alba's artistic abilities, Petrochenkov remarked that "her focus on Chicano popular culture and popular art is unique." Lois A. Marchino, writing in *The Oxford Companion to Women's Writing,* concurred, "The poetry of protest was the first genre to emerge, and poets have continued to examine ethnicity and culture and to experiment with language. Chicana poet, Alicia Gaspar de Alba has provided historical awareness and inspiration."

Issues of Identity Are a Primary Focus

In addition to Chicano studies, Gaspar de Alba is also interested in issues of identity. She currently teaches a course in "Barrio Popular Culture," in which she investigates the cultural politics of the barrio as expressed by Chicano art, literature, film, and other cultural production, particularly manifested in Chicano iconography, legends, and rituals. She also teaches a course in "Chicana Lesbian Literature," which is the first course taught at UCLA that is devoted exclusively to the literature of Chicana lesbians. Alicia developed the first Chicana/Lesbian course at UCLA back in 1994. Subject material explores issues of identity, family, sexuality, religion, and personal memoirs of Chicana lesbians. She has also devoted her time to several UCLA boards and committees, including the Faculty Advisory Committee, Library Committee, and Faculty Advisory Board. Most recently, she serves as an external reader for the Dissertation Committee and on the editorial board for Chicana/Latina Research Center. Regarding one of the works that Gaspar de Alba shares with two Chicana poets, *Three Times a Woman: Chicana Poetry,* an essay in *Bilingual Review* that addresses Gaspar de Alba's use of language: "Alicia Gaspar de Alba cultivates a poetry of paradox that explores the borders between politics and the sexes."

Gaspar de Alba has participated in many lectures and presentations since 1985. In 1994, she presented "Out of the House, the Halo, and the Whore's Mask: The Gender Politics of the CARA Exhibition" for the Symposium on Chicano Aesthetics, at UCLA. On another occasion in 1995, as the keynote speaker, she delivered "Alter-Nativity and the CARA Exhibition" for the IUP Latino Graduate Student Qualitative Research Seminar at the Smithsonian Institution. She was also involved in a 1996 panel presentation in a "Live Interview with Sor Juana Ines de la Cruz," a conference on Latin American Women Writers at the University of New Mexico. Most recently, Gaspar de Alba presented "Lesbian Drag: The Separatist Habit of Sor Juana Ines de la Cruz" for the Feminist Research Seminar at UCLA and "Between Sameness and Otherness: The Smithsonian Discovers' Chicano/a Art" for the Cultural Studies Academic Exchange Session at the conference of Ford Fellows in Washington, DC

Gaspar de Alba's academic publication *Chicano Art: Inside/Outside the Master's House: Cultural Politics and the CARA Exhibition* studies Chicano art through resistance and affirmation from 1965 to 1985. The CARA Exhibition was a controversial exhibition that travelled to museums in Los Angeles, Denver, San Francisco, Washington, DC, and other cities in the early 1990s. She recently returned from a conference on Chicano literature in Granada, Spain, where her work was featured. She is currently working on a seventeenth-century historical novel that is set in Boston during the witchcraft trials and features a mestiza protagonist.

Current Address: The César Chávez Center for Interdisciplinary Instruction in Chicana and Chicano Studies, Univ. of California, Los Angeles, 67 Kinsey Hall, Box 951559, Los Angeles, CA 90095–1559.

Sources:

CLNet Home Page. Available at http://latino.sscnet.ucla.edu/people/gaspar.a.html.

Excellence Through Diversity: Profiles of Forty-two Ford Foundation Fellows. Available at http://www2.nas.edu/fo/2132.html.

Kubiac, Brenda. Letter to and telephone conversation with Alicia Gaspar de Alba, March 13, 19, and April 16-18, 1998.

Marchino, Lois A. *The Oxford Companion to Women's Writing in the United States,* edited by Cathy N. Davidson and Linda Wagner-Martin. New York: Oxford University Press, 1995.

Marga Gomez
Comedienne, playwright, actress, activist

Selected discography:

Hung Like a Fly, (CD) Uproar Entertainment, 1997; (cassette) University of Puerto Rico Press, 1997.

Selected filmography:

Sphere. Warner Brothers, 1998.

Overview

Successfully merging artistic genres and categories, Marga Gomez is a multitalented entertainer who has forged a career as a stand-up comic, actor, writer, and performance artist. The daughter of a Cuban comedian and a Puerto Rican exotic dancer, Gomez bills herself as an "exotic

Marga Gomez

comedian." Like her comic idol, Lily Tomlin, Gomez is adept at creating a bevy of outrageous characters onstage. Gomez is known for her ability to shift easily from comic one-liners to dramatic disclosure and has received critical acclaim in the 1990s as one of the outstanding practitioners of the dramatic monologue form. She is also a recognized leader in the growing field of gay and lesbian comedy.

Early Life and Career

Marga Gomez, who prefers not to disclose her age, was born in the 1950s to two well-known New York City performers, Margo (who danced under the name Margo the Exotic) and Wilfredo Gomez (known onstage as Willy Chevalier). Growing up in the upper Manhattan neighborhood known as Washington Heights, she entered show business as a child performer, appearing onstage with her parents for the first time at age seven. The Hispanic American theatrical world provided an unconventional and influential backdrop for Gomez's early years; she would later chronicle her formative childhood experiences in performance pieces such as *Memory Tricks* and *A Line around the Block.*

Gomez's parents divorced in the mid-1960s, when Gomez was 12 years old, and the fame and financial security they had previously earned in the theater began to dissolve. Gomez went to live with her mother in Massapequa, Long Island, and saw her father on weekends. Gomez had attended an inner-city Catholic school as a child; during her adolescence, she attended a high school where she was the only Hispanic American student. Suburban Long Island felt isolating to Gomez, and she became shy and introverted. On graduating from high school, Gomez went to Oswego State College in upstate New York, where she first came out as a lesbian. After studying English and political science for two years, Gomez flunked out of college and moved to Binghamton, New York, where she became involved in a lesbian feminist community.

Career Starts in San Francisco

Gomez moved to San Francisco in the early 1980s, where she attempted to get involved in acting. She joined Lilith, a feminist theater ensemble, and toured Europe and the West Coast extensively for three years. Gomez credits this experience with giving her theatrical monologues and stand-up material a feminist edge. Gomez also spent a season with the San Francisco Mime Troupe and was one of the original members of the Hispanic American comedy group Culture Clash. During this time, Gomez developed her stand-up routine—a mixture of off-beat characterizations, quirky social commentary, and sexual politics.

By 1988 Gomez had acquired a loyal following and won the Cabaret Gold Award as Entertainer of the Year from the San Francisco Council on Entertainment. Gomez has performed at countless events across the country and has been a featured performer on numerous television shows. In addition to her work for television, Gomez made a brief appearance in the feature film *Batman Forever.*

Performance Monologues Win Kudos

In 1991, as a result of an offer from the University of California San Diego Multi-Cultural Theater Festival, Gomez created the full-length performance monologue, *Memory Tricks,* the first in a series of performance pieces written and performed by Gomez, along with *Marga Gomez Is Pretty, Witty & Gay,* and *A Line around the Block.* It is this body of work that has brought Gomez her greatest critical attention, including rave reviews, international media focus, honors, and awards. The tragicomic story of Marga's relationship with her flamboyant mother, *Memory Tricks* traces the emotional path from her mother's days as a showgirl to her struggle with aging and Alzheimer's disease. Gomez probes the difficult emotions surrounding the mother-daughter relationship—in this case, a relationship in which the child must play mother to her own parent.

Following its six-week sold-out run at the Marsh Performance Space in San Francisco, *Memory Tricks* was twice chosen to be a part of the prestigious Solo Mio festival at Life on the Water Theater in San Francisco. Gomez was invited to perform a one-hour version of *Memory Tricks* as part of the New York Shakespeare Festival's Festival of New Voices in 1992, followed by a limited engagement of the complete piece in April 1993. It has since been performed all over the United States, Canada, and Europe.

Gomez's next performance piece, *Marga Gomez Is Pretty, Witty & Gay,* opened at Josie's Cabaret in San Francisco in October 1991 to packed houses. The work has played across the United States, and in March 1993 it was included as part of the Whitney Museum's Biennial Performance Series. The work's title is a send-up of the song, "I Feel Pretty" from *West Side Story;* it also marks the fact that Gomez has been an out performer for most of her career. Although Gomez's lesbianism is only indirectly mentioned in *Memory Tricks, Marga Gomez Is Pretty, Witty & Gay,* is packed with lesbian humor, including a hilarious sketch describing a fantasy relationship between Anais Nin and Minnie Mouse. During the show, Gomez overturns a common stereotype of gays and lesbians with the line, "We do not recruit, we impress."

Latin Memories Form *A Line around the Block*

Gomez began performing *A Line around the Block,* a companion piece to *Memory Tricks,* in 1994. The work was co-commissioned by the Mark Taper Forum in Los Angeles and The New World Theater at the University of Massachusetts in Amherst. *A Line around the Block* had its creative beginnings in a sketch entitled "The 13 Minutos," which formed part of the theater group Culture Clash's show, *Carpa Clash,* at the Mark Taper Forum. Gomez won Theater LA's 1993-1994 Ovation Award as Best Featured Actress in a Play for her work in *Carpa Clash.*

A Line around the Block is a remembrance of Gomez's father, Willy Chevalier, as well as a bittersweet look back at the Hispanic American theatrical world of the 1950s and 1960s. Gomez has credited her father with giving her the desire and the determination to go into show business. In both *Memory Tricks* and *A Line around the Block,* Gomez pays tribute to her parents by showing the limits placed on their talents by discrimination against Hispanic Americans. Despite her own assimilated background, the immigrant experience of her parents and Hispanic American culture have been major influences on Gomez's work. Gomez sees the strength of her writing coming from being an outsider in two worlds: a gay in the Hispanic American world, a Hispanic American in the gay world. Playhouse International optioned Gomez's screenplay of *Memory Tricks,* which has been expanded to include several players in order to be made into a feature film. Gomez has also contributed written material to several books: *Out, Loud, & Laughing; Out of Character;* and *Contemporary Plays by Women of Color.* In 1997, Gomez released her first compact disc recording, *Hung Like a Fly,* based upon new stand-up material. Dubbed a lesbian Lenny Bruce by comedian Robin Williams, Gomez has garnered national acclaim for her humor. She has performed stand-up comedy on a number of nationally telecast programs, including: Rosie O'Donnell's *Stand-Up Spotlight* on VH-1, with Whoopie Goldberg on Public Television's *Comedy Tonight,* the *Good Times Cafe* on

the Arts and Entertainment Network, HBO's *On the Ledge* and *Comic Relief VI,* Comedy Central's *Out There,* and Showtime's *Latino Laugh Festival.* Currently, Marga Gomez is dividing her time between coasts as she continues with all her pursuits. With her many talents and powerful presence, this rising star—an inspiration to both the gay and lesbian and Hispanic American communities—is just beginning to shine.

Sources:

Guthmann, Edward. "A Chip Off the Old Block." *San Francisco Chronicle,* November 5, 1995.

Horowitz, Simi. "Marga Gomez." *New York Native,* May 10, 1993.

Janovy, C. J. ". . . A lesbian Lenny Bruce." *Pitch Weekly,* October 23-30, 1997.

Pollon, Zélie. "Marga Gomez Is Definitely Going Places." *Deneuve,* October 1994: pp. 24-27, 54.

Reser, Phil. "Marga Gomez Lifting Spirits, A Family Tradition." *San Francisco Hot Ticket,* September 1988.

Troy, Patricia. "Marga Gomez," *Venice,* April 1994.

Valdes, David. "Pretty Wonderful." *Bay Windows,* May 12/ May 18 1994.

West, Blake. "Marga Gomez Goes Public," *Metroline,* February 2-15, 1995.

Irma Flores Gonzales
(1942–)
Organization executive, community activist, consultant, filmmaker

Selected filmography:

Oregon's Chicanos: A Culture in Conflict. Independent Film, 1985.

Overview

Irma Flores Gonzales, chair of the board of directors of the National Council of La Raza (NCLR) and civil rights activist, has helped many people through the years. NCLR is the largest Hispanic constituency-based organization and leading think tank, based in Washington, DC. It serves Hispanic people around the world, with particular success in Central and Latin America, fueling the growth of business and bringing long-sought hope of economic survival. *Hispanic Business* magazine has commented that NCLR is ". . . by all accounts the most effective Hispanic organization." Few would doubt that this success is due to the commitment of people as capable as Flores Gonzales.

Learns Important Family Values

Irma Flores Gonzales was born in El Paso, Texas, on April 11, 1942, to first generation Mexican Americans. In addition to their own five children, her parents raised the three children of a cousin killed in an auto accident. Flores Gonzales' father was an engineer, and the family enjoyed a comfortable middle-class lifestyle. A good Catholic education and a large, close-knit family contributed to her very happy childhood. She knew little of the struggle of farm workers while growing up in El Paso.

Flores Gonzales initially intended to become a teacher when she first entered college. When she married and moved to Portland, Oregon in 1970, however, she took a job with the government in order to help support her husband and young daughter while he finished his education. Flores Gonzales' position as a civil rights officer with the Western Regional Office of Personnel Management marked the beginning of her career in public service. In the course of her work, Flores Gonzales established a relationship with the Colegio Cesar Chavez, a private, four-year, liberal arts college in Mount Angel, Oregon. Initially, she was a member of the college's board of trustees and, from 1979 until 1985, served as college president.

Increases the Size of Her Family

During the late 1970's, Flores Gonzales decided to adopt a child. After attempts to adopt a child in the United States were unsuccessful, she traveled to Colombia. When she found a boy in whom she was interested, Flores Gonzales soon discovered that he had two brothers who also needed a home. After careful thought, she decided to adopt all three boys. Although raising four children was not without difficulty, Flores Gonzales considers motherhood as one of her greatest accomplishments.

In 1985, Flores Gonzales was appointed by the police chief to develop and implement community policing in Portland. That same year, *Oregon* magazine named her one of the state's most influential women for her work in producing and writing a documentary film entitled, *Oregon's Chicanos: A Culture in Conflict.* Combining Flores Gonzales' interest in filmmaking with her work as a Hispanic American advocate, the film dealt with the challenges and hardships faced by Oregon's Chicanos as they make the transition from rural to urban life.

When Oregon Governor Neil Goldschmidt named her as head of the Oregon State Community Services Agency in 1987, Flores Gonzales was responsible for managing its $250 million allotment. Her agency oversaw all federal and state-funded poverty programs, including housing assistance, food stamps, and energy assistance. She also managed innovative programs to develop small businesses within Native American and farmworker communities.

Resolves to Live Life and Enjoy It!

In 1989, Flores Gonzales faced the battle of her life when she was diagnosed with advanced renal cancer. She participated in a series of experimental treatments for persons with renal cancer. Of the 58 persons who participated in the treatments, Flores Gonzales was the only one to be cured of the disease. While she credits aggressive treatment for her cure, her physicians point to her "iron will" as the primary reason for her return to good health. During her illness, Flores Gonzales vowed that if she survived, she would dedicate her life to those things she loved to do. Working with people and helping to find solutions to their problems are among her greatest loves.

Resumes Important Work in Activism

Since recovering from cancer in 1992, Flores Gonzales has resumed her work as a community activist. In addition to her work with the NCLR, she serves as a community needs consultant for the W.K. Kellogg Foundation, an organization that focuses on the needs of Hispanic communities throughout the Americas, and as an advisor for the Families, Neighborhoods, and Community Development Special Programs division. She is also acting director of the Transitions Project, which provides housing assistance, alcohol and drug counseling, and other services to homeless adults in Portland. She is a founding board member of the Oregon Council of La Raza, a leading advocacy organization for Oregon's Hispanic community, as well as a board member for the Center for Community Change, the Hispanic Association for Corporate Responsibility, and the Northwest Multicultural Institute.

Current Address: National Council of La Raza (NCLR), 1111 19th St., NW, Ste. 1000, Washington, DC 20036.

Sources:

Gonzales, Irma Flores. *National Council of La Raza Biography Sheet.* Washington, D.C.: National Council of La Raza Headquarters, 1998.
Spear, Jane. Telephone conversation with Irma Flores Gonzales, May 7, 1998.

González Parsons, Lucy
See Parsons, Lucy González

Gracis Vidal de Santos Silas, María Africa
See Móntez, María

Stephanie Gonzales

(1950–)

State government official

"The number one priority of this office is public service," said Stephanie Gonzales, New Mexico's twenty-first secretary of state. Elected in 1990 after serving as deputy secretary of state, Gonzales took the oath of office on January 1, 1991, and was re-elected for a second four-year term in 1994. This important position lies directly behind the governor and lieutenant governor, whose duties the secretary must perform in their absence.

Responds To Community Needs

As part of the responsibilities of her office, Gonzales is chief elections officer and oversees the entire election process, beginning with maintaining a computerized list of registered voters and testing voting machines. She also oversees the campaign finance reports and financial disclosures by candidates and other state officials, initiates campaign finance reform, regulates lobbyist laws, and provides public access to vital records through the Internet. In addition to her duties as secretary of state, Gonzales was appointed in 1993 by President Clinton to the Commission

Stephanie Gonzales

on White House Fellowships, and serves as an *ex officio* board member of the New Mexico Public Employees Retirement Association. She is also on the boards of both the National Association of Secretaries of State and the New Mexico AIDS Service and serves as a council member of League of United Latin American Citizens (LULAC) and the National Association of Latino Elected and Appointed Officials.

Gonzales views her role as secretary of state as a servant to the public. "When someone comes to us with a question or need, we make sure that person is directed to an individual or agency that can give them an answer," she said in a telephone interview. "We have a reputation for being responsive to people's needs."

Learns by Experience

A graduate of the Loretto Academy for Girls in Santa Fe, Gonzales had no special degree or formal training in politics. She did, however, have perhaps the most important training of all—the example of her parents. Gonzales was born in Santa Fe, NM on August 12, 1950. Her father, Herbert Martines, a native of Mexico, came to the United States as an infant when his parents moved to a small village in southeastern San Antonio. Her mother, Beatrice Abeyta, was born in northern New Mexico. "Mom and Dad are my mentors," said Gonzales. "My mother was a full-time homemaker, and my father a truck driver. He later established himself in a career selling insurance. My parents were always involved in politics on a local level. I grew up stuffing envelopes and was going door-to-door distributing campaign literature by the age of ten or 11. I guess politics is in my blood."

Gonzales left school at the age of 18, married at the age of 20, and had 2 sons. While working as office manager for a general practitioner from 1973 to 1986, she remained politically active, volunteering in her local community. Because of her political involvement, she was asked to consider an appointment to the position of deputy secretary of state. She accepted the appointment in 1987 and remained in that position for the full four-year term. It would prove to be the first of many steps in the political arena. That experience inspired Gonzales to seek an elected position. "I really liked what I was doing and felt I was doing a good job, so I decided to run for secretary of state," she said. "I was considered the underdog in that election. I had no name recognition and no money. One of my opponents was a well-known former city councilor of Albuquerque, and the second outspent me three-to-one." But Gonzales drew on the training her parents had given her as a child. "I met the voters one-on-one," she said. "I targeted certain areas of the state with consistent voters who where likely to vote again, and personally took my message to them. And my message was clear—that I could 'hit the ground running.'" Her persistence and hard work paid off when she won the election.

The decision to run for secretary of state was a difficult one to make. Gonzales said, "I sometimes wondered, 'What am I doing?' But I knew I could serve the citizens of New Mexico well." So well did she serve the citizens, they reelected her in 1994. "I will leave my office [in 1998] knowing my pledges to the public have been fulfilled," she said. But Gonzales does not take all the credit for a job well done. "I am surrounded by very competent people who are a lot smarter than I am, and that makes my job easier," she said.

Participates on Other Levels

Each year in her appointed role to the commission of White House Fellowships, Gonzales and about 30 other appointed commissioners interview 40 or 45 young women and men from across the nation. These young adults have been selected through nationwide interviews to travel to Washington, DC, for the final interview. "Of these finalists, we select 15 to 18 to serve a 12-month fellowship," she said. "This is not an internship. This is an opportunity for brilliant young women and men to work side-by-side with cabinet members or deputy cabinet members at the highest levels of federal government."

Gonzales has been profiled in *The Hispanic-American Almanac, Who's Who in America, Who's Who in American Politics, Who's Who of American Women, Who's Who among Hispanic Americans,* and *Who's Who in the West.* One of the organizations Gonzales is active in is the New Mexico AIDS Service. As a board member, she is committed to increasing public awareness of the severity of the disease. "On a personal level, I am very active. I participate in walks and fund-raising events, and give what I can financially," she said.

Family is very important to Gonzales. She and her family suffered a tremendous tragedy in 1988 when her oldest son, then a teen, was killed by a drunk driver. Her youngest son, Adan, now 25, and his wife, Jennifer, have two children, Rebecca Lynn aged 5 and Sarah Nicole, 21 months.

Works Toward the Future

Gonzales is now embarking on another level of her career. With her second term in office nearing an end, she is gearing up to run for lieutenant governor of the state. "Once again, this will be a grass roots campaign," she said. "This is the hardest race. There are two other individuals campaigning—a woman out of Albuquerque who is wealthy, and a gentleman currently in the house of representatives for New Mexico who has access to money. But I'm going to work very hard at attaining that position," she said.

Current Address: Office of the Secretary of State, State Capitol Rm. 420, Santa Fe, NM 87503.

Sources:

The Hispanic American Almanac. Detroit: Gale Research, 1993, p. 334.

Thompson, Märie L. Telephone conversation with and biographical information from Stephanie Gonzales, March 20, 1998.

Diana Gonzalez
(1957–)
News correspondent

From plane crashes to hurricanes to Cuban refugees, veteran television news reporter Diana Gonzalez has excelled at covering some of the country's most compelling stories of the past five years. As one of the top minority correspondents in the nation, she is proud that her hard work has led to national exposure and is aware that other Hispanic Americans—especially Hispanic American women—look up to her. Gonzalez has proven that she is more than able to live up to those expectations.

Diana Gonzalez

Gonzales was born in Havana, Cuba, on July 19, 1957, to Raul and Maria Gonzalez. In 1960, with sister Liliana, the Gonzalez family moved to Miami a year after Fidel Castro overthrew the government of Fulgencio Batista in a military coup in January of 1959. Her father returned to Cuba with a military contingent that took part in the April 17, 1961, Bay of Pigs Invasion. Following the defeat of the U.S.-trained Cuban exiles by the Cuban army, Raul Gonzalez was imprisoned in his native country for two years. He was released from prison in 1963 and returned to his family in Miami.

Shows Early Interest in Journalism

Diana Gonzalez's interest in broadcast journalism began at a young age, when family friend Alma Walker, the public affairs director at WPLG-TV in Miami, interviewed the young teen for a report on Cuban refugees. It had been ten years since Gonzalez and her family had fled Cuba. The interview sparked an interest with Gonzalez, and Walker went on to become her mentor, helping Gonzalez obtain internships in the broadcasting industry. With Walker's support, Gonzalez went on to pursue her interest academically.

Gonzalez spent her college career at the University of Florida in Gainesville. While a student, she worked as a booth announcer for WUTF-TV, the local Public Broadcasting System (PBS) affiliate. She also completed an internship as a weekend general assignment reporter for WJXT-TV in Jacksonville. The job earned her college credit and a small stipend. But more importantly, this "phenomenal experience" gave her practical training that enabled her to envision what life in broadcast journalism would be like. Those on-air WJXT stories formed her resumé tape, which led directly to her first professional job.

In 1978, Gonzalez received her bachelor's degree in broadcast journalism. Shortly thereafter, she landed her first professional job in Miami with WTVJ-TV (then a CBS affiliate). She was a news reporter for the station and hosted a weekend magazine show *Montage*. In 1983, Gonzalez moved to the rival ABC station, WPLG-TV, and worked as a medical reporter and midday anchor until 1993. Her work during this period earned her two Florida Emmys in 1983 and 1986, an Award for Excellence in Medical Journalism in 1985, and the Maggie and Regional Emmy Awards in 1990.

Covers Wave of Cuban Refugees

In July of 1993, she was hired at CBS as a national correspondent for its network news, and worked out of the Miami bureau. In 1994 Gonzalez covered the mass exodus of thousands of refugees from Cuba. Following Cuban leader Fidel Castro's approval of the exodus, the refugees—called "rafters" because many left Cuba on rafts—hoped to cross the Florida straits and immigrate to the United States. President Bill Clinton, however, enacted new policies that prohibited refugees from receiving asylum in the United States. Instead, over 25,000 rafters were seized at sea and detained at the U.S. Naval Station in Guantanamo Bay, Cuba. Describing the experience as "very emotional," Gonzalez harkened back to her family's experience as Cuban immigrants. "I witnessed such a degree of desperation in these people fleeing Cuba," she recalled.

While much of the reporting of this story was difficult, there were parts that Gonzalez found quite exciting. She flew with the "Brothers to the Rescue," a humanitarian group of pilots who scoured the straits of Florida in search of rafters. "Once the rafters were located, the pilots would swoop down and drop supplies. It was very exciting to cover these volunteers who risked so much for people they did not even know," said Gonzalez.

Teams with Dan Rather

In October of 1995, Gonzalez was part of the CBS news team, which included anchor Dan Rather, that reported on one of the year's biggest weather stories. With winds of 135 mph, Hurricane Opal made its destructive path through the Deep South into the Florida Panhandle. Heavy rains and overflowing rivers created chaos, forcing over 30,000 people to seek aid in Red Cross shelters. The two were assigned to cover Florida, with Gonzalez in Pensacola and Rather in Panama Beach. The CBS news coverage of Hurricane Opal earned Rather, Gonzalez, and other journalists a National Emmy Award nomination. In February of 1996, Gonzalez covered the return of Pope John Paul II to Nicaragua.

One of the most difficult experiences of Gonzalez's career was when she covered the Mother's Day weekend crash of ValuJet Flight 592 in the Florida Everglades in 1996. One hundred nine people died when a DC-9 bound for Atlanta crashed into a swampy area on May 11, just 15 miles from Miami International Airport. Gonzalez reported live from the crash scene. It was an area infested with snakes and alligators and, because the swampy waters did not circulate, the plane's flammable fuel had saturated the surroundings. The long-time Miami correspondent remembered that the experience was so horrible because "it happened in our own backyard." The chaos of the scene stayed with her. "There were alligators around, there was the difficulty of talking with the grieving families, and there was the responsibility of having to get the facts of the crash straight."

In September of 1996, Gonzalez returned to WTVJ-TV (now an NBC affiliate), where she is currently a news reporter. In her new position she continues the tradition of excellence that has been a hallmark of her career. Gonzalez is divorced and lives in Miami with her two children.

Current Address: WTVJ, Miami-Fort Lauderdale, 316 N. Miami Ave., Miami, FL 33218.

Sources:

Baker, Beth. Telephone interviews with Diana Gonzalez, March 19-20, 1998.

Gonzalez, Diana. Biographical press release. WTVJ-TV.

Larson, Erik. "Death in the Everglades." *Time,* May 20, 1996, p. 30.

Latino Link Home Page. Available at http://www.latinolink.com.

Red Cross Home Page. Available at http://www.redcross.org.

Van Biema, David. "Snuffed Out While Embracing the World." *Time,* July 29, 1996, p. 40.

Village Life News Magazine Home Page. Available at http://www.villagelife.org.

Myrtle Gonzalez
(1891–1918)
Actress

Selected filmography:

Her Husband's Friend. Vitagraph, 1913.
The White Feather. Vitagraph, 1913.
The Little Sheriff. Vitagraph, 1914.
The Choice. Vitagraph, 1914.
Captain Alvarez. Vitagraph, 1914.
Tainted Money. Vitagraph, 1914.
His Wife and his Work. Vitagraph, 1914.
The Masked Dancer. Vitagraph, 1914.
Millions for Defense. Vitagraph, 1914.
The Level. Selig, 1914.
Sisters. Selig, 1914.
Ward's Claim. Selig, 1914.
Anne of the Mines. Vitagraph, 1914.
The Quarrel. Vitagraph, 1915.
The Man from the Desert. Vitagraph, 1915.
His Golden Grain. Vitagraph, 1915.
The Game of Life. Vitagraph, 1915.
The Ebony Casket. Vitagraph, 1915.
A Child of the North. Vitagraph, 1915.
The Chalice of Courage. Vitagraph, 1915.
The Offending Kiss. Vitagraph, 1915.
The Legend of the Lone Tree. Vitagraph, 1915.
Her Last Flirtation. Vitagraph, 1915.
Inside Facts. Universal, 1915.
Does It End Right?. Universal, 1915.
The Bride of Nancy Lee. Universal, 1915.
The Terrible Truth. Universal, 1915.
The Girl of Lost Lake. Universal, 1916.
The Gambler. Universal, 1916.
A Fool's Gold. Universal, 1916.

The End of the Rainbow. Universal, 1916.
The Brink. Universal, 1916.
Bill's Wife. Universal, 1916.
Lonesomeness. Universal, 1916.
Miss Blossom. Universal, 1916.
It Happened in Honolulu. Universal, 1916.
Missy. Universal, 1916.
The Secret Foe. Universal, 1916.
A Romance of Billy Goat Hill. Universal, 1916.
The Secret of the Swamp. Universal, 1916.
The Pinnacle. Universal, 1916.
The Wise Man and the Fool. Universal, 1916.
Mutiny. Universal, 1917.
God's Crucible. Universal, 1917.
Southern Justice. Universal, 1917.
The Show-Down. Universal, 1917.
The Greater Law. Universal, 1917.

Overview

Silent screen actress Myrtle Gonzalez became the first Hispanic American female star of the silent screen. She made more than 40 films during her short career. She died at the young age of 27, her life cut tragically short by influenza.

Grows Up in Los Angeles

Gonzalez was born to a Los Angeles grocer on September 23, 1891. She was a native Mexican Californian and grew up in Los Angeles. Gonzalez began her film career as a stock player, acting in assorted roles. Her screen debut came in *Ghosts* in 1911. Her star truly began to rise when Gonzalez joined Vitagraph Pictures in 1913. She was assigned to the company's Western unit in Los Angeles, although the main studio was in Brooklyn. Her first role for Vitagraph was in *Her Husband's Friend* in 1913. Her fame grew rapidly, and she soon became the first Hispanic American female star of the silent screen, and one of the most popular draws of the silent era.

Appears in More Than Forty Films

Gonzalez played numerous roles, appearing in more than 40 films in the years 1913 to 1917. Many of these films were Western dramas. She frequently played strong-willed heroines, and most often shared the screen in her Westerns with William Duncan. The two worked well together and appeared jointly in over a dozen films, including 1913's *The Choice,* 1914's *The Level* and *Anne of the Mines,* and 1915's *The Quarrel, The Game of Life, The Ebony Casket,* and *The Offending Kiss.*

Some of Gonzalez's best known films include *Deception* in 1913, *The Masked Dancer* and *Captain Alvarez* the following year, and *The Chalice of Courage* and *A Natural Man* both in 1915.

Suffers Untimely Death

At the height of her career, Gonzelez's life was cut short. She died from influenza, exacerbated by a heart condition. She passed away on October 22, 1918, at the age of 27. Had she lived, her popularity as an actress likely would have continued. She was a marquee player for the film company Vitagraph, which had big plans for her future on screen. Her legacy as the first Hispanic American female star of silent era endures, as does her work on the silver screen.

Sources:

Hispanic Threads In America. Available at: http://www.ma.iup.edu/Pueblo/latino_cultures/contrib.html.

Keller, Gary D. *A Biographical Handbook of Hispanics and United States Film.* Tempe, AZ: Bilingual Press, 1997.

Rainey, Buck. *Sweethearts of the Sage: Biographies and Filmographies of 258 Actresses Appearing in Western Movies.* Jefferson, NC: McFarland & Company, 1992.

Reyes, Luis, and Peter Rubie. *Hispanics in Hollywood.* New York: Garland Publishing, 1994.

Rodriguez, Clara E., ed. *Latin Looks: Images of Latinas and Latinos in the U.S. Media.* Boulder, CO: Westview Press, 1997.

The Internet Movie Database. Available at: http://us.imdb.com/Name?Gonzalez,+Myrtle.

Truitt, Evelyn Mack. *Who Was Who On Screen.* New York: R. R. Bowker, 1977.

Jovita González de Mireles
(1899–1983)
Editor, author, historian, organization president

Selected writings:

Mi Libro de Español, 3 volumes: volumes 1 and 2 by González de Mireles, E. E. Mireles, and R. B. Fisher; volume 3 by González de Mireles and E. E. Mireles. Benson, 1941-1943.

El Español Elemental, 6 volumes, by González de Mireles and E. E. Mireles. Benson, 1949.

Overview

Jovita González de Mireles is one of the significant female writers of the first half of the twentieth century. History and fiction converge in her essays as she describes the life, customs, and beliefs of her people along the Mexican border. At a time when minorities and women had little opportunities to advance in the academic world, González de Mireles received respect from her peers by the breadth and depth of her scholarly work.

Enjoys Privileged Upbringing

Born in Roma, TX, in 1899, Jovita González belonged to a prominent Spanish family descended from the original settlers of what became the American Southwest. She was raised on her grandfather's ranch in the Rio Grande valley. The ranch had come to her family when her great-great-grandfather, as one of the *agraciados* (grantees), received a land grant from the Spanish crown in the northern frontier of New Spain. At a time when education was a precious commodity for minority group members, Jovita González obtained a B.A. with a teaching certificate in history and Spanish at Lady of the Lake College in San Antonio. After teaching at Saint Mary's Hall in San Antonio, she continued her education at the University of Texas at Austin and graduated with a master of arts on August 19, 1930. Her master's thesis, "Social Life in Cameron, Starr and Zapata Counties," is a well-documented study of the history and the inhabitants of those counties. While at the University of Texas in 1925, she became acquainted with J. Frank Dobie at the Texas Folk-Lore Society. With Dobie's encouragement she initiated her research work on the Mexican folklore of Texas and became a prominent member of the society. She was elected president of the Texas Folk-Lore Society in 1930. On April 17–18, 1931, and April 22, 1932, she presided over the annual meetings of the society held respectively in San Antonio and in Austin. González's essays and folkloric tableaux appeared periodically from 1927 through 1940 in various publications of the Texas Folk-Lore Society and in the *Southwest Review.* She was also associated with the League of United Latin American Citizens (LULAC), one of the earliest Hispanic organizations that attempted to formulate a Hispanic ideology in regard to the socioeconomic situation of the Hispanic. She became vice-president and president of LULAC, and her essays appeared in the early 1930s in *LULAC News,* a publication of the organization. In her master's thesis she dedicates a section of chapter 5 to LULAC and discusses its creation, purpose, and constitution.

Teaches at High School

González married Edmundo E. Mireles, who also worked in the field of education. He was president of the Educational Committee of LULAC in 1937. In 1940 she and her husband were in Corpus Christi, TX, where he was coordinator of the Spanish programs in the public school system. After W. B. Ray High School in Corpus Christi was founded in 1959, González de Mireles taught Spanish and history there and sponsored the activities of the Pan American Club. She remained at Ray High School until her retirement in 1966.

Besides being one of the earliest Hispanic women folklorists, González de Mireles had a keen interest in the pedagogical aspects of the Spanish language at the elementary level. She assisted her husband in the production of the three-volume series *Mi Libro de Español* (My Spanish

Book, 1941-1943) and the six-volume reader *El Español Elemental* (Elementary Spanish, 1949).

Writes to Promote Understanding Between Races

Although González de Mireles produced her essays and her picturesque folkloric tableaux using an upper-class point of view, she shows an awareness of the socioeconomic realities of the Hispanic population of the Southwest. In her master's thesis and in some of her essays she points out that some of the conflicts that have arisen among the border inhabitants were produced by the Anglo-American colonization of that region. She states that Anglo Americans, who consider the Texas-Mexicans of the border counties as interlopers and undesirable aliens, should reflect on the following facts: that the majority of those Mexicans were living in what is today Texas long before Texas was Texas; that Mexicans were in those territories long before many Americans crowded the decks of immigrant ships; that a great number of Mexicans along the border did not come as immigrants but were the descendants of people granted land by Charles V, the Spanish king.

González de Mireles hoped that through her writings she would promote a better understanding between two culturally and ideologically opposed races, the Mexicans and the Anglo Americans. Her folkloric sketches are humorous, lively, and colorful. They usually begin with a description of a character who is later the subject of an event or series of events. For example, González de Mireles's "Folk-Lore of the Texas-Mexican Vaquero" (1927) discusses the frontier vaquero (cowboy), an extraordinary type of range man born and bred in Texas; yet he is either unknown to most people or considered an undesirable character. She says that this vaquero is the product of both the Native American and the Spanish conquistador. From his Indian ancestors, he inherited his love for the open prairie and for his freedom, as well as his melancholy and his fatalistic view of life. From the Spaniards he derived his courteous personality, a love for music and poetry, and religious devotion. The life of the vaquero revolves around myths through which he attempts to understand nature. He has, for example, the myth of "El Cenizo" (a silvery shrub which produces white, pink, and lavender flowers), which tells the story of how this plant was a gift of the Virgin Mary to the vaqueros during a drought. Since this plant appeared on the prairie on Ash Wednesday, it was called El Cenizo (The Ashen One). "The Mocking Bird" is another vaquero story that relates how this bird became endowed with white feathers on its wings at a time when all creatures spoke a common language: Spanish. "El Cardo Santo" (The Thistle) was a gift to Antonio, a vaquero who disliked flowers with thorns and criticized nature for creating beauty that one could not gather without pricking one's hands. "The Guadalupana Vine" is a tale that centers on a South Texas vine which has medicinal properties. Legends of ghosts and treasures abound among the vaqueros, states González.

The great majority of the legends deal with buried treasures in southern Texas which the Spaniards left behind during Indian raids. In the legend of the Chimeneas Ranch (Chimney Ranch), the ranch is haunted by the spirits of the former owners who frighten the vaqueros at night-fall. Along with all these tales, González de Mireles includes several folk songs and epic compositions that come from the border vaqueros.

Portrays Folklore of Pastoral Peoples

"Tales and Songs of the Texas-Mexicans" (1930) concentrates on the folklore among the pastoral people of the border lands. In addition, the narrator laments that the goatherds and the old-style vaqueros are becoming extinct and that their traditions are viewed with contempt by young Hispanics. The essay is divided into two parts, "Folk Tales" and "Songs." Vaquero tales, says the narrator, are humorous and somewhat realistic while goatherd stories are mystical and focus on nature. There are two goatherds that stand out in the narrator's mind, Tío Patricio and Chón. They are depicted in a picturesque manner in González's charming, straightforward style: "Chón was little, black, and ugly; his wrinkled, withered face resembled a bat's, and his sharp eyes blinked with the regularity and solemnity of a toad's. He was a little heathen, a materialist who could see and understand nothing beyond his goats. On the other hand, Tío Patricio was a mystic, a visionary who saw in nature the handiwork of his Creator." When these two characters visited the narrator's family ranch, all rejoiced, for their visit meant tales from Tío Patricio and songs from Chón. The latter produced extremely brief compositions; hence at the ranch emerged the following saying: "Es corta como la canción de Chón" (It is short like Chón's song). In addition, this collection includes the following narratives: "Tío Patricio," "The Carpenter," "The Cicada," "The Cardinal," "The Dove," "Ambrosio the Indian," "The First Cactus Blossom," "The Gift of the Pitahaya," and "The Devil on the Border." The section of the essay entitled "Songs" includes "Remigio Treviño," the earliest *tragedia o corrido* (Mexican ballad) on Texas soil that González de Mireles found. The ballad relates the story of Remigio Treviño, a soldier stationed at Camargo who in the early 1860s decided to expel the Americans who were settling along the border. He succeeded in killing ten Americans, but in 1863 he was captured while raiding Rio Grande City and was later hanged. Other songs included are "The Tío Pancho Malo Song" (Mean Uncle Pancho Song), "El Sombrero Ancho" (The Broad-Brimmed Hat), "Coplas Del Payo" (The Rustic's Song), "El Rancho Grande" (The Big Ranch), "La Palomita" (The Little Dove), and "La Triguñita" (The Pretty Brunette).

Comments on the History of Texas Mexicans

In "America Invades the Border Towns," which appeared in the *Southwest Review* (Summer 1930), González de Mireles comments on the rude awakening experienced by the inhabitants along the Texas border at the beginning of the twentieth century. In those parts, Texas-Mexicans had lived quite happily, unaware that they could be considered foreigners and experience racial discrimination. With an insurgence of Anglo Americans from the North and the Middle West, the border towns underwent serious economic changes. Middle-class shopkeepers and grocers went out of business when the new commerce opened chain grocery stores and devised new methods of merchandising. Mexican people began to be banished from public places and social events. Such treatment caused extreme anger and resentment, but many Mexicans realized that they had to assimilate into the American way of life. Their children, who up to that time had gone to Mexican schools, began attending American schools where they were penalized for speaking Spanish. González de Mireles states that the only Mexicans who benefited from the arrival of Americans were the *peones* (agricultural laborers and farmhands), for the new system meant higher wages for them and a simple change of masters. The border situation during the 1930s disturbed González de Mireles, and she hoped that the Americanization of young people might bring an understanding between the Texas-Mexicans and the Anglo Americans.

Creates Colorful Characters

In 1932 González de Mireles published two series of short sketches under the title "Among My People." The first series appeared in the *Southwest Review* in January, and the second series was included in J. Frank Dobie's *Tone the Bell Easy.* The following narratives comprise the first series: "Juan, El Loco" (The Mad John), "Don José Maria," and "Don Tomás." These three tableaux are portrayals of picturesque border characters. The narrator reminisces about the old border communities, which were changed forever by the American way of life. One could still find areas, however, where the language and traditions remained untouched. From one of these areas emerged Juan, El Loco, a strange shepherd whose only worldly possessions were a comb and a broken mirror. He claimed that he had witches inside him ordering him about, a belief supported by the narrator: "It was said by the *vaqueros* and the *rancheros* that he became worse on Fridays and when the moon was full." In the second sketch, Don José María was one of the richest and most pretentious landowners of the lower Rio Grande Valley. He lived like a feudal lord and exercised his authority over his family and his land. However, Don José María would become a lamb when his wife, Doña Margarita, spoke to him. The third sketch, "Don Tomás," provides a glimpse of a man whose absolute patriarchal authority came to an end with the arrival of American law and order.

The second series is made up of "Shelling Corn by Moon Light," "Pedro the Hunter," "The Mail Carrier," "The Perennial Lover," and "Tío Pancho Malo" (Bad Uncle Pancho). "Shelling Corn by Moon Light," recalls the late summer nights when the ranch help congregated at the Big House to shell corn and tell ghost stories. In the second sketch, Pedro the hunter was a famous man among border folk because he spoke English and had seen the world. He had worked on the plantations of the South, had seen the "Tren Volador" (The Swift Train), and had been in Houston. However, Pedro had returned home longing for the familiar sights and smells of the border countryside. "The Mail Carrier" focuses on the character of Tío Esteban (Uncle Esteban), who not only delivered mail, but knew and told "All the scandal of the two counties through which he passed." He was also the Cupid of the area, for he promoted love affairs and even delivered letters free of charge for lovers. "The Perennial Lover" is the story of Carlitos, a man who was in the habit of writing love letters every spring to all eligible ladies. One year, much to his astonishment, a lady accepted his advances and he had to marry her. Finally, the tale of Tio Pancho Malo portrays an old man whose nonconformity with the ways of the world earned him the nickname of "Malo" (Bad).

"The Bullet-Swallower" (1935) depicts a character whose partly paralyzed right arm ended in a clawlike hand with dirty fingers. This deformity and a partially closed eye were the result of numerous fights. Squatting on the floor, he told wild stories about border feuds, bandits, and smugglers while making vicious gestures in the air with an antique knife. According to the narrator, this man was born in the wrong time, for he would have made an excellent conquistador, or perhaps a knight in a chivalry novel. The anecdote, narrated in the first person, reveals that the character was called "Antonio Traga Balas" (Anthony the Bullet-Swallower) because he had been shot in the mouth by a Texas Ranger but had survived the ordeal. On another occasion he was almost frightened to death when he helped a man to die in peace in a miserable shack and went to find some neighbors to come watch the corpse with him until the burial. Not finding anyone to help him, he returned to the shack, which was in flames. At this point of the story González de Mireles's descriptive talent is made evident: "I ran inside. The sight that met my eyes was one I shall ever see. I was nailed to the floor with terror. The corpse, its hair a flaming mass, was sitting up in the coffin where it had so peacefully lain all day. Its glassy, opaque eyes stared into space with a look that saw nothing and its mouth was convulsed into a most horrible grin. I stood there paralyzed by the horror of the scene."

Recounts Spanish Conquest

"Latin Americans" is an essay by González de Mireles included in a 1937 Prentice-Hall publication on the United States minority population, *Our Racial and National Minorities,* edited by Francis J. Brown and Joseph Slabey Roucek. González de Mireles's participation in this early study of American minority groups indicates the professional respect she had acquired in her time. Her entry is documented with interviews and, following an introduction, is divided into three sections: "Cultural Differentiation and Assimilation," "Organizations," and "Contribution to American Life." Utilizing a historical, upper-class perspective, González de Mireles introduces the study by discussing the social class system that Spanish conquistadors implanted in the New World. The *criollos,* descendants of the early Spanish colonizers, were at the top of the socioeconomic structure. The *mestizos,* people of Indian and Spanish ancestry, were next. Their social position varied according to their percentage of Spanish blood, measured by the color of their skin. At the bottom of the social totem pole were the *peones,* who were direct descendants of the Indians. This hierarchy was applied to all Latin Americans regardless of their location in the New World.

González de Mireles also includes a historical account of the presence of Spain in what later became United States territory. The explorations of Juan Ponce de León in Florida, the remarkable journey of Alvar Núñez Cabeza de Vaca from the Gulf of Mexico to the Gulf of California, and the great explorations of Francisco Vázquez de Coronado through the southwestern territories are emphasized. To González de Mireles, all Latin Americans are similar in spirit, for they have been marked by the procedures of the Spanish explorations and conquest. She believed the motto of the National University of Mexico, "Through my race speaks my spirit," might as well be the motto for all Latin Americans in the United States. The annexation of the Spanish Southwest to the United States, which took place with the Treaty of Guadalupe Hidalgo in 1848, was an extremely painful experience for the Latin Americans, especially those of the gentry class who were proud of their Spanish heritage and aristocratic stock. Having lived isolated for centuries, exercising a patriarchal way of life, they considered Americans vandals who had deprived their mother country of a large territorial mass.

González de Mireles provides a review of the Mexican immigration that began with the Mexican Revolution of 1910. Different from the old inhabitants of the Southwest, these immigrants belonged to the underprivileged class and were uneducated to the point of illiteracy; from them came the migrant workers, who face poverty on a daily basis. González de Mireles testifies that these people maintain a fatalistic attitude toward life as a direct result of their Indian heritage.

Emphasizes Latin American Contributions

González de Mireles emphasizes the multiple contributions of Latin Americans to American life and culture in regard to architecture, art, artisan products, film, music, and language. The greatest contribution, however, is the literary influence of Latin American legends, traditions, and ballads, which emerge in American literature. Concluding that Latin American influence in the United States has been constructive, González de Mireles seriously questions why Anglo Americans, who are enthusiastic about Spanish art and culture, have yet to accept the Latin Americans in their midst.

Although they tend to stereotype Chicanos, Jovita González de Mireles's essays and folkloric tableaux are invaluable in the study of the evolutionary process of Hispanic literature. In an epoch when it was almost impossible for Hispanics to stand out in the American intellectual scene, González de Mireles was singled out as a woman of talent. Probably one of the earliest folklorists in the field of Hispanic studies, she will remain one of the most prominent Hispanic figures in the first half of the twentieth century.

Sources:

Mexican American Literature. New York: Harcourt Brace Jovanovich, 1989.

Velázquez-Treviño, Gloria Louise. "Cultural Ambivalence in Early Chicano Prose Fiction." Ph.D. dissertation, Stanford University, 1985.

Velázquez-Treviño, Gloria Louise. "Jovita González: una voz de resistencia cultural en la temprana narrativa chicana," in *Mujer y literatura mexicana y chicana: culturas en contacto: primer coloquio fronterizo 22, 23 y 24 de abril de 1987.* Tijuana, B.C.: El Colegio de la Frontera Norte, 1988, pp. 76-83.

Christine Granados
(1969–)
Editor

Christine Granados is a young, Hispanic American journalist who has made significant contributions to the popular culture of Hispanic American women as contributing editor of the bilingual magazine, *Moderna.* She is an example of many modern Hispanic women in America, women who have been Anglicized from a young age and have had to carve out a new identity within their blended community.

Grows Up in Anglicized Environment

Grandados was born on January 8, 1969 and raised in El Paso, Texas. She is a third-generation Hispanic who recently began investigating her own family heritage. Her father's family came from the Texas border area of Terlingua when it was still a part of Mexico. Her maternal great-grandmother emigrated from the Chihuahua region of

Mexico. The youngest of four children, Granados grew up in a household where both English and Spanish were spoken, however, she never learned to speak Spanish. During Granados's childhood, public schools discouraged knowledge of a second language. Today, Granados is making a concerted effort to learn Spanish and speak it fluently. She is also the first member of her family to acquire a college degree.

Granados credits her mother with inspiring her interest in print journalism. In an editorial in the Winter 1997 issue of *Moderna*, she recalls watching her mother prepare for an evening on the town. "I was mesmerized by her sense of style and beauty. Her jet-black cropped hair and olive complexion made her favorite pair of beige hot pants with matching tunic and platforms look exotic. She introduced me to the world of fashion." Together, they would scour issues of *Vogue* and *Harper's Bazaar* looking for fashions by their favorite Hispanic designers, Oscar de la Renta and Carolina Herrera. Her mother often raved about the feminine styles of the Dominican and Venezuelan fashion mavens.

Gains Support for Journalism Career

Granados's high school journalism teacher, Mrs. Love, supported her interest in journalism and helped her to develop excellent writing skills. She also cites Toni Morrison as her favorite author and inspiration. Another important influence was Ray Hagar, the progressive sports editor of the *Austin American-Statesman*. Because Granados was active in high school softball, soccer, and volleyball, Hagar offered to make her the *Statesman*'s first female sports reporter. She covered national and local sports events and was generally accepted by the local teams. For nine years, she worked as a reporter for newspapers in Texas and California. In addition to the *Austin American-Statesman*, she wrote for the *Long Beach Press-Telegram* and *The El Paso Times*. She also covered the 1992 presidential elections, worked as a police reporter, and wrote full-length feature stories.

Edits Magazine for Hispanic American Women

In 1995, Granados's career path led her to the fledgling *Moderna* magazine, where she accepted a position as a freelance writer. After only five months on the job, Granados was promoted to editor. In March of 1997 *Moderna*, which first appeared as an insert in *Hispanic* magazine, began publication as a national quarterly. *Moderna*, which means "modern woman" in Spanish, is a fashion, beauty, and health magazine for Hispanic American women. It is different from other mainstream women's magazines because it is bilingual and includes phrases that combine both languages into a derivative known as "Spanglish." The use of "Spanglish" provides readers who are proficient in English with the opportunity to improve their Spanish language skills. As editor of *Moderna*, Granados supervised the production staff, developed magazine style and content, and solicited clients for national advertising. She also wrote feature articles such as "Tough Enough for Hollywood," which explored the life and career of the Hispanic actress Constance Marie.

Granados is well known for authoring a controversial article entitled "How Latina Are You?" which describes how Hispanic American women are guilty of stereotyping each other. One example of this concerns the debate over what to call people of Spanish-American heritage. To Granados, it is a moot point. As she remarked in Ramon Renteria's article in *The El Paso Times*, "I'm not a good Chicana, but I can get the attitude. I call myself Latina, Latino, Mexican-American, Hispanic. Nothing offends me." The same disparity applies to the misconception that most Hispanics are Catholic. "I'm agnostic. Everybody just assumes I go to church every Sunday and that I'm a Catholic." Granados also finds it difficult to be a prominent woman within the Hispanic community. Hispanic women are not encouraged to appear too proud or intelligent because this interferes with traditional family values. Outward signs of personal success are also not considered attractive qualities for a Hispanic woman.

In 1997, Granados was invited to participate as a panelist at the Elizabeth Cady Stanton/Susan B. Anthony Conversations on Contemporary Issues, which was sponsored by the Susan B. Anthony University Center of the University of Rochester. As a participant at this event, Granados was challenged to discover the role that Hispanic American women play in the feminist movement. In her March/April, 1998 editorial for *Moderna*, Granados writes, "With the help of authors Ana Castillo and Afda Hurado, I discovered that Latinas are creating our own brand of feminism. Not only are we helping to redefine the American standard of beauty, eating habits and family ties, we are finally staking our claim in the United States."

Pursues Advanced Degree in Creative Writing

Christine Granados stepped down as editor of *Moderna* in 1998 to pursue her master's degree in creative writing. However, she continues to serve as contributing editor. Her goal is to eventually write a book about growing up as a Hispanic girl in El Paso. She is married to Ken Estencooke and lives in Rockdale, Texas.

Sources:

Grey, Joe. "Christine Granados: Spanish, English or Spanglish, *Moderna* editor gives Latinas a choice. *Texas Business,* April, 1997, p. 14.

Renteria, Ramon. 'No Hablo Español': Hispanics fight stereotypes based on skin color, surnames. *The El Paso Times,* n.d.

Jackie Guerra
(1967–)
Actress, comedienne, activist

Selected filmography:

Dave's World. CBS-TV., 1994.
First Time Out. WB-TV, 1995.
Selena. Warner Bros., 1997.

Overview

Actress and comedienne Jackie Guerra is the first Latina to star in her own television series. Guerra worked as a union organizer and political consultant before turning to stand-up comedy. She quickly got her own television series. Guerra has since moved on to feature films, appearing in *Selena.* She is presently developing her own talk and variety show.

Early Life and Career

Guerra was born to poor Mexican immigrants in San Diego in 1967. Her father worked his way up the ladder in the company that owns Jack-in-the-Box restaurants, starting as a dishwasher. Guerra grew up in Los Angeles, but has also lived in Mexico and Brazil. She attended college at Yale and completed her degree in political science back home at University of California, San Diego.

Guerra worked for the Democratic Party on political campaigns and, as a union organizer, working with César Chávez at one point. Her first experience with comedy came in 1992, when she took the microphone at an amateur night competition. She won the evening's contest and pursued a career in stand-up comedy. She toured the college comedy circuit, where her political and issue-oriented humor was well-received.

After a recurring role on the CBS comedy *Dave's World,* Columbia Pictures Television tapped Guerra to head up her own situation comedy, aptly titled *First Time Out,* on the newly-created Warner Brothers Network. She became the first Latina to star in her own prime-time series. While the show did not find an audience and lasted only thirteen episodes, Guerra described the series to N. F. Mendoza of the *Los Angeles Times* as a celebration of "life in LA . . . show[ing] women of all shapes, sizes, creeds, backgrounds [that] they can make it and not wait for some guy in armor to take them away."

Guerra appeared on the big screen in 1996 in the biography of slain singer Selena. Guerra played Selena's sister Suzette. The story was close to Guerra's heart. She told *The Dallas Morning News,* "A lot of us were enamored of the story and had lived through the rising of Selena's star as fans. But I don't think any of us were prepared for the emotional impact that being part of this movie was going to have."

Breaking Down Barriers

Guerra realizes that stereotyping is prevalent for Latinos in the film industry. As she said in *Variety,* "The natural tendency is for casting directors to call me in for Latina roles . . . They're looking for someone with an accent, or somebody who looks like the Latinos of our pop culture understanding. And I think that as a country we still have a border mentality." Guerra told the *Los Angeles Times* that she feels Latinos can learn from the struggle of African Americans in Hollywood. "What we are learning from the African American community is you can work without having to shuck and jive. You can make money shucking and jiving but why? It doesn't feel good to get rich playing something you're not proud of."

Guerra knows that to overcome these obstacles, Latin-themed shows and movies must be successful in the ratings and at the box office. Guerra knew if people did not see *Selena* early in its release, it would not last in theaters. She explained to the *Rocky Mountain News* that, "When films like *Selena* come to the theaters, we have to show our presence so Hollywood knows Latinos support Latino projects. We need to stand up and say, 'Presente!'"

Guerra believes the Latin community must support its own and, at the same time, become part of the mainstream entertainment community. She explained to the *Los Angeles Times,* "While we have to create and nurture our own and stick together, we still have to work with everyone else. We have to have a collaborative, not a confrontational, attitude. Staying true to our experience and perspective is the change." She looks forward to the day when Latin actors are considered for all roles, no matter their ethnicity. "Until we're playing Jewish roles, Italian roles, WASP roles in mainstream movies, anyone who casts Marisa Tomei [in *The Perez Family*] as Cuban has got a lot to answer for."

Guerra has also had to face another obstacle: her battle with her weight and an eating disorder. She remembers thinking she "was the grossest person in the world." She was chastised by producers to lose weight. She told the *Orange County Register,* "For 13 years of my life I was bulimic and very sick, in and out of programs all the time, always going back, very close to dying at one point. It's still a huge issue for me, every day of my life. I sat next to supermodel Cindy Crawford on a plane recently and I realized her thighs were the size of my forearm." Guerra says she still struggles with ". . . the emotions that related to eating and dieting and purging."

Guerra felt uncomfortable with some of the weight jokes on her series; however, Guerra was not given sufficient creative control to eliminate them. She felt it was more important to compromise on issues of control so that one day members of her ethnically-diverse cast and crew could move up to positions of greater influence. She hopes one day to be a producer herself.

Personal Life

Guerra enjoys cooking, particularly Mexican food. She spends her free time watching films, especially foreign movies and classics. Guerra admitted to the *Los Angeles Times* that she also likes "campy stuff, like *Valley of the Dolls*." She enjoys shopping in "weird places" like Tijuana and East L.A.

Awards and Charitable Work

Guerra has devoted her time to many worthy causes. In 1997 she supported the struggle of the United Farm Workers in their pursuit of a fair contract with the strawberry industry. She has also supported youth alcohol prevention programs in Los Angeles, as well as the Association for the Advancement of Mexican Americans.

Guerra was nominated for the National Council of La Raza's 1998 American Latino Media Arts Award for her work in *Selena*. Guerra is currently developing a variety and talk show of her own. While she faces stiff competition in this arena, Guerra has always been ready to face challenges. As Guerra told *The Tampa Tribune* she has followed her own advice to have fun and not ". . . waste time or energy on negative people." And with her characteristic humor, she also warns people to "avoid excessive housework."

Sources:

Aguilar, Louis. "Release of 'Selena' Film Bringing Big Expectations From Hollywood." *The Fort-Worth Star-Telegram*, March 26, 1997, p. 2.

Cabrera, Cloe. "Hispanic Notables Reveal Resolutions." *The Tampa Tribune*, June 1, 1996, p. 1.

Chagollan, Steve. "Hollywood's One-Way Mirror." *Variety*, November 17, 1997, p. 5.

"County Scan." *The Orange County Register*, July 21, 1997, p. B3.

Davies, Jonathan. "Six ALMA noms Go To 'Selena.'" *The Hollywood Reporter*, March 13, 1998.

Dougherty, Robin. "When The Spanish Language Is Spoken On Prime Time TV Today, There's No More 'Splainin' To Do, Yiddish Already Blazed That Trail." *Chicago Tribune*, April 3, 1997, p. 1.

Guerra, Jackie. "My Favorite Weekend." *Los Angeles Times*, April 3, 1997, p. F7.

Guthrie, Marisa. "TV Book; Plugged In." *The Boston Herald*, July 20, 1997, p. 4.

Gutierrez, Eric. "In The Game At Last; A New Generation Is Boldly Defying The Old Stereotype Of The Hollywood Latina As Maid Or Seductress." *Los Angeles Times*, March 16, 1997, p. 3.

———. "Awakening Giant?; Latinos in Film Industry Rally Their Own Support." *Variety*, April 27, 1997, p. 27.

Hodge, Shelby. "Excellence Acknowledged; Mexican American Group Honors Community Standouts." *The Houston Chronicle*, February 17, 1997, p. 3.

Littlefield, Kinney. "Glorying In The Single Life, Latina Style: Jackie Guerra's Fight Against Type." *The Record*, September 24, 1995, p. 4.

Mendoza, N. F. "Guerra Gets Counted On 'First Time Out.'" *Los Angeles Times*, September 23, 1995, p. 8D.

Rebac, Lydia. "Breaking Down Barriers; Hispanic Actress, Stand-Up Uses Humor and Her New Series To Bring Diverse Groups Together." *Fort Lauderdale Sun-Sentinel*, September 23, 1995, p. 1D.

Schneider, Karen S. et al. "Mission Impossible." *People*, June 3, 1996, p. 64.

Slewinski, Christy. "'Out'-Of-The-Ordinary Sitcom." *New York Daily News*, November 16, 1995, p. 106.

"Strawberry Chain." *City News Service*, August 27, 1997.

Sumner, Jane. "Selena Reborn." *The Dallas Morning News*, November 17, 1996, p. 1C.

Vasquez, Sherri. "Denver Hispanics Sing the Praises of 'Selena' at Premiere." *Rocky Mountain News*, March 24, 1997, p. 18D.

Guerrero Fuentes, Tina
See **Fuentes, Tina Guerrero**

Gutiérrez, Margarita Isabel
See **Gutiérrez, Margo**

Margo Gutiérrez
(1952–)
Librarian, bibliographer, editor

Selected writings:

Sourcebook on Central American Refugee Policy. Edited with Milton H. Jamail and Chandler Stolp. University of Texas and the Central America Resource Center, 1985.

The Border Guide: Institutions and Organizations of the United States-Mexico Borderlands. Edited with Milton H. Jamail. Center for Mexican American Studies, University of Texas at Austin, 1992.

Encyclopedia of Mexican American Civil Rights. Edited with Matt Meier. Greenwood Press, Forthcoming.

Overview

Margo Gutiérrez is the Mexican American and Latino Studies librarian and bibliographer at the University of Texas at Austin. The Benson Latin American Collection is housed in the Mexican American and Latino Studies Library and was established in 1974. Its purpose is to provide information on Mexican American and U.S. Latino history and culture to both students and the faculty of the Center for Mexican American Studies. Gutiérrez is responsible for ordering materials for this collection and also provides specialized reference services and bibliographic instruction.

Spends Formative Years in Arizona

Gutiérrez was born Margarita Isabel Gutiérrez in Tucson, Arizona, on June 11, 1952. She was called Margo from birth since her grandmother's name was also Margarita. Her father, Francisco Yslas Gutiérrez, was a butcher; her mother, Maria Velia Jimenez, owned and operated a small grocery store. Gutiérrez lived in Tucson until 1982, except for a year she spent in Guadalajara, Jalisco, Mexico. She also traveled extensively, sometimes for research, in countries such as Guatemala, Honduras, Belize, and Nicaragua. In 1978, she married Milton H. Jamail, a Ph.D. university lecturer on Latino politics and freelance journalist, and a year later received her bachelor of arts degree in Latin American studies from the University of Arizona. She obtained a master of library science degree from the same institution in 1980. Her area of concentration in her master's degree was providing library services for Spanish-speaking people and reference sources in the social sciences.

After obtaining her M.L.S., Gutiérrez worked as a cataloger at the University of Arizona until 1982, then obtained a position as the readers' services librarian at Texas Lutheran College in Seguin from 1982-84. Here she and her husband had their first son, Gabriel Enrique Jamail-Gutiérrez, who was born in 1983. They moved to Austin in 1984 and a year later had another son, Jorge Samir Jamail-Gutiérrez. Gutiérrez started her position at the Benson Latin American Collection at the University of Texas at Austin in 1987 and continued her education by obtaining a master of arts degree in Latin American studies at the University of Texas in 1989.

Receives Professional Recognition

Gutiérrez has been the recipient of numerous awards recognizing her outstanding academic work and her contributions to the field of library science and Mexican American and Latino studies. These include two research grants from the University of Arizona in 1980, a Graduate Opportunity Program fellowship for graduate study at the University of Texas at Austin from 1982-84, a Minority Graduate Development Award from the American Lutheran Church in 1986-87, and the Charles Wilson Hackett Award for outstanding graduate student in the area of Latin American studies from the Austin chapter of the Pan American Roundtable in 1989. In addition, she received the Director's Staff Honors Award from the General Libraries at the University of Texas at Austin in 1997.

Gutiérrez has been active in many professional organizations, including the National Association for Chicana and Chicano Studies, the American Library Association (1987-91), and the liaison with Mexican Libraries Subcommittee of the International Relations Committee (1990-91). She was also chair of the Reference and Adult Services divisional committee for library services to the Spanish-speaking from 1987-88, and in 1999 will serve as a program committee member of the Texas Library Association.

Creates Publications and Presentations

Gutiérrez has compiled many bibliographies on Mexican Americans and Mexican American studies for the Benson Latin American Collection, including *Mexican American Biographical Sources* (1997), *Mexican Americans in Texas: Notable Works, 1990-1996* (1997), *The Anti-Immigrant Backlash: Selected Sources* (1996), and *La Chicana: Work, Family, Education and Gender* (1995), among others. She has also published articles, such as "The Mexican American Library Program and Its Archival Collections," in *Nahuatl to Rayuela: The Latin American Collection at Texas,* edited by Dave Oliphant (University of Texas, 1992); "Israel's Military Role in Central America," with Milton Jamail in *Central America and the Middle East: The Internationalization of the Crises,* edited by Damián J. Fernández (Florida International Press, 1990); and "What the Academic Library Needs: Point of View of a Chicana Library Student," in *Final Report and Working Papers, SALALM XXV* (Seminar on the Acquisition of Latin American Library Materials, 1981).

With her husband, Gutiérrez also wrote a book titled *The Border Guide: Institutions and Organizations of the United States-Mexico Borderlands,* published in 1992. In this book, Gutiérrez and Jamail list organizations and institutions located along the entire stretch of the U.S.-Mexico border and provide short histories and descriptions of the major twin cities along the border. Louis Mendoza of *Modern Fiction Studies* stated that the guide is "an extremely useful source for anyone interested in conducting border studies or who could benefit from a brief introduction to the communities along the border." Gutiérrez also has a forthcoming book, written with Matt Meier, titled *Encyclopedia of Mexican American Civil Rights.*

In addition, Gutiérrez is active in presenting papers on the Mexican American Library Program to professional organizations such as the Society of Southwest Archivists, the National Association for Chicano Studies, and the Southwest Council of Latin American Studies. With her background and experience, Gutiérrez can certainly be called an expert in the field of Mexican American and Latino reference sources.

Witnesses Changes in the Field

Gutiérrez commented on the changes she has seen in her field in *CIRD Bibliographer Newsletter* when she said, "Before I came to this position over ten years ago, my predecessors had concentrated primarily on collecting materials related to Mexican Americans or Chicanos concentrated in the southwestern U.S. Today, the focus of collection development efforts is much broader. . . . Immigration is still an issue, but it's not just from Mexico anymore, nor are Latin American immigrants confined to the traditional receiving states of California and Texas." Acquisitions and collection development are just one part of Gutiérrez's job, but she said, "The 'Latinization' . . . of the U.S. keeps me awfully busy."

In the same publication Gutiérrez stated that she is ". . . proud of the accomplishments of the Mexican American Library Program in making this component of the General Libraries among the finest in the country. . . " and ". . . to be affiliated with this gem of a collection is truly awesome." According to Gutiérrez, the Mexican American Library Program is one of the top three in the country, along with the University of California at Berkeley and the University of California at Los Angeles.

Current Address: Benson Latin American Collection, Mexican American and Latino Studies Library, Univ. of Texas at Austin, Austin, TX 78713-7619.

Sources:

Bethel, Kari. Telephone conversation and correspondence with Margo Gutiérrez, March 1998.
CIRD Bibliographer Newsletter. January 1998.
CLNet Home Page. Available at http://www.latino.sscnet.-ucla.edu/library/services.malp.html.
Mendoza, Louis. "The Border Between Us: Contact Zone or Battle Zone?" *Modern Fiction Studies.* Spring 1994, pp. 133-136.
The University of Texas at Austin Library Online Home Page. Available at http://www.lib.utexas.edu/subject/area/mals.html.

Sandra Guzmán
Editor

Sandra Guzmán is editor-in-chief of *Latina* magazine, the first bilingual lifestyle magazine for Hispanic women. As editor, she provides a much needed forum for the Hispanic American female voice nationwide.

Sandra Guzmán

Guzmán was born in Puerto Rico, where her mother, Lydia, was a *madre de leche,* or wet nurse, to many local children in Las Cucharas, the tiny fishing village in southern Puerto Rico where they lived. When young Sandra objected to her mother's role as a wet nurse, her mother explained that she was blessed with plenty of healthy milk and that there was enough for her own babies and everybody else's. As a result, many young mothers sought Lydia for help with nourishing their infants. The Guzmán family eventually left Puerto Rico and settled in Jersey City, New Jersey. Guzmán graduated from Rutgers University where she received a bachelor of arts degree in history and philosophy.

Begins Journalism Career at *El Diario/La Prensa*

Guzmán began her journalism career as a reporter for *El Diario/La Prensa,* the oldest and most widely circulated Spanish-language newspaper in New York City. During her tenure at *El Diario/La Prensa,* she was an investigative reporter and wrote about education and city politics. She later served as senior spokeswoman to the former New York City Controller, Elizabeth Holtzman.

Breaks Ground on Hispanic Television

After leaving *El Diario/La Prensa,* Guzmán joined WNJU-TV, Telemundo's local affiliate in New York, where she worked as assignment manager and public affairs producer for the evening news. During her career at WNJU-TV, the news program received high ratings in the competitive Spanish-language media market. She moved on to become public affairs producer of *Enfoque 47* and produced a program entitled *Embargo Contra Cuba*, which analyzed the controversial U.S. embargo of Cuba. The program won high acclaim and earned Guzmán an Emmy Award from the New York Chapter of the National Academy of Television Arts and Sciences in 1995. It also marked the first time that a program on Telemundo received this prestigious award.

Following her success with *Enfoque 47*, Guzmán accepted a position as segment producer for Fox 5's *Good Day, New York*, one of New York's top-rated morning programs. Guzmán wrote and produced segments that depicted urban life in New York within the various Hispanic cultures. It is this insight and incisiveness that Guzmán brings to her current position as editor of *Latina* magazine.

Magazine Focuses on Hispanic Women's Issues

Every article in *Latina* is published in both English and Spanish, and many of the advertisements are in Spanish. The articles in the magazine tackle mainstream issues with an emphasis on how they relate to Hispanic women. For example, in her Editor's Letter for the April, 1998 issue of *Latina*, Guzmán addresses the problem of conflicting nutritional values. "Imagine, a so-called nutritious program that tells me I can't eat *arroz con pollo* or *pasteles*. As far as I'm concerned, that's anti-Latino, and I won't go for it. *Nuestra comida* is chock-full of nutrition, so what are those 'experts' talking about, anyway?" She also mentions an item in the same issue that dramatizes a Hispanic American female's story of family pressure, ". . . first to marry than to have *bebecitos*. I'm sure you'll relate to the writer's plight."

Guzmán's leadership abilities and contributions to her community have been recognized. In 1998, she was among seven Rutgers University alumni to receive special honors for outstanding leadership in their communities and contributions to the arts. Her commitment to excellence in her journalistic endeavors will certainly hold *Latina* in good stead.

Current Address: Latina, 1500 Broadway, Ste. 700, New York, NY 10036.

Sources:

Guzmán, Sandra. Editor's Letter, *Latina*, April, 1998.
Guzmán, Sandra. Editor's Letter, *Latina*, May, 1998.

H

Laura Harring
(1964–)
Actress

Selected filmography:

The Alamo: Thirteen Days to Glory (TV movie). 1987.
General Hospital (TV series). 1990.
The Forbidden Dance. 1990.
Dead Women in Lingerie. 1991.
Rio Diablo. 1993.
Exit to Eden. 1994.
Sunset Beach (TV series). 1997.

Early Life

Laura Harring's life and career have been marked by the highs and lows so characteristic of Hispanic American women who seek to excel in the performing arts. As the first Hispanic Miss USA, Harring had many open doors into the entertainment industry. However, Harring has had to fight Hollywood stereotypes of Hispanic Americans to win decent roles. In spite of the lack of quality roles for Hispanic American actresses, this talented actress has demonstrated that she is equally at home in television and movie roles.

Leads Colorful Life

Laura Harring's life has been as colorful as some of the roles she has played. The daughter of Maria, a secretary who later became a psychotherapist, and an farmer, Raymond, she was born Laura Martinez-Herring on March 3, 1964, in Los Mochis, a city in western Mexico, the second of three sisters. Her parents divorced in 1971, and her mother later married Gaston Lima, a Cuban lawyer and doctor, and the family relocated to San Antonio. The couple prospered in real estate, and life was comfortable until 1976, when tragedy struck during a family outing. Caught in a bizarre highway shooting incident, 12-year old Laura was grazed by a stray bullet to the head, leaving a wound that required 13 stitches. Young Laura escaped death "by a few millimeters," according to her sister Rita in an interview with *People Weekly.* Recovering from her injury, she went on to graduate from Aiglon College, a Swiss boarding school, in 1982. Selected to participate in a special program, Harring worked in a manual labor program in India. Always adventurous, she backpacked through Asia and found herself the unwilling object of the affections of her employer, a Philippine restaurateur. For eight months he refused to let her leave, withholding her passport until her mother cabled that she intended to "come and get her." Harring returned to Texas, but postponed college because she arrived too late to enroll that school year.

Becomes First Hispanic Miss USA

A reversal of fortune led Harring to enter show business: the family lost extensive cattle ranch holdings in Mexico as a result of agrarian reform legislation. While working in a boutique, Harring was enticed to enter a beauty pageant for a trip to Europe and won the Miss El Paso title and then the Miss USA title in 1985. As the first Hispanic American Miss USA, she enjoyed the spotlight.

Traditionally the pageant is a springboard for young women's careers, especially in acting. "Winning opened a lot of doors for me," she told *People Weekly.* As she crowned the new Miss USA at the before television cameras, Harring was being scouted by network representatives. She was selected to audition for an NBC television movie, *The Alamo: Thirteen Days to Glory,* starring the acclaimed Puerto Rican actor Raul Julia as Santa Ana. She played Julia's lover, and while her part was small, it was a showcase role in a prestigious project.

Encounters Stereotypes

Harring seemed to have a bright future in show business, but the beautiful Hispanic American newcomer quickly encountered an old problem in the entertainment industry—the dearth of good roles for and about Hispanic American women. Although the numbers and quality of opportunities for women in the industry have improved over the years, Hispanic American women have not generally shared the gains of other minorities. Hispanic American women often find themselves restricted to stereotyped parts such as domestics, exotic beauties, spitfires, and victims. They seldom have an opportunity to audition for roles that reach beyond the token images portrayed in the U.S. media. According to Clara E. Rodriguez in the book *Latin Looks: Images of Latinas and Latinos in the U.S. Media,* "What makes Latina images different is that there are so few images, that they are so narrow, and that lately they are so consistently narrow and lower class. . . ." Harring had a taste of this stereotyping when she joined the cast of *General Hospital*, one of daytime television's most highly-rated soaps, in 1990. Her character was focus of the first Hispanic storyline in daytime drama. While Harring found the experience rewarding and the exposure helpful to her career, she was discontented with the role as written. "I was a victim all the time, and I hate that," she told *New York Times* reporter Justine Elias, describing her role as Carla Greco, a Central American refugee.

Harring's movie roles were likewise constricted to stereotypes. She made her feature film debut as Nisa, a Brazilian princess in *The Forbidden Dance* in 1990, and the critics were not kind to her or to the film. The plot had Nisa travel to the United States, work briefly as a maid, fall in love with her employer's son, and battle a malevolent corporation with him to save the rainforest. The climactic scene featured her doing the lambada on national television, appealing to U.S. citizens to join a boycott of the corporation. In 1991, she appeared as Marcia in the oddly titled *Dead Women in Lingerie,* a spoof about a serial killer who targets immigrant seamstresses. Another role that did not do credit to her ability or intelligence was a supporting part in the widely panned 1994 film *Exit to Eden*. Audiences avoided the adaptation of Anne Rice's novel about kinky sex despite the presence of popular stars Rosie O'Donnell, Dana Delany, and Dan Ackroyd.

Television has provided frequent opportunities for Harring to guest star in series and in television movies. Her credits include an appearance on the popular *Baywatch* series, as well as *Silk Stalkings* and *Flipper*. The year 1993 brought another high-profile television movie, *Rio Diablo*. Notable as a vehicle for country singers Kenny Rogers, Naomi Judd, and Travis Tritt, Harring played Tritt's stolen bride in the film. She was also in the original cast of producer Aaron Spelling's series *Sunset Beach* in 1997. Harring played the "smart and feisty" policewoman Paula Stevens. In a *New York Times* interview, she expressed her appreciation for a more substantial part than the one she had played on *General Hospital*: "When I joined *Sunset Beach*, I said, 'I'm not going to be a pushover anymore. I may wear a little more hair spray than most cops, but police are normal people with real, full lives.'" Her role on the show ended in December of 1997.

Harring believes better roles will come her way, citing Meryl Streep as the actress she most admires. She was briefly married to Count Carl Edward von Bismarck from 1987 to 1989. The marriage ended over Harring's insistence on pursuing her own career. She lives in Brentwood, CA, and enjoys painting, dancing, and writing poetry.

Sources:

Elias, Justine. "Establishing a Soap is No Day at the Beach." *New York Times,* February 23, 1997.

Lipton, Michael A. and John Griffiths. "Riding Waves: Sunset Beach Vixen Laura Harring Knows About Ups and Downs." *People Weekly,* October 27, 1997, pp. 65-66.

Rodriguez, Clara E., ed. *Latin Looks: Images of Latinas and Latinos in the U.S. Media.* Boulder: Westview Press, 1997.

Tucker, Ken. "Rio Diablo" (review). *Entertainment Weekly,* February 26, 1993, p. 49.

Salma Hayek
(1968–)
Actress, model, media executive, entrepreneur

Selected filmography:

The Sinbad Show. Fox, 1993.
Mi vida loca. Cineville, Inc., 1994. Also known as *My Crazy Life.*
El Callegon de los Milagros. Almeda Films, 1995.
Desperado. Columbia Pictures, 1995.
Fair Game. Warner Bros., 1995.
Fled. Metro Goldwyn Mayer, 1996.
From Dusk Till Dawn. Miramax Films, 1996.
Breaking Up, 1997.
The Hunchback. TNT, 1997.
Fools Rush In. Columbia Pictures, 1997.
54. Redeemable Pictures/Miramax Films, 1998.
Dogma. Miramax Films, 1998.
The Velocity of Gary, 1998.
The Wild, Wild West, Warner Bros., 1998.
Frida. Trimark Pictures, 1999.

Overview

Salma Hayek is the first Mexican Hollywood actress to have a leading role in an U.S. film since the 1930s. The young star shared top billing in the 1997 romantic comedy *Fools Rush In* and has appeared in films with such Hollywood celebrities as Antonio Banderas (*Desperado,* 1995) and Quentin Tarantino (*From Dusk Till Dawn,* 1996). She has been nominated for her film performances in both Mexican and U.S. movie award ceremonies, and she beat out Madonna for the title role in a film about Mexican artist Frida Kahlo. Apart from her acting career, she is considered to be one of the symbolic leaders in Mexico's NAFTA generation, a politically influential group of young adults.

Hayek was born September 26, 1968, in Coatzacoalcos, Veracruz, Mexico, the daughter of a Mexican mother and Lebanese father. The hot climate of a Mexican Gulf Coast port where local beaches were often closed because of

Salma Hayek

chemical spills from the local oil refinery was an incentive to many youngsters to flee into air-conditioned theaters; but Hayek's love of film was a true passion. Her dreams of becoming a movie star developed at an early age, and trips to the matinee with her father were regular Sunday afternoon events. When she was a teen, her affluent family sent her to the United States to attend a Roman Catholic boarding school in Louisiana; but she was expelled for playing pranks. Later, she studied international relations and drama at the Universidad Iberoamericana in Mexico City.

Gets Started in Acting

By the time Hayek was in her early twenties she was a successful soap opera star on Mexican television. Her first real acting role was in the soap *Nuevo Amanecer.* In 1989 she was starring in the title role of the television series, *Teresa.* Her performance as Teresa won her several awards, including the Premio TV y Novela and the Heraldo, Mexico's equivalent of the Emmy. Despite a successful television career in her native country, Hayek longed for Hollywood. She told Laura Lopez in *Time,* "I didn't want to act in soap operas the rest of my life. I wasn't interested in [social] position but in artistic integrity." Determined to chase after her dream, in 1991 Hayek shocked her fans by moving to Los Angeles with meager English-language skills, little money, and no job offers. The United States was a different world, and the former Mexican soap star did not find success quickly. She told Michael Atkinson in *Interview,* "I knocked on many doors and got turned down

many times." For the next three years, Hayek struggled for bit parts and improved her English at Shakespearean workshops. She returned to Mexico briefly to play a sweet-natured barrio woman who becomes a prostitute in the acclaimed film *El Callegon de los Milagros*(1995). Hayek's performance earned her an Ariel nomination for best actress (Mexico's version of the American Academy Awards).

U.S. Film Career Takes Off

After appearing in a regular role on *The Sinbad Show,* a short-lived television series, Hayek's luck in the United States eventually turned. Her first big break came in 1994, when she managed to get a one-line part in the film, *Mi vida loca.* Afterwards, appearing on a Spanish-language talk show in Los Angeles, Hayek told the host that although she wanted to do U.S. films, there were not any roles available for Latin women—something she intended to change. Director Robert Rodriguez and his producer wife, Elizabeth Avellan, saw Hayek on the talk show and called her to audition for *Desperado,* the sequel to the highly praised *El Mariachi.* She got the part. Hayek told *Entertainment Weekly,* "No one else believed in me then, and I had nearly lost faith in myself. But they [Rodriguez and Avellan] saw something that others didn't. . . ."

In 1995's *Desperado,* Hayek was featured opposite Spanish actor Antonio Banderas. A steamy love scene with Banderas favored her with a "Best Kiss" nomination at the MTV Movie Awards. More important, her role in this film caught the attention of other Hollywood directors. She went on to parts in movies such as *Fair Game* (1995) and the action-comedy *Fled* (1996), in which she appeared as the smart, soft-hearted hostage of escaped convicts played by Laurence Fishburne and Stephen Baldwin. (Commenting on Hayek, Fishburne stated, "Salma has the kind of comedic timing that people like Lucille Ball had.") In Robert Rodriguez/Quentin Tarantino-directed *From Dusk Till Dawn* (1996), Hayek had a provocative cameo as a snake-charming, bikini-wearing vampire called Satanico Pandemonium—a role that some in the Latin community felt to be a waste of Hayek's talent.

Although Hayek seems grateful to have had parts in all her features, she is aware of being typecast as the "spitfire," or "Latin vamp" characters to which many women of her ethnicity have been limited. As her career grows, Hayek sees herself in a wider variety of roles. Her more recent film and television characters have proved her versatility. In the film *Breaking Up* (1997), she played a character not written particularly for an Hispanic American woman. In TNT's *The Hunchback,* she starred as Esmeralda. But it was not until the romantic comedy *Fools Rush In* that Hayek starred in her first major motion picture as the leading lady.

Released on Valentine's Day in 1997 to mixed reviews, *Fools Rush In* is a story about a Mexican American woman named Isabel (Hayek) and an Anglo young man (played by

Matthew Perry of the television series *Friends* fame) who have a one-night stand that results in Isabel's pregnancy—which leads to a hasty Las Vegas marriage. The story revolves around the newlyweds adjusting to conflicts in cultures. Hayek sought the part of Isabel for nearly three years. Once she had it, she advised director Andy Tennant to include a scene in which Isabel lights candles in a church while discussing her pregnancy with her mother. Hayek argued that any Roman Catholic Mexican woman would discuss such an issue with her mother—and Tennant agreed. "What Salma brings. . . is production smarts," Tennant told Lopez. "She's not just concerned with herself and her role, but with the whole production. She looks at material like a studio executive, which is rare. Most actresses just aren't interested."

NAFTA Generation

Both Hollywood and Mexico admire Hayek for her professional intelligence and ambition. Outside film stardom, however, she is considered a leader in what is known as Mexico's NAFTA generation. Named after 1994's North American Free Trade Agreement, the NAFTA generation is emerging as Mexico's largest group of young adults poised to shape the future of that country since the 1920s. *Time* magazine said of Hayek, "[She is] a strong-minded individualist who is willing to trash the rules and thumb her nose at Mexico's autocratic elite—a rebel without an ideological cause. . . . She is more than an opinionated starlet." Hayek, however, is uncomfortable with her connection to the NAFTA generation. She told Tim Padgett in *Time*, "I don't think I represent them as much as I'm just part of them. We shouldn't be bitter toward Mexico: our generation should be about having the choices our parents didn't have, whether it's politics or movies."

Signs Contract with Revlon

Hayek seems to have it all: success, brains, and beauty. In 1996 she was chosen by *People* magazine as among the 50 most beautiful people in the world. She signed a contract with cosmetics manufacturer Revlon in 1997 to appear in their commercials and ads. Although she does not believe in working out at the gym ("You're practically eating other people's sweat," she is often quoted to have remarked), beauty regimens and rituals are not unpracticed. As a child, Hayek's grandmother would shave Hayek's hair and clip her eyebrows in the belief that the ritual would provide a more luxurious regrowth. And, with the exception of an occasional cigar, Hayek claims not to smoke or do drugs, and she rarely drinks alcohol.

Aims for Lifetime of Movies

"I aim for a lifetime of movies," Hayek told Michael Atkinson. With several films already lined up in her future, her career does not seem to be slowing down. Hayek will appear in the following films scheduled for production or release in 1998: *54,* a Mark Christopher debut film about the legendary Studio 54 disco in New York City at the height of its glory; *Dogma,* a supernatural comedy by director Kevin Smith; a wrenching love story by director Dan Ireland titled *The Velocity of Gary; The Wild, Wild West,* a Barry Sonnenfeld film that co-stars Will Smith and Kevin Kline and is based loosely on the 1960s television adventure series; and *Frida,* a Roberto Sneider film in which Hayek will portray the famous Mexican painter Frida Kahlo. As Laura Winters expressed in an interview that appeared in the June issue of *Elle,* "She is now finally getting the chance to show her range and to play roles that demonstrate her emotional versatility as an actress. . . ."

An intelligent, beautiful, and respected actress, Hayek has come a long way since arriving in the United States. For example, she has formed her own film production company, Ventanarosa, and has been involved for a long time on the creative level with the Frida Kahlo film. She told Padgett, "When I got to Hollywood, being Mexican was considered so uncool. . . . If I have my way, that's going to change." Hayek is clearly doing her part.

Sources:

Atkinson, Michael. "Take a Hayek!" *Interview,* February 1997, p. 112.

Dam, Julie K.L. "Beauty Plus Brains Steering Her Own Course to Stardom." *Time,* July 7, 1996, p. 66.

"Fled Features Masterful Collaboration. . . ." *New York Voice Inc./Harlem USA,* July 24, 1996, p. 18.

Guardado, Sandra. "Love Bridges Different Cultures." *El Sol Del Valle,* February 20, 1997, p. 4.

Mournian, Thomas. "Salma Mousse." *Los Angeles Magazine,* August 1996, p. 85.

Padgett, Tim. "Salma, the Free Spirit. . . ." *Time,* April 14, 1997, p. 42.

"Salma Hayek." *People,* May 6, 1996, p. 168.

Winters, Laura. "She's Gotta Have It." *Elle,* June 1998, pp. 122–126.

Ester Hernández
(1944–)
Artist, civil rights activist, women's rights activist

Ester Hernández is an activist in the Chicano art movement, using the art forms of printmaking, murals, and pastels. In a personal statement about her work, she talked

Ester Hernández

about counteracting negative images of her countrywomen "... to visually depict the dignity, strength, experiences, and dreams of Chicana/Latina women. As a Chicana artist, I believe it is important to produce and disseminate positive images of our varied lives...." Now living and working in San Francisco, CA, her works have been exhibited throughout the United States, Latin America, Europe, Africa, and Russia. She has been artist-in-residence for many years in the Oakland schools and senior art programs and has received numerous awards and grants for her work.

Hernández was born in 1944 in the Sierra Nevada foothills in the central San Joaquin Valley of California, the sixth child of farmworker parents. Her mother, Luz Medina, practiced the family art of embroidery brought from North Central Mexico and her father, Simon Hernández, raised in Texas and of Yaqui heritage, was an amateur photographer and visual artist. Her maternal grandfather was a master carpenter who made religious sculptures in his spare time. With this family and community heritage, Hernández believes, "My background has taught me that we Chicanos must continually strive for beauty and spirituality. This beauty—found in both nature and the arts—is the seed that uplifts our spirit and nourishes our souls."

Hernández describes her early childhood awakening to the creative process. At the age of two, she fell in the mud wearing a fancy dress for a family party. The next day she noticed the impression she had left was still there. In *The Art of Provocation* Hernández recalled, "I began to think

about mud as something more than just mud, but as something I could actually shape and the shape would last. I spent a lot of time looking at it, manipulating it, and even eating it. That one moment of play triggered a way of dealing with the world around me."

Impressed by Chicano Courage and Conviction

Since the 1930s, Hernández's parents have been active in the union movement, striving for better conditions and rights for migrant farmworkers. The movement became more politicized in the early 1960s when César Chávez organized farmworker strikes. In 1965, Hernández watched Chávez, Dolores Huerta, and leaders of the United Farm Workers Union march through her hometown and stand against the police and ranchers, protesting for justice and human rights. Hernández, along with many other Chicano artists, was impressed by their courage and conviction and found a cause for her artistic voice. Later, some of these works were organized by the Wight Art Gallery at UCLA and exhibited in a nine-city tour titled "Chicano Art: Resistance and Affirmation, 1965-1985, (CARA)."

Hernández was educated at Laney College and Grove Street College in Oakland, CA, where she learned mural painting and screen-printing from Malaquais Montoya. At the University of California at Berkeley, she studied art and Chicano studies and received a B.A. in art. She also joined a group of Chicana artists known as the Mujeres Muralistas, or the Women Muralists. In 1976, Hernández was awarded a California Arts Council artist-in-residence at a bilingual school in East Oakland, where she taught ceramics, papermaking, printmaking, and mural painting based on Mexican traditions. This commitment to teaching in the community, whether at schools, senior centers, or with the disabled, remains important to her.

Deconstructs Icons

The 1976 etching, *Libertad*, begins Hernández's singular artistic device of taking familiar icons and deconstructing them to articulate the hidden meaning. Here, she portrays herself chiseling away the foundations of the Statue of Liberty to reveal the Mayan stele upon which it is built. Issues of colonialism and lack of human rights, especially freedom, for the indigenous Mesoamerican cultures upon which European colonists built their culture, are conveyed with irony and defiance. Similarly, her 1976 aquatint *La Virgen de Guadalupe Defendiendo Los Derechos de Los Xicanos* or *The Virgin of Guadalupe Defending Chicano Rights*, draws from her early devotion as a *Guadalupana* or follower of the Virgin of Guadalupe, and explodes the myth of the feminine power as passive and contained. Here, the Virgin steps out of her halo and offers a karate kick in defense of Chicano/a social justice. The ancient Indian mother, Tonantzin, newly conceived as the Virgin Mary, continues to intercede for the people in their struggle for economic and political power, and, in Ester Hernández's vision, with humor and defiance. These two pieces are considered the first examples of Chicana feminist art.

Creates Mournful Testaments

Hernández's 1981 screen-print, *Sun Mad* has become a cultural icon for the farmworkers plight. The familiar Sun Maid(c) raisin box displays the smiling young girl as a skeletal horror offering her grapes replete with pesticides and harvested under acute labor conditions. This symbol is a mournful testament to the illnesses and physical hardships suffered by Hernández's family and the entire community of farmworkers whose water and food has been contaminated with poisonous chemicals. It also, for the first time, raised the consciousness of consumers to the health hazards of agricultural pesticides. Hernández's elegy to the Chicano/a struggle culminates in her 1984 screen-print, *Tejido de Los Desaparecidos,* the *Weaving of the Disappeared.* Her model is the shawl or *rebozo* of the native Indian peoples of Mesoamerica. The rebozo is a woman's wrap that acts as head covering, baby carrier, or rifle holder, and symbolizes the maternal care fostered in the indigenous family and community. Hernández takes the pattern, or *ikat,* of the shawl and weaves in images of death and civil war. Death heads, helicopters, and skeletons form the texture of the shroud of all those who have disappeared and died in the wars of Central and South America.

Bridges Nature and Spirit

The sacred feminine continued to dominate Hernández's work in the late 1980s as she created images that sought to bridge the chasm between nature and spirit. The 1986 print *Mis Madres* shows the native creator Mother, Tonantzin, holding the world gently in her uplifted hand. The Virgin of Guadalupe is re-created again, but in more intimate form. *Cosmic Cruise* shows young Ester, her mother, and grandmother (in her rebozo) riding in a Model T driven by the Virgin. In *La Ofrenda,* the religious icon of the Virgin is tattooed on the bare back of Hernández's friend Renee, and a hand offers a single rose. This embodiment of the sacred means, to Hernández, that ". . . much of our cultural legacy, we literally carry on our backs." To others, the message is more expansive. "The artist has brought the icon into a new age of liberation and defiance in this print as she blurs the line between human and the divine," says scholar and critic Amalia Mesa-Bains.

In the last ten years, Ester Hernández has also included in her art those women who have been influential in her life. The 1987 pastel work, *If This Is Death, I Like It,* shows the death head of honored Mexican artist Frida Kahlo wearing a watermelon slice hat. This piece is currently in the private collection of author Alice Walker. Another favorite subject is the legendary Mexican singer, Lydia Mendoza. As Hernández says in *The Art of Provocation,* "She gave me advice about how hard life is, but if you find something you really want, then do it. . . .I chose to honor her strength, beauty, dignity, and perseverance." More recently, Hernández has been focusing her work on a Mexican performance artist, Astrid Hadad, who "makes fun of all the Mexican stereotypes of women. She is very perceptive and fascinating."

The Hispanic American art of Ester Hernández continues to exhibit around the United States, notably in a long-running show called "Ceremony of Spirit: Nation and Memory in Contemporary Latino Art." More recently, her *Sun Mad* images appear in an ongoing traveling art exhibit of the Smithsonian Institute titled, "Poster: American Style." In 1997, she produced a film called *Sun Mad—The Video.* Hernández is also featured in episode two of the PBS video *Chicano! History of the Mexican American Civil Rights Movement.* Hernández draws inspiration from the strength of the women around her and in her own personal story. She concluded the same article saying, "When I focus on these powerful women, I hope that by looking at them . . . I will have a better understanding of them and myself."

Current Address: 1263 Hampshire St., San Francisco, CA 94110.

Sources:

Baker, Kenneth. "Chicano Art Hits Town." *San Francisco Chronicle,* June 27, 1991, p. E1.

CARA (Chicano Art: Resistance & Affirmation) catalog. Los Angeles: Wight Art Gallery, University of California, 1991.

Ceremony of Spirit catalog. San Francisco: Mexican Museum, 1994.

Mesa-Bains, Amalia. "The Art of Provocation: Ester Hernández. A Retrospective." CN Gorman Museum, Native American Studies, University of California-Davis, 1993.

———. "Domestic Allegories." *Artes Del Otro México: Fuentes y Significados. Exhibition Tour: 1993-1995* catalog. Chicago: Mexican Fine Arts Museum, 1993.

———. "Ester Hernández—Artist Monograph Series." San Francisco, CA: Galleria de La Raza, 1988.

Shackelford, Penelope. "Chicana's heritage is all of ours." *The Davis Enterprise/Winters Express,* October 26, 1995.

Inés Hernández-Avila
(1947–)
Poet, professor, critic

Selected writings:

Con Razón Corazón. San Antonio: M & A Editions, 1987.

Overview

Inés Hernández-Avila is a writer whose entire work reflects her dual heritage as a Chicana and a Nez Percé. Her poetry expresses the richness of both cultures, and her distinctive and powerful voice is considered one of the most important among Chicana poets. Inés Hernández is a poet, critic, and professor who has succeeded in academia with a long and diverse record of accomplishment. In her book *Con Razón, Corazón,* published in 1987, she set the tone for her career with this declaration: "I know what I want Inés to be, what I say she is, and I feel a responsibility to act upon that—*es todo* [that's all]. I am also painfully aware of my weaknesses, at the same time it occurs to me that some have called me arrogant. Our egos are vulnerable to presumption, I believe." This characteristic frankness is one of Hernández-Avila's strengths as a poet and critic. She has said that her heritage and sense of social responsibility are her inspiration. Some of her work is autobiographical; she often writes of her parents and the strong influence each has had on her.

Works as Professor and Poet

Born in Galveston, TX, on February 28, 1947, Hernández-Avila is the daughter of Janet Tzilimamuh Andrews Hernández, a Nimipu, or Nez Percé, Indian, and Rodolpho Hernández. She studied at the University of Houston and received her B.A. in 1970, an M.A. in 1972, and a doctorate in English in 1984. In 1970 and 1971, she taught high school English in La Marque, TX, and from 1971 to 1976 she worked on her doctorate after receiving the Ford Foundation Doctoral Fellowship for American Indians. While she was an assistant professor of English at the University of Texas, she was the editor of *Hembra,* a Chicano journal. She said, "I believe my poetry mirrors an awareness of myself as an individual and as a member of a collective voice (of which the Chicano-Chicana voice is only a part) which is seeking a more humanistic society." During graduate school, Hernández-Avila moved to California to further her interest in Native American studies. In time she advanced to chair of the Native American Studies Department at the University of California at Davis. As a performer and a writer, she draws on ritual by chanting and lighting candles to begin readings. Her style incorporates the rhythm of prayers and the point-counterpoint of short lines, recalling its roots in the oral tradition of Native Americans. She has been published in numerous publications, notably *Americas Review, Calyx,* and *Third Woman.*

Writes Fiction and Poetry

Hernández-Avila is a prolific and original writer. "Enedina's Story" (1994) is a rich and robust stew of a story that highlights the author's ability to inspire a strong sensory response in her readers. Two friends spend an afternoon preparing food for a reading/political meeting/performance. While the food simmers enticingly, the two friends, Enedina and Marina, cook, gossip, and confess. Men are an important part of the discussion, but politics and their pasts are of equal interest. "Enedina's Story" allows us a look into their lives, which are shaped by their political experiences as Chicanas as much as they are by relationships. Hernández-Avila's women are strong, humorous, and thoughtful; the reader feels as if they are in the kitchen with them and enjoying the experience.

"Para Teresa" is a very personal poem that has received much critical attention and has been anthologized several times. The speaker is a Chicana girl who is ridiculed for her studious nature by Teresa and the tough and cynical *pachucas.* She defends herself against their accusations that she is a traitor to the race: "My Contest was to prove/ beyond any doubt/that we were not only equal but/ superior to them/That was why I studied./If I could do it, we all could." At the end of the poem, the narrator, now older, remembers and claims understanding and sisterhood with Teresa. Hernández-Avila is deft at code-switching, using a mixture of English and Spanish, and "Para Teresa" uses this device to great effect. Much of her early work is in Spanish, but more has been written in English since 1977.

"To Other Women Who Were Ugly Once" is a strong indictment of the cultural brainwashing of women. Hernández-Avila's angry denunciation of the media cult fostered especially by women's magazines is applicable to any woman, but for women of color has the added twist given their invisibility in a predominantly white culture. "Do you remember how we used to panic/ when Cosmo, Vogue and Mademoiselle/ladies/would Glamour-us out of existence/. . ." A resolute feminist, Hernández-Avila concludes: "My resistance to this type of/ existence/ grows stronger every day." For Hernández-Avila, her feminism is integral to her writing. In "Soy Guerrilla," or "I am a Warrior Woman," she recalls the figure of La Adelita, a popular literary heroine of the Chicano Renaissance of the 1970s. Tey Diana Rebolledo links Hernández-Avila with this literary tradition of Mexican literature. The *soldaderes,* or women guerrillas, figure prominently, acting as warriors alongside their men: "It is clear that an identification exists between the revolutionary fighter for justice, land and food, and contemporary writers who believe that the pen and the sword are related." As a warrior woman, Hernández-Avila is most effective in the poem "With Due Respects to La Llorona"—a call to activism. She herself has lived a life of activism, having been a member of La Raza Unida and the Chicanos Artistas a Azatlan, as well as the Mexican American Youth Organization.

Celebrates Mestiza Heritage

Hernández-Avila is an enrolled member of the Colville Federated Tribes of Nespelem, Washington. The dual consciousness of Native American and Chicana cultures makes her writing strong and passionately political. Her mother's example helped Hernández-Avila resist prejudice and taught her to celebrate her mestiza heritage. As a Native American woman, Hernández-Avila often reflects on spirituality. One poem, "Steps of Cleansing," explores the experience of "days of woman cleansing" and "the balancing of purification/that leads me to remembrance/ . . . " and speaks of unity and love for "the mother earth." She mentions totemic animals such as hawks, bears, and turtles, and traditional ritual that evoke a mythic level that deepens her poetry and twines it with feminist thought in a graceful expression of her relationship to nature. Similarly, she celebrates the female self—strong and resilient, with a focus on the metaphor of the womb, which she sees as a place of spiritual and physical power. Her critical work explores the politics of the relationship between Chicanas/os and Native Americans, and her poetry expresses its soul.

Sources:

Castillo-Speed, Lillian. *Latina: Women's Voices from the Borderlands.* New York: Touchstone Books, 1995.

Fisher, Dexter. *The Third Woman: Minority Women Writers of the United States.* New York: Houghton Mifflin, 1980.

Hernández-Avila, Inés. "Steps of Cleansing." *Americas Review,* Fall/Winter, 1995, p. 118.

Rebolledo, Tey Diana. *Women Singing in the Snow.* Tucson: University of Arizona Press, 1995.

Rebolledo, Tey Diana, and Eliana S. Rivero. *Infinite Divisions: An Anthology of Chicana Literature.* Tucson: University of Arizona Press, 1993.

María Herrera-Sobek

(1943–)

Professor, editor, poet, author

Selected writings:

The Bracero Experience: Elitelore Versus Folklore. UCLA Latin American Center Publications, 1979.

Beyond Stereotypes: The Critical Analysis of Chicana Literature (edited). Bilingual Press, 1985.

Chicana Creativity and Criticism: Charting New Frontiers in American Literature (edited). Arte Publico Press, 1988.

Gender and Print Culture: New Perspectives on International Ballad Studies (edited), 1991.

The Mexican Corrido: A Feminist Analysis. Indiana University Press, 1992.

Reconstructing a Chicano/a Literary Heritage (edited). University of Arizona Press, 1993.

Northward Bound: The Mexican Immigrant Experience in Ballad and Sound. Indiana University Press, 1993.

Chicana (W)Rites: On Word and Film (edited). Third Woman Press, 1995.

Culture Across Borders: The Popular Culture of Mexican Immigration to the United States (edited). University of Arizona Press, 1998.

"Volume IV" of *Recovering the U.S. Hispanic Literary Heritage* (edited), forthcoming.

Santa Barraza: The Life and Work of a Mexica/Tejana Artist, (edited), forthcoming.

Overview

María Herrera-Sobek has spent much of her life bridging two worlds. As a child, she and the grandparents who raised her traveled frequently between Mexico and the United States. Then, as now, Herrera-Sobek serves as a bridge between the majority white American culture and her Hispanic heritage. She is the first Chicana to be tenured at the University of California at Irvine and, in 1997, became the first Luis Leal Endowed Chair in the Chicano Studies Department at the University of California, Santa Barbara.

Loves Reading

It has been a long time since Herrera-Sobek's first poem was published in *Revista Chicano Riquena* (Spring, 1978). Since then, she has edited dozens of books, published several of her own, and penned articles, papers, and poems. Herrera-Sobek said in a telephone interview, "I started writing poetry when I was a child, and the teachers would just make a big deal out of it, so I would think it was

María Herrera-Sobek

something worthwhile pursuing, very flattered that my teachers thought I was writing something worth their praise. I guess that's what initiated my interest. I just began to like poetry, always reading poetry books when I was a little girl."

In fact, Herrera-Sobek's reading skills earned her early recognition. At the age of three, she learned to read Spanish and began reading the newspaper to the residents of Reynosa, Mexico, a border city near Rio Hondo where her grandparents were agricultural workers toiling in the fields. At the age of 13, Herrera-Sobek's love of reading and literature was sealed by a gift: a poetry book, *The One Hundred Best Poems in the Spanish Language,* which introduced her to the world of bilingual writing. From that point on, Herrera-Sobek wrote poems in both Spanish and English.

Studies Two Languages

Herrera-Sobek attended Northward Elementary School and Northward Junior High School in Rio Hondo. She began writing in English, but became bilingual as she grew older. In 1957, Herrera-Sobek's family relocated to Gilbert, AZ, where she enrolled in Gilbert High School. In high school, she began collecting poems she had scribbled in various tablets. She graduated with honors in 1961 and was class valedictorian. Herrera-Sobek's education continued at Arizona State University in Tempe, from which she received a B.S. in chemistry in 1965. After graduation she spent several years of working in a biochemstry laboratory at the University of California in Los Angeles, until she was accepted into UCLA's graduate program in Latin American studies in 1969. Herrera-Sobek earned a M.A. in 1971, and a Ph.D. in Hispanic languages and literature in 1975.

Herrera-Sobek describes her writing as "very philosophical and very metaphysical. I explored themes of death; I was very concerned with death. My two grandparents adopted me, they passed away, one in the 1970s, one in the 1980s; [I was] exploring the meaning of life." The death of her grandmother inspired a collection of poems that appeared in an anthology titled *Three Times A Woman,* published by Bilingual Press. Most recently, Herrera-Sobek has focused her writing on poems regarding the Vietnam War, ". . . how I experienced it and how Chicanos around me experienced it." Five of her poems on the Vietnam experience have been accepted for publication in a forthcoming anthology edited by Jorge Mariscal.

Devotes Life to Teaching/Writing

Herrera-Sobek has devoted her life to teaching and writing. Her first academic appointment came from California State University, Northridge, where she worked from 1972 until 1975. After that, she secured a spot in the Spanish and Portuguese Department at the University of California, working there for 21 years. While at UCI, Herrera-Sobek co-founded the Chicano Studies Program,

the Latin American Studies Program, and helped develop the Women's Studies Program. She was the first Chicana to win tenure and to become full professor at that university.

In 1979, Herrera-Sobek's first work titled *The Bracero Experience: Elitelore Versus Folklore* was published. During the 1980s, Herrera-Sobek edited two critical works on Chicana literature: *Beyond Stereotypes: The Critical Analysis of Chicana Literature;* and *Chicana Creativity and Criticism: Charting New Frontiers in American Literature.* She followed these efforts with numerous other works in the 1990s, including: *Gender and Print Culture: New Perspectives on International Ballad Studies, The Mexican Corrido: A Feminist Analysis, Reconstructing a Chicano/a Literary Heritage, Northward Bound: The Mexican Immigrant Experience in Ballad and Sound, Chicana (W)Rites: On Word and Film,* and *Culture Across Borders: The Popular Culture of Mexican Immigration to the United States.* Two forthcoming titles, to which Herrera-Sobek serves as editor, include: "Volume IV" of *Recovering the U.S. Hispanic Literary Heritage;* and *Santa Barraza: The Life and Work of a Mexica/Tejana Artist.*

Her love of writing led her to share her gift with others. Since 1997, Herrera-Sobek has served as a professor in the Chicano Studies Department at UC-Santa Barbara, where she teaches courses on such subjects as feminist theory, Chicana writers, Hispanic/Chicano oral traditions, and colonial literature of the Southwest. During the 1998-99 academic year, she plans to teach creative writing.

Receives Numerous Honors

Throughout her career, Herrera-Sobek has held four visiting professorships, including one at Stanford and another at Harvard; received upwards of twenty grants, scholarships, and distinctions; been honored with ten awards for writing and teaching; directed literary contests and university departments; and published extensively. Herrera-Sobek continues to distinguish herself as both a writer and a teacher in her endeavors.

Current Address: Chicano Studies Dept., Univ. of California, Santa Barbara, Santa Barbara, CA 93106.

Sources:

Cohn, Lynne M. Telephone interview with María Herrera-Sobek, March 1998.

Herring, Laura Martinez
   See **Harring, Laura**

Hinojosa, Letitia
   See **Hinojosa, Tish**

Tish Hinojosa
(1955–)
Singer, songwriter, instrumental musician

Selected discography:

Taos to Tennessee. Watermelon, 1987.
Homeland. A&M, 1989.
Culture Swing. A&M, 1990.
Aquella Noche. Watermelon, 1991.
Memorabilia Navideña. Watermelon, 1991.
Culture Swing. Rounder, 1992.
Destiny's Gate. Warner Bros., 1994.
Frontejas. Rounder, 1995.
Cada Niño/Every Child. Rounder, 1996.
Dreaming from the Labyrinth/Soñar del Laberinton. Warner, 1996.
The Best of the Sandia: Watermelon 1991-1992. Watermelon, 1997.

Selected filmography:

True Believers: The Musical Family of Rounder Records, 1994.

Overview

Singer and songwriter Tish Hinojosa does not so much cross musical borders as ignore them. Her music combines sounds and styles from American folk music, Nashville's country-western, traditional Mexican genres, and Tejano conjunto music, or Mexican American music from Texas. She writes everything from love songs to protest songs, ballads to dance tunes. Her exciting and interesting genre-bending style has also delayed her success somewhat, for recording companies like neat classifications, which Hinojosa's music defies. She started singing professionally in the 1970s and began recording albums in the 1980s, but only started receiving regular national attention in the 1990s.

Listens to Variety of Music

The youngest of 13 children born to immigrant parents on December 6, 1955, Hinojosa listened to many different kinds of sounds during her childhood. Her older brothers and sisters listened to folk and popular music of the 1960s—by artists like Joan Baez and Judy Collins. Her parents listened to the radio stations playing Mexican music. "I love the music of the traditional aspect of our community," she told *Hispanic.* "Conjunto music, the ballads, and the romantic singer/songwriter songs—the older music from Mexico that my parents like a lot—made a very positive impression."

Hinojosa began singing while in high school after her mother bought her a guitar. She explained to the *Dallas*

Morning News: "It was just the $20 guitar you get down [in Mexico] at the Mercado. But I was really, really proud, and I still have that guitar."

In music, Hinojosa found something all her own. "Finally," she declared to the *Dallas Morning News,* "I [had] found something I could do myself. I wasn't just tagging along with my sisters somewhere." She also discovered that she had a special gift. She was singing one day at school with her friends, she told the newspaper, "and I started singing one song. They all just sat there kind of quietly, and they said: 'You know that you can sing?'" She did not read musical notation, but taught herself songs by ear from records. Her sister Linda Gonzalez described the process to the *Dallas Morning News:* "She'd sit in her room and play a record over and over again until she could pick the notes out. She never took guitar lessons."

Begins Musical Career

After graduating from high school, Hinojosa started performing around town, recording popular tunes in Spanish for a leading Tejano label, and singing jingles in Spanish for radio commercials. After a few years without moving ahead in her career, she moved first to New Mexico and then to Nashville, seeking new music and new opportunities. She traveled around the country to perform at colleges and coffee houses; she began learning the country-western hits of singers like Emmylou Harris and Roseanne Cash; and she landed a job singing demo tapes for the Mel Tillis Publishing Company. After two years in Nashville without signing a record deal, she moved back home to San Antonio to regroup. In the following years, she began to sing more of her own songs, and in 1987, released a privately-recorded collection entitled *Taos to Tennessee.*

During these years, Hinojosa had trouble landing a major recording label because of her eclectic sound. No one could quite categorize her music. She sang folk music, country-western songs, and conjunto songs; many of her own compositions synthesized traits from all these styles. To critics outside Nashville she was too country, to others inside Nashville, she was not country enough.

That Hinojosa didn't fit any mold gave the record companies a good excuse to ignore her for a few years. "There's so much talk now about artists who have fallen between the cracks," she told the *Los Angeles Times.* "So many of the singer-songwriters just don't fit into niches in Nashville or in pop music anymore. I guess I'm one of those. But I feel like I'm in good company, because I like a lot of people that are in the same crack that I'm in."

Hinojosa's record *Taos to Tennessee* sold well locally, received some notice, and started turning her career around. Two years later, she recorded her first major-label album, *Homeland,* for A&M records. The album contains the sounds and songs typical for Hinojosa—a combination of country-western, folk, and conjunto, presented in both Spanish and English.

Benefits from Music Label Switch

While *Homeland* garnered rave reviews, Hinojosa relationship with A&M did not last. Only a week before the company was due to release her second album there was a management shake-up, and they dropped her from their register. "It was one of those hard, fast lessons about what major record labels are about," she told the *Los Angeles Times*. "It's one of those confusing things. I'm not sure if and who to blame, and why there's people there that I never heard from again and while I was there they acted like they were real good friends. It was kind of a strange little thing."

The end of Hinojosa's association with A&M had a positive side, however, for she recorded the material for the her second album all over again, but this time in Austin rather than in Hollywood. Hinojosa was extremely pleased with the results. "What we got is a lot more personal record," she explained to the *Los Angeles Times*. It's a lot more of me, a lot more of Texas. The sound is a lot more real, my sound. . . . In L.A. it was a lot less time spent on a lot more frills. And what we did in Texas, a lot more heart went into it, a lot more time and thought." *Culture Swing* was finally released in 1992 by the independent folk-oriented label Rounder Records. *The New York Times* praised the work, calling its typical combination of Spanish and English, folk, country, and conjunto sounds a "panoramic musical landscape."

Hinojosa's fortune seemed to change again after the production of *Culture Swing*. She began writing new material with a new sound. "I was going in all kinds of directions," she explained in *Hispanic*. "It's real personal, but on a different level than *Culture Swing*." This new sound caught the ear of the Warner Brothers label. "Originally, the new album was to have been my second for Rounder Records, the label that released *Culture Swing*,, she continued in *Hispanic*. "But the flavor of the recording took a different direction. It still had some Spanish language in it and a bit of Spanish sensitivity, but lyrically and musically, it stretched out further. I don't want to call it pop, because that's too general a term, but a major label sensed its potential and signed me to a long-term contract."

Later Works

In the winter of 1994, Warner Brothers released *Destiny's Gate*. *Entertainment Weekly* music reviewer Bob Cannon referred to it as ". . . another exotic blend of TexMex, folk, and country, with [Hinojosa's] sensual soprano adding depth to everything she touches." Her next recording titled *Frontejas* also won favorable reviews. "Her passion for the music of the border region of Mexico and Texas is presented with missionary zeal," wrote *Hispanic*. ". . . it is the purity and sincerity of Hinojosa's sweet, expressive voice that makes *Frontejas* such a remarkable and highly recommended work." Hinojosa also found time to perform live with the 1995 Border Tour, a collection of Texas musicians representing various musical genres.

After *Destiny's Gate*, Hinojosa began working on a bilingual children's album titled *Cada Niño/Every Child*.Traditional Mexican songs performed by Hinojosa in a folk/rock style, *Publishers Weekly* stated that the 1996 recording was "[n]ot frenzied or raucous. . . a good pick for quiet times and thoughtful children." That same year, Hinojosa released another album titled *Dreaming From the Labyrinth/Soñar del Laberinton*, which the *Phoenix New Times* referred to as, ". . . the most provocative and accomplished recording of the Austin singer/songwriter's career. As the title implies, the recording is suffused with elegant dream imagery."

Supports Bilingual Education

During 1996, Hinojosa also began working on behalf of the National Association for Bilingual Education as well as the National Latino Children's Agenda in an effort to support bilingual education. Relating to her own childhood experience of speaking Spanish and English, Hinojosa stated, "Children shouldn't be made to feel that their language is something that needs to be taken away from them or washed away, as if it's some form of defect."

It is evident that despite the conflicts and problems her unique musical style has engendered for her, Hinojosa has no plans to change her musical approach. As she stated in a Manazo Music press kit, "When you resist pop formulas for your own artistic vision, the twists are sometimes confusing, but now I'm seeing the wonderful results of not straying from a true road."

Current Address: Manazo Music Mgmt., PO Box 3304, Austin, TX 78764.

Sources:

Armstrong, Robin. Additional information provided by Manazo Music Management, 1994.

Billboard, December 5, 1992.

"Cada Niño/Every Child." *Publishers Weekly*, June 17, 1996, p.32.

Cannon, Bob. "Destiny's Gate." *Entertainment Weekly*, May 27, 1994, p. 88.

Chicago Tribune, February 14, 1993.

Dallas Morning News, May 29, 1994.

Hispanic, January 1994.

Howard, Lee. "Native Tongues: Tish Hinojosa finds her way through *el laberinto*." *Phoenix News Times*. Available at http://www.phoenixnewtimes.com/1996/060696/music2.html.

Los Angeles Times, November 26, 1992.
People, July 11, 1994.
Pulse!, April 1993.
Ramirez, Juan. "Music." *Hispanic,* July 31, 1995, p. 84.
Spin, February 1993.
Stereo Review, May 1993.
The New York Times, December 6, 1992.

Washington Post, November 25, 1992.

Hughes, Grace Flores
    See **Flores-Hughes, Grace**

I-K

India
See **La India**

Susana Jaime-Mena
(1952–)
Painter, sculptor

Susana Jaime-Mena has come to be known for minimalism in her work. However, as she has progressed through the years since deciding to devote her life to art, Jaime-Mena keeps surpassing her own previous simplicity. The sensualism for which she has come to be known, within the abstract realm, continually emerges from each new body of work, looking different each time, as it explores still other aspects

Susana Jaime-Mena

of the motions of the life that moves inside and around her. The path she has followed through the evolution of her work has been driven by no less than the quest in her soul to understand the entropy inherent in the universe and the place it holds in human perceptions.

Develops Early Passion for Art

Susana Jaime-Mena was born in Buenos Aires on October 21, 1952. Her father, Antonio Jaime-Mena, had been born in Spain and became a highly successful business leader. Her mother, Aydee Bruno, was a first generation Argentinean born to Italian immigrants. As the youngest of three children (she also has an older half-brother from her father's previous marriage), Jaime-Mena enjoyed an affluent upper middle-class lifestyle, including 12 years of Catholic schooling and a weekend house in the country. During those weekends in the country, she witnessed her father enjoying life as a "Sunday painter," as he escaped from the many demands of his work. His artistic talents were so accomplished that he even sold his paintings to friends. As a child and young adult, Jaime-Mena also found great pleasure in painting and drawing and wanted to become an artist. However, her parents encouraged her to choose a career that would provide a more substantial income. Bowing to her parents' wishes, she entered university to study economics and English. She earned her degree and began teaching English.

Accepts New Mission in United States

Although she had embarked upon a stable career as an English teacher, Jaime-Mena could no longer contain her desire to become an artist. She moved to New York City in 1980 and enrolled in the Art Students League. In 1982, she moved on to the School of Visual Arts, where she earned a bachelor's degree in fine arts in 1982 and a master's degree in fine arts in 1987. Since her early days in New York, Jaime-Mena's work showed increasing maturity and promise. She was awarded the Louis Bouche Memorial Merit Scholarship in 1982, followed by a grant from the Rhodes Family Awards in 1985. In 1990, she won a highly coveted award from the Pollack-Krasner Foundation. Jaime-Mena moved to Miami in 1996, but continued to exhibit her works in New York City and in cities throughout the world.

Heals Emotional Wounds through Art

Although Jaime-Mena's artistic works had earned her awards and international acclaim, she feared that the pursuit of artistic fulfillment had cost her the respect and admiration of her parents. Those fears would remain until her mother came to visit her at work in her studio. During the long hours together, Jaime-Mena and her mother forged a close bond of love and mutual respect greater than they had ever known before. Two years after the visit, her mother developed terminal pancreatic cancer. She rushed back to Argentina and was at her mother's side when she died. Although her mother's death had brought her work to a temporary standstill, Jaime-Mena emerged from her grief with a deeper artistic vision.

When she speaks of her art, Jaime-Mena could be mistaken for a quantum physicist—the words "entropy" and "dynamics" flow from her as easily as "color" and "form." She draws from her rich cultural heritage to breathe life into all three essential states of being—the soul, the mind, and the body. Her struggle represents no less than the pureness of joy she derives from them.

Current Address: 1775 SW 16th Ave., Miami, FL 33145.

Sources:

Spear, Jane. Telephone conversation and resume from Susana Jaime-Mena, April 28, 1998.

Katy Jurado
(1927–)
Actress

Selected filmography:

Bullfighter And The Lady. Republic, 1951.
The Brute. 1952.
High Noon. United Artists, 1952.
Arrowhead. Paramount, 1953.
San Antone. Republic, 1953.
Broken Lance. 20th Century Fox, 1954.
The Racers. 20th Century Fox, 1955.
Trial. MGM, 1955.
Man From Del Rio. United Artists, 1956.
Trapeze. United Artists, 1956.
Dragoon Wells Massacre. Allied Artists, 1957.
The Badlanders. MGM, 1958.
One-Eyed Jacks. Paramount, 1961.
Barabbas. Columbia, 1962.
Smoky. 20th Century Fox, 1966.
A Covenant With Death. Warner Bros., 1967.
Stay Away, Joe. MGM, 1968.
Any Second Now. NBC-TV, 1969.
The Wild Bunch. Warner Bros., 1969.
The Bridge In The Jungle. 1970.
A Little Game. ABC-TV, 1971.

Once Upon A Scoundrel. 1973.
Pat Garrett And Billy The Kid. MGM, 1973.
The Children Of Sanchez. 1978.
The Widow Montiel. 1979.
Evita Peron. NBC-TV, 1981.
Under The Volcano. 20th Century Fox, 1984.
Lady Blue. ABC-TV, 1985.
The Fearmaker. 1989.

Overview

Actress Katy Jurado, born Maria Cristina Estella Marcela Jurado Garcia, on January 16, 1927, in Guadalajara, Mexico, was a regular in Western films of the 1950s and 1960s. She worked with many Hollywood legends, including Gary Cooper in *High Noon*, Spencer Tracy in *Broken Lance*, and Marlon Brando in *One-Eyed Jacks*, and such respected directors as Fred Zinneman (*High Noon*), Sam Peckinpah (*The Wild Bunch* and *Pat Garrett and Billy the Kid*) and John Huston (*Under the Volcano*). She was nominated for an Academy Award for Best Supporting Actress for her work in 1954's *Broken Lance*. More recently, she has appeared in both film and television work, including 1989's *The Fearmaker*, and on the ABC-comedy *a.k.a. Pablo*. Jurado currently lives and works in Mexico.

Early Life and Career

One of three children, Jurado was born to a wealthy family in Mexico. Jurado had a privileged childhood. Both

Katy Jurado

her maternal and paternal families were wealthy, at one time owning much of the land that became the state of Texas. Both families lost much of their wealth during the Mexican revolution, but Jurado still lived well. Her father was a cattle baron and orange farmer, and her mother was a well-known opera singer. Her mother gave up the stage to marry and raise a family. Jurado's cousin, Emilio Pontes Gil, was president of Mexico beginning in 1928.

Famous Mexican director Emilio Fernandez discovered Jurado when she was still a teenager. He gave her a leading role in a major Mexican film and, over her parents' objections, Jurado became an actress. She quickly became a star of the Mexican cinema, appearing in more than 30 Spanish-language films. Her popularity with audiences also landed her a radio show in Mexico.

Hollywood

Following a successful career in Mexican films, Jurado came to Hollywood as a writer for Mexican publications. She was motion picture and gossip columnist for several Mexican magazines and newspapers. It was not long before Hollywood noticed this talented actress, particularly after her work in such Mexican features as *The Brute* and an excellent version of *The Pearl*, based on the classic John Steinbeck story. Her first appearance in an American film came in 1951's *The Bullfighter and the Lady*, opposite Gilbert Roland. Jurado stayed close to home, as the film was made on location in Mexico. At that time, Jurado did not even speak English. Jurado memorized and delivered her lines phonetically. Despite this handicap, her strong performance brought her to the attention of Hollywood producer Stanley Kramer. Kramer cast her in the classic Western *High Noon*. Jurado quickly learned to speak English for the role, studying and taking classes two hours a day for two months. The time was well-spent. Jurado delivered another powerful performance in one of the most memorable films of the era, playing the former love of reluctant hero Will Kane.

Jurado continued to appear in numerous Westerns, including 1954's *Broken Lance* with Spencer Tracy, 1961's *One-Eyed Jacks* with star and director Marlon Brando, and Sam Peckinpah's classic *The Wild Bunch* in 1969. She again worked with Peckinpah on his ill-received 1973 revisionist Western *Pat Garrett and Billy the Kid*. Jurado also appeared in many non-Western studio films during the 1950s and 1960s. These included *Trapeze* in 1956 with Tony Curtis and Burt Lancaster, 1958's *Fun in Acapulco* and 1969's *Stay Away, Joe*, both with Elvis Presley. Jurado later appeared in director John Huston's acclaimed 1984 drama *Under The Volcano* with Albert Finney.

Jurado appeared on television in the 1981 miniseries *Evita Peron* with Faye Dunaway, and in made-for-television movies such as *Lady Blue* in 1985. In 1984, Jurado appeared in the short-lived ABC television series *a.k.a. Pablo* with comedian Paul Rodriguez. Since then, she has made sporadic appearances in film and spends most of her time in her native Mexico.

Personal Life

At a young age and, against her parents' wishes, Jurado married a Mexican actor and writer named Victor Velazquez. Together, they had a son and a daughter. The marriage ended in divorce, and the children remained with Jurado's family in Mexico when she traveled to the United States to work. In 1959, Jurado married actor Ernest Borgnine, with whom she co-starred in *The Badlanders* the previous year. The marriage lasted only five years, and the couple divorced in 1964.

In 1968, Jurado became depressed and attempted suicide by ingesting sleeping pills. She had left a suicide note for her family and was discovered in time to save her life. After her suicide attempt, she revived both her personal and professional lives and, in 1972, married again, on a private island she owned off the coast of southern Mexico. Jurado again appeared on television and in films during the 1970s. Sadly, tragedy struck in 1981 when Jurado's son died in an automobile accident at the age of 35.

In 1985, Jurado was named film promotion commissioner for the Mexican state of Morelos. In that position, Jurado issued filming permits, found locations for movies, and arranged accommodations for film crews. The position provided Jurado with the opportunity to do what she loves most, helping to arrange and develop national and international motion pictures in her beloved Mexico. In 1998, Jurado completed a timely Spanish-language film for director Arturo Ripstein called *El Evangelio de las Maravillas* about a millennium sect.

Awards

Jurado has been honored repeatedly for her film work and her tireless support of Latino causes. She received an Ariel, the Mexican equivalent of the Oscar, for her work in her third Mexican motion picture, as well as an Ariel nomination for her role in *The Brute*. Jurado was recognized for her work in the 1954 Western *Broken Lance*. She was also nominated for an Academy Award for that film, but lost to Eva Marie Saint. In 1985, Jurado was honored with the El Angel Award by the Bilingual Foundation of the Arts Ole Theatre, a Latino performing arts institution in Los Angeles. This award honors outstanding performers of Hispanic heritage. In 1992, Jurado was honored at the Golden Boot Awards, which reward those involved in Western films. In her acceptance speech, Jurado said, "It is not one person who makes a movie, it's the actors and producers and directors who make good films. And I hope in the future that people will make good pictures for love, not money." In 1997, she received a special gold Ariel at the Mexican Film Awards. Though normally award recipients are not allowed to make comments during the ceremony, Jurado took the microphone and gave a vigorous defense of Mexican performers and the under-appreciated Mexican film industry.

While Jurado was often unjustly dismissed by critics as an average actress, she has given many noteworthy screen performances. In her starring roles, she lit up the screen with her exotic beauty, and she provided depth and humanity to supporting characters. She became an icon of the classic Western films of the 1950s. She has continued to work tirelessly in support of recognition for Mexican performers and Mexican films. Her love of the art of film is as evident on-screen as it is in her work off-screen.

Sources:

All Movie Guide. Available at http://allmovie.com/amg/ movie_Root.html.
Burman, John. "Western Posse Vows To Ride On." *The Hollywood Reporter,* August 17, 1992, p. 34.
"Entertainment Briefs." *BPI Entertainment News Wire,* August 7, 1992.
Katz, Ephraim. *The Film Encyclopedia.* New York: Harper Collins, 1979.
Loper, Mary Lou. "On View: Previewing The Golden Thimble Exhibit." *Los Angeles Times,* May 5, 1985, p. 39.
Monaco, James, ed. *Baseline's Encyclopedia of Film,* New York: Perigee, 1991.
Peterson, Bettelou. "TV Week." *Chicago Tribune,* February 21, 1988, p. 25C.
Rainey, Buck. *Sweethearts of the Sage: Biographies and Filmographies of 258 Actresses Appearing in Western Movies.* Jefferson, North Carolina: McFarland & Company, Inc., 1992.
"Spicy Films On The Plate." *Variety,* March 23, 1998, p. 69.
Sutter, Mary. "'Cilantro and Parsley' Flavor Ariel Awards." *Variety,* December 8, 1997, p. 26.

Eugenia Kalnay
(1942–)
Meteorologist, professor

Meteorologist Eugenia Kalnay weathered a stormy political climate in Argentina to become one of the top meteorologists in America. The complex field of operational numerical weather prediction improved significantly under her ten-year tenure as head of the Environmental Modeling Center (EMC), one of the National Centers for Environmental Prediction (NCEP). In 1997, Kalnay became the first Hispanic senior executive in the U.S. Department of Commerce to receive the Presidential Rank Award for Meritorious Achievement, earned for her leadership in the improvement of computer models that help render accurate and timely weather forecasts.

Eugenia Kalnay

Kalnay, who is very democratic in her work philosophies, comes by her views naturally. In search of a more democratic society, her father, Jorge Kalnay, left his native Hungary just after World War I to ride the European immigration wave to Argentina, where he met and married Swiss-born Susana Zwicky. The seventh of eight children, Kalnay was born in Buenos Aires on October 1, 1942.

Argentine president Juan Domingo Perón came into power in 1946, bringing about sweeping changes and socialist reforms that redistributed the country's wealth to include workers and women. The Kalnay family experienced a corresponding change of fortune. "Before Perón," recalled Kalnay in a telephone interview, "the society was much more divided into rich and poor. After [Perón gained power, my family] went from having lots of servants . . . to me helping my mother do the shopping and cleaning." A series of military regimes rose and fell in Argentina during the decades following Perón's downfall. As a girl, Kalnay often discussed the times with her father, an internationally-known architect. "We liked to talk about philosophy and the world," Kalnay said in the interview. "We were very close." Her father died in 1957.

Tough times followed. Kalnay's mother had to work long hours to earn money to raise the children. "I remember occasionally putting cardboard inside my worn-out shoes," Kalnay recalled. "Yet growing up in Argentina was very good for me because despite the common perception of Latin countries, women are in a much more egalitarian situation. There was never any doubt that an intelligent girl should go to college to study science or another professional career. Also, fortunately, in Argentina college was free." Kalnay planned to major in physics as a freshman at the University of Buenos Aires until her mother intervened by registering her to compete for a scholarship in meteorology. Her mother, who did not have the opportunity to finish high school, realized that meteorology would be a good area for future employment. Kalnay won first place in the scholarship competition and received a degree in meteorology in 1965, earning the highest grades at the University of Buenos Aires' School of Sciences.

Begins Career in Meteorology

Defying her mother's order that she remain single until she earned a Ph.D., Kalnay married the summer before heading off to the Massachusetts Institute of Technology (MIT). The overwhelmingly male classes at MIT were a surprise to Kalnay because in Buenos Aires female students made up half the science classes. As the lone female in the School of Meteorology, she also became its first pregnant student. In January of 1970, she gave birth to Jorge Rodrigo Rivas. She received her doctorate from MIT the following year. Kalnay then returned to South America as an assistant professor at the national university in Uruguay. In 1973, when the military took power in Uruguay, Kalnay went back to MIT as a research associate.

After several promotions, Kalnay was offered a position as senior research meteorologist at the modeling and simulation lab run by the National Aeronautics and Space Administration (NASA). The job with NASA, however, required U.S. citizenship. Kalnay became a United States citizen in 1978, not only to work at NASA, but because she also abhorred the military dictatorship in Argentina. Each time she visited that country, she dutifully reported to a local police station to renew her passport. "It was scary," she recalled. The armed forces had launched a civil war against leftists. Between 1976 and 1982, some 20,000 Argentines vanished, never to be heard from again. "I had many friends disappear," Kalnay said. She eventually realized that she would never permanently return to her "motherland." Kalnay remarried in 1981 to Malise Cooper Dick, a transport economist at the World Bank.

Becomes a Leader in Her Field

By 1984, Kalnay commanded the Global Modeling and Simulation Branch of NASA. It was there that she started developing her consensus-building skills. Kalnay's greatest challenge came as the director of the EMC/NCEP. Using computer models of the atmosphere and oceans, the EMC tracks huge amounts of meteorological data and makes

weather, marine, and climate predictions for the National Weather Service and its worldwide counterparts. Accurately forecasting major storms saves lives and contributes to the national economy. Yet EMC/NCEP did not always have such a fine reputation. "When I joined in 1987, the EMC was considered a backwater place, way behind in science and technology," Kalnay commented in the interview. "Now it is the best operational center in the United States, and maybe the second best in the world." During Kalnay's tenure, NCEP became a pioneer in both the fundamental science and the practical applications of forecasting. She helped develop many successful projects, including coastal ocean forecasting, three- and four-dimensional variational data assimilation, and seasonal and interannual dynamical prediction. The scientist's greatest satisfaction, however, came from working with people. "People say that I have a special ability to recognize talent," she said. "It was wonderful to see young people develop and mature into outstanding scientists, which is what we needed."

In 1997, Kalnay decided to step down from her position as director of EMC to return to being a full-time scientist at the University of Oklahoma. She holds the only chaired professorship in meteorology in a state university and retains her position as a senior scientist with NCEP. Explaining her decision to step down as NCEP's director, Kalnay said, "I had put all my energy into the job for ten years. Originally I had planned to be director only for three years or so, and was worried about staying too long. As my husband reminds me: Power corrupts."

Current Address: Energy Center, University of Oklahoma, 100 E. Boyd, Ste. 1310, Norman, OK 73019–0470.

Sources:

Elliot, Jim. "Eugenia Kalnay Receives Presidential Rank Award." *AMS (American Meteorological Society) Newsletter,* January 1997.
Worhach, Denise. Telephone interview with Eugenia Kalnay, April 1, 1998.

Komaroff, Lydia Villa
See Villa-Komaroff, Lydia

Kravitz, Rhonda A. Rios
See Rios-Kravitz, Rhonda A.

L

La Chata Noloesca
See Escalona, Beatriz

Diana LaCome

Entrepreneur, consultant, community activist

Diana LaCome is one of the most respected executive managers and organizational consultants in the United States. She has directed and assisted a wide range of private and public sector organizations and has consistently used her talents to help empower the disenfranchised. LaCome's social, professional and political interests are reflected in the scope of her volunteer work, which includes serving on the advisory boards of transportation, criminal justice, human rights, and broadcasting organizations.

Extended Family Influences LaCome

LaCome has experienced much acclaim and success since her humble beginnings in Questa, NM. Her maternal grandparents, Fermin and Ursula Herrera, both hard-working and compassionate people, raised her, giving LaCome the very best they could. They passed along to her lessons that would later help her in her adult life, and fostered in her a desire to see projects through to their conclusion—an invaluable lesson that would becomes crucial in her adult professional life. She graduated from high school and attended San Francisco City College, receiving an associate's degree in criminology in 1971. LaCome then transferred to California State University at San Francisco, receiving a bachelor's degree in sociology in 1973. She completed her postsecondary education by taking graduate courses in public administration at California State University at Hayward in 1978-79. Before completing her undergraduate studies, she earned a nomination for inclusion in *Who's Who in American Politics* in 1978.

Begins Corporate Training Career

LaCome wasted no time in pursuing her dream. In 1979, shortly after graduation, she became director of field operations for the National Concilio of America. LaCome's

responsibilities in this position included the organization and incorporation of four local Hispanic community organizations operating in California, recruitment and training of organizational directors and the planning and implementation of training and technical services. She also became a trustee for the United Way fundraising organization in 1980. LaCome's early work as an association executive earned her recognition as among the Outstanding Young Women of America in 1981.

LaCome continued to sharpen her educational background. She completed the IBM Corporate Executive Management Training Program in Tarrytown, NY, in 1982. Two years later, she became a consultant for the San Francisco Community College District. In this capacity she collaborated with the U.S. Department of Commerce's Minority Business Development Agency, minority chambers of commerce, trade associations, and businesses to plan, organize and coordinate a six-month program of conferences, workshops, and seminars on minority business. LaCome began consulting in the private sector when she planned and coordinated a women and minority enterprise conference for the City of San Jose Business Conference in 1985. She launched her own entrepreneurial career in January of 1987, founding the Hispanic Development Corporation. LaCome entered the field of public interest broadcasting and telecommunications in 1987, joining KNTV Channel 11 in San Jose, CA, as a member of the Hispanic Advisory Board and becoming a member of the statewide multilingual council of Pacific Bell.

Becomes Involved in Business and Community Activism

Increasingly, LaCome's activist reputation became widely known in the business and social justice communities. She was viewed as someone who could make things happen and effect positive change. It was no mere coincidence that various organizations sought to have this rising star on their committees. She became a member of the Hispanic Advisory Committee of the Oakland Athletics Baseball Club and a member of the board of the National Concilio of America in 1989. Her entrepreneurial career also continued to blossom with the founding of P.R. Plus Enterprises, a small business consulting partnership. In 1990, LaCome joined the advisory councils of the California Department of Transportation and the California Department of Corrections. Her involvement in the public sector continued to grow during the next four years, as she accepted positions on the advisory councils of the California Department of General Services, the Santa Clara County Traffic Authority and Bay Area Rapid Transit (BART). LaCome became further involved in community development and social justice when she became project director for the San Francisco/Oakland Minority Business Development Center in 1992. She accepted the position of project manager of the NEDA Project of the California Department of Corrections in 1994. LaCome furthered her professional development by completing the Total Quality Management Training Program conducted in Fresno, CA, in 1993. She extended her involvement in the promotion of minority business by becoming executive director of the California Business Council for Equal Opportunity in June of 1994. In this capacity she directed strategic planning, fundraising, public relations and formulation and implementation of educational programs for the organization. Her accomplishments as both a businesswoman and as a social activist led her to be named one of five "Women of the Year" by the Mexican American Opportunity Foundation of Los Angeles in 1995.

Enters Business and Politics

Drawing on her experiences with public sector enterprise development and transportation projects, LaCome became program manager of Caltrans Supportive Services for NEDA San Joaquin, Inc. in 1996. In this position she planned and directed searches and referrals for contractors to provide the engineering, construction, and architectural services required by the Cypress Freeway reconstruction project and coordinated training and technical assistance programs for selected contractors. LaCome re-entered politics in 1996, co-founding Californians for Equality, a political action committee working to defeat California Ballot Proposition 209, which sought to eliminate affirmative action programs within the state. *Hispanic Business Magazine* named LaCome as among the "200 Most Influential Hispanics in the United States" in 1996, in recognition of her continuing efforts in the public and private sectors.

LaCome remains active as the founder and president of P.R. Plus Enterprises, and as a co-founder and partner in Syntonics International LLC, a firm which provides executive, management, customer service, and conflict resolution training programs to businesses. She also serves as a board member for the United Minority Business Enterpreneurs, Inc. and the California Business Council for Equal Opportunity. She continues to seek management positions in both the public and private sectors that allow her to apply her corporate, administrative and organizational skills to business and problems.

Current Address: P.R. Plus, Enterprises, 25037 Copa de Oro Dr., #203, Hayward, CA 94545.

Sources:

Eldridge, Grant. Curriculum vitae and other materials supplied by Diana LaCome, April 1998.

La India
(1970–)
Singer, songwriter

Selected discography:

Llegó La India. Soho Sounds, 1992.
Yemaya y Ochun. Soho Latino, 1994.
Dicen Que Soy. Soho Latino, 1994.
India: Mega Mix. UNI/RMM Records, 1996
Sobre El Fuego. RMM, 1997.

Overview

Transforming herself from the house singer, India, to the salsa diva, "La India," this Nuyorican singer from the Bronx created a tremendously successful career for herself at a very young age. She first joined the hot urban trend of house music and hip hop and then helped a new generation blaze a trail into the music usually associated with their parents: salsa. As the popularity of salsa returned, La India's star rose, but she did not stop there. Her singing career continues to evolve and mature, always striking a balance between cultural traditions and music's cutting edge.

Born Linda Belle Caballero in 1970 in Rio Piedras, Puerto Rico, India moved as a baby to the tough "La Candela" or "the candle" section of New York City's Bronx. Her cigar-smoking grandmother was a strong influence who taught her to be independent and free. It was a lesson the young girl would take to heart. In grade school, India met Louie Vega, forming a friendship that lasted through high school, and the two became involved in the urban "street" music scene. Vega produced large parties with house music, which India would advertise. The friendship subsequently evolved into a business partnership and, later, marriage.

Attains Early Success

Caballero's fine-featured beauty earned her the nickname "India" as a child, and a modeling career by the time she was 15 years old. But music was her main interest. Her career began as a house singer under the tutelage of Jellybean Benitez, who had little respect for the salsa India grew to love. By age 14, she was singing backup for the Latin hip hop group TKA, scoring many top ten dance hits, such as "I Can't Get No Sleep," which hit number one on the dance charts. At age 19, she married Louie Vega, who was by then a disc jockey and record producer and was known as "Little" Louie Vega. When she signed a contract with Warner Brothers in the 1980s, she seemed poised to follow in the footsteps of singers like Madonna, who translated the vibrant rhythms of the street into a highly commercial form of pop dance music. After one 1990 album of English-language dance music, *Breaking Night,* however, India decided to expand her horizons—and return to her own cultural roots. "I felt pressure to follow in Madonna's footsteps, and I didn't want to base my career on sex," she said in an interview with the *New York Times.* "So I began to change how I saw myself."

Rediscovers Salsa

The famous keyboardist and salsa band leader Eddie Palmieri was looking for a female singer, and when he strolled into Vega's studio one day India's vocalizations impressed him. Her work with Palmieri reminded listeners of Celia Cruz, an Afro-Cuban singer with a robust style, considered by many to be the queen of salsa. Although it took some time before India felt as comfortable in Spanish as she did in English, in 1992 Palmieri produced India's salsa album *Llegó La India,* on Soho Sounds. It quickly received praise as one of the year's best salsa albums. Most critics responded favorably to the hard-edged, full-voiced style of the transformed "La India".

La India was creatively inspired by trading in the synthesizers of dance music for the horns and percussion of salsa. Yet her exploration of the rich variety of musical cultures had only begun. In 1994, La India and Vega released *Yemaya y Ochun,* an album of dance tunes that paid homage to the Santeria chants that underlie much of Afro-Caribbean music. That same year, La India released *Dicen Que Soy,* a very popular album that remained in the Billboard Top Ten Latin Chart for months. The album's title song proclaimed a strong, independent attitude as the singer listed things that people said about her, concluding firmly, "I don't care."

Offers Strong Female Voice

Singing in Spanish and English, La India presents herself as a true "Nuyorican," part of an urban generation of hip, bilingual, bicultural Hispanic Americans. Her music pays tribute to the cultural inheritance of traditional Latin genres like salsa, even as it participates in the contemporary urban dance trends that generate much commercial pop music. Her audience includes a large proportion of women, alienated by much of salsa's traditional "macho ladykiller" attitude. La India's songs take strong positions in typically female situations; when singing about taking control of her life and relationships, loving who she is, not depending on men, and demanding to be treated with respect, she gives voice to a particularly Hispanic American feminist awareness. "Women see me as a figure they can respect," she said in a *Chicago Tribune* interview. They

know I've been through a lot. I'm not going to let no man put me under." The titles of La India's songs confirm this sentiment: In "Qué Ganas Que No Verte Nunca Más," or "What A Joy Not To Have To See You Anymore," she acts like the opposite of an abandoned woman, while in "Ella o Yo," or "Her or Me," the singer insists that the man to whom she sings cannot treat her badly by having two women.

La India's self-assertive personal style has also contributed to her success as the voice of a new generation. Known for her striking appearance, set off with sexy clothes and manicured nails, she also manages to undermine her own diva image by smoking cigars as she sings, a gesture quickly borrowed by Madonna, among others. While her beauty is strongly feminine, the cigar represents a claim to power and authority traditionally thought to be masculine. But it is more than a pose: as a composer and arranger of her own songs who works closely with her producers, La India keeps control of her creative process as well as her image.

Heads in New Directions

Always eager to learn more and experiment with different forms, La India varies her musical style as well as the people with whom she works. In 1996, she collaborated with legendary mambo bandleader Tito Puente and the swing institution, the Count Basie Orchestra, to produce *Jazzin'* for RMM Records, an English language version of swing classics such as "Love for Sale" and "Crazy He Calls Me" with a Latin twist. Accompanied by a traditional swing orchestra, La India's strong, clear voice provides an intriguing contrast to the often softer, passive style of the traditional chanteuse, while Puente's syncopation gives the tunes a Latin flair. In addition La India's fourth album, *India: Mega Mix,* was released to the public.

In 1996, La India and Vega divorced, but remained on friendly terms, continuing to work together. *Sobre el Fuego,* her 1997 release from RMM Records, has been widely praised as a sign that La India is maturing as a singer and songwriter. She continues to exploit the stunningly wide range of her voice. On the album, she sings a duet with salsa queen Celia Cruz, a gesture which many take as a sign that if Cruz is the reigning queen of salsa, La India is her princess and heir to the crown. In the duet, the older singer offers advice to the younger about staying true to oneself. It is advice that La India seems to have followed. "There's so many things I want to do," she told the *Los Angeles Times.* "I don't want to do them to be different or just for a challenge, but because my heart and soul tell them to."

Sources:

Obejas, Achy. "La India: She Adds a Feminist Fillip to Salsa's Macho Beat." *Chicago Tribune,* October 31, 1997, Tempo, p. 1.

Oumano, Elena. "She's S-S-S-Smokin'!" *Los Angeles Times,* August 14, 1994, Calendar, p.3.

Pareles, Jon. "Pop Review: Seasoning the Kiss-Off with Salsa and Soul. *The New York Times,* December 31, 1997, section E, p. 10.

Torres, Richard. "Sonidos Latinos: La India Finds Her True Salsa Muse." *Newsday,* October 19, 1997, p. D35.

Watrous, Peter. "Flocking to Salsa, No Longer Hispanic Fogy Music.*New York Times,* June 6, 1994, p. C11.

Susan Leal

(1949–)

Municipal government official

Susan Leal, city and county treasurer of San Francisco, is a woman of many distinctions. She is only the second Hispanic American woman in the United States to become the city and county treasurer of a major city, following in the footsteps of Mariam Santos of Chicago, who was the first Hispanic American woman to attain that elected position. Before that, Leal was the first Hispanic American woman to sit on the eleven-member San Francisco board of supervisors. She broke down another barrier as well: she was the first gay or lesbian person of color to serve on the board.

Making Preparations

Leal was born on October 11, 1949, in San Francisco to Mexican parents. She graduated in 1967 from Presentation High School, an all-girls Catholic high school in that city. Her pursuit of higher education took her across the Bay to the University of California at Berkeley, where she received her B.A. in economics in 1971 and a law degree in 1975. Following law school, she left scenic California for the historic, but politically-charged Washington, DC. There she served as counsel to the U.S. House Energy and Commerce Committee's Subcommittee on Oversight and Investigations. In that capacity she directed drug safety and consumer protection investigations of the Food and Drug Administration, dealing daily with issues of fraud and waste in public and private health care. That exposure early in her career to reports of a misguided and mismanaged health care system had a profound impact. For that reason, health care administration and operation remained a key focus of Leal's attention for years to come. In her work with Al Gore, who then held a seat in Congress, she sought to uncover the wrongdoing that plagued health care throughout the United States.

Returning Home

In 1982, Leal left the nation's capital to become a senior consultant to the California State Assembly's Committee on Ways and Means. She had the tedious task of drafting the assembly's health budget. Two years later, Leal entered the private sector, becoming vice president of a nationally recognized company and assisting corporations and unions throughout the United States in health care management.

Even though Leal expressed little interest in running for an elected position or seeking a public service appointment, it was "not surprising" when her career turned toward public office. In June of 1993, San Francisco mayor Frank Jordan called Leal to request that she fill a seat left vacant when Roberta Achtenberg left the board to become assistant secretary of the federal Housing and Urban Development Department. She accepted, thus launching her career in city government. A year later, she actively sought election to the four-year seat; she won with over 100,000 votes cast across the city.

Leal's foray into the city's finances began when she chaired the board's finance committee. Leal was responsible for preparing and balancing the city's $3.4 billion

Susan Leal

budget. Leal also served as a member of the San Francisco Transportation Authority at this time. Her project to improve the Mission District's lighting was realized when she successfully secured $450,000 from the U.S. Department of Transportation.

Her initial work on this project, as well as her successful campaign to upgrade what is regarded as the "busiest busline in the West," the Mission 14, brought Leal the honor of being named "No. 1 Elected Leader" by the San Francisco Mission Merchants Association's "Greater Mission Awards" in 1996. Known as the "Mission Miracle Mile," this is the cultural shopping center for the Hispanic American population of San Francisco. As Leal stated in accepting her award, "This street has a proud, rich history as one of the most vibrant in the city. Mission Street will be a jewel in our city once again." Additionally, Leal helped defeat the voter-initiated ballot measure calling for the repeal of the renaming of Army Street to César Chávez Boulevard.

The Employee Benefits and Practices Measure, or Proposition E, came for a vote before the board of supervisors in 1996. Leal stood as the lone member to vote against it, but she was vindicated in November. Even thought the mayor placed it on the ballot and organized labor supported it, voters soundly rejected it. Once again Leal, as she had so often done in the past, went the distance to stand her ground in the midst of political opposition.

Representing the People

Leal's willingness to stand by her convictions earned her the endorsement of many during her 1997 campaign for the position of treasurer. In an editorial in strong support of her election, the *San Francisco Chronicle* noted that, "Leal, who has both an economics and law degree, has sharpened her financial skills in private business and at City Hall. She had headed the Board's Finance Committee and developed a wide understanding of municipal finances. Her experience should enable her to run a fair-sized city office with an independent spirit. . . she has gone her own way in disputes with the present and past two mayors. . ."

Leal entered the office of city and county treasurer with the goal of making it more efficient. She considers her role as the city's banker and investment officer, as well as manager of the Tax Collector's Office, a public trust. Leal has set four priorities for the Treasurer's Office: to seek the best return on investments with the lowest risk; to make investments consistent with San Francisco's socially responsible values; to modernize the Treasurer and Tax Collector's Office to make it more consumer friendly; and to ensure the fair and efficient collection of taxes and fees.

When asked what accomplishment she considers to be her greatest since sitting in public office, Leal answered confidently: "I think it is the funding of city-wide child care by using city money entirely without the use of federal or state dollars." This and her other work in directing money in caring for the city's children brought Leal her most treasured honor, that of being named as the "City Legislator of the Year" in 1997 by San Francisco's largest child advocacy group. Leal continues to pursue her work as a caretaker of the people's money.

Current Address: Office of the Treasurer, City and County of San Francisco, 875 Stevenson St., Rms. 250, San Francisco, CA 94102.

Sources:

Leal, Susan. Treasurer's official biographical information sheet, 1998.

Mission Merchant Association and Greater Chamber of Commerce Association Page. Available at http://www.carnaval.com/mma/awards/mma awards.htm.

San Francisco Elections Page. Available at www.ci.sf.ca.us.

San Francisco Treasurer's Homepage. Available at http://www.citysearch7.com/E/V/SFOCA/1000/23/20.

Spear, Jane. Telephone conversation with Susan Leal, March 27, 1998.

Nancy León
(1944–)
Organization president

Nancy León has spent most of her career as an outspoken advocate for improved education and leadership development within the Hispanic community. Following her early activities in English as a Second Language (ESL), bilingual, and migrant education programs in California, León gradually began to focus on empowering more Hispanic American women to take on leadership roles. As president of the National Hispana Leadership Institute (NHLI) since 1993, León has encouraged hundreds of young women to become leaders and to serve as mentors to other Hispanic American women. She has frequently stated that it is the responsibility of Hispanic American women who have achieved leadership positions to remem-

Nancy León

ber their communities and to help other women while moving up the ladder.

Spends Early Career in Educational Programs

Nancy León, whose parents were a farmworker and homemaker, grew up in California during the 1950s and early 1960s, at a time when most Hispanic American women were encouraged to marry and have children, rather than attend college. However, León did not follow the traditional route. After receiving a B.S. at California Polytechnic State University (1968) and an M.A. in multicultural education at Pepperdine University (1978), León became a teacher and then an administrator at several English as a second language (ESL), bilingual, and migrant education programs in California. While a teacher, León met her first mentor, a Hispanic American woman who urged León to become an administrator so that she could have more influence over educational policy. This encouragement not only convinced León to change her own career path, but also led her eventually to become president of an organization that has helped many other Hispanic American women to find mentors.

Through the early 1990s, León focused on migrant education, serving as director of the Monterey County Office of Migrant Education from 1986 to 1992. During this time she also served on the boards of numerous community-based organizations, such as the Second Chance Gang Prevention Program.

Directs Her Attention to Hispanic American Women Issues

While working in Monterey County in 1988, León was awarded a one-year fellowship at the National Hispana Leadership Institute, then located in Washington, DC. This time proved to be another turning point in her career. She joined a group of promising Hispanic American women who spent a year developing special community projects, returned to their communities, and mentored other aspiring women. "Yo Puedo" (I Can), developed by León, was a program to improve self-esteem and leadership skills in middle and secondary school migrant students who hoped to attend college. Her program was so successful that it achieved national recognition, and in 1991 she was given the Congressional Award. In 1993, after serving as a board member of NHLI and president of its alumnae association, León became the president of NHLI, a position she still held in 1998.

NHLI, which is now located in Alexandria, VA, and has become a nationally known organization for training Hispanic American female leaders, had an unlikely start. In 1984 the Coors Brewing Company (originally as a marketing effort following boycotts by several minority groups) decided to do outreach to Hispanic American women. The company asked a group of Hispanic American women (including Maria Elena Toraño, a former Carter administration official) to serve as consultants on how it could help Hispanic American women. As Toraño later recalled for *Hispanic Outlook in Higher Education,* "We discovered one issue that cuts across the lives of all Hispanic American women — the need to develop leadership abilities." The consultants proposed that Coors fund a program that would increase Hispanic American female participation in decision-making, especially on the national level.

Coors agreed to sponsor the initial round of a one-year fellowship program for Hispanic American women who had already demonstrated their involvement in community leadership. In 1986 Coors contributed $300,000 as an initial grant for the pilot project, which was called the Coors National Hispana Leadership Initiative. After the pilot year, a national advisory committee was formed to create an ongoing organization, renamed the National Hispana Leadership Institute.

In succeeding years many other sponsors joined Coors, and by early 1998 almost 200 Hispanic American women had completed fellowships. Private and corporate grants absorb most of the cost of the program, and scholarships are available for women who need additional financial assistance. Many of the participants have come from public sector management positions and have been the first in their families to graduate from college. NHLI also publishes a quarterly newsletter and offers many activities for its alumnae so that they can continue to be part of an ongoing community.

In October 1997, NHLI celebrated its tenth anniversary with a conference and award ceremony that included a wide variety of speakers from within the Hispanic American female community. Discussion sessions included topics such as small business strategies, political campaigning, technology, and personal development.

Advocates Mentoring and Breaking Hispanic American Female Stereotypes

León has placed a strong emphasis on having fellows in the NHLI program serve as mentors to other women in the community. As quoted in *Hispanic Outlook in Higher Education,* she believes that, "We cannot forget our communities when we get educated and move up. . . .We cannot forget that we got here on the shoulders of other women." And she sees that her work can be helpful beyond the Hispanic American female community. In 1997 NHLI formed an alliance with the Asian-Pacific-American Leadership Institute, in order to share NHLI's experience in setting up mentoring programs. The two groups spent several days together, sharing their experiences and ideas. In 1998 NHLI has similar plans for forming coalitions with Native American and African American women's organizations.

León also sees how Hispanic American women have faced the double obstacles of racism and sexism, and she has addressed gender issues within the Hispanic community. She often has been outspoken in suggesting that Hispanic American women break out of stereotypical roles. Noting in *Hispanic Link* that families have different expectations for boys and girls, she stated that Hispanic American women must be just as highly educated as Hispanic American men, since many Hispanic American women will end up heading families and having business careers. When asked to comment on the Hollywood-fed stereotype of "luscious Latinas" for *Hispanic,* León said that there was no room in the business world for this image and that few professional Hispanic American women promote it. She went on to attribute this harmful stereotype's existence to another entity as well as Hollywood: women's magazines: "I hate women's magazines. Practically every ad in fashion magazines presents women as sex objects, and we're the only ones, as consumers of these products, who can change that." At the same time, she is a staunch believer in the need for both men and women in the Hispanic community to develop as leaders and for both to value traits such as nurturance and spirituality. As she noted in an article written for *Hispanic,* "Before we can lead others, we have to lead ourselves. . . .Resolving the issue of leadership is not just a 'woman' thing."

León also is convinced that Hispanic American women, after long being involved in grassroots political efforts, are just beginning to reap the benefits. In an article she wrote for *Hispanic Link,* León pointed proudly to the rising Hispanic American female political figures on the national front who began their careers in community activities such as the PTA, child care programs, environmental causes, and scholarship drives. Through these activities carried on over so many years, León believes that Hispanic American women have created solid relationships with their communities and, as a result, are now being entrusted with increasingly important political offices.

Current Address: National Hispana Leadership Institute, 1901 N. Moore St., Ste. 206 , Arlington, VA 22209.

Sources:

Alma-Bonilla, Yara I. "Latina Groups Refine Methods, Keep Goals." *Hispanic Link,* September 21, 1997. Available at http://www.latinolink.com.

León, Nancy. "Latina's Ladder to Political Success Is Anchored in Barrio Deeds." *Hispanic Link,* February 16, 1997. Available at http://www.latinolink.com.

———. "A Model for Latina Leadership." *Hispanic,* March 1996, p. 80.

McDowell, Melody. "National Hispana President Credits Mentoring for Success." *Minority Business News USA,* October 15, 1997, p. 36.

Menard, Valerie. "Luscious Latinas: Hispanic Stars Break Stereotypes." *Hispanic,* June 1997. Available at http://www.azcentral.com/hispanic.

National Hispana Leadership Institute Home Page. Available at http://www.incacorp.com/nhli.

Pinto Alicea, Ines. "Focus on the National Hispana Leadership Institute." *Hispanic Outlook in Higher Education,* February 1, 1994, p. 6.

Tania León
(1943–)
Conductor, music director, composer

A multi-faceted musician, Tania León is an international figure in the music world. She has carved a niche for herself in contemporary music as a composer, conductor, and music director, in the process receiving numerous commissions and awards. Tania León "has distinguished herself as a proponent of music without category beyond a standard of excellence," remarked long-time music commentator Howard Mandel in an article for *Ear Magazine.* "Her enthusiasm for contemporary composers regardless of gender, race, or national origin indicates an all-embracing worldview as befits a warm, lively woman who accepts no imposed limits to her own activity."

Spends Early Years in Cuba

The daughter of Oscar León Mederos and Dora Ferran, León was born in Havana, Cuba, on May 14, 1943, of a

Tania León

mixed ethnic background. Her ancestors hailed from China, Nigeria, France, and Spain. In Havana León studied piano, violin, and music theory, earning multiple bachelors degrees and a masters degree in music from the Carlos Alfredo Peyrellado Conservatory. While still a student she wrote her first compositions—boleros, bossa novas, and popular music. From 1964 to 1967 León performed as a piano soloist in her native country and acted as music director for a television station in Havana.

León immigrated to New York City in 1967. Two years later, she accidentally met Arthur Mitchell, who asked her to accompany on piano his new dance troupe—Dance Theater of Harlem. León improvised music to fulfill Mitchell's rehearsal needs, and before long Mitchell offered León the music directorship of the troupe, a position she held until 1980. In addition to her artistic managerial activities, León began composing works for the troupe, such as *Tones,* which she and Mitchell collaborated on in 1970. The ballets *The Beloved* and *Dougla* quickly followed. *Dougla,* in particular, met with success, becoming a regular part of the repertoire of European dance companies.

Takes Up the Baton

Although composing was well within the realm of imagination for León, at the time there were no women conductors, so she did not consider conducting a viable career choice. "Women conducting a symphony orchestra? Taboo. It was completely unheard of," León recalled to

Mandel. "It never crossed my mind." Yet when the Dance Theater of Harlem performed at the Festival of Two Worlds in Spoleto, Italy, in 1971, León was unexpectedly given the opportunity to conduct the Julliard Orchestra, which was accompanying the troupe. "I was encouraged by Arthur Mitchell and Gian-Carlo Menotti to work with the orchestra," reminisced León to Anne Lundy in the *Black Perspective in Music.* "They encouraged me to do that, and I had never done it in my life. It was my very first time, but I picked up the baton, and I conducted the performance."

Upon returning to the United States, León began to study conducting formally with Laszlo Halasz, one of the founders of the New York City Opera. Encouraged, she enrolled at the Julliard School of Music to study with Vincent LaSilva. While working with the Dance Theater, León earned a bachelors degree in music and then a masters degree in composition from New York University. Three years later, León studied at the Berkshire Music Center at Tanglewood with many guest conductors, among them the world famous Leonard Bernstein and Seiji Ozawa.

León's conducting activities extended far beyond the Dance Theater. At the invitation of composer-conductor Lukas Foss, she founded the Brooklyn Philharmonic Community Concert Series in 1977, which she conducted for the next 11 years. León also served as the music director-conductor of the 1978 Broadway production of *The Wiz* and the *Dance in America* series for public television. In 1979 she directed Robert Wilson's *Death, Destruction, and Detroit,* and several years later she composed and directed the music for the plays *Maggie Magalita* and *The Golden Window.* After leaving her position with the Dance Theater, León appeared as a guest conductor at venues in the United States and Puerto Rico. León saw this as a pioneering time for her, and she faced problems "like any pioneer would," she told *Ebony.* "It's not common for a woman of my skin color to conduct serious music, so I have to know the score inside out, or work twice as hard as male conductors."

Finds Musical Voice

In the mid-1980s, León began to express her diverse musical background in her compositions. She assimilated gospel and jazz, as well as Latin American and African elements into pieces, creating a highly rhythmic and colorful signature sound. For example, in Carabali, a piece for orchestra, León employed rhythms and improvisation from Cuban jazz, in a far-ranging blend of tonal colors and rhythmic patterns. Explaining that the Carabali are Africans who fought off slave traders to become known as an indomitable people, León described in *Peer-Southern Concert Music* the piece named *Carabali* as "a symbol of a spirit that cannot be broken." León added, "I have tried to convey such an image by creating a body of sounds propelled by a persistent rhythmic language." Upon the premier of the work, a reviewer for the *Cincinnati Enquirer* remarked, "Highly intellectual, and a demanding piece for both orchestra and conductor, Carabali is both accessible and powerful."

León's compositions garnered praise and soon earned her recognition as a new voice in the music world. In 1985 she was awarded a residency at the Lincoln Center Institute in New York City and won the Dean Dixon Conducting Award. She also joined the composition faculty of the Brooklyn College Conservatory, where she was made full professor in 1994.

In the 1990s, León hit her stride, with a steady stream of residencies, guest conducting appearances, and commissions for new pieces. In the fall of 1992, she conducted the Johannesburg Symphony during the Dance Theater of Harlem's historic trip to South Africa, when the company became the first multi-racial arts group to perform and teach there in modern times. León has been invited to appear as a guest conductor-composer at Harvard University, Yale University, the Cleveland Institute, the Ravinia Festival in Chicago, the Bellagio Center in Italy, the Gewandhausorchester Leipzig and the Beethovenhalle Orchestra in Germany, and elsewhere.

In 1993 León accepted a three-year appointment as Revson Composer Fellow for the New York Philharmonic. Her responsibilities included advising conductor Kurt Masur on contemporary music, which she believes puts off many potential listeners. The antidote, according to León, is using orchestras in community outreach; otherwise, audiences for classical music will continue to dwindle, seriously threatening its existence. "An orchestra, for me, is an educational institution, and each orchestra member is a specialist, as well as a teacher," León explained in the *I.S.A.M. Newsletter* (Institute for Studies in American Music). "It is terribly important that we walk constantly into schools and community centers to offer master classes that expose our youngsters to the art of music." "If all of us—players, conductors, administrators—reassess our priorities and devote some time to community work, we will take important steps toward rebuilding our image and our audiences," she added. León has long put her words into action, beginning with the Brooklyn Philharmonic Community Concert Series in the late 1970s and extending to the master classes she taught at the Hamburg Musikschule in Germany in 1995.

Starts Latin American Music Festival

León also acts as artistic director for the concert series on Latin American music sponsored by the American Composers Orchestra (ACO). She cited a historical precedent for the series in the interest by North Americans in Latin American music during the 1930s, 1940s, and 1950s. However, this interest fizzled out in the 1960s with the heightening of North-South political tensions. León would like to see the interest in Latin American works rekindled. She was instrumental in organizing the American Composers Orchestra's Sonidos de las Americas—Sounds of the

Americas—festival, which first took place in February of 1994 in New York City. As early as 1991, she and ACO Managing Director Jesse Rosen had traveled to Central and South America to search out new sounds. "We met with composers, with leaders in contemporary music in Venezuela, Brazil, Argentina, and Mexico," León recounted to Octavio Roca of *Symphony Magazine*. "The first thing we realized is just how much is out there—and how rich the variety." With such diverse music available, León and Rosen decided to focus the first annual festival on the music of Mexico. By festival time, they had organized, with the help of the Mexican Cultural Institute and the cooperation of Carnegie Hall, concerts, symposia, and master classes dealing with the works of Mexican composers. Calling the festival "long overdue," León voiced her aspirations to Roca. "Maybe in future years more orchestras can model programs after this one, and we will have a new movement of interconnections between countries, so that whole communities of composers can be known. Now that the door is open, this program can continue." León plans for future festivals to spotlight the music of other Latin American countries.

León's composing process seems to mirror her life in its complexity. Like all creative activity, composing is a process of bringing together disparate elements to create a whole. "My ideas have to do with my present," León told a *Symphony Magazine* reporter. "They come when I least expect it, in the street, sitting at home, in the car. Ideas start tapping in anywhere, anytime. They wake me up and all of a sudden I'm hearing an entire orchestra playing something." The composer keeps a notebook available to jot down her ideas as they come. She can be inspired by such varied events as a visit to a museum or getting stuck in a traffic jam. León collects these varied musical ideas, which she crafts into a commissioned work based on the parameters of the piece. She prefers to work on a single composition at a time.

One commission seemed so daunting at first that León almost turned it down—an opera. "When I had the invitation to write an opera, I almost slammed down the telephone. I just couldn't deal with it," the composer was quoted as saying in the *I.S.A.M. Newsletter*. Fortunately León reconsidered, for the award-winning *Scourge of Hyacinths* was the result. Adapted from a radio play by Nobel Prize-winning dramatist Wole Soyinka of Nigeria, the opera deals with the plight of three political prisoners in an unnamed dictatorship. The fate of the prisoners is linked to a goddess of the native Yoruban religion, the music of which León remembered from her childhood. The hyacinths represent corruption and literally and figuratively prevent the protagonists from escaping their horrible fate. The opera's 12 quick scenes play continuously, with León's lightly orchestrated and highly rhythmic music propelling the action. León herself conducted the premier performances in Munich, Germany, in May of 1994. For *Scourge of Hyacinths*, she won the BMW Prize for Best Composition at the Munich Biennale for New Music Theater. In 1999, the opera will be co-produced by the Grand Théâtre de Genève and the Opéra de Nancy et de Lorraine, with León conducting. Also, the Dortmund Opera has commissioned a new opera from León based on a short story by Isabel Allende. Her other recent commissions include a major multi-media work entitled *Drummin*, which premiered in November of 1997 at the Lincoln Theatre in Miami; *Sol de Doce* for the men's vocal ensemble Chanticleer, with poetry by Pedro Mir; *Singing Sepia*, a song cycle in collaboration with poet Rita Dove for the chamber ensemble Continuum; *Para Viola y Orquesta*, premiered by a consortium of four U.S. orchestras; and *Hechizos* (Spells), commissioned and premiered by Frankfurt's Ensemble Modern in March 1995.

Receives Numerous Awards

Winning prizes is nothing new for León. She has received awards for her compositions from Chamber Music America, Readers' Digest, ASCAP, Cintas, Meet the Composer, and Women of Hope. She has also been awarded grants from the National Endowment for the Arts, the Copland Fund, Rockefeller Foundation, and the American Academy of Arts and Letters, which have allowed for recordings to be made of her works. *Indigena*, a compact disc of León's chamber music was released on the CRI label. A compact disc that includes *Bata* and *Carabali* is available from the Louisville Orchestra's First Edition Records. Other pieces can be found on the Albany Records, Newport Classic, Leonarda, and Mode labels.

Considering herself a global citizen, León does not like to be categorized by race or gender. "I have come to a place where I have no citizenship and I have a global consciousness," she once told *Ear Magazine*. And as a global citizen, she desires to bridge the gap between Latin American and European music, a lofty—some would say impossible—aspiration. Yet León is not easily deterred from pursuing her goals. "My chosen purpose in life is to be a musician, a composer, a conductor," she told Lundy. "This is the way I am making my contribution to mankind" and for these contributions, she wishes to be judged.

Current Address: Kaylor Management, Inc., 130 W. 57th St., Ste. 8G, New York, NY 10019.

Sources:

Adams, J., et al. "Remaking American Opera." *I.S.A.M. Newsletter*, Spring 1995, p. 2.
American Record Guide, January/February 1995, p. 48.
Ashley, R. "Music and Money: Two Discussions." *Ear Magazine*, April 1991, pp. 21-29.
Bakers Biographical Dictionary of Musicians. New York: Schirmer, 1992.
Brooks, Iris. "An American in Paris and Other Expatriate Composers Speak Out." *Ear Magazine*, October 1989, p. 32.
Cincinnati Enquirer, January 19, 1992, p. B4.
Cohen, Aaron I. Volume 1 of *International Encyclopedia of Women Composers*. Books & Music, 1987.
Ebony, February 1989, pp. 54-62.
"Festivals (Munich's Biennale)." *Musical Opinion*, June/July/August 1994, p. 211.
"Future Music." *Ear Magazine*, 1986-1987, p. 16.
"Kabiosile." *Symphony Magazine*, 1988, p. 27.
Kaylor Management, Inc. Biographical information. January 1998.
Kiraly, P. "Musical Melding." *Symphony Magazine*, October 1991, p. 29.
Lundy, A. "Conversations with Three Symphonic Conductors." *Black Perspective in Music*, Fall 1988, pp. 213-225.
Mandel, Howard. "Tania León: Beyond Borders." *Ear Magazine*, January 1989, pp. 12-13.
"Momentum: For Solo Piano." *Notes: Quarterly Journal of the Music Library Association*, 1988, pp. 581-82.
New York Times, December 10, 1991, p. C19.
The Norton/Grove Dictionary of Women Composers. New York: W.W. Norton, 1995.
Peer-Southern Concert Music, fall 1992, pp. 1-2.
Peer-Southern Concert Music, winter 1994-95, p. 4.
Roca, Octavio. "Sonidos de las Americas: Mexico-The Sound of America." *Symphony Magazine*, May/June 1994, pp. 38-44.
San Francisco Chronicle, October 10, 1994, p. E3.
Schiff, D., et al. "Americanizing the American Orchestra." *I.S.A.M. Newsletter*, Fall 1933, pp. 9-10.
Schlueter, Paul. "The Western Wind. " *American Record Guide*, July/August 1992, p. 279.
Silsbury, E. "Munich Biennale: Sublime and Ridiculous." *Opera*, festival 1994, pp. 101-102.
Southern, Eileen. *Biographical Dictionary of Afro-American and African Musicians*. Westport, CT: Greenwood Press, 1982.

Levins Morales, Aurora
See **Morales, Aurora Levins**

Sheila Lichacz
(1942–)
Artist, diplomat

Sheila Lichacz's simple but monumental paintings have earned her acclaim as an artist and prestige as a diplomat. Appointed ambassador-at-large for the Republic of Panama, she resides in Miami, FL, where she creates works that

Sheila Lichacz

are both modern in style and deeply spiritual in content. Uninterested in the affluent, trend-driven contemporary art world, Lichacz exhibits her work in a gallery in downtown Miami, but does not market in other areas. Instead of focusing on the commercial aspects of art, she works in the hope that her painting will communicate her joyous spiritual message to as many people as possible.

Lichacz was born in 1942 in Monagrillo, Panama, a place usually considered to have been the birthplace of ceramics sometime around 3000 BC. The Mesoamerican history and culture of her birthplace impressed Lichacz from an early age; she remembers finding pottery shards as a little girl while playing in the Rio Santa Maria, the river that flowed near her family's ranch. She was also fascinated by the Mesoamerican potter who worked in the village near her home, a woman who taught her to make miniature pots using clay from the river. Combined with her devout Catholic faith, these early impressions are the strongest influences on her art.

Lichacz did not become an artist immediately. After a happy and peaceful childhood, she attended Our Lady of the Lake University in San Antonio, TX, where she met and married John Lichacz, an officer in the United States Air Force. After Lichacz earned her B.S. in home economics in 1965, the couple moved to Puerto Rico, where she earned an M.A. in education at the Inter-American University in San Germán. In 1970, she gave birth to a daughter, Gina Marie.

Discovers Painting

Returning to Panama, Lichacz began substitute teaching and working as a counselor in the Panama Canal Zone schools, while her husband became chief of protocol for the United States Air Force Southern Air Command. One day, while working as a guidance counselor, a student spit in Lichacz's face, telling her that Americans did not want Panamanians in the Canal Zone. Deeply shaken, Lichacz decided she could not teach anymore. Instead, she enrolled in an art class at Canal Zone College. According to Lichacz, the instructor did not like her paintings of trees or landscapes, but when she decided to paint a clay pot, the teacher was suddenly impressed. From that day on, Lichacz developed her technique, using abstract and inanimate forms to combine cultural memory with deep beliefs. As she grew more confident, the size of her paintings increased, until she began working in a monumental scale unusual for women artists.

Artwork Depicts Pre-Columbian Pottery

Lichacz's subjects, all very simply rendered in vivid color, include fruits, vegetables, and leaves, along with the ceramic pots that are representative of her birthplace. The pots also become dynamic symbols for the life process and for the articles of faith the artist professes. Vessels made from earth, the pots suggest the physical fertility of women as well as the creative impulse of art. In some paintings, pots are shown emerging from a larger pot or from a large shell; Lichacz's treatment of these organic forms is reminiscent of the flower paintings of Georgia O'Keefe. But Lichacz's pots are dynamic, often depicted in a sequence that suggests the processes of birth and maturation. The wide, dark mouths of the *tinajas,* or large earthenware pots, and gourds used to carry water called *tulas* suggest a rich interior that makes them into symbols for the soul.

At the same time, Lichacz's titles and compositions serve to connect her paintings with biblical themes. *Dancing and Cana* and *Miracle at Cana,* for instance, show groupings of pots that remind the viewer of the vessels of water that Jesus, in the Gospel of John, turns into wine. But the way the pots seem to dance with joy suggests that they represent the witnesses to the miracle as well—themselves vessels of a higher presence. These biblical referents help place the work in the religious context Lichacz desires. Painting is a religious process for her: on each canvas she begins by inscribing the letters "AM+GD," which stand for the Latin phrase *Ad Majorem Gloriam Dei* meaning "for the greater glory of God."

Achieves Success as Painter

In 1977, Lichacz began exhibiting her paintings in Panama. That same year, one of her paintings was presented to King Juan Carlos of Spain by the government of Panama. By 1980, the President of Panama named her "Pride of Panama and the Americas." In 1983, she was commissioned by the Archdiocese in Panama to paint a gift for Pope John Paul II. Her painting *Voices of the Americas* depicted 31 pots, representing the 31 Latin American nations, that seem to look up at a golden cross. It became part of the Vatican Museum's permanent collection and led to Lichacz's two private audiences with the Pope. At the first audience, Lichacz showed the Pope a collection of photographs of her work, including a tapestry she had created by collecting and sewing together handmade Indian *molas,* or layered fabrics, in the shape of a cross. When the Pope admired the tapestry, she offered it to him as a gift and he accepted, a moment Lichacz sees as the highlight of her artistic career.

Lichacz's first exhibit in the United States was at the Museum of Modern Art of Latin America in Washington, DC, in 1981. With her husband retired from the Air Force and managing her artistic career, the couple moved back to the United States. More individual exhibitions followed at galleries in Santa Fe, Los Angeles, and Miami, among others. Many university galleries exhibited her works, including the University of California at Irvine and Harvard University. She maintained her international presence as well: one of her paintings was presented as a gift to the president of Peru by the government of Panama, and in 1994 she was commissioned to design the poster for the Summit of the Americas. In 1995, she was named ambassador-at-large by the president of Panama. In 1996 she became the first woman to be honored with the Hispanic Achievement Award in the International Friendship Award category.

Recently, Lichacz has created a series of collage paintings using thousands of pre-Columbian pottery shards she has collected over the years. She exhibits them in her Miami studio space, but they are not for sale, because she wants to keep them on view together. Her love for the pre-Columbian culture of her birthplace led her to become instrumental in saving the ancient shell mounds in Monagrillo when they were being vandalized by people wanting to make adobe for new buildings.

Makes the Most of Her Life

Lichacz's works express the depth of her religious belief, as well as her love for the Mesoamerican culture of Panama. In their exuberant joy, they are also testaments to her love of life, an emotion that has been shaped by a series of benign but life-threatening brain tumors, which required eight surgeries to remove. In a statement about her work, she said, "The reason my work is so spiritual is that without faith, I never would have survived. None of us are going to live forever. We are all going. A nun told me when I was a freshman in college, 'Make the most of yourself, because you will never happen again.' That is the philosophy of my life."

Sources:

Conwell, Douglas. "Sheila Lichacz at the Vatican." *Southwest Profile,* April 1984, p. 12.
Johnson, Jan. "The Gospel in Clay Pots." *Virtue,* January/ February 1997, p. 20.
Johnson, Jan. "Shards of Redemption." *Christianity Today,* February 5, 1996, p. 44.

Graciela Limón
(1938–)
Author, professor

Selected writings:

In Search of Bernabé. Houston: Arte Publico Press, 1993.
The Memories of Ana Calderón. Houston: Arte Publico Press, 1994.
Song of the Hummingbird. Houston: Arte Publico Press, 1996.
The Day of the Moon. Houston: Arte Publico Press, forthcoming.

Overview

Graciela Limón, a powerful and uncompromising voice in Chicana literature, has made a distinct and impressive contribution with her novels. With her first novel, *In Search of Bernabé,* which received the Before Columbus American Book Award and was named a Notable Book of 1993, she emerged as an authentic talent. Limón has not stopped writing since, producing two more published novels in three years and adding to the body of her critical work through the publication of scholarly essays.

Dreams of Becoming a Writer

Limón, the daughter of Mexican immigrants, was born in East Los Angeles on August 2, 1938. As a child, she dreamed of becoming a writer, but her insecurity over her abilities made the dream seem too far-fetched. However, when she was 12, a novel about Joan of Arc captured her imagination and she became a ferocious reader of historical novels. By the time she was 20, Limón's literary aspirations were firmly in place.

Limón attended Marymount College in Palos Verdes Estates, CA, earning a B.A. in Spanish literature in 1965. She then attended the University of the Americas in Mexico City, where in 1969 she was awarded her master of arts in the same field. She returned to California for her doctoral degree in Latin American literature from the

University of California at Los Angeles. An assistant professor in the modern language department at Loyola Marymount University from 1969, she was made an associate professor when she received her Ph.D. in 1975, and a professor in 1980, the same year she was made chair of the Department of Chicana and Chicano Studies.

Becomes a Novelist

Limón's career as an academic allowed her to be part of the growth of Chicano studies as a discipline, and her position as chair of the Chicana and Chicano Studies Department of Loyola Marymount University and professor of U.S. Hispanic literature provides her with the opportunity to teach and write in the community that is so much a part of her work. As a Hispanic American writer, her writing decidedly reflects Lillian Castillo-Speed's description of Hispanic American literature: "... Readers are intrigued by a literature that can claim antecedents in the Spanish-language Latin American literary tradition, the English-language literature of immigrants to America, feminist literature, and the literature of the emerging voices of America's ethnic minorities." Limón's early ambition to be a novelist finally became a reality when her critical essays were rejected by editors for being more creative than critical. Fortunately, her belief in her talent persisted and she turned to fiction. She published her first novel, *In Search of Bernabé,* to wide critical acclaim in 1993. The *New York Times Book Review* stated, "Graciela Limón's first novel, *In Search of Bernabé,* leaves the reader with that special hunger that can be created only by a newly discovered writer. Ms. Limón's prose is self-assured and engrossing. *In Search of Bernabé* deserves a large audience." The novel grew out of Limón's 1990 visit to El Salvador as part of a delegation to investigate the killing of Jesuit priests the previous year. Her ability to translate the suffering of that country within a family saga of a mother and her two lost sons made *Bernabé* a powerful indictment of the death squads and of U.S. involvement in that tragedy. This began Limón's relationship with Arte Publico Press, the most prestigious publisher of Hispanic literature in the United States and the publisher of all three of her novels.

Publishes *The Memories of Ana Calderón*

Limón's second novel, *The Memories of Ana Calderón,* (1994) vividly traces the title character from a Mexican seaside childhood abruptly ended by her mother's death, to a hellish migrant camp, and finally to California and Los Angeles. In spite of her father's ever-present anger and the loss of her son, Ana grows into a woman of substance. In this book, Limón also displays her remarkable gift for blending Spanish into the text in such a way that even a non-speaker can appreciate the richness of the mother tongue. Her vision embraces many diverse characters, all original and quite memorable. *The Memories of Ana Calderón* received a mixed reception from critics, but the book attempts a great deal and succeeds in portraying an unforgettable woman.

Releases *Song of the Hummingbird*

Limón's third book, *Song of the Hummingbird* (1996), is a lyrical and elegant expression of hidden history. The novel tells the story of Huitzitzilín, a princess, then slave and concubine who witnesses the Spanish conquest of her people. Calling *Hummingbird* "downright hypnotic," the *Washington Post* praised Limón's vision of pre-Colombian Mexico and the resilient spirit of her people.

Depicts Strong Female Characters in Her Writings

Limón's fiction is best known for its strong women: Huitzitzilín, the Aztec woman who shows us her world through "the eyes of the conquered;" the indomitable Luz Delcano, a mother searching for her lost son in a land of death, and Ana Calderón, the resilient heroine of an epic tale of a woman's life. Limón has a special gift for depicting the inner life of children, showing how dreams of the future are translated into a harsh reality. For example, young Ana Calderon's vision of a life as a dancer is her refuge; when that dream dies, a love of learning takes its place and sustains her.

Limón is amused by the idea that reviews have made much of her "late" start as a novelist; it is clear that her fiction is a reflection of a mature individual and her style is unaffected and original. Despite a successful academic career, her prose has none of the pretensions sometimes expressed by novelists from academia. Ellen McCracken, author of *New Latina Narrative: The Feminine Space of Postmodern Ethnicity* said of her: "Limón has quickly established herself as one of the key voices in the new Chicana fiction of the post-Chicano Movement period. Crossing the literal and figurative borders of the Americas geographically and chronologically, her novels bring the issues of feminism, social justice, popular religiosity, and transborder cultural identity to larger national concerns about the dynamics of multiculturalism."

A warm and gracious person, Limón does not take herself too seriously. She is proud of her academic achievement and success as a novelist. In addition to her creative work, which has been widely anthologized, she has also published reviews and critical work on Mexican, Latin American, and Caribbean literature. She is presently at work on a fourth novel, *The Day of the Moon,* to be published in 1999.

Current Address: 740 North Bradshawe St., Montebello, CA 90640.

Sources:

Castillo-Speed, Lillian, ed. *Latina: Women's Voices from the Borderlands.* New York: Touchstone Books, 1995.

Hanly, Elizabeth. "Song of the Hummingbird." *Washington Post Book Review,* April 28, 1996.

McCracken, Ellen. *New Latina Narrative: The Feminine Space of Postmodern Ethnicity.* Tucson: University of Arizona, forthcoming.

Stavans, Ilan. "Questions of Legitimacy," *The New York Times Book Review,* November 14, 1993, p. 66.

Sylvia S. Lizárraga
(1925–)
Author, professor

Sylvia Lizárraga's abiding concern with sociopolitical issues and the struggle for social change has been her major preoccupation as a creative writer, essayist, and teacher. Known primarily for her short stories, Lizárraga also has published numerous essays on topics related to Hispanic literature and issues of racial and gender discrimination. Once a high school dropout, she rose through the academic ranks to become an instructor at the University of California at Berkeley.

Struggles to Complete Education

Born in Mazatlán, Sinaloa, Mexico, Lizárraga is the daughter of Pedro M. and Carmen Sarmiento. A successful blacksmith in Mazatlán, Pedro Sarmiento believed in the value of education and secured math and English tutors for his children. In 1940, at the age of fifteen, Sylvia Sarmiento married Roberto Lizárraga, and their first two children, Alba and Bobby, were born before their move to San Diego, CA, in 1946. Their two younger children, Marta and Esteban, were born in California. In 1957, when their youngest child started kindergarten, Lizárraga enrolled full-time at Midway High School for adults, beginning an uphill battle against her husband, family, and friends, who thought her desire to go to school was a sign of insanity. She completed high school in two years and graduated with her oldest daughter. At the suggestion of one of her teachers she applied to San Diego State University and entered in September of 1959; unfortunately, an automobile accident in November made it impossible for her to continue.

It was not until 1968, after Alba married, Bobby left for Vietnam, and Marta moved to her own apartment, that Sylvia Lizárraga, at the age of 43, returned to college. Her intense interest in all subjects prompted her to take every introductory course offered at Southwestern Junior College in Chula Vista, CA, graduating in 1970 with highest honors and twice the required number of units. That summer she traveled throughout Europe and upon her return decided to continue her education. She completed a B.A. in Spanish at San Diego State University in 1972 and an M.A. and Ph.D. at the University of California, San Diego, in 1976 and 1979 respectively. She held a Ford Foundation Fellowship from 1973 to 1978 and has taught at the University of California, Berkeley, since 1979.

Short Stories Focus on Women

One of Lizárraga's first published short stories, "De recuerdos" (From Memories), won first place in the 1972 San Diego State University Literary Contest. The story juxtaposes the playful world of children—in which a young brother insists that his sister be treated as an equal by the neighborhood boys—and the harshly realistic, although metaphorical, world of the town's madwoman who cannot understand the basis of inequalities.

While participating in the Chicano Literary Workshop at the University of California, San Diego, Lizárraga produced the majority of her seven short stories that appear in the anthology *Requisa treinta y dos.* The focus of the collection is life and the working conditions in the Southern California border region. Lizárraga focuses primarily, though not exclusively, on women in various social roles: mothers, adolescents, documented and undocumented workers, community organizers. The skillful narration of small, apparently insignificant, everyday occurrences in the lives of these characters reveals a complex yet subtle treatment of socioeconomic factors that affect their lives: physical and psychological abuse, social inequities, racial and sexual discrimination. Characteristic of Lizárraga's narrative is its attempt to draw a critical and analytical response from the reader, prompted by the juxtaposition of a character's perception of his or her situation to an omniscient narration exposing a multidimensional, objective reality which reveals the contradictions. Interior monologues and stream-of-consciousness techniques enable the characters to arrive at self-knowledge through an understanding of their circumstances.

For example, the protagonists of "Silver Lake Road" and "Management" are indigent single mothers who struggle daily to make ends meet. The pressing economic considerations of the single mother in "Silver Lake Road" provide the background to her rape by a young man she has compassionately given a lift to the border. Her economic straits and their alleviation pall next to the violence and helplessness she experiences as she is raped. In "Management" the protagonist reflects on the details of an interview for a job as a waitress at a prosperous Mexican restaurant owned by an assimilated Mexican and his Anglo wife. She realizes that dressing in a "Mexican costume" while enduring condescending attitudes and ill-treatment was too high a price to pay for the meager salary.

Explores Problems of Adolescents and Discrimination

Some of the consequences of the socioeconomic and psychological problems confronted by adolescents are dealt with in Lizárraga's short stories "Coming Out," "Monarchy," and "The Moment." In "Coming Out" a dying 15-year old orphan girl reveals in a stream of consciousness her innocent assessment of her adoptive mother and pimp boyfriend. The questions asked of her by a hospital employee as the girl is being admitted to the hospital trigger thoughts of a childhood of love with her parents but also of deprivation. "Monarchy" is an anecdote which, through irony and satire, comments on the inequities of social class and their perpetuation through seemingly insignificant extracurricular activities in school. The story reveals how these activities are devised to favor economically advantaged girls and to keep poorer girls distracted from their studies with a competition they will never win. "The Moment" describes the alienation suffered by a young student due to language barriers and lack of support from his teachers. As the story develops, the student reaches a level of consciousness which permits him to realize he is not entirely at fault for his lack of comprehension in the classroom.

In these short stories Lizárraga's characters are not militant nor do they speak about massive social protest. Rather, by means of a strong narrative and deft portrayal of her characters, she exposes discrimination and its effects on them. She comments metaphorically on the effects of discrimination on the consciousness of those discriminated against in the widely published 1981 short story "Don." The story centers on a young girl's mysteriously acquired capacity to remain invisible before the world in spite of her attempts to have others acknowledge her presence. Perplexed by the fact that some people "genuinely" cannot see her, the anonymous narrator wonders how she could have inadvertently acquired this curious talent.

Lizárraga's creative work includes two short stories, "¿Qué tenía que ver con ellos?" (What Did It Have to Do With Them?, 1987) and "Unidos" (United), in which she experiments with narrative technique by taking on the forceful and critical tone characteristic of her essays. Those essays examine the limitations of various critical methods, especially when applied to Hispanic literature and the portrayal of Hispanic women in literature by Hispanic male authors, among other topics. Her 1988 study, "Hacia una teoría para la liberación de la mujer" (Toward a Women's Liberation Theory), contributes to the developing dialogue of feminist theory which takes into account gender, class, and race.

Lizárraga's writings, creative and critical, depict an oppressed minority and argue for a reexamination of reality in order to change it. They challenge readers to rethink their perceptions and understanding of reality. Unfortunately, Lizárraga's work has received scant critical atten-tion. But, as María Herrera-Sobek has noted in her essay-review of *Requisa treinta y dos,* Lizárraga's literary contributions stand out both for her excellent artistic elaboration as well as for the perspective she offers.

Sources:

Herrera-Sobek, María. "Literatura y sociedad: la problemática del chicano/mexicano en los Estados Unidos a través de la obra literaria." *Bilingual Review,* September-December 1984, pp. 83-87.

Sánchez, Rosaura. "Chicana Prose Writers: The Case of Gina Valdés and Sylvia Lizárraga," in *Beyond Stereotypes: The Critical Analysis of Chicana Literature,* edited by María Herrera-Sobek. Binghamton: Bilingual/Editorial Bilingüe, 1985, pp. 60-70.

Rebecca Lobo
(1973–)
Basketball player, author

Selected writings:

The Home Team. New York: Kodansha America, 1996.

Overview

When people recount the early years of the Women's National Basketball Association (WNBA) and recall the names of some of the leagues' notable players, Rebecca Lobo will be remembered along with the best of them. She is a champion rebounder, both on and off the court. She has excelled in academics and sports, a winning combination that is not easily matched by her peers. Lobo was chosen the All-American center in 1995, the year her team, the University of Connecticut women's basketball team won the 1995 NCAA Championship with a 35-0 season. She holds the honor of being the only Big East basketball player to have simultaneously earned the titles of Scholar-Athlete of the Year and Big East Player of the Year, capturing those titles not once but twice. She is definitely making a lasting impact in the league.

Lobo was born in Connecticut and lived there for her first two years. Lobo, who grew to a statuesque 6 feet 4 inch tall, athletic-minded woman, was raised in Southwick, MA. Her Cuban American father and her mother encouraged

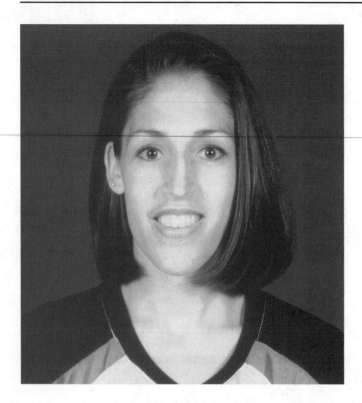

Rebecca Lobo

Rebecca and her older siblings, Jason and Rachel, to be independent. One lesson in perseverance that Lobo never forgot was when she was struggling with her tap dancing in the third grade. It was too much of a challenge, and she wanted to quit. Her mother, however, would not let her, and Lobo learned to take on challenges rather than run away from them.

The decision to be a basketball player was an easy one for Lobo. She first developed an affinity for the game at an early age. In her book, *The Home Team,* co-written with her mother, Ruth-Ann, Lobo recalls that she had career goals even in the third grade when she wrote a letter to the general manager of the Boston Celtics, informing him that she was going to be, "the first girl to play for the Boston Celtics." The combination of her love for basketball and her upbringing, which taught her not to give up, helped her through tough times when she encountered hurdles while playing in the Olympics and then in her professional career.

Women's Basketball Becomes More Popular

Success, however, has not always come easy. Professional basketball, like so many other male-dominated sports, did not accommodate women's teams. Diehard basketball fans seemed to have little interest in watching two women-only teams attempt jump shots, block rebounds, and shoot free-throws. But during her college years Lobo began to see a change. An increasing number of sports fans began to develop an interest and appreciation for women's basketball. When she first saw the University of Connecticut play, only some of the bleachers were used, and maybe a couple thousand spectators showed up for a game on a good night. By the time Lobo became a senior in college, every home game was sold out and some 9,000 fans filled the stands. In fact, more Connecticut viewers watched the Huskies's championship game than the Superbowl.

Joins Olympic Team

Lobo's interest in basketball did not diminish when she graduated from college. In fact, it was only the beginning of her passion for the sport. At age 22, Lobo became the youngest member to play on the U.S. Olympic team in the 1996 Atlanta Summer Olympics. Interestingly enough, the transition from being a top college basketball player to the youngest player on the Olympic team was tougher than she had anticipated. Her nickname on the team was 'Rookie'. Even the team's coach, Tara VanDerveer, was initially leery of taking on Lobo because she felt that Lobo was not as physical a center as she wanted. It did not take Lobo very long to realize that this was a step up to a different level of basketball playing. She compared the experience to being back at college as a freshman again, having to prove herself. But Lobo convinced even the most skeptical of critics that she had what it takes to be an Olympic star, when she led her undefeated team to a gold medal.

Though the Olympics were a highlight for Lobo, the experience was one of many professional achievements. At age 23, Lobo became one of the first two women signed in the fledgling WNBA. Lobo led her team, the New York Liberty, all the way to the very first WNBA finals, where they took the championship. During her first season with the New York Liberty in 1997, Lobo scored the team-high point amounts several times and was a significant factor on the defensive side of the basketball court.

Copes with Mother's Cancer

Lobo's life has not been without its setbacks. When she was a junior in college, she learned that her mother had breast cancer. The news was devastating to Lobo and, in a report, she was said to have considered quitting basketball because of her mother's illness. In her book, Lobo denies ever having such thoughts. In fact, it was basketball that kept Lobo focused. From the time she was a child tossing a ball at a garage-mounted hoop, basketball was her escape, her way of coping with life's problems. During her mother's battle with cancer, Lobo says that basketball was the only thing that kept her together. "I almost laughed when I read that in her article. I wonder if the reporter would understand if I told her that basketball was what saved me during that time," Lobo wrote. "I wonder if she could comprehend the fact that practicing or playing was the only time I could completely free my mind of everything that was going on; that my mother's illness would not enter my mind at all as long as I was on the court playing this simple game."

Lobo has now joined her mother in encouraging women to get regular mammograms in hopes of detecting breast cancer at a stage where it is most easily treated. This mission has taken her across the country and has raised 1.4 million dollars for cancer research. Lobo also volunteers for the Children's Miracle Network where she signs autographs, visits children, and helps to raise funds. Because of these endeavors and other causes that Lobo takes part, *USA WEEKEND* magazine voted her among the most caring athletes in their fifth annual awards in 1997. She continues to show that on the basketball court as well as in life, she gives 100 percent.

Current Address: New York Liberty, Madison Square Garden, Penn Plaza, New York, NY 10121.

Sources:

ESPN Home Page. Available at http://espn.sportszone.com/editors/atlanta96/bios/wbask/lobo.html.
Hispanic OnLine Home Page. Availabe at http://www.hisp.com/aug95/thirty.html.
Lobo, Rebecca, and RuthAnn Lobo. *The Home Team.* New York: Kodansha America, Inc., 1996.
National Basketball Association Home Page. Available at http://www.nba.com/news_feat/lobo_award.html.
National Basketball Association Home Page. Available at http://www.nba.com/playerfile/Rebecca_Lobo.html.
Vilona, Bill. "Rebecca Lobo." *Gannett News Service,* July 21, 1996, p. S12.

Longeaux Vásquez, Enriqueta
   See **Vásquez, Enriqueta Longeaux**

Lopez, Constance Marie
   See **Marie, Constance**

Jennifer Lopez
(1970–)
Actress

Selected filmography:

In Living Color. FOX-TV, 1990-1993.

Second Chances. CBS-TV series, 1993.
Hotel Malibu (TV series), 1994.
Money Train. Columbia Pictures, 1995.
My Family/Mi Familia. New Line Cinema, 1995.
Jack. Buena Vista/Hollywood Pictures, 1996.
Blood & Wine. Fox Searchlight, 1996.
Selena. Katz/Q Productions Inc.-Esparza/Warner Brothers, 1997.
Anaconda. Sony Pictures Entertainment/Columbia Pictures CL Cine, 1997.
U-Turn. Sony Pictures Entertainment/TriStar Pictures/Phoenix, 1997.
Out of Sight. Universal Pictures, 1998.

Overview

Jennifer Lopez is one of a new crop of multi–talented Hispanic American actors who are breaking the racial barriers in Hollywood and earning their way into mainstream, big-budget productions. In a fairly short period of time, Lopez moved up the ladder of fame from dancing to television to movies. Now a star in her own right, Lopez has the luxury of choosing her projects in a field where Hispanic American actors have traditionally been typecast.

Dreams of Performing as Actress

Born in New York on July 24, 1970, to parents of Puerto Rican descent, Lopez has dreamed of becoming a performer since as far back as she can remember. She recalled that

Jennifer Lopez

while growing up in the Bronx she found few if any Hispanic American role models in the media. Fascinated by *West Side Story,* she said Rita Moreno was the only person with whom she could identify. When Lopez was five, her mother, a kindergarten teacher, got her started with dance lessons, and she took them every weekend. As she got older, Lopez pursued these lessons on her own and began to dance professionally on the musical stage. She traveled abroad with the European tour of *Golden Musicals of Broadway* and with the Japanese tour of *Synchronicity.* She also appeared in regional productions of *Jesus Christ Superstar.*

Begins Career in Television

Meanwhile, Lopez decided to audition for a part as one of Rosie Perez's "Fly Girl" dancers on Fox's hit TV comedy series *In Living Color.* She got the job in competition against two thousand other candidates. Lopez was reluctant to take on the part of a dancer since she hoped to break into acting, but a lucrative contract convinced her to take the part. This role and the exposure it brought Lopez gave her the first big break in her acting career. After her stint with *In Living Color,* two more television roles followed: a CBS series, *Second Chances,* in which she costarred with Connie Selleca and Megan Fallows, and *Hotel Malibu.* Her work in television opened the door to the movie industry, and in 1995 she won a small role in *My Family/Mi Familia,* directed by Gregory Nava. Francis Ford Coppola produced this critically acclaimed movie that covers three generations in the life of an Hispanic American family.

Gains Starring Roles

In one of her first major roles, Lopez costarred with Woody Harrelson and Wesley Snipes in the 1995 movie *Money Train,* a film that netted her better reviews than the two stars. She played Grace, a New York City transit cop who is used as a decoy in a money scam. Her character was very close to her own cultural background. The movie's director, Joseph Ruben, said of Lopez: "Grace had to be first of all believable as a street cop. You had to believe that she grew up in New York City, that she was a tough, strong New York cop. On top of that, she had to be one hell of an actor with humor and a lot of spirit. Jennifer fit the bill. She's the real thing." There was a lot of competition for the non-Hispanic American role, and Lopez won it.

Her performances in *Mi Familia* and *Money Train* brought Lopez once again to the attention of Francis Ford Coppola. He was directing a new comedy, *Jack,* about a ten-year old boy with a rare disorder that gives him the physical appearance of a man. In the movie, Robin Williams, who plays the boy, falls in love with his teacher, played by Lopez. In February of 1997, Lopez played opposite Jack Nicholson in *Blood and Wine,* a well-received film about a wine merchant (Nicholson) who has marital problems and takes Lopez as his mistress.

Stars in Popular Movie *Selena*

The following month, Lopez played Mexican American Selena Quintanilla Perez, a dazzlingly popular Mexican singer, who was slain at the age of 23 by a former president of her fan club. Selena was noted for her Tejano music, a combination of rock, R&B, pop, polka, and traditional Latin fare, and had released one platinum album and two gold albums. Charming and talented, she was on the path to superstardom before her untimely death. Noted actor Edward James Olmos played Selena's father, a frustrated musician who pushes his children hard to succeed. No major motion picture with a Hispanic American theme ever opened in so many theaters. Lopez easily won over the competition for her role, for which she reportedly received $1 million.

Lopez acknowledged that *Selena,* which received rave reviews from critics and moviegoers alike, was an important movie for her: "Kids loved the movie and they introduced it to their parents and grandparents." The character she plays parallels some of her own life, and it is a role with which she easily identifies. "Though I'm Puerto Rican from the Bronx and she was a Mexican in Texas, we've both been treated the same way as minorities and as women," she said in an interview. Lopez said that Selena and she were at similar stages in their careers, enjoying success but not hugely popular. They also had similar personalities. Lopez's admiration for Selena is also obvious with quotes like: "I used her as an example when I was making this movie. . . She was always herself. . . She was Latin, she had dark hair, and she dyed it even darker." Lopez's director, Gregory Nava, said that casting Lopez gave him a head start as a director because she was immensely popular. This movie also proved the setting for another important turn of events: Lopez's boyfriend Ojani Noa, a Cuban-born waiter she had met in Miami, gave her a surprise proposal at a wrap party for *Selena.* They were married in early 1997, a few weeks before the movie was released.

Film Roles Continue to Increase

In April of 1997, Lopez played the lead role in *Anaconda,* which also starred John Voight, Eric Stoltz, and Ice Cube. In the fall of 1997, she costarred with Sean Penn and Nick Nolte in Oliver Stone's dark comedy/melodrama *U-Turn,* based on the novel *Stray Dogs* by John Ridley. Penn plays a small-time gambler who is driving to Las Vegas to pay off a debt. His car breaks down, and he gets stuck in a small town in Arizona. There he meets Lopez's sexy character, who tries to hire him to kill her husband so she can escape an abusive marriage. One of her most recent movies was *Out of Sight,* the film version of Elmore Leonard's novel. In the film, which was directed by Steven Soderbergh (director of *sex, lies, and videotape*), Lopez played a U.S. federal marshal who falls in love with the man (George Clooney) who takes her hostage during a prison break. Afterwards, she is charged with leading the manhunt to track down Clooney's character. Reportedly, Lopez beat out several of Hollywood's most popular young actresses for the role.

Although she is immensely proud of her Hispanic American heritage, Lopez and her management are anxious to avoid having her perceived by casting agents as only suitable for Hispanic American roles. *Selena* director Nava bemoaned the Hollywood tendency to typecast, particularly when it comes to ethnicity: "That whole mentality comes out of a mind-set people have of what it means to be Latino. We're still very much pigeonholed as types as opposed to individual talents. Actors, like writers, directors, and everyone else, have to fight notions of what we should be like in order to be who we are. Our work and our talent is shattering these concepts, but they're still out there."

Gains Greater Recognition

Jennifer Lopez was selected by editors at *People* for inclusion in the magazine's feature "The 50 Most Beautiful People in the World 1997." *Hispanic* magazine named Lopez among the "25 Most Powerful Hispanics" in Hollywood. The Hispanic American publication surveyed all aspects of the acting industry, in front of the screen as well as behind. It stated that Hispanic American actors and Hispanic American-based themes are making a positive impact and opening up new opportunities, adding that there is still a long way to go.

While many Hispanic actors still struggle to achieve recognition, Lopez seems to have overcome the curse of typecasting. Of her near-meteoric rise in the movie business, Lopez said in an interview: "God is watching over me, that's all I can say. He has a plan for me. I've been really lucky. And I work hard."

Sources:

Celebsite Home Page. Available at http://www.celebsite.com/people/jenniferlopez/.

Gutierrez, Eric. "In the Game at Last: A New Generation Is Boldly Defying the Old Stereotype of the Hollywood Latina as Maid or Seductress." *Los Angeles Times,* March 16, 1997, p. 3.

Hispanstar Home Page. Available at http://www.hispanstar.com./influentials96/res100dir-t+.html.

Hobson, Louis B. "Lopez Takes the Heat." *Calgary Sun,* October 5, 1997.

The Internet Movie Database Home Page. Available at http://us.imdb.com/Aname?Lopez,+Jennifer.

Mr. Showbiz Home Page. Available at http://www.mrshowbiz.com/interviews/296_1.html.

Stoynoff, Natasha. "Fallen Star: Jennifer Lopez Thinks About What Could Have Been in Selena." *Toronto Sun,* March 16, 1997.

Thompson, Bob. "U-Turn Star a Straight Shooter." *Toronto Sun,* October 1, 1997.

Josefina López
Playwright, poet

Selected writings:

Simply Maria or the American Dream. Play.
Food for the Dead. Play.
Real Women Have Curves. Play.
Raw & Ready: Poetic Thoughts. Self–published, 1997.

Overview

At the age of three, Josefina López knew that she was going to be a writer. "I've always known it," she declared in the *Ann Arbor News.* By the age of 17, this confident young woman had written her first nationally-renowned play, *Simply Maria.* She was just 21 years old when another of her plays, *Real Women Have Curves,* was produced in various cities across the United States. Before most young people have even chosen careers, López had become a fresh and exciting new presence in the theater. Reflecting on the possible reasons behind her success, she concluded in the *Los Angeles Times,* "I've taken our beautiful hot and fiery colors of Mexico and mixed them with American feminism and freedom of speech.

Josefina López

Born in Mexico

Josefina López was born in Cerritos, a town in the Mexican state of San Luis Potosi. Seeking a better life, her parents moved their eight children to Los Angeles when Josefina was just six years old. The journey to the United States was frightening for the little girl; she was allowed to cross the border only because she was using her sister's U.S. birth certificate. Her parents had green cards but Josefina did not and, consequently, her childhood years were marred by the fear of being sent back to Mexico. As a teenager, she had to lie about having a social security number in order to gain employment. This precarious status left her feeling as if she did not fit into U.S. society.

Garners National Acclaim for Debut Effort

While the nightmarish existence of living as an undocumented person in an inhospitable country has left its mark on López, the young playwright might contend that her fears have worked to her advantage. After seeing Luis Valdez's moving play *I Don't Have to Show You No Stinking Badges,* the teenage López was inspired to write her own story, which she entitled *Simply Maria, or the American Dream.* A frank look at López's life as a young Mexican in the United States that examines how difficult it can be to reconcile loyalty to one's heritage with the hope of achieving the American Dream, *Simply Maria* is not a typical interpretation of the adolescent experience. "I wrote *Maria* because I had to," she explained in the *Los Angeles Times.* "I just poured out my guts."

López entered *Simply Maria* in two contests—the Young Playwrights Festival in New York, in which she was a semifinalist, and San Diego's Gaslamp Quarter Theatre California Young Playwrights Project, in which she captured first place. *Simply Maria* was subsequently produced in San Diego in January of 1988.

López's blossoming talent attracted a great deal of attention. In 1990, an adaptation of her play aired on public television and won the Vocal Program Award for Excellence in the children's category. Since 1990, López has written two other plays of note—*Food for the Dead,* which deals with homosexuality and machismo, and *Real Women Have Curves,* which is about López's experiences working in a sewing factory. In the *Ann Arbor News,* López remarked that *Real Women Have Curves* "deals with empowerment and self-pride, and acceptance by women of their physical selves and their inner selves." She went on to note that the latter title "is a little exaggerated in terms of some of its comedy, but it's very realistic in its emotions." *Real Women Have Curves* has met with favorable reviews in the many different cities in which it has been produced. A critic writing for the Ann Arbor-based *Current* observed, "This ambitious play thumbs up its nose at societal presumptions that women are supposed to be tall, modelesque, and painfully nipped at the waist, while delivering other powerful messages." In 1997, López published *Raw & Ready:*

Poetic Thoughts, a book of poems dealing with cultural identification, love, and sexual politics.

Produces Television Series Pilots

Although she has been recognized as a promising young playwright, López has decided to expand her horizons and create television shows. Teaming with Jon Mercedes III, she founded Mercedes/López Productions and landed agreements to develop three television series pilots. The first series, a sitcom entitled *The Chavez Family,* is a collaborative effort with notable producer Norman Lear and Paramount TV. López is also working on a drama entitled *Innercity HSTA,* which she describes as "Fame meets Beverly Hills 90210." Lastly, she hopes to produce *La Fiesta,* a comedy-variety show featuring Latin music.

Sources:

Ann Arbor News, April 3, 1992, pp. D1-2.
Avila, Alex. "25 Most Powerful Hispanics in Hollywood." *Ethnic News Watch.* Stamford, CT: SoftLine Information, Inc., April 30, 1996, p. 20.
Canto, Minerva. "Latina Playwright Crafts TV Series." *Detroit Free Press,* May 7, 1998.
Cole, Melanie. "30 Under Thirty: Stand Back, World, Here Comes Generation Equis." *Ethnic News Watch.* Stamford, CT: SoftLine Information, Inc., August 31, 1995, p. 22.
Current, April, 1992, p. 23.
Los Angeles Times, July 29, 1990, section CAL, pp. 48+.

Lourdes Lopez
(1958–)
Dancer

Lourdes Lopez rose against the odds to become a premier dancer in the New York City Ballet. Until 1997, she was a principal dancer in this leading ballet company. Lopez achieved this status while juggling roles as mother and wife, a rare combination for ballerinas at the height of their careers.

Lopez was born in Havana, Cuba, in 1958, a year before Fidel Castro assumed power. Her father was an army officer who fought against Castro's rebel forces. These were turbulent times, full of uncertainties and hostilities—not an environment conducive for raising a family. So in 1959, as the socialist Castro rose to power, the Lopez family moved to United States, choosing Miami as their new home. Her father managed to find work as an accountant for Ecuatoriana Airlines.

Enrolls in Dance

As a child, Lopez did not show signs of being a gifted dancer. In fact, at age five, Lopez was diagnosed as flat-footed and pidgeon-toed, requiring orthopedic shoes. On top of that, she had very weak muscles in her legs. To address the weak muscles, an orthopedic surgeon advised Lopez's family to enroll her in dance lessons to build her strength. It was love at first twirl. By the time she was eight, the young dancer was studying with a private coach for an hour and a half a day, six days a week. When she was ten, she showed so much promise that her mother decided to take her to New York to audition for scholarships for ballet school.

The trip was financially difficult for the Lopez family, but they were very supportive of their daughter. "My mother's always been there with me," she told a reporter for the *Miami Herald* later. "She's not pushy like a stage mother. It's just that she said, 'If you want to be a dancer, I'm behind you all the way.'" Lopez won scholarships to three different schools and chose the School of American Ballet (SAB). At age 11, she began attending the school in the summers. Her family spent the summers in New York City to support her in her pursuit of her dream.

Lopez returned to the SAB every summer until she was 14 years old. At that point she decided to spend all of her time studying in New York and moved in with her older sister, who was a college student at New York University. Lopez attended the Professional Children's School while studying full-time at the SAB.

Auditions for the New York City Ballet

When she was 16 years old, Lopez's hard work began to pay off. She was among the few chosen from the SAB's 500 young students to join the New York City Ballet's corps de ballet. In the dance community this role is equivalent to the chorus in an opera. This was a key opportunity for Lopez to become part of the one of the world's most prestigious ballet companies. The artistic director and force behind the dance troupe was the legendary George Balanchine, an imposing genius who launched the SAB and the City Ballet. Balanchine was already widely recognized as one of the greatest choreographers in the history of dance. Although the world-famous Jerome Robbins was also one of the City Ballet's choreographers, dancers in the company knew that their future depended upon pleasing the imperious Balanchine. Demanding and uncompromising, he was known to view his ballerinas as physical embodiments of grace and beauty—the soul of ballet.

In the corps, Lopez played background roles, such as the third swan from the left in the back row of Balanchine's

Swan Lake. Even so, her talents were recognized, and she was admired for her clean lines, dark-eyed beauty, and strong physique. As a girl, Lopez had feared that she might grow up the "wrong shape" for classical ballet, which requires a willowy physique. By carefully watching her diet, she ensured that her five-foot, six-inch frame stayed slender to fit the image of an ideal ballerina. Although her shoulders became broader than the average ballet dancer's, she used this to her advantage, underscoring her movement with a physical strength that was markedly different from other dancers. Lopez was also noted for her acting abilities. The ease and vibrancy with which she communicated her characters' emotions stood out in the City Ballet, which was so focused on precision that the corps was often compared to a machine.

Earns Promotion to Soloist

After another four years of hard work, Lopez was cast in small solo roles. In 1980, at the age of twenty-two, she was promoted to the rank of soloist, one of a group of fourteen dancers who come between the corps and the principal dancers in rank. They receive higher salaries and dressing rooms with their names on the door and do not dance in corps roles anymore. Rather, each soloist is assigned to some principal roles each year.

As a soloist, Lopez received opportunities to demonstrate her talents. She danced opposite rising star (and later director of the City Ballet) Peter Martins in *Stravinsky Violin Concerto*. One reviewer wrote that Lopez "danced the brisk opening passages with a charmingly playful air, and brought an air of intriguing sensuality to the *pas de deux* with Peter Martins." Whereas the former dancer had appeared vulnerable in this role, the reviewer concluded that "Lopez met Martins more as an equal, and a very different chemistry emerged."

Lopez danced a variety of roles as a soloist, continuing to improve her technique, especially increasing her ability to dance the quick, allegro steps required of Balanchine dancers. In 1984, she was promoted to the rank of principal dancer. Now, as a prima ballerina, she could step into the spotlight and perform the leading roles in a wide range of new and beloved ballets. As a soloist, Lopez's work had taken her all over the world and she joined company tours to France, England, Germany, Denmark, and China.

Becomes Prima Ballerina

George Balanchine had died in 1983, and the New York City Ballet began to change. No longer guided by Balanchine's fervent classicism, the dancers began to be challenged by more modern techniques and choreography. Lopez's repertory included lead roles in classical ballets such as *La Somnambula, Divertimento #1, Sernade, Stars and Stripes, Firebird,* and *The Four Seasons.* But she also created roles in pieces choreographed by Peter Martins, including *Sonate di Scarlatti* and *Rejouissance.* A far cry from her classical roots, she created a role in *Rhapsody in Blue,* a piece danced to George Gershwin's well-known music and choreographed by Lar Lubovitch, a modern dance choreographer. For that piece, Lopez worked at learning to dance without classical ballet point shoes.

Faces New Challenges

In 1987, Lopez married Lionel Saporta, an attorney with his own practice. Two years later, she suffered a career-threatening injury after a bump on her heel damaged her tendon. Doctors suggested surgery. Instead of worrying about the long recuperation period and the chance that she might never be able to dance as well again, Lopez decided to take advantage of the time off. "There were two things I always wanted," she told an interviewer. "I had always wanted to go to school, and I had always wanted to have a child. I ended up doing both." Lopez enrolled in Fordham University and took courses. She had always had an interest in child psychology, but had never had the time to explore it. And in 1989, she gave birth to a daughter, Adriel.

The challenge of having a baby is one that few ballet dancers dare take. Unsure of how pregnancy will affect their fitness, they worry that they might lose the few precious years they have of peak performance. Lopez shared these fears, but discovered them to be unfounded. After her daughter was born, she was nearly as fit as ever, in part because she had continued her classes throughout her pregnancy. It took some time to regain her old sense of balance, however. Still, two months after giving birth, she was back in class. One year later, she was back in her role as principal dancer. Before long, she had a new fan in the audience: daughter Adriel. Asked to comment on the challenge of juggling such an intense artistic career and motherhood, Lopez simply responded "It's hard, but the rewards are great."

In 1993, Lopez was among the central figures in a 16-city national tour billed as "Principal Dancers of the New York City Ballet." She continued to create new and favorite roles as a principal dancer until 1997, when she retired from the City Ballet to take on other challenges.

Sources:

Flatow, Sheryl. "Ballerina Mother." *Playbill,* December 1992, p. 52.
Manhattan Magazine, 1989, p. 58.
Roberts, Pat. "Working Toward a Level of Beauty." *Miami Herald,* October 3, 1975, p. 1D.
Solway, Diane. "City Ballet Moves to an American Beat." *New York Times,* April 24, 1988, section 2, p. 1.
Switzer, Ellen Eichenwald. *Dancers! Horizons in American Dance.* New York: Atheneum, 1982.

Yolanda López
(1942–)
Artist, professor, women's rights activist

Yolanda López's controversial painting *Portrait of the Artist: Our Lady of Guadalupe* shows a muscular young woman jogging out of her halo. Feminists have lauded the painting, reproduced as a poster, while traditional Catholics have criticized it as sacrilegious. López, however, is more concerned about raising the consciousness of women with her art than she is about pleasing the status quo. In spite of the controversy that her work has generated, she continues to create works of art fashioned by her feminist aesthetic.

López was born in San Diego, CA, in 1942, the oldest of three sisters. As a single parent, her mother supported the family for thirty years by working at an industrial sewing machine. López's maternal grandparents, who had fled Mexico in 1916, lived with the family.

Since Spanish was the language spoken at home, López initially had trouble understanding English at school and had to repeat the first grade. Drawing, however, came easily to her. "I've always made drawings," she told Betty LaDuke, author of the 1992 book *Women Artists: Multi-Cultural Visions.* "In first grade there was a chalkboard, and, while the boys drew airplanes and bombs, I did little farm animals with straw hats."

Teachers recognized López's talent and encouraged her to apply to the College of Marin, north of San Francisco, where she was accepted. She also attended San Francisco State University. As the civil rights movement swept across college campuses, López joined in efforts to promote ethnic studies programs and minority scholarships. In 1968, she took part in San Francisco State University's Third World Strike.

López dropped out of college and moved to San Francisco's Latino Mission District, where she combined social work and political activism with art. She worked as a community artist with a group called Los Seis de la Raza. "The streets were my gallery," she told LaDuke. "I saw my work everywhere, and unsigned."

Creates Feminist Work

After nine years of intense political activity, however, López felt burnt out and moved back to San Diego to complete her bachelor of arts degree. In 1973, with the help of a Ford Foundation fellowship, she began graduate work at the University of California at San Diego. Her three-part graduate art project focused on the relation of

Chicano women to mainstream U.S. society. First, she presented a series of larger-than-life drawings titled *Three Generations of Mujeres.* These realistic, non-idealized drawings of her own grandmother, Victoria F. Franco; mother, Margaret S. Stewart; and herself as the daughter, work against stereotypical images of Mexican American women. "Qualities of a life lived with dignity and self-respect are not limited to my family," López told LaDuke. "They are qualities shared by many women who are not part of the majority culture's concept of being female or feminine."

The second part of her graduate exhibit: a series of self-portraits titled *A Donde Va Chicana?* or *Where Are You Going Chicana?* López shows herself dressed in shorts and a T-shirt as a runner, jogging to lose weight and gain control of her body. In *Feminist Studies,* she described the series as "a woman calling on her body in an assertive and physically disciplined manner as a power ally," adding, "Endurance is one of our greatest survival tools."

Focuses on Our Lady of Guadalupe

For the third part of the exhibit, López focused on Our Lady of Guadalupe as a means for creating symbolic transformation. While condemning the mythic image of the Virgin that has served to immobilize women, she saw in Our Lady of Guadalupe remnants of the Aztec earth and fertility goddess. "Essentially, she [the Virgin of Guadalupe] is beautiful, serene and passive," López wrote in a 1978 statement about her work. "She has no emotional life or texture of her own. . . .Because I feel living, breathing women also deserve respect and love lavished on Guadalupe, I have chosen to transform the image. Taking symbols of her power and virtue I have transferred them to portraits of women I know."

In *Mother: Our Lady of Guadalupe,* López portrays a tired and bespectacled woman at her sewing machine stitching gold stars of hope on Guadalupe's blue robe. She is lit up by rays of light normally associated with the Virgin as a tribute to all hard-working women. Next, in *Grandmother: Our Lady of Guadalupe,* López portrays her grandmother holding a snakeskin and a knife to symbolize her enduring connection with the earth. She, too, is lit up by rays of light. Finally, in *Portait of the Artist: Our Lady of Guadalupe,* López shows herself as an active and confident woman, wearing the blue cape with the stars draped over one shoulder and holding the snake in her other hand. She is smiling and leaping forward, treading on the back of an overturned angel. Gone is the traditional image of the angel with outstretched arms ushering in the Virgin.

Work Generates Controversy

Some traditional Catholics viewed López's last installment in the series as sacreligious. In the article "Yolanda López's Art Hits 'Twitch Meter' to Fight Stereotypes," Lili Wright detailed the controversy for *The Salt Lake Tribune* on May 14, 1995. López's picture evoked such strong feelings that a worker in a printshop reportedly refused to photograph it. "You can mess around with my woman, my car, anything—but you don't touch my lady," the worker was quoted in *The Salt Lake Tribune.*

The controversy reportedly spread to Mexico after the feminist magazine *Fem* published López's images. The magazine office received bomb threats, and vandals trashed several Mexico City kiosks. "People either really were excited and loved it or were disturbed by it," López said in *The Salt Lake Tribune.*. "That's when I knew I was on to something. It hit the twitch meter." *Portrait of the Artist: Our Lady of Guadalupe* was reproduced as a poster to announce the event "Issues in Chicana Scholarship" at the University of California, Irvine, in 1993. It remains an important image in feminist Chicana art.

Continues Bringing Art to the Community

After receiving her master of fine arts degree in 1978, López embarked on a career combining art, education, and community activism. She has taught in the ethnic studies department at the University of California, Berkeley, delivered slide shows and lectures, brought her installations to various local and national exhibits, and generated enthusiasm for community arts events. In 1989, she organized a three-day multimedia event, "The Mission Is Bitchin'," featuring art, poetry, music, dance, comedy, and panel discussions. A *San Francisco Chronicle* review on May 28, 1989, described the Mission neighborhood as "a mixture of swagger, style[,] and visual vitality."

The following year, López's installation *Things I Never told My Son about Being a Mexican* and accompanying video, *When You Think of Mexico* appeared at "The Decade Show" in New York City. In his review of the show for *Arts Magazine,* Giulio V. Blanc wrote, "The video. . . is typical of López's devastating critique of the patronizing ethnocentrism that is encoded in so many images that the United States produces of Mexico and Latin America as a whole."

Sources:

Blanc, Giulio V. "When You Think of Mexico: Latin American Women in The Decade Show." *Arts Magazine,* April 1990, pp. 17-18.
Chicana and Chicano Space Home Page. Available at: http://mati.eas.asu/edu:8421/~getty/html_pages/YLópezlssOutl.html.
Cockcroft, Eva Sperling. "Portrait of the Artist as the Virgin of Guadalupe." *Art in America,* June 1992, p. 90.
LaDuke, Betty. "Yolanda López: Breaking Chicana Stereotypes." *Feminist Studies,* Spring 1994, pp. 117-122.

Yolanda Luera
(1953–)
Poet, author

Selected writings:

Solitaria J. La Jolla, CA: Lalo, 1986.

Overview

Yolanda Luera, a talented, promising poet and fiction writer of the United States-Mexico border, has stepped to the forefront of Hispanic literature today. Publishing exclusively in Spanish, she has a keen sense of the pain of the life of the poor, especially of women, and of the language and wisdom of the common people, as well as their will to endure. Her writing is artistically salted with a wry, picaresque sense of humor.

Struggles to Complete Education

In 1950 Luera's parents, Pedro Luera and Amada Salas de Luera, moved from Sinaloa and Durango in northern Mexico to Mexicali, where she was born on March 4, 1953. The family moved to Tijuana in 1958 and lived there until 1970. Her education in Mexico, after the sixth grade, included secretarial school for six months, after which she worked for a pittance from 1967 to 1968 at a lithography shop, and the following year with one of Tijuana's leading paint manufacturing and wholesale companies. Later her family settled in San Ysidro, CA. Her cousins who were attending the University of California, San Diego (UCSD), introduced her to the high school equivalency program. Before getting her high school degree, and while still struggling to master the English language, she worked as a babysitter and field hand. Encouraged by friends and family, she found her way to San Luis Obispo, CA, in 1971, and earned her high school general education diploma. One month after she began her studies at San Diego State University in 1972, they were interrupted by a serious auto accident that left her unable to walk for a year. On August 26, 1972, she married Ernesto Padilla in San Diego, and they moved back to San Luis Obispo, where she renewed her studies, this time at California Polytechnic. Yolanda decided to suspend her studies during her pregnancy with her first child, Mayela. Ernesto and Yolanda have two other children, Gabriela and Santiago. Her years in the United States as a working woman and her determination to write and to achieve academic excellence make her a paradigm of the Hispanic woman who creates new personal and literary realities. She is now a naturalized citizen of the United States.

With the encouragement and support of her husband, Luera published her first book of poems, *Solitaria J,* in 1986. Written in Spanish, as are her other publications to date, these collected poems have been translated into English by James Hoggard. She is an unpretentious artist and takes her place among the new generation of poets who speak forthrightly to the world with compelling honesty and insight.

Blends Mexican and American Qualities in Writing

Like Sergio Elizondo, Lucha Corpi, and other Hispanic writers who lived their formative years in Mexico, Luera demonstrates an attraction to the folklore and traditions of Mexico while writing within the context of her experience in the United States. Critic Gabriel Trujillo Muñoz includes her among notable women writers of the U.S.-Mexico border area who began to write in the late 1970s and continued through the 1980s. Their themes, according to Trujillo Muñoz, include dealing with "the family circle, love relationships, and their vision of the reality of the border which they live and experience in all of its complexity and magnitude" (translated from Spanish). Prior to the 1970s the women of the borderlands were essentially limited to writing society columns, recipes, and advice to the lovelorn in newspapers.

Throughout her academic career, Luera has given expression to her talent as a poet and short story writer, publishing as opportunities have presented themselves. She is a serious reader, and, aside from mainstream Latin Americans and other writers to whom she has been exposed in the course of her regular studies in literature, she has been greatly influenced by Lorna D. Cervantes, as well as by Carmen Tafolla, Xelina Rojas-Urista, Margarita Luna Robles, Emily López, and Ana Castillo, whom she admires greatly.

Some of her publications have been prompted by writer-friends who have given her feedback throughout the years, notably Tafolla, who has written a sensitive and poetic appreciation in English in her introduction to *Solitaria J:* "That uncommon letter 'J,' once the proud Mexicano 'X,' then changed, so arbitrarily, so colonizingly, from the rhythmic sonete-sound of 'sh' to the forced breath of a 'J,' punctuated like some upside-down exclamation mark, with no thought for its implications or consequences, even its name an obscenity [lesbian], is a reflection of our own personal history; we have had our Indian 'X' conquered, we stand alone, without our heritage, without even our identity, trying to survive in the barrio of our forgotten and sacrificed x's, with nothing but a solitary 'j' standing there watching us, blank faced."

Getting *de allí a aquí* (from there to here) is a dominant theme of Luera's writing. She and her readers are in the process—at once bridges and wayfarers, in evolution—of becoming, of struggling through the irrationality of society and social institutions, toward the discovery of a common humanity.

Finds Poetic Voice in Family and Community

Trujillo Muñoz praises Luera for her portrayal of the family, and in particular of other women in families, as a means of self-definition. As an example, he quotes "Amada" from *Solitaria J* (translated from Spanish): "I want to be happy, says my mother/ She suffers my father who slobbers alcohol each weekend./ Suffers my sadly retarded sister enjoying her candies beneath the bed. And suffers my grandmother in her last drop-by-drop years, who left off being the matriarch and became just a sick grandmother."

Luera is also a poet of the community. Her social awakening began when she was a young girl experiencing some of the injustices of society against minorities. Her mother, a farm worker, introduced her to the marches of César Chávez when they came through the area in the early 1970s. As Luera listened to the people, she began to discover a sense of community. In 1974 she met Chilean exiles at UCSD after the assassination of Salvador Allende. She writes of them (translated from Spanish): "There are burials/ which bear flowers,/ bear grief only,/ not a body." She speaks of social injustices, of being forced to the margins of a male-dominated society, of fears—the fear of nuclear annihilation and of the uncertainty of life.

In one of the first poems in her collection, "Vida para siempre" (Life without End), Luera speaks of Benjamina, who lives "encerrada / en una tarjeta postal / con sello extranjero (enclosed / in a postcard / with a foreign stamp): "She noted that her eyes/ no longer showed colors,/ just shadows/ black and white./ Alone just the beating of her heart/ thudding in her breast/ insistent as a beggar woman" (translated from Spanish).

Commenting on Luera's poem "El que entre locos anda" (He Who Walks among the Mad), Salvador Reza, editor of *Voz Fronteriza* (the newspaper of UCSD), wrote: "In her poetry, Luera shows us that she belongs to that group of "healthy consciousness" considered mad by certain sectors of "Here," and she gives a rallying cry to all those men and women, solitary "consciences," to unite and open the doors of the insane asylum in which we live" (translated from Spanish). In this poem there is a suppressed rage against the enforced conformity to which people submit in their hypocrisy and posing.

Keeps It Simple

Luera refuses labored metaphors and contrived insights. "My context," she says, "is simple. This is my principal concern: to be brief, to be direct. It is essential that I communicate what is basic—with economy, with simplicity." She uses everyday images to make her point with unspoiled originality, as in the poem from which the collection takes its name, "Una solitaria J": "I wish I could lie/ like the heathen calendar/ which rushes about madly screaming the names/ of all the unbaptized saints" (translated from Spanish).

Luera speaks with modesty and humor of her poems as "mis toothless y pelones hijos; but you have to love them porque te cuestan!" (My toothless and baldheaded children; but you have to love them because they have cost you dearly!). Her next book of poetry, she says, may be in English.

Expands into Fiction

Luera is also a promising fiction writer and is presently working on a collection of short stories, *La mujer que esperó sentada* (The Woman Who Waited Sitting). She took third place in the Thirteenth Chicano Literary Contest with her 1987 story "De Domingo a Domingo" (Sunday after Sunday), published in 1988 in *Irvine Chicano Literary Prize, 1985-1987*. In this woman's narrative, Casimira de Díaz is preparing for her customary Sunday visit to her sick grandmother. Casimira stands naked before the mirror making a frank and humorous appraisal of her 33-year old body. She sees herself growing older, changing as are her children and her language while San Diego insinuates itself into her Mexican reality. She drives through the numbing monotony of traffic to her grandmother who is hooked to life-support systems that drip glucose. The grandmother is the focus of Casimira's tender remembrances of another reality they shared when Casimira was a child.

In "La Chirrionera" Luera presents an adaptation of a folktale from Mexican oral tradition, making it a part of literature. The story as told to her by her grandmother from Durango tells of La Chirrionera, a snake with a very long tail it uses to enchant children while it drinks the milk from their nursing mothers. Luera develops the story, using images of water and of a woman singing a siren song. This unusual story filled with symbols of life and death, along with traditional, stereotypical negative images of women, is not intended, she says, as a variant of the tale of La Llorona (The Weeping Woman) from Aztec and Mexican tradition. The story opens with the first-person narrative of the protagonist Toño—no one knows where he came from—left behind in a town abandoned by the people, who have given him an herb, *la dormilona* (the sleepyhead), which is making him swell up and break out in boils. At first, when children disappeared from town, people blamed La Chirrionera. But later they discovered that it was Toño who killed the children left in his care by the old Chona, the oldest woman in town, and that he fed them to La Chirrionera. He has been left behind so that La Chirrionera will have only him to devour when the snake enters the town. The story closes with Toño recalling the useless parting words of the priest, urging him to think good thoughts and think about something else, as a breathy smell of warm milk and monstrous swelling eyes engulf him.

Yolanda Luera's fiction and poetry present an imaginative voice, which speaks for those on both sides of the border, with a strong sense of respect and love for traditions. She still aspires to obtaining a doctorate in literature and hopes some day to extend her travels beyond the little she has seen of Europe—including Madrid, Barcelona, Paris, and London. If it were possible, she would live for a year in Brazil, away from the United States and Mexico, to learn Portuguese and to work on a novel in the land of Jorge Amado, one of her favorite writers. But wherever she travels, she is analyzing and contrasting what she discovers with what is on the border and in Mexico City.

Sources:

Tafolla, Carmen. Introduction to Luera's *Solitaria J* La Jolla, CA: Lalo, 1986.
Trujillo Muñoz, Gabriel. "La literatura contemporánea: El punto de vista femenino." *Ranura del Ojo,* Summer 1988, pp. 6-14.

M

Magaña, Leticia Márquez
See Márquez-Magaña, Leticia

Mares Asip, Patricia
See Asip, Patricia Mares

Margo
(1917–1985)
Actress, dancer, community activist

Selected filmography:

Crime Without Passion. 1934.
Rumba. 1935.
Robin Hood of El Dorado. 1936.
Winterset. 1936.
Lost Horizon. 1937.
A Miracle on Main Street. 1940.
The Leopard Man. 1943.
Behind the Rising Sun. 1943.
Gangway for Tomorrow. 1943.
The Falcon in Mexico. 1944.
Viva Zapata! 1952.
I'll Cry Tomorrow. 1955.
From Hell to Texas. 1958.
Who's Got the Action? 1962.

Overview

Margo, the beautiful and versatile actress of Hollywood's Golden Age, was born Marie Marguerita Guadalupe Teresa Estela Bolado Castilla y O'Donnell on May 10, 1917, in Mexico City. The daughter of a prominent Spanish surgeon, Dr. Amedia Bolado, Margo was raised in the United States. A lively, precocious child, she first appeared on stage as a dancer at age six in Mexico City. Her debut in the United States came five years later at the Mexican Theater in Los Angeles. A sensational dancer, Margo

Margo

joined Eduardo Cansino's Spanish dancing school as a child and took classes throughout her teens. Cansino, a choreographer for Hollywood and an acclaimed Spanish dancer, had other famous pupils including his daughter Margarita, later known as screen siren Rita Hayworth, and actress Betty Grable. Spanish dance was in vogue in Hollywood, and Cansino, known as a tough taskmaster, worked his pupils hard. While Margarita was cowed by her father, Margo was more resilient. According to Cansino's son, Vernon, in *Rita Hayworth: The Time, the Place and the Woman*, Margo "would take it because she could go home, curse him in the street, and come back the next day saying, 'O Maestro, you're marvellous.'" The niece of Cuban orchestra leader and film personality Xavier Cugat, she performed with his band as a specialty dancer in Mexican nightclubs and at the elegant Waldorf-Astoria hotel's Starlight Roof. Margo was the lead dancer in her uncle's act when Cugat introduced the rhumba, which became a national dance sensation. She also performed with George Raft in a dance act at the Paramount Theater in New York.

Profiled in *Collier's* as "The Girl With One Name," Margo received rave reviews for her Broadway debut as Miriamne at the age of 17 in Maxwell Anderson's *Winterset,* a role she recreated in the 1936 film version. The drama intentionally evoked the sensational Sacco-Vanzetti case of the 1920s. In the film, her character is shot and killed, whereas in the original play Miriamne survives. She remained active in the theater, performing in productions of *Faust* in 1938, followed by *The Streets of Paris* and *Seventh Heaven* in 1939. That year she also danced in the ballet *El Amor Brujo* with Mexico's National Symphony Orchestra. Other notable performances were in *The World We Make* in 1941, *Tanyard Street,* and *A Bell for Adano* in 1944.

Begins Film Career

Margo's career as a film actress began in 1934 with a showy part in *Crime Without Passion,* with Claude Rains. Cast as a tragic murder victim, Margo's performance was praised. This proved to be the first in a long series of similar roles, and, like many Hollywood actresses, she struggled against typecasting. Her talents as a dancer were next displayed in the 1935 film, *Rumba.* Her role in *Robin Hood of El Dorado* (1936) was initially the leading female character, Juanita, but she was abruptly recast in a smaller role as Rosita, whose murder motivates the hero's vengeance. Margo's best-known role was as a Tibetan girl, Maria, in Frank Capra's *Lost Horizon* (1937). Capra praised Margo's performance, calling her "brilliant," and her career seemed ready to catapult after the success. However, after her next film, *A Miracle on Main Street,* a "B" movie in which she starred as a carnival dancer who finds an abandoned baby on Christmas Eve, it would be three years before she appeared on screen again. *The Leopard Man,* a cult favorite based on Val Lewton's thriller novel, reinforced Margo's reputation as an exotic. Similar roles followed: *Behind the Rising Sun, Gangway for Tomorrow,* (both in 1943) and *The Falcon in Mexico* (1944). None of these films, however, advanced her career.

Marriage Brings Happiness

Margo avoided the tempestuous lifestyle common in the entertainment world. She was the second of three wives, from 1937 to 1940, of Frances Lederer, the Czech-born stage and screen actor best known as the doomed Alwa Schoen in G.B. Pabst's classic silent film *Pandora's Box.* She became an American citizen in 1942, and three years later married actor Eddie Albert in St. Patrick's Cathedral in New York City. The couple was devoted to one another, and had, by all accounts, one of Hollywood's most successful marriages. During the 1950s, they performed a song-and-dance night club revue created for them by director Herbert Ross. They had one son, Edward, born February 20, 1951, and an adopted daughter, Maria. Edward reflected on his childhood for the *New York Times* in 1972, revealing that his mother had run afoul of the Hollywood establishment. "My mom was blacklisted for appearing at an anti-Franco rally; she was branded a Communist, was

spat upon in the streets, and had to have a bodyguard." His father's film career was affected as well, and only somewhat recovered after his military service in the Pacific during World War II. Later, Albert became a television star in the 1960s sitcom, *Green Acres,* which eased financial strains on the family. Margo acted intermittently in the 1950s and 1960s, most notably in *Viva Zapata!,* directed by Elia Kazan, and starring Marlon Brando and Anthony Quinn. She also had a supporting role in the Lillian Roth story, *I'll Cry Tomorrow,* starring Susan Hayward as the alcoholic singer. *From Hell to Texas,* made in 1958, and *Who's Got the Action?,* a 1962 comedy starring Dean Martin and Lana Turner, were the last two films of her career.

Margo continued to work as an acting coach; one of her pupils, Anthony Pena, is a long-time cast member of the daytime drama *The Young and the Restless.* Margo was dedicated to helping Hispanics succeed in the arts, and her kindness and generosity helped many young people advance their careers.

Acts as Patron of the Arts

In the 1960s, Margo turned her attention to the community, becoming a leading advocate for the arts in Los Angeles as well as on the national scene. She served on the National Council on the Arts, was a steering committee member of the President's Committee on the Arts and Humanities, and a member of the Presidential Task Force on the Arts and Humanities. In California, she was active in the State Arts Council, and served on the board of the Music Center Theater Group, as well as the vice-chairperson of the Los Angeles Two Hundred Committee, which fostered cultural exchanges between Los Angeles and Mexico. With Frank Lopez, a noted labor union organizer, she led a successful campaign to save a historic boathouse in East Los Angeles's Lincoln Park which became Plaza de la Raza, a thriving community-based arts and education center.

When Margo died on July 17, 1985, the National Endowment for the Arts chairperson eulogized her at a memorial service at the Plaza de la Raza, recalling her remarkable life and personality: ". . . she was earthy and poetic, softhearted and tough-minded, a romantic and a pragmatist, a potential cynic who lived by faith, a Latin Yankee." Plaza de la Raza honored her by naming a theater for her, and celebrates her memory in a semi-annual family-oriented cultural festival.

Sources:

Capra, Frank. *The Name Above the Title.* New York: MacMillan, 1971.

Hodsoll, Francis S. M. "Obituary." *American Film,* October, 1985, p. 88.

Katz, Ephraim. *The Film Encyclopedia.* New York: HarperCollins, 1994.

Kobal, John. *Rita Hayworth: The Time, The Place and The Woman*. New York: W. W. Norton, 1977.

New York Encyclopedia of Film. New York: Times Books, 1984.

Plaza de la Raza Home Page. Available at http://www.plazaraza.org/about/index.htm.

Springer, John. *They Had Faces Then*. Secaucus, NJ: Citadel Press, 1974.

Within Our Gates: Ethnicity in American Feature Films, 1911-1960. Berkeley: University of California Press, 1997.

Constance Marie

(1969–)

Actress, dancer

Selected filmography:

Santa Barbara. NBC-TV, 1984.
Salsa. 1988.
Dirty Dancing. (Television series) 1988.
12:01. (Television movie) 1993.
Island City. (Television movie) 1994.
Fast Company. (Television movie) 1995.
Mi Familia/My Family. New Line Cinema, 1995.
Selena. Q Productions, Inc. 1997.
Union Square. NBC-TV, 1997.

Overview

As an actress, Constance Marie has made a career out of her ability to take on diverse challenges in her profession and be noticed. Jokingly attributing her success in movies and television to "on-the-job training," she is a talent on the rise. Her work in such critically acclaimed films as *Mi Familia* and *Selena* has helped her to develop into one of the premiere Hispanic American actresses of the 1990s.

Dreams of Acting

Born Constance Marie Lopez in East Los Angeles on September 9, 1969, she was raised by her artist mother in West Hollywood. She and her younger brother, Michael Christopher, had a knockabout childhood during which Constance Marie often had to defend her sibling in street fights. An article in *Moderna* described her as "a hard-nosed scrapper who struck terror into little boys."

Enters Show Business as Dancer

Marie began her dancing career on singer David Bowie's "Glass Spider" tour. In 1988, Marie was spotted by choreographer Kenny Ortega and cast as a dancer in her first film, *Salsa*. The movie featured music greats Tito Puente and Celia Cruz, and was the story of a mechanic who wants

a dancing career. While the film was energetic, it failed to create the excitement generated by the box office hit *Dirty Dancing*, the inspiration of many dance films. Nevertheless, Constance Marie was on her way, and hoped to break into acting roles. She hated the toll dance injuries took on her body, and feared being typecast as a dancer. Marie got her wish when Ortega cast her in the television series *Dirty Dancing* playing the part Cynthia Rhodes had played in the film. Crediting Ortega for her start as an actress, Marie told *NBC Live Transcripts*, ". . . he gave me an opportunity and encouraged me to do something I'd never done before. . . and pushed me." Calling acting "a natural transition from dancing," Constance Marie began to be considered a promising young talent. Marie went on to join the cast of the daytime drama *Santa Barbara* as the new love interest of the popular lead character, Cruz. When her character was killed in an explosion, Marie took away with her a valuable skill learned from the grueling schedule of soaps: "Soap operas definitely taught me how to remember the words, shooting an hour episode every day," she said in an interview with *NBC Live Transcripts*. But in spite of her acting abilities, the actress has often encountered the same typecasting that has plagued Latinos in Hollywood for decades. Even being considered for non-stereotypical roles is difficult: "Once you're in, you not only have to be better than everyone else but you have to rise above your best and be brilliant because of how we are perceived," she was quoted as saying in *Moderna*.

Finds Success in Films

As a director who has spent his career making films about Latinos and with Latino casts, Gregory Nava recognized that Constance Marie was a versatile talent and cast her in an important role in *Mi Familia* (1995), his highly acclaimed multi-generational saga. Calling the role of Toni Sanchez her favorite, Constance Marie garnered favorable critical attention for her portrayal of the ex-nun turned activist. Nava had to fight studio executives to cast Constance Marie because they wanted a better-known actress in the part. Nava told a reporter for *Moderna*, "I knew she would be sensational. She was so extraordinary. Her tape was brilliant. When the studio executives saw her, they were wowed by her." Nava next cast her as Marcela Quintanilla, the devoted mother of slain Tejano superstar Selena, played by Jennifer Lopez, in one of 1997's most awaited releases. Although her part was less showy than the role of Toni Sanchez in *Mi Familia*, it was just as challenging. Marie worked closely with the real Marcela to perfect her character, and spent hours being made up to look 20 years older.

Furthers Career in Television

The busy actress has worked steadily in television. Her television movie credits include *12:01*, an acclaimed thriller (1993); *Island City* (1994), and *Fast Company* (1995). She received favorable attention as a guest star on ABC's hit series *Spin City*, playing Gaby Sanchez, a new love interest for Michael J. Fox's character. Other television appearances include: *Jake and the Fatman, Reasonable Doubts, The Sentinel* and *Maloney. Union Square,* a 1997 sitcom based in a New York eatery with an ensemble cast featured Constance Marie as Gabriella Valdez, a Chicana Texas transplant hoping to make it big on Broadway. The show failed to catch on, but Constance earned the praise of the executive producer Fred Barron: "She is wonderful. She's very smart and beautiful." In the same *Moderna* interview, Nava observed that "Constance is great for television. Very few actors can master both the big screen and TV. She has that 'threatening quality' as we say in the business, that is great for the big screen. But she is also the kind of performer you love to have in your home every week."

True to Herself

With her success, Constance Marie has not forgotten her roots, and makes giving back a priority. She has worked with the homeless and gives motivational speeches in schools. Her attitude towards life and her career is a resilient and characteristically honest one: "An actor has to have the hide of a rhinoceros and the soul of a rose," she said in a *Moderna* interview. She shares her home with her cat Homey and enjoys dancing, gardening, and practicing yoga.

Sources:

Chicago Sun-Times Home Page. Available at http://www.suntimes.com/ebert/ebert_reviews/1997/03/032103.html.
Granados, Christine. "Tough Enough for Hollywood." *Moderna,* Fall, 1997.
Hollywood Online Home Page. Available at http://www.hollywood.online.com.
Joyner, Will. "The New Season in Review." *New York Times,* September 25, 1997.
NBC Television Home Page. Available at http://205.173.92.140/tvcentral/shows/unionsquare/biomarie.html.

Christine Marín
(1943–)
Archivist, curator, educator, scholar

Selected writings:

A Spokesman of the Mexican American Revolution Movement: Rodolfo "Corky" Gonzales and the Fight for Chicano Liberation, 1966-1972. R. & E. Research Associates, 1977.
Latinos in Museums: A Heritage Reclaimed. With co-editor Antonio Jose Rios-Bustamante. Krieger Press, 1998.

Christine Marín

Overview

Christine Marín is the archivist and curator of the Chicano Research Collection at the Hayden Library at Arizona State University in Tempe, Arizona. She has been recognized for her work with the collection and her research and writing on the subject of Mexican American history and Mexican Americans in the Southwest United States.

An Arizona Native

Christine Marín was born on December 28, 1943, in Globe, Arizona. Her father, Lupe Trujillo Marín, was a copper miner, and her mother, Eulalia Renteria Marín, was a homemaker. Marín earned a B.A. in English from Arizona State in 1974 and a M.A. in twentieth century American history from the same institution in 1982. In addition to her work with the Chicano Research Collection, Marín has contributed to the field of Chicano studies through teaching, researching, and writing.

Begins in Adjunct Faculty Position

Marín's teaching career began as an adjunct faculty associate in the Arizona State Women's Studies Program. From 1986 to 1995 she taught such courses as "La Chicana" and "Women in the Southwest." She occupied the same position in the Department of Chicana and Chicano Studies in 1997, teaching the course "Issues in Chicana/Chicano Studies Gender."

A Career as Archivist and Curator

In 1989 Marín was hired as the curator and assistant archivist for the Chicano Research Collection. She served as the unit head of the collection and was responsible for acquiring, evaluating, and coding materials; coordinating the conversion of the card catalog for the collection to a database; and providing intellectual access to departmental collections and materials. She was also the subject specialist for the Chicano Research Collection and for the Spanish Language Books for Children Curriculum Collection. Marín was promoted to associate archivist in 1991, a position in which she continued and expanded upon the duties she had performed for the previous two years. Additional responsibilities in her new position include coordinating the activities of a graduate student for the Chicano Research Collection, working with faculty in order to coordinate their needs with the library's goals, and keeping up-to-date on the latest developments in resources available electronically. Marín stated that the most important aspect of her position is obtaining materials and processing them so they are available for users of the collection.

Active in Professional Organizations

Marín has been a member of various organizations related to her field. She served on the advisory board of the Arizona Chicano Mobile Institutes in Phoenix from 1972-75, and was a member of the Arizona Historical Society in Tucson. Other organizations in which Marín has been involved include REFORMA (Library Services to the Spanish Speaking), the American Association for State and Local History, the National Association for Chicano Studies, the Society of American Archivists, and the National Council of Public History. Marín also has served as an editorial consultant to *La Revista Bilingue* (*The Bilingual Review*), published by the Bilingual Review Press at Arizona State University since 1993.

Publications and Presentations

Marín has published articles and book reviews in various periodicals, including *Journal of Arizona History, Journal of the West, Journal of the Southwest,* and *New Mexico Historical Review.* Her work also appears in *Perspectives in Mexican American Studies* and *Encyclopedia of the American West.* Much of Marín's work relates to the history of Mexican Americans in the Southwest. Some of her published articles include: "They Sought Work and Found Hell: The Hanigan Case of Arizona" (*Perspectives in Mexican American Studies,* Volume 6, 1997); "Arizona Mining Strikes" (*Encyclopedia of the American West,* Volume 1, 1996); and "Mexican Americans on the Home Front: Community Organizations in Arizona During World War II" (*Perspectives in*

Mexican American Studies, Volume 4, 1993). "The Power of Language: From the Back of the Bus to the Ivory Tower" is due to appear in *Chicanas and Language: Reconstruction, Reflection, and Innovation,* edited by D. Letticia Galindo and Maria Dolores Gonzales Velasquez (University of Arizona Press). Marín also has a monograph in process titled *Latinos in Museums: A Heritage Reclaimed* (Kreiger Press). Earlier in her career, Marín wrote a book titled *A Spokesman of the Mexican American Revolution Movement: Rodolfo "Corky" Gonzales and the Fight for Chicano Liberation, 1966-1972,* which was published in 1977 by R. & E. Research Associates.

In addition to publishing her research, Marín has made many presentations throughout the state of Arizona at conferences, meetings, and lecture series. Just a few of her many presentations include "Arizona's Hispanic Women of Importance" (1998), "The Chicano Movement and its Legacy" (1998), "Mexican Americans in Arizona Mining History" (1997), and "History and Genealogy: A True Partnership" (1995). In 1993 she presented professional papers at the National Association for Chicano Studies Annual Conference in San Jose, California, and the Berkshire Conference on the History of Women in New York. In 1994 she presented at the American Historical Association Annual Meeting in San Francisco, the Annual Southwest Labor Studies Conference in Santa Cruz, California, and the Western History Association Annual Conference in Albuquerque.

Awards and Recognitions

In 1996, Marín received the Faculty/Scholar AACHE (Arizona Association of Chicanos/Hispanics for Higher Education) Award. The previous year she was awarded the Arizona Humanities Council's Distinguished Scholar of the Year Award. Marín was cited in *The National Directory of Chicano Faculty and Research* and *Latin American Research Review* in 1975. More recently, she has appeared in *Chicano Scholars and Writers* and *Who's Who in Library and Information Services* (1982). Edward C. Oetting, head of archives and manuscripts at the Arizona State University Libraries, wrote that the Chicano Research Collection ". . . has been nurtured and built almost exclusively through Ms. Marín's administrations" and that she has made a great contribution to the university through her work with students and her "perseverance and vision" in working with the Chicano Research Collection.

Future Plans

Marín expects to receive her Ph.D. from Arizona State University in the field of Mexican American history, with specialization in twentieth-century American history, in 1998. She then plans to continue her archivist work part-time and teach students at the university level in either the history or the Chicano/Chicana studies department. Marín continues to conduct research in the Southwest United States and write about issues concerning Mexican Americans.

Current Address: Chicano Research Collection, Dept. of Archives and Manuscripts, Univ. Libraries, Arizona State Univ., PO Box 871006, Tempe, AZ 85287-1006.

Sources:

Bethel, Kari. Correspondence and telephone conversation with Christine Marín, March, 1998.

Lee, Joel M. ed., *Who's Who in Library and Information Services,* Chicago: American Library Association, 1982.

Martinez, Julio A., ed., *Chicano Scholars and Writers: A Biobibliographical Dictionary,* Metuchen, N.J.: Scarecrow Press, 1979.

Leticia Márquez-Magaña

(1963–)

Genetics researcher, professor

Biology professor Leticia Márquez-Magaña routinely mixes genetics research with progressive teaching methods, a concoction that earned her a $500,000 National Science Foundation (NSF) Career Award in 1996. No

Leticia Márquez-Magaña

stranger to honors, that same year Márquez-Magaña won a coveted NSF Postdoctoral Fellowship, which is bestowed upon just ten researchers annually. She proudly counts herself as one of five Hispanic biology professors at San Francisco State University (SFSU), the highest concentration of Hispanic scientists in the 23-campus California State University system. Well aware of the controversies surrounding genetic engineering and the artificial manipulation of DNA, Márquez-Magaña developed an undergraduate curriculum that examines the ethics involved in her own research, as well as in the scientific discoveries which spawned the Genetic Revolution. The NSF grant also underwrites an innovative mentoring program for graduate students. "Traditionally, educators have unnecessarily mystified science," said Márquez-Magaña in a 1997 SFSU press release. "As a mentor, I want to enable students to reach their full potential by empowering them to participate in their own learning within a collaborative environment."

Parents' Desire for Education Motivates Márquez-Magaña

As an undergraduate in the 1980s, Márquez-Magaña herself had no role model in the sciences. She credits her parents' frustrated desire to become educated with motivating her to succeed academically. Márquez-Magaña's Mexican father had been working and living in the United States for a few years by the time her Mexican mother immigrated to California in the summer of 1963 when she was eight months pregnant. Leticia Maria Márquez was born in Sacramento on August 15, 1963. Although she was born a U.S. citizen, Márquez-Magaña claims to have "de corazon de una Mexicana" (the heart of a Mexican woman). She attended public elementary schools, but since her first language was Spanish, her parents felt that she could learn more in a private Catholic school environment where she could receive more personal attention from the teacher. Her father, a construction laborer, and her mother, a cannery worker, had to work very hard in order to send their four children to private school. After breaking through the language barrier, Márquez-Magaña graduated at the top of her class from the all-girls Bishop Manogue High School.

However, the valedictorian quickly dropped from the top as a freshman at Stanford University. In the rigorous academic environment of one of the top universities in the country, Márquez-Magaña found that classes were not so easy, and she needed a few years to learn how to study. In the frustration of this period, she considered switching from her science major and foregoing her dream of a graduate school education. By the beginning of her senior year, however, she began to perform well in her courses and by the end of her year in graduate school, she was being recruited for doctoral programs. Márquez-Magaña's belief that a role model would have alleviated many of the problems she encountered in school spurred her on to become a role model herself to aspiring minority scientists. Márquez-Magaña earned her masters degree in biological sciences from Stanford in 1986. She went on to doctoral studies, funded through an NSF minority fellowship, at the University of California, Berkeley. One of her research projects focused on the cloning and sequencing of genes. She earned a Ph.D. in 1991.

Immediately afterward Márquez-Magaña married Tómas Magaña, a fellow graduate student and Chicano who would later become a pediatric medical doctor. Following a long honeymoon and vacation, Márquez-Magaña returned to Stanford Medical Center to conduct postdoctoral research on the role of a mammalian enzyme in insulin degradation.

Teaches at San Francisco State University

SFSU hired Márquez-Magaña as an assistant professor in 1994. Along with her research duties, she teaches courses in microbial genetics, molecular biology, and microbiology. She believes that, as an educator, her overall goal is to empower her students to become active participants in their education. To this end, she not only presents information in class, but she also tells students why the information is important and relevant, how it was experimentally obtained, and how they can use the information for their own educational goals. It is her hope that this process will demystify scientific concepts and make them more tangible for the students. By implementing investigative and collaborative learning strategies she allows the students to construct their own knowledge instead of being receptacles for transmitted knowledge.

Success Connects to Service

Part of the sweetness of her success comes from Márquez-Magaña's desire to share her success with others. She has participated in several programs dedicated to increasing the number of women and minority students in the sciences. She has also given research presentations to fledgling scientists, spoken on panels for interested students, and participated in workshops designed to empower the new undergraduate or graduate student with the information to succeed in their respective program.

Current Address: Dept. of Biology, San Francisco State Univ., 1600 Holloway Ave., San Francisco, CA 94132.

Sources:

Bush, Merrik, "Growth of Hispanic Professors Represents the Changing Face of Science at San Francisco State University." SFSU Public Affairs Press Releases, March 3, 1997.
Márquez-Magaña, Leticia. Brief autobiography included in a booklet distributed at the annual conference of the Society for the Advancement of Chicanos and Native Americans, 1991.

Patricia Preciado Martin
(1939–)
Author

Selected writings:

The Bellringer of San Augustin. Pajarito Publications, 1980.
Images and Conversations: Mexican Americans Recall a Southwestern Past. University of Arizona Press, 1983.
Days of Plenty, Days of Want. Bilingual Review Press, 1988.
Songs My Mother Sang to Me. University of Arizona Press, 1992.
El Milagro and other stories. University of Arizona Press, 1996.

Overview

If it were not for Patricia Preciado Martin, the residents of Tucson might not know as much about the rich Mexican American history within the city's borders. Preciado Martin began spinning stories when her two children were young; on camping trips, she would make up stories in the evenings to entertain them. Ten children's stories later, Preciado Martin became interested in chronicling the stories and histories of Mexican Americans in Tucson, AZ. Three published books into her carefully evolving career as a writer and historian, Preciado Martin has been heralded as a local documentarian and notable voice for the oft-ignored Mexican American population in Arizona. "I think it's very important that Mexican Americans feel a sense of place because we're always told to go back from where we came," said Preciado Martin during a telephone interview.

Preciado Martin was born and raised in Tucson, AZ. She graduated with honors and a B.A. in elementary education from the University of Arizona in 1960 and has been active in the Mexican American community of Tucson, including development of the Mexican Heritage Project at the Arizona Historical Society. Preciado Martin taught at the junior high and high school levels during the 1960s. During this decade she also joined the Peace Corps and served in Belize, where she met her husband of 35 years, Jim Martin.

Her first book, *The Bellringer of San Augustin*, a bilingual children's book, was published in 1980 for the International Year of the Child. In 1983, the University of Arizona Press published *Images and Conversations: Mexican Americans Recall a Southwestern Past*, which won the Virginia McCormick Scully Award for the best history book by a Chicana or Native American woman. The photographs that accompanied Preciado Martin's tales in this tome were shot by the late Louis Carlos Bernal, an acclaimed photographer of the Tucson barrio. Several of the writings in Preciado Martin's collection of short stories, *Days of Plenty, Days of Want* (1988), have won short story contests, including a contest at the Mexican American Studies and Research Center in Tucson and a second prize at the Chicano Short Story

Patricia Preciado Martin

Contest at the University of California at Irvine; a folktale earned a prize from the International Year of the Child. *Songs My Mother Sang to Me* (1992), an oral history of the lives of ten Mexican American women, and Preciado Martin's most recent book, *El Milagro and Other Stories* (1996), were both published by the University of Arizona Press. The latter has been compared to Laura Esquivel's *Like Water for Chocolate* in the way that it mixes food, family, and tradition. It is based on the people and places Martin recalls from her childhood in Tucson in the 1950s.

Patricia Preciado Martin has not sought a career of prestige and fame nor of notoriety. She weaves the stories of Mexican Americans and their history in Arizona into eloquent collections for personal satisfaction and to fill the gap left in historical accounts of native Arizonans; if the books sell, that is a plus in Preciado Martin's mind.

Preciado Martin began chronicling the Mexican American history of Tucson through folktales she had been told when she was young. So she began to walk through the barrios (neighborhoods), asking Mexican Americans their versions of local folktales. During the telephone interview, she said, "What happened was, these older people would tell me the folktale and then they would want to keep talking about their lives. So I realized no one had ever interviewed our Mexican American elders here, and our history goes back to the sixteenth century, if you count some of the explorers that were here before the settlements. I became extremely interested in this. I had interviewed an

elderly aunt and with her history, my sister and I found our great-great-grandparents' ranch in Mexico. Oral history is a great way to document your history. That kind of validated for me the importance of oral history; not only family history, but community history."

In the stories Preciado Martin heard, Mexican American mothers and grandmothers figured prominently, which led her toward her next book, *Songs My Mother Sang To Me*. She said that it is not necessarily a book about women, but rather "a book by women about history." "No one had ever written or documented the contributions of Mexican American women," she said. "We were mostly portrayed, and are still, as ladies of the night and not much else really, and I knew that my own family history was not like that. I felt that Mexican American women had really been short-changed; she was as much a pioneer as any other ethnic group of women."

Songs My Mother Sang To Me tells the stories of ten Mexican American women from southern and central Arizona. Preciado Martin emphasized the roles of Mexican American women, especially "women's work." "I want to destroy the stereotype that Mexican women did nothing but hang out in the cantinas." Even Preciado Martin was surprised by what she found. "Mexican women were midwives and healers and seamstresses and laundresses, but also politicians, journalists, creative writers, and poets. They were. . . teachers, perhaps not in the traditional ways but they were religious leaders, the leaders of their culture. They did everything a man did, including building houses, fences," said Preciado Martin.

The book was difficult for Preciado Martin to research. In the postscript to the book's preface, she wrote: "This book was also motivated by very personal feelings—a love and respect for the richness and power of my Mexican heritage and an abiding love for the memory of my maternal grandmother, Mercedes Rascon Romero. My Grandmother Mercedes, a mestiza of Tarahumara lineage, came to Clifton, Arizona, from Guerrero, Chihuahua, as a young bride in the late 1800s. She lived in El Barrio de los Alacranes in a home that my Grandfather Exiquio built. The house still stands where she bore and raised her children. She was tall-five feet and ten inches—and elegant. She was known for her beauty, her gentility, her spirituality, her generosity, her skill as a seamstress and cook, and her musical ability." Preciado Martin's grandmother died during the Great Depression and was buried in what used to be a segregated cemetery in Clarkdale, AZ. Preciado Martin never knew her grandmother, but in writing and researching this book, she in a way was looking for her own history.

Preciado Martin likes to use the women from *Songs My Mother Sang To Me* as role models for young people. She often gives oral history presentations to young Mexican Americans, "to give people a sense, all of us Mexican Americans, who grew up with discrimination, prejudice, to show we do have a sense of place here, a sense of continuity, place, belonging, a sense of gratitude for what our forefathers have gone through to get us where we are today. We're still struggling, but I think we're better off than they were and we're better off because of them," Preciado Martin said.

Preciado Martin does not write for prestige or power, though she has received several literary awards, and certainly not for money. She willingly admits that the money earned from the sale of her tomes is mere "beer money," and credits her husband for financially supporting the family enough to allow her to pursue her historical documentation and writing. She regularly calls on her adult children as editors and critics; "They're my best literary critics," she said. "They're very honest with me, and they truly do love my writing." Preciado Martin has a book of love stories planned for future release.

Current Address: 1735 E. Entrada Nueve, Tucson, AZ 85718.

Sources:

Christie, Joyce. "Writer sees courage, poetry in histories of early-day Mexican-American women," *Yuma Daily Sun*, April 29, 1993.

Cohn, Lynne M. Telephone interview with Patricia Preciado Martin, March 13, 1998.

"Generations." *Tucson Daily Citizen*, Sept. 15, 1992.

Martin, Patricia Preciado.*Images and Conversations: Mexican Americans Recall a Southwestern Past*. Tucson: University of Arizona Press, 1983.

————.*Songs My Mother Sang to Me*. Tucson: University of Arizona Press, 1992.

————.*El Milagro and Other Stories*. Tucson: University of Arizona Press, 1996.

Prezelski, Carmen Villa. "Patricia P. Martin preserves memories."*Tucson Citizen*, Feb. 27, 1996.

Ross, Deborah. "Loving tales of everyday lives." *The Phoenix Gazette*, Oct. 5, 1993.

Severson, Ed. "Barrio vignettes." *Arizona Daily Star*, April 18, 1996.

Julie A. Martines
(1966–)
Construction service executive, entrepreneur

Entrepreneur Julie Martines has to think a minute when asked how she motivates her employees. "It's probably my own work ethic," she said. "I lead by example." At

Julie Martines

the age of 25, Martines took the lead in her own life and started her own business. Entering a field dominated by men, she began leasing, selling, and servicing construction equipment. She named her Chicago-based company WillRent, Inc., and, as its president and chief executive officer, has taken it from ground zero in 1991 to more than $2.5 million in 1997. Martines, who has seven employees, said in a telephone interview, "I am not a boss that holds people's hands or looks over their shoulder. I give my employees freedom to take the route they think is appropriate for each situation, and I believe they do much better in that type of environment." Martines said in an interview with *Latina*, magazine, "You have to prove yourself—you have to do that every day in business. But because of gender or race, some of us have to do it a little more."

Finds Business Niche

Martines was born on June 16, 1966, in Winfield, IL, the younger of two sisters. Her parents, both born in the United States, started their own business in heavy machinery more than thirty years ago. After she graduated from the University of Wisconsin-Madison with a bachelor of science degree, Martines went to work doing interior architecture, design, and space planning with a Chicago firm in their real estate services/tenant development department which managed 11 corporate office buildings in the downtown and surrounding areas. In 1991, economic conditions caused a decline in that industry, and Martines, who always had a strong desire to own her own business, decided this was a good time to step out on her own. "I wasn't particular about what I did. I just wanted to be doing my own thing, making my own decisions, and working for myself. I grew up in a family-owned business. That's what I saw every day. I just thought that was what everyone did. Oh, I saw the struggles and the challenges my parents had, but I also saw the rewards," she said. Martines, who worked all through high school and college, feels her two years of experience as an employee were important to her successful entrepreneurial endeavor. "I would recommend to anyone wanting to start their own business that they work for someone else first," she said.

Takes Initiative

In Martines's particular endeavor, experience and determination needed a partner—money. She said, "This business is capital-intensive. I needed a quarter of a million dollars to purchase my initial inventory." As a base, she used her personal savings and applied for a loan through the Small Business Administration. While awaiting its approval, the bank with which she was working approved an interim loan. She worked very hard at laying a good foundation. "I tried not to reinvent the wheel," she said. "I got advice from my family, fellow business owners, and did a tremendous amount of networking. I attended receptions and functions and met with people who had been in similar situations to me."

Martines applied her talents to every aspect of her business—from marketing and advertising to reviewing equipment inventory, from working with new customers to strategic planning. Soon, her investment and hard work was reaping rewards. In an interview with *Hispanic Business*, she said, "A lot of our success has to do with the opportunities that Mayor Daley provided within the city. He and his people have said flat out that they believe in providing opportunities for minority and women-owned businesses." However, taking advantage of opportunities requires vision backed with action. Martines obviously has both qualities, coupled with courage. In an interview in *Hispanic*, magazine, Martines said, "I love working for myself. I have never worked so hard in my life, but the results are well worth it! I encourage women of any age to do whatever they can to establish themselves, learn skills, and gain independence so they can be financially and personally rewarded through their own achievements."

Recognizes Opportunities for Hispanics

Martines believes the market is wide open for Hispanic American women with the vision and drive. A *USA Weekend* article supports her view when referring to a study from the National Foundation for Women Business Owners. The study shows that, of eight million businesses in the United States owned by women, thirteen percent are owned by African Americans, Latin Americans, Asian Americans,

and Native Americans. The article also reports that the number of people employed by minority women has more than tripled in the last ten years. "There is a tremendous amount of opportunity out there for women, particularly in non-traditional fields," Martines said in a telephone interview. "My advice to women is that they come out of their shell—get involved. People are looking under rocks for women, particularly Hispanic women, in non-traditional fields. Opportunities are so much greater in areas where not everyone and their brother are doing it."

Involves Herself in Community

Apart from her busy career, Martines finds time to volunteer in professional and civic organizations. She is a board member of Casa Central, City of Chicago-Gary Regional Airport Authority, the Federation of Women Contractors (of which she is also vice president), and the Hispanic American Construction Industry Association, and is a member of the Mexican American Chamber of Commerce. "Although I am in a handful of organizations at any one time," she said, "I concentrate most of my energy on one for a couple of years so I can do my best for that organization. Then I change focus. This gives new people an opportunity to provide their expertise—to get new blood into the organization."

Embraces Strong Values

Martines, who rides horses in her leisure time, recently embarked on an exciting personal endeavor. She married Patrick McKevit, who came to the United States from Northern Ireland 11 years ago. They share not only a love of horses, but also a heritage of immigration and strong work ethic. "My experience with so many of the Spanish community—and my husband and the members of his family who have also come to the States—is that, out of sheer necessity, they have to hustle and work hard just to feed and clothe and shelter themselves and their families. So they begin with that work ethic and drive," she said. "I find many Americans just don't have that drive. They take for granted what they have here—but they certainly do have opportunity."

Current Address: Will Rent Inc., 3228 S. Wood St., Chicago, IL 60608.

Sources:

Chambers, Veronica. "Minority Women: The New Bosses." *USA Weekend,* October/November, 1997, p. 24.
Cole, Melanie. "30 Under Thirty: Stand Back, World, Here Comes Generation Equis." *Hispanic,* August 31, 1995, p. 22.
Mendosa, Rick. "The 10 Best Cities for New Hispanic Entrepreneurs." *Hispanic Business,* May, 1994, pp. 41-49
"Paying the Rent—Y Más!" *Latina,* August, 1997, p. 16.

Thompson, Märie L. Telephone conversation and bio-graphical material from Julie A. Martines, April, 1998.

Elizabeth Martinez
(1943–)
Entrepreneur, consultant, librarian, author

Elizabeth Martinez was born April 14, 1943, in Pomona, California, where she grew up in the poorest part of town. "I was a library kid," she recalled in an interview for the *Orange County Register.* "Books were a kind of escape. I visited places I'd never seen." Her local children's librarian developed an interest in her, and encouraged her to read and learn about the world; Martinez ended up going to the library as much for the librarian as for the books. After graduating from high school with excellent grades, "I was turned down at the local private college because of my ethnic background," she told Vachon. But she tried again, entered the University of California at Los Angeles in 1961, and received her bachelor of arts in Latin American studies in 1965. The following year, Martinez secured her master's in library and information science from the University of Southern California (USC) in Los Angeles (she later obtained a certificate in management from USC in 1978, and an executive management program certificate from the University of California at Irvine in 1986). "I more or less chose this career by accident, because I did not want to be a teacher," Martinez commented in her interview with Vachon. She was determined to make a difference in people's lives, and realized that she could accomplish that by being a librarian. In 1966, Martinez joined Los Angeles County Public Library as California's first Mexican American librarian. One day, a young Hispanic girl brought her mother to the library to meet Martinez. "'See mom, she looks just like me,'" the child said. "You never understand how much a role model you are until something like this happens," remarked Martinez in her *Orange County Register* interview.

In 1972, the Los Angeles County Public Library promoted Martinez to the position of regional administrative librarian for the west and central county regions. During the following seven years she administered 12 to 15 libraries with a personal budget of more than $1 million. Among other accomplishments, Martinez established a Chicano resource center in East Los Angeles and an Asian cultural center in Montebello; she also developed a multilingual telephone information center. From 1974 until 1976, Martinez lectured at the California State University's School of Library Science at Fullerton, served on its advisory committee, and contributed to the school's success in obtaining a federal grant for the creation of a Mexican American librarians' institute.

Supervises Construction of New Libraries

After serving for a short period of time as the Los Angeles County Public Library's chief of public services, Martinez accepted the position of county librarian for the Orange County Public Library in 1979. She handled the system's $24-million budget and oversaw its 600 employees. During her tenure, Martinez also supervised the construction of eight new community libraries, including the San Juan Capistrano regional library (its concept earned architect Michael Graves national and international acclaim); implemented one of the largest computerized circulation control systems; established multicultural services and a books-by-mail loan service; created the Friends of the Library Foundation; and set an annual recognition day for the library's friends and volunteers. In June of 1990, Martinez returned to the Los Angeles Public Library as city librarian.

As city librarian for Los Angeles, California, Elizabeth Martinez administered an operating budget of more than $37 million and supervised a staff of 1,200 employees assigned to 63 library branches. In addition to the library's existing branches, Martinez supervised the construction of 26 new branches, including the central library built at an estimated cost of $212 million. Martinez, who started her career as a children's librarian, was the only Hispanic woman heading one of the largest library systems in the United States. She admitted that her ascent to the position of administrative head was arduous. "Being a woman, and a Mexican American woman at that, I had to be the best at all times in order to gain professional acceptance," she explained in a telephone interview with Michelle Vachon. "I was perceived as representing all Hispanics, and strongly felt the responsibility of showing what the entire Hispanic population could accomplish." In 1966, there were only five Mexican American librarians in the country and "we all knew each other." "One of my efforts since I became a librarian has been to recruit more Hispanics into the profession," related Martinez in the *Los Angeles Times.* "There are very few Hispanics who go into the library profession, and one of the reasons is that they don't have a tradition of library services in their community."

Heads the American Library Association

In 1994, Martinez was selected to become executive director of the American Library Association (ALA). Despite a promising beginning, her tenure as executive director was marred by infighting within the association, vocal disagreements regarding Martinez's salary and compensation package, and concerns about her leadership abilities. Weary of the bitter controversy and verbal attacks, Martinez announced her resignation in July of 1996. However, she remained in office until July 31, 1997. In a 1997 interview with *American Libraries,* Martinez listed the ALA Goals 2000 initiative, a comprehensive five-year plan to prepare the library profession and the ALA for the 21st century, as one of her proudest accomplishments as ALA director. She also remarked to *American Libraries,* "I am also very proud of the role that ALA played in the formation of the Gates Library Foundation, which will connect public libraries in low-income communities to the Internet and train librarians in technology and electronic resources. . . I was honored to represent ALA at the national level with government, foundations, corporations, and the public."

Founds Own Consulting Firm

Martinez created her own consulting firm, Woven Future, in 1998. The firm provides strategic directions and facilitates partnerships between corporations, foundations, and government and public institutions. The goal of these partnerships is to focus the future of technology and education in such a way as to best benefit communities, cultural institutions, and libraries.

Earns Numerous Awards and Honors

Martinez's achievements have earned her numerous awards throughout her career. She received the George I. Sanchez Award from the National Association of Spanish Speaking Librarians in 1976, the Edmund D. Edelman Certificate of Commendation from the Los Angeles County Board of Supervisors in 1977, the Hispanic Women's Recognition Award from Orange County's League of United Latin American Citizens in 1982, Orange County's Women of Achievement award in 1988, and Orange County's Women's Alert Award in 1990. The Hispanic Book Distributors named Martinez as Hispanic librarian of the year in 1990, and since 1987, by governor's appointment, she sits on the board of trustees of the California State Summer School for the Arts.

Martinez has written extensively on racism. In a 1988 article published in *Library Journal,* she stressed that "Racism is an epidemic, like AIDS. It . . . permeates every aspect of our society." Mentioning incidents from her personal life—"I didn't look 'American'"—she concluded: "I continue to be an optimist—a cautious, sometimes suspicious, but still vigilant optimist. And my message is this: Now that we know what was, and what is, think about what if? What if we worked together to overcome racial bias?. . . What if we dialogued and learned about each other so as to lessen sensitivity and hostility? What if we gave each other the benefit of the doubt?. . . What if we begin today?"

Sources:

"Why It's So Difficult to be Executive Director of ALA." *American Libraries,* September 1997, pp. 66-67.
Los Angeles Times, (Orange County edition), April 7, 1986, pp. V1, V3.
Orange County Register, March 15, 1989, pp. K1, K4; September 12, 1989, p. B2.
Vachon, Michelle. Interview with Elizabeth Martinez, August 28, 1992.

Elizabeth Sutherland Martinez
(1925–)
Author, journalist, civil rights activist

Selected writings:

Letters from Mississippi. New York: McGraw-Hill, 1965.
The Youngest Revolution: A Personal Report on Cuba. Dial Press, 1969.
Viva La Raza! The Struggle of the Mexican-American People. Co-authored with Enriqueta Longeaux y Vásquez. Doubleday, 1974.
500 Years of Chicano History in Pictures (500 Años del Pueblo Chicano). SouthWest Organizing Project, 1991.
De Colores Means All of Us: Chicana Views for a Multi-Colored Century. South End Press, 1998.

Overview

Elizabeth Martinez still remembers experiencing discrimination as a child, when she had to sit at the back of a Washington, DC, bus. In the 1960s Martinez was one of the first Chicanas to become involved in the African American civil rights movement, spending the summer of 1964 in Mississippi; three civil rights workers were murdered while she was there. By the 1970s, she also had become active in the farmworkers' movement led by César Chávez and the Native American occupation at Wounded Knee, as well as the budding Chicano movement. In later years Martinez began to work on forming alliances among people of color and was exploring the role of women in these movements. Her books and articles often include personal accounts of her own experiences as a Chicana, as well as documenting historical movements.

Becomes Activist in the 1960s

Born Elizabeth Sutherland in 1925 in Washington, DC, Elizabeth "Betita" Martinez soon learned about discrimination. At the time the nation's capitol was segregated, and she remembers how she and her father, along with the black passengers, were told to move to the back of the city bus. Martinez graduated from Swarthmore College and then spent five years at the United Nations, as a researcher on African issues. After working as an editor at the publishing firm Simon and Schuster, Martinez became books and arts editor at *The Nation.*

In 1960 Martinez had become involved with the Student Nonviolent Coordinating Committee (SNCC) and was deeply disturbed when four black children were killed by a bomb in an Alabama church. During the summer of 1964, she decided to spend several weeks in Mississippi, where freedom riders had gathered to support the African American civil rights movement: that summer would change the course of Martinez' life. She spent her time in Mississippi talking to volunteers working all over the state to register voters. Most of the freedom riders were white college students who had travelled to Mississippi. Three of the student volunteers—Andrew Goodman, James Chaney, and Michael Schwerner—were murdered during the summer, and many others were beaten or arrested. Martinez chronicled the experiences of the freedom riders in *Letters from Mississippi,* a collection of letters written by the volunteers, which she edited. She also began to work full-time for SNCC, spending the next three years directing its New York office. At the time she was one of only a few Chicanas involved in the African American civil rights movement.

Joins Other Civil Rights Movements

In the later 1960s, Martinez started to focus on additional civil rights struggles. She was sent to California by SNCC in 1965 to represent the organization at the United Farm Workers of America march led by César and Helen Chávez and Dolores Huerta. This was her first political experience in the midst of people who shared her roots. Martinez also travelled to Cuba and spent a summer interviewing people about their lives under the relatively new Castro government. To get first-hand knowledge, she lived and worked in an agricultural camp for young women on the Isle of Pines. This experience is recounted by Martinez in *The Youngest Revolution: A Personal Report on Cuba.*

By 1968, Martinez had decided to focus her attention on the Chicano movement, and she travelled to Albuquerque, New Mexico, where she became involved with the Alianza Federal Pueblos Libres (National Alliance of Free Pueblos). Although she had intended only to visit for a few weeks, she remained in Albuquerque for the next eight years. While there she helped to found and publish a pioneering newspaper, *El Grito del Norte (The Cry of the North).* Attending both the first Chicano Youth Liberation Conference in Denver, Colorado, in 1969 and the 1972 National Convention of La Raza Unida in El Paso, Texas, helped to solidify Martinez' commitment to the Chicano movement. In 1974 her book *Viva La Raza! The Struggle of the Mexican-American People* was published.

Martinez and other Chicanos went to Wounded Knee, South Dakota, in 1973, to participate in the commemoration of the 1890 siege during which hundreds of Sioux had been killed by U.S. soldiers. The demonstrators took over several buildings on the Pine Ridge reservation and found themselves surrounded by hundreds of federal agents with military equipment. The modern-day siege ended peacefully, but participants were observed and often harassed by federal agents for years afterward.

Focuses on Solidarity Among People of Color

In the 1990s Martinez, now living near San Francisco, continued to write and work on civil rights and human rights issues. Her writings look back at her involvement in both the African American civil rights movement and the Chicano movement and encourage alliance among people of color. In 1993's "Beyond Black/White: The Racisms of Our Time," Martinez urges increased attention to a variety of civil rights and human rights issues, noting that she could find little mention in historical books chronicling the 1960s about African American civil rights movement, but even less about the Chicano, Native American, and Asian American movements of those times. She believes that, in civil rights movements, "liberation has similar meanings . . . : an end to racist oppression, the birth of collective self-respect, and a dream of social justice." In 1995's "Affirming Women's Rights," Martinez emphasized that women of color have a key role in preserving their rights that grew out of the movements of the 1960s, particularly at a time when affirmative action is under attack.

Martinez was featured in an episode of the 1996 PBS series, *Chicano! History of the Mexican American Civil Rights Movement.* During that year she and author Elena Featherston went on a national "Black and Brown Get-Down" tour. Her pictorial history, *500 Years of Chicano History in Pictures (500 Años del Pueblo Chicano),* became the target of censorship in 1997, when teachers in a New Mexico school district were ordered to stop teaching Chicano history. Her most recent book, *De Colores Means All of Us: Chicana Views for a Multi-Colored Century,* looks at solidarity and diversity from a woman's perspective.

Sources:

"Elizabeth Martinez." *Chicano! Biographies.* Available at http://www.pbs.org./chicano/bios/martinez.html.

Gonzales, Patricia, and Roberto Rodriguez. "A Woman Warrior Recalls the Birth of a Movement." Reprinted at *Indigenous Peoples' Literature Home Page.* Available at http://www.indians.org/welker/indios10.htm.

Martinez, Elizabeth Sutherland. "Affirming Women's Rights." *Social Justice,* Fall, 1995, p. 64.

———. "Beyond Black/White: The Racisms of Our Time." *Social Justice,* Spring-Summer 1993, p. 22.

Santisteban, Ray. "Chicano History Censored." *The Progressive*, May 1997, p. 15.

Luz Josefina Martinez-Miranda
(1956–)
Physicist, instrumental musician

Luz Josefina Martinez-Miranda is a leading physicist in the field of materials science, which studies the properties of materials such as crystal. Martinez-Miranda has made significant contributions to her field and garners the respect of her colleagues. Her commitment to research has resulted in her being honored with several distinguished fellowships and awards.

Martinez-Miranda was born September 8, 1956, in Bethesda, MD, the daughter of Puerto Rican American chemists who came to the United States for career purposes. She was raised in the United States until she reached kindergarten, when her family returned to Puerto Rico to live in Toa Baja, a small town 12 miles west of San Juan. In high school, a favorite teacher inspired Martinez-Miranda to choose physics as a career. "I was quite inclined to be a scientist since my parents were chemists," she said during a telephone interview. "Even when I was little, my brother and I would play games in which we would pretend to be working in a chemistry lab." True to her calling, Martinez-Miranda received a B.S. in physics from the University of Puerto Rico in 1977, and an M.S. in physics from the same university two years later.

Arrives in the United States to Study Physics

Because universities in Puerto Rico did not have many resources for the study of experimental physics, Martinez-Miranda studied materials science at the Massachusetts Institute of Technology, receiving a Ph.D. in condensed matter physics in 1985. For the next two years, she performed research as a postdoctoral fellow at the University of California at Berkeley. In 1987, she went to the University of Pennsylvania to serve as an assistant professor in the department of electrical engineering, with a secondary appointment in materials science and engineering. She was recognized by the state of Pennsylvania in 1988 as an Outstanding Young Woman of America for her contributions to scientific research.

It was at the University of Pennsylvania that Martinez-Miranda first received a faculty appointment. She was finally teaching and doing research, as she had always wanted. "I like to make the research we do come alive to the students," she remarked. "I actually use research I've done in the lab to illustrate concepts in their textbooks. It makes science seem a part of the real world." Martinez-Miranda left Pennsylvania in 1994 to become a visiting professor at the Department of Physics and Liquid Crystals Institute at Kent State University. In 1995, she became assistant professor in the materials and nuclear engineering department at the University of Maryland.

Delves into the Properties of Crystals

In her research, Martinez-Miranda studies phase transformation in materials—or the movement of materials from liquid to solid. Some of her latest work involves the way liquid crystal molecules arrange themselves when they come into contact with another surface, a science that makes it possible to have digital displays on electric clocks. According to Martinez-Miranda, the more uniform the crystal is, the easier it is to create a clear display that is easily read by a consumer. This science also has applications to the production of computer and television monitors. Large corporations, such as General Motors and Ford, use knowledge of crystals to create computerized displays on automobile dashboards that help drivers map a route to any destination in a city.

Martinez-Miranda has won a number of awards for her work. In 1979 she garnered a National Science Foundation minority graduate fellowship. In 1985, she received the Massachusetts Institute of Technology Edward L. Horton Fellowship Award. In 1988 she was honored with the Career Advancement Award from the National Science Foundation. Active in her profession, her resume boasts numerous articles featured in scholarly journals, membership in several professional organization and societies, and positions that include serving as a summer faculty fellow at both the Naval Research Laboratory in Washington, DC, and the Sandia National Laboratories in Albuquerque, NM.

Partakes in a Creative Secondary Career

Materials science is not Martinez-Miranda's only passion. At the same time she was studying science, she was also developing her love for music. In 1979, the same year she earned a master's degree in physics, she was awarded a bachelor's degree in music performance from the Conservatory of Music of Puerto Rico. In many ways, Martinez-Miranda views music and physics as quite similar. "Music depends a lot on math, physics, and engineering. For when you play, the quality of the music often changes because of the room design, acoustics, and the transfer of sound. Both music and science are areas of knowledge with a set of rules you have to follow. So in a very real way, they're similar. But at the same time, music feeds my creative side as physics can't." The musically-inclined physicist plays both the piano and the harpsichord and regularly performs in early music or Baroque chamber groups.

Sources:

Boughton, Barbara. Telephone conversation with Luz Josefina Martinez-Miranda, March 23, 1998.

Martinez Tucker, Sara
See **Tucker, Sara Martinez**

Milagros Mateu
(1947–)
Education program manager

In her 1997 bid to enter graduate school at George Washington University, Milagros "Millie" Mateu described

Milagros Mateu

herself as a five-foot tall, 120-pound, 50–year-old dichotomy. She explained in a telephone interview, "I have always maneuvered between two cultures, used two languages, and negotiated the many customs and mores of each." For more than 25 years, Mateu has wielded her bicultural talents in a variety of settings—college campuses, government agencies, and nonprofit organizations—to help students, employees, and immigrants thrive. She currently heads an Hispanic education program at the National Aeronautics and Space Administration (NASA), as part of its ongoing efforts to encourage disadvantaged students to study math and science. In 1996, Mateu created an award-winning mentoring project, funded by NASA, that involves seven community colleges and universities in heavily Hispanic communities across the nation. "I'm very proud to say that I work for NASA," said Mateu. "When I got to see my first shuttle launch, it proved very emotional. It made me proud to be an American. It made me think about how my parents would have felt had they been able to be with me."

Gains Strength from Parents' Examples

Mateu's parents, both born in Puerto Rico, moved to New York City in the 1940s to seek a better life. "They made a lot of sacrifices to come to the mainland," said Mateu. She was born on December 11, 1947, the youngest of five children born to née Constancia DeLeon, a homemaker, and Juan Mateu, an accountant turned Episcopalian priest. The Puerto Rican family experienced the harsh realities of living in a poor neighborhood on the west side of Manhattan in the 1950s. "My parents had some very rough times," recalled Mateu. She explained that heart trouble plagued her father, bouncing him in and out of jobs and hospitals. Yet her father knew others had it much worse. True to his calling, he started a health clinic and later a soup kitchen on the lower east side. His daughter said, "He was very avant-garde in that way. This was in the fifties, when no one was doing that kind of thing." His advanced thinking also extended to family matters. "Even though we were poor," said Mateu, "my parents valued education." She realizes that others in her Puerto Rican community never got that far. "They were just trying to survive." The emphasis her parents continually placed on education was the single biggest influence in her life.

Returns to Puerto Rico

A real turning point came when the whole Mateu family moved back "home" to be near family as her father convalesced. Her Puerto Rican homecoming started with "tons of relatives hugging and kissing at the airport." Mateu immediately recognized the beauty of the culture. "People were very warm and caring. It just opened up a whole new world for me." The 12-year old Mateu went to a private school on a hardship scholarship and soon became fluent in Spanish. Freed from prejudice and overcrowded classrooms, Mateu excelled in school for the first time in her life. In New York, "Teachers never expected very much of me as a student." By contrast, in Puerto Rico, "I was on the honor roll, despite the fact that I worked part-time." Her father lived long enough to see Mateu earn kudos in school and enroll in college, but he died in 1966. Her mother lived until 1993.

Pursues Education

As an undergraduate at the Inter-American University in Puerto Rico, Mateu majored in sociology. She married in her junior year and received a bachelor of arts degree in 1970. That same year she gave birth to her only child, a daughter named Tehani Collazo. Mateu then returned to New York City to continue her studies while working part-time. She earned a master of arts degree from Columbia University in 1972, followed by a master's degree in educational administration from Fordham University in 1977. In her proposal for a doctorate twenty years later, Mateu explained how her academic progression related to her application to an executive leadership program in human resource development: "Sociology gave me an appreciation for systems and dilemmas; art and education cultivated my creative thinking and educational administration allowed me to integrate these two fields to creatively manage systems in the workplace."

Starts Career at Montclair State College

Her early career path gave her great personal satisfaction. At Montclair State College in New Jersey, she ran a bilingual program for three years. "Some of the students worked in factories by day and attended school at night and on weekends," said Mateu. "These people were poor and struggling. I had tremendous admiration for what they were doing to better themselves." Some were professionals, exiled from Cuba, trying to revalidate Cuban credentials through course work while learning English. That experience strengthened Mateu's views on the need for bilingual education in the United States. "Instead of looking at bilingual education as a remedial program, this country should look at it as something that all citizens should have, not just as a transitional program. All Americans should be encouraged to learn a second language." Mateu has always advised youngsters, especially Hispanics, "to gain exposure to as many things as possible." Through the years, she also offered career advice to her daughter: "Do something you truly love doing, something you truly believe in. And be the best you can be at it."

Finds New Challenges with Justice Department

Having recently divorced, Mateu moved with her daughter to Massachusetts for a government post in 1977. "I researched which school system had the best reading and math scores," Mateu said, following her family tradition of prizing education. "We wound up in Brookline, which was basically a Jewish community." Mateu worried unnecessarily about her Puerto Rican child in this unfamiliar territory. "It was fine. She was very well received." By 1992, after Mateu's job with the Federal Aviation Administration (FAA) in Boston ceased to be challenging, she moved to Washington, DC, to advance her career, now that her daughter was grown. For the next two years, Mateu worked for the U.S. Department of Justice as an assistant manager in the international criminal investigative training program. Her job entailed extensive travel throughout Latin America, overseeing programs that taught foreign government officials how to create and enforce democratic laws.

Mateu's growing managerial skills eventually led her to a position at NASA, where she runs the Hispanic education program, as well as teaching and running a curriculum enhancement program. Of the $33 million NASA dedicates for the Hispanic education program, one million dollars a year goes to the Hispanic Association of Colleges and Universities to fund Proyecto Access, which was created by Mateu. The project offers academic enrichment activities and motivational exercises for disadvantaged youths during their summer break. She said, "It has the potential to do a lot of good for the young professionals who run the programs and for the youngsters who become involved." Mateu considers this consortium of government and educational institutions one of her greatest professional achievements.

When asked for the personal philosophy that guides her success, Mateu said, "When opportunities present themselves, I have been willing to meet the challenge." She has always put her faith "in hard work, preparation, and education. And I believe in myself without being too smug." Looking back and taking stock, Mateu said, "The common thread in my career and life is education." She finds great comfort knowing her parents "would have felt good about my work in educational institutions in America, [supporting] all of those things that they held dear."

Current Address: Office of Equal Opportunity Program, Minority Univ. Research and Education Div., National Aeronautics and Space Administration—Code EU, Washington, DC 20546.

Sources:

Mateu, Milagros. "Statement of Purpose For George Washington University Executive Leadership in Human Resource Development." September, 1997.

Worhach, Denise. Telephone interview with Milagros Mateu, April 1, 1998.

Mateu, Millie
See Mateu, Milagros

Mena, Susana Jaime
See **Jaime-Mena, Susana**

Olga A. Mendez

State senator

After winning a special election in 1978 to represent the 28th state senatorial district of New York, Olga A. Mendez became the first Puerto Rican woman elected to a state legislature in the United States. She won with an astounding 89 percent of the vote in a district encompassing an area of New York City that includes sections of the Bronx, East and Central Harlem, Roosevelt Island, and upper Washington Heights. Subsequent victories have been equally impressive with nine consecutive reelections realizing ever-increasing margins. In 1994 she won reelection with 90 percent of the vote, a success that Mendez recognizes as a testament to her goal of taking the interests of every one of her constituents to heart.

Chooses An Unlikely Path

Mendez was born in the city of Mayaguez, Puerto Rico. She received her B.S. from the University of Puerto Rico and, in 1960, was awarded a M.A. in psychology from the Teacher's College at Columbia University. After successfully defending her doctoral dissertation in educational psychology in 1975, Mendez received her Ph.D. from Yeshiva University. Before entering the political arena, Mendez served as a research psychologist at Albert Einstein Medical College, as well as an associate professor at the State University of New York at Stonybrook. Interestingly enough, Mendez had never taken a political science course during her time in college.

Mendez's devotion to people has been the binding thread for all of her activities and causes. Prior to election to public office, Mendez devoted herself to volunteer work with organizations that promoted a government for all the people in every sense of the phrase. The passion of her convictions was displayed in voter registration efforts extending beyond her own district and state and reaching throughout the United States.

Exhibits Dedication to Representative Government

Mendez's dedication and commitment to representative government paved a worthy path for recognition, and many honors and appointments were bestowed upon her. Prior to her 1978 New York state senate election, Senator Mendez was an elected delegate to the 1972 Democratic Convention for Democratic presidential candidate Senator George McGovern, serving as whip to what was then the 19th congressional district. Ensuing presidential election years found Mendez serving as a delegate to the Democratic conventions in 1980, 1984, and 1988, the year she was appointed a delegate for the Reverend Jesse Jackson. At the convention she had the honor of nominating the charismatic Jackson for president of the United States. Moreover, her honors extend well beyond the boundaries of the Democratic Party. Other elections and appointments have included: delegate to the National Conference of Women in Houston; member of the board of Community School District Number 4 in East Harlem; chairperson of the executive committee of Manhattan County; and delegate to the White House Conference on Families.

Becomes Obvious Senatorial Choice

In 1978 a seat in the New York Senate became unexpectedly available when Senator Herman Medio resigned to join Mayor Koch's cabinet in New York City. His resignation was followed by the resignation of Roberto Garcia, who chose to fill a congressional post. The political musical chairs gave Mendez a unique opportunity to emerge as the candidate of choice. She has been overcoming political hurdles ever since her first election to the Senate. In addition to her distinguished status as the first Puerto Rican woman elected to the New York State Senate, Mendez has attained other positions of distinction in government. The newly-formed Senate Democratic Puerto Rican and Hispanic Task Force in 1989 chose her as its first president. She was elected secretary of the Senate Minority Conference in 1984, the first Puerto Rican woman again, to hold that position. In 1993, she was unanimously chosen as chairperson of the Minority Conference, yet another first for a Puerto Rican woman in New York.

Senator Mendez holds several standing committee assignments in the legislature. Also in her official capacity, she serves as a member of the Senate Minority Task Force on Women's Issues, the Women's Legislative Caucus, executive board member for the Center for Women in Government, the Harlem Urban Development Corporation, Task Force for Women in the Courts, the Senate Minority Task Force on Affordable Housing, the Legislative Commission on Science and Technology, and the Child Care 2000 Task Force.

Overcomes Personal Tragedy

When she was diagnosed with breast cancer in 1993, Mendez faced the disease as she has faced so many challenges. Pausing briefly to reflect on what impact this dreaded disease would have on her life, she said in an interview, "The phrase 'I never promised you a rose garden' entered my head. I knew it wasn't going to be easy." Immediately, Mendez thought about what it meant to other women, especially African American and Hispanic American women living in her community. The disease raised her awareness in so many ways. She discovered that the rate of breast cancer among those two populations were higher than for all other groups of women. She was compelled to do something about it, so she created a widespread information literature campaign among members of her district. She also set out to form an organization known as The First Saturday in October, a cooperation of all area clinics and hospitals providing free mammograms to women in need. It is her stated goal that women, for themselves first, and in their role as caretakers for their families, must realize that "a woman is more than the sum of her parts, and must work in loving herself." As of early 1998, following successful surgery and other treatment, Mendez has been declared "cancer-free" for five years.

For Senator Olga Mendez public recognition from her official tasks represents only a fraction of what fills her life. The activities of her official appointment calendar will likely remain full, too numerous to tally the many commitments and causes she battles. Each day, however, Mendez can be found working behind the scenes, quietly influencing change in New York. Indeed, nothing is insignificant to Mendez when it comes to representing her constituents.

Current Address: New York State Capitol, 420 State Capitol Bldg., Albany, NY 12247.

Sources:

East Harlem Page. Available at http:www.east-harlem.com/stsenate.htm.

New York State Senate Democrats Page. Available at http://www.nydems.org/senate/mendez.html.

Spear, Jane. Telephone conversation with Olga Mendez, March 23, 1998.

Who's Who in American Politics, 14th edition, 1993-94. New York: Reed Publishing, 1993.

Conchita Maria Mendoza

Conchita Maria Mendoza
(1948–)
Physician, organization executive

Dr. Conchita Maria Mendoza is a noted geriatrician and chief of the Division of Geriatrics at Long Island College Hospital in Brooklyn, New York. She was active in MADRE, an organization that supports women in Central America and the Caribbean, and has led several medical teams on trips to El Salvador and Nicaragua. Throughout her career, she has demonstrated her commitment to helping those who do not have access to adequate health care.

Born in Havana, Cuba

Mendoza was born June 22, 1948, in Havana, Cuba, the daughter of Miguel Mendoza, an electrical engineer, and Conchita Menocal, who worked as a sales clerk in this country. The family emigrated when Mendoza was 12 years old and settled in Red Bank, New Jersey, a small town on the state's north shore. Mendoza attended Manhattanville College, graduating with a B.A. in 1970. During her college years, she became politically involved in Vietnam War protests and in the Latin American rights movement. "At first I was very involved in the Puerto Rican liberation movement, but then also I started getting more interested in Cuba," she said during a phone interview. "I eventually went to Cuba and saw that the revolution had not been so bad. So I became a supporter of Castro." Mendoza currently supports her fellow Cubans as president of the Cuban-American Health Professionals Association. The association sends medical literature, medicine, and other medical supplies to Cuba.

Mendoza's concern for people without access to adequate health care spurred her decision to become a doctor. She attended Boston University School of Medicine and received her M.D. in 1977. She completed her residency at King's County Hospital and the Health Science Center of the State University of New York in Brooklyn.

After completing her residency in 1980, a friend persuaded Mendoza to work with the U.S. Public Health

Service in Borinken Neighborhood Health Center in East Harlem. "It was a real community clinic," she remarked. "And at that time, the communities in New York were doing health care the right way. The clinic was run by community boards, and they understood the concept of community needs. All the health care was provided in teams—there would be a doctor, a nurse practitioner, a health educator, and a social worker that would see each patient. So the problems in the patient's life that were contributing to his or her illness would be dealt with."

Begins Work in Geriatrics

At the time Mendoza began to specialize in geriatrics, there was no formal specialty in that field. In fact, it was not until years later that the American Board of Internal Medicine declared geriatrics a specialty, started training doctors, and established an exam to certify geriatricians. Because she had been a practicing physician for years in the field of geriatrics, Mendoza was allowed to take the test, which she easily passed.

Between 1982 and 1990, Mendoza was a clinical instructor at New York Medical College and a clinical instructor at the Health Science Center of the State University of New York in Brooklyn from 1988 to 1989. She became a clinical assistant professor in 1989, at the same time working as an attending physician at Kings County Hospital in Brooklyn. Mendoza was medical director of ambulatory care at the Gouverneur Diagnostic and Treatment Center from 1990 to 1991, and attending physician at the Ambulatory Care Network of Bronx-Lebanon Hospital Center from 1991 to 1993. She also taught geriatrics to the residents in internal medicine and was a clinical instructor at the Albert Einstein College of Medicine from 1991 to 1994.

In 1993, Mendoza was selected as an attending physician in the Division of Geriatrics, Department of Medicine of the Bronx-Lebanon Hospital Center, where she stayed until 1994. She was then offered the position of associate chief in the Division of Geriatrics, Department of Medicine at the Long Island College Hospital. Mendoza later became chief of the Division of Geriatrics, a position she currently holds. She also teaches residents about geriatrics at Long Island College Hospital, a task she enjoys.

Heads Medical Teams Traveling to Central America

Mendoza is politically active and worked with MADRE, a support group for women in Central America and the Caribbean. She founded MADRE's Health Professionals Committee and headed several medical delegations to Nicaragua and El Salvador. "We would go into the war zone (in Nicaragua) and offer health care to the women," she stated. "In both Nicaragua and El Salvador, the women had lots of complaints. They were living in such terrible situations that they suffered severe depression and stress-related conditions such as backaches. Some of them didn't feel like living anymore. It was difficult in such a short time

to solve their medical problems. But we paid attention to their troubles and needs, did solidarity work, and tried to make them feel good, even if it was for a brief period of time."

Mendoza has been divorced twice and has one son, Jaime Hickey-Mendoza. Mendoza plans to marry Cesar Perales, a vice-president at Presbyterian Hospital in Manhattan and former deputy mayor for health under New York Mayor David Dinkins. Mendoza loves being a geriatrician and dealing with her patients. "People who live to be 80 or 90 are very special people. They have wonderful life histories. They're the kind of people who are concerned about good health, because in order to reach old age they had to do something right," she said. "I learn more from my patients than they learn from me." Mendoza works from 8 a.m. until 7 p.m. every day. "It's hard to do everything in just 40 hours."

Current Address: Dept. of Internal Medicine, Div. of Geriatrics, The Long Island College Hospital, 339 Hicks St., Brooklyn, NY 11201.

Sources:

Boughton, Barbara. Telephone conversation with Conchita Maria Mendoza, MD, April 2, 1998.

Theresa Annette Mendoza
(1955–)
Emergency manager, civil engineer

Theresa Annette Mendoza is a civil engineer who heads the nationwide U.S. Army Corps of Engineer's Readiness Support Center, which guides the Corps in its response to disasters. Mendoza has helped to direct the Corps efforts in disasters such as the Northridge Earthquake in Los Angeles and Hurricane Andrew in Miami. She oversees a budget of $1.3 million.

Family Emphasizes Mexican Heritage

Mendoza was born in Oakland, California, on November 28, 1955, to a Mexican American family that emphasized their cultural heritage. Her mother Mary, worked as a manager of the bakery in a local Lucky's grocery store while her father, Jose, was a sheet metal worker. She has two younger brothers.

During her youth, Mendoza kept the cultural traditions of her family alive by participating in a Mexican dance troupe and "Banda de Guerra," a drum and bugle corps

Theresa Annette Mendoza

dedicated to the music of Mexico. She was an above-average student in high school. "I was well-rounded—not a bookworm," she said during a 1998 interview in her office in San Francisco.

From an early age, Mendoza was fascinated by structures and her favorite subjects were science and math. One of her hobbies was collecting information about the pyramids. Her cousins in Mexico were electrical engineers, and she resolved that she too would become an engineer.

Develops Interests in Hydrology, Civil Engineering

Mendoza attended San Jose State University where she earned a BS degree in civil engineering in 1979. During her college years, she became more interested in hydrology than electricity and decided to pursue a degree in civil rather than electrical engineering. After graduation, Mendoza worked as an intern engineer for 15 months with the State of California, Department of Transportation (CALTRANS). Her job included preparation of air and noise environmental impact reports and archaeological site evaluations. In 1980, she took on a job with the U.S. Army Corps of Engineers in San Francisco, where she started to specialize in hydrology, and worked on soils testing projects and quantity estimates for needed dredging materials, among other tasks.

From 1982 to 1986, she worked as a hydraulic engineer in the Corps. Serving as project manager for the Novato

flood insurance study, she developed plans flood control projects, performed studies on flood plains and was responsible for the study's budget. In 1986, Mendoza made her first foray into management when she became chief of emergency management. In 1989, she also served concurrently as manager for the Damage Survey Reports Office. In addition to doing flood control work, she took charge of a project that would develop a coordinated and effective earthquake response for the San Francisco Bay area. This effort began after the Loma Prieta earthquake that toppled the San Francisco Bay Bridge in 1989. Mendoza was instrumental in developing a plan for an earthquake center. "One year later the plan I developed in 1990 for earthquakes was adopted for our entire organization and implemented nationwide," she said during the interview. "I was then selected to be the active chief of the Corps emergency response nationwide."

Heads Earthquake Preparedness Center

In 1992 she became the chief of the Earthquake Preparedness Center and worked with officials from the Federal Emergency Management Agency (FEMA) to plan emergency response in 13 cities in the United States considered high risk for earthquakes. As chief, Mendoza developed a plan to use Corps personnel, called advisors, to direct onsite assistance in the event of a disaster. Besides repairing critical structures, they worked to ensure that communities got potable water and that debris would be cleared. "It was a one-of-a-kind program—the first of its kind in the nation," Mendoza said.

In 1997, Mendoza assumed her present job as chief of the Corps' Engineer's Readiness Support Center and developed the curriculum and training methods for the program. She leads the Corps' effort to train specialized teams, including engineers, to provide hands-on assistance with such immediate needs as restoration of power, temporary housing, and water during all natural disasters. Her efforts proved especially effective when the teams she helped devise provided help with rehooking the power supply and bringing in potable water during Hurricane Andrew.

Earns Recognition as Emergency Manager of the Year

In 1988, Mendoza was selected as Emergency Manager of the Year by the Corps. "It was a real surprise," she said. "I was the only female chief of emergency management who had ever got the award. So it was quite an honor." Yet Mendoza prefers not to use her gender or her nationality to obtain recognition, she said. And she has never experienced discrimination as an engineer and a woman. "I've always advanced through merit, not through nationality or gender," she added. "Of course, things are easier for women today. When I was in college there were five women engineering students, and we were expected to do well. But I was lucky, because there had been women before me in engineering who had paved the road," she said. In 1993 Mendoza also received the Hispanic Engineer Award for professional achievement in government. She was selected for Commanders Awards from the U.S. Corps of Engineers for her work in the Loma Prieta Earthquake in 1997, the Northridge Earthquake in 1994, and the California floods in 1997.

Active in Avocational Interests

Aside from her job, Mendoza is active in her Catholic parish in Oakland. She also sponsors three underprivileged children in Bolivia, Columbia, and India through the Christian Children's Fund. As well as engineering, Mendoza has a passion for travel and learning new languages. She has traveled throughout the United States, Mexico, Europe, Asia, and the South Pacific. "I'm also a Walt Disney movie fanatic," she said with a laugh.

Current Address: Readiness Support Center, U.S. Army Corps of Engineers, Dept. of the Army, 333 Market St., Rm. 1026, San Francisco, CA 94105–2195.

Sources:

Boughton, Barbara. Telephone conversation with Theresa Annette Mendoza, April 24, 1998.

Beatriz Michelena
(1890–1942)
Actress, singer

Selected filmography:

Salomy Jane. California Motion Picture Corporation, 1914.
Mrs. Wiggs of the Cabage Patch. California Motion Picture Corporation, 1914.
Mignon. California Motion Picture Corporation, 1915.
The Lily of Poverty Flat. California Motion Picture Corporation, 1915.
Phyllis of the Sierras. California Motion Picture Corporation, 1915.
Salvation Nell. California Motion Picture Corporation, 1915.
The Price Woman Pays. California Motion Picture Corporation, 1919.

Overview

Beatriz Michelena, born in 1890, was one of the earliest stars of the silent screen. The actress was enticed to the screen after World War I hampered her opera career. She was the headliner for the Motion Picture Corporation of America, founded by herself and her husband George

Middleton. Michelena starred in 16 silent films during the period 1914 to 1919.

Grows Up in Talented Family

Beatriz Michelena was part of a talented family. Her father, Fernando Michelena was one of the great operatic tenors of his day. Her sister Vera Michelena was also an actress. The sisters would play near the old Tivoli Opera House in San Francisco where their father would perform.

Michelena's father nurtured her singing skills and hoped she would follow in his footsteps on the operatic stage. She diligently studied the opera throughout her formative years. She appeared in musical productions such as "A Girl From Dixie," "The Tik-Tok Man of Oz," and "The Princess Chic." She also enthralled vaudeville audiences with her singing.

However, when war broke out, Michelena's plans to continue her studies in Europe were thwarted. She lamented her situation to Roberta Courtlandt, saying, "Dad promised to take me to Europe to complete my musical studies, and perhaps make a debut abroad. But just as we were ready to go, the war came—this horrible, horrible war. But we didn't think it would last long, and I still hoped. But now there doesn't seem to be any end to it. But I am still hoping."

Turns to Silent Films

As the war dragged on, Michelena channeled her energies to other pursuits. Ironically, this aspiring opera singer, who valued her voice above all else, turned to the silent world of film. The California Motion Picture Company offered her a place at its head, and Michelena became the company's marquee star. She was reluctant at first, unable to imagine herself acting without an audience. She thought this would be like rehearsal, and, Michelena said, she had always thought herself "a poor rehearser." After consulting with her father, whom she considered a teacher and advisor, and receiving his approval, she decided to accept the position. Her father thought it would be an excellent opportunity for Michelena to prepare for her operatic debut. Seeing herself on film would allow her to evaluate her performances by viewing them on screen and, thus, correct any faults.

Performs Own Film Stuntwork

Michelena also overcame doubts that work in film would be too strenuous. Although most singers of the day went to great lengths to protect their voices, avoiding outdoor activities, Michelena embraced these, believing the exercise improved her health and voice. She swam the Mohave River in *Salomy Jane*, rode on horseback, and "ran around barefooted in *Mignon* in all kinds of weather." She concluded that "being an outdoor girl and living a healthy, normal life as a screen actress improve[d] the voice."

Michelena debuted in the Bret Harte romantic Western *Salomy Jane,* and the dark-eyed beauty was an immediate hit on the screen. Her enthusiastic performance garnered her critical reviews. Even without the use of her voice, she was able to convincingly convey pain and happiness on the silent screen. She made 16 movies in her short career between 1914 and 1919, including *Mignon* and *The Lily of Poverty Flats.*

Michelena was a hit in silent films, and she enjoyed the work. She told Waldemar Young that "I have fallen in love with the work. To me it has all been a wonderful self-revealment." She enjoyed working on locations in California and described the still plentiful trees and wilderness of early twentieth-century California as inspirational, adding, "No one with the smallest spark of acting fire could resist this. Given a picturesque character to portray and an interesting story to develop in this environment, one can not help but make it real and vivid." She enjoyed having her work seen by the broad audience that film allowed. She told Young, "We play to millions of people here, where they play to thousands in the so-called 'regular theater.'"

Michelena continued to long for the opera, telling Courtlandt it was the "highest aim of [her] life." When asked what her greatest ambition was, she responded, "To become a wonderful grand opera singer." She said her movie career was "merely a preparation for what is to come." Michelena continually studied scores of famous operas and traveled to Los Angeles to hear the singers who performed there. She said she "never missed an opportunity to improve her voice."

Enjoys Personal Interests

Michelena lived in a Swiss chalet in the San Rafael Hills, not far from the California Motion Picture Studio where she worked. She spent her leisure time surrounded by the flowers and shrubs that lined her estate. She also kept several pets, including two birds and a prize-winning wolfhound. She was married to producer and director George Middleton, with whom she ran the California Motion Picture Company. When not studying her scripts or preparing costumes for her film productions, Michelena continued to study opera, her first love, whenever time allowed. But her greatest successes came on the screen. She brought a spark to her roles. Although she could never use her voice to thrill the millions of silent filmgoers as she had theater-goers in the past, she used her dark eyes and expressive features to convey emotions from the silent screen. She died in 1942 at the age of 52.

Sources:

City Wide Web. Available at http://www.citywideweb.com/sanrafael/srhistory.html.

Courtlandt, Roberta. "At Home with a Bret Harte Heroine."*Motion Picture Classics,* August 1917, p. 59.

The Internet Movie Database. Available at http://us.imdb.com/Bio?Michelena,+Beatriz.

Michelena, Beatriz. "How I Became a Photo Player." *Motion Picture Classics,* February, 1916, p. 39.

Rodriguez, Clara E., ed. *Latin Looks: Images of Latinas and Latinos in the U.S. Media.* Boulder, Colorado: Westview Press, 1997.

"A Sprite of Romantic Drama: Beatriz Michelena." *Motion Picture Magazine,* July, 1915, p. 88.

Truitt, Evelyn Mack. *Who Was Who On Screen.* New York: R. R. Bowker Co., 1977.

Young, Waldemar. "A Prima Donna Of The Screen: An Interview with Beatriz Michelena, a Picture Recruit from the Operatic Stage." *New York Dramatic Mirror,* July 1, 1914, p. 25.

Natacha Seijas Millán
County government official

Natacha Seijas Millán, commissioner of District 13 in Miami-Dade County, Florida, is both a politician and a social activist. As an advocate, she has set out on a quest to make a difference in the lives of the downtrodden and has

Natacha Seijas Millán

received many accolades in the process. As a politician, she has had to weather controversy, criticism, and power struggles. Through it all, Millán has remained true to her principles and has used her influence to win many victories for minorities in her district.

Millán was first elected in 1993 and re-elected without opposition in 1996. From 1987 until her election in 1993, she served on the Hialeah City Council. She is vice-president of the YMCA and executive director of the Hialeah branch. In 1994 she was convening chair of the Women's Hemispheric Conference. In her present position, much of the city of Hialeah and Miami Lakes are in her jurisdiction. As part of her responsibilities, she serves as chairperson of the aviation planning and operations committee and is a member of committees that affect infrastructure, the environment, the budget, finance, public protection, and health care. She also serves on the governing board of the Hialeah Hospital.

Takes Responsibility for the Lives of Others

Millán was born in Havana, Cuba, and moved to the United States in the late 1950s. During her lengthy career, she has focused on the groups she feels are most neglected: minorities, women, children and the elderly. She authored two programs that were accepted by the county, providing greater opportunity for certified firms owned and operated by women and minorities to participate in county contracts. The programs are entitled "Women Business Enterprise Program" and "Hispanic Business Enterprise Program." Also, in an effort to protect and create a safer environment for those segments of the population that are particularly vulnerable or under-represented, Millán has sponsored, developed, and implemented programs within the county government. She was instrumental in creating designated parking spaces in conveniently located areas of malls and large shopping centers for vehicles carrying small children. In addition, she has developed programs to assist victims of domestic violence, led the effort to implement state-wide reporting of abuse of the elderly and a corresponding system of response to these reports, and has published educational materials in the form of brochures and videos that offer advice on the legal rights of the mentally ill. She also sponsored a measure in which local charities receive the first opportunity to obtain surplus or obsolete county equipment and other property.

Along with her accomplishments on behalf of these specific groups, Millán has achieved much for the population of her county in general. As chairperson of the Construction, Development, and Utilities Committee from 1993 to 1996, she was responsible for major service departments including the Water and Sewer Authority; Planning, Development, and Regulation; Solid Waste; and Building Code Compliance. During her tenure as chair of this committee, the county experienced lower residential garbage collection fees, stabilization of long-term financing of landfills, initiation of the rebuilding of the water and sewer system, and expanded code enforcement in neighborhoods.

Receives Numerous Honors

Millán is a public servant who has received many honors and awards from a diverse range of organizations, including the Clara Barton Founders Award of the North Dade Chapter of the American Red Cross; Woman of Impact Merit Award, 1996 from the Women's History Month Coalition; Woman of the Year Award from the Coalition of Hispanic American Women; Woman of Distinction Award from the Girl Scouts Council of Tropical Florida; Outstanding National Woman of the Year Award from the Latin Business and Professional Women's Club; and Distinguished Service Award from the National Association of Cuban-American Women.

Current Address: Metro-Dade Center, 111 NW 1st St., Miami, FL 33128–1963.

Sources:

Miami-Dade County Home Page. Available at http://www.metro-dade.com.

Miranda, Luz Josefina Martinez
See **Martinez-Miranda, Luz Josefina**

Maria Robledo Montecel
(1953–)
Executive director

Selected writings:

Hispanic Families as Valued Partners: An Educator's Guide. Intercultural Development Research Association, 1993.

Overview

Maria Robledo Montecel has dedicated her life's work to promoting equity and excellence in education for young people in the United States, especially those who are poor

Maria Robledo Montecel

or are minorities. As executive director of the Intercultural Development Research Association (IDRA), she has fought for the rights of minority students and implemented programs to aid the development of bilingual education. Robledo Montecel is concerned with high school dropout rates, especially as they relate to the Hispanic community, and has conducted extensive research into a solution to that problem.

Robledo Montecel was born on January 14, 1953, in Laredo, TX, to Ismael Robledo Martinez and Paula Benavides Lopez. She graduated from Our Lady of the Lake University/ Worden School of Social Services in 1972 magna cum laude. During her undergraduate years, she was inducted into the Alpha Chi Society. After graduation, she attended Antioch College, where she received her M.Ed. with honors in 1975 and was awarded a high achievement commendation. She continued her education at the University of Wisconsin, where she received both a women and minority research fellow from the National Institute of Education and a Title VII doctoral fellow with the university. She earned her Ph.D. in urban education in 1985.

Enters Educational Career

Throughout her years of schooling, Robledo Montecel consistently worked in the field of education, from developing surveys designed to gauge assistance to client school systems to serving as director of the Bilingual Education

Cost Analysis Project for the Intercultural Development Research Association in San Antonio, TX. After completing her Ph.D., she served as the director for the Center for the Prevention and Recovery of Dropouts (1985-1988), where she helped develop a predictive model for identifying dropouts in major urban school systems, in addition to starting several dropout prevention tutoring programs. She was a principal investigator and project director of the Texas School Dropout Survey project, the first statewide study of dropouts in Texas. According to an *Ethnic NewsWatch* article in 1994, this study found that the dropout rate for native-born Hispanics was higher than that of immigrants. Robledo Montecel said that her team "found, in fact, that 85 percent of the Texas Hispanic dropouts ages 16 to 24 were born here. Also contrary to the recent GAO [Government Accounting Organization] report, our study found that recent immigrants were less likely to drop out of school than those born here. One reason is because they did not view themselves in the negative terms that those who were born here did." Since 1989, Robledo Montecel has served as director of the Valued Youth Program, a national research and demonstration project that offers training and technical assistance for teachers to help reduce the dropout rate among young people, and as director of training and technical assistance for the Intercultural Development Research Association (IDRA).

Heads the Intercultural Development Research Association

In 1992, Robledo Montecel took on the position of executive director of IDRA, a non-profit research and public education organization dedicated to creating education that works for all children. IDRA's goal is to create and implement cutting-edge educational policies, including a commitment to gender and minority equity. They have also provided schools with the tools for improving bilingual education and have operated one of only two evaluation assistance centers for limited-English-proficient students in the United States. Other areas of concentration for IDRA include teacher retention, early childhood education, dropout prevention, adult literacy, and immigrant education.

As executive director of IDRA, Robledo Montecel has written extensively about how to improve schools. Her publications have consistently focused on dropout rates of minorities, especially Hispanics, and what government, schools, and parents can do to alleviate the problem. In her testimony to the U.S. House of Representatives Committee on Education and the Workforce, Robledo Montecel told them that as adults, "right now, we are failing our children." She went on to explain that "[i]n this country, more than one in ten Hispanic students drops out of school every year. According to a Census Bureau report released last month, the high school dropout rate among Hispanics rose to 11.6 percent in 1995." This rate was more than twice that for the country as a whole. She then pointed out that "of all students who drop out of school, half are Hispanic."

The response to the problem, said Robledo Montecel, must be a combination of strategies that include the schools, families, and communities as well as the students. In addition, she pointed out that any strategy must include an informed public policy, in terms of costs per student. According to Robledo Montecel, these costs will be more than made up for by the reduction in other services which are often utilized by dropouts. "Benefits include reduced dependence on welfare programs (unemployment insurance) and reduced anti-social behavior such as drug and alcohol abuse, criminal activity and related expenses," she said.

Makes Education a Lifelong Commitment

Robledo Montecel's commitment to education reaches beyond her daily work life. She serves on the boards of the Hispanic Chamber of Commerce, the Mexican-American Solidarity Foundation, and was a founding board member of CIVICUS World Alliance for Citizen Participation. CIVICUS is an international organization dedicated to "civil society, voluntary action, pluralism, philanthropy, and community service." She has also served as a volunteer advocate for the Alamo Area Rape Crisis Center, the chair of the San Antonio 2000 Lifelong Learning Council, and a consultant on the Education of Immigrant Students for the Mellon Foundation. She served on the Race and Ethnic Studies Institute's National Advisory Council at Texas A&M and was co-chair of the 1996 International Youth Service Conference in San Antonio.

In addition to her own publications, Robledo Montecel has served on the editorial boards of *The Journal of At-Risk Issues* and *Texas Researcher*. She has also been invited as an expert to speak on Hispanic educational issues for both the White House Initiative on Educational Excellence for Hispanic Americans (1995) and the House of Representatives Committee on Education and the Workforce (1997). Her dedication to education and Hispanics has not gone unnoticed. In 1997, she was awarded the *La Prensa* Hispanic Heritage Education Award and was named among the "100 Influential Hispanics" by *Hispanic Business*.

Current Address: Intercultural Development Research Assn., 5835 Callaghan Rd., Ste. 350, San Antonio, TX 78228-1190.

Sources:

Carbo, Rosie. "Students: Risk Factors for Dropping Out." *Hispanic Outlook on Higher Education*, November 15, 1994, p. 7.
Hispanic Dropouts: Prevention & Recovery. Available at http: www.handsnet.org/handsnet2/Articles/art.871937914.
Who's Who in America. 49th edition. New York: Marquis Who's Who, 1995, p. 2931.

María Móntez
(1920–1951)
Actress

Selected filmography:

The Invisible Woman. 1940.
Boss of Bullion City. 1941.
That Night in Rio. 1941.
Raiders of the Desert. 1941.
South of Tahiti. Universal Pictures, 1941.
Arabian Nights. Universal Pictures, 1942.
Ali Baba and the Forty Thieves. 1944.
The Exile. 1947.
Siren of Atlantis. United Artists, 1948.
The Wicked City. 1951.
Thief of Venice. 1952.

Overview

María Móntez played the role of the sexy screen siren in such 1940s action adventures as *Arabian Nights, Gypsy Wildcat,* and *Cobra Woman.* Móntez was known for the revealing nature of her costumes as much as for her acting talent. Her alluring publicity photos served as pin-ups in barracks around the world during World War II.

María Móntez

The auburn-haired actress was born María Africa Gracis Vidal de Santos Silas on June 6, 1920, in Ciudad Trujillo, the Dominican Republic, to Teresa Vidal de Santos Silas and Ysidro Gracis. Her father, the Spanish consul to the Dominican Republic, had consular posts in South America, France, and Great Britain. María had five brothers and four sisters and learned to speak and read English and French as well as Spanish.

Changes Life Pattern

Móntez's parents sent her to a convent school, from which she tried to run away. She nevertheless completed her education and moved to Belfast, where she performed small parts in a theatrical group and, at the age of 17, married William G. MacFeeters, an Irish officer in the British army. Before long, María became bored with life in Belfast and traveled to London, Paris, and, finally, New York. MacFeeters cabled her to come home, but Móntez told him she wanted to stay a while longer. Finally, MacFeeters came to New York to retrieve his wife. When she refused to go, saying that she was in love with another man and wanted a career, MacFeeters gallantly wished her well.

With MacFeeters gone, Móntez cavorted with eligible bachelors and found work as a model for top photographers and illustrators. Artist McClelland Barclay chose her as his model of the complete sophisticated woman. Móntez took a screen test after a Hollywood talent scout suggested one. The movie production company RKO liked the results and paid for a three-month course in speech to eliminate her accent. Her agent, meanwhile, shrewdly negotiated a better deal with Universal Pictures. Universal changed her last name to Móntez to evoke memories of the nineteenth-century dancer and femme fatale Lola Móntez, mistress to King Louis I of Bavaria.

Begins Film Career

Móntez began her film career with the grade-Z Western *Boss of Bullion City,* released in 1941. She then landed parts in *The Invisible Woman, That Night in Rio,* and *Raiders of the Desert.* In *South of Tahiti* she appeared in a sarong. "This proved to be of historical importance," wrote Kyle Crichton in 1942 in *Colliers.* "Theater owners broke out in perspiration, there was the happy clank of silver on box-office ledges and writers were set to work changing drawing-room scenarios into jungle stories." In 1942, Móntez appeared as the scantily-clad dancing girl in *Arabian Nights.* She spent six hours a day for three months learning the Oriental-style dance. The role called for her to be imprisoned in a harem guarded by leopards. She managed to escape on horseback with her male co-star. In 1944, she appeared in another Arabian-themed movie, *Ali Baba and the Forty Thieves.* Móntez's admirers credited her with making such lines as "I am here to tempt the hearts of men" seem seductive and believable. Many of her movies contained steamy scenes in bathtubs or swimming pools.

"Out of 15 pictures, in about 13 either I have been in a bath or a [swim]," she told *The Saturday Evening Post.* "My studio gives the public their money's worth." In well-dressed Hollywood circles, Móntez was famous for wearing low-cut gowns. She shunned alcohol, however, because she believed that women who depended on their health and beauty should not drink.

Reaches Stardom

Within two years, Móntez had become a top star. In 1943, she received the Order of Juan Pablo Duart and the Order of Trujillo award for promoting friendly relations between the United States and the Dominican Republic and outstanding female achievement. On July 13, 1943, she married the French actor Jean-Pierre Aumont. The event was well publicized, as was the birth of their daughter, María Christina, on February 14, 1946.

Móntez's fiery temper became the talk of Hollywood. "For, though María is a ball of fire in the studio, in her own drawing room she is Halley's comet colliding with a super nova," observed the *Saturday Evening Post.* "It has been said that. . . 'You either like Móntez with a deep, whole-souled liking or you can't take her, with or without a chaser. Hers is a personality that defies indecision.'"

Career Declines

Móntez predicted that within five years she would win an Academy Award. But the prediction never came true, nor did her attempts to win more challenging dramatic roles. "Every time I begin to emote, I look up and there is a horse-stealing my scene," she complained in the *Saturday Evening Post.* As World War II drew to a close in 1945, so, too, did Móntez's career. Escapism gave way to realism, and the exotically-costumed Móntez suddenly seemed out of place. Her part as mistress to Charles II in *The Exile,* starring Douglas Fairbanks, Jr., was so insignificant that it was usually cut when shown on television.

Together with Aumont, she financed and acted in *Siren of Atlantis,* her last Hollywood-made picture. She played the part of Antinea, the most beautiful and seductive woman in the history of the world. Antinea's first 53 boyfriends had died of love. The movie concerned her 54th and 55th boyfriends. The boyfriend played by Aumont defeated his rival to emerge as the love of Antinea's life. *Siren of Atlantis,* released in 1948, did less than expected at the box office. Móntez and Aumont left Hollywood and settled in France. Móntez acted in the French film *The Wicked City* and the Italian film *The Thief of Venice.*

In January of 1951, Móntez briefly visited Hollywood in connection with her suit for $38,000 of back salary for *Siren of Atlantis.* She then returned to Paris to appear in a play written by her husband. Increasingly, Móntez worried about her weight. She told her friends that she exercised, did yoga, and took extremely hot baths with reducing salts to keep her weight to 125 pounds.

On September 7, 1951, Móntez was planning to have lunch with her two sisters, Anita and Teresita, but wanted to take her hot bath first. The two sisters waited downstairs in Móntez's home in Suresnes, a suburb of Paris. Finally, becoming worried, Anita knocked on the bathroom door and called to her sister, but there was no answer. Móntez had suffered a heart attack and was unconscious. Attempts to revive her failed. Aumont, who was at work on location, returned home, where he collapsed in grief. María Móntez was dead at the age of 31.

Sources:

Crichton, Kyle. "Born to Act." *Colliers*, April 4, 1942, p. 7.

Dickens, Homer. "María Móntez." *Films in Review,* January 1963, pp. 59-60.

Halliwell, Leslie. *The Filmgoer's Companion.* New York: Hill & Wang, 1974.

"María Móntez, 31, Dies Suddenly." *New York Times,* September 8, 1951, p. 8.

Martin, Pete. "Dominican Dynamite." *Saturday Evening Post,* June 28, 1945, p. 29.

"Móntez: In *Arabian Nights* She Does the Single Veil." *Life,* September 28, 1942, p. 69.

Schuster, Mel, ed. *Motion Picture Performers.* Metuchen, NJ: Scarecrow Press, 1971.

Smith, John M. and Tim Cawkwell, eds. *The World Encyclopedia of the Film.* A. & W. Visual Library, 1972.

Truitt, Evelyn Mack. *Who Was Who On Screen.* New Providence, NJ: R.R. Bowker Co., 1983.

"Transition." *Newsweek,* September 17, 1951, p. 63.

Weaver, John T., ed. *Forty Years of Screen Credits 1929-1969.* Metuchen, NJ: Scarecrow Press, 1970.

Linda L. Montoya

Linda L. Montoya
(1947–)
Photographer, entrepreneur

For Linda Montoya, photographing people is an intimate form of communication. "People let down all the walls around them and let me inside," Montoya said in a telephone interview. Her photographs of people and places have appeared in magazines, books, galleries, and museums since 1981, and one, "Chapel in Chimayo," hangs on permanent exhibition in the capitol building in Santa Fe, NM. In an article on cross-culturalism for *THE magazine,*

Christine Hemp commented that Montoya's photos, ". . . lead us into a new way of seeing."

Lives in Two Cultures

The daughter of Nora and Ruben Montoya, Linda Montoya was born in Santa Fe on September 6, 1947, with a rich Spanish heritage. Her father, a metallurgist, is also a *santero,* or a carver of saints, as well as a descendant of an early colonial governor. One of her mother's ancestors, Manuel Abeyta, built El Santuario de Chimayo, her hometown in northern New Mexico. Montoya grew up in a family caught between two cultures, as they attempted to retain their Hispanic heritage while living in the predominantly Anglo culture of the United States. Montoya grew up understanding Spanish, but spoke only English. Her cousins translated when she spent summers with her Spanish-speaking grandparents in Chimayo.

After graduating from high school, Montoya spent a year at New Mexico State University. Then, as a young bride in 1967, she followed her husband to Massachusetts, and worked as a secretary while he studied at Amherst College and attended graduate school at Northeastern University. "In Boston, I was feeling out of kilter with my identity," she said. "I talked like the people there, but I felt differently." She became increasingly interested in the arts and began taking courses—first, a photography class at the Art Institute of Boston, and then art history and sculpture through Harvard University's extension program.

Begins Career in Photography

With the break-up of her marriage, Montoya returned to New Mexico in September of 1973. A wealthy friend who was supportive of her artistic endeavors gave her a photographic enlarger and money for classes. Montoya's family also rallied to her side, helping her build a darkroom at her grandmother's house in Santa Fe. Meanwhile, she took photography classes at the College of Santa Fe and worked as the manager and printer of a photo lab. By 1981, Montoya was able to work full-time as a professional photographer.

Explores Her Cultural Identity

Frustrated by her attempts to learn Spanish as an adult, Montoya listened to the advice of a friend and took an extended trip to Mexico in January of 1984. The trip taught her about herself as a person in addition to helping her overcome the language barrier. She later told a reporter for the *Albuquerque Journal* that "For me, going to Mexico was like finding my roots. Though I'm not Mexican, I'm from that background." She and a friend traveled to remote parts of Mexico where some people had never seen a camera and hid their faces when Montoya tried to take their picture. One day she wanted to photograph a group of Indian women selling handmade clothes outside a church in San Cristobal de las Casas. She found, however, that one girl, Rosa, did not want to have her picture taken. Montoya assured her that she would never take a picture without her permission and let Rosa look through the camera. Gradually, Rosa began to trust her and, ultimately, brought other women for Montoya to photograph, as well. Montoya told the *Albuquerque Journal,* "I let them touch my camera, let them play with it. . . .The only way I can do my portraits is to know my subjects. Anytime I've done it without knowing them, I've felt that I was intruding on their souls. That's why I feel good about these photos. I know these people."

Publishes Prominent Work

Throughout the 1980s, Montoya published and exhibited her work. In 1985, she did black and white developing and printing for Robert Altman's film, *Fool for Love,* and, in 1987, a collection of Mexican Indian portraits became part of the permanent exhibit of the First National Bank of Albuquerque.

Captures Beauty in All People

Like her mother, Montoya looks for the bright side of people. "There's too much darkness," she said in a telephone interview. She tells people not to worry about their wrinkles. Unlike a glamour photographer, she photographs people the way they are rather than the way they might prefer to be. "Some people come in, and they've been told they have to be beautiful or handsome, that they can't be too fat or too skinny" she said. "I try to make them feel that we all have beauty inside of ourselves."

In the spring of 1998, a gallery in Frankfurt, Germany, exhibited a collection of Montoya's photographs. That summer, she moved from Santa Fe to Las Cruces, NM, to develop a connection with New Mexico State University and find new sources of stimulation. "I'm basically documenting my life," she said. "I don't know how many people get to do that."

Current Address: L.M. Images, 1210 Lujan St., Santa Fe, NM 87505.

Sources:

Axelrod-Contrada, Joan. Telephone conversation with Linda Montoya, April, 1998.
Drabanski, Emily. "Montoya's Photographs Touch People's Lives." *New Mexico Magazine,* July, 1988, pp. 31-35.
Evans, Karen. "A Journey of the Heart." *Impact: Albuquerque Journal Magazine,* November 20, 1984, pp. 4-9.
Hemp, Christine. "Critical Reflections: Vision of Life, Land, and Water: The 1996 Hispanic Biennial of Contemporary Art." *THE Magazine,* March, 1996, p. 37.

Velma Montoya

Organization executive, state government official

When she was appointed to a twelve-year term as a regent of the University of California, Velma Montoya began the latest stage of a life devoted to community service. As a member of the governing board of one of the largest universities in the country, with nine campuses throughout the state and more than an $11 billion budget, Montoya can call on a wealth of experience teaching on the university level and working in many areas of public policy. Throughout her career she has devoted herself to the welfare of the Hispanic community and has been recognized many times for her contributions.

Born in East Los Angeles, Montoya is the daughter of Mexican immigrants, Consuelo and Jose Montoya. She grew up there with her brother, Joe, and was the first member of her extended family to graduate from high

Velma Montoya

school. She went to Occidental College in Los Angeles on scholarships and graduated in 1959. An excellent student, she was inducted into Phi Beta Kappa in her junior year, as well as two other honorary societies. She declined a Fulbright scholarship, but did study at St. Hugh's College, Oxford as one of the first group of Marshall scholars, after earning an M.A. in international relations from the Fletcher School of Law and Diplomacy in 1960. She married Earl A. Thompson in 1961, and they have one child, Bret. She turned to the study of economics and got a second MA from Stanford University in 1965 and taught economics at the California State University at Los Angeles. In 1973 she began working as a staff economist for the nonprofit Rand Corporation think tank, where she continued until 1982. During this period she finished her Ph.D. in economics at the University of California at Los Angeles, getting her degree in 1977. During this time she also helped found the Republican National Hispanic Assembly of California.

In 1982 she went to Washington, DC, to work as assistant director for strategy at the White House Office of Policy Development, the first Hispanic American to serve in that office. Later she served as an expert economist in the Office of Regulatory Analysis of the Occupational Safety and Health Administration (OSHA). She returned to the Los Angeles area and began teaching in 1985. She was director of studies in public policy at Chapman University School of Business in Orange, and she then taught at Pepperdine University and California State Polytechnic University. In 1990 she was appointed by President George

Bush to the Occupational Safety and Health Review Commission, an independent agency created by Congress to decide workplace safety and health disputes between employers and OSHA. As commissioner she helped make it easier for employers without attorneys to appear before the Commission, and she requested that employees be provided meaningful opportunities to participate in protecting their workplace safety and health. Her term expired in 1997. Governor Pete Wilson of California appointed her to the University of California Board of Regents in 1994.

Montoya has been active in the affairs of the Hispanic community all of her life. As mentioned, she was a founding member of the Republican National Hispanic Assembly of California, as well as a member of the Hispanic advisory panel of the National Commission for Employment Policy from 1981 to 1982. She was president of the Hispanic American Public Policy Institute from 1984 to 1990. She served on the Census Advisory Committee on Hispanic Population for the U.S. Census of 1990 and serves on the Advisory Committee of the U. S. Senate Republican Conference Task Force on Hispanic Affairs. She was also a member of the Hispanic National Policy Forum and of the National Executive Advisory Board for the *Harvard Journal of Hispanic Policy*. In 1997 she was elected president of the National Council of Hispanic Women. It is little wonder that *Hispanic Business* magazine named her among the "100 Most Influential Hispanics" in 1982, 1990, and 1997.

Her service has not been confined to the Hispanic community, however. Among many other activities, she became a member of the board of trustees of the Salesian Boys and Girls Club of East Los Angeles in 1989 and the advisory board of the National Rehabilitation Hospital of Los Angeles in 1991. She has served on various boards and committees of the California State Bar Court, the Industrial Research Institute for Pacific Nations, Veterans in Community Service, and numerous other organizations. Besides the recognition by *Hispanic Business* magazine, she was named Woman of the Year by both the East Los Angeles Community Union in 1979 and the Mexican American Opportunities Foundation in 1983. She has been listed in *Outstanding Young Women of America, Who's Who of Emerging Leaders in America*, *Who's Who of American Women*, *Who's Who among Hispanic Americans*, *Who's Who in the West*, and *Who's Who in America*.

Although she describes herself as a conservative in fiscal matters and a moderate on social issues, she has proven to be an independent-minded regent. She voted against the controversial proposal to end affirmative action in hiring and contracts, although she favors maintaining affirmative action in student admissions at the University. Despite her opposition, however, the proposal passed. In 1997 she abstained on a vote to extend health benefits for partners of gay employees of the University, and her abstention allowed the measure to pass, to the chagrin of Governor

Pete Wilson. She is well-regarded by the other regents, who elected her vice-chairman of the Board in 1997.

During her career Montoya has also published regularly in journals on economics and public policy as well expressing her opinions in editorials in such publications as the *Los Angeles Times* and *The Washington Times*. She was also a contributor to *The Mexican American People*, by Leo Grebler, et al, published by the Free Press.

Current Address: The Regents of the University of California, 7095 Hollywood Blvd., #520, Hollywood, CA 90028.

Sources:

"100 Most Influential Hispanics," *Hispanic Business*, October, 1997.

Weiss, Kenneth R. "Regent Explains Abstention on Benefits Vote," *Los Angeles Times*, November 23, 1997.

Who's Who in American Politics, 15th edition, 1995-1996. New Providence, NJ, Marquis Who's Who, 1995.

Who's Who of American Women, 20th edition, 1997-1998. New Providence, NJ, Marquis Who's Who, 1996.

Cherríe Moraga
(1952–)
Author, editor, women's rights activist

Selected writings:

This Bridge Called My Back: Writings by Radical Women of Color. Edited with Gloria Anzaldúa. Persephone Press, 1981. Also published under the title *Esta puente, mi espalda: Voces de mujeres tercermundistas en los Estados Unidos.* Spanish translation by Ana Castillo and Norma Alarcón. ISM Press, 1988.

Cuentos: Stories by Latinas. Edited with with Alma Gómez and Mariana Romo-Carmona. the Kitchen Table/Women of Color Press, 1983.

Loving in the War Years/Lo que nunca paso por los labios. South End Press, 1983.

Giving Up the Ghost: Teatro in Two Acts. West End Press, 1986.

The Last Generation. South End Press, 1993.

The Sexuality of Latinas. Edited with Norma Alarcón and Ana Castillo. Third Woman Press, 1993.

Waiting In the Wings: Portrait of a Queer Motherhood. Firebrand Books, 1997.

Overview

Frank and undaunted, Cherríe Moraga has managed to express feelings that many Hispanic women share. Although she is lighter-skinned and did not experience the pain of prejudice that some Hispanics face, Moraga had to cope with another type of discrimination: homophobia. As a lesbian, Moraga began to understand what her darker-skinned mother had always felt, and this realization, coupled with her passion for writing, incited Moraga to textually communicate the feelings that generations of minorities, regardless of specific race, gender, or sexual orientation, have experienced. The results of Moraga's hard work, a book of poems, collections of writings by other minorities and feminists, and several plays, have startled readers and made U.S. literary history; in addition to encouraging women and minorities, especially Hispanics and Chicanas, to seriously consider their cultural and sexual situations, she has assisted other culturally cognizant writers to revise the norm in contemporary literature. Moraga was as a central figure in feminist, lesbian, Chicana, and U.S. literature during the decade of the 1980s.

Grows up with Bicultural Influences

Moraga was born on September 25, 1952, in Whittier, California. As the offspring of a biracial marriage, she was influenced by two cultures. Her father's family was from Missouri and Canada, and her mother's family was from California, Arizona, and Sonora, Mexico. Moraga's family moved to live near her mother's relatives in San Gabriel, California, when she was nine years old. Like Moraga, Southern California is the product of Mexican and Anglo influence. Moraga was surrounded by the Spanish language, and a mixture of Spanish and English, as well as English; she experienced Mexican customs at home, and American traditions in school.

Moraga was a good student; she intended to become a teacher. In college, however, when Moraga began to study writing, her aspirations began to change. The people who wrote fascinated her as much as writing itself; she began to develop a love for art and artists. Despite this new interest in art and writing, Moraga was determined to finish school and become a teacher. When she earned her bachelor of arts from a small private college in Hollywood in 1974, she became one of the few people in her family to hold a degree.

Reveals Sexual Preference

Following graduation, Moraga began to teach. Her first job was as an instructor of English at a private, Los Angeles high school. Moraga might have kept teaching if she had not enrolled in a writing class through the Los Angeles Women's Building. This class stimulated her artistic instincts, and she became more and more enthusiastic about her writing. At the same time she began to blossom as a writer, Moraga "came out" as a lesbian. As she no longer had anything to hide from herself or others, Moraga was finally able to express herself freely; some of her first works were lesbian love poems.

Although Moraga was happy with her personal revelation and progress as a writer, she soon found that not everyone would be willing to accept her textual expression of her sexuality. Some of the first challenges she received as an open lesbian were from members of her inspirational writing group. These members argued that, in her writing, Moraga should not refer to her lover as "she." A reading audience, they said, expected loving, sexual relationships to be heterosexual—homosexual intimations would be unsettling. Instead of persuading Moraga to write a lie, however, the reading group incited Moraga to write specifically as a lesbian and about homosexual issues. Moraga decided to commit herself to writing what she wanted to write—her readers would just have to change their expectations.

Moves to San Francisco

Moraga's commitment to at least try to become a serious writer conflicted with her job as a teacher. She had taught for two years when she left the profession and Southern California for San Francisco in 1977. In San Francisco, she could avoid the influence of her family and immerse herself in a community that is known for its liberal attitude as well as its artistic atmosphere. Moraga promised herself that, if she did not excel as a writer after a year of total devotion to the art, she would return to teaching.

The year in San Francisco proved to be rewarding. As Moraga supported herself with odd jobs and unemployment, she read and wrote. Finally, she had the time to explore the world of lesbian literature. Books such as Radclyffe Hall's 1928 *The Well of Loneliness* and the works of Djuna Barnes inspired and enlightened Moraga. She also found time to talk with other aspiring artists, lesbians, and feminists in cafés. This diverse community of women supported Moraga's endeavor to write. Her poetry began to mature.

Begins Writing Career

By the time Moraga's year was up, she had written enough outstanding poems to read in front of an audience. With the Los Angeles poet Eloise Klein Healy, she read to a packed coffeehouse. Moraga realized that she was more than a writer—she was a good writer; she had something valid to say, and she knew how to say it. She also found that, as she had hoped, audiences would appreciate the contents of her poems as much as her poetic voice. Moraga's success after this first year assured her that she should continue to write.

At this point in her career, Moraga began to think and write more about being, specifically, a lesbian of color. She was not just a lesbian, she was a Chicana lesbian. Instead of just being discriminated against for being a woman, or of Mexican American descent, she could experience prejudice for her sexual orientation as well. This sort of bias could come from anyone, even other women, feminists, and lesbians. One poet, Judy Grahn, wrote of being a

lesbian of color. Her poems spoke to Moraga; they expressed something that she had been trying to pinpoint herself, and they did so simply and elegantly. Determined to meet this inspirational poet, Moraga arranged a meeting. At this meeting, Grahn gave Moraga a piece of advice that she still follows. Yvonne Yarbro-Bejarano, writing in the *Dictionary of Literary Biography*, quoted Grahn as saying, "do what nobody else can do, which is to write exactly from your own voice, the voices you heard growing up." Grahn's advice, as well as her political orientation, gave Moraga a new direction.

By the time Moraga was ready to begin her thesis for her master's degree in feminist writing at San Francisco State University, she was also ready to tackle the issue of being a feminist and/or lesbian of color. She did so by agreeing to work with Gloria Anzaldúa as she collected writings of women of color for a book. The women included essays, poems, letters, and conversations that discussed feminism and lesbianism from the perspectives of women of color in the book; they even added a foreword by the well-known writer, Toni Cade Bambara. The result of this collaboration not only fulfilled Moraga's thesis requirement, but also made her a recognizable figure in the feminist world and stimulated the minds of women of color.

Receives Recognition and Honors

Moraga received her master's degree in 1980, and *This Bridge Called My Back: Writings by Radical Women of Color* was published the next year. This "groundbreaking collection of Third World feminist theory," as Barbara Smith called it in the *New England Review*, was "solidly based in personal recollection and self-revelation." A critic for *Ms.* magazine commented, "The Bridge marks a commitment of women of color to their own feminism—a movement based not on separatism but on coalition. . . " *This Bridge Called My Back* was republished in 1983, and it won the 1986 Before Columbus Foundation American Book Award. A revised, bilingual edition of the book was published as *Esta puente, mi espalda: Voces de mujeres tercermundistas en los Estados Unidos* in 1988.

Moraga included a preface, two poems and one essay in the book she edited. The essay, entitled, "La Güera," deals with the writer's anxiety over being a lesbian as well as a minority, her guilt for not understanding the prejudice her mother faced, and, most importantly, her anger that such bias would occur at all in the free society the United States claims to be. "It wasn't until I acknowledged and confronted my own lesbianism in the flesh, that my heartfelt identification with and empathy for my mother's oppression—due to being poor, uneducated, and Chicana—was realized," writes Moraga in "La Güera." "My lesbianism is the avenue through which I have learned the most about silence and oppression, and it continues to be the most tactile reminder to me that we are not free human beings." "In this country," she continued," lesbianism is a poverty—

as is being brown, as is being a woman, as is being just plain poor."

The anger, frustration, and the knowledge that change must be instigated by the oppressed themselves that are found in Moraga's essay also appear in her poems in *This Bridge*. In "For the Color of My Mother," which Moraga had written during her first year in San Francisco, the poet speaks of the anguish that her mother had never expressed, and by doing so gave her mother a voice. She wrote: "I am a white girl gone brown to the blood color/of my mother/speaking for her. . . ." In "The Welder," Moraga expresses her belief in solidarity and empowerment. "I am a welder./Not an alchemist./I am interested in the blend of common elements to make/ a common thing. . . . I am the welder./ I understand the capacity of heat' to change the shape of things. . . . I am the welder./I am taking the power into my own hands." Moraga not only advocates action in her poems, she is politically active herself.

Travels to the East Coast

In 1981, while attempting to find a publisher for her thesis, Moraga went to Boston and then to New York. The feminist scene in these cities was exciting at the time, and Moraga found many feminists and Hispanics (especially Puerto Ricans) who shared her ideas. It was not long before she became politically involved in her new communities. She spent time with local activists, joined an organization which sought to end sexual violence, and co-founded the Kitchen Table/Women of Color Press, which would allow still more feminists and women of color to express themselves textually.

When Moraga edited one of the group's first published books, *Cuentos: Stories by Latinas,* with Alma Gómez and Mariana Romo-Carmona, she once again broke ground for Hispanic feminists and lesbians. Like *This Bridge, Cuentos* was a revolutionary anthology: it was the first collection of writings by feminist Latinas. Also, once again, Moraga included some of her own work in an anthology. The two stories in *Cuentos*, "Sin luz," and "Pesadilla" deal with sexuality, racism, homophobia, and the attempts of women to cope with all three.

In "Sin luz," which means "without light," a young girl married to an old man has trouble feeling anything, physically or emotionally. Although she never feels fulfilled with her marriage, the girl becomes pregnant. The loss of her baby at seven months thus has various symbolic implications: Can a child be created without love, or light? Is a homosexual union, which cannot produce a child, different from a union which is neither loving nor fruitful? Moraga's other story, "Pesadilla," or nightmare, describes a fictional lesbian relationship. In it, Cecilia, a Chicana, and Deborah, a black woman, attempt to love each other and live together despite the interruptions of the pervasive outside world. The symbolic violation which occurs when a man breaks into their apartment and paints homophobic slurs on the walls penetrates the souls of the women and almost spoils the love between them.

Moraga's next project was to collect some of the work that she had produced herself since just before she left Southern California. The result of this effort was *Loving in the War Years: (Lo que nunca pasó por sus labios)*. As Raymund Paredes in the *Rocky Mountain Review* wrote, the pieces in this collection are "notable for their passion and intelligence." Included in *Loving* is the poem, "For the Color of My Mother," and the essay, "A Long Line of Vendidas." This latter piece, written while Moraga was in New York, discusses Chicana sexuality in light of the Chicana's cultural heritage. According to Moraga, Chicanas were always taught to think of the needs of their men before their own; Chicana's must understand their particular situation, and free themselves from this sexual and cultural oppression. Once again, Moraga had given American literature another first. As Yarbro-Bejarano noted, *Loving in the War Years* was the first published book of writing by an avowed Chicana lesbian.

Expresses Lesbian Themes in Plays

Moraga's desire to express her feelings and ideas about being a minority as well as a lesbian intensified. She began to work on a play. *Giving Up the Ghost; Teatro in Two Acts* was read in mid-1984 at a feminist theater in Minneapolis, and later that year Moraga took her play to INTAR, the Hispanic-American Arts Center in New York City. At INTAR, the playwright-residency program directed by the renowned Off-Broadway playwright María Irene Fornes, Moraga began to develop the specific skill needed to produce a good play and started working on other plays and musicals.

Moraga's experience at INTAR contributed to her success as a playwright. *Giving Up the Ghost: Teatro in Two Acts* was published by West End Press in 1986, and has been produced twice, in 1987 in San Francisco and in Seattle. Moraga has written two other plays that have not been published, *La extranjera*, which she wrote in 1985, and *Shadow of a Man*, which she wrote in 1988. Another of Moraga's plays, *Heroes and Saints*, was produced in Los Angeles in 1989.

Giving Up the Ghost is Moraga's most celebrated play. In this work, Amalia and Marisa share a homosexual relationship after Marisa is raped and Amalia's male lover dies. The play is set in an East Los Angeles barrio, and has an English script peppered with Spanish; it seems to accurately reflect the Chicana culture the audience expects. The homosexual relationship, however, as well as Moraga's symbolic treatment of it, makes the play remarkable. Raymund A. Paredes, in the *Rocky Mountain Review,* succinctly describes this underlying symbolism. He writes, "*Giving Up the Ghost* represents the most radical element of contemporary Chicana writing. Moraga portrays heterosexual love as inherently abusive, an act of violent penetration which in the context of the excessively masculine culture of Mexican Americans becomes more brutal still." Despite the negative aspects of the culture, explains Paredes, Moraga "clings to her ethnic identity fiercely, demanding in her work that the culture transform itself in behalf of women's rights of self-determination."

Returns to Teaching Career

In 1986, Moraga returned to teaching. This time, however, she instructed students in the art of writing instead of in English. At the Chicano Studies Department at the University of California at Berkeley, Moraga could finally combine her initial desire to teach, her passion for writing, and her study of Chicana culture. She could also live in the intellectually stimulating San Francisco Bay area. Although she is teaching, Moraga continued to write: in 1989, she worked on a collection of poems entitled, *Dreaming of Other Planets*. In 1993 she released *The Last Generation*, a work published by South End Press, and collaborated with Norma Alarcón and Ana Castillo on *The Sexuality of Latinas*, published by Third Woman Press. Moraga is also working to develop her knowledge of theater, and to stage some of the plays she has written.

In 1996, Moraga participated in a panel discussion entitled "Across the Great Divide: Immigration, the Arts and American Culture." This panel was convened to discuss the anti-immigration policies prevalent in America during the 1990s, such as California Proposition 187, which would deny schooling to unregistered immigrant children. In 1997, Moraga published her most recent book entitled *Waiting in the Wings: Portrait of a Queer Motherhood*. Moraga maintains her determination to speak out against various kinds of oppression while upholding the Chicano culture she has both chided and cherished.

Sources:

Dictionary of Literary Biography, Vol. 82, Gale, 1989.
Essence, January 1982, p. 17.
Lomelí, Francisco A. and Carl R. Shirley, eds.
Moraga, Cherríe, and Gloria Anzaldúa, editors,*This Bridge Called My Back: Writings by Radical Women of Color*, Persephone Press, 1981, revised bilingual edition (edited with Ana Castillo) published as *Esta puente, mi espalda: Voces de mujeres tercermundistas en los Estados Unidos*, Spanish translation by Castillo and Norma Alarcón. ISM Press, 1988.
Mother Jones, January-February, 1991, p. 15.
Ms., March, 1992, p. 39.
New England Review, summer, 1983, pp. 586-87.
Rocky Mountain Review of Language and Literature, Volume 41, number 1-2, 1987, pp. 125-28.

Aurora Levins Morales
(1954–)
Author, professor, lecturer, activist

Selected writings:

La Poblacion, 1979.
Canto Libre, 1980.
Step by Step, 1981.
Getting Home Alive. Firebrand, 1986.
Medicine Stories: History, Culture, and the Politics of Integrity. South End Press, 1998.
Remedios. Beacon Press, 1998.

Overview

Writer, lecturer, historian, and activist Aurora Levins Morales was born on February 24, 1954, in Castañer, Puerto Rico. Levins Morales, whose surname reflects her Jewish-Puerto Rican heritage, expresses her own cultural experience and the experiences of others through short historical fiction vignettes. In addition to her fiction, Levins works part-time as a professor at the University of Minnesota, writing and speaking on the subjects of history, culture, and politics. Levins Morales holds an M.A. and Ph.D. from The Union Institute in Cincinnati, OH. Her speaking engagements at universities, colleges, and for organizations cover a wide spectrum of topics, including feminism, history, cultural politics, activism, and creative writing. Since 1981, she has been an independent consultant on training and educational resource development in community building.

Early Life and Career

At age five, Aurora's mother taught her how to read, and at seven she began writing poetry. When Aurora was 13-years old, her family moved from Indiera, Puerto Rico, to Chicago, where she remained until she began to pursue an education at Franconia College in New Hampshire in 1972. She then moved to Oakland, CA, to complete her undergraduate studies in creative writing and ethnic studies and began giving readings and publishing her writing. In her early career, dating back to 1974, Levins Morales worked as a research assistant for a marine biology and island ecology project for the Department of Natural Resources of Puerto Rico. In other work-related experiences, Levins Morales worked as a news reporter and documentary producer for the Pacifica Radio Station, KPFA, in Berkeley, CA. (KPFA had a Third World news bureau in East Oakland, CA.) She also researched local and international news on Latin American and U.S. Latino topics, such as the domestic social movements.

While pursuing her educational goals, Levins Morales received numerous literary and academic honors including the President's Circle of Scholars Award in 1997 from the Union Institute. In 1993, she received an honorable mention from the Ford Foundation pre-doctoral fellowships for minorities. She also received the Ardella Mills Prize for journalistic prose and honorable mention for fiction from Mills College in 1989, among others, during her academic years.

Influences on Writing and Activism

For Aurora Levins Morales, the telling of stories, as they relate to personal experience and political heritage, is the best way to understand how past events influence the future. She has been speaking nationally for the past 18 years on topics ranging from dismantling privilege to feminism and racism to radical Jewish heritage. In addition, she writes and speaks about multicultural histories of resistance, feminism, cultural activism, and the ways that racism, anti-semitism, sexism, class, and other systems of oppression interlock. Morales said in an interview with the author, "Writers have to be leaders in their communities." She makes no apologies for what some people might describe as radical revolutionary thinking.

When Levins Morales writes, she does not think consciously of a particular audience but rather considers the issues which are critical to her at that moment. Another influence on her writing is her loyalty to the rural Puerto Rican community that she grew up in and, in particular, the women in that community. She also feels a strong responsibility to young Puerto Ricans who have very little access to any literature that reflects the realities of their lives. According to Levins Morales, "The vast majority of the popular culture's portrayal of Puerto Ricans is extremely stereotyped and oppressive." Levins Morales, as a fiction writer, focuses on writing material that can be used by Hispanic communities in their struggle for survival and identity. As an activist, she frequently writes on issues that challenge the "politically correct" and has demonstrated a willingness to engage in conflict and controversy.

Levins Morales spent five years from 1991 to 1996 extensively researching Puerto Rican women's history that pertained to the histories of West African, Spanish, and Caribbean women. Using primary and secondary sources, she questioned complex theoretical issues, such as under-documented populations complex social interactions, and political implications of representation in writing the history of multiple oppressed peoples. In fact, Levins Morales was a founding member of the Latina Feminist Comparative Research Group, formed in 1993. For two years, the group examined issues in Hispanic American feminist research. The group received the Rockefeller Foundation grant in 1995 to continue its research in the area of feminist theory. The group's compiled research is currently under consideration for publication by a university press.

Publications

Levins Morales has had her essays, poems, and short stories published in various journals and magazines, including the *Americas Review, Ms., Coming Up,* and *Gay Community News.* Her work has also appeared in various anthologies by women of color: *This Bridge Called My Back: Writings by Radical Women of Color* in 1981, which was the first anthology of Hispanic American women writers published in the United States, and *Cuentos: Stories by Latinas* in 1983, which is now a standard text in women's and ethnic studies. In 1986, her literary works included *Getting Home Alive,* a narration in prose and poetry about identity, family, and the immigrant experience that she co-authored with her mother, Rosario Morales. *Getting Home Alive* has been widely used as a college text; *Publisher's Weekly* referred to it as "serious, literary and passionate." Forthcoming in 1998 is a collection of essays featured in *Medicine Stories: History, Culture and the Politics of Integrity* and *Remedios,* which is a prose poetry work of history.

Levins Morales co-wrote three multi-media plays depicting Latin American history and culture, produced by La Peña Cultural Center in Berkeley, CA., where she worked as an arts administrator and educator. These include: *La Poblacion* (1979), *Canto Libre* (1980), and *Step by Step* (1981). Since 1989 Morales has been a frequent contributor to *The Women's Review of Books and Bridges: A Journal for Jewish Feminists and our Friends.* She is currently working on *Malascrianzas,* a collection of short stories with Rosario Morales, and *Indiera,* consisting of poetry, essays, and original art work documenting the history of a small coffee-growing community in rural Puerto Rico, co-authored with her father, Ricardo Levins Morales. Levins Morales currently divides her time between Berkley, CA, and, also Minneapolis, MN. She continues to write and speak on issues that are important to her and her culture.

Current Address: 3637 17th Ave., S., Minneapolis, MN 55407.

Sources:

Kubiac, Brenda. Letter to and telephone conversation with Aurora Levins Morales, March 1998.
Mutter, John. "Getting Home Alive." *Publishers Weekly,* November 14, 1986, p. 57.
Torrens, James S. "U.S. Latino Writers—the Searchers." *America,* July 25, 1992, p. 41.
Turner, Faythe, ed. *Puerto Rican Writers at Home in the USA: An Anthology.* Seattle: Open Hand Publishers, 1991.

Carmela Patricia Morales
(1965–)
Cancer researcher

Carmela Patricia Morales is a distinguished cancer researcher and young scientist who specializes in hepatology and cancers of the gastrointestinal tract. Last year she was one of six minority physicians to receive a Robert Wood Johnson fellow—a $315,000 grant which will fund Morales' research on telomerase, a protein present in many cancers, for four years.

Morales was born in El Paso, Texas, on May 9, 1965, the daughter of a middle-class family struggling to achieve the American dream. Her mother worked in the family photography business, and her father unloaded baggage at the Greyhound bus station. An outstanding student in the parochial grade school and high school that she attended in El Paso, Morales was determined to make her family proud.

Discovers Interest in Medical Research

Morales entered Texas A&M University in College Station, Texas. In her third year she participated in a research and educational program for promising students at the University of Texas Medical School. A biochemistry major, she planned to become a physician. But her third-year workshop in the medical school taught her that research was also a potential career—a career for which she was well-suited.

"I liked the fact that as a researcher you designed strategies to solve interesting problems in unique and creative ways," she said recently in a telephone interview. "At the same time I was able to apply things I was learning in college as a biochemistry major."

Morales eventually went on to attend the University of Texas Southwestern Medical School, receiving her M.D. degree, and then became part of the junior faculty and a research fellow, where she concentrated on working on questions in cell biology and neuroscience, all relating to the progression of some cancers, especially gastrointestinal(G.I.)cancers.

Researches Proteins Present in Cancer Cells

Morales was in the right place at the right time. The lab she joined at the University of Texas had already shown that the protein telomerase was present in a large variety of cancers—and in very high levels. Yet, normal cells contained little of this substance. Morales and her fellow researchers also knew that telomerase was very important in G.I. cancers—specifically, in helping to make cancer cells in this region of the body immortal.

G.I. cancers are also very easily studied. A G.I. cancer in a human patient is readily accessible by using an endoscope to look at and take samples of the cancer. An endoscope is a lighted tube that a doctor inserts into the patient's body through a surgical cut or a natural opening such as the anus.

The problem in treating such cancers is that they are often detected at a late stage, making them harder to cure. In fact, the current technique used for diagnosis only detects half of all G.I. cancers. But by trying to detect the presence of telomerase, Morales felt, scientists could then pick up most gastrointestinal cancers. When Morales did studies on three sorts of cancers—colon cancer, pancreatic cancer and esophageal cancer—she did indeed find that a test devised to pick up the presence of telomerase accurately diagnosed better than 90 percent of the cancers. "The encouraging thing about this research is that now we may even be able to predict the likelihood of these cancers developing in certain patients—that is, which patients are a higher risk. Her research paper on this study was published in the journal,*Cancer* in August, 1998.

The test Morales used to detect the cancerous tissue employs a probe made of microscopic human RNA. The RNA probe is also radioactive—and the researcher manipulates it, touching the probe to the cancerous tissue. The probe lights up if telomerase is present, as the RNA binds to the telomerase.

Receives Highly Sought Award

Morales is enthusiastic about these discoveries and grateful for the support of the award from the Robert Wood Johnson Foundation. The money makes it possible for her to spend most of her time in the lab, doing the work she loves—research that helps bring the scientific community nearer to answering questions about cancer.

Gains Knowledge from Mentors

Morales has had many mentors along the way, but she has especially gained knowledge from her contacts with Prof. Jerry Shay and Prof. Jennifer Cuthbert at the University of Texas. Shay heads the telomerase lab, and Cuthbert heads the division of internal medicine and is a hepatologist. "Women in gastroenterology and hepatology are very uncommon. So it's encouraging for me to see someone like Dr. Cuthbert who's such a wonderful role model. Dr. Shay has also been very important in my career development. He's given me a real intellectual understanding of the role of telomerase in cancer."

Morales is also a role model herself. As well as the Robert Wood Johnson Foundation Award, she has won awards from the American Association for Cancer Research and from the Department of Internal Medicine at the University of Texas.

As she continues to forge forward in her demanding research career, Morales also finds time to be a wife and mother of a five-month-old baby. "You learn how to be very efficient in managing your time," she said. Her husband is cardiologist Juan Escobar, a doctor in private practice in Dallas.

Morales plans to continue her research career and hopes to eventually attain a position as part of the full-time faculty in university academic medicine. "I'm very positive about the future of women in medical research. In the future I want to continue providing intellectual insights into the nature of cancer and to continue learning what it means to be a good scientist," she said.

Current Address: Dept. of Cell Biology and Neuroscience, Southwestern Medical Ctr. at Dallas, Univ. of Texas, 5323 Harry Hines Blvd., K2.500, Dallas, TX 75235-9039.

Sources:

Boughton, Barbara A. Telephone conversation with Carmela Patricia Morales, March 11, 1998

Sylvia Morales

Sylvia Morales

Filmmaker, media executive, entrepreneur

Selected filmography:

Chicana. 1979.
Los Lobos: And a Time to Dance. PBS, 1984.
Esperanza. American Film Institute.
SIDA Is AIDS. PBS, 1988.
Values: Sexuality and the Family.
Faith Even to the Fire. Sylvan Productions, 1992.
"Struggle in the Fields." *Chicano! History of the Mexican American Civil Rights Movement* series. PBS, 1996.

Overview

A well-known documentary film producer and director, Sylvia Morales has made a significant contribution to broadening American understanding of what it means to be a Mexican American or Chicano. As the producer of the

second of four episodes of the landmark public television production *Chicano! History of the Mexican American Civil Rights Movement* in 1996, Morales brought to the American public the story of farm workers' efforts to form a national labor union. Her other documentaries also highlight the Hispanic experience both from a historical and modern perspective.

The second episode of *Chicano!*, entitled "Struggle in the Fields," documents the campaign led by César Chávez, an advocate of nonviolence, to protect the rights of farm workers, many of whom were Mexican Americans or illegal Mexican aliens. Morales's film documents the 1965 strike against California grape growers by farm workers demanding better working conditions and fair wages. The film follows the national boycott of California-grown table grapes led by Chávez that led eventually to the first union contracts in farm labor history. That victory was followed by an even more important milestone in the farm labor fight: the passage of the California Labor Relations Act.

Early Films Receive Critical Praise

One of Morales's earliest contributions to the world of documentary film came in 1979 with the release of the prophetically titled *Chicana,* which chronicled the changing roles of women in Hispanic (particularly Mexican American) society from pre-Columbian times through the late 1970s. It was critically well received. She followed

Chicana with a film profile of the East Los Angeles-based musical group Los Lobos. Entitled *Los Lobos: And a Time to Dance,* the documentary was first aired by the Public Broadcasting System in 1984.

In a one-hour narrative drama entitled *Esperanza,* which Morales directed under the Women Filmmakers Program of the American Film Institute, she explored the struggle of a young immigrant girl to survive when her mother is arrested. *SIDA Is AIDS,* a one-hour documentary broadcast in both Spanish and English, was produced by Morales for PBS. She followed this with a half-hour documentary entitled *Values: Sexuality and the Family. Values,* also produced in both Spanish and English versions, examined health issues facing the Hispanic American community.

Forms Production Company

In 1988, Morales formed Sylvan Productions. One of Sylvan's earliest and most successful productions was a documentary entitled *Faith Even to the Fire,* coproduced by Morales with Jean Victor. This Emmy-nominated program chronicles the lives of three contemporary American Catholic nuns, struggling for social justice even when it brings them into conflict at times with the teachings of their church. Examined in detail are the lives of Sister Rosa Marth Zarate, a nun of Mexican ancestry who works with and organizes Hispanic Americans in California's San Bernardino County; Sister Marie de Pores Taylor, an African American nun who is a political and community activist in Oakland, CA; and Sister Judy Vaughan, an Irish American nun who was almost expelled from her order because of her pro-choice position. In the course of the film, the three speak out about the problems of sexism, classism, and racism within the Catholic church and what they are doing to combat it. This hour-long documentary film, first broadcast by PBS, won the Silver Apple Award at the 1993 National Educational Film & Video Festival.

Among Morales's other documentary films are "Union Maids" and "Modern Mothers," both of which were produced for the Turner Broadcasting series *A Century of Women.* Morales also produced a film called *Tuesday's Child Is Full of Grace* for PBS. As a director, Morales has produced a body of work that both hits directly to the center of important issues, and treats those issues with compassion and equity.

Sources:

Filmakers Library Home Page. Available at http://www.filmakers.com/WOMEN4.html.
Kanellos, Nicolás, ed. *The Hispanic Almanac: From Columbus to Corporate America.* Detroit: Visible Ink Press, 1994., p. 552.
PBS Home Page. Available at http://www.pbs.org/chicano/bios/morales.html.

Cecilia Muñoz
(1962–)
Organization vice president, lobbyist, civil rights activist

Whether fighting immigration legislation or testifying before Congress, Cecilia Muñoz has been an intense, prominent voice on behalf of Hispanic American rights. As vice president for the Office of Research, Advocacy and Legislation at the National Council of La Raza (NCLR), a nonprofit organization established to improve opportunities for Hispanics, she oversees all legislative activities that cover issues of great importance to Hispanic Americans. Colleagues call her "a ferocious advocate."

Cecilia Muñoz was born in Detroit, Michigan, on July 27, 1962, the youngest of four children. Her parents had moved to the United States from La Paz, Bolivia, so that her father, an automotive engineer, could go to the University of Michigan. When she was three, the family moved to Livonia, a growing, middle-class, white Detroit suburb. Muñoz attended the University of Michigan in Ann Arbor and completed her undergraduate degrees in English and Latin studies in 1984. Her time at the university reminded

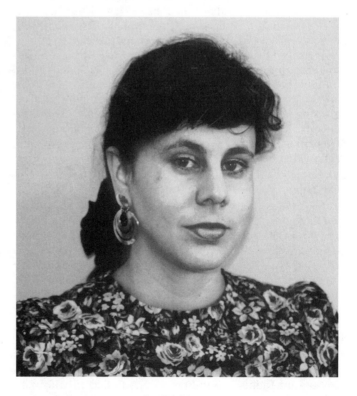

Cecilia Muñoz

her of her youth in Livonia, where Hispanics were in the minority. But, as a side job, she worked as a tutor to Hispanic American inmates at the state prison in nearby Jackson, an experience that helped her get closer to her Hispanic culture. Following graduation, Muñoz continued her education at the University of California at Berkeley, where she obtained her master's degree.

Muñoz moved from California to Chicago to work for the Roman Catholic Archdiocese of Chicago as head of the Legalization Outreach Program for Catholic Charities. Following the 1986 enactment by President Ronald Reagan of the Immigration Reform and Control Act—an amnesty program that allowed undocumented immigrants who met certain criteria (such as having lived continuously in the United States) to become legal U.S. residents—Muñoz helped more than five thousand immigrants obtain legal citizenship in the United States. Working double-digit hours, she operated 12 field offices throughout metropolitan Chicago, an intense experience. The racism and sexism she confronted in her job gave her greater empathy in working with immigrants.

National Council of La Raza

In 1988, Muñoz began her work at NCLR as the senior immigration policy analyst. She had developed a real interest in working for an institution that focused on Hispanic Americans, and she picked a prominent one. Formed in 1968, the National Council of La Raza bills itself as "the largest constituency-based national Hispanic organization, serving all Hispanic nationality groups in all regions of the country." Media outlets have viewed the NCLR's Policy Analysis Center as the pre-eminent Hispanic think tank, a voice for all Hispanic Americans. It seeks to reduce poverty and discrimination and to improve opportunities for Hispanic Americans by strengthening Hispanic community-based organizations through assistance in such areas as management and resource development; it also gives its perspective on a variety of public policy issues, to encourage the adoption of programs that will better serve Hispanics. Muñoz currently is in charge of all legislative actions handled by the policy staff.

Controversy Over Welfare Reform

On August 22, 1996, President Bill Clinton signed into law the strictest federal welfare reform law in years. It had major implications for legal immigrants who were not citizens. They became ineligible for food stamps and Supplemental Security Income (SSI), the latter of which assists aged, blind, and disabled individuals. The cost savings from these cutbacks was estimated to be between 20 and 30 billion dollars over six years.

Immigrant advocate groups and charitable organizations, such as the NCLR, Northern California Coalition for Immigrant Rights in San Francisco, and Second Harvest, felt that the law was too harsh and unfair. Immigrants who came to the United States legally yet, who were not citizens, would be cut off from immigrant public assistance programs. This was especially critical to refugees who come to the United States with little money and few possessions, and who typically need several years for an adequate transition to their new surroundings. Advocates claimed it was unfair to change the rules and cut off benefits to those who had come to the United States legally.

The NCLR demonstrated the suffering these cutbacks created. The organization put a human face on the misery by presenting individuals who spoke at a press conference of the direct personal impact of these cost-cutting measures. Speaking on behalf of the NCLR, Muñoz stated, "We have no other choice but to demonstrate the human cost of these policies. And the human cost is extraordinary." It was predicted that an estimated one million immigrants would be adversely affected by rescinding food stamps. "Many of these immigrants are working men and women who supplement their income with food stamps in order to provide food for their families," stated Muñoz in an article in *The Orange County Register.*

The public lobbying ultimately proved successful. In July of 1997, less than a year after Clinton originally signed the bill, lawmakers softened their legal mandates by allowing some legal immigrants to continue their SSI benefits. According to Muñoz, "The lesson of the last year seems to be you can only make policy change to undo terrible wrongs after people have died or after people have entered situations that are just excruciatingly painful to watch." Muñoz believes that the decision to withhold food stamps should also have been reversed. She has spoken out for its reinstatement: "It was unfair to deny SSI to immigrants and apply this change in the law retroactively. It's equally unfair to do the same with food stamps." Some attributed the tough immigration law to the fact that it was an election year. Mark Krikorian of the Center for Immigration Studies said, "The election year having passed and the special-interest groups concerned having mounted a very large and very effective lobbying campaign, Congress pulled back."

Fighting Against Discrimination

The height of irony—but an example of the kind of issue on which Muñoz works the hardest—occurred on March 21, 1997, when Muñoz was twice asked on the telephone about her citizenship, just prior to her attendance at a White House briefing on immigration. Although the White House claimed that, for security reasons, a new policy required visitors to give their date of birth, Social Security number, and citizenship, Muñoz seemed to be singled out. According to fellow attendees Frank Sharry, executive director of the National Immigration Forum, a Washington nonprofit advocacy group, neither he nor Josh Bernstein, policy analyst at the National Immigration Law Center, were questioned. "There are laws against this stuff in the workplace," asserted Sharry in a *Washington Post* article. "This selective questioning of people is based on what, the number of vowels in their name?" An angry Muñoz said "[I had] smoke coming out of my ears. I hit the ceiling. This is exactly what we're fighting against."

The negative image of immigrants is something Muñoz battles every day. In 1997, a coalition of immigration reform groups set out to reduce legal immigration and eliminate illegal immigration. The Federation for American Immigration Reform (FAIR) claimed that "large numbers of immigrants make all our problems worse." Arizonans for Immigration Reform said in a *Arizona Republic* article that immigrants represent "an invasion that will destroy our country's sovereignty if something is not done about it." Muñoz countered these claims in the same article by pointing out the United States has largely "benefited from its generous tradition of welcoming immigrants." Indeed, an earlier report by the National Research Council concluded "immigrants are a net boost to the U.S. economy, adding up to ten billion dollars each year." Muñoz theorizes that anti-immigrant groups "try to find out what people in a certain area are concerned about and then try to link those concerns to immigration." In California, she said, the depressed economy was often blamed on immigrants; in Arizona, fast growth was their fault. Muñoz feels these criticisms stem from people worrying "about Latinos being culturally different."

Acts as Tough Advocate

Muñoz greets her visitors graciously. Fellow workers describe her as modest. In addition, she speaks warmly of her family—husband Amit Muñoz-Pandya, a human rights lawyer, and daughters Cristina and Meera. But she fights hard "doing the work I always wanted to do." As colleague Sharry says, Muñoz is as "tough and determined an advocate as you can find. She doesn't back down an inch."

Current Address: National Council of La Raza, 1111 19th St., NW, Ste. 1000, Washington, DC 20036.

Sources:

"Congress Weakens Immigration Policies." Associated Press. December 1, 1997. Available at http://www.lubbockonline.com/news.

Eversley, Melanie. "A Leading Authority: Detroit Native Speaks Out Proudly for Latino Issues." *Detroit Free Press.* November 3, 1997.

Hayward, Brad. "Welfare Reform Has Legal Immigrants Wary." *Sacramento Bee.* September 4, 1996.

"Immigrants Add $10 Billion to Economy Annually, Study Says." *Washington Times.* May 19, 1997. Available at http://web.lexis-nexis.com.

McDonnell, Patrick J. "Proposed Cutbacks in Aid Alarm Legal Immigrants." *Los Angeles Times.* July 30, 1996, p. A1.

Mittelstadt, Michelle. "Nearly 1 Million Cut from Food Stamp Rolls." The Associated Press. August 25, 1997. Available at http://amarillonet.com/stories/082597/million.html.

National Council of La Raza. Mission Statement.

Navarrette, Ruben, Jr. "Groups Ask for Cuts in Immigrants." *Arizona Republic.* November 11, 1997. Available at http://www.azcentral.com/hispanic.

Sample, Herbert A. "Activists Want Food Stamps Restored to Immigrants." *Orange County Register.* August 22, 1997, p. A15.

Sun, Lena H. "White House Queries Activist on Citizenship." *Washington Post.* March 21, 1997, p. A28.

Nakata, Lorraine Garcia
See **Garcia-Nakata, Lorraine**

Jackie F. Nespral
(1966–)
Television anchor, reporter

A former co-anchor on the weekend NBC *Today* show in New York City, Jackie Nespral gave up her high profile position in 1996 to return to her native Miami, Florida. As an anchor/reporter on WTVJ-6, she says she has the "best of both worlds." She is in front of the television cameras but also is able to spend more time with her family.

Seeks Television Career

Jacqueline Frances Nespral was born on April 21, 1966, in Miami, to Jose Francisco and Sonia M. Valdez de Nespral. She graduated from the University of Miami in 1989 with a B.S. degree in psychology and a minor in communications. She also completed two years of postgraduate work in print and broadcast journalism at Florida International University. Despite her major in psychology, she turned to television.

Nespral began her career in 1986 as a spokesperson for Univision. During 1989-90, she went in front of the camera as a weather anchor for Dynamic Cablevision. Next she reported for Television Marti and anchored a one-hour live national newscast *Noticias y mas* for the UnivisionNetwork.

Makes Major Career Decision

By 1992, Nespral had found her way to the "big time" on NBC television. With co-anchor Scott Simon, they replaced Mary Alice Williams and Garrick Utley as hosts of the Saturday and Sunday editions of the *Today* show. Nespral became known for her perceptive interviews with well-known figures from the political scene and the entertainment world. She received an Easter Seal award for her story about the struggle of one family to have their learn-ing-disabled child educated in the public schools. Covering such events as the peace talks in El Salvador or Hurricane Andrew in the South kept Nespral on the move. However, her busy on-camera life often separated Nespral from her family, which includes her husband, Armando Luis Hassun, a surgeon at Columbia Kendall Hospital in Miami, their daughter, Frances Jacqueline, and son, Armando, Jr., living in Florida. Her weekend job in New York meant spending at least four days away from her family. In January of 1996, Nespral made a huge career decision. She left the top New York market for a job as an anchor/reporter with Miami station WTVJ-6.

Gains Honors

The honors for Nespral's work, both in front of and away from the cameras, include: the Statue of Liberty Commission Award from the New York City Commission in 1986; Miami Key to the City in 1987; and the Easter Seals EDI Award in 1993. She also received honorable mention from the American Women in Radio and Television for her work reporting the controversy regarding the distribution of the so-called morning-after pill for contraceptive use.

Current Address: WTVJ-6, 316 N. Miami Ave., Miami, FL 33128.

Sources:

Blue, Rose. Telephone interview with Nespral aide, March 10, 1998.

Hispanic OnLine. Available at http://www.hisp.com/aug95/thirty.html.

Unterburger, Amy L. *Who's Who Among Hispanic Americans.* 3rd ed. Detroit: Gale Research, 1994.

Elvia Elisa Niebla
(1945–)
Environmental scientist

Elvia Elisa Niebla is an environmental scientist who has made notable contributions to the study of forests. Her work centers on directing vital scientific studies on the impact of acid rain, pollution, and climate change on U.S. trees and soils. She has also helped to alleviate discrimination against Hispanic Americans in the United States and made it easier for many Hispanic Americans to obtain government employment.

Niebla was born March 12, 1945, in Nogales, Mexico, the youngest of four children. Her father, Fernando Niebla, was a clerk in a brokerage that imported produce. When she was six-years old, her family moved to the Arizona side of Nogales. "I always say we crossed the street and changed countries," she laughed during an interview. Niebla admitted that she was interested in science at an early age. "I felt science was like a puzzle, and I like working with puzzles. Science answered lots of important questions."

Develops Interest in Environmental Issues

After junior college, Niebla attended the University of Arizona, where she received a bachelor's degree in zoology in 1967, followed by a master's degree in education a year later. For a while she was a public school teacher in Claremont, CA, a city west of Los Angeles. Developing an interest in environmental issues, she returned to studies at the University of Arizona after three years of teaching, and earned a Ph.D. in soil chemistry in 1979. Her specialty was soil contamination.

Niebla began a career as a physical scientist at the University of Arizona during the 1970s. She was then employed by the National Park Service from 1979 to 1984. For the next five years, she worked at the Environmental Protection Agency (EPA) as a soil chemist and, with other scientists, wrote U.S. regulations on sludge (waste products) used to amend soil and grow crops. She defended the regulations to the EPA Science Advisory Board and various interest groups, including environmentalists and industry organizations. For her work on the regulations, Niebla was awarded the Bronze Medal for Commendable Service, one of the EPA's highest awards.

In 1984, Niebla obtained her M.B.A. from the University of Northern Colorado, boosting her career in government. "I was increasingly in a position of managing departments--having to do strategic planning, budget formulation, and deal with personnel issues. I needed first the theoretical knowledge that comes from an M.B.A., as well as five years as a director in the National Park Service to hone my practical skills." Highly regarded for her knowledge and dedication, Niebla was named national coordinator of the USDA Forest Service's Global Change Research Program in 1989.

Studies Destruction of Forests

As an administrator, Niebla coordinates studies on the impact of fuel emissions and climate changes on U.S. forests. The data from these studies is collected to allow Congress to decide what kind of environmental legislation is needed to help reduce pollution. Niebla explained the importance of these studies: "It's definitely been proven that human activities are affecting the forests—changing the climate and killing off trees. And that means there are a lot of changes taking place very quickly in the forests. Species migrate, causing further harm, because they no longer carry seeds to different areas in the forest, supporting new growth. Whether or not our forests will survive is an open question."

Like many scientists, Niebla believes the key to controlling the damage to our forests is reducing greenhouse gases, atmospheric gases that result from automobile fuel emissions. The processing of garbage in the United States also contributes to air and water pollution. "It's not very well accepted, but the real answer to cutting down on harmful pollution is to use less fuel, or use more energy efficient machinery and cars. Recycling is also helpful because the less energy we use to process garbage, the better," Niebla declared.

Addresses Employment Inequities of Hispanic Americans

Another of Niebla's concerns is employment discrimination practices against Hispanic Americans. In 1984 her work in preventing discrimination earned her the Hispanic Employment Manager of the Year Award from the U.S. Office of Personnel Management. The award recognized Niebla's efforts to remedy inequities in federal government hiring procedures, which she claims effectively barred Hispanic Americans from employment. "Everyone would say 'We don't have Hispanics in government because we can't find Hispanics who are 'qualified'," she said in the interview. "So I decided to test that theory." With a group of other federal employees, she administered the federal employment test to high school seniors in an area of Arizona stretching from Nogales to Tucson. "The problem was that many Hispanics were poor, and the test was previously only given in Phoenix. And many Hispanics in Arizona could not afford the cost of a trip to Phoenix," she explained. The results of the newly administered test, however, showed that Hispanic Americans in areas other than Phoenix were quite capable of holding down federal jobs. After Niebla's investigation concluded, testing sites in Arizona were increased to give minorities better access to them.

In 1997, Niebla was selected as a Brookings congressional fellow and worked as a legislative assistant to Rep. Ed Pastor of Arizona, researching issues on environmental justice, border affairs, education, and Hispanic American concerns. Her weekly participation in House of Representatives Hispanic Caucus meetings helped resolve many important issues affecting Hispanic Americans. "It was a tremendous opportunity to learn the workings of the legislative branch of the government from the inside," she said.

Niebla, who has a large extended family, credits her mother, Marina, as her primary source of inspiration. "She always told me I could do anything. She encouraged me to be curious." Her favorite algebra teacher in high school was another mentor. He stayed after school to teach her calculus—a subject that was not offered in Niebla's school—because he felt she had promise. "He was one of those teachers who encouraged me to do a bit more than everyone else—to strive a little harder."

Sources:

Boughton, Barbara. Telephone conversation with Elvia Elisa Niebla, March 28, 1998.
Who's Who in the West 19th edition, 1984-1985. Wilmette, IL: Marquis Who's Who, 1983.

Sonia M. Nieto

Sonia M. Nieto

(1943–)

Professor, author, editor

Selected writings:

Affirming Diversity: The Sociopolitical Context of Multicultural Education. Longman, 1992.
The Education of Latinos in Massachusetts: Research and Policy Consideration. Co-edited with Ralph Rivera. Gaston Institute, 1993.
The Light in Their Eyes: Student Learning, Teacher Transformation, and Multicultural Education. Teachers College Press, forthcoming 1999.

Overview

Sonia Nieto is a professor of education at the University of Massachusetts and an expert on bilingual and multicultural education. She has written and edited several books, contributed numerous essays to scholarly journals, and presented many papers to educational conferences and meetings. Nieto's work focuses on multicultural and bilingual education, the education of Hispanic Americans, curriculum reform, and Puerto Rican children's literature. She is also a powerful advocate for comprehensive multicultural education in U.S. schools.

Spends Early Years in Brooklyn

Nieto was born on September 25, 1943, in Brooklyn, New York. She was one of three children born to Federico Cortes and Esther Mercado, Puerto Rican immigrants who owned a small grocery store in Brooklyn. Nieto attended New York City public schools. She received a B.S. degree in elementary education from St. Johns University in 1965. She earned her M.A. degree in Spanish and Hispanic literature from the New York University Graduate Program in Madrid, Spain, in 1966.

Enters Career in Teaching

Upon returning from Spain in 1966, Nieto taught English and Spanish in a Brooklyn junior high school. She was the first Puerto Rican teacher in the school, and she quickly discovered that ethnic boundaries applied to both students and teachers. In a panel discussion subsequently published in the *Harvard Educational Review,* she recalled, "What I find interesting in looking back, and I don't think I thought about it too much then, was the fact that they not only labeled the kids, but they also labeled me. So I was known as the NE [non-English] teacher. . . . Ethnicity for me at that point meant that I could be labeled in a negative way."

In 1967, Nieto married Angel Nieto, a teacher and children's book author. They have two daughters, Alicia and Marisa. Nieto went on to teach fourth grade in the first bilingual school in the Northeast at Bronx's Public School 25, one of the first to be funded by the Title VII program. In 1972, Nieto took her first position in higher education as instructor and deputy chairperson of the Department of Puerto Rican Studies at Brooklyn College, where she worked in a joint program in bilingual education with the School of Education. In 1975, she moved with her family to Massachusetts. She earned her doctoral degree in education, concentrating in curriculum studies with a special emphasis on multicultural and bilingual education, from the University of Massachusetts in 1979. Nieto joined the faculty at the University of Massachusetts at Amherst in 1980 as an assistant professor. In 1993, she became a full professor.

Receives Numerous Awards

Over the course of her career as scholar, educator, and advocate, Nieto has received numerous awards and honors. She received the Human and Civil Rights Award from the Massachusetts Teachers Association in 1989. In 1991, she was honored with the Outstanding Accomplishment in Higher Education Award from the Hispanic Caucus of the American Association of Higher Education. She has also been awarded the Drylongso Award for Anti-Racist Activists from Community Change of Boston (1995) and the Teacher of the Year Award from the Hispanic Educators for Multicultural Education (1997). In addition, Nieto received an Annenberg Institute Fellowship for 1997-99.

Works as an Advocate and Community Leader

Nieto has served on numerous commissions, panels, and advisory boards from the local to the international level. These include the Massachusetts Advocacy Center, an advisory committee for California Tomorrow, and the National Advisory Boards of both Facing History and Educators for Social Responsibility. She was a member of the Puerto Rican Educators Association from 1971 to 1975. Other professional memberships include the National Education for Bilingual Education, the Massachusetts Association for Bilingual Education, and Phi Delta Kappa. She also served as a committee member of the American Educational Research Association from 1995 to 1997 and has served on the editorial board since 1997.

Publishes *Affirming Diversity*

Nieto published her most comprehensive work in 1992 entitled *Affirming Diversity: The Sociopolitical Context of Multicultural Education*. In this defining work, Nieto wrote,

"Multicultural education cannot be understood in a vacuum but rather must be seen in its personal, social, historical, and political context." She explores the sociopolitical dimensions of race, ethnicity, and language in relationship to education. Emphasizing the complexity of influences that determine success or failure in the classroom, Nieto explores the benefits of, and necessity for, multicultural education in the United States.

Affirming Diversity is organized into two sections. The first part is humanized by the stories told by ten young people from various cultural backgrounds. Nieto used these stories to form and highlight her conceptual framework. The second part more closely resembles a standard textbook, including chapter overviews, discussion, and questions for reflection. In this section of the book, Nieto attempts to deliver a new vision of multicultural education to educators. A reviewer in the *Harvard Educational Review* stated, "Overall, *Affirming Diversity* is a powerful and beautifully written work that captures the knowledge, experiences, questions, and wisdom of a Puerto Rican scholar and practitioner committed to academic excellence, educational equity, and social change."

Involved in Forthcoming Projects

Nieto's next book, *The Light in Their Eyes: Student Learning, Teacher Transformation, and Multicultural Education*, will be published in 1999. Author of many scholarly articles, her latest contribution, "Fact and Fiction: Stories of Puerto Ricans in U.S. Schools," will appear in a special issue of the *Harvard Educational Review*, which focuses on the education of Puerto Ricans. Nieto is also editing a forthcoming book entitled *Puerto Rican Students in U.S. Schools*.

During a roundtable discussion published in the *Harvard Educational Review*, Nieto advocated for understanding ethnicity that is "a step closer to the real-life complexity of identity." For Nieto, identity is developed from a multitude of factors. "On a personal level for me, ethnicity means my language and it means my languages. And how I combine my languages, and how I express myself. And it's a primary part of my identity, but it's only a part. It means my birth family, and my home, and my childhood memories, and the senses and smells of my past and also of my present."

Current Address: School of Education, Furcolo Hall, Univ. of Massachusetts, Amherst, Amherst, MA 01003.

Sources:

"Affirming Diversity: The Sociopolitical Context of Multicultural Education." *Harvard Educational Review,* Spring 1994, pp. 112-113.
Bethel, Kari. Correspondence with Sonia Nieto, April 1998.

Clark, Sanza B. "The Schooling of Cultural and Ethnic Subordinate Groups." *Comparative Education Review,* February 1993, pp. 62-68.

Gordon, Beverly M. "Affirming Diversity: The Sociopolitical Context of Multicultural Education." *Journal of Negro Education,* Summer 1992, pp. 440-443.

Hale, Sylvia. "Affirming Diversity: The Sociopolitical Context of Multicultural Education." *Canadian Review of Sociology and Anthropology,* May 1997, pp. 228-230.

Trueba, Enrique. "Ethnicity and Education Forum: What Difference Does Difference Make?" *Harvard Educational Review,* Summer 1997, pp. 169-187.

Who's Who in the East, 24th ed. New Providence, NJ: Marquis, 1992.

Josephina Niggli
(1910–1983)
Author, playwright

Selected writings:

Mexican Silhouettes. Silhouette Press, 1931.
Mexican Folk Plays. University of North Carolina Press, 1938.
Mexican Village. University of North Carolina Press, 1945.
Step Down, Elder Brother. Rinehart, 1947.
A Miracle for Mexico. New York Graphic Society, 1964.

Overview

Novelist and playwright Josephina Niggli was best known for eschewing popular stereotypes to capture the true flavor of northern Mexican culture, particularly in her novel *Mexican Village.* In his study of Chicano literature as published in *MELUS,* Raymond A. Paredes declared, "*Mexican Village* stands as a major transitional work in the development of Chicano fiction. . . . Niggli's greatest achievement was to delineate an important aspect of Mexican American experience and to create a distinctive ambience for its presentation."

Begins Writing in Youth

Niggli started writing early, encouraged by her parents and teachers. An only child, Niggli was born to Frederick Ferdinand and Goldie Morgan, a cement plant manager and a concert violinist, respectively, on July 13, 1910, in Monterrey, Mexico. The Mexican Revolution, which erupted the year of Josephina's birth, drove the family to San Antonio, Texas, in 1913, in search of safety. "Little Niggli," as Josephina was nicknamed, was home-schooled until her teenage years, when she attended Main Avenue High School in San Antonio.

At age 15, Niggli enrolled in San Antonio's Incarnate Word College. While there, she won second place in a short story contest held by *Ladies' Home Journal.* Niggli went on to publish other pieces in magazines such as *Mexican Life, Collier's,* and *The Writer.* For local radio station KTSA, she wrote radio plays that proved to be quite popular. In 1928, Niggli's father paid to have a collection of her poems published under the title *Mexican Silhouettes;* shortly after publication, the chapbook won the National Catholic College Poetry Contest.

Joins Theatrical Troupe

After earning her bachelor of arts degree in 1931, Niggli studied playwriting with Coates Gwynne, director of the San Antonio Little Theatre. Gwynne quickly recognized Niggli's talent and encouraged her to continue her education. Four years later, Niggli entered the University of North Carolina at Chapel Hill, where she began her fruitful association with the Carolina Playmakers. Displaying her versatility, she wrote, directed, designed costumes, and acted in the folk-oriented plays that were the company's specialty. During her years at Chapel Hill, Niggli wrote some of her best plays, including *Tooth or Shave, The Cry of Dolores, The Red Velvet Goat, Azteca, Sunday Costs Five Pesos, Soldadera,* and *The Singing Valley*—all written from 1935 to 1936.

Niggli's plays ranged from lighthearted, folkloric comedies to serious historical dramas. For example, the farcical *Tooth or Shave* portrays two married couples who disagree about appearances, while *Soldadera* depicts the efforts of women soldiers during the Mexican Revolution. *The Singing Valley,* which served as the thesis for Niggli's master of arts degree, revolves around a father who brings his U.S.-reared children to Mexico, the land of his birth.

During the middle and late 1930s, Niggli won two fellowships in dramaturgy from the Rockefeller Foundation. She also worked at the Theatre of the National University of Mexico under playwriter Rodolfo Usigli. In 1938, Niggli lived in New York City on a fellowship of the Bureau of New Plays, allowing her to attend many theatrical productions as she honed her own craft. After returning to Chapel Hill the following year, she worked as a script editor for the Carolina Playmakers radio division. The next decade found Niggli creating several more plays, among them *The Ring of General Macias,* about a Mexican family fighting revolutionary forces in its homeland, and *Miracle at Blaise,* dealing with a Hispanic American woman's participation in the French Resistance during World War II. While teaching English and drama at the University of North Carolina, Niggli made time—in the mornings before classes and on weekends—to work on her novel *Mexican Village.*

First Novel Wins Acclaim

In 1945, *Mexican Village* received the Mayflower Cup Award for "best book of the year by a North Carolinian."

The work was translated into several languages, and in 1953, a movie based on the novel was developed; Niggli worked on the screenplay of the film version, which was called *Sombrero.* Commenting more than thirty years later on Niggli's novel, Raymond Paredes remarked in *MELUS:* "In its sensitive evocation of rural life, its emotionalism, and affectionate portrayal of exotic experiences and personalities, the book culminated the romantic tradition in Mexican American writing. But *Mexican Village* also pointed forward to an emerging school of realism, confronting such issues as racism, the oppression of women, and the failure of the Mexican Revolution."

Niggli's second novel was published two years later. Critically and popularly well received, *Step Down Elder Brother* intertwines a love story with commentary on the rise of the middle class in Monterrey, Mexico. Niggli considered the new work to be more important than *Mexican Village* because of its social content.

Winning another fellowship in 1950 allowed Niggli to visit the Abbey Theatre in Dublin, Ireland, where she studied performances. Four years later she repeated the process at the Old Vic School in Bristol, England. In 1956, Niggli accepted a professorship at Western Carolina University. She taught English and drama for one year before being named department head, a post she held until her retirement in 1975. In 1964 Niggli published a young adult book, *A Miracle for Mexico.* It would be her last literary work; Niggli died in 1983.

Sources:

Contemporary Authors-Permanent Series, volume 2. Detroit: Gale, 1978.
Dictionary of Literary Biography Yearbook: 1980, edited by Karen L. Rood, Jean W. Ross, and Richard Ziegfeld. Detroit: Gale, 1981.
Hispanic Writers, edited by Bryan Ryan. Detroit: Gale, 1991.
MELUS, Summer 1978, pp. 71-110.
Spearman, Walter. *The Carolina Playmakers: The First Fifty Years.* Chapel Hill: University of North Carolina Press, 1970.
Yale Review, Spring 1948, p. 576.

Ana Nogales

(1953–)

Psychologist, author, columnist, television commentator

Selected writings:

Dr. Ana Nogales' Book of Love, Sex, and Relationships: A Guide for Latino Couples. Broadway Books, 1998.

Ana Nogales

Overview

Ana Nogales, a practicing psychologist, author, weekly columnist, and television personality, serves the Hispanic American community as few people do. Nogales believes that even amid the diversity of the cultures that represent the Hispanic community at large, there are more similarities than differences among them. If her best-selling book, *Dr. Nogales' Book of Love, Sex and Relationships: A Guide for Latino Couples,* or the number of people who seek her advice weekly through her newspaper column and television appearances are any indication, Nogales combines the qualities and expertise of the consummate professional with those of the trusted neighbor and friend. She opens her ears—and heart—to help other Hispanic Americans solve problems that are often unique to their community.

Leaves One Home for Another

Ana Nogales was born in Buenos Aires, Argentina, on June 26, 1953. Both of her parents were immigrants from Poland who had settled in Argentina. Nogales grew up in a loving home and was encouraged at a young age to cultivate an interest in people. Although she was an exceptional student in math and physics, she never intended to pursue either as a career. Rather, she was drawn toward the education field and received her elementary teaching credential from the Escuela Normal No. 1 de Profesoras in 1968. She eventually accepted a position as an instructor and director of the psychology department at a private college. Nogales has also served as co-director of UPA, Children's Recreational Groups, an educational psychologist for a kindergarten, and an instructor at the Top Level Institute. After Nogales received her master's degree in psychology from John F. Kennedy University in Buenos Aires in 1975, she entered private practice and conducted both individual and group psychotherapy sessions. In 1979, Nogales left Argentina and settled in Southern California.

Takes to the Airwaves

Upon her arrival in the United States, Nogales began working on a doctorate in psychology. She continued her private practice and also spent two years as the clinical supervisor of an outpatient alcoholism treatment program. By the time Nogales received her doctorate in psychology from United States International University in 1982, she had already starting appearing as a guest expert on television talk shows, such as *Cristina* and *Sevcec,* on the Spanish networks Univision and Telemundo and on radio shows broadcast by CNN, Radio Express, and local stations. In 1983 Nogales became co-host of *El y Ella,* a television program dealing with the various psychological problems found in marriage and family life. Although she was quickly becoming a media celebrity, Nogales continued to build a successful private practice specializing in individual, marital and family psychotherapy, psychological and educational evaluations, seminars, and workshops. She opened offices in Los Angeles and Santa Ana, California and provides psychological services for the Orange County Social Services Agency.

In 1992, Nogales began hosting her own daily radio call-in show, *Aqui Entre Nous,* which offered Hispanic American callers information, practical suggestions for solving personal problems, and a sympathetic ear. *Aqui Entre Nous* moved to television in 1994. In a 1994 *Los Angeles Times* article by Leila Cobo-Hanlon, Nogales explained the importance of *Aqui Entre Nous,* "There is an incredible need in the Hispanic community to have a place to ask. In general, due to government budget cuts, people now have less access to mental health professionals, and the problem is greater when they need help in Spanish. So Spanish speakers have nowhere to go, especially in emergency cases. Mine is an open line to help people in Spanish, and it's the only one." In 1995, broadcasts of *Aqui Entre Nous* ended. One year later, Nogales began hosting a segment on psychological issues for KVEA-TV's 11:00 news broadcast. She appears periodically on television segments whenever expert psychological commentary is needed.

Writes for a Special Cause

In 1997, Nogales' column entitled *Aqui Entre Nous* began appearing in two weekly Spanish-language newspapers, *Para Ti* and *La Opinion.* Like her earlier radio and television shows of the same name, the *Aqui Entre Nous* column covers psychological issues of interest to Hispanic Americans. No subject is considered out-of-bounds or off-limits.

In 1998, Nogales published her book, *Dr. Ana Nogales' Book of Love, Sex, and Relationships.* She concurrently released a Spanish-language edition, *Amor, Intimidad y Sexo: Una Guia Para la Pareja Latino.* In the book, Nogales discusses issues such as domestic violence, parenting difficulties, and sexual problems that are found in Hispanic American relationships. She also offers practical exercises that readers can use to improve the relationships in their lives. In the introduction to her book, Nogales argues that problems encountered within the Hispanic American community often reflect long-held cultural traditions and religious beliefs. Those aspects of Hispanic culture that make it so special and vibrant can also become problematic. She writes, "As Latin Americans, we face additional challenges when it comes to relationships. Our cultural values frequently clash with those of the mainstream culture, and we must cope with a unique set of social pressures." Since its publication, *Dr. Ana Nogales' Book of Love, Sex, and Relationships* has received generally favorable reviews.

Ana Nogales lives in Yorba Linda, California, and is married to Alex Nogales, a first generation Mexican American. They have three children. Nogales enjoys a close relationship with her parents, siblings, and large extended family, something that she believes exemplifies one of the greatest strengths of Hispanic culture.

Current Address: 3550 Wilshire Blvd., Ste. 670, Los Angeles, CA 90010.

Sources:

Cobo-Hanlon, Leila. *Los Angeles Times,* 1994.

Nogales, Dr. Ana, with Bellotti, Laura Golden *Dr. Ana Nogales' Book of Love, Sex, and Relationships: A Guide for Latino Couples.* New York: Broadway Books, 1998.

Spear, Jane. Telephone conversations and curriculum vitae from Dr. Ana Nogales, May, 1998.

Stier, Debbie, publicist. Press Release for *Dr. Ana Nogales' Book of Love, Sex, and Relationships.* Broadway Books, 1998.

Antonia Novello

(1944–)

International diplomat, former U.S. surgeon general, physician

In 1990, Antonia Novello was the first female minority to be appointed surgeon general in the United States. As the number one health advocate in the nation, Novello led a crusade against underage drinking and smoking, fighting especially hard against beer and cigarette advertisements

Antonia Novello

that seemed to target teen audiences. Now a public health advocate with UNICEF, she continues to stand firm on her beliefs and fight for what she believes in.

Novello was born in Fajardo, Puerto Rico, on August 23, 1944. She and her brother were raised by their mother, a school teacher, after their parents' divorce. Novello suffered from a painful congenital colon condition until she was 18–years old, when it was finally corrected. She has said that one of the reasons she became a doctor was to help others who were suffering as she had. Novello received both her B.S. and M.D. degrees from the University of Puerto Rico, where she was—as described by her teacher Dr. Ivan Pelegrina in the *Detroit Free Press*—"one of our brightest students." Ana Flores Coello appears to have been a major motivating force in her daughter's life at this stage; Novello told *Glamour:* "I wasn't allowed to work until I graduated from medical school because my mother felt that once I earned money I might be sidetracked by material rewards before I got to my real work."

Develops Early Interest in Pediatric Care

Novello did get to her "real work," beginning with an internship and residency in pediatrics from 1970 through 1973 at the University of Michigan (UM) Medical Center in Ann Arbor. She served as a fellow in pediatric nephrology at UM in 1973 and 1974, and she remembered this "first job" in *Glamour* as critical in her eventual decision to enter government work; she "learned how many people slip

through the cracks." Monitoring the progress of patients waiting for kidney transplants, Novello was dismayed at the number who could not be helped. Those cases in which she, personally, was powerless to help were especially affecting: "You become a true caring physician when you're able to share the pain."

In 1971 Novello was the first woman to receive the UM Pediatrics Department's Intern of the Year award. Her classmate Dr. Samuel Sefton, who is now a neonatologist in Kalamazoo, MI, told the *Detroit Free Press,* "It was difficult for women to be accepted [in the medical field] then, and I always was impressed with the way she handled situations." Barbara Lanese, head nurse (then and now) of the UM perinatal unit, concurred with Sefton: "[Antonia] was a resident when female physicians weren't as readily accepted as they are today. . . . She was a wonderful physician, and she was warm, friendly and well-respected. She was able to break the tension just by the kind of person she is."

In 1974 Novello joined the staff of Georgetown University Hospital in Washington, DC, as a pediatric nephrology fellow. She served as a project officer at the NIH's National Institute of Arthritis, Metabolism and Digestive Diseases in 1978 and 1979, a staff physician at NIH from 1979 through 1980, and the executive secretary in the Division of Research Grants at NIH from 1981 through 1986. She earned a master's degree in public health from Johns Hopkins University in 1982.

From 1986 until her appointment as surgeon general, Novello served as deputy director of the National Institute of Child Health and Human Development, where she nurtured a special interest in children with AIDS. Concurrently, Novello was a clinical professor of pediatrics at Georgetown University Hospital. Her colleague there, pediatric department chairman Dr. Owen Rennert, told the *New York Times* that Novello "is tremendously concerned about the medical and social problems of children and she has a way of drawing others into that concern." In 1982 and 1983 Novello was a congressional fellow on the staff of the Labor and Human Resources Committee chaired by Senator Orrin Hatch, a Republican from Utah. As reported in the *Washington Post,* Hatch later commented that she had "given good advice on several bills . . . including legislation on organ transplants and cigarette warning labels."

Accepts Appointment to Surgeon General Post

When C. Everett Koop announced in late 1989 that he would retire from the post of U.S. surgeon general, speculation about who his predecessor would be was particularly lively. During his eight-year tenure, Dr. Koop played an unusually prominent role in American public life, elevating the previously soft-spoken voice of the surgeon general to a forceful, opinionated one that demanded attention. Koop gained national prominence and respect by speaking out on controversial issues, sometimes colliding openly with the views of the administrations of presidents Ronald

Reagan and George Bush on such topics as sex education and the use of condoms to prevent the spread of AIDS.

This was a time of controversy and hostility between some scientists involved in public health issues and the Bush administration. Several candidates for top jobs at such organizations as the NIH, the Center for Disease Control, and the Health Care Financing Administration had withdrawn their names from consideration, complaining that their interviews had included questions about their views on abortion and on the use of fetal tissue in research (another controversial practice opposed by the Bush White House). Dr. Burton Lee, the President's personal physician, might have been a contender for surgeon general, but took himself out of the running because his views on abortion did not coincide with Bush's. In so doing, he echoed the administration's contention that it is important and appropriate that the appointee defend Bush's positions with conviction.

During Novello's two-hour interview, she was able to convince administration officials that her view on abortion was the approved one. Some observers speculated that Novello's reputation for cooperative, dedicated, and essentially low-key work made her a particularly desirable choice after the outspoken reign of Dr. Koop. Yet Novello claimed at a press conference covered in the *Washington Post* that "as long as the data can be trusted and is not just hearsay, I'll say it like it is. . . . I was never told I have to keep a low profile. I really intend to be like Dr. Koop when the data is there."

When Novello was chosen for the surgeon general post, many observers noted that following in the illustrious footsteps of Dr. Koop would not be easy. The first woman and the first Hispanic to hold the position, Novello brought with her a reputation for hard work and dedication, but her ability to fight for her convictions was unproven. But Novello claimed, as reported in the *Washington Post* several months after she was sworn in, "I'm for the people who deserve help . . . how I vote is not relevant. I think that as a woman, as a Hispanic, as a member of a minority [group]. . . I bring a lot of sensitivity to the job." Voicing a concern that echoed in other quarters, California Democratic Representative Henry Waxman told the *Post*, "I hope she's a fighter, because it's a bad time for infant mortality, for AIDS, for the homeless, for the uninsured, and this administration hasn't shown much interest in these problems . . . she can do a lot."

As head of the 5,700 commissioned officers of the Public Health Service, Novello promised to focus her energies on AIDS-infected children, smoking (she opposes particularly the glamorous portrayal of smoking in advertisements) and such women's health issues as breast cancer and heterosexual AIDS. Other areas of concern for Novello include teenage drinking, drinking and driving, and the stigma of mental illness.

Strives for Better Health Care

The position of surgeon general is an essentially public role, and Novello—who received several hundred invitations to speak per month—spent much of her time on the road, promoting the cause of better health. She talked with Louis Sullivan, Secretary of Health and Human Services, three or four times a week and met with him monthly. Sullivan, with whom Novello pledged to work closely, described her (as quoted in the *Detroit Free Press*) as "a very commanding woman who has a tremendous ability to reach out to communities."

Novello's own perception of the potential power and impact of her new job became more sharply defined, she told the *Washington Post*, when she visited her birthplace, Puerto Rico, shortly after becoming surgeon general: "When I got off the plane, kids from my mother's school lined both sides of the road handing me flowers. . . . I went to the VA hospital to speak. When the veterans saw my gold braid [she is a vice admiral in the Public Health Service] they all stood and saluted. . . . I realized that for these people, for women, I have to be good as a doctor, I have to be good as a surgeon general, I have to be everything."

After her appointment to the surgeon general post in 1990, Novello addressed and attempted to solve many of the problems which concern her, including teenage drinking. In late 1991, she met with some of the largest beer and wine companies in the United States and asked them to stop aiming their advertising at children and teenagers. "The ads have youth believing that instead of getting up early, exercising, going to school, playing a sport or learning to be a team player, all they have to do to fit is learn to drink the right alcohol," remarked Novello during a press conference covered in the *New York Times*.

In addition to her attempts to lessen teenage drinking problems, Novello also aspired to provide better health care for children, women, and minorities. As she stated in an *Hispanic* interview shortly after her appointment: "I hope that being the first woman and minority surgeon general since the post came into being—and the visibility the post confers—enables me to reach many individuals with my message of empowerment for women, children, and minorities." By the time she left the post in 1993, Novello had educated millions on how to live healthier lives, and she has not stopped spreading her message since her 'retirement.' After leaving government service, Novello began to work with UNICEF as a special representative for health and nutrition.

Current Address: UNICEF, 1315 31st St., NW, Washington, DC 20007.

Sources:

Anstett, Patricia. "America's Doctor Surgeon General Breaks Old Barriers." *Detroit Free Press,* October 30, 1990, p. 1C.

Cohen, Charles E. "Butt Out, Guido Sarducci! Surgeon General Antonia Novello, Your Sister-in-Law, Wants Everyone to Quit Smoking." *People,* December 17, 1990, pp. 109–110.

Cohn, Victor. "Novello: 'I Intend to be Like Dr. Koop.'" *Washington Post,* May 8, 1990, p. 17.

Glamour, August, 1990.

Hilts, Philip. "Alcohol Ads Criticized as Appealing to Children." *New York Times,* November 5, 1991, p. A16.

Hilts, Philip. "President Picks Hispanic Woman to Become U.S. Surgeon General." *New York Times,* October 18, 1989, p. A20.

Hispanic, January/February, 1990, p. 20.

Howes, Kelly King. *Dictionary of Hispanic Biography,* Detroit: Gale Research, 1995.

Leary, Warren E. "A Surgeon General Nominee." *New York Times,* November 2, 1989, p. B18.

"New Criticism for Heileman." *New York Times,* June 27, 1991, p. D20.

Parade, November 11, 1990.

Quindlen, Anna. "The War on Drinks." *New York Times,* November 6, 1991, p. A25.

Specter, Michael. "Woman Picked as Surgeon General." *Washington Post,* October 18, 1989, p. A9.

"Surgeon General: Abortion Foe." *Newsweek,* October 30, 1989, p. 84.

Thompson, Larry. "The Debate Over Choosing Health Officials." *Washington Post,* October 24, 1989, p. 6.

Who's Who of American Women, 1997–1998. New Providence, NJ: Marquis Who's Who, 1998.

Wolford, Tonya E. "Beyond Nursing." *Hispanic,* October 1991, p. 15.

Ellen Ochoa

Ellen Ochoa

(1958–)

Astronaut, aerospace specialist

A specialist in optics and optical recognition in robotics, Ellen Ochoa is noted both for her distinguished work in inventions and patents and for her role in American space exploration. Among her optical systems innovations are a device that detects flaws and image recognition apparatus. In the late 1980s she began working with the National Aeronautics and Space Administration (NASA) as an optical specialist. After leading a project team, Ochoa was selected for NASA's space flight program. She made her first flight on the space shuttle Discovery in April of 1993, becoming the first Hispanic woman astronaut.

The third of five children of Rosanne (Deardorff) and Joseph Ochoa, Ellen Ochoa was born May 10, 1958, in Los Angeles. She grew up in La Mesa, CA; her father was a manager of a retail store and her mother was a homemaker. Ochoa attended Grossmont High School in La Mesa and then studied physics at San Diego State University. She completed her bachelor's degree in 1980 and was named valedictorian of her graduating class; she then moved to the department of electrical engineering at Stanford University. She received her master's degree in 1981 and her doctorate in 1985, working with Joseph W. Goodman and Lambertus Hesselink . The topic of her dissertation was real-time intensity inversion using four-wave mixing in photorefractive crystals. While completing her doctoral research she developed and patented a real-time optical inspection technique for defect detection. In an interview with Marianne Fedunkiw, Ochoa said that she considers this her most important scientific achievement so far.

In 1985 she joined Sandia National Laboratories in Livermore, CA, where she became a member of the technical staff in the Imaging Technology Division. Her research centered on developing optical filters for noise removal and optical methods for distortion-invariant object recognition. She was coauthor of two more patents based on her work at Sandia, one for an optical system for nonlinear median filtering of images and another for a distortion-invariant optical pattern recognition system.

Becomes an Astronaut for NASA

It was during her graduate studies that Ochoa began considering a career as an astronaut. She told Fedunkiw that friends were applying who encouraged her to join them; ironically, she was the only one from her group of friends to make it into space. Her career at NASA began in 1988 as a group leader in the photonic processing group of the Intelligent Systems Technology Branch, located at the NASA Ames Research Center in Moffett Field, California. She worked as the technical lead for a group of eight people researching optical-image and data-processing techniques for space-based robotics. Six months later she moved on to become chief of the Intelligent Systems Technology Branch. Then in January of 1990 she was chosen for the astronaut class, becoming an astronaut in July of 1991.

Ochoa's first flight began April 8, 1993, on the orbiter Discovery. She was mission specialist on the STS-56 Atmospheric Research flight, which was carrying the Atmospheric Laboratory for Applications and Science, known as Atlas-2. She was responsible for their primary payload, the Spartan 201 Satellite, and she operated the robotic arm to deploy and retrieve it. This satellite made forty-eight hours of independent solar observations to measure solar output and determine how the solar wind is produced. Ochoa was the lone female member of the five-person team which made 148 orbits of the earth.

Ochoa's technical assignments have also included flight-software verification in the Shuttle Avionics Integration Laboratory (SAIL), where she was crew representative for robotics development, testing and training, as well as crew representative for flight-software and computer-hardware development. Ochoa's next flight was on the STS-66 Atmospheric Laboratory for Applications and Science-3 (ATLAS-3) flight in 1994. ATLAS-3 continued the Spacelab flight series to study the Sun's energy during an eleven-year solar cycle; the primary purpose of this was to learn how changes in the irradiance of the Sun affect the Earth's environment and climate. On this mission Ochoa acted as payload commander. All told, Ochoa has logged more than 480 hours in space. Starting in 1995, she worked as Assistant for Station to the Chief of the Astronaut Office, directing crew involvement in the development and operation of the International Space Station. She hopes to be a crew member on a shuttle mission involved in the construction of this very important station. Dr. Ochoa is currently a CapCom, the individual who communicates with the crew onboard space shuttle missions.

Receives Honors for Achievements

Ochoa is a member of the Optical Society of America and the American Institute of Aeronautics and Astronautics. She has received a number of awards from NASA including the NASA Group Achievement Award for Photonics Technology in 1991, the NASA Space Flight Medal in 1993, and the NASA Outstanding Leadership Award. In 1994, she received the Women in Science and Engineering (WISE) Engineering Achievement Award. She has also been recognized many times by the Hispanic community. Ochoa was the 1990 recipient of the National Hispanic Quincentennial Commission Pride Award. She was also given *Hispanic* magazine's 1991 Hispanic Achievement Science Award, and in 1993 she won the Congressional Hispanic Caucus Medallion of Excellence Role Model Award. She is the recipient of the Albert Baez Award for Outstanding Technical Contribution to Humanity.

Speaks to Hispanic Students as Role Model

Outside of her space research, Ochoa counts music and sports as hobbies. She is an accomplished classical flautist—in 1983 she was the Student Soloist Award Winner in the Stanford Symphony Orchestra. She also has her private pilot's license and in training for space missions flies "back seat" in T-38 aircraft. Ochoa also finds time to honor many requests to speak to students, particularly Hispanic American students. "I see it as an opportunity to talk about the importance of education and doing the best you can at everything you do," she said during an interview for *Latina* magazine. "Being a role model was certainly not my original intent for wanting to be an astronaut, but it's an added benefit."

Ochoa is married to Coe Fulmer Miles, a computer research engineer. They have no children.

Sources:

Biographical data on Ellen Ochoa, NASA Johnson Space Center, August 1993.

Fedunkiw, Marianne. Interview with Ellen Ochoa, March 18, 1994.

Hispanic Awareness Month Home Page. Available at http://www.ornl.gov/HR/hispanic.htm.

López, Nora. "La Primera Astronaut." *Latina,* May 1998, pp.62.

Missions Highlights STS-56, NASA Johnson Space Center, May 1993.

Margarite Fernández Olmos
(1949–)
Author, editor, professor

Selected writings:

La cuentística de Juan Bosch: un análisis estético-cultural. Editora Alfa & Omega, 1982.

Contemporary Women Authors of Latin America: Introductory Essays and *New Translations* Co-edited with Doris Meyer. Brooklyn College Press, 1984.

Sobre la literatura puertorriqueña de aquí y de allá: aproximaciones feministas. Editora Alfa & Omega, 1989.

Pleasure in the Word: Erotic Writing by Latin American Women Co-edited with Lizbeth Paravisini-Gebert. White Pine Press, 1993.

Remaking a Lost Harmony: Short Stories from the Hispanic Caribbean Co-edited with Lizbeth Paravisini-Gebert. White Pine Press, 1995.

The Latino Reader: An American Literary Tradition Co-edited with Harold Augenbraum. Houghton Mifflin, 1997.

Sacred Possessions: Vodou, Santeria and Obeah & the Caribbean Co-edited with Lizbeth Paravisini-Gebert. Rutgers University Press, 1997.

Overview

Margarite Fernández Olmos has devoted much of her writing and teaching career to awakening interest in Latin American women writers. As a professor in the department of modern languages at Brooklyn College in New York, she has been influential in the development of texts related to this oft-neglected group of writers. Her extensive research worked as a catalyst to bring Latin American writing to the forefront of the academic world.

Receives Valuable Encouragement from Parents

Fernández Olmos' parents, Peter Fernández and Virginia Ortiz, both immigrated to New York City from Puerto Rico. Her father, born in Ponce, had arrived in the 1920s as a teenager along with his seven brothers and sisters after they were orphaned. Her mother, raised in the Puerto

Margarite Fernández Olmos

Rican mountain town of Barranquitas where her family owned a small coffee farm, came to New York at the age of 17 to join an uncle who had come to the United States earlier. Peter and Virginia met and married in the 1930s. Even cosmopolitan New York was not immune from discrimination, Peter discovered. Returning from service in World War II, Peter was refused an apartment by a landlord who said he did not rent to "Spanish people."

Margarite Fernández Olmos was born February 24, 1949. When she was three, Fernández Olmos's parents moved her and her younger sister Jeannie to a new home in the small beach town of Keansburg, NJ, about an hour away from New York. Though they were met with initial mistrust by their new neighbors who were unsettled by the arrival of people of a different ethnicity, the family was eventually accepted, and they forged strong friendships in the community. Of her years growing up in Keansburg, Fernández Olmos recalled in an interview: "My mother's constant prodding and my father's exaggerated pride in his children led me to seek every honor, attempt every prize in order to prove not only myself but my family's rightful place in that working-class society."

Finds Inspiration in Bilingual Childhood

Fernández Olmos childhood included a series of visits to assorted aunts, uncles, and cousins scattered all over the Northeast. She and her sister found further inspiration in the achievements of some of their older cousins, including one who became the first mainland Puerto Rican to attend West Point. Others in the extended family had not fared as well and struggled to survive in some of the worst ghettos of the Northeast. Memories of her bilingual childhood include lazy days on the Jersey shore and hectic parties in Manhattan, where aunts and uncles chattered in Spanish and danced to the latest mambos of Perez Prado, while in another room Margarite and her cousins shared rice and beans and secrets communicated in English.

After finishing grammar school at St. Ann's in Keansburg, Fernández Olmos attended classes at nearby Red Bank Catholic High School. Although she credits the school with giving her a sound education, she said high school heightened her awareness of class differences while teaching her little about cultural differences. This all changed when she began studies at New Jersey's Montclair State College (now Montclair State University). There, she was introduced to the first of many Hispanic professors who would become role models and mentors. Although her first career choice was fashion design, she was forced to find an alternative because the college did not offer a degree in design. By default, she opted for a major in Spanish language and literature. Inspired by the success of her mother's cousin, Dr. Theresa Ortiz de Hadjopoulos, she decided to become a college professor. Her junior year was spent at the University of Madrid. She has said that this was the most rewarding of all her college years "and one that affirmed my cultural identity: a year in Spain quickly teaches a Puerto Rican that she is not Spanish, as we used to be called by many Americans before they became more ethnically aware."

Graduating cum laude from Montclair State in 1970, Fernández Olmos won a Ford Foundation fellowship. She was attracted to New York University's master's degree program in Madrid because it afforded her an opportunity to return to Spain. It was during her graduate year in the Spanish capital that she met her future husband, Enrique Olmos, a native Dominican who was living in Madrid at the time. After receiving her master's degree in 1972, she decided to pursue a doctorate at NYU. Back in New York, NYU Professor Haydee Vitali, who was passionate about the field of Caribbean and Latin American studies, influenced and shaped Fernández Olmos's career. A 1977 car trip through much of Latin America with her husband helped to confirm her decision to dedicate her research to the varied literatures and cultures of the region.

Joins Brooklyn College as Instructor

After working as an adjunct lecturer at a number of New York City area colleges and universities, Fernández Olmos decided it was time to bring some order to her life by getting one job in one place. Spotting an ad in the *New York Times* one Sunday in 1976, she applied for and landed the position of instructor in the department of modern languages and literatures at Brooklyn College, an arm of the City University of New York. She continued as an instructor until 1981, when she was named an assistant professor. In 1984, she was named an associate professor, followed in 1990 by promotion to a full professorship, a post in which she continues to serve.

For most of her academic and writing career, Fernández Olmos has concentrated on the exploration of Latin American and Caribbean literatures and cultures, Hispanic American studies, Afro-Caribbean culture, and the writing of Latin American women. Her very first book, based on her doctoral dissertation, examined the artistry of Juan Bosch, the former president of the Dominican Republic. A major literary figure, Bosch had been largely overlooked by scholars before the publication of her *La cuentística de Juan Bosch: un análisis estético-cultural* in 1982. Though they earlier may have been deterred by political considerations having little to do with Bosch's literary accomplishments, in the wake of Fernández Olmos's book more and more scholars began to weigh in with their own critical reviews of Bosch's work.

Becomes Fascinated by Latin American Women Writers

At the same time she was finishing her research and writing on Bosch, Fernández Olmos was becoming increasingly fascinated by the subject of Latin American women's writing. In collaboration with Brooklyn College colleague Doris Meyer, she edited in 1983 *Contemporary Women Authors of Latin America: Introductory Essays* and *New Translations,* a two-volume work they collected largely to fulfill a classroom need. There was a decided lack of translated material available for a special topics course on Latin American women authors the two had created at Brooklyn College. In the early 1980s, the subject had been largely ignored by scholars, leaving the two little choice but to create their own texts. The resulting work laid the groundwork for others to explore this area of research, which by the mid-1990s had become an established field of study. Fernández Olmos's personal essay contribution to *Introductory Essays* was a study of Puerto Rican authors Rosario Ferré and Ana Lydia Vega that generated critical interest in the work of both women.

A continuing passion for Fernández Olmos has been the literature of Puerto Rico. In 1989, a collection of essays that she had written on the subject over the years was published in *Sobre la literatura puertorriqueña de aquí y de allá: aproximaciones feministas.* Her essays, which examine the writings of both island-based Puerto Ricans and those who have emigrated to the U.S. mainland, highlight some of the similarities and contrasts between the two groups that through the years have been either ignored or dismissed. Her longtime interest in Puerto Rican literature stems from an invitation in 1982 to contribute an essay on Puerto Rican women writers in the United States to the journal, *Third Woman.*

Finds Reward in Collaborative Works

One of the unforeseen bonuses of Fernández Olmos's work with Doris Meyer was the discovery that collaborative research can be "extremely rewarding, productive, and even enjoyable." Working next with Lizabeth Paravisini-Gebert, she co-edited *El placer de la palabra* in 1991, which two years later was translated into English and published as *Pleasure in the Word: Erotic Writing by Latin American Women.* The two broke new ground in their exploration of the expressions of sexuality in the books of Latin American women authors. Other researchers had extensively reviewed eroticism in the literature of European and North American writers. However, not much effort had been made to examine such writing by Latin American women. The book's later offering as a Paperback Book Club selection gave it an audience beyond the academic and critical community. Working again with Paravisini-Gebert on her next project, Fernández Olmos translated and co-edited a collection of short stories from the Spanish-speaking Caribbean. Entitled *Remaking a Lost Harmony: Short Stories from the Hispanic Caribbean,* the product of their second collaboration was published in 1995.

When Fernández Olmos was invited to teach a seminar on Hispanic American writing for New York City English and Spanish high school teachers during the 1995-1996 school year, she once again discovered that there was no existing text "that could present the full history and complexity of this important American literary tradition." This set the stage for the research and writing that resulted in the publication of *The Latino Reader: An American Literary Tradition from 1542 to the Present,* a work on which she collaborated with Harold Augenbraum. A critical anthology addressing the entire range of the Hispanic American tradition, from Cabeza de Vaca to such contemporary authors as Oscar Hijuelos, *The Latino Reader* was published in 1997 by Houghton Mifflin.

Once again collaborating with Paravisini-Gebert, Fernández Olmos next undertook an exploration of the little studied contribution of Afro-Latino peoples to the national cultures of the Caribbean and Latin America. As far back as the late 1970s, Fernández Olmos had taken steps to broaden her understanding of the role played by African-based traditions in the culture of the Dominican Republic. Her interest in this important contribution, not only to Dominican culture but also to the cultures of many Caribbean and Latin American countries, has been reflected in her writing, her classes, and the cultural events she promotes. She has said she recognizes the "need to eliminate a Eurocentric view and acknowledge the durability and pervasive resonance of African and indigenous traditions in the definition of national cultures in the Americas." In 1997, the research of Paravisini-Gebert and Fernández Olmos culminated in the publication of *Sacred Possessions: Vodou, Santeria and Obeah & the Caribbean.*

Current Address: 105 Mimosa Ln., Staten Island, NY 10312.

Sources:

Amerman, Donald. Letter from Margarite Fernández Olmos, April 20, 1998.
Jaime, Collyer. "400 Years of Writing in 'Latino Reader.'" *Phiadelphia Inquirer,* May 4, 1997.

Dyana Ortelli

Comedienne, actress, civil rights activist

Selected filmography:

Little Treasure. TriStar Pictures, 1985.
Three Amigos! Orion Pictures Corp., 1986.

Shattered Spirits. TV, 1986.
Born in East L.A. 1987.
Marblehead Manor. Syndicated TV, 1987.
La Bamba. Columbia Pictures, 1987.
Alienator. Prism Pictures, 1989.
Dollman. Full Moon Entertainment, 1991.
American Me. 1992.
The Rockford Files: If The Frame Fits . . . CBS-TV, 1996.
Columbo: A Trace of Murder. ABC-TV, 1997.

Overview

Actress, comedienne, and activist Dyana Ortelli has appeared in such popular films as *La Bamba* and *American Me.* She has frequently made guest appearances on television programs like *NYPD Blue* and *Seinfeld.* Ortelli has also made a name for herself as a stand-up comic, regularly appearing at Los Angeles area comedy clubs. In addition to her entertainment work, Ortelli has been a strong advocate for the cause of Hispanic Americans in the entertainment industry.

Appears in Film and Television

Known to her friends as La Ortelli, Dyana Ortelli has appeared on screen with some of Hollywood's biggest stars. She joined Chevy Chase, Steve Martin, and Martin Short in 1986's *Three Amigos,* worked with Cheech Marin in *Born in East L.A.,* with Lou Diamond Phillips in *La Bamba,* both in 1987, and with Edward James Olmos in *American Me* in 1992.

In addition to her film roles, Ortelli has made guest appearances on numerous popular television shows, including *Seinfeld, NYPD Blue, Amen, Matlock,* and *Hill Street Blues.* She has appeared on the children's television show *Pepe Plata* on the Spanish language network Univision, and has hosted the program *Transit 2000* in Los Angeles. Ortelli has also been featured in numerous Spanish radio and television commercial voice-overs for the likes of Sears, Sprint, and Toyota. These roles, however, were often small, and Ortelli has felt limited. While she acknowledged for *Latin Heat* that "the quality of Latino roles is improving," Ortelli feels there is still a long way to go. Ortelli said that until recently, her choice of roles was limited to maids, hookers, and criminals.

Becomes Stand-Up Comedienne

With mounting frustration over the lack of quality roles for Hispanic American actresses, Ortelli turned to stand-up comedy as an outlet for her creativity and a platform for her views. She created the character Ramona from Pamona, performing regularly at comedy clubs. As related in *Latin Heat,* Ortelli viewed stand-up as a way to "make a lot of noise to wake up the industry." Complaining about Hollywood stereotypes, she added, "I'm 100 percent Mexican and damn proud of it, and if you're Mexican and you're an actor in Hollywood, you get to play all the un-people - undocumented, unemployed, uneducated, on-drugs." Ortelli went on to quip, "In fact, I played so many Mexican maids, I'd get up every morning and clean my neighbor's house just to get in character for the next big role!"

Ortelli is also part of the comedy group of Hispanic American comediennes known as The Hot and Spicy Mamitas, whose goal is to shatter stereotypes about Hispanic American women. Other members of the troupe include Sully Diaz, Marilyn Martinez, Lydia Nicole, and Ludo Vikaa.

Remains an Activist in Hispanic American Entertainment Community

Ortelli has been a vocal advocate for Hispanic Americans in the film industry. Ortelli described the problems facing Hispanic Americans in Hollywood to Marc Berman for *Daily Variety*: "The images we see of our people are frightening—they are criminals, maids, and prostitutes. Hispanics don't get cast as doctors and lawyers. We never get to play a significant and dignified role in our culture." Ortelli was active in the protest against the casting of a non-Hispanic American female to play the role of Mexican artist Frida Kahlo in a biographical film. Ortelli lamented to Andy Marx for the *Los Angeles Times*, "She's our biggest hero, a woman who symbolizes Mexican pride, and they didn't even cast a Latino in the role." Because of the opposition spearheaded by Ortelli, including the picketing of New Line Cinema's offices by women dressed as Kahlo, the company decided to withdraw its financing for the film, and the film was put on hold indefinitely.

Ortelli explained the reasons for the protests against the film, telling Marc Berman, "We're going ahead because [the film] is an example in Hollywood of the exclusion of Hispanics. Whether the project goes or not, they still are guilty of discriminating against Hispanics." Ortelli's group issued a statement saying, "Hispanics do not endorse the idea that an actor has to be from the minority he portrays. However, the entertainment industry has systematically denied Hispanics the opportunity to portray significant roles outside their cultural group. Now Hispanics are excluded from significant roles within their cultural group."

Nevertheless, Ortelli realized the irony of stopping a production that did use much Hispanic American talent and told the story of an important Mexicana role model. Ortelli told David J. Fox for the *Los Angeles Times*, "It was never our intention to stop the movie . . . I just felt . . . they should be careful about choosing the right actress." Ortelli stills hopes the film can one day be made, with Hispanic Americans playing significant parts. The activist work of

Ortelli and others, however, has produced positive results: Mexican film actress Salma Hayek has been signed to portray Frida Kahlo in this resurrected film project. The film is scheduled for production in late 1998.

In addition to her work for Hispanic American performers, Ortelli has been involved in other worthy causes. She served as a presenter at the Golden Eagle Awards, given in recognition of Hispanic American achievements in the entertainment industry, and has donated her time to the National Read-In, which supports donations of books to schools that serve disadvantaged students.

Ortelli has made the most of the roles available to her, with memorable appearances on stage, television and film. She has blazed a trail for Hispanic Americans in Hollywood, both through her talents on-screen and her relentless pursuit of equality off-screen.

Sources:

Berman, Marc. "'Frida' On Shelf." *Daily Variety*, August 18, 1992, p.1.
———. "Latinos Decry H'w'd Casting Practices." *Daily Variety*, August 7, 1992, p.3.
———. "Protest Still On After NL Drops 'Frida.'" *Daily Variety*, August 6, 1992, p.3.
Fox, David J. "Valdez's 'Frida' On Hold." *Los Angeles Times*, August 18, 1992, p. F1.
Green, Judith. "An Activist Director's Unlikely Role." *The Record*, September 9, 1992, p. D11.
The Internet Movie Database. Available at: http://us.imdb.com/Bio?Ortelli,+Dyana.
Kahn, Joseph P. "Waltham West." *Boston Globe*, August 3, 1992, Living, p. 31.
Kellner, Elena. "Is 'Evita' in Madonna's Future?" *Los Angeles Times*, September 13, 1990, Nuestro Tiempo, p.8.
"Kellogg USA teams up with Dr. Seuss and National Center for Family Literacy" *Business Wire*, January 14, 1993.
Latin Heat. Available at: http://www.dreams.com/content/base/issue1.03/LatinHeat/Ortelli.
———. *Latino Women in Comedy.* Available at: http://www.dreams.com/content/base/issue1.01/html/body_women_in_comedy.phtml.
———. "Letters to the Editor" *Daily Variety*, August 31, 1992.
Ortelli, Dyana. "Film Industry Discrimination." *L.A. Times*, September 19, 1992, p. B7.
Snow, Shauna. "Film Clips." *Los Angeles Times*, August 2, 1992, p.19.
———. "Olmos Film Tops Eagle Awards." *Los Angeles Times*, June 8, 1992, p. F1.

Ortiz Cofer, Judith
See Cofer, Judith Ortiz

Concha Ortiz y Pino de Kleven
(1910–)
State representative, rancher

The Grande Dame of New Mexico

A descendant of the Ortiz and Pino families, among the earliest Hispanic settlers in northern New Mexico in the seventeenth century, Concha Ortiz y Pino de Kleven was born in Galisteo on May 20, 1910. Raised at her family's Galisteo ranch, about 70 miles northeast of Albuquerque, she became the child her father groomed to carry on the family tradition of serving in the New Mexico state legislature.

One of Concha's ancestors, Nicolas Pino, was a leader of a December, 1846 rebellion just after the U.S. conquest of New Mexico. After the rebellion was put down, Nicolas vowed that, given time to learn a new language and a new form of government, a member of every generation of the Pino family would run for election to the legislature. And so it was, beginning with Facundo Pino, who was first elected to the House in 1855 and later became speaker of the House and president of the Senate. Concha's father served in the state legislature, and he asked her to be the family member of her generation to enter public service.

From a very early age, Concha showed greater interest in her father's role as a state legislator than any of her siblings. Her older brother, Frank, was busy running the family ranch while his father tended to legislative affairs. It was Concha who tagged along with her father to meetings of the state's movers and shakers. She sat next to him in the legislature for a whole session, building an interest in and enthusiasm for government. "I loved my father," she recalled in an interview with the *Albuquerque Journal.* "Dad understood me. I would dream of things that I wanted to do to save society, and he would support me. And I think he used me for his own dream . . . to have a son to be very active in all these things."

Another Powerful Influence

Another powerful influence on young Concha was her paternal grandmother, Doña Josefa, who was probably most responsible for shaping her social conscience. "My grandma, she was the brains, the heart and soul of the village," she remembered. "Talk about the miracle of the loaves and the fishes. How she supported so many people. . . . Anyone who needed a place to live was welcome there."

Though Concha early on began to develop a sense of responsibility to her family and her fellow New Mexicans, there nevertheless was a lighter side to her years growing up in Galisteo. She remembered fondly planting a wildflower garden, delivering soup in buckets to the needy, and climbing into bed with Doña Josefa to share dinner on a tray. One Halloween, Concha and some friends tipped outhouses into an arroyo, a move designed to take advantage of a federal government project to replace the old outhouses with newer models.

One of the least happy of her childhood memories is her recollection of her years at the Loretto Academy, a Santa Fe convent school where she spent the winters. "I never liked the convent," she said. "The sisters called me 'Cochinita' (little pig) instead of 'Conchita.' When she finally graduated from Loretto, the nuns' final words to her father were: "You've wasted your time and money, Mr. Pino. She hasn't learned anything."

With her father's financial assistance, Concha's first undertaking after leaving the convent was a vocational school to teach traditional Hispanic arts. Her father supplied a small house in the family compound and paid for a teacher. At first, she admitted, the school was more about having fun and less about teaching the arts. However, when her father cracked down, Concha began to get serious. The products students turned out in this "hacienda de genado" eventually led to the establishment of vocational schools for the arts around the state.

Wins Election to State House

Concha's turn to represent her family in the state legislature came in the mid-1930s. Running as a Democrat, she was elected to two three-year terms (1936-1942) in the state House of Representatives. During her second term, she became the first female majority whip in the country. She proposed legislation on bilingual education and helped earn women the right to serve on juries in her native state.

After leaving the House at the age of 32, Concha headed for Albuquerque where she signed up for classes at the University of New Mexico. There she met international law professor Victor Kleven, a handsome young widower whom she married in 1943. She recalled in an interview with the *Albuquerque Journal* that it was Victor's mind that first attracted her to him. "The thing about Victor was he had such a beautiful mind, such a fair mind. And it was such fun to open a book and say, 'Victor, I don't understand this. What's it all about?'"

In the early 1950s, after her father's death, family duty summoned Concha back to the family ranch. Under a court order, which emerged from litigation over the disposition and preservation of the ranch, Concha was named to operate the 100,000-acre property. The ranch was in desperate need of rejuvenation, a project that Concha attacked with a vengeance, installing new fences, new windmills, and a new spirit. By 1956, the ranch was prospering and Concha and Victor were finishing a home they had built there. Upon its completion, Victor came up from his teaching post in Albuquerque for a celebration. That evening, he died of a cerebral hemorrhage. The couple had been married 13 years.

After Victor's death, Concha leased the ranch and returned to Albuquerque, where she threw herself into the good works that had been such a big part of her life from her early days in Galisteo. Through the years she has served on the boards of the Albuquerque Symphony Orchestra, Amigos de las Americas, Lovelace Medical Foundation, the Newgate Project, the Conference of Christians and Jews, and the New Mexico Arts Commission, among others. She was appointed by President John F. Kennedy to the National Council of Upward Bound; by President Lyndon B. Johnson to the National Commission on Architectural Barriers; and by President Gerald R. Ford to the National Endowment for the Humanities.

Active in later years, Concha received a number of honors, including her installation in 1990 into the City of Albuquerque's Senior Citizens Hall of Fame and a Lifetime Achievement Award in 1992 from the Albuquerque Hispanic Quincentennial Committee. In 1993, she received the Board of Directors Award from the Historical Society of New Mexico, and the Archdiocese of Santa Fe awarded her the Papal Honor of the Holy Order of the Sepulcher in 1995.

Sources:

Barela, Margaret. "High Ideals Motivate Galisteo's Grande Dame." *New Mexico Magazine,* January, 1993, pp. 54-59.

Gomez, Eduardo. "Homenaje a Concha Ortiz y Pino de Kleven." *El Puente,* Spring, 1997, p. 7.

Meyer, Connie. "Concha Ortiz y Pino de Kleven." *Century,* July 15, 1981, pp. 14-17.

Seidman, Carrie. "The Grande Dame of New Mexico." *Albuquerque Journal Sage Magazine,* October, 1996, pp. 9-12.

Woods, Annie. "Birthday Celebration to Benefit Santuario de Guadalupe." *The New Mexican,* May 20, 1990, p. C-9.

P-Q

Lucy González Parsons
(1853–1942)
Revolutionary, activist, author, publisher, entrepreneur

Selected writings:

Life of Albert Parsons, 1889.
The Famous Speeches of the Eight Chicago Anarchists in Court, 1910.

Overview

A multidimensional pioneer, Lucy González Parsons not only was one of the first minority activists to associate openly with left radical social movements, she emerged as a leader in organizations primarily composed of white males. In her associations with anarchist, socialist, and communist organizations, González Parsons took up the causes of workers, women, and minorities, as well as the homeless and unemployed.

Lucy González Parsons's origins are shrouded in mystery. Much of the mystery is due to her own conflicting accounts of her place of birth, name, date of marriage, and national origins. The best record dating her birth indicates sometime in March of 1853, and her birthplace was probably on a plantation in Hill County, Texas. She publicly denied her African ancestry and claimed only a Native American and Mexican mixed heritage. According to Carolyn Ashbaugh in *Lucy Parsons, American Revolutionary,* however, there is a very strong probability that she was born a slave, and there is historical evidence that she lived with a former slave of African descent, Oliver Gathing, before her union with Albert Parsons in 1871.

Albert Parsons, a confederate soldier in his youth, was a radical Republican and was the subject of violent mob attacks both as a result of his politics and his marriage to a woman of darker hue. (Albert Parsons was white.) Texas's hostile environment as a Ku Klux Klan stronghold made the couple's departure imperative, and in 1873 they took up residence in Chicago.

Experiences Chicago Labor Unrest

Albert and Lucy Parsons arrived in Chicago during a period stamped by an economic crisis and intense labor unrest. The clashes between workers, whose material conditions had eroded drastically, and capitalists, who had enlisted armed support, were daily public encounters. Albert Parsons was a printer by trade, and the couple made their home in a poor working class community. Living among Chicago's impoverished yet militant workers was the catalyst for the Parsons' political transformation from radical Republicanism to radical labor movement activism. The Parsons had two children: Albert Richard, born in 1879, and Lula Eda, born in 1881. Lula Eda died in 1889 from lympodenomia.

Their initial association with the political left was through the Social Democratic Party and the First International, founded by Karl Marx and Frederick Engels. It was through this contact that the Parsons became aware of the socialist ideology of Marxism. Their ties to these groups, however, were short-lived, since both organizations were disbanded in 1876, the year the Parsons became affiliated. In the wake of the dissolution of the Social Democratic Party and the First International, they joined the Workingmen's Party of the United States.

Minority Socialists Emerge

The Chicago chapter of the Workingmen's Party (WPUSA) held many of its meetings in the Parsons' home. Albert, as a representative of the WPUSA, vied in the 1877 local elections for ward alderman. The year 1877 was a crucial turning point in the history of the United States. It marked the end of the Reconstruction era and the start of the first general strike ever witnessed in this country, the great railroad strike of 1877. While the WPUSA did not start the strike, it was the most active political party to lend organized support to it. It attempted to infuse the strike with socialist propaganda. Out of the strike and the political womb of the WPUSA were born the first minority socialists in the United States, Lucy González Parsons and Peter H. Clark. Clark had joined the Workingmen's Party in March of 1877 and was affiliated with the Cincinnati branch.

While the party's work around the strike had considerably enhanced its visibility and membership roll, a political division resulted in the formation of a new party in December of 1877, the Socialistic Labor Party. (In 1892, the name became the Socialist Labor Party.) The SLP organ, the

Socialist, became a means for González Parsons to express her views on the struggles of the working class. In addition to poems, she penned articles denouncing the capitalist class and describing the plight of the workers. González Parsons combined writing for the *Socialist,* speaking for the Working Women's Union, and motherhood. The Working Women's Union, founded some time in the mid-1870s, pressed women's issues before the SLP and demanded women's suffrage as a party platform item, as well as equal pay for men and women.

By the early 1880s, both González Parsons and Peter H. Clark had left the SLP. Clark departed due to the neglect of a specific program addressing the issue of black people, while González Parsons left to join the International Working People's Association. The IWPA was an anarchist organization; it called for the abolition of the state, cooperative production, and autonomy of workers through voluntary association. The foremost problem of the SLP, in González Parsons's view, was its reformism; that is, its peaceful approach to transforming capitalist social relations.

Advocates Violent Overthrow of Capitalism

The IWPA was open to all methods that would lead to the overthrow of capitalism. According to Carolyn Ashbaugh, she stated: "Let every dirty, lousy tramp arm himself with a revolver or knife on the steps of the palace of the rich and stab or shoot their owners as they come out. Let us kill them without mercy, and let it be a war of extermination and without pity." González Parsons had no illusions about the peaceful transfer of power, nor any belief in the peaceful coexistence of capitalism and labor. However, she did cling to one of the SLP's illusions, that racism would immediately be eradicated in class struggle. The SLP believed further that the origin of racist violence was not in racism, but in the dependency of minorities as workers.

Though González Parsons belittled the complexity of the relationship of racism to capitalism, she, unlike most minority leaders in 1886, called for armed resistance. According to Foner, she made the point, "You are not absolutely defenseless. For the torch of the incendiary, which has been known with impunity, cannot be wrested from you."

This statement is most revolutionary and radical, especially when placed in the context of minority political leadership. For example, the year 1886 was the high tide of Booker T. Washington's accommodationist posture. On May 1, 1886, González Parsons was a key leader in the strike at Haymarket Square, Chicago, for an eight-hour work day. The strike ultimately resulted in a bombing and the arrest of Albert Parsons and seven other activists. Lucy González Parsons attempted to rally a defense of the "Haymarket Eight" and made over 40 speeches in a tour of 17 states as part of this effort. In 1887, however, Albert Parsons was executed, along with three of his comrades.

González Parsons Founds Newspaper

The added tragedy of the death of her daughter shortly following her husband's execution did not discourage González Parsons's involvement in radical politics. In 1892 she started her own paper, *Freedom,* which covered such issues as lynching and peonage of black sharecroppers. By 1905, she became a founding member of the Industrial Workers of the World. The IWW's political line espoused the independence of trade unions and their control of the wealth and power. González Parsons insisted that women, Mexican migrant workers, other minorities, and even the unemployed, be full and equal members of the IWW. She also worked closely with William "Big Bill" Haywood and Elizabeth "The Rebel Girl" Gurly Flynn, both of whom later joined the Communist Party.

Organizing the homeless and unemployed, González Parsons led significant battles in San Francisco in 1914 and Chicago in 1915. The cause of political prisoners became a central focus for her in the 1920s and she joined the International Defense Fund. She was involved in the cases of Tom Mooney, the trade unionist, the "Scottsboro Boys," and Angelo Herndon. She was elected to serve on the national committee of the ILD in 1927. In 1939, she became a member of the Communist Party.

In 1942 González Parsons died in a fire in her home, which was subsequently ransacked by government authorities. Papers, books, and other sources that captured the long life of a veteran of the political movements of the left were removed. Lucy González Parsons's legacy was preserved, however, by the younger members of the Communist Party, for whom she had been a source of knowledge, experience, and political wisdom.

Sources:

Ashbaugh, Carolyn. *Lucy Parsons, American Revolutionary.* Chicago: Charles H. Kerr Publishing Company, 1976.

Foner, Philip S. *American Socialism and Black Americans.* Westport, Conn.: Greenwood Press, 1977.

Hine, Darlene Clark, ed. *Black Women in America.* Brooklyn: Carlson Publishing, 1993.

Katz, William L. *The Black West.* Seattle: Open Hand Publishing, 1987.

Parsons, Lucy, ed. *Famous Speeches of the Eight Chicago Anarchists.* New York: Arno Press and the New York Times, 1969.

Salem, Dorothy, ed. *African American Women: A Biographical Dictionary.* New York: Garland, 1993.

Perales, Mirta de
See **de Perales, Mirta**

Ana Maria Perera
(1925–)
Publisher, editor, author, women's rights activist, civil rights activist

Selected writings:

Martí and Education for the People. University of Havana Press, 1948.
Psychological Bases of Education for Democracy. University of Havana Press, 1950.
Status of Women in the USA, Mexico and Central America Pan American Union, 1953.
Freedom and Freedom of Choice. Oriente Press, 1956.

Overview

Ana Maria Perera has dedicated a long career to improving the lives of Hispanic women and other minorities.

Ana Maria Perera

In addition to founding the National Association of Cuban-American Women (NACAW), she served for some 30 years in top administrative positions in the U.S. government, particularly in the Department of Education. Perera currently serves as associate publisher and senior editor of *Temas* magazine, a Spanish-language publication based in New York. "I like to work in a quiet way," she said in a telephone interview. "I don't want to show off. You can do a lot and accomplish a lot if you don't care who gets the credit."

Perera was born June 3, 1925, in Santiago de Cuba, the daughter of Carlos F. Perera, a journalist, and Ana Moya Lora, an educator. She received her B.A. from Baldor Academy in Cuba, then attended graduate school at the University of Havana. In 1946, she received her master's degree in social work and, in 1949, a doctorate in education.

As a young woman, Perera embarked on a career in diplomacy. "I fully understood that if I prepared myself for a good position in the diplomatic service, I would have the opportunity to travel, experience other cultures, and learn new things that would help me serve my country and others," she said in the Coalition of Hispanic American Women's newsletter, reprinted in the *Congressional Record* on May 17, 1991.

Perera began her professional career as a member of the technical staff of the Organization of American States' Education Division (OAS). Then, from 1950 to 1959, she worked in Cuba's permanent mission to the United Nations. In the 1960s, she served as a correspondent for the German Press Agency and as an assistant professor in the Defense Language Institute of the Department of the Army. She married Alberto Garces, an office manager, on August 3, 1960, in New York City. The couple divorced in 1967. Perera became a U.S. citizen on August 11, 1967. In 1968, she began her work as a government official.

Improves Opportunities for Women and Minorities

For the next 26 years, Perera worked to improve opportunities for women and minorities in employment and education. "I believe that all issues that hurt women hurt minority women even more," Perera wrote in a personal statement for *Minority American Women: A Biographical Directory* compiled by Fisk University librarian Jessie Carney Smith. "We suffer double discrimination—once for being female and once for being a member of a minority group."

Founds National Association of Cuban-American Women

In 1972, Perera founded the National Association of Cuban-American Women, her favorite project. Unlike most organizations, NACAW opened up its membership to more than just its core constituency. Perera included women from all Spanish-speaking countries—not just Cuba—because she believes there is strength in numbers. "The more united we were, the stronger we could be," she said. NACAW encourages Cuban-American and other minority women to pursue educational and career opportunities. In addition to helping disadvantaged students attend college, NACAW conducts seminars on women's issues and presents annual awards to outstanding Cuban-Americans and other Hispanic leaders. According to Perera, NACAW currently has close to 6,000 members.

Administers Government Programs

As an administrator for such government departments as Labor, Employment, and Training Administration and Health, Education, and Welfare, Perera fought against discrimination in employment and education. She helped to monitor compliance with the Women's Educational Equity Act and to compile a report detailing the troubled state of education in America. She also administered regulations mandating equal rights for women in sports. The Department of Education recognized her work on four separate occasions. Perera even had her picture taken with former U.S. presidents Ronald Reagan and George Bush.

Perera has participated in some 50 other civic and community organizations, including National Conference of Puerto Rican Women, Americans for Justice on the Job, and Committee on the Concerns of Blacks and Hispanics. She also helped create the Committee for Cuban Political Prisoners. "My message to Hispanic American women is to advance as much as possible in the field of technology," she said in the Coalition of Hispanic American Women's newsletter. "It is no longer enough to pursue social or political science careers. In addition, women need to learn computer systems. However, above all, they need to protect the spiritual values that strengthen democracy."

Joins *Temas Magazine*

On May 13, 1994, Perera retired from the U.S. Department of Education. Her doctor advised her to just take it easy and slow down. Instead, she decided to work even harder as associate publisher and editor of the Spanish-language *Temas* Magazine. Begun as a small, pamphlet-sized publication in 1950, *Temas* has grown into a national magazine with a circulation of over 110,000. Many of its feature stories are reprinted in reading packages for high schools and universities. "As associate publisher and editor for *Temas* magazine, Ana Maria Perera has been able to communicate and touch the lives of her fellow Hispanic brothers and sisters," wrote a writer for *Hola! Hispanic Resource Guide.* "Mrs. Perera has worked tirelessly to en-

hance and change the lives of Hispanic women as we approach the 21st century." In addition to her work on *Temas* Perera has published four books: *Martí and Education for the People, Psychological Bases of Education for Democracy, Status of Women in the USA, Mexico and Central America,* and *Freedom and Freedom of Choice.*

Current Address: National Assn. of Cuban-American Women of the USA, Inc. (NACAW-USA, Inc.), PO Box 11012, Washington, DC 20008.

Sources:

"Ana Maria Perera: Leader for Hispanic Women's Rights." *Congressional Record.* May 17, 1991.
Axelrod-Contrada, Joan. Telephone conversation with Ana Maria Perera, May 1998.
Giuliani, Rudolph W. Proclamation: *Temas Magazine* 45th Anniversary Day, November 30, 1995.
Hola! Hispanic Resource Guide. Floral Park, NY: DanEd Enterprises, Inc., 1998.
"In Honor of *Temas Magazine* and Ana Maria Perera for Excellent Service to the Hispanic Community." *Congressional Record.* September 30, 1996.

Hilda Perera
(1926–)
Author

Selected writings:

Biografía de Lincoln. Instituto Cultural Cubano-Norteamericano, 1947.
Cuentos de Apolo, Editorial Lex, 1947, 3rd edition. Franhil Enterprises, Inc.; 1975, 4th edition, Editorial Everest, 1983.
Aspectos de La Voragine. Editorial Manigua, 1956.
Ortografía, Imprenta Lázaro y Hno., 1956, 12th edition. Minerva Books, 1977.
Cuentos de Adli y Luas. Editorial Lex, 1960.
Mañana es 26. Imprenta Lázaro y Hno., 1960.
Una niña bajo tres banderas. Editora Nacional de Cuba, 1960.
Cómo escribir para adultos recién alfabetizados. Comisión Nacional Cubana de la UNESCO, 1961.
La lectura (Colección manuales técnicos). Biblioteca Nacional "José Martí," 1961.
Ortografía básica. Comisión Nacional Cubana de la UNESCO, 1961.

Acentuación y puntuación (first three editions originally published in Havana, Cuba), 4th edition. Minerva Books, 1966.

Idapo: El sincretismo en los cuentos negros de Lydia Cabrera. Ediciones Universal, 1971.

El sitio de nadie. Editorial Planeta, 1972.

Cuentos para chicos y grandes. Editorial Miñón 1976.

Felices Pascuas. Editorial Planeta, 1977.

Podría ser que una vez. Editorial Everest, 1981.

Plantado (novel). Editorial Planeta, 1981, 2nd edition, Barcelona, Spain: Plaza y Janés, 1985.

Pericopín. Editorial Everest, 1981, new edition, 1997.

Rana Ranita. Editorial Everest, 1981 English translation published as *Froggie Frogette,* New York: Lectorum Publications, 1997.

(With Dr. Mana Fraga) *La pata Pita* (pre-primer; includes teacher's manual and workbook). Minerva Books, 1981, revised edition, 1995.

Pepin y el abuelo. Editorial Everest, 1982, new edition, 1997.

Mai. Editorial Santa Maria 1983.

(With Dr. Fraga) *La pata Pita vuelve.* Minerva Books, 1984, revised edition, 1998.

Kike. Editorial Santa Maria, 1984, English translation by the author's daughter, Hilda Gonzales S., and W. Hampton published as *Kiki: A Cuban Boy's Adventures in America.* Pickering Press, 1992.

La fuga de los juguetes. Editorial Everest, 1986.

Los Robledal. Editorial Diana 1987.

Mumú. Editorial Bruño, 1990.

La jaula del unicornio. Editorial Noguer, 1991.

Javi. Editorial Everest, 1991.

El burrito que quería ser azul. Editorial Everest, 1992.

Tomasin y el cerdito. Editorial Everest, 1992.

La noche de Ina. Ediciones Libertarias, 1993.

Perdido. Fondo de Cultural Económica, 1994.

El automóvil del abuelo. Editorial Everest, 1995.

El duende y el mar. Centro de Información y Desarrollo de la Comunicación y la Literatura Infantiles, 1995.

La media roja (published as part of *Un barco cargado de . . . cuentos*). Ediciones S-M 1996.

Volver a empezar. Rigby, 1997.

De encuentros y despedidas. Ediciones Cocodrilo Verde, 1997.

To Begin Again. Rigby, 1997.

Overview

Dr. Hilda Perera is one of the most prestigious Spanish-language writers working today. A native Cuban living in Miami, Florida, since 1964, she has written extensively on topics ranging from children's fiction to literary criticism to Cuban politics and the Castro revolution. Not only has she twice been awarded Spain's illustrious Premio Lazarillo—the Spanish equivalent of the Newbery Award—she received the Hispanic Heritage Award and was also nominated for the Nobel Prize in literature in 1993. In a recent interview she credits her writing career to the support provided by her parents and teachers while she was growing up in

Havana, Cuba. "My family was completely devoted to us—my sister and I—and they were very understanding about any vocation we might have," she said. "I didn't seem to show any particular talents for writing until I was about twelve. Then I wrote something and it caught the attention of the teacher, and from then on they started asking me to write. I won a very important prize when I was 17 in an international contest, and then I started writing on the same subject. Finally it came out as a book when I was 21 years old."

Earns Educational Opportunity through Middle-Class Roots

Perera's personal circumstances helped her gain an education that was more varied than that of many other Cubans. "Mine was an upper-middle class family," Perera explained. "My father was a Supreme Court judge in Cuba and my mother just was a mother, which was plenty. I went to an Episcopalian school because my mother was very keen on our studying English when we were young. She saw that it was most important for us to speak English and that's why she sent us to this private school." "The cathedral school prepared us very well; it was very tough," she continued. "I was really very well prepared for high school and college, and besides that I studied like a fiend. I enjoyed studying tremendously. My favorite subjects were literature (of course), and chemistry, and algebra."

Perera put her knowledge of English to good use in preparing her manuscript biography of Abraham Lincoln, which became her first published book. *Biografia de Lincoln,* she explained in her interview, was written specifically in order to win a scholarship from the Cuban American Institute in Havana. The scholarship allowed her to attend Western College for Women (now part of Miami University in Oxford, Ohio) in 1946. "I was very fond of Western. It was a wonderful experience," she said. "I loved having contact with so many people from so many different countries."

Perera had already been working in a literature program at the University of Havana for three years by the time she started at Western College. "I majored in English because they gave me credit for the subjects I had studied in Havana so I could complete the degree in one year, but it was an awful effort," she explained. "I had to make up all the English requirements in one year. That was quite tough, because I hadn't had English since the fifth grade. But I was grateful for the opportunity to make up for all those years that I had not had English. The instructors were very good, very helpful."

"As soon as I graduated from both Western College and the University of Havana," Perera continued, "I went to look for a job, and on the first day I got one with Ruston Academy. There I started teaching Spanish to English speakers, and later I became head of the Spanish department. Ruston Academy gave me liberty to continue to study—the headmaster was very understanding." Perera stayed with the institution until it was closed in 1959. Afterwards she gave specialist courses in education at the Library of Havana and worked for the Cuban National Commission of UNESCO until 1962. "This person who was very well placed in the Communist Party happened to be a friend of mine," she explained. "He offered me the secretariat of UNESCO, but I told him, 'Look, if I accept a post from you I'll have to cater to your taste and to your opinions, and I don't want that,' and he said, 'So why don't you take a post as consultant, and you will be totally free.' I accepted that. I wrote a book on alphabetization for UNESCO called *Cómo escribir para adultos recién alfabetizados.*"

Produces Cuban Revolutionary Work

Like many other Cubans, Perera initially welcomed Fidel Castro's overthrowing of the corrupt Bautista regime in 1959. She was honored by the Ministry of Education in 1960 when she won the National Children's Book Contest with her collection *Cuentos de Adli y Luas.* In 1962, however, she decided "that the revolution wasn't for me. Castro ruined so many lives. . . . I was all for the revolution in the beginning, from 1960 through 1961. . . but then I started seeing things I didn't like, and that's when I decided to withdraw. It was very painful. Many of my friends were in prison without writs of *habeas corpus* to set them free. Finally, I had written a novel about the revolution called *Tomorrow is 26* (*Mañana es 26*). After I had written it the police came to my house and took it away. Apparently they wanted *Tomorrow is Communism*, not *Tomorrow is 26*." In 1964 Perera and her family made the decision to leave the country. "My mother was still living at that time; my father had died. Curiously enough, she was the one that took the lead in leaving the country, because she said that it was not Cuba any more. I was very much against Bautista, but I never thought the revolution would turn out the way that it did," she said.

Leaving Cuba after the revolution proved difficult for Perera. "Being a writer I had been put in certain positions I had to resign from, and I had a great deal of trouble getting out," she stated. "First we went to Mexico for a few months. It was easier to get papers of residence in Mexico than in the United States. Since I was a writer, and the United States is very careful about which writers it admits, the consulate in Mexico went through the whole of my work to be sure that there wasn't any communism involved. But it wasn't too much trouble. It was worse getting out of Cuba." Perera wrote about her reactions to the communist revolution in Cuba in the novel *El sitio de nadie*, which, she revealed, was a bestseller in Spain for two years. It was also named first runner-up at the 1972 Planeta International Novel Contest.

Begins New Career in the United States

After living in Mexico for a few months, Perera relocated to the United States and began building a new career for herself as a writer and critic. She attended the University of Miami, earning a master's degree there in 1970 with a thesis, *Idapo: El sincretismo en los cuentos negros de Lydia Cabrera*, on the works of ethnologist Lydia Cabrera. Perera had already produced one book on Cabrera's work, *Aspectos de La Voragine*, which was published in Cuba in 1956. The new work "'Idapo' means 'syncretism'; it's an African word, because Lydia used to work on African cultures," Perera explained. "She was a very charming person. She was very funny, and I enjoyed talking to her. It occurred to me that since she had so many books and so many things I could work on, if I was already her friend then I could get more out of her."

Although Perera had published several collections of children's stories while she was still living in Cuba, including *Cuentos de Apolo* and *Cuentos de Adli y Luas*, her reputation as an author of books for children expanded greatly after her move to the United States. "I had two children and they started asking for stories, so I started making stories for them. That was the beginning," she explained. "Then I went on by myself when they grew up. They loved stories about animals, so I started with that, and then I went on to write about children. I kept those stories, and eventually they won the most important prize in Spanish given to a Spanish author, called the Premio Lazarillo. They gave me that prize twice: once for *Cuentos para chicos y grandes*, and the second time for a book called *Podría ser que una vez.*"

Much of Perera's most recent work for children and young adults has concentrated on stories about children, several of which have been translated into English. "*Mai*, is for young adults and has been a best-seller in Spain; it sold over 180,000 copies there," she explained. "That's a lot in Spain; it's not anything here in the United States, but in Spain it's a lot. I translated it into English, and I've sent it out recently to see if I can get it published." *Rana Ranita*, translated as *Froggie Froggette*. is a fantastic animal story that, she said, "has been very successful in the Spanish version, especially in California." *Pericopín* was shortlisted as one of the ten best books of 1980 by the Catholic Commission of Children's Literature in Spain. One of the most popular of her English translations is the story called *Kike* in its Spanish version and *Kiki: A Cuban Boy's Adventures in America* in English translation. It tells the story of a young boy and his brother and cousins who find themselves refugees in the United States without the ability to speak the language or the skills to survive in the society. "It was based on the experiences of many of the boys I knew who had come by themselves," Perera explained. "It was quite a tragic experience."

Gains Honors and Recognition for Her Work

Besides fiction, Perera has also published texts and workbooks designed to teach Spanish to young children.

Working with Dr. Mana Fraga, she created *La pata Pita* and *La pata Pita vuelve,* two of the most popular Spanish-language pre-primers in the Americas. They have been used extensively in public schools throughout the United States and in Puerto Rico. They are also the subject of a special education thesis that studies their effectiveness in teaching children in regular and advanced-learning courses to read. Since their original publication in the early 1980s, the books have gone through several editions. Although both *La pata Pita* and *La pata Pita vuelve* are published in the United States, "practically all my works have been published in Spain," Perera explained. "Spain offered me the opportunity. When you win a prize like the Premio Lazarillo, all the doors are open, and I decided to take advantage of that."

Many of Perera's works have been nominated or have received other honors, including runner-up awards in the Planeta International Novel Contest for *El sitio de nadie* in 1972, *Felices Pascuas* in 1977, and *Los Robledal* in 1986. *Los Robledal* was also runner-up at the 1987 Novedades Diana International Novel Contest in Mexico. Her best-known honors, however, came in 1992 and 1993. In July of 1992 she received a special prize from the Instituto de Cultura de Sur de la Florida for her literary achievements. In that same month Xavier Suárez, the mayor of the city of Miami, honored Perera with a special certificate in recognition of her contributions to children's literature. At the same time Stephen P. Clark, the Commissioner of Florida, proclaimed Hilda Perera Day, partly in celebration and recognition of Perera's many prizes and awards, but also to honor her textbooks that are used in the Florida public schools. In 1993, she explained, "ten professors nominated me for a Nobel Prize for my body of work. It was the same year I received the Spanish Heritage award and, although I didn't really expect anything of it, I was very honored that they thought of me. It was very exciting."

Current Address: 8371 SW 5th St., Miami, FL 33144.

Sources:

"Review of *Froggie, Froggette.*" *Publishers Weekly,* May 26, 1997, pp. 85-86.
"Review of *Kiki: A Cuban Boy's Adventures in America.*" *Booklist,* December 15, 1992, pp. 738-39.
"Review of *Kiki: A Cuban Boy's Adventures in America.*" *School Library Journal,* February, 1993, p. 94.
Schon, Isabel, ed. *Contemporary Spanish-Speaking Writers and Illustrators for Children and Young Adults: A Biographical Dictionary.* Westport, CT: Greenwood Press, 1994.
Shepherd, Kenneth R. Telephone interview with Hilda Perera, April 6, 1998.

Edith A. Perez
(1956–)
Physician, cancer researcher, medical manager, lecturer

Dr. Edith A. Perez is a distinguished physician and leader in clinical breast cancer research. She heads the hematology/oncology program at the Mayo Clinic in Jacksonville, FL. Her commitment to eradicating cancer through new and better treatments has earned her a place with today's top medical researchers.

Born April 30, 1956, in Humacao, Puerto Rico, the daughter of Ruben Perez, a grocery store clerk, and Edith Maldonado, a librarian, Perez recalls a quiet childhood filled with the pleasure of reading. Shortly before Perez entered college at age 16, her grandmother died of a heart attack. It was then that Perez decided she wanted to be a physician. "I thought if I had been a doctor, I could have saved her," she reflected in a telephone interview. At the same time, Perez was becoming aware of the problems people with cancer faced. "Patients with cancer usually had a very poor prognosis," she said. "And at that time there wasn't even much doctors could do to provide symptomat-

Edith A. Perez

ic relief. I decided I wanted to tackle this problem—to go to medical school in order to treat and cure cancer."

Studies at University of Puerto Rico

Perez studied biology at the University of Puerto Rico in Rio Piedras and graduated cum laude with a B.S. in 1975. She attended medical school at the University of Puerto Rico in San Juan, graduating in 1979 with an M.D. During her fourth year in residency, Perez decided to perform research in internal medicine at Loma Linda University in California. Her stint at Loma Linda persuaded her that she should pursue both patient care and research. "I liked the idea that I could research and work on developing cures for cancer. At the same time I liked the people contact of having a practice."

After working for two years as a general internist in the Division of National Health Services Corp. to pay back a government scholarship, Perez began to specialize in hematology at the University of California at Davis in 1984. For the next three years, she immersed herself in research and later became an assistant professor of medicine at the university. From 1989 to 1995, she also served as director of clinical oncology studies at the Veterans' Affairs Outpatient Clinic in Martinez, CA, and volunteered for one year in the Army Reserve. In 1994, Perez became an associate professor of medicine at the university. The following year, she moved to Florida and joined the staff of the Mayo Clinic in Jacksonville, where she currently serves as director of clinical trials in the division of hematology and oncology as well as the director of the breast cancer program.

Describes Medical Practice at Mayo

Perez considers it an honor to practice at Mayo, and according to her, it is one of the best hospitals in the world. She claims to spend about 80 percent of her time seeing patients and another 50 percent performing research. "I am working 130 percent of the time, and much of my research is done after hours," she remarked. She finds research fascinating, having helped develop new agents that eliminate the nausea and vomiting many patients experience after chemotherapy treatment. She has also developed a new combination of drugs that has proven to be highly effective in destroying breast cancer cells. Her study results have been submitted to several medical journals.

In addition to her research, Perez serves on several women's health committees and reviews manuscripts for a number of medical journals. Her membership in professional societies includes the American Association for the Advancement of Science, the American Society of Clinical Oncology, the American Association for Cancer Research, and the American Society of Hematology. She is also a fellow of the American College of Physicians.

Perez travels the globe to speak to both doctors and lay groups about new developments in genetics and breast cancer treatment. She gets satisfaction from educating other doctors about new therapies and alerting the public to preventive steps against cancer. Naturally, she enjoys witnessing some of her patients defeat cancer. She sees her roles as an educator, a physician, and a researcher as complementary.

Receives Numerous Awards

Perez has received a number of awards, including a National Health Service Corps scholarship and an American Association for Cancer Research-National Cancer Institute Travel Award. Yet, the award she for which she is most proud is a $500 Elks scholarship that she won while in high school in 1972. "To me that was a lot of money. It meant a lot to me. I felt that I had been singled out—that I was special." Today, Perez relaxes from her busy schedule by playing tennis, jogging, traveling, and going to the opera. She admitted, however: "Mostly I devote myself to my work. I love what I do. I feel very rewarded by it."

Current Address: Mayo Clinic, 4500 San Pablo Rd., Jacksonville, FL 32224.

Sources:

Boughton, Barbara. Telephone conversation with Edith A. Perez, MD, April 2, 1998.

Who's Who of American Women, 13th edition, 1983-1984. Wilmette, IL: Marquis Who's Who, 1983.

Who's Who of American Women, 14th edition, 1985-1986. Wilmette, IL: Marquis Who's Who, 1984.

Who's Who of American Women, 15th edition, 1987-1988. Wilmette, IL: Marquis Who's Who, 1986.

Who's Who of Emerging Leaders in America, 1st edition, 1987-1988. Wilmette, IL: Marquis Who's Who, 1987.

Minerva Peréz
(1955–)
Televison anchor, news correspondent

Minerva Peréz is making a mark in television journalism. Across Texas and parts of Arizona and California, Peréz has used the power of television to inform and enlighten viewers in the western states. While she has logged time at a number of key stations, she currently can be seen on KTRK-TV in Houston, TX, where she serves as a weekend co-anchor and veteran reporter. The unpredictable and often hectic schedule has not prevented her from playing an active role in the community, as she is involved

Minerva Peréz

in a variety of projects, most notably literacy and personal development programs.

Prepares For A Career in Television

Texas is home to Peréz, who was born in San Juan, TX, on October 25, 1955. She remained in southern Texas throughout her formative years. Peréz knew early on what career path she would follow, as she had a flair for verbal and visual communication. In 1980, she received a bachelor's degree in mass communications and Spanish from the University of Texas-Pan American. Her degree was a formidable combination, as bilingual reporters are a scarce group, but in high demand. Adding Spanish to her studies broadened Peréz's reporting capabilities beyond English-speaking subjects, and added an invaluable dimension to her reporting talents. Early on, she was rewarded for her dedication and foresight. For three of the years she was in college, Peréz received the Don Mallory Mass Communications Memorial Scholarship.

Peréz established a good foundation while in college and was able to land an internship with KUTV radio in Edinburg, TX. The real world experience combined with her studies helped to further prepare Peréz for life outside of college. In 1979, a year before graduating from the University of Texas, Peréz began her career as a broadcast journalist by serving as a reporter, producer, and news anchor with KGBT-TV, a small station in Harlington, TX. By 1982, she had already evolved into a celebrity, and was ready to make

the transition to a larger television market. Peréz relocated to San Antonio, TX, as a news reporter and morning anchor with KMOL-TV. A big opportunity came when Peréz joined KVUE-TV in the state capitol of Austin in 1984, giving her insight into legislative procedures. A year later, she accepted a position with KRLD-TV in Dallas.

Explores Career Opportunities

In 1986 Peréz left Texas to become a new reporter with KPNX-TV in Phoenix, AZ. She remained in that position for just one year before becoming a reporter and news anchor with KTLA-TV in Los Angeles. Her outstanding talent as a television journalist was recognized in 1987, when she received the Spot News Coverage Associated Press Media Award and a Los Angeles Press Club Award. Peréz's professional horizons expanded when she became host of a community affairs program. She proved so capable in her new role that she received an Emmy Award nomination for Best Host of a Community Affairs Program, and a Golden Mike Media Award for Best Series in 1990. While serving as a journalist in Los Angeles, Peréz covered many memorable events, including the Whittier Earthquake, the Rodney King beating, the visit of Pope John Paul II to Los Angeles, and the George Bush presidential campaign of 1990. She also tracked the "Hollywood scene."

Heads Back Home

After some six years of chasing stories in Arizona and California, Peréz decided to return to Texas, this time joining KTRK-TV of Houston in 1992 as a reporter and weekend anchor. Her continuing commitment to professional excellence and community service led to the creation of the Minerva Peréz Communications Scholarship by the Montebello Hispanic Coalition. Peréz's regional and national reputation continues to grow, with features on her life and activities appearing in publications, including *Vanidades, Nuestras Vidas,* and various textbooks profiling prominent Hispanic Americans.

Peréz continues to pursue career advancement while maintaining an active schedule of community service. She holds positions on the advisory and governing boards of multiple organizations, including Houston's Mayor's Council on Literacy, the Houston Read Commission, the Harris County Children's Assessment Center, the Morales Foundation, the Houston Association of Hispanic Media Professionals, and the Houston Independent School District's Primary Prevention Program (PPP). She also retains an honorary board position with the Puente Learning Center, a literacy program for children and youth living in the East Los Angeles area.

Current Address: KTRK-TV, 3310 Bissonnet, Houston, TX 77005.

Sources:

Kanellos, Nicolás. *The Hispanic American Almanac.* Detroit: Gale Research, 1993.

Eldridge, Grant. Curriculum vitae and other materials from Minerva Peréz, April 1998.

Pérez, Selena Quintanilla
See **Selena**

Perez Ferguson, Anita
See **Ferguson, Anita Perez**

Preciado Martin, Patricia
See **Martin, Patricia Preciado**

Victoria Principal
(1950–)
Actress, author, entrepreneur

Selected filmography:

The Life and Times of Judge Roy Bean, 1972.
The Naked Ape, 1973.
Earthquake, 1974.
Last Hours Before Morning (TV movie), 1975.
Vigilante Force, 1975.
I Will, I Will. . . For Now, 1976.
The Night They Took Miss Beautiful (TV movie), 1977.
Fantasy Island, ABC-TV, 1977.
Dallas, CBS-TV, 1978-87.
Pleasure Palace (TV movie), 1980.
Not Just Another Affair (TV movie), 1982.
Mistress (TV movie), 1987.
Naked Lie (TV movie), 1989.
Blind Witness (TV movie), 1989.
Sparks: The Price of Passion (TV movie), 1990.

Don't Touch My Daughter (TV movie), 1991.
The Burden of Proof (TV movie), 1992.
Seduction: Three Tales from the 'Inner Sanctum' (TV movie), 1992.
River of Rage: The Taking of Maggie Keene (TV movie), 1993.
Beyond Obsession (TV movie), 1994.
Dancing in the Dark (TV movie), 1995.
The Abduction (TV movie), 1996.
Michael Kael in Katango, 1997.
Love in Another Town (TV movie), 1997.

Selected writings:

The Body Principal. New York, 1983.

Overview

An actress in films and television, especially known as the star of the long-running television series *Dallas,* Victoria Principal also became a Hollywood producer, entertainment executive, and health fitness expert. She lives by two guiding principles for success: Be wary of flatterers who pretend to be friends and ignore rumors.

Discovers Show Business

The daughter of Victor and Ree Veal Principal, Victoria was born in Fukuoka, Japan, on January 3, 1950. She grew up, however, in the southeastern United States and attended Miami-Dade Community College in Florida. She soon found work as a model and began appearing in television commercials.

In 1972, Principal got her first movie role, *The Life and Times of Judge Roy Bean,* starring Paul Newman and Ava Gardner. This tongue-in-cheek Western was well received. From there, she played in *The Naked Ape* (1973); *Earthquake,* a 1974 film with Charlton Heston and Ava Gardner; *Vigilante Force,* about California oilfields, with Kris Kristofferson (1976); and *I Will, I Will . . . For Now,* a 1976 satire with Elliot Gould and Diane Keaton.

From movies, Principal went to television. She appeared in the popular series *Fantasy Island,* starring Ricardo Montalbán, in 1977. During that period she was also on the TV screen in: *Last Hours Before Morning* (1975), *The Night They Stole Miss Beautiful* (1977), *Pleasure Palace* (1980), *Not Just Another Affair* (1982), *Naked Lie* (1989), and *Blind Witness* (1989). But Principal really became a name and face to television audiences when she joined the cast of the mega-hit TV-series *Dallas,* remaining from 1978 to 1987.

Becomes Author and Fitness Expert

Being successful and beautiful was not enough for Principal, so in the 1980s she turned her attention to the fitness scene with the publication of *The Body Principal: The Exer-*

cise Program for Life (1983). The book offers a safe and effective 30-day diet plan, as well as a realistic maintenance program, for a trim, healthy body.

Principal's introduction to the benefits of exercise occurred when she injured her knee while playing football on vacation in Hawaii in 1977. Back in Los Angeles, she was told that surgery would be needed to repair her weakened quadriceps muscle, which is the muscle in front of the thigh. Hoping to avoid an operation, she consulted another orthopedic surgeon, who put her in a cast and warned her that she must limit her physical activities for up to six months. In order to shorten the "downtime," Principal embarked on an exercise plan. It worked. At the end of three months, she was walking in high heel shoes, although it took a year to play sports again. Now, Principal exercises every day and is happy to do so. She writes books, does commercials, and goes on television to encourage others to take care of their health and to keep their bodies fit and strong.

Still not content with her busy life, Principal entered the lucrative cosmetics market in the 1990s. With Aida Thibiant, well known in the Beverly Hills salon field, she created Principal Secret, an enormously successful skin care infomercial. This treatment line of cosmetics grossed some $40 million during its first three years on the air. Cosmetics sales account for some 10 percent of all infomercial sales in a single year, and Victoria Principal's contribution has been called the most successful skin care infomercial on television. In 1995, Principal, along with other well-known names in the fitness field such as Jane Fonda and Richard Simmons, was honored at the Fourth Annual NIMA International (formerly National Infomercial Marketing Association) awards. She was named Best Female Presenter for her "Principal Secret IV" infomercial, which also took Best Documercial.

Busy with fitness and cosmetics, Principal still is seen on prime-time television. In 1990, she starred in the TV movie *Sparks: The Price of Passion,* and in 1991, *Don't Touch My Daughter.* In 1992, she gave her viewers a few chills when she starred in *Seduction: Three Tales from the Inner Sanctum.* In 1993, a CBS-TV special cast her in the movie *River of Rage: The Taking of Maggie Keene.* Also, in the 1990s, Principal took on a new challenge, producing her own films in Hollywood.

Sources:

"Fitness Titans Jake Steinfeld, Richard Simmons and Jane Fonda, along with Victoria Principal, Big Winners at Fourth Annual 'NIMA Awards'." *PR Newswire,* September 21, 1995, p. 92.
James Gadberry, Rebecca. "Cosmetics loom large in the infomercials game." *Drug & Cosmetic Industry,* November 1994, pp. 46-50.
Who's Who of American Women. Wilmette, IL: Marquis Who's Who, 1988.

Guadalupe C. Quintanilla
(1937–)
Professor, organization president, community activist, chairperson

Guadalupe C. Quintanilla began life labelled as 'mentally retarded' because of the language barrier she encountered in an American school as a Spanish-speaking student. However, her determination to receive an education was unflagging, and she eventually earned a Ph.D. in education as well as a top administrative position with the University of Houston. Not content with overcoming the language barrier on her own, Quintanilla set up an influential Spanish language program within Houston's police and fire departments in order to improve relations between the city's workers and the large Hispanic population.

Struggles to Acquire Education

Guadalupe C. Quintanilla was born in the tiny village of Ojinaga in the Mexican state of Chihuahua on October 25, 1937. Known as Lupita as a child, she was raised by her poor but loving grandparents after her parents divorced. From a very early age, Lupita discovered that learning did

Guadalupe C. Quintanilla

not come easily to her. She was labeled a slow learner and had to struggle to acquire the education she knew was essential to getting out of the poverty into which she had been born.

When she was 13, her grandparents sent Quintanilla to Brownsville, TX, to live with her father. He enrolled her in school, where she found herself by far the oldest student in a first grade class, a placement dictated by her poor performance on an English-language intelligence test. Stung by the embarrassment and humiliation of her dilemma—a 13-year old surrounded by fellow students of six and seven-Lupita found she was doing little more in school than hanging posters and papers on the wall and escorting younger girls to the restroom. Miserable, she begged her father to let her drop out of school. Reluctantly, he agreed.

When she was only 16, Quintanilla married a Mexican American dental technician and settled happily into the role of housewife. Within five years, she and her husband had three children, two boys, Victor and Mario, and a girl, Martha. Content with her existence as wife and mother, it seemed at that point in her life to matter little that her education had been cut woefully short. Several years later, however, in 1967, Quintanilla became alarmed at the consistently poor grades her sons were bringing home from school. A visit to their elementary school quickly revealed the problem. The teacher labelled the boys 'slow learners,' and the principal said they were being hindered by hearing only Spanish at home.

Devastated to learn that her children were facing some of the same humiliation that had made her school days so miserable, Quintanilla resolved to do something to remedy the situation. She knew in her heart that her boys were as smart as other students, but they needed her help at home in order to do well in school. It was essential that she learn English so that she could help them with their schoolwork. She tried at first to read her children's schoolbooks, using a dictionary frequently to look up the meaning of words that were unfamiliar. But it was no use, she soon decided; as she said in a *Reader's Digest* article, "I needed to be taught."

Heads to College

When Quintanilla begged a high school English teacher to let her sit in on a freshman English class, she was told that her records showed her to be mentally retarded and therefore not eligible even to audit the class. In desperation, Quintanilla returned to the principal of her sons' elementary school for advice. To her surprise, the principal recommended that Quintanilla try to get into a course or two at Brownsville's junior college, Texas Southmost College. With no high school diploma, Quintanilla could not even get an appointment to see the college registrar. Determined, however, to plead her case, she staked out his car in the parking lot until he left for the day. Impressed by her obvious determination, he agreed to let her take four

basic courses. She was warned that failure to pass those courses would spell the end of this educational experiment.

And so, at the age of 27, Quintanilla began her pursuit of a higher education, struggling to balance her studies and her responsibilities as a wife and mother. She rode two buses to school in the morning, returned home at noon to make lunch for her husband, headed back to school for afternoon classes, and then took the two-bus trip home in time to welcome her children when they returned from school. She arose at 4 a.m. to do her homework. Despite the huge workload, she made the dean's list in her very first semester at Texas Southmost and discovered that she had an enormous appetite for learning. Not content with the offerings at the Brownsville junior college, she enrolled at four-year Pan American University in Edinburg, TX, carpooling there on Tuesdays and Thursdays for classes. On Mondays, Wednesdays, and Fridays, she continued to attend classes at Texas Southmost. At the end of three years, she had earned an associate's degree from Texas Southmost as well as a bachelor of science degree from Pan American.

Overcomes Stereotypes

In some ways, though, these were difficult years for Quintanilla. Despite the joy she found in the adventure of learning, she was nagged by feelings of guilt. In the *Reader's Digest* interview, she said, "The traditional Hispanic woman in me said, 'You're neglecting your family.' I knew I was breaking away from their expectations. But I needed this education—for myself and for my children." There was no question that her children's feelings for her were changing. They loved her as they always had, but they were developing an intense pride in her accomplishments. And as her education expanded, she brought what she had learned home to her children, trying to help them over some of the hurdles they had encountered in their studies. Before long, the boys were moved out of remedial classes and back into the mainstream.

After completing her studies at Texas Southmost and Pan American, Quintanilla moved with her children to Houston, where her father now lived. She planned to take classes in Spanish literature at the University of Houston. Before long, she decided to pursue a master's degree in the subject at the university. Because money was tight, she graded exams and worked as a teaching fellow in order to bring in some extra cash. At night, she taught a conversational Spanish course at the local YWCA. When she completed her master's program and received her degree in 1971, the university approached her with a job offer. The school planned to establish a new program for Mexican American studies and wanted Quintanilla as interim director. She rebuffed school authorities, telling them, as reported in *Reader's Digest*, "I don't want an interim post. If I'm going to take the headaches of a new program, I want to cure those headaches." She got a permanent position and soon was learning the ropes of administrative duties. As had been the case for most of her adult educational experiences, she proved a quick study. Not content with the training she was picking up on the job, however, Quintanilla soon decided to pursue a doctorate in education.

Rises in Her Field

It was an ambitious undertaking, and Quintanilla recalls the next few years as very tough indeed. Not only did she have her full-time administrative job for the university and a full academic load in her doctoral studies, but she also continued to teach at the university as well as two nights a week at the YWCA. She juggled all of these responsibilities without shortchanging her children. She made it a point to be at home to greet them when they returned from school each day, and she never missed any of the school events in which her children were involved.

After receiving her doctorate, Quintanilla in 1977 became the first Hispanic woman to receive a one-year fellowship from the American Council on Education, a fellowship that she served at the University of Houston as an administrative intern in the chancellor's office. At the end of her fellowship year, she was named assistant provost for undergraduate affairs. In 1981, she was promoted to assistant provost of the university, which at that time had a student body of more than 30 thousand. Always modest about her job, when anyone asks her what she does, Quintanilla usually replies simply, "I'm with the University of Houston." She maintains a healthy sense of humor about herself, which was apparent in her introduction of then-Vice President George W. Bush at a Houston speaking engagement in the 1980s. "My first language is Spanish, so sometimes I can get confused by English 'js' and 'ys.' I hesitate to tell you where the vice president attended college, because he may wind up having gone to jail instead of Yale."

Helps Her Community

One of Quintanilla's most significant civic contributions has been in improving cross-cultural communications among many of her fellow Hispanics with limited English skills and members of police and fire departments, particularly in Houston. During the late 1970s, she was struck by a newspaper report of a tragic Chicago fire in which a number of Hispanics had perished because they failed to understand the escape instructions that firefighters shouted to them in English. She realized that a similar tragedy could easily occur in Houston, which is home to a large population of Hispanics, many of whom speak little English. The need for improved communications between Houston's police and the city's Hispanics was particularly keen during this period because relations between the two groups were poor. The city's Latinos accused police of brutality and indifference, and their resentment boiled over into a riot.

Into this somewhat hostile environment came Quintanilla and her offer to set up a Spanish language course for Houston's police officers and firefighters. She argued that such a program would help improve communications between law enforcement personnel and the very large Hispanic population of the city. In making her case for such a program, she told police and fire officials, "Here's why we need the course. You tell me that most Mexicans are liars, but frequently they may be giving you the right answer to a wrong question. You pick up a man whom we'll call Juan Gomez Perez. You ask him, 'What's your name?' He says, 'Juan.' 'No,' you say, 'your last name.' He answers, 'Perez.' He's honest. But what you really wanted was his surname, which is Gomez. The computer gives you nothing about a Juan Perez, whom you know by sight and know has been picked up for driving without a license. 'He lied,' you say. But he didn't." Her arguments persuaded police who quickly agreed to her proposal. Firefighters later joined the program.

Many of the city's Hispanics were critical of Quintanilla's proposal to work with the police, suggesting that she was a "tio taco," the Chicano equivalent of an Uncle Tom. However, even obscene phone calls and death threats failed to scare her off, so convinced was she that her language program could reduce existing tensions in the city. Thousands of Houston policemen and firefighters have taken her language course, which has been praised by training officers from the Federal Bureau of Investigation. After her groundbreaking efforts in her community, she was named by President Reagan to the advisory board of the National Institute of Justice.

Continues to Contribute

Today, Quintanilla serves as president of the Cross-Cultural Communication Center of Houston, while continuing her academic career as an associate professor in the Department of Hispanic and Classical Languages at the University of Houston. Her cross-cultural communications program in Houston was cited by both the Department of Defense and the Department of Justice as the best of its kind in the United States. She was invited to provide similar training to members of the 16 law enforcement agencies responsible for security during the Pan American Games.

Earns Prestigious Acclaim

Quintanilla has received a number of presidential appointments and honors over the years, including a nomination in 1983 to the U.S. Commission on Civil Rights. In 1990, she was nominated by President George Bush to be Attorney General of the United States, an honor she declined in order to continue her service to the University of Houston. In 1991, she was appointed to the National Commission on Education Excellence for Hispanic Americans, a group she now serves as vice-chair. She has been inducted into both the National Hispanic Hall of Fame and the Hispanic Women's Hall of Fame.

Current Address: Cross Cultural Communication Center, 7115 Richwood, Houston, TX 77087.

Sources:

Amerman, Donald. Letter from Guadalupe C. Quintanilla, April 1, 1998.

Blank, Joseph P. "The Triumph of Guadalupe Quintanilla." *Reader's Digest,* June, 1984, pp. 2-6.
Kanellos, Nicolás, ed. "Guadalupe C. Quintanilla." *The Hispanic-American Almanac.* Detroit: Gale Research Inc., 1993, p. 734.

Quintanilla-Pérez, Selena
See **Selena**

R

Carmen Ramos
(1961–)
Entrepreneur, business executive, consultant

Carmen Ramos is founder and chief executive officer of Quality Management Resources, Inc. (QMRI), a Washington, DC-based corporation serving organizations in the development of long-term market and management strategic planning. QMRI's clients include local and federal government agencies, non-profit organizations, and multinational corporations. "The greatest satisfaction of my line of work is the ability to cultivate a more effective and dynamic working environment that produces better results," Ramos explained in a telephone interview. "In looking at today's ever-changing environment, management is faced with continuous challenges." In her job, she provides the assistance necessary for businesses and agencies to carry through long-term strategies and optimize their business potential. In a rapidly changing corporate culture, the decisions made by the business community today will have far-reaching impact on the global economy. Ramos, without question, is playing a key role in defining the economic role of these agencies and companies well into the 21st-century.

Credits Success to Family

Ramos' success story begins in Arecibo, Puerto Rico, where she was born in 1961, and continues in Florida, where she was raised. Her father, William, was a chef. Her mother, Rosalina, worked as a cashier at an elementary school. Ramos credits much of her success to her upbringing, which she said was "full of love and tough expectations." The benefits of this early environment are also enjoyed by her brother, William A. Ramos, a legislative aide to the commissioner of Dade County, FL, and her sister Marisol O. Ramos, assistant to the chief of staff for the mayor of Rochester, NY.

Ramos' early dreams were to become a jazz singer, but she set that aside and attended Barry University in Miami, FL. (She still hopes to someday sing in small jazz clubs just for the fun of it.) While at the university, Ramos majored in management. During her formal training, Ramos began to form opinions about how best to address issues of management consulting and marketing educational programs. Early on, she believed that the focus should be on the overall management of a system and not just bottom-line financial results. All too often, corporate America implemented short-term strategies that successfully boosted quarterly-profits, but did little to contribute to the overall health and long-term growth of the business. Ramos desired to change this corporate strategy by recommending training programs that include the works of such management and productivity gurus as Dr. W.E. Deming, Peter Drucker, Peter Senge, and Stephen Covey, to name a few.

After graduating from college in 1983, Ramos joined the Miami office of Citibank/Citicorp as a loan assistant. Two years later, she was promoted to account executive at Citibank International's personal banking division. In that position, she managed the personal banking investments of customers from Central America and the Caribbean. Ramos feels that "hands-on" experience in the corporate world added significant value to her formal education.

In 1986, Ramos became director of quality, training, and marketing for Citibank's international personal banking division, and was responsible for implementing strategies to build profitability and customer loyalty. Her key activities included customer research throughout Latin America, staff training and development, and product and business development. "During this time I developed a keen sense for the critical success factors in changing the culture of organizations and creating employee-focused and customer-driven institutions. As a result, I started providing consulting and training to businesses—both public and private—interested in enhancing corporate competitiveness," Ramos said.

Establishes Her Own Company

Ramos' consulting activities motivated her to leave Citibank and strike out on her own. In 1991, she founded QMRI in Miami. The company has five basic corporate values that allow for successful implementation of organizational objectives. They include: identifying the best methods and strategies, both short- and long-term, in the entire process of transformation; applying years of experience gained through analyzing and solving similar problems for other organizations and adapting proven techniques to new situations; understanding the sensitive human situations that are often so crucial to the transformation of an organization and consciousness of the fact that improvement seldom occurs unless human beings are persuaded to appreciate how suggested strategies will ultimately affect and benefit them; taking the time necessary to fully concentrate on developing strategies that will meet the needs of customers and seeking to serve as a vehicle for clients to optimize their working environment while creating innovative methods to enhance the long-term objectives of an organization; and, finally, introducing new methods and techniques which create internal and external short- and long-term successes and providing support toward the creation of effective, far-reaching new solutions.

Moves to the Nation's Capitol

In 1992, Ramos moved QMRI's base of operations to Washington, DC, to be closer to her husband, Jeffrey Watson, who, at the time, was working on Bill Clinton's presidential campaign. Watson was later appointed a special assistant to the President for intergovernmental affairs. Ramos found life in the nation's capitol noticeably different from that of Florida. "Miami has a more 'fun' focus; though business is serious, the environment is much warmer and more open. Washington, DC, is about being serious and approaching business and life with a different kind of intensity," she commented.

QMRI's clients come from both the public and private sectors. Among them are Georgetown University's Center for Intercultural Education and Development, for which QMRI developed a curriculum and management system for professors who administer the program locally in Panama, Nicaragua, Guatemala, and El Salvador; the U. S. Department of Energy for which QMRI served as facilitator to an employee team in developing an agency-wide training plan and implementation strategy; and CAC Ramsey, for which QMRI conducted customer satisfaction interviews to assess satisfaction with service quality and evaluated customer related job functions in order to streamline processes. Other clients include the Colorado Public Schools, First Union National Bank, Metropolitan Dade-County, the Library of Congress, and Norwest Financial Mortgage Company. In 1997, *Hispanic* magazine placed Ramos as number 12 on its list of the top 100 Hispanic entrepreneurs. According to *Hispanic,* QMRI's revenues climbed from $275,000 in 1995 to $650,000 in 1996, representing a growth rate of 136 percent.

Ramos explained that "my being Hispanic is something that is embedded in everything that I do. I am tremendously proud of being a Puerto Rican woman and can see how my culture, its values, and traditions, have helped me shape who I am and how I think. I believe my company may provide the same services if it were run by a non-Hispanic, but it would not have the same flair, intensity, or multicultural/international focus." Her work has not gone unnoticed. Ramos was the 1998 president-elect and 1999 president of the Greater Washington Ibero-American Chamber of Commerce.

Ramos and her husband, who is president of J. Watson and Company, a governmental relations and economic development consulting firm, reside in Washington, DC, with their two sons, Alejandro and Ariel. In her spare time, Ramos enjoys reading, singing, music, art, and learning languages. She is a volunteer consultant to the National Women's Business Center in Washington, DC, where she provides training sessions and counseling on business planning for women interested in starting their own businesses. She has also taught mid-level management at Georgetown University. Ramos told *Hispanic* magazine, "I have maintained the undeniable belief that if I have perseverance, I will learn what I need to learn and meet the people I need to meet to make my goals a reality."

Current Address: Quality Management Resources, Inc., 1400 16th St., NW, Ste. 210, Washington, DC 20036.

Sources:

Hispanic, April 1997, p. 30.

Kalfatovic, Mary. Telephone interview with Carmen Ramos, 1998.

Romo, Carlos. "Ten Who Dared: Hispanic Entrepreneurs Who Have Succeeded Against the Odds." *Hispanic* November 30, 1996, p. 30.

Katherine Quintana Ranck
(1942–)
Author, organization executive

Selected writings:

Portrait of Doña Elena. Tonatiuh-Quinto Sol, 1982.

Overview

Narrative description is Katherine Quintana Ranck's greatest asset as a writer. Her works powerfully preserve a fast-disappearing traditional lifestyle once typical in the villages of rural New Mexico. The last of eleven children, she was born Katherine Quintana on October 4, 1942 in Santa Fe to Ramón Trujillo Quintana and Lebradita Romero Quintana. Her maternal grandmother, Sofia Madrid Romero, was the inspiration for Ranck's first published work, *Portrait of Doña Elena* (1982). As a young girl, Ranck was an avid reader, pulling books at random from library shelves and thus discovering the classics by accident. Her years at Leah Harvey Junior High School in Santa Fe were vital in her formation as a writer, due to the influence and encouragement of eighth-grade teacher William Gill, who introduced Ranck to the formal study of literature and critiqued her first manuscript. Immediately after graduating from high school at age seventeen, she married James Phillip Ranck in 1960. In 1968 they moved to the San Diego area and now reside in National City, California. In 1970, James Ranck suffered a massive coronary. Subsequent medical expenses and an uncertain financial future sent his wife job hunting, with bilingualism as her only marketable skill. Working at various medical-related clerical jobs, she was willing to accept the least popular nighttime schedules, because these allowed her to be home with her two children in the daytime, when she was needed the most. Ranck enrolled at Southwestern College in nearby Chula Vista, California, to upgrade her job skills, earning an associate degree in child development in 1978. She is currently director of child development programs for the National City Public Schools and is pursuing a graduate degree at National University in San Diego. The Rancks have two adult children, Kimberly and Lance, and a granddaughter, Kimberly Marie. Katherine Quintana Ranck's favorite pastimes include visiting small galleries that display the arts of the Southwest and reading literary works depicting the beauty of rural New Mexico and its peoples.

Ranck's works are psychologically oriented whether narrated in the first or third person. Her fine descriptions are colored by the emotional involvement of the narrator and invite the sensory participation of the reader. Ranck's poetic prose tends to charm the reader into continuing with the work despite the lack of action, movement, or intricate story line.

Portrait of Doña Elena evolved from a creative-writing class Ranck took at Southwestern College under the guidance of instructor Joan Oppenheimer. When Ranck wrote a character sketch of her maternal grandmother, who had died in 1967 at the age of eighty-nine, the family would not let Ranck rest until the details were fleshed out into a complete work. In writing the short novel, Ranck reached back into her fond memories of childhood visits to her grandmother's rural New Mexican home in the village of Nambé, and she synthesized them into her first published literary work. Ranck recalled sensory impressions of her grandmother's wooden stove, water well, the homemade pies and freshly baked bread in the old family home, as well as the warmth of an extended family living under the gentle protection of a revered matriarch. Ranck says of her novel, "Images were what I wrote, a portrait of the land and people I loved. The story line became a necessity, thin strands upon which to weave a tapestry." Protagonist-narrator Constance (Consuelo) Trujillo Sorensen is a Minnesota-raised artist who visits Nambé for the first time in search of her cultural roots. Persuading Doña Elena to sit for a portrait, Constance finds herself in a Hispanic environment that is initially uncomfortable, culturally and linguistically. Her emotional conflicts are resolved through the compassion of Doña Elena's family and the artistic and emotional support of grandson Roberto, a fellow artist and kindred spirit who leads her to a sense of artistic completion and personal well-being. The story is told through the eyes of an artist, thus conveying picturesque descriptions of the

land itself and of the traditional types who sit for portraits, representing a bygone era. The book is mostly in English with a sprinkling of Spanish terms that are explained simply. It can be enjoyed on a variety of levels and is appropriate reading even for young adults.

"Relics," published in 1984, evolved from a short-story contest at the Santa Barbara Writers' Conference in 1978. It is also an intensely sensorial work. Ranck explains, "In the short story 'Relics' I provide only the images; the reader is free to provide his own story. Perhaps that is why it took five years to find a publisher for it. No one wants to work harder than the author when reading a story." The theme again centers on internal conflict and a sense of incompleteness.

Much of Ranck's creative work is unpublished, most of it having been written for young children. On a regular basis she creates stories to be used in the instructional programs for the National City School District day-care and preschool centers. When still a classroom teacher, she often encouraged her students to create fiction orally, which she would then record and invite students to illustrate.

In her professional capacity as a child-development specialist, Ranck has written several articles for local newspapers, advising parents in matters related to their preschoolers. Her recent promotion to director of the program has added responsibilities, making her involvement in children's literature somewhat less frequent, although she can still manage at times to write stories for others to tell.

Katherine Quintana Ranck's publishing hiatus in recent years is due in part to her husband's heart condition, which has required two transplant surgeries, and partly to the demands a career in education has on her time and creative energies. She looks forward to the time when she can once again return to her literary endeavors and pursue the publication of several in-progress works.

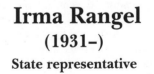

Irma Rangel
(1931–)
State representative

Irma Rangel is the first Mexican American woman elected to the Texas House of Representatives and the first Mexican American woman to serve as chair of the Mexican American Legislative Caucus, as well as chair of the House Committee on Higher Education. In 1969, when she graduated from law school, she was only the sixth Mexican American woman licensed to practice law in the nation. In 1977

Irma Rangel

and 1979, President Jimmy Carter appointed her to the Judicial Nominating Panel for the U.S. Court of Appeals. Rangel is a tireless advocate for the disadvantaged, and her work has been recognized by numerous civic groups.

Learns From Example

Rangel remembers her early life well, especially her parents Presciliano and Herminia Rangel. Both were orphaned at an early age: Presciliano at 5 and Herminia at 11. While poverty and illiteracy could have been obstacles too difficult to surmount, Rangel's parents overcame the deficits of their early lives and served as firsthand examples to young Rangel of how hard work could lead to success.

Rangel's father worked as a cotton picker when he was young. He never went to school and could not speak English, but he refused to be held back by his lack of education. He was determined to succeed, and he did, first becoming a barber's apprentice and later buying the store where he spent hours learning his new trade. He went on to expand into other fields, such as appliance sales and real estate, becoming one of the most successful and politically influential Mexican Americans in his community. Rangel's mother also became a prominent business owner, first selling dresses from the family car, then moving to the house, and finally owning the Three Sisters Dress Shop.

Success did not change the Rangel family, as they never forgot their humble beginnings. Her parents strongly be-

lieved in showing compassion for people who were less fortunate, less successful, or less able. To this end, Rangel remembers her father taking her and her two sisters to his ranch to pick cotton for a week, just so they would know what it was like to be field workers. That experience made a powerful impact on the Rangel sisters. They would not take anything for granted and, moreover, learned a lasting lesson: not everyone can achieve success on their own; some will need a little bit of help. For that reason, the Rangel sisters, Minnie Rangel Henderson and Olga Rangel Lumley, all entered public service of some kind. While many Mexican American girls married young and never considered higher education as a viable option, Rangel's parents continually stressed the virtues of education and independence.

At first, Rangel sought a professional career as a teacher, but her parents urged her to get a degree in business administration. She graduated with her business degree from Texas A&M University-Kingsville (then known as Texas A&I University) in 1952. Although she first took teaching jobs in nearby southern Texas towns of Robstown and Alice, in 1956, she accepted a job teaching English to the children of oil company employees in Caracas, Venezuela. After returning to the United States, she taught briefly in the Menlo Park Independent School District. During the summer of 1965, after returning to Venezuela to serve with the Teacher Corps, she decided to follow the dream she had been nursing all along.

Since childhood, Rangel wanted to become an attorney, but had held back because she was worried she would fail. As an adult, she became more confident in her abilities and so, at age 35, she enrolled in St. Mary's University School of Law in San Antonio, TX, and received her degree in 1969. From 1969 until 1971, she worked as a law clerk for Judge Adrian Spears in San Antonio. In 1971 she accepted a position as an assistant district attorney in Nueces County, TX—but only after she negotiated for a salary that was equal to that of males in the same position. During this time she began to form many of the views that would be the foundation for her political career.

When Rangel began work as a Nueces County assistant district attorney in Corpus Christi, she also joined the boards of the Corpus Christi YWCA and the Family Counseling Services. Through her job and her board positions, Rangel started to become aware of the social plights of impoverished families, paying particular attention to issues that affect women. These problems included abortion, which was illegal at the time, with many young women considering suicide their only alternative to childbirth. She also determined that the government's lack of respect for families on welfare in South Texas contributed to juvenile delinquency. Not coincidentally, much of Rangel's later legislation focused on education and the family. Even though she followed the Catholic religion, Rangel also became a staunch supporter of abortion rights.

Heads into Politics

After a year as assistant district attorney, Rangel decided to move her professional life back home and, in 1973, became a partner in a Kingsville law firm, Garcia and Rangel. Before long other politically active Mexican American women encouraged her to run for the state legislature in 1976. She ran for a seat in the Texas House of Representatives and won. She has since served as a representative for several Texas districts in a political career that spans over two decades.

During this time she has been an effective politician. Much of her legislation is designed to assist women, the elderly, migrant workers, and abuse victims. For instance, her legislation created family violence centers and helped to establish domestic violence and aggravated domestic violence as offenses for spouse assault. But when asked about the achievement of which she is most proud, Rangel points to her introduction of House Bill 1755 that she designed to provide employment and educational programs for mothers with dependent children. More than just a quick fix, Rangel's vision was a way to help break multigenerational cycles of poverty and help families get off welfare.

Work Receives Honors

Some of the honors and awards she has won include: Selection as a Fellow of the State Bar of Texas in 1984; induction into the Texas Women's Hall of Fame in 1994 by Texas governor Ann Richards; "Legislator of the Year," awarded by the Mexican American Bar Association in El Paso, TX, in 1997; and "Woman of the Year," in 1998 by the Texas Young Democrats. Whether serving as vice-chair of the Texas advisory committee of the U.S. Commission on Civil Rights, working as an attorney in private practice, battling for the environment, or serving her constituents, Irma Rangel has been a tireless supporter of human rights and a champion for those without champions.

Current Address: Texas House of Representatives, PO Box 2910, Austin, TX 78768-2910.

Sources:

Crawford, Ann Fears, and Crystal Sasse Ragsdale. *Women In Texas: Their Lives, Their Experiences, Their Accomplishments.* Burnet: Eakin Press, 1982.

Grant, Mary Lee. "Rep. Irma Rangel won't forget roots." *Kingsville Record,* July 11, 1993, p. 1.

"Irma Rangel announces for reelection." *The Kingsville Record,* December 21, 1997, p. 1A.

Rangel, Irma. Resume, 1998.

Ray, Steve. "Upbringing shaped Rangel's career: Kingsville lawmaker enters Hall of Fame." *Corpus Christi Caller Times,* January 30, 1994, p. A12.

Esther G. Renteria
(1939–)
Organization president, chairperson, civil rights activist

Esther Renteria has been a print and television news reporter, a talk show hostess, and a public relations executive. She has funneled much of her activist work through the National Hispanic Media Coalition, where she served as national chairperson. She has led the crusade for more positive and broader exposure of Hispanic Americans in all facets of the media.

Spends Early Years in East Los Angeles

Renteria was born in East Los Angeles in 1939. She attended East Los Angeles College, then received her B.A. degree from California State University at Los Angeles. Renteria began her career as a reporter for the *Alhambra Post Advocate* in 1959. She then moved on to the *East Los Angeles Tribune and Gazette,* where she was a reporter from 1962 to 1968.

Following her newspaper work, Renteria moved on to broadcast journalism. She became a news writer for KNX-TV in Los Angeles in 1968. She moved in front of the camera to host *Ahora!,* a public television program she also produced in 1969. Renteria then served as public information director for East Los Angeles College from 1970 to 1983. In 1983, she established her own public relations firm.

Founds National Hispanic Media Coalition

Renteria helped found the National Hispanic Media Coalition (NHMC) in 1986. She is currently national chair emeritus. The Coalition seeks to improve the portrayal of Hispanic Americans in the media and increase the numbers of Hispanic Americans working in all areas of the media. The NHMC fought numerous battles on behalf of Hispanic Americans. After failed meetings with Los Angeles television stations regarding their hiring of Hispanics, the NHMC challenged the license renewals of stations that failed to properly recruit and employ Hispanic Americans. Renteria questioned the stations' policies, pointing out to Jube Shiver, Jr., in the *Los Angeles Times,* "One Los Angeles station had no Hispanic employees at all. Others are doing really dumb things like advertising in English in La Opinion [a Los Angeles Spanish-language newspaper]." Although the Coalition was unable to prevent the stations from renewing their licenses, it did bring attention to the needs of the often-ignored Hispanic community.

Renteria is also concerned about the portrayals of Hispanic Americans on television and in film. She told Julie

Lew for the *Washington Post,* "We represent one character out of every fifty roles on television. We are two times more likely to be a stereotype than a white character, and three times more likely than a black." Frustrated by the proliferation of bad Hispanic American role models on television, and the effect such portrayals have on youngsters, Renteria indicated to Ray Richmond of the *Orange County Register* that Hispanic Americans are portrayed on television as maids, gardeners, drug dealers, pimps, prostitutes, gang members, and illegal immigrants. "None of those jobs requires a high school diploma, so we don't see ourselves as needing one."

Renteria is most concerned about the next generation. As she told Harry F. Waters for *Newsweek,* "Television tells children where they are in society. If you're not on TV, you're not important. And right now, we're still very unimportant." Renteria thinks visibility of Hispanics on television is important because Hispanic children "need the self-esteem of seeing themselves on TV," while non-Hispanic children "need to see [Hispanics] to know how to interact with them, to know we're all different but we're all the same, to eliminate the fear of the unknown."

Despite promises from the major networks, Renteria indicated to Greg Braxton for the *Los Angeles Times,* "It's the same old thing. Hispanic writers are not being hired . . . and Hispanic actors and actresses are not being hired." Renteria feels the only solution is increased Hispanic ownership of television stations and production companies.

Founds Rainbow Broadcasting

To gain a Hispanic American foothold in broadcasting at the ownership level, Renteria was one of the founders and president of Rainbow Broadcasting, an Hispanic group of broadcasters and civic leaders that sought to challenge several Los Angeles stations' right to television license renewal. The group was unable to obtain a station license, but their challenge did cause the Los Angeles stations to carefully evaluate their employment policies with regard to Hispanic Americans.

Plays Important Role in Media Activism

Renteria has constantly challenged the media to live up to its promises of egalitarian coverage for all groups. To this end, Renteria has led numerous protests against media outlets that have failed to do this. Renteria's groups have threatened boycotts of Hispanic American viewers during critical ratings periods to force Los Angeles stations to change their hiring and employment practices to more accurately reflect the make-up of Hispanic Americans in the community. She has fought to have offensive billboards removed in Los Angeles, to stop ethnically derogatory radio programming in Jackson, Michigan, to stop the airing of old "Dick Tracy" cartoons that negatively depicted Hispanic and Asian Americans, and demanded an

apology from radio disc jockey Howard Stern, after he made insulting remarks about slain Tejano singer Selena.

Renteria has also taken aim at Spanish-language media giant Univision. When the station moved its headquarters from California to Miami, Renteria voiced her concern to Maria Newman, a writer for the *Los Angeles Times.* She said, "If you are going to serve your constituency, you need to be where they are. . . . I don't see how you can be based in Miami, 3,000 miles away from most of your viewership." In addition, when a group of investors largely financed by Mexican nationals sought to purchase Univision from Hallmark Cards, Renteria protested the move. Renteria feared the deal would lead to importation of programming from Latin America, leaving little room for original programming that directly served the Hispanic American community. Fearing the move would lead to foreign domination of Spanish-language broadcasting in the United States, Renteria remarked to Kathleen Murray for a *New York Times* article, "Hispanic Americans need more about the Americanization process. There's nothing to help them mainstream."

Renteria married her husband Martin Renteria in 1971. They have two sons, Christopher and David. Renteria currently lives and works in Southern California.

Current Address: National Hispanic Media Coalition (NHMC), 3550 Wilshire Blvd., Ste. 670, Los Angeles, CA 90010.

Sources:

Braxton, Greg. "Networks, Studios Won't Discuss Minority Reports." *Los Angeles Times,* June 17, 1993, p. F2.

Brennan, Steve. "Hispanics Urge FCC to Prevent Univision Sale." *Hollywood Reporter,* June 19, 1992.

Crowe, Jerry. "Advertiser's React to Stern's Comments." *Los Angeles Times,* April 13, 1995, p. F2.

———. "Latinos to Stern: Apology is Not Accepted." *Los Angeles Times,* April 11, 1995, p. F2.

Elber, Lynn. "Non-black Minorities Don't Even Get the Chance to be Insulted on U.S. TV." *Toronto Star,* November 24, 1992, p.C6.

Lew, Julie. "Hispanics and the Hollywood Hustle." *Washington Post,* September 1, 1991, p. G1.

Murray, Kathleen. "Banging the Drums as Spanish TV Comes of Age." *New York Times,* April 10, 1994, Section 3, p. 10.

National Hispanic Media Coalition. Available at: http://www.latinoweb/nhmc/.

NHMC Wins Major Case Against KCAL-TV, Channel 9. Available at http://www.latinoweb.com/nhmc/nhmcnews/positivep2.htm.

Newman, Maria. "Move to Miami Is Matter of Time, Univision Says." *Los Angeles Times,* September 6, 1990, p. F1.

Parker, Donna. "Pickets Target Stern, KLSX." *Hollywood Reporter,* July 14, 1995.

Puig, Claudia. "Activists Fear Foreign Share in Univision."
    Los Angeles Times, April 30, 1992, p. 1.
———. "Latino Group Asks FCC to Block Sale of Univision."
    Los Angeles Times, June 19, 1992, p. D2.
———. "Study No Surprise for Latinos." *Los Angeles Times,*
    September 8, 1994, p. F1.
Richmond, Ray. "Are Networks Tuning Out Hispanic
    Culture?." *Orange County Register,* August 9, 1992, p. H4.
Robb, David. "Parody on Radio Ires Hispanics." *Hollywood
    Reporter,* January 5, 1995.
Shiver, Jube, Jr. "Minorities Target Licenses of 11 Radio
    Stations." *Los Angeles Times,* November 1, 1990, p. D2.
Shuster, Fred. "Pair of Mexican DJs Unite Youth of Bakers-
    field." *Albany Times-Union,* December 15, 1994, p .6.
Smaus, Robert. "Disney's KCAL Comes Under Fire." *Los
    Angeles Times,* July 5, 1990, p. F1.
Unterburger, Amy L., ed. *Who's Who Among Hispanic Ameri-
    cans.* Detroit: Gale Research, 1992.
Valle, Victor. "Latino Group Challenges TV Licenses." *Los
    Angeles Times,* November 2, 1988, p. 1.
———. "Latino Coalition's Bid for KTTV." *Los Angeles
    Times,* November 10, 1988, p. 1.
Waters, Harry F. "Listening to Their Latin Beat." *News-
    week,* March 28, 1994, p. 42.
Wharton, Dennis. "Mich. Station Draws Ire of Hispanic
    Org." *Daily Variety,* January 5, 1995, p. 40.
Who's Who in the West. Wilmette, IL: Macmillan, 1987.

Guadalupe A. Reyes
(1918–)
Community activist, organization executive

Advocate for Families

Guadalupe A. Reyes is an advocate for disabled people and their families, and the founder of two Chicago-based organizations which provide resources to help them improve their lives. She was born in 1918, the daughter of a migrant worker. A mother of nine of her own children, Reyes understood the importance of a supportive and caring community. Not finding the community she needed in Chicago, she set out to create one.

Recognizes a Need and Fulfills It

Reyes first founded Esperanza (Hope), a school for children with disabilities. Initially, Reyes created the school as a grass-roots effort which originated when her own son, whose early bout with spinal meningitis caused severe disability, needed an alternative to expensive private education. When she saw no options available, she decided to create a school for disabled children. Esperanza was founded in 1969 when Reyes held meetings for parents of handicapped children in a small office. Since then, the school has flourished. One year after the first meetings, the state approved the program as a tuition-free school for children with multiple handicaps. Now serving around 280 people, Esperanza School and Community Services provides intervention, job training, counseling, and support services, in addition to education, for both children and adults with disabilities.

Continues Community Service

In 1973, Reyes founded a second program for adults with disabilities called El Valor (Courage). El Valor's mission is to encourage independence in individuals with disabilities by helping them develop practical skills for daily life. With a staff of almost 200 full-time and part-time employees, El Valor provides community housing and bilingual and bicultural vocational training, advanced degree programs, and job placement for approximately 1,200 families in the Chicago area. El Valor has been accredited by the Commission on Accreditation of Rehabilitation Facilities (CARF) and has received numerous awards for its programs, including the Chicago Community Trust Titus Management Award, the Helen Cody Baker Social Service Communication Award, and the *Chicago Sun-Times* QUEST Award for excellence in education programs. It has also received the August W. Christmann Award for outstanding employment and residential programs, the "A+ Award" from the Department of Education for its unique program, and the Northern Illinois University award for outstanding contributions in educational outreach to minority communities.

El Valor also spawned a program called Tocar el Futuro, (Touch the Future) an educational model which demonstrates that people from an inner-city background "can achieve excellence as a norm and that the inclusion of children with disabilities in a regular classroom setting benefits all children" (El Valor Home Page). This program has allowed El Valor to create three educational centers in urban Chicago communities, providing early education programs for 1,500 children, enrichment programs for 6,000 family members, and advanced degree programs for 250 working minorities.

Accepts National Honors

Through the programs offered by El Valor and Esperanza, Reyes has heightened national public awareness regarding the importance of early learning for children, parental involvement, and opportunities for disabled and low-income individuals. In 1996, Reyes was recognized for this achievement by *Hispanic Magazine* with an Hispanic Achievement Award, which honors Hispanic Americans who have made significant contributions in their fields and have had a positive impact on the Hispanic community.

Current Address: El Valor, 1850 W. 21st St., Chicago, IL 60608.

Sources:

El Valor Corporation Home Page. Available at http://www.iarf.org/members/elvalor.htm.

Hispanic Magazine Online. Available at http://www.hisp.com/oct96/reyes.html.

Skalka, Patricia. "Make the Dream Grow!"*Reader's Digest,* July 1988, pp. 64-68.

Thelma T. Reyna
(1946–)
Principal, author, community activist

Thelma T. Reyna is a committed educator, an accomplished scholar, and an active member of her community. The principal of South Pasadena High School in South Pasadena, California, since 1996, Reyna has never strayed far from the classroom. She earned degrees in English and education, became, in the words of the eminent African American scholar Dr. Robin D. G. Kelly, "one of the world's greatest teachers," and went on to pursue a career

Thelma T. Reyna

in secondary school administration. Reyna has also published creative writing, including short stories, essays, and poetry, as well as a number of research studies and pedagogical articles.

Family Roots Are Multicultural

Reyna was born on June 2, 1946, in the small town of Kingsville, Texas, to Raul Clemente Tellez, Sr., and Mary Guerra Tellez, both civil servants. Her parents brought up their nine children with the help of an extended family, members of which sometimes shared their household. Reyna's grandmother lived with the family for many years. "My family life was turbulent, even though I generally consider my childhood to have been a happy one," Reyna stated in *Growing Up Chicana/o.* Though she is proud to call herself a Hispanic American, Reyna considers her ethnic heritage to be typically American. Her background includes Native American and Irish, as well as Mexican and Spanish. Reyna is third-generation American on her mother's side of the family and second-generation on her father's. She grew up in a Spanish-speaking household and began learning English in elementary school. "I highly cherish my bilingual, bicultural heritage," Reyna said. "I find that the older I get, the more I cherish my roots."

Studies and Teaches

Education played a formative and lasting role in Reyna's life. She attended Henrietta M. King High School in Kingsville and then went on to college at Texas A&I University. In May of 1968 Reyna graduated with a B.A. degree and a double major in English and journalism. She pursued her interest in literature by continuing at Texas A&I, enrolling in its master's program in English. She graduated in August of 1969, having also completed a minor in psychology.

Reyna began her career with her family's best interests in mind. When they began to look for teaching positions Reyna and her husband, Victor, who was also a high school teacher, had already had their first child, Victor, and Reyna was pregnant with their daughter Christina. They chose to work in California because at the time the state's teachers enjoyed the best working conditions and earned the highest incomes in the country; in Reyna's native state of Texas, both conditions and wages were rated among the lowest. Reyna's first job put to use what she had learned about both English literature and human psychology. She became an English teacher at South Pasadena High School, where she taught grades nine through twelve for the next sixteen years. Reyna made a passionate and devoted teacher and she has remained deeply committed to her community at large and to South Pasadena High in particular. In 1976 the California State PTSA honored her for outstanding service to children and youth. In 1982 she was recognized by Quill and Scroll International Honorary Society with a faculty award. She has also been remembered as an inspiration by many of her students.

Teacher Becomes Administrator

As Reyna continued to teach her English classes, she became increasingly interested in how the educational institution worked together as a whole. Between 1984 and 1986, she mentored other teachers at the high school. During this period, she was also hard at work on her second master's degree, this time in educational administration. She graduated from the program at California State University with honors in September of 1986. Reyna put her new knowledge of educational administration together with her years of classroom experience when she took her next position, that of dean of students at Blair High in Pasadena. Over the next decade, Reyna held a number of assistant principal positions throughout the Pasadena public schools. During the 1992-1993 school year Reyna acted as assistant principal of student affairs at Marshall Fundamental Secondary School, then took a job as assistant principal of curriculum and instruction at John Muir High School for the following two years. She returned to Blair High in 1995 to oversee its curriculum and instruction. In July of 1996 Reyna was named principal of South Pasadena High School.

Despite the fact that Reyna's active and successful career absorbed much of her energy, she has continued to pursue her own scholarly interests. Both reflected her passionate interest in the local school system. She has published pedagogical and educational articles in district publications and conducted independent research studies at the district level as part of her academic program. In August of 1994 Reyna received her doctorate in administration from the University of California, Los Angeles, with a specialization in curriculum and teaching studies. Her doctoral dissertation was entitled "A Comparison of Male and Female Public School Administrators Regarding Their Upward Mobility: Mentors, Sponsors, and Networks."

Reyna's writings are not limited to an academic audience. In addition to her scholarly studies, Reyna has published creative writing on regional, national, and international levels. Her short stories, essays, and poetry have appeared in anthologies, magazines, and journals. Reyna has published in forums that reflect her cultural background and interests, including collections such as *Growing Up Chicana/o* (1993), *New Voices in Literature, Language, and Composition* (1978), and *The Grito del Sol Collection* (1984). "Almost everything I have published is an account of something straight out of my childhood," she wrote in an introduction to her short story "Una Edad Muy Tierna, M'ija" in *Growing Up Chicana/o*. Referring to the death of her brother in Vietnam at age 18 as well as those of her beloved maternal grandparents, she went on to say that

"loss was a reality that colored many of my perceptions about growing up, and it was an inevitable companion to love."

Reyna lives with her husband in Pasadena. She is active in her community. She has sat on Pasadena's Human Rights Commission since 1996 and served as a city mayor's appointee on the Charter Reform Task Force in 1997 and 1998. She is also a member of the Association of California School Administrators and the Kiwanis Club. In his book *Race Rebels* former student Robin D. G. Kelly described as "simply unparalleled" Reyna's "extraordinary commitment to public education and to struggling colored city kids."

Current Address: South Pasadena High School, 1401 Fremont Ave., South Pasadena, CA 91030.

Sources:

Hardy, Sarah Madsen. Telephone interview with Thelma T. Reyna, May 14, 1998.
Kelly, Robin D. G. *Race Rebels: Culture, Politics, and the Black Working Class.* New York: Free Press, 1994.
López, Tiffany Ana, ed. *Growing Up Chicana/o.* New York: William Morrow, 1993.
Who's Who in American Education, 1988-89. New York: National Reference Institute, 1989.

Felisa Rincón de Gautier
(1897–1994)
Mayor, community activist, women's rights activist

Felisa Rincón de Gautier was the first woman to be elected *alcaldesa* of San Juan, the largest city on the commonwealth island of Puerto Rico. From 1946 to 1969 Doña Fela, as her supporters called her, led the city in a series of widely-publicized social reforms. "Mrs. Rincón de Gautier was a co-founder of the Popular Democratic Party, which led the island's transition from a rural to an industrial society, and a women's rights advocate," explained *New York Times* contributor Mireya Navarro. "With her trademark turban and fan, she visited the sick, sheltered hurricane refugees in her home, held a weekly open house to hear constituents' complaints, and had snow flown in from the states in the winter as a gift to Puerto Rican children." "She was scorned as a cross between Boss Tweed and Marie Antoinette by her enemies," stated a *Time* magazine

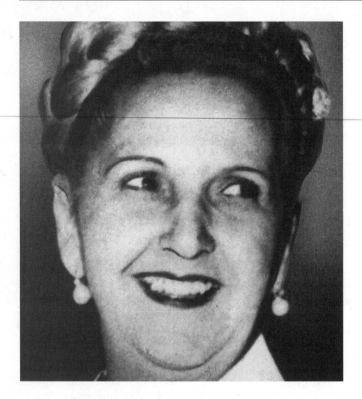

Felisa Rincón de Gautier

obituary, but, the writer added, she was also greatly loved by the poor people of the city that she served. Even after her death in 1994, she continued to influence Puerto Rican politics. All three of the candidates in the 1996 election for mayor of San Juan, for example, evoked the memory of Rincón de Gautier in their campaigns.

Born in Difficult Circumstances

Felisa Rincón was born in Ceiba, Puerto Rico, on January 9, 1897—only a year before Spain ceded the island to the United States as one of the conditions ending the Spanish-American War. Her mother, Rita Marrero Rivera de Rincón, died when Felisa was eleven. Her father, the lawyer Enrique Rincón Plumey, was unable to bring up his eight children by himself, and Felisa, the oldest child, left high school in her junior year in order to care for her younger brothers and sisters. After her father's finances improved, Felisa moved to New York City for a short time, working as a seamstress in a posh dress shop on Fifth Avenue. When she returned home, she borrowed money to start her own business and soon became owner of a series of several different retail stores, including flower and clothing shops.

In 1932 Felisa became actively involved in Puerto Rican politics. When the island came under U.S. control in 1898, the island's citizens were left in a political limbo. They were no longer Spanish citizens, but they did not have the rights of U.S. citizens either. Since then, the residents of the

island have been divided three political camps: those who want complete independence for Puerto Rico (autonomy), those who want statehood (assimilation), and those who want some intermediate position. In 1917, after much lobbying by the Resident Commissioner Luis Muñoz Rivera, the forces who favored statehood gained an important victory when the U.S. Congress passed the Jones Act, which gave Puerto Ricans U.S. citizenship. Women received the vote in 1932. Felisa, who had campaigned vigorously for the right of women to vote, was fifth in line at the next elections.

The party that Felisa first joined was the Liberal party, which sought independence from the United States. She became active in San Juan politics, holding the office of party leader in the city. In 1936, the party approached her to stand for a senatorial seat. However one of the party's leaders, Luis Muñoz Marín (son of the former Resident Commissioner), believed that independence would not best serve the interests of all Puerto Ricans. He split from the Liberal party and formed the Popular Democratic party in 1938. Felisa followed his example, and in 1940 she became president of the party's San Juan committee. In March of that year she married the lawyer Genaro A. Gautier, who served as assistant attorney general of Puerto Rico and secretary general of the Popular Democratic party.

Felisa Rincón de Gautier was approached several times during the 1940s by the San Juan Board of Commissioners, who offered her the position of city manager. She declined twice, in 1940 and 1944, before finally accepting the job when the incumbent mayor Don Roberto Sanchez Vilella resigned in 1946. She was elected to the position in 1948 and was reelected four more times before retiring from the post in 1968. Much of her political support came from the poorest residents of the city, whom she organized into a powerful voting block in the Popular Democratic Party. "She worked hard to please the electorate," recalled Eric Pace in the *New York Times.* "'My opponents campaign just before elections and then they disappear,' she once said. 'I start campaigning the day after the election and never stop.'"

Develops Program of Public Works

The *alcaldesa* responded to the needs of her supporters in a series of public works. One of her earliest campaigns cleaned up and rehabilitated a number of San Juan slums, continuing work begun by federal housing authority projects during the Great Depression. She also oversaw the construction of new schools, hospitals, housing projects, sanitation facilities, and generally expanded care for underprivileged people, both young and elderly. She also brought a personal touch to the mayoral office, holding open forums every Wednesday at city hall, at which any citizen could bring a complaint or petition before her directly. In 1948, after the first election for the office of governor in which the residents of Puerto Rico were allowed to vote, Rincón de Gautier hosted a party for thousands of the poor children of San Juan, seeing to it that all of them received gifts in honor of the Feast of the Three Kings (January 6). Later she became famous for importing "planeloads of snow for Christmas parties" for local children, Pace recalled. "She maintained that personal touch even as San Juan grew, from a population of 180,000 when she first took office to 600,000 by 1961, when she was still meeting once a week with residents who needed advice or assistance."

Rincón de Gautier also gained notoriety for the number of relatives she appointed to city offices. Her sister Josefina served as deputy mayor during Rincón de Gautier's trips outside San Juan. A *1954 Saturday Evening Post* article suggested that during the early 1950s more than a dozen members of the *alcaldesa*'s extended family held positions in the city government. She remained unaffected by comments from her political opponents who charged her with nepotism. "After detractors said she had given city jobs to too many of her relatives," reported Pace, "she replied: 'I wish I had 20 more nieces. They work better—for less.'"

Rincón de Gautier won worldwide attention and honors for her campaigns on behalf of the poor and underprivileged. She made two Central and South American tours on behalf of the U.S. Department of State in 1953 and 1956, speaking on behalf of education programs and explaining the unique relationship between the commonwealth of Puerto Rico and the mainland United States. In 1954 she was named "Woman of the Americas" by the United Women of America. She accepted honorary degrees in law, humanities, and arts from Mount Mary College, Temple University, and the Universidad de Puerto Rico. In addition, she received the Spanish Golden Medal of Honor, the French Joan of Arc Medal, the Israeli Order of Merit, the Vatican's Pope Pius XII Medal and the Cruz del Santo Sepulcro de Jerusalem, the Madeline Borg Award from the Philanthropic Hebrew Federation of New York, and the Jane Addams Medal from the Federated Women's Clubs of America before she retired from office in 1968.

Even after she left office Felisa Rincón de Gautier remained active in U.S. politics. She was a member of the U.S. Democratic Party's National Committee and continued to serve as a delegate to national conventions until 1992, when she made her last political appearance at the age of 95. She was incapacitated only during the final months of her life, and she died in a San Juan nursing home after suffering a heart attack on September 16, 1994.

Sources:

Candee, Marjorie Dent, ed. *Current Biography Yearbook 1956.* New York: H. W. Wilson, 1957.

Graham, Judith, ed. *Current Biography Yearbook 1994.* New York: H. W. Wilson, 1994.

Gruber, Ruth. *Felisa Rincón de Gautier.* New York: Crowell, 1972.

LaCossitt, Henry. "The Mayor Wears Flowers in Her Hair."*Saturday Evening Post,* May 22, 1954, p. 38.

Lofaro, Michael Quinn, et al. "Obituary." *Time,* October 3, 1994, p. 29.

Navarro, Mireya. "Three candidates wage tough campaign in drive to become San Juan's second female mayor." *New York Times,* September 29, 1996, p. 16.

Pace, Eric. "Felisa Rincón de Gautier, 97, Mayor of San Juan." *New York Times,* September 19, 1994, p. D9.

Rhonda A. Rios-Kravitz
(1949–)
Educational administrator, librarian, community activist

Rhonda A. Rios-Kravitz has spent much of her career as a strong advocate for underprivileged students and women of color. She has worked as a librarian for over twenty years and has served the Sacramento community, where she is currently access services librarian and department head at California State University, Sacramento. Rios-Kravitz has created her own combination of activism and community service in helping to design programs and library services for underrepresented students in the community. Her work has gained her recognition on many levels. A widely published author, she has written about issues in library administration and management, minorities in library science, and medical libraries.

Rises in Library Field

Rios-Kravitz, born April 15, 1949, is the granddaughter of migrant farm workers from Mexico; her parents were also poor. She grew up in the housing projects in Hunters Point, San Francisco, with parents who instilled in their daughter an appreciation for education and achievement. The high value that her family placed on education motivated her to go to college, and she received a bachelor's degree from California State University, Sacramento, in 1974. Rios-Kravitz received her master's degree in library science from Simmons College in Boston in 1979. She began to practice librarianship at the Belmont Memorial Library in Massachusetts in 1977. From there, she moved to a position as library research consultant for the department of library science at Simmons College in 1979. Rios-Kravitz also served as part-time reference librarian at the Francis A. Countway Library of Medicine at Harvard University in 1982 and 1983, and served in two different capacities for Massachusetts General Hospital from 1979 through 1987. She was the reference librarian, and then assistant director for library consult services, for the MGH

Health Sciences Library and the associate and assistant librarian for the Palmer Davis Library at the School of Nursing. In 1987, Rios-Kravitz moved to California and served in the California State Library as Ethnic Services Consultant from 1987 through 1990. She then took her present post at California State University in Sacramento.

Serves Community

Rios-Kravitz is a devoted community servant both as an extension of and in addition to her career. Her commitment to providing services to students who might not otherwise have them, and her desire to foster innovation in public policy to support these students have motivated her to engage in community activities and initiatives. She is an active member of the American Library Association, chairing the Racial and Ethnic Diversity Committee in 1994, and she is currently a member of the Recruitment Assembly. During her membership in the California Library Association, Rios-Kravitz has been the chair of both the Mentoring and Leadership Committee and of the Cultural Diversity Committee. She was also named assembly member, a statewide elected position, from 1993 to 1996.

The service Rios-Kravitz provides extends beyond her profession and into the educational community of California State University at Sacramento. She supports curriculum and faculty development as well as multicultural causes, notably as a founding member of Education Excellence Through Diversity (ED-X), an ad hoc committee of faculty, staff, and students who support diversity and affirmative action, and on the Committee for Diversity Awards, which presents grants to underrepresented students and faculty. She has also been an academic senator (1993-1996), the affirmative action representative for the library (1995-present), and a member of Beyond the Canon: New Strategies for Pedagogy and Curriculum (1991-1994). She is currently co-chair of the Association of Mexican American Educators, a member of the Council on University Planning, and a member of the Faculty Policies Committee.

Rios-Kravitz has done substantial and significant work with the organization REFORMA, the National Association to Promote Library Service to the Spanish-speaking. REFORMA was established in 1971 to help encourage library services for Hispanics nationwide. A member since 1987, Rios-Kravitz has served both as vice-president and president of this organization. REFORMA helps recruit and retain bilingual and bicultural librarians with scholarships and mentorship programs. The organization promotes collection development, which includes Spanish-language and Hispanic materials, and the development of library services and programs which focus on the needs of the Hispanic community. It seeks to educate the Hispanic population about the availability of library services, and it conducts an annual scholarship drive which awards scholarships to library school students interested in working with Hispanics.

Rios-Kravitz reached beyond her community and heritage to serve in the capacity of delegate to the 41st Commission on the Status of Women at the United Nations in New York City in March of 1997. She also served as a delegate to the Non-Governmental Organization (NGO) Fourth World Conference on Women in August and September of 1995 in Beijing, China.

Receives Honors

It is not surprising that Rios-Kravitz has been recognized for the service she has provided for the past 20 years. She was awarded the YWCA Outstanding Women Award in Higher Education for Sacramento, which recognizes community contributions and the promotion of cross-cultural understanding. It also recognizes women who advocate policies promoting productive and self-sufficient lives for women and their families. As the recipient of the Association of College and Research Libraries Initiative Fund in 1995, Rios-Kravitz was granted funds to develop a survey to examine what creates barriers to the advancement of the careers of academic librarians. Six hundred surveys were sent to librarians nationwide, 300 of whom were members of ethnic library organizations. Rios-Kravitz is also the recipient of the National Women of Color Day March First Award from CSUS Multicultural Center, awarded for diversity in library scholarship and service.

Former Congresswoman Barbara Jordan once asked, "When do any of us do enough?" In response, Rios-Kravitz takes up this challenge and writes, "In these times of educational crisis, I feel compelled to seek additional avenues to make effective change. . . . Today's educational policies do not adequately address the issues of equity. A student from a poor neighborhood does not share the educational privileges of a child from a rich neighborhood. Students from underrepresented groups have less first-hand knowledge about what careers are available to them. It is difficult, if not impossible, to be a winner in an unfair race. . . . I seek to change policies and practices that negatively affect underrepresented students' eligibility, application, admissions, and enrollment." This has been the driving goal for Rios-Kravitz, and these values are exemplified in the long-term service which she has provided to the Hispanic community.

Current Address: Library, California State Univ., Sacramento, 2000 Jed Smith Dr., Sacramento, CA 95819.

Sources:

CLNET Home Page. Available at http://latino.sscnet.ucla.edu.library/reforma/refointr.htm.

Cooper, Amy. Letter to Rhonda A. Rios-Kravitz, March 1998.

"Local Women's Network at World Confab." *Sacramento Observer,* November 1, 1995, p. A8.

"REFORMA": *The ALA Yearbook of Library and Information Services.* Chicago: American Library Association, 1990.

"Rios-Kravitz, Rhonda A." *The ALA Yearbook of Library and Information Services.* Chicago: American Library Association, 1990.

Marina Rivera
(1942–)
Poet, entrepreneur, tutor

Selected writings:

Mestiza. Grilled Flowers, 1977.
Sobra. Casa Editorial, 1977.
*Fingers of Silence.*Brushfire, 1981.
Half a Caramel and a Cluster of Chile Pequin, 1984.

Overview

In Marina Rivera's first book of poetry, *Mestiza,* she writes poetry "con una vigorosa belleza de imágenes que se clavan en ánimo" (with vigorous beautiful images that penetrate the soul), according to Eliana Rivero (*Palabra,* Spring 1979). *Mestiza* was published in 1977, as was Rivera's second book of poetry, *Sobra.*. Rivera has also published poems in various anthologies and periodicals. Much of her poetry deals with her experience growing up as a Chicana in an Anglo-American world, although she addresses universal themes as well.

A Difficult Beginning

Rivera was born on February 9, 1942, in Superior, Arizona, a small town east of Phoenix. Her father is a naturalized citizen who was born in Mexico and brought to the United States as an infant when his mother crossed the border to escape the turmoil of the Mexican revolution. Her mother, also of a Mexican family, was born and raised in eastern Arizona.

Rivera and her brother moved with their parents to Phoenix when she was still a small child. Her father, a World War II veteran, was entitled to housing project assistance, and they lived in a predominantly white neighborhood. She and her brother did well in school, but because of their ethnic background, they were excluded from social events. They also struggled with the language barrier. In school they were expected to speak only English, and as a result they lost their ease with the Spanish language and were teased about this by their Spanish-speaking relatives.

Claiming an Education

Thanks to the Vesta Club, a group dedicated to helping Chicanos attend college, and to academic scholarships, Rivera was able to go to undergraduate school at Northern Arizona University in Flagstaff. She was cited in *Who's Who in American Colleges and Universities* in 1963. In 1964 she graduated summa cum laude with a bachelor of arts degree in English and a minor in French. Rivera then attended graduate school at the University of Arizona, where she received a master of arts degree in public speaking in 1966. As a graduate student, Rivera participated in a group called the Poetry Center. She was a member of the board of directors for a year and participated in many of the readings and programs. She also met her husband through this forum, from whom she has since become divorced. Rivera returned to the University of Arizona later and earned a master of fine arts in poetry writing in 1981.

A Successful Teaching Career

Rivera first worked as a teacher while in graduate school at the University of Arizona, where she was a teaching assistant for two years. From there, she moved into high schools, teaching English, speech, and creative writing in various locations in Arizona, California, and Texas. She belonged to the Tucson Education Association and the National Education Association. She stated in *Dictionary of Literary Biography,* "I have been either a teacher or a student all of my life." In 1982, however, she left her position as English teacher for the Special Projects High School for Advanced Studies at Tucson High School and moved to a small community behind the Catalina Mountains. She started a small upholstery business and began providing language tutoring services to corporate families who had come from Spain.

Two Books of Poetry in the Same Year

Although Rivera first started writing poetry when she was in high school, it was not until 1972 that her poems began to be published. They first appeared in small magazines throughout the Southwest. Then, in 1977, Rivera published her two collections, *Mestiza* (bilingual poetry) and *Sobra* (poetry in English). The poems for these books were drawn from her most significant work from 1972 to 1977. The poems in *Mestiza* often address the experience of living as a Chicana in an Anglo-American world. Rivera stated in *Dictionary of Literary Biography,* "I came to know the best in both cultures and the worst in both." The themes of racial prejudice and identity are intermixed with more personal themes. For example, one poem deals with Rivera's grief over her brother's death; another addresses a family conflict. Nature and animals are also important in the poems in *Mestiza,* both for their own sake and as symbols.

Sobra contains some of the same themes and images, but the poems in this volume are more introspective and personal. One reviewer of *Sobra* in *Booklist* stated that Rivera "is less concerned with telling the story than with letting the reader glimpse a private world in shades of gray, of words and themes that do not always have clear meanings" and that she "uses these abilities to communicate and is highly successful."

Poetry for a Cause

Rivera went on to publish other works as well. In 1981 she published, with several others, the chapbook *Fingers of Silence*. She has also published poems in several anthologies, including: *I Had Been Hungry All These Years: An Anthology of Women's Poetry* (1975); *The Face of Poetry* (1976); and *Southwest: A Contemporary Anthology* (1977). Her poems have appeared in periodicals, such as *Caracol, Revista Chicano-Riqueña, Palabra,* and *Denver Quarterly.* Another collection of poems, titled *The Celia Poems,* is yet to be published. Rivera stated in *The Third Woman,* "I give all my profits from poetry to a group which gives scholarships to talented Chicano youth who otherwise would not have funds to continue in school." Rivera is referring to the Vesta Club, the same organization that helped her attend college.

In regards to her purpose, Rivera stated in *Dictionary of Literary Biography,* "If my work says anything it tries to say 'look deeply, choose the reflection of your own heart, no matter the color in those eyes.'" Rivera continues to write poetry while supporting herself mainly through her tutoring services and upholstery work. In 1984 she completed another collection of poetry titled *Half a Caramel and a Cluster of Chile Pequin.*

Sources:

"Book review." *Booklist,* April 15, 1978.

Fisher, Dexter, ed. *The Third Woman: Minority Woman Writers of the United States.* Boston: Houghton Mifflin, 1980.

Lomelí, Francisco A. and Carl A. Shirley, eds. *Dictionary of Literary Biography* Volume 122, "Chicano Writers," second series. Detroit: Gale, 1992.

Martinez, Julio A., ed. *Chicano Scholars and Writers.* Metuchen, NJ: Scarecrow Press, 1979.

Migdalia Rivera
Executive director

Crusader for Latino Advancement

Born in Humacao, Puerto Rico, Migdalia "Millie" Rivera has been the executive director of the Latino Institute since the end of 1988. Under her leadership, the organization has seen its stature increase exponentially, both in the

Migdalia Rivera

Chicago metropolitan area, where it is headquartered, and across the nation. It is widely recognized today as the Midwest's leading Latino policy and leadership development institute. Rivera brings to the Latino Institute a great deal of experience as a manager of human and financial resources. Both before and since coming to the institute, she has developed considerable expertise in organizational development, the planning and evaluation of programs, and fundraising.

Under the guidance of Rivera, the Latino Institute has proven its effectiveness in addressing issues of equity in the areas of education, political empowerment, economic development, housing, and health. This has been accomplished through research and policy analysis, advocacy, and leadership development. Rivera's commitment to the institute's mission of justice through empowerment and self-determination began when she came to work in a staff position in the mid-1980s. She moved quickly through middle and senior management positions before assuming the executive directorship in 1988.

Works for Aspira Inc.

Before coming to the Latino Institute, Rivera gathered a good working knowledge of both the nonprofit and for-profit sectors. For Aspira Inc. of Illinois, a nonprofit organization, she worked to develop leadership for Latino youth. Impressed by the work she had done in Illinois, the New York City chapter of Aspira lured her to the Big Apple to become the coordinator of adult educational opportunities. She later returned to Chicago, taking a job in the for-profit sector at New Frontier Development Corporation. She had only been at New Frontier a short time when she was promoted to liaison between housing development and management.

Active in Civic and National Affairs

Rivera is bicultural and bilingual in English and Spanish. A graduate of Cornell University, she has done much in her life's work to raise public consciousness and awareness of such important issues as education and race relations, as well as the importance of civic participation. A fierce defender of Latino civil rights, she actively demonstrated against the *Chicago Sun-Times* in February of 1997 after the newspaper ran a series of articles about the controversial ways in which the city's Roberto Clemente High School was using antipoverty funds. Rivera protested that the newspaper had unfairly linked school officials with the violent Puerto Rican independence group FALN. "The *Chicago Sun-Times* represents the free press. But in this series of reports, it opted to use the power of its free speech to try to deny to a community its right to assembly, association, and free speech."

Extremely active in both civic and national affairs, Rivera is a member of several boards of directors, including the Alliance of Latinos and Jews, Alivio Medical Center, HispanoCare, Leadership for Quality Education, and the National Puerto Rican Coalition. She also serves on the executive committee of the Illinois Immigrant Policy Project and is a member of the Chicago Committee of the Chicago Council on Foreign Relations. Recently she was appointed to the board of directors of the Federal Reserve Bank of Chicago.

Rivera is particularly proud of the alliance the Latino Institute has forged with the Jewish Federation-Jewish United Fund of Metropolitan Chicago to lobby in Springfield, the state capital, for immigrant aid. The two groups successfully argued for the passage of a new state law which counteracts some of the cuts passed in the national Welfare Reform Act. Of the groups' cooperative effort, Rivera said, "This relationship is quite remarkable, very exciting, and holds great potential for the future."

Among the many awards Rivera has received are the 1996 National Hispanic Community Service Award, presented jointly by *Hispanic* magazine and Shell Oil Company, and the Hispanic Heritage Award, which was given to her by WSNS-TV, the city of Chicago, and the Chicago Park District. The Midwest Women's Center selected her among the "Top 10 Most Distinguished Women in Chicago," while *Hispanic* magazine named her among the "100 Most Influential Hispanics" in the nation.

Current Address: Latino Institute, 14 E. Jackson, Ste. 1220, Chicago, IL 60604.

Sources:

Amerman, Donald. Letter from Migdalia Rivera, February 24, 1998.

Fitzgerald, Mark. "Picketing the *Chicago Sun-Times.*" *Editor & Publisher,* March 15, 1997, p. 11.

Hispanic Magazine Home Page. Available at http://www.hisp.com/oct96/rivera.html.

Rivera, Millie
   See **Rivera, Migdalia**

Eliana Suarez Rivero
(1942–)
Poet, editor, professor

Selected writings:

El gran amor de Pablo Neruda: estudio crítico de su poesía (The Great Love of Pablo Neruda: A Critical Study of His Poetry). Plaza Mayor, 1971.

Eliana Suarez Rivero

De cal y arena (Of Lime and Sand). Aldebaran, 1975.
Cuerpos breves (Brief Bodies). Scorpion, 1976.
Siete poetas. Scorpion, 1978.

Overview

Eliana Rivero is a professor of Spanish at the University of Arizona at Tucson. In addition, she has written poetry, edited her own book, and co-edited an anthology of Chicana literature. Her most important contributions are in the areas of Latin American and U.S. Hispanic literatures and women's literature and feminist criticism.

From Cuba to the United States

Rivero was born in Artemisa, Cuba, on November 7, 1942, to Mario J. Suarez, an accountant, and Maria (Rivero) Suarez. She grew up on the narrowest portion of Cuba in the Pinar del Río province. Her grandfather and great aunts and uncles had come to this area from the Canary Islands and from southern Spain. Rivero began her collegiate education in 1958, attending Virginia Intermount College for one year. She then attended the University of Havana from 1959-60 and immigrated to the United States in 1961.

Earns Notable Education

In 1964 Rivero graduated cum laude from the University of Miami in Coral Gables, Florida, with a B.A. in Spanish. After receiving a master's degree, she earned her Ph.D. in Latin American literature from the same university in 1967. As a student, Rivero received numerous awards, including the Burton Wilson Award for Outstanding Undergraduate in Romance Languages (University of Miami) and the Panamerican Airways Latin American Division Award for Outstanding Student in Spanish, both in 1964. She received the Maytag Fellowship for Graduate Studies at the University of Miami from 1965-67. Also in 1967, Rivero married Angel Rivero (a Sears Roebuck Company manager) on July 28. They have one daughter, Elisabet.

An Active Professional

In 1967, Rivero was hired as an assistant professor of Spanish at the University of Arizona in Tucson, where she continued to advance in her teaching and writing career to full professor in the Spanish department. Since starting her career as a professor and writer, Rivero has been involved in many different professional organizations, including the Modern Language Association of America, the American Association of Teachers of Spanish and Portuguese, the American Association of University Professors, the Pacific Coast Council for Latin American Studies, and the Rocky Mountain Council of Latin American Studies, for which she was a member of the executive board. She was also a faculty adviser for Chapter Pi, Sigma Delta Pi from 1967-74; an adviser to *Movimiento Estudiantil Chicano de Aztlan* for cultural activities from 1976-77; a council member of Instituto Internacional de Literatura Iberoamericana from 1975-1977; a member of the Mexican American Studies Committee at the University of Arizona, beginning in 1975; and co-editor of Scorpion Press, a small press for Chicana and Latina women in Tucson. Rivero earned the American Council of Learned Societies Travel Grant in 1975.

Feeling Different

Rivero spent many years feeling out of place in the predominantly Anglo-American United States. She said in *Michigan Quarterly Review,* "Even though I had been living in the United States since 1961, earned my college degrees here, married and started a family in this country, I still saw myself as quite 'different.' On the border, looking in and out." In reaction to this feeling, Rivero said she ". . . dived headlong into assimilation," assuming whatever accent was prevalent depending on where she was at the time. It was not until 1983 that Rivero began her formal work comparatively studying and compiling the works of Chicana, U.S. Puerto Rican, and Cuban American women. Her choice of women authors was based on the fact that she saw in their writings the same quest for identity, the same feeling of "otherness," that she herself had experienced.

A Variety of Endeavors

Rivero published her first of many articles in 1966 in *Hispania.* Her major works include a book titled *El gran amor de Pablo Neruda: estudio crítico de su poesía (The Great Love of Pablo Neruda: A Critical Study of His Poetry,* 1971), and two books of poetry, *De cal y arena (Of Lime and Sand,* 1975) and *Cuerpos breves (Brief Bodies,* 1977). Her first book, *El gran amor de Pablo Neruda,* was well received. D.L. Shaw wrote in *Modern Language Review* that ". . . the value of Professor Rivero's book, coming as it does after sundry chronological surveys of Neruda's vast output, lies in the fact that it attempts to explore synthetically a major aspect of his diction, his use of recurrent symbols, in order to uncover the bed-rock of his poetic personality." Shaw also stated that Rivero is able ". . . to knit her conclusions together into a comprehensive interpretation which is the first of its kind on Neruda. . . " and called the book "useful and welcome."

Rivero is also co-editor (with Jose A. Balseiro) of *El cabellero de las espuelas de oro,* published in 1968, and (with Tey Diana Rebolledo) of *Infinite Divisions: An Anthology of Chicana Literature,* published in 1993. *Infinite Divisions* is an anthology of poetry and prose written by Mexican American women and seeks to ". . . reflect the development of a Chicana consciousness from its first seeds to the present. . . ," according to a review in *Publisher's Weekly.* The first section is titled "Foremothers" and contains transcriptions of stories gathered from elderly women who were once the storytellers of the community as early as the nineteenth century. A review in *Booklist* called this "wonderful, enlightening reading" and said that ". . . the hefty collection will satisfy more than one taste, whether literary, historical, or even sociological."

Rivero has also contributed numerous articles and reviews to periodicals such as *Hispania, Alaluz, Explicacion de textos literarios, Revista,* and *Iberoamericana.* Rivero stated in the *Contemporary Authors* series, "I have gone more and more into creative writing, but I find that critical commentary adds to my knowledge of the phenomena of poetry in particular and language in general."

In describing her quest for self-identity, so often expressed in her writing, Rivero said in *Michigan Quarterly Review* that since the mid-1980s she has ". . . fully traveled the road back to 'recubanization' . . . Yes, I am a Cuban by origin and culture . . . but I have lived elsewhere for most of my life. . . . I am a hybrid."

Current Address: Dept. of Spanish and Portuguese, Modern Languages Bldg., Rm. 545, Univ. of Arizona at Tucson, Tucson, AZ 85721.

Sources:

Maratos, Daniel C. and Marnesba D. Hill. *Cuban Exile Writers: A Biobibliographic Handbook.* Metuchen, NJ: Scarecrow Press, 1986.
Martinez, Julio A., ed. *Chicano Scholars and Writers: A Biobibliographical Dictionary.* Metuchen, NJ: Scarecrow Press, 1979.
Press, Jaques Cattell, ed. *Directory of American Scholars,* eighth edition, Volume III. New York: R.R. Bowker, 1982.
Publishers Weekly, May 17, 1993, p. 74.
Rivero, Eliana S. "'Fronterisleña,' Border Islander."*Michigan Quarterly Review,* Fall 1994, pp. 669-674.
Shaw, D.L. "Book Review." *Modern Language Review,* October 1972, pp. 932-933.

Emyré Barrios Robinson

(1926–)

Entrepreneur, business executive

Emyré Barrios Robinson was one of the first women to achieve the rank of top executive in a space research company. For ten years, from 1980 to 1990, she ran Barrios Technology, a contract company that used non-engineering personnel to do the repetitive engineering tasks necessary to design space shuttle flights. Although she did not have engineering expertise, she was adept at running a business and inspiring employees, a talent for which she has received numerous national awards.

Barrios Robinson was born on March 23, 1926, the daughter of Ignacio Barrios, a physician, and Emyré Pacheco de Barrios. Both her mother and father emigrated to El Paso, TX, from Mexico, and were married in the United States. Along with her two brothers, Barrios Robinson was raised in a traditional Mexican environment, and she did not learn English until she began kindergarten. After graduating from high school in El Paso, she studied for two years at the University of California at Los Angeles. There she met and married Harold MacBride, and she left school to start a family. They had three children—Theresa, Deborah, and Ronald—before divorcing. She was remarried in August of 1958, to Donald MacChesney Robinson, and they had one child, Diane.

Develops Interest in Space Technology

When her children were old enough to go to school, Barrios Robinson took the opportunity to return to college. She graduated with a bachelor of arts degree from the University of Houston in 1971. Barrios Robinson's husband, an engineer working for McDonnell-Douglas on space shuttle flights, influenced her to consider space technology when she began looking for a job. In 1973 she was hired as an associate technical editor for Kentron International, where she helped transcribe the tapes that recorded communications between astronauts on the space shuttle and the ground crew.

Eventually Barrios Robinson was promoted to supervisor and then data services manager, a position in which she managed 41 other employees, most of whom were technical editors. In 1978, she became business manager and learned how to evaluate Kentron's costs for NASA work project proposals. While acting as business manager, she became aware that NASA was thinking of shifting some of its mission planning calculations from engineers to other people with good mathematical skills but no engineering degree. As a result, NASA asked for proposals from its contractors.

Starts Barrios Technology

Barrios Robinson realized that this could be her golden opportunity to start her own business. She sought out engineers who were technically qualified and wanted to join her in forming a new corporation. Seven engineers joined Barrios Robinson, who did the accounting in submitting the winning proposal. They were awarded a $1.8 million contract for 2 years, which subsequently was renewed. In 1980, she left Kentron and incorporated Barrios

Technology. "It was a dream come true for me," said Barrios Robinson during a telephone interview from her home in Dickinson, near Houston. She started with six people—all non-engineers—who were good in math, and who had taken at least trigonometry and calculus in college. One had a bachelor's degree in biology, for example, and another had a music degree. They often worked in mission control at NASA and became deeply involved in creating the software and math computation for the space shuttle. "It was very exciting for them to be involved in the space shuttle program, so they developed a deep commitment to the project," Barrios Robinson said.

By 1990, Barrios Robinson's business expertise had helped build the company to 525 employees and $25.5 million in revenues. At that time, she broadened the company's scope to take contracts from NASA for instrument calibration in addition to flight design. Later that year, Barrios Robinson realized she needed to turn over the reins of the company to someone else, as she was approaching the age of 65. A decisive woman, she sold a portion of her shares that year, and, in 1992, sold the balance to one of the engineers who had helped found the company. Barrios Robinson stayed on as president, but by 1994, when she turned 68, she retired completely. "It was time to slow down and give the younger folks a chance to run the company," she said.

During her career, Barrios Robinson made significant contributions to the company, as well as to Houston and its business community. She has received numerous awards, including Small Business Contractor of the Year from the Small Business Administration in 1982, and NASA's Excellence Award for Quality and Production in 1989 and 1990. Her company was also selected as one of the "best companies for women" in a book of that title from Simon & Schuster in 1988. In addition, she was named among the top 500 Hispanic businesses in the nation for 5 consecutive years. "My goal was always the bottom line," she said. "I allowed the technical people to run that aspect of the company. But I always expected very high performance from everyone. When we reached a goal, I would move the goal posts and ask for higher standards from my employees," she said. "All in all, it was a joy to create and work for Barrios Technology. Everyone was so committed."

Founds Condor Trading International

Always on the move, Barrios Robinson has not been inactive since leaving Barrios Technology. After she retired, Barrios Robinson helped found a new venture, an import/export company called Condor Trading International, Ltd., which imports fresh produce from Latin America. She is a majority owner, as well as chief executive officer and chairperson of the board.

Barrios Robinson is very active in the community and has served on the boards of many Houston organizations for more than 12 years. She sits on the dean's executive advisory board at the University of Houston's College of Business Administration and is part of the dean's advisory council for that university's College of Technology. She also serves on the boards of the Greater Houston Women's Foundation, the San Jacinto Girl Scouts Council, and the Arts Alliance Center at Clear Lake. One of her most cherished awards came from the Girl Scouts when she was selected as "A Woman of Distinction." Barrios Robinson was 1 of only 15 women in Houston to receive the award and 1 of 80 in Texas. "I love working with young people and the Girl Scouts, so the award was very special to me," Barrios Robinson said.

Current Address: Condor Trading International Ltd., 17511 El Camino Real, Ste. 144 , Houston, TX 77058.

Sources:

Boughton, Barbara. Telephone conversation with Emyré Barrios Robinson, April 22, 1998.

Robledo Montecel, Maria
See **Montecel, Maria Robledo**

Belen B. Robles
Organization president

As the first woman president of the nation's oldest and largest Hispanic civil rights organization, Belen B. Robles has been a leader in the fight to improve the lot of Hispanic Americans throughout the United States. In her role as the head of the League of United Latin American Citizens (LULAC), Robles is responsible for ensuring that the Hispanic American voice is heard by the federal government, and that Hispanic American rights are upheld in U.S. communities. Her extensive involvement with various committees and organizations has made Robles into one of the most influential figures in the arena of political activism.

The League of United Latin American Citizens (LULAC), headquartered in El Paso, TX, was founded in the late 1920s as an organization to advocate improved conditions for the Hispanic community. Robles first became involved in the work of the organization nearly forty years ago and held a variety of elected and appointed positions within LULAC before assuming the group's presidency. These posts have included the chair of the organization's Nation-

Belen B. Robles

al Educational Service Centers, national director for civil rights, national director for women's activities, and national secretary.

In addition to her involvement with LULAC, Robles has spent much of her professional career working with the U.S. Immigration and Naturalization Service and the U.S. Customs Service. In that arena, she has served as supervisor of the El Paso International Airport; chief inspector of the Bridge of the Americas, linking El Paso and Ciudad Juarez in the Mexican state of Chihuahua across the Rio Grande River; director of community relations for the El Paso district of the U.S. Customs Service; and deputy director for inspection and control. Her current post with Customs is as chief inspector for cargo operations at the Bridge of the Americas.

Makes Significant Achievements

During her presidency of the League, Robles has been credited with a number of achievements, including organizing the group's first education summit in Chicago and its first civil rights symposium in Dallas. In June of 1997, at LULAC's annual convention in Los Angeles, she joined civil rights activist Rev. Jesse Jackson in calling for a Justice Department investigation into whether California's Proposition 209 violates federal law. As the League's president, she represented all Hispanic Americans at the International Summit of the Americas held in Miami. Robles also organized a conference to assess Republican legislators'

Contract with America and its impact on the Hispanic American community. The conference came up with its own answer to the GOP proposal. Robles announced: "LULAC's 'Commitment with America' represents the basic principles that Hispanics have held dear for centuries, such as strong family values, fiscal responsibility, and reduction of government waste. But we will not tolerate being singled out as the scapegoats for this country's economic problems. Instead, we will vigorously challenge those legislators and public officials who continue to attack Hispanics."

Active in Numerous Organizations

Robles's involvement in community affairs extends beyond LULAC to a number of other organizations she has served as an executive or member. These include the El Paso Hispanic Chamber, for which she once served as director; the National Hispanic Leadership Agenda as vice chair; and SER Jobs for Progress, also as vice chair. She has been a member of the executive committee of Foundation Solidaridad Mexico-American A.C. and a board member of both the National Hispanic Corporate Council and the Martin Luther King Jr. Federal Holiday Commission. Robles is a member of the Hispanic Leadership Institute and an honorary member of Rotary International. At the federal level, Robles is an active member of the Immigration and Naturalization Service/U.S. Border Patrol Merger panel and the Better Relations with Mexico Committee. She also chaired an advisory committee to the commissioner of the Immigration and Naturalization Service.

Leadership Earns Accolades

Robles has been recognized as an outstanding leader in helping Hispanic Americans obtain civil and social justice in the United States. At the May 17-18, 1996, Colorado state convention of LULAC, she told the audience that the beating of two Mexican nationals by California highway patrolmen in Riverside County earlier that year was "the tip of the proverbial iceberg" of the way law enforcement officers treat Hispanics in the United States. She charged that most police officers "don't have the same respect for our people as they do for the majority population."

Among the honors Robles has received are the Chamizal Medallion, awarded by President Lyndon B. Johnson, and the Sustained Superior Performance Award from the U.S. Customs Service. She has been named among the "10 Outstanding Women in Federal Service," among the "100 Most Influential Hispanics in the United States" by *Hispanic Business* magazine in October of 1997, and among the "25 Most Powerful Hispanics in Washington" by *Hispanic* magazine in November of 1997.

Robles is married to Ramiro Robles and is the mother of three children, Ramiro Jr., Carlos Francisco, and Mary Helen LoPresti. Robles is equally at home speaking English or Spanish. Throughout her lifelong involvement in community affairs, she has played an active role in ensuring that the culture, history, and economic conditions of Hispanic Americans are not overlooked in the corridors of power.

Current Address: League of United Latin American Citizens, 221 N. Kansas, Ste. 1200 , El Paso, TX 79901.

Sources:

Alvarez, Frank. "LULAC Pledges 'Commitment' with America." *La Prensa de San Antonio,* July 7, 1995.

Amerman, Donald. Letter from Belen Robles, February 27, 1998.

Hispanstar Home Page. Available at http://www.hispanstar.com./influentials96/res100dir-t+.html.

Yzaguirre, Raul. "What Latino Leaders Say." *El Sol del Valle,* August 3, 1995.

Mary Rodas
(1975–)
Marketing executive

A contributor in *Hispanic* magazine declared Mary Rodas to be "the Latina equivalent of Tom Hanks' character in the movie *Big.*" At the age of four, Rodas became a product tester for toy manufacturer Catco, Inc. By the time she entered New York University in 1994, she had held the position of vice president of marketingat Catco, Inc. for four years. At that time she had two offices in Manhattan, a chauffeur-driven limousine, and a stock portfolio. In a 1993 *Detroit News* article, Barry Rohan wrote, "She collects about $200,000 a year in salary and benefits as a corporate executive and recently was on a short *New York Times* list of people who became millionaires through the recession. Not bad for a 17-year old high school student." By 1998 Rodas was also vice-president of artists and repertoire at Deco Disc Industries, the company for which she developed a new form of CD packaging.

Success Comes out of Poverty

The daughter of poor immigrants, Rodas's success is in marked contrast to the life her parents led. Her parents left El Salvador in 1971 to seek a better life in the United States. The couple spoke little English and took relatively low-paying jobs. "When my parents came to this country," Rodas told Ines Pinto Alicea in *The Hispanic Outlook in Higher Education,* "they had the feeling that the next generation would do better." Rodas was born in New Jersey on Christmas Day in 1975. Pinto Alicea noted that the Rodas

family was so poor that they had to save "for months to buy a Barbie doll."

Rodas's business career began in the early 1980s, when her father took her on his inspection tours of the Union City, NJ, apartment building where he was superintendent. Catco, Inc. founder Donald Spector explained to *New York Daily News* journalist Sonia Reyes, "Her father came to [my] apartment to do some work. I had tiled my own kitchen and used a chipped tile behind the kitchen door, thinking no one would see it. But Mary caught it, reprimanded me, and told me I didn't lay the tiles down right. Right then, I knew she was special." Her eye for detail impressed Spector so much that he appointed her as an official toy tester at his company. By 1990, at the age of 14, Rodas was the youngest corporate vice president in America.

Demonstrates Special Talents for a Difficult Position

Spector realized that what made Rodas special was her ability to pinpoint potential problems with toys and clearly express criticisms. She became a consultant and market researcher who took Spector's new toys to school to see how her friends liked them. Rodas also provided important feedback on the way products appeared to children—ways that did not occur to the adults who designed and manufactured them. "I would tell him how to improve products from a kid's perspective," Rodas told Alicea. For example, when asked her opinion about a doll with a birthmark, Rodas told Spector to remove it "because it looked like a pimple." "Mary has caused the company to change direction more than once with her comments and insight," Catco president Barbara Carver told *Sales & Marketing Management.* "Though she may not really know it, Mary has an instinct and natural interest in her products that most people just don't have."

Rodas's young age also gave her a special rapport with Catco's target market. "What's cool to Rodas and her contemporaries is potentially lucrative to Catco," McGeehan quoted Carver as saying. Rodas admits her ability to communicate with youngsters has a lot to do with her age. Some believe, however, that the rapport Rodas has established with children will continue long after she leaves Catco.

Adds to Creation of Balzac Product Line

Catco fully recognized Rodas's value as a marketer and consultant when they conceived the Balzac Balloon Ball in the late 1980s. The Balloon Ball, a virtually puncture-proof cloth bag that can be inflated like a balloon, became very popular in the United States and abroad during the early 1990s. Catco credited Rodas with giving the toy a broad appeal and a wide market that sold ten million units worldwide by 1994. "Originally, the cloth ball was a white fabric," Reyes explained. "But when Mary suggested bright neon colors because kids get bored with white, the company complied with her wishes." She also suggested uses for the toy that the original designers had not thought of, such as filling it with water, rice, or coins in order to change its weight and behavior. "She was instrumental in every stage of its development—from color selection to packaging to television commercials," declared Cohen. "In fact, her face has come to represent Balzac. She appears in commercials and promotional materials for the product and has traveled to countries such as Italy, France, and England, promoting it."

The Balzac Balloon Ball became Catco's signature product and launched a number of other Balzac merchandise, including clothing, watches, and other toys. In 1993, Rodas helped design and promote Balzac Glop, which Rodas called "the craziest and wildest candy the world has ever seen." Catco released Glop in conjunction with the Henry Heide Company of New Brunswick, the same company that owns the Jujubes and Jujyfruits lines of candies. Rodas said that it was inspired by the way young people play with chewing gum. "A lot of kids like slimy things," she told Reyes. "Do you ever notice how kids love to play with their bubble gum by pulling it in and out of their mouths?"

The third major product that Rodas helped Spector develop and market was the Deco Disc, a cardboard compact disc holder less fragile and more environmentally friendly than the traditional plastic jewel cases. *Record* reported: "When Rodas saw the initial designs for Catco's patented decorative packaging for compact discs, she had a free-form notion. Instead of being rectangular and resembling greeting cards, the cardboard disc-holders—Deco Discs—could be cut in different shapes, like holiday ornaments." Carver said in the article, "For a kid, this is so much more user-friendly. We see this as being huge for a collectible market." When Rodas test-marketed the Deco Discs among her friends at school, the young Catco executive found that her friends went wild over them.

Balances Education and Career

The same success that brought money to Rodas and her family also imposed restrictions on her. She was eventually faced with the problem of trying to get a high school education while working as a corporate executive. It was difficult to balance her professional life with school. "She briefly attended a Catholic school in New Jersey, but the school officials and her classmates did not accept her work or schedule," Pinto Alicea said. Eventually Rodas was placed in the Professional Children's School in New York City, where her classmates included other young people with careers. The school's flexible schedule allowed her to keep up with her studies as well as her work at Catco, Inc.

In the fall of 1994, Rodas enrolled as a freshman at New York University. Her coworkers at Catco originally believed that she would begin preparing for a career in politics or in psychiatry. By her senior year, however, she had decided to major in film. "She said she decided not to study business because it would be 'going backwards,'"

reported Pinto Alicea, "and that studying film would give her a different perspective by putting her behind the camera instead of in front of it." Rodas also began to contribute her time to public service organizations. She became chair of the March of Dimes' national youth program and a member of the board of directors of Lebanon Hospital in the Bronx.

Despite her school schedule, Rodas continues to work for Catco and Deco Disc Industries, the company that Spector founded to promote the packaging that she helped design. Surprisingly, before she turned 21, her age made it very difficult to get a bank loan, even as a Catco executive. In August of 1997, however, Rodas successfully negotiated a $750,000 line of credit with New York-based MTB Bank for Catco's latest product: inflatable plush balls called "BlowUps."

Sources:

Cohen, Andy. "Whiz Kid." *Sales & Marketing Management,* July, 1994, pp. 92-93.

Cole, Melanie. "30 under Thirty: Stand Back, World, Here Comes Generation Equis." *Hispanic,* August 31, 1995, p. 22.

McGeehan, Patrick. "A Millionaire at 17: Teen Helps Toy Maker Branch Out." *Record,* June 30, 1993.

Pinto Alicea, Ines. "Students: Teenager Sheds Briefcase for Backpack." *Hispanic Outlook in Higher Education,* September 15, 1994, p. 8.

Reyes, Sonia. "She's 'Big' Player in Toy Industry." *New York Daily News,* February 16, 1994, sec. 1, p. 31.

Rohan, Barry. "Teenage Tycoon: For 17-Year-Old Mary Rodas, Toys Are Big and Profitable." *Detroit News,* November 25, 1993, sec. F, p. 1.

Sullivan, Joanna. "Young Toy Executive Finally Manages to Convince a Bank She's Not Just Playing Around." *American Banker,* August 25, 1997, p. 9.

Sylvia Rodríguez

(1947–)

Professor, anthropologist, author

Selected writings:

The Matachines Dance: Ritual Symbolism and Interethnic Relations in the Rio Grande Valley. Albuquerque: University of New Mexico Press, 1996.

Overview

Sylvia Rodríguez assumes the varied roles of teacher, researcher, and author, as associate professor of anthropology at the University of New Mexico (UNM), a post she has held since leaving a teaching position at UCLA in 1988. Her research focus is on interethnic relations in the U.S.-Mexico borderlands, with particular emphasis on Hispano-Pueblo-Anglo relations in the Upper Rio Grande Valley of New Mexico in the twentieth century. Her work in this area has made her a standout in the field of anthropology.

Becomes Distinguished Professor of Anthropology

Rodríguez holds a B.A. from Barnard College and Ph.D. from Stanford University. She has published articles on the impact of tourism and resort development on ethnic identity, representations of ethnicity, and ethnic relations, and on art, public culture, and cultural politics. She has also conducted research and written on land and water issues as they relate to ethnic relations in New Mexico. Her three current ethnographic research projects deal with the Taos water rights adjudication. Her publications have won several awards, including, most recently, the 1997 Chicago Folklore Prize, and Regional Library Association 1997 Southwest Book Award, both for her book, *The Matachines Dance: Ritual Symbolism and Interethnic Relations in the Upper Rio Grande Valley* (UNM Press, 1996). She teaches courses on the principles of cultural anthropology, the U.S. Southwest, comparative ethnic and minority relations, peoples of Mexico, Spanish-speaking peoples of the borderlands, and ethnographic methods.

Born in Taos, NM, Rodríguez attended Catholic and public schools, graduating from Verde Valley High School in Sedona, AZ. Her parents, Alfredo Antonio Rodríguez and Grace Graham King, raised Rodríguez and her older sister, Anita. After graduation, Rodríguez was hired as an assistant professor in the department of sociology-anthropology at Carleton College from 1977-1981, while pursuing her Ph.D. from Stanford University. Rodríguez then moved to California where she worked as an assistant professor in the department of anthropology at UCLA from 1983-1988. She returned to New Mexico in 1988 and joined the faculty as an assistant professor of anthropology at the University of New Mexico until she was offered the position as the associate professor of anthropology in 1992. While in the classroom, she explores topics such as people and cultures of Mesoamerica, women in cross-cultural perspective, comparative minority relations, problems and practice in ethnography and ethnicity in the U.S. southwest, to name a few.

Rodríguez's professional affiliations include: American Anthropological Association, American Ethnological Society, Society for Cultural Anthropology, National Association for Chicano Studies, Association of Latina and Latino Anthropologists, where she was a member of the organizing committee's executive board from 1990-92, Committee on Anthropology in Predominantly Minority Institutions within the American Anthropological Association (C.A.P.M.I.) from 1992-93; American Folklore Society, and American Studies Association.

Sought-After Public Speaker

Since 1978 Sylvia Rodríguez has been an invited speaker for presentations, professional meetings, and college assemblies. Most recently, she served on the panel for the Southwestern Political Science Association meeting and viewed a video documentary called *This Town is Not for Sale!* On another occasion, Rodríguez's article "Tourism, Whiteness, and the Vanishing Anglo," was presented at a conference titled "Seeing and Being Seen: Tourism in the American West." She also presided over the National Trust for Historic Preservation Conference on October 17, 1997, which covered the topic "The Architecture of Tourism and Resistance in Taos." Her knowledge and insight has placed her into other nonacademic invited talks, presentations, and workshops as well. For example, her article "The Matachines Dance in the Upper Rio Grande Valley" was presented to the East Mountain Historical Society, Tijeras, and also the South Broadway Cultural Center.

Extensive research over the past 30 years that began while she attended Stanford University has been the source of numerous articles, chapters, and journals. Rodríguez's research began in 1968 in a counterculture commune in northern New Mexico for six months. Through her research, she has become a valuable source of information which she, in turn, shares with others in her teaching, lectures, and writing. She has participated as an expert witness and consultant on topics such as the impact of commercial development in the community and the use of land in New Mexico. In 1997, she received a grant from the Southwest Hispanic Institute for water rights adjudication for the Taos project. Rodríguez began her research in this area back in 1995, and it remains an important issue of concern for her.

Earns Awards for Work

Rodríguez received the Edward H. Spicer Award for her article, "Reconstructed Ethnicity in Contemporary Taos," that was published in the *Journal of the Southwest* in 1990. In this article she discussed folklore, the United States, New Mexico and Taos, and their connection with tourism. Rodríguez also won acclaim for a 1993 essay entitled, "The Tourist Gaze, Gentrification, and the Commodification of Subjectivity in Taos." She earned the Snead-Wertheim Endowed Lectureship in Anthropology and History from the University of New Mexico in 1996. In addition, editorial boards sought Rodríguez's expertise. She has presided on such boards as the *Journal of the Southwest, Frontiers, Cultural Anthropology,* and most recently *Aztlan.* She is also a standing member of the New Mexico Press Committee.

Some works that are currently in progress are a video documentary, *This Town is Not for Sale: The 1994 Santa Fe Mayoral Election,* an article and chapter on "Tourism, Whiteness and the Vanishing Anglo," and a report on "Acequia Custom and Practice in the Taos Valley." Environmental concerns remain important to Rodríguez as she plays an active role in her community.

Current Address: Dept. of Anthropology, University of New Mexico, Albuquerque, NM 87131.

Sources:

Kubiac, Brenda. Biographical information material from and telephone conversation with Sylvia Rodríguez, March 11-13, 1998.

University of New Mexico Home Page. Available at http://www.unm.edu/~anthro/vitae/s_rodr.html.

Teresa Rodriguez

Television host, news correspondent, producer

In 1982 Teresa Rodriguez became the first Hispanic American ever to anchor a national newscast. She reached this landmark when she landed the job as host of *Noticiero,* a prime-time Spanish-language news show produced by the Spanish International Newsweek (SIN), now known as

Teresa Rodriguez

Univision. In the years since, she has won a number of prestigious awards for her coverage of socially and culturally relevant stories. She is the recipient of at least seven Emmys with Univision and is a member of the National Association of Hispanic Journalists. Currently Rodriguez is the anchor, correspondent, and executive producer of Univision's only news magazine special, *Aqui y Ahora con Teresa Rodriguez,* as well as a special host for Univision's national news program, *Noticiera Univision.* Throughout her career she has been committed to communicating with the Hispanic American community about their most current and pressing concerns.

Wins Broadcast Journalism Award

Reviewing a list of Rodriguez's achievements and awards might lead to the conclusion that Rodriguez always had the ambition to work in television news. Upon graduating from college magna cum laude in her first major, marketing, and with a perfect 4.0 grade point in her second, economics, Rodriguez had her sights set on law school. But another opportunity steered Rodriguez toward her future in television news. "I received the coveted *Wall Street Journal* Award for Excellence in Economics. It was the first time that a female Hispanic American had won such an award. That award opened doors to my first job in broadcasting," said Rodriguez in a letter to the author. When WPBT-Channel 2 Miami was looking for a business reporter, the award made Rodriquez stand out, and she landed the job. Ever since, she has been a broadcast journalist. Rodriguez takes her own experiences as a lesson, stating, "I believe strongly in education and try to stress how important that is whenever I speak to kids at schools, fairs, et cetera."

Rodriguez's next challenge was to anchor live news, which she did up to three times a day over the next several years. She worked at CBS and NBC affiliates in Miami, as well as at SIN, where she became the first Hispanic American, male or female, to perform as main anchor for a prime-time national news program. As an anchor she covered a range of nationally and internationally significant news stories, including Pope John Paul II's visit to the United States, the 1984 presidential election, and Hurricane Andrew, for which Rodriguez was co-recipient of the prestigious George Foster Peabody Broadcasting Award in 1992.

Demonstrates Flair for Features

While working as an anchor at the local NBC affiliate Rodriguez sometimes substituted for Connie Chung on NBC's national news magazine show *Sunrise.* Shortly thereafter, NBC offered her a job as the regular host of *Sunrise,* seeking to replace Chung. Rodriguez turned down the offer in order to stay in Miami. She made this decision in part because she wanted to raise a family in Miami, but also because Univision offered her the opportunity to become more involved in features.

Rodriguez became the creator, executive producer, and host of a magazine-style news show called *Portada,* which was broadcast not only in the United States but also in 18 Latin American countries. She had always had an interest in feature reporting, as evidenced in several special reports that she did early in her career. She hosted an award-winning series called *America through Spanish Eyes,* which discussed the Hispanic American experience in an effort to increase awareness of the particular challenges and problems Hispanic Americans face. She also presented a special made by the Public Broadcasting Network in Los Angeles, which was simulcast on Univision in Spanish, entitled "SIDA is AIDS." These examples illustrate some of Rodriguez's most notable work on subjects pertinent to the Hispanic American community. Rodriguez has continued that commitment at Univision. She hosted "Callejon sin Salida" or "Blind Alley," a special about the educational crisis of Hispanic Americans in the United States, and "Huellas de un Milagro" or "Footprints of a Miracle," concerning sightings of the Virgin Mary, both of which won Emmys.

Currently Rodriguez is the host, correspondent, and executive producer of *Aqui y Ahora,* a news magazine that focuses on issues most relevant to Hispanic Americans. In addition, she hosts two special segments on Univision's national newscast—an in-depth report on current events and issues and a one-on-one interview with notable newsmakers. She is also the spokesperson for *La Familia de Hoy,* a series of vignettes aired on Univision that take up pressing social issues such as immunization and voter registration.

Stresses Education and Ethnic Pride

Rodriguez's career has been characterized by a drive to achieve and a commitment to her community, which she attributes to her upbringing. She was born in Cuba, and when she was only nine-months old immigrated to the United States, where she has lived ever since. "My mother and father never went past an eight-grade education and I owe them my love of books and the determination to make it in life," Rodriguez wrote in a letter to Sarah Madsen Hardy. "Now that I have my own family, I cannot stress how important an education is, as well as being bilingual and being proud of your roots."

Current Address: Aqui y Ahora con Teresa Rodriquez-Univision, 9405 NW 41st St., Miami, FL 33178.

Sources:

Madsen Hardy, Sarah. Letter from Teresa Rodriguez, March 23, 1998.
Palmisano, Joseph M. Letter from Univision, February 23, 1998.

Lola Rodríguez de Tío
(1843–1924)
Poet, nationalist, women's rights activist

Selected writings:

Mis Cantares. 1876.
Claros y Nieblas. 1885.
Mi Libro de Cuba. 1893.

Overview

A revered figure in both Cuban and Puerto Rican history, Lola Rodríguez de Tío was born September 14, 1843, in San Germain, Puerto Rico. Born into the island's ruling class, she was the daughter of Don Sebastian Rodríguez de Astudillo, Dean of the Magistracy of Puerto Rico and Doña Carmen Ponce de León, a descendant of Ponce de León, the explorer and first governor of the colony. Rodríguez was a bright child who showed early promise as a poet. Her education in religious schools and by private tutors was guided by her mother, who was described in the *Enciclopedia Puertorriqueña Ilustrada* as "an educated, well-read woman with a fine spirit and the wide-awake intelligence of a child." It was rare for women to be educated in Puerto Rico; most women, especially poor women, were illiterate. It was rarer still for a woman to be an intellectual, but Rodríguez was supported and encouraged in her progress as a poet by poet Ursula Cardona de Quinones. Her understanding of the disparity of opportunity for women made her one of Latin America's most influential early feminists.

Becomes Revolutionary Poet and Patriot

Rodríguez de Tío married at age 20; her husband, Bonacio Tío Segarra, was a respected and influential journalist and poet. Partners in life and politics, the couple were a thorn in the side of the government. As a colony, Puerto Rico had been long abused, suffering corruption and brutality under Spain's colonial governors. Puerto Rico's visionary patriot, Eugenio María de Hostos (1839-1903), was an important influence on Rodríguez de Tío. Hostos spent most of his life in exile. His eloquent writings inspired many others to call for independence from Spain. Rodríguez de Tío's home in Mayaguez became a salon where the leading intellectuals, including Hostos, discussed politics and called for revolution. Forthright in her opposition, she boldly challenged the government.

The work for which Rodríguez de Tío is best known, and which caused her to be deported, was "La Borinquena." In 1868, she composed a fiery lyric for a traditional melody; she read it aloud at a literary gathering at her home to immediate acclaim. It begins: "Awake, Borinquenos, for they've given the signal!/Awake from your sleep, for it's time to fight!" "La Borinquena" became Puerto Rico's national anthem, but Rodríguez de Tío's lyrics were later replaced with the more sentimental lyrics of Manuel Fernandez Juncos. The Lares Uprising of 1868 brought about a repressive response from the government—Rodríguez de Tío and her husband were given hours to leave the island. They went into exile in Caracas, Venezuela where Hostos was already living. They grew closer to Hostos during their time in Venezuela; Rodríguez de Tío was a bridesmaid at his wedding in 1878.

Finally, the family was allowed to return to Puerto Rico in 1885, but once again, Rodríguez de Tío's writing infuriated the government. "Nochebuena," a tribute to political prisoners, was published in 1887, the "terrible year" of the "Componte." Rodríguez de Tío and her family were exiled in 1889 to Cuba, never again to live in Puerto Rico. However, she devoted the rest of her life to achieving independence for both her homeland and Cuba.

Finds A Second Homeland

Their political activity for Cuban independence caused Rodríguez de Tío and her husband to be expelled from Havana in 1892. They joined a group of Cuban exiles in New York City, where Rodríguez de Tío met Jose Marti, the legendary Cuban patriot and poet. This period in her life was one of intense political activity—the group of political exiles created the Cuban Revolutionary Party in 1895. Jose Marti regarded Rodríguez de Tío as an equal in art and in politics. When Marti was killed in Cuba in 1895, the exiles carried on their efforts through political clubs. Rodríguez de Tío was elected president of "Rius Rivera" in 1896, and secretary of another club, "Caridad," in 1897. She and her family returned to Cuba in 1899 after the Spanish-American War, and she devoted the rest of her life to social justice and the betterment of the condition of women in Cuba.

Rodríguez de Tío is considered a leading literary figure and a national hero: she was named to the Cuban Academy of Arts and Letters in 1910 and Patron of the Galician Beneficent Society in 1911. She continued to be active in politics, and served as inspector general of the private schools in Havana, as well as in the Ministry of Education. Like many other feminists of her time, Rodríguez de Tío also sought to reform women's fashions. Federico Ribes Tovar described her attire in *Enciclopedia Puertorriqueña Ilustrada*: "This strange woman with her radical thoughts, wore a skirt of a very peculiar design, like an Amazon's, and wore a blouse with a high neckline and a wide bow tie, and her hair was cut like a man's." He also reported that she was considered to be devout, a fine wife and mother, and an "exemplary friend."

Referred to as "Daughter of the Isles"

Rodríguez de Tío's importance as a poet is a matter of dispute among literary critics, but her place in Puerto Rican letters is not. Referred to in the *Encyclopedia of Latin American Literature* as that country's "most distinguished 19th-century lyric poet," her style is sometimes dismissed as derivative, but her verses are well-known and very influential. No less an authority than Ruben Dario, considered Spanish America's greatest modern poet, praised Rodríguez de Tío, calling her "the Daughter of the Isles."

As a disciple of Romanticism, Rodríguez de Tío was influenced by Spanish Golden Age poets and the traditional stanza. She published three books: *Mis Cantares,* in 1876 (*My Songs*); *Claros y Nieblas,* in 1885(*Bright Intervals and Mist*); and *Mi Libro de Cuba,* in 1893 (*My Book on Cuba*). One of her most famous verses, "Cuba and Puerto Rico" was quoted by Fidel Castro in a 1966 speech: "Cuba and Puerto Rico are/of one bird, the two wings;/they receive flowers and bullets/in the same heart." However, he mistakenly attributed it to Jose Marti. Rodríguez de Tío's poem does capture her affection for both Puerto Rico and her adopted homeland: it concludes: "What a lot if in the illusion/ that glows red in a thousand tones,/ Lola's muse dreams/ with fervent fantasy/ of making one single homeland/ of this land and of mine." She died on November 10, 1924, in Havana at the age of 81.

Sources:

Babin, Maria Teresa, and Stan Steiner. *Borinquen: An Anthology of Puerto Rican Literature.* New York: Vintage Books, 1974.

Marques, Rene. *The Docile Puerto Rican.* Philadelphia: Temple University Press, 1976.

Smith, Verity, ed. "Puerto Rico." *Encyclopedia of Latin American Literature.* Chicago: Fitzroy Dearborn, 1997.

Tío, Carlos F. Mendoza. *Contribución al Estudio de la Obra Poetica de Lola Rodríguez de Tío.* San Juan, 1974.

Tío, Carlos F. Mendoza. "Lola Rodríguez de Tío." *Investigaciónes Literarias, Vols. I-III.* San Juan, 1974.

Tovar, Federico Ribes. "Lola Rodríguez de Tío." *Enciclopedia Puertorriquena Ilustrada.* New York: Plus Ultra Educational Publications, Inc., 1970.

Lin Romero
(1947–)
Poet, teacher

Selected writings:

Happy Songs, Bleeding Hearts. Toltecas en Aztlán, 1974.

Overview

Lin Romero's family originally lived in New York, but her father—believing Mexico would be a wholesome place to raise children—moved the family to Mexico City where the future Chicana poet was born on October 15, 1947. She received her early education at the bilingual American School Foundation. At seventeen she went to California and studied at San Francisco State University, the University of California, Los Angeles, and California State University, Los Angeles, where she graduated. At UCLA she wrote the poems included in Michael Victor Sedano's doctoral dissertation, "Chicanismo in Selected Poetry From the Chicano Movement, 1969-1972." In the epilogue of *Happy Songs, Bleeding Hearts* (1974), the reader learns Romero had experienced the "transient urban life of Mexico City" as well as that of Los Angeles. Roberto Sifuentes calls Romero's collection a "poetic chronicle" that presents "the last tear being dropped by a Chicano group for the indios lacandones," the Indians of the Yucatán peninsula of Mexico. Lin was a member of a group funded by the Centro de Estudios Xicanos de UCLA, and *Happy Songs, Bleeding Hearts* is her account of the group's trip into the land of the Lacandones, ". . . the ones who still live true and free con la tierra [with the earth] we thought, we hoped." The brief book is a combination of poignant, revealing photos, and prose and verse that mingles English with Spanish and an occasional Mayan phrase.

Commenting on *Happy Songs, Bleeding Hearts* in *Chicano Literature* (1982), Charles M. Tatum declares that the "book title aptly catches the duality of the collective experience: beneath the happy sounds of song and dance reside both the memory and daily encounters with poverty and other forms of human suffering." Before visiting the jungle home of the Lacandones, the "last true people," Romero's group stopped at the town of San Cristóbal de las Casas in Chiapas, Mexico. At least seven tribes of Indians lived there, and Romero describes their circumstances as bleak: "Indios, people dying from hunger, disease, alcoholism, physical exhaustion and spiritual grief." Romero ridicules attempts by the Mexican government to help the Indians by incorporating them into a rapidly changing society. The poet decries the fact that the Indians are being convinced to give up their old ways and dress in modern clothes, exchanging their talent for embroidery and weaving in order to work as maids, street sweepers, and construction workers, struggling just to get basic necessities.

The tone of *Happy Songs, Bleeding Hearts* changes when the group heads into the jungle lands of the Lacandones, the last remnant "of the once great Mayan empire." As their plane approaches, the poet anticipates that they "will hear cantos like never before / never again / cantos de sol y agua" [of the sun and water]. The group is welcomed by the leader of the Lacandones, tours their palm-tree houses, and shares a dinner with them of tortillas, chili, and fruit, but the poet is saddened when she sees the missionaries and anthropologists who "swallow the people alive / to return to Europe / burp them up / receive an applause." Despite this exploitation, the Lacandones were a jolly, generous people who shared what little they possessed with their guests.

Romero's journey, however, left her with a burden— "the burden of knowledge that our quest to gather truth and beauty found truth: dead bodies." This touching account of her visit to the dying people includes photographs of the pensive, stoic, questioning eyes and faces of young and old. These are pictures of musicians and leaders, women with plaited hair and children with unkempt tresses, all impassively awaiting their fate as they go about their daily rounds of marketing, gossiping, and praying.

Reflecting on her career during an interview, Romero revealed that she began writing poetry when she was in the sixth grade. Later she was influenced by several people connected with the Chicano movement— of San Diego. Since the student uprisings at San Francisco State University in the late 1960s, Romero has been invited to participate in poetry readings. From San Francisco to San Diego, from Berkeley to Stanford, she has consistently contributed to Cinco de Mayo and other commemorative celebrations.

Romero admits that the bulk of her poems have not been published due to her own lack of organization. Nevertheless, some twenty have appeared in magazines and anthologies. A study of these poems reveals her desire for a new free world of Aztlán. She challenges her readers to return to their past and to recognize the value of the roots of la Raza (the Race) and challenges herself to be a means of peace.

Since 1994, Lin Romero has been part of the Taco Shop Poets, a band of writers and musicians based in in the San Diego, California, and Tijuana, Mexico, that recite bilingual poetry and perform rituals and experimental music at taquerias, cafes, cultural centers, galleries, academic settings, and street corners. The Taco Shop Poets have been referred to as a "raffish band of scribes. . . who want to bring poetry to the people and people to the poetry."

Sources:

Sedano, Michael Victor. "Chicanismo in Selected Poetry From the Chicano Movement 1969-1972: A Rhetorical Study," Ph.D. dissertation, University of Southern California, Los Angeles, June 1980.

Sifuentes, Roberto Sifuentes. "Essay," in *A Decade of Chicano Literature (1970-1979)*. Santa Barbara: Causa, 1982, p. 61.

Taco Shop Poets Homepage. Available at http://www.n2.net/ecruse/progsTacoShop.html.

Romero Cash, Marie
See **Cash, Marie Romero**

Romo, Gilda Cruz
See **Cruz-Romo, Gilda**

Rossana Rosado
(1961–)
Editor, journalist

Born in New York City in 1961 to parents of Puerto Rican descent, Rossana Rosado has spent most of her career as a journalist. In radio, television, and print journalism, she has distinguished herself for the excellence of her work. In 1994 she became the first Puerto Rican and woman to be named editor-in-chief of *El Diario/La Prensa,* the largest Spanish-language daily newspaper in the United States.

Journalism Career Begins

A graduate of Adlai E. Stevenson High School in the Bronx, Rosado attended Pace University in White Plains, New York, where she received a bachelor's degree in journalism in 1983. Her career in journalism began in 1982 at New York radio station WCBS-FM, where she served as an assistant to the director. She moved from that job to an associate producership at WNYC-TV 31. She then returned to WCBS, this time to the AM broadcast operation, where she worked as a desk assistant. Her first experience at *El Diario/La Prensa* came in 1986 when she served as metro editor. From 1988 until 1992, she worked at WPIX-TV, first as a producer of public affairs programming and later as public service director. In that post, she was responsible for the creation and placement of hundreds of public service announcements a week. While at WPIX-TV, she won several prestigious awards, including an Emmy for the production of a public service campaign called "Care for Kids." She also won the New York State Broadcaster's Award and the Folio Award.

Former Editor is Murdered

During her first stint at *El Diario/La Prensa,* Rosado worked under editor Manuel de Dios Unanue, who in March of 1992 was murdered in an Elmhurst, Queens, restaurant apparently on the orders of Colombia's Cali cocaine cartel. When de Dios was posthumously honored in 1994 by the Inter-American Press Association with its grand prize for press freedom, Rosado hailed de Dios's "extraordinary commitment to his craft" for his courageous crusade against the scourge of large-scale drug peddling in Latino communities. She said that "those of us who knew him always expected he'd be killed. There was almost a zaniness to Manuel, one step beyond crusading. He was absolutely the most prominent American journalist to expose the cartels."

Takes Significant Leadership Roles

Rosado has also demonstrated her talents outside of the field of journalism. In 1992, Rosado took a detour into the public sector, serving as vice president for public affairs at the New York City Health & Hospitals Corporation. In that position, she was responsible for the overall marketing and promotion of the corporation's services and facilities, which at that time included six hospitals and eleven primary health-care centers.

In 1994 Rosado was named editor-in-chief of *El Diario/La Prensa.* In addition to her duties as editor, she serves as general manager for news and sales, overseeing the national retail and classified advertising departments of the newspaper as well. Under Rosado's direction, the newspaper began publication in 1996 of a Sunday edition for the first time in its lengthy history. The newspaper invested $1 million in staff, equipment, and promotional advertising in support of the Sunday edition. At the time of the launch, Rosado announced the Sunday edition would feature a 20-page color feature supplement called "Siete Dias" ("Seven Days") that would include the previous week's news from all Latin American nations with a sizable population in New York.

Married to Jaime Quinones since March of 1990, Rosado is the mother of a son, Jaime Jr. She is a board member of the Harlem-Dowling Child Care Center. In both her professional and personal affiliations, Rosado has proven her leadership abilities, and will most certainly continue to do so in the future.

Sources:

Brock, Pope. "Trouble: Journalist Manuel de Dios Unanue Took On Drug Lords and Corrupt Politicians. One Had Him Killed. A Crusader Falls." *People,* March 30, 1992, p. 53.
"El Diario Launches Sunday Edition." *Editor & Publisher,* April 27, 1996, p. 50.
Moses, Paul. "Writers Honor Slain Editor." *Newsday,* July 20, 1994, p. A15.
Rosado, Rossana. Letter to author, March 2, 1998.

Rosich, Vanna Marie
See **White, Vanna**

Rothe de Vallbona, Rima Gretel
See **de Vallbona, Rima**

Vicki Lynn Ruiz
(1955–)
Professor, historian, author, editor

Selected writings:

Working for Wages: Mexican Women in the Southwest, 1930-1980. Southwest Institute for Research on Women, 1984.

Cannery Women, Cannery Lives. Mexican Women, Unionization, and the California Food Processing Industry, 1930-1950. University of New Mexico Press, c1987.

Women on the United States-Mexico Border: Responses to Change Edited with Susan Tiano, Allen & Unwin, 1987.

Western Women: Their Land, Their Lives. Edited with Lillian Schlissel and Janice Monk, University of New Mexico Press, c1988.

Unequal Sisters: A Multicultural Reader in U.S. Women's History Edited with Ellen Carol DuBois, Routledge, 1990.

From Out of the Shadows: Mexican Women in the Twentieth Century. Oxford University Press, 1997.

Overview

Vicki Lynn Ruiz has risen to the top of her profession, fueled, she told interviewer Tom Pendergast, "by insomnia and a drive to succeed." Ruiz, an oral historian who has attempted to understand the lives of Mexican American women in the twentieth century, has done extensive research on the subject. She is the author of two books and has served as a co-editor of several anthologies.

Ruiz's interest in Mexican history springs directly from her past. She was born on May 21, 1955, in Atlanta, Georgia, the daughter of Robert Mercer and Ermina Ruiz. Robert's parents were furious that he had married a Hispanic woman and disowned him. Ermina was proud of her heritage and enjoyed sharing it with her children. Besides recounting stories of working in the coal mines and beet fields of southern Colorado, she told them of her father, who had come to the United States during the Mexican Revolution and was once an active member of the Industrial Workers of the World (a radical union that was organized between 1905 and 1920), and of her mother, a proud woman whose family had emigrated to Colorado from New Mexico early in the nineteenth century.

Ruiz, however, grew up in Florida, far from her Mexican roots. Her father owned a large sport fishing boat and supported the family by taking tourists on deep-sea fishing trips. During her childhood, Ruiz participated in the family business by stocking local hotel lobbies with flyers and selling fishing trip tickets. Because of the seasonal nature of the family business, the family moved back and forth frequently between Marathon and Panama City. Ruiz told Pendergast, "I grew up on the water, and I particularly loved the time we would spend in the Florida Keys." The family's nomadic existence meant that Ruiz attended many different schools as a child, but by the time she reached the eighth grade, her mother insisted that they stay in one place.

Living in what Ruiz only half-affectionately calls the "Redneck Riviera"—Panama City, Florida—posed its share of difficulties. Some local parents did not want their sons dating a Mexican girl, and Ruiz was denied a Daughter of the Confederacy academic scholarship because she could not trace her ancestry to the pre-Civil War South. By the time she finished high school, she knew she wanted to escape her small town, and education provided the quickest way out.

Examines Role of Women Cannery Workers

Ruiz attended Gulf Coast Community College and graduated with an associate of science degree in 1975. She entered Florida State University and graduated with a bachelor of science degree (summa cum laude) in 1977. After graduation, she initially wanted to become a high school teacher, but her professors convinced her to pursue graduate studies instead. "I applied to Stanford University on a whim," she related to Pendergast, "and a professor named Al Camarillo called me and told me he would support my application." Camarillo proved to be a huge source of support and guidance for Ruiz, introducing her to the history of the women's cannery unions in California and Luisa Moreno, an early union organizer who had been deported from the United States for her activism. "I went to Guadalajara, Mexico, to interview Moreno," Ruiz said, "and I came back knowing what I would study."

In 1978, Ruiz received her master's degree in history from Stanford and then earned a doctorate in history, also from Stanford, in 1982. Her doctoral dissertation, which examined the plight of Mexican American cannery workers and their pursuit of unionization, was published by the University of New Mexico Press in 1987 under the title *Cannery Women, Cannery Lives: Mexican Women, Unionization, and the California Food Processing Industry, 1939-1950.* In a *Southwestern Historical Quarterly* review, Yolanda G. Romero called the book "an outstanding addition to the historical literature on labor," and William Flores, writing in the *Oral History Review,* deemed it "essential reading for anyone engaged in research on Chicanos and Mexicans, on cannery workers, and more broadly on issues of gender and work."

Ruiz's first academic post was at the University of Texas in El Paso. "I felt lucky that there was a job in my field," she told Pendergast, "and I kept thinking how lucky I was to be teaching, because I was learning so much from my students." She left El Paso in 1985 for the University of California at Davis, where she enjoyed the support of a community of Chicano scholars, and stayed at Davis until 1992. She then accepted a position at the Claremont

Graduate School near Los Angeles as the Andrew W. Mellon All-Clermont Professor in the Humanities. In 1995, Ruiz became a professor of history and women's studies at Arizona State University and remained in that post until 1996.

Continues to Research Mexican Women's History

During this entire period, Ruiz continued to work in the field of Mexican American women's history, co-editing *Women on the United States-Mexico Border: Responses to Change* and *Western Women: Their Land, Their Lives.* In 1997, she published her latest work *From Out of the Shadows: Mexican Women in the Twentieth Century.* Through the use of interviews, oral histories, and archives, *From Out of the Shadows* chronicles the triumphs and struggles of Mexican women during the twentieth century. As Ruiz relates in an issue of *The Chronicle of Higher Education,* "My book focuses on how these women, rather than being passive victims of poverty, sexism, and racism, have shaped their own lives and culture through mutual assistance and collective action."

Throughout her career, Ruiz has been the recipient of numerous awards. She received a Critics Choice Award from the Educational Studies Association in 1991 for her work as co-editor of *Unequal Sisters: a Multicultural Reader in U.S. Women's History.* That same year, the National Women's Political Caucus presented Ruiz with a Distinguished Achievement Award for her book *Cannery Women, Cannery Lives: Mexican Women, Unionization, and the California Food Processing Industry, 1930-1950.* In 1992, she earned the Chicana/Latina Research Project Scholar Award. Ruiz was honored in 1994 with a Community Service Award from the Chicano/Latino Studies Department at Cal State Long Beach. During her career at the University of California, Davis, she received an Outstanding Faculty Award and an Honored Faculty Award.

Ruiz cites Luisa Moreno as one of her role models for her strength and bravery in organizing women in the California food processing industry. But she reserves the greatest praise for her mother, whose enthusiasm for life never wavered despite the fact that she often had to work long hours at difficult jobs to help support her family. "My mother was a survivor," Ruiz recalled, "and she found great joy in working and helping out. She is also a wonderful storyteller."

Ruiz is the mother of two boys, Miguel and Daniel, from her first marriage, which lasted from 1979 until 1990. She married Victor Becerra in 1992.

Current Address: Dept. of Chicana/o, Arizona State Univ., Tempe, AZ 85287.

Sources:

American Historical Review, April, 1989.

Journal of American History, June, 1988; December, 1988; December, 1989; December 1990.

Ms., July/August, 1990.

New Republic, October 22, 1990.

Oral History Review spring, 1989.

Pendergast, Tom. Telephone interview with Vicki Ruiz, September 9, 1992.

Scanlon, Jennifer, and Sharon Cosner. *American Women Historians, 1700s-1900s: A Biographical Dictionary.* Westport, CT: Greenwood Press, 1996.

Southwestern Historical Quarterly, April, 1989.

"What 15 Leading Historians Are Working on Now." *The Chronicle of Higher Education,* January 9, 1998.

S

Theresa Saldana
(1955–)
Actress, community activist

Selected writings:

Beyond Survival. Bantam Books, 1986.

Selected filmography:

Nunzio. 1978.
I Wanna Hold Your Hand. 1978.
Home Movies. 1979.
Defiance. 1980.
Sophia Loren: Her Own Story (TV movie). 1980.
Raging Bull. 1980.
Victims for Victims: The Theresa Saldana Story (TV movie). 1984.
The Commish (TV series). 1991-1996.
All My Children. (TV series). 1996.

Theresa Saldana

Overview

Theresa Saldana has had a varied and distinguished career as an actress on stage, screen, and television. However, a grisly attack on her life by a deranged fan brought her career to a halt, as she recovered emotionally and physically in a years-long struggle. Now fully recovered, Saldana's life is back on track as she proves that she has both talent and resiliency.

Describing herself as a "Puerto Rican-Italian," in *Parade* magazine, the Brooklyn native was adopted when she was five days old and raised by Divina and Tony Saldana. A devout Catholic, she attended parochial school for twelve years and showed an early commitment to a career in the performing arts. Encouraged by her parents, she studied dance and voice and was a pupil of the renowned acting coach Sanford Meisner. After a successful stint on the New York stage, she moved to Los Angeles to pursue a career in film and television. Her 1978 film debut in *Nunzio* was well received and led to a role later that year in Robert Zemeckis' *I Wanna Hold Your Hand,* a Hollywood treatment of Beatlemania on the Ed Sullivan Show. In 1979 she appeared as Judy in *Home Movies,* directed by Brian DePalma, a quirky farce about filmmaking. She won the plum part of Sophia Loren's sister Maria in the popular 1980 television film *Sophia Loren: Her Own Story,* and that same year won her first co-starring role in *Defiance,* with Jan-Michael Vincent, a story of young love and gang violence in New York City. Her real breakthrough part was the role of Leonore LaMotta in Martin Scorsese's critically acclaimed *Raging Bull.* Saldana gained favorable attention playing the sister-in-law of Robert DeNiro's character in the Oscar-winning film. Her small part made a big impression on Hollywood, and as a young, happily married woman in her third year of college, she was leading, by her own account, "a happy and fulfilling life."

Suffers Attack by Stalker

The accomplished young actress made headlines on March 15, 1982, when, on her way to an acting class, she was attacked in front of her home and stabbed repeatedly by Arthur Jackson, a deranged Scottish drifter. Jackson had first seen Saldana in *Defiance,* and his obsession with her led him to Los Angeles. He stalked her, posing as a representative of director Martin Scorsese, obtaining information from her unwitting family and manager. In a journal filled with minute handwritten details of his search for Saldana, Jackson wrote of his need to "send to Heaven" a "beautiful angel too good for this world." Her condition was extremely grave, but she survived the attack and spent two years making a full recovery through grueling physical therapy and counseling.

Becomes Advocate for Crime Victims

In her book, *Beyond Survival,* Saldana detailed her healing and triumph over fear. ". . . The assault on my body lasted only a few minutes, just long enough to bring me to the brink of death. But the assault on my mind, my heart, my soul was to last far, far longer. . . . The purpose of my book is not to make others suffer vicariously through my agony but, rather, to show how essential it is to create something positive out of an ugly, wrenchingly painful experience." During her recovery she founded Victims for Victims, a victims' rights organization that calls attention to the plight of crime victims who are too often inadequately protected by existing laws and whose suffering is intensified by medical bills and inadequate insurance. Saldana, understanding from her own experience that the trauma of crime victims was long-lasting and profound, undertook a campaign to publicize the need for tougher laws and more compassionate treatment of victims. She also portrayed herself in the 1984 television movie, *Victims for Victims: The Theresa Saldana Story,* which graphically recreated her attack and recovery. The film helped raise awareness of the victims' rights movement, to which Saldana devoted herself by promoting her book. Her advocacy was recognized with a presidential commendation for outstanding service on behalf of crime victims. With Gavin de Becker, a security expert who helped draft the legislation, Saldana successfully lobbied to toughen California law to deter stalkers. Jackson, who had never stopped threatening Saldana, was released from a California prison after serving 14 years; he was, however, immediately extradited to Scotland where he is presently serving a life sentence for murder in connection with a robbery.

Saldana's personal life was significantly damaged by the attack. Her first marriage to substance abuse counselor Fred Feliciano came apart as a result of the strain of her convalescence. Saldana's mother was deeply depressed for a year following the attack, and her father was so disturbed by Jackson's repeated death threats to his daughter that he suffered a heart attack and died. At Jackson's second trial in 1990, Saldana stated that ". . . what I would like more than anything in my life is to shed my career as a victim, once and for all, and just be able to return to my own life and to my career without being further harassed. . . ." Once Jackson was returned to prison in Scotland, Saldana was at last able to live without constant fear.

Begins a New Life

Saldana put her attack and its aftermath behind her and moved forward in her career. Family life is most important to her, however; she is married to actor Phil Peters and they have a daughter, Tianna. Placing her family first, she has limited her career in order to spend more time with them. Even so, Saldana received popular and critical acclaim for her five-year run as Rachel Scali in the ABC series *The Commish.* She was nominated for a Golden Globe Award and, in 1996, received a Bravo Award for her role in that series. In 1997, she joined the cast of daytime drama *All My Children* for a limited role as mystery woman Christina Vargas/Diane Martinez.

Although she is no longer active in Victim for Victims, Saldana continues to have a special informal ministry to the sick and takes her daughter with her. She told *Catholic Digest* magazine, "I know, having been there, how much it means to be visited in the hospital." Honored by the Southern California Motion Picture Council for lifetime achievement and cited at the 1998 American Latino Media Arts Awards for her positive portrayal of a Hispanic woman in *All My Children,* Saldana has regained a happy and vibrant life and continues to be professionally active on her own terms.

Sources:

Brady, James. "In Step With: Theresa Saldana." *Parade,* January 24, 1993.

Klein, Dianne. "A Crime Without End." *Los Angeles Times,* June 2, 1989.

Markman, Ronald, and Ron Labreque. *Obsessed: The Stalking of Theresa Saldana.* New York: William Morrow, 1994.

Saldana, Theresa. *Beyond Survival.* New York: Bantam Books, 1986.

Stauffer, Kathleen. "Theresa Saldana: An Actress, Her Daughter, and a Life Full of Miracles." *Catholic Digest,* November, 1997, pp. 18-34.

Maria Elena Salinas
Television anchor

Delivers the News

For millions of Americans, it is not Tom Brokaw or Dan Rather who are invited into the home each evening via television to deliver the world's news. Rather, the millions of Americans for whom Spanish is their first language depend each night upon Maria Elena Salinas to fill them in on current events around the globe. Since 1987, when she joined the Univision television network as co-anchor of the network's nightly *Noticiero Univision,* Salinas has been an influential force in Spanish-language news broadcasting in this country and much of Latin America. Miami-based Univision's network reaches beyond the borders of the United States to Mexico, Central America, and South America.

Before taking on her duties as news co-anchor at Univision, Salinas developed a reputation as a hard-hitting broadcast journalist in the sprawling Los Angeles Spanish-language market. Salinas began her career in television in 1981 as a news reporter at KMEX. She also served as host of community affairs program there before assuming the post of news anchor. Immediately before joining Univision, she worked as news anchor at the network's Los Angeles broadcast affiliate KMEX-TV, Channel 34.

During her years as news co-anchor at Univision, Salinas has interviewed and profiled most of the movers and shakers in Latin American politics, including Mexican presidents Ernesto Zedillo and Carlos Salinas de Gortari, Argentine President Carlos Menem, Peruvian President Alberto Fujimori, Violeta Chamorro and Daniel Ortega of Nicaragua, Panama's General Manuel Antonio Noriega, and Chilean strongman Augusto Pinochet. She has also interviewed U.S. presidents George Bush and Bill Clinton.

Covers Wide Variety of Events

In addition to her interviews with some of the most powerful politicians in the Americas, Salinas has covered a wide variety of events during her television news career. She has reported on the superpower summits of the Cold War period, electoral battles throughout Latin America, and the last four presidential elections in the United States. Away from politics she has covered the devastation wrought by natural disasters, including Hurricane Andrew's 1992 visit to South Florida. She has brought human interest stories to the attention of her viewers as well as reporting on the achievements of Hispanic American communities throughout the nation. Salinas has paid particular attention to continuing controversies over immigration. During Pope John Paul II's January trip to Cuba in 1998, Salinas and her Univision news co-anchor Jorge Ramos spent a week on location in Cuba to cover the pontiff's activities and services throughout the island nation as well as the reaction of the Cuban people to the precedent-setting visit. Of the Latin American market for news from sources other than the government, Salinas said recently: "There are hundreds of millions of people who are hungry for information, for independent information. I think that's why now everybody wants to have a piece of the pie. The pie is really big, and it's really good."

Married to Elliott Rodriquez, Salinas has two children and makes her home in Miami, headquarters of Univision. She was a founding member of the National Association of Hispanic Journalists (NAHJ) and a former board member of the California Chicano News Media Association. When

NAHJ honored Felix Gutierrez, executive director of The Freedom Forum Pacific Coast Center in Oakland, CA, as the "padrino (godfather) of Latino journalists," Salinas presented him with a plaque and praised him for his work as an educator, activist, and scholar.

Current Address: Univision, 9405 NW 41st St., Miami, FL 33178.

Sources:

Amerman, Donald. Letter from Maria Elena Salinas, February 23, 1998.
CNN Financial Network Home Page. Available at http://cnnfn.com/news/9606/27/cbs_spanish/index.htm.
The Freedom Forum Home Page. Available at http://www.freedomforum.org/FreedomForum/resources/general_pubs/fweekly/arc hive/fw061995.html.
Jackson, Terry. "How TV Will Blanket Big Event." *Miami Herald,* January 18, 1998.

Elisa Maria Sánchez
Organization president

Born and raised in the tiny New Mexico mining town of Central, Elisa Maria Sánchez has mostly positive recollections of life in the copper mining region. Central, now known as Santa Clara, was a predominantly Chicano community in a county plagued by segregation, but the injustices only served to pull the Hispanic Americans together as church and school became the dominant spheres of social activity. From these culturally-rich roots Sánchez grew up to president of MANA, A National Latina Organization.

Community Supports Cultural Pride

Looking back on her childhood, Sánchez wrote in the late 1980s: "I sang in the church choir and participated in a myriad of activities with all my girlfriends. My early school years could have been filled with problems but weren't by a quirk of fate. All the Mexican teachers hired by the local school district were sent to Central or a farm community nearby. Unwittingly, the district sent us role models." Those role models and supportive Anglo teachers created a positive educational environment for Sánchez and her fellow students. "Our school curriculum included New Mexico history filled with the likes of Cabeza de Baca, Coronado, and Cortez," she recalled. This early pride was supplemented with an appreciation for the culture of her Spanish and Mexican forebears. Students in Central studied Mexican music and dance and applied what they learned in a celebration of Hispanic American culture. "I remember how beautiful and proud I felt dressed in my *china poblana*," Sánchez stated.

Experiences Discrimination

Sánchez's first brush with overt discrimination occurred when she entered high school. Guidance counselors pointedly avoided recommending college preparatory courses for Chicano students. She recalled that one of her first acts of public rebellion was to defy her counselor and insist that she needed the appropriate courses to prepare for higher education. Her own parents had little education, her mother attending school through the eighth grade and her father finishing only one semester of high school. However, both parents made clear to Sánchez and her sister that they were expected to get a college education.

In high school and beyond, there were many signals from the majority community that were ". . . designed to diminish us as human beings," but Sánchez recalled that it left no real scars on her soul. She credits her upbringing for helping her to grow into adulthood basically unscathed emotionally. Both of her parents were very loving, she said, always challenging her ". . . to get involved, to do different things, to be creative, and to expand my knowledge. Their message was that there was truly nothing that I couldn't do,"—something she came in time to believe without question.

Parents Strongly Influence Sánchez

Though her parents divorced when Sánchez was about ten, both her mother and her father remained strong influences in her life as she went through school. She remembers her mother as "a very unique individual and a tremendous motivator. Even before I entered school she had exposed me to a wide range of ideas through books. She filled our home with them. Among them were the classics, like the *Odyssey*. She succeeded in creating in me a curiosity about everything." Her mother would read to her each afternoon as she put her down for a nap. "I remember those times as rituals," Sánchez wrote. "If I didn't understand something, she would patiently explain it to me. I traveled the world with Odysseus and navigated the Mississippi with Mark Twain. My home and life today reflect this period. I have a deep respect for books and ideas."

After her parents divorced, her father moved away from rural New Mexico to Los Angeles. Sánchez recalled that he never missed a support payment through her years of public school and college. At the beginning of each school year and on major holidays, he sent packages of beautiful clothes for his daughters. All of this was done on his salary as a laborer. "I remember him driving me to Los Angeles City College for my first day of college, so proud I thought

he would burst." Sánchez earned a B.A. and an M.A. from Western New Mexico University in Silver City. She also has an M.P.A. from Baruch College of the City University of New York, which was earned through the National Urban Fellows program, and is a graduate of the Gallup Leadership Institute in Lincoln, Nebraska.

Another profound influence on Sánchez as she was growing up was her mother's activism. As the chair of the women's auxiliary of a mining, mill, and smelter workers union, her mother led members of the auxiliary onto the picket line when a Taft-Hartley injunction barred the workers themselves from picketing during a strike in the late 1940s. "Although a child, I marched with my mother, licked stamps for mailings, and made sandwiches for those on the picket lines," Sánchez recalled. "I experienced a solidarity I strive for even today because I saw what could be accomplished when people work together, trust each other, and struggle for a common goal." That strike later became the subject of a film entitled *Salt of the Earth,* and Sánchez's mother appeared prominently in the film.

Experiences Civil Rights Movement

Sánchez's first real experience as an activist came in the South during the civil rights struggle in the 1960s. Although she was a Chicana, she was subjected to verbal abuse and taunts because of the cause she championed. "Being called a 'nigger' during that volatile time allowed me to get a feel for what it's like to be black. I also learned that, while our histories may vary, discrimination smells, tastes, and feels the same to those who experience it. All minorities, it seems to me, live with one foot in the barrio or ghetto and the other on a banana peel."

Returning to New Mexico and Grant County in the early 1970s, Sánchez decided to run for elective office, becoming the first woman to run for the post of county commissioner. She recalled in the late 1980s: "I ran a straightforward, honest, and issues-oriented campaign. I didn't win, but it's interesting to look back at that campaign. I was talking about waste disposal, water, the environment, and diversity—all critical issues now being addressed by the county."

Reflects on 1970s Hispanic Activism

Sánchez remembers the mid-1970s as a time of great excitement and hope for the future. Living in Washington, DC, during the presidential administration of Jimmy Carter, she was stimulated by the high level of Hispanic activism. She recalled that many Hispanic Americans held positions of influence in the administration and elsewhere in Washington. At the time, Sánchez was president of MANA. "The synergism of our board was something to experience," she recalled. "Playing off of each other, we challenged ourselves to greater thinking. We questioned old concepts, defied past practices, and in the process forged a truly national organization with a unique philosophy for Chicanas by Chicanas."

MANA is a national organization whose goals are: The development of the leadership talents and skills of Latinas; elimination of barriers to opportunity and advancement; and service to the community. Sánchez led the organization as its president from 1977 through 1979 and again in the mid-1990s returned to take the helm. She was reelected to that post in 1996. She is leading MANA in its transition from a volunteer-led organization to a staffed national community service organization of informed activists. Among the initiatives announced during her most recent tenure have been Latina Vote '96, a partnership with the Women's Vote Project that registered voters and helped Latinas gain citizenship in 1996. Reacting in October of 1997 to a national survey that showed that women do not realize their full potential as a force in U.S. elections, Sánchez said, "Clearly elections must be more user-friendly if larger numbers of women are to participate." The National Hermanitas Project, a local mentoring project aimed at keeping middle-school girls in school is another initiative announced during Sánchez's most recent tenure. Another program launched under MANA's broad theme of Rebuilding Latino Communities for the 21st Century has been AvanZamos, a project to improve the leadership skills of community leaders.

Returns to California

Between the end of the 1970s and 1994, when Sánchez returned to MANA as its president, she spent much of her time in the San Diego area where, among other things, she served as project director for Trade and Economic Development in San Diego County's Department of Transborder Affairs. In that position, she was a catalyst in the developing field of transborder economic development. One of her responsibilities was the monitoring of the Mexican maquiladora industry and the assessment of its impact on San Diego County's economy and infrastructure. Sánchez advised the county board of supervisors on border economic development and trade policy. Prior to taking on her duties in transborder affairs, she was special assistant to the chief administrative officer of San Diego County.

While in the San Diego area, Sánchez became involved in the activities of the local MANA chapter, serving as the first coordinator of its Hermanitas Program and chair of the chapter's first annual conference. In 1992, she was elected chapter president. Her community activism in San Diego was not limited to MANA. She served on the boards of the San Diego-Imperial Counties Girl Scout Council, the San Diego Community College District Facilities Corporation, and Planned Parenthood of San Diego and Riverside Counties. She was also a member of the advisory board for the Leadership Training Institute of the Chicano Fed-

eration. She was appointed commissioner of the City of San Diego International Affairs Board and Greater San Diego Visitors and Tourism Bureau.

Reflects on Activist Career

Looking back on her career, Sánchez observed, "My professional and volunteer experiences haven't always been easy, but they've been exciting and fulfilling. I have been the first Hispanic or Chicana in almost every position I've ever held. I've lived in various parts of the country, and I've traveled and worked internationally. Some of my colleagues have viewed me as an affirmative action hire who wasn't qualified for the job. I've managed to prove them wrong each time. Other times, my own people have tried to put me down, and I have overcome that opposition by remaining true to my own principles and values. And I've had the good fortune to work with men and women of all colors who accepted me as an equal. I've also been fortunate to have met and developed friendships with men and women all over the country who have been strong supporters throughout my career."

Though there are many challenges that lie ahead for them, Sánchez sees hope that Hispanic Americans can take more of a role in the ethical and moral leadership of this country if they remain true to themselves and exemplify their traditional values. Most importantly, she suggests, there needs to be a greater focus on the future and less preoccupation with the past. "We are caught in the rhetoric and roots of our past rather than using the strengths of our Spanish and Indian roots to move toward change and the future."

In 1997, Sánchez received a high honor from her peers in the federal government. She was awarded the Medallion of Excellence by the Congressional Hispanic Caucus Institute for advancing the status of all Hispanic American women.

Current Address: MANA, A National Latina Organization, 1725 K St., NW, Ste. 501, Washington, DC 20006.

Sources:

Amerman, Donald. Letter to Elisa Maria Sánchez, February 27, 1998.
"MANA Makes History with New Board." *MANA Home Page.* Available at http://www.hermana.org/news4.htm
"100 Influentials Directory" *HispanStar Home Page* Available at http://www.hispanstar.com./influentials96/res100dir-t+.html
Shepherd, Scott. "Women Voters Underrate Their Power, Survey Says; Females Perceive Obstacles in Getting to Polls." *Rocky Mountain News,* October 15, 1997, p. 36A.

Loretta Sanchez

(1960–)

Federal representative

Loretta Sanchez grew up in Anaheim, California. Born to Mexican immigrants, Sanchez learned English in the Head Start program. As an adult, she went on to become a financial analyst and lived a relatively quiet and secure life until the early 1990s, when she became disillusioned with the Republican Party's stand on immigration and women's issues and switched political parties. In 1996, she ran for the House of Representatives against ultra-conservative California congressman Robert Dornan and narrowly defeated him. The election was contested for over a year by Dornan, who claimed Sanchez had won because illegal immigrants had voted for her, but Sanchez ultimately was declared the victor. When Sanchez is not in Washington, she and her husband Stephen Brixey reside in Garden Grove, California.

Grows Up in Immigrant Family

Loretta Sanchez was one of seven children born to Mexican immigrant parents in California. Spanish was spoken in her home, and she did not learn to speak English

Loretta Sanchez

until she was enrolled in a Head Start program for disadvantaged children. In 1965 her parents moved to Anaheim, then a largely white community. Immediately some neighbors moved out rather than live near a Hispanic family. (Many years later, a woman who had moved from the house next door apologized to Sanchez's mother for thinking that the Sanchez children "would bring ours down.")

All of the Sanchez children were outstanding students, a fact that Sanchez attributes to her parents' efforts. Her mother volunteered to help with school activities, and her father insisted that the children study and follow strict rules, so that they could avoid the discrimination he had encountered when he came to California. Every week he would choose a chapter from a book in Spanish, and all of the children had to prepare book reports to be read aloud.

Enters Career as Businesswoman

Sanchez graduated from Chapman University (CA), where she received a B.A. in economics, was named Student of the Year, and obtained an M.B.A. in finance from American University (DC). She first worked for the Orange County Transportation Authority (1984-87), then a new planning agency, where her first successful project (and the agency's) involved raising funds for highway emergency call boxes. Later she embarked on a career as a financial analyst, specializing in working with public agencies. During this time Orange County's government declared bankruptcy due to risky investments. However, Sanchez was not involved with any of these bad deals, having chosen her business partners carefully. Sanchez married a securities trader, Stephen Brixey, and (until her campaign for Congress in 1996) often used her husband's non-Hispanic surname in her professional life.

Although Sanchez was professionally and personally active in many civic projects in the 1980s and early 1990s, she was not then considered a major activist within the Hispanic community. Much of her work involved planning and financing for schools, police stations, and libraries. However, she did work on many general community activities: helping to have a freeway sound barrier built in her Anaheim neighborhood (1990); corporate fundraising to carry out summer school courses and to sponsor college scholarships at her old junior high school (1993); and helping to set up KinderCaminata, a program in which kindergarten students from low-income families were introduced to a community college near their homes (1994). In 1995, a group of 10,000 kindergartners and their parents spent a day at the college through KinderCaminata. She also ran a financial consulting business called "Amigo Advisors."

Becomes Politicized during 1992 Election

Until the early 1990s, Sanchez had not been heavily involved in politics. She was a registered Republican voter, and she and her husband lived an upper-middle-class lifestyle in a Southern California suburb. However, the national election of 1992 changed that pattern completely. Sanchez was deeply disturbed by the rhetoric at the Republican National Convention; she saw it as anti-immigrant and anti-female, among other shortcomings. Although Sanchez was fiscally conservative in her outlook, much of the rhetoric at the convention was decidedly in opposition to her social principles. Sanchez is pro-choice, opposed to anti-gay discrimination, and in favor of helping welfare recipients to obtain jobs before taking away their benefits.

As a result, Sanchez switched her party affiliation to Democrat, and soon afterward she entered her first political race. She ran for a city council race but as a newcomer was easily defeated, coming in eighth out of sixteen candidates. But she was not dissuaded from further political campaigns by this loss. Instead, she decided to run for the U.S. House of Representatives in 1996, challenging a man who had held the seat for nine terms, Robert Dornan.

Unexpectedly Elected to Congress

On many issues, Robert Dornan was more in tune with the district that he represented than his challenger, Sanchez. California's 46th District in Orange County had been stereotypically viewed as a conservative, rich, and largely white community. However, by 1996 the district had a large lower-middle-class population. It also was almost 50 percent Mexican American (many not registered to vote) and 12 percent Asian (with a large Vietnamese population). Many of the Hispanic and Asian residents came from a traditional Catholic background and held pro-life and anti-gay views.

Robert Dornan was a man who totally supported these conservative views. He went well beyond mere support, however. While in Congress, he developed a reputation for extreme outspokenness—for instance, publicly deriding President Clinton and making frequent derogatory comments about gays, particularly those with AIDS. He also supported California's Proposition 187, which targeted the state's large immigrant population, although he was not one of the key parties involved in its passage. In fact, Dornan publicly mentioned that his wife was going to vote against it. He had soundly defeated Robert Bañuelos, a Hispanic activist, in the 1992 election. At the same time, only about one-third of the eligible population usually voted, and only about the same amount of registered voters were Hispanic, which also might help to explain Dornan's repeated re-elections.

Dornan briefly campaigned for president in 1996, but his efforts proved extremely unsuccessful, and he withdrew from the race. He then turned to his re-election campaign for Congress, deeply in debt following his bid for the presidency. By the time Dornan entered the campaign, Sanchez already had raised substantial campaign funds (including funds from Democrats out-of-state who hoped to defeat the ultra-conservative spokesman Dornan), and

had been making frequent appearances throughout the district. Rather than focus on her Hispanic background and controversial issues such as immigration, Sanchez talked about "bread and butter" issues: education, Social Security, and jobs. She described herself in a *Los Angeles Magazine* interview as "a very traditional career woman, not a partisan animal" and as "fiscally conservative and socially progressive." When the election results were counted in November, there had been a major upset: Sanchez had beaten Dornan, by fewer than 1,000 votes.

Election to Congress Bitterly Challenged

Given the narrow margin of votes by which Sanchez defeated Dornan, it was not surprising that he requested a recount. However, Dornan's challenge went far beyond this request. He claimed that Sanchez's victory occurred because of voter fraud, saying that Hispanics who were non-citizens and even illegal immigrants had voted for his opponent. A California grand jury did consider the possibility that a local Hispanic group had registered noncitizens during a voter drive, but it found insufficient evidence to bring any indictments. Because of Dornan's protests, the U.S. House of Representatives Oversight Committee launched an investigation into the election, which lasted for over a year.

Sanchez was surprised to find Dornan apparently making plans to resume his work in Congress, even though the investigation was not completed. On several occasions when she went to the House floor for a vote, Dornan also was present, sitting with his Republican colleagues. He also made frequent media appearances in which he made derogatory statements about Sanchez, such as calling her a "lapsed Catholic" (according to the *New York Times*). As a way of claiming her office space, Sanchez placed some models of B-2 bombers outside of the door to show that she was the legitimate successor to Dornan, who had been nicknamed "B-1 Bob" because of his support for the controversial B-1 bomber program.

Many political observers believe that Dornan's tactics seriously backfired within his district. While Sanchez had not had a high profile in the Hispanic community before the election, people already infuriated by California's passage of Proposition 187 saw the election investigation as an attack on Hispanics in general. Her popularity skyrocketed, while criticism of Dornan within the Hispanic community escalated. According to a *Los Angeles Times* poll conducted during the investigation, Dornan's favorability rating was only 27 percent among Hispanic voters. Vietnamese American voters likewise were being investigated, to their equal displeasure.

In February 1998, over a year after the election, the House Oversight Committee task force conducting the investigation dismissed the election fraud charges. After checking Orange County voter records against Immigration and Naturalization Service records, the task force found that 748 voters had been illegally registered immigrants, not enough to overturn the election. Dornan subsequently announced his plans to run for re-election in 1998. But, because of the damage done among ethnic voters by his charges against Sanchez, what might have been an easy campaign to regain his seat was likely to become a highly charged and nasty battle.

Maintains Activist Position in Congress

During her first term in Congress, Sanchez served on several committees and task forces. She was a member of the House Committee on Education and the Workforce, as well as its Postsecondary Education Subcommittee and Oversight and Investigations Subcommittee. As the first "Head Start kid" in Congress, she hoped to expand higher educational opportunities for disadvantaged children and to facilitate the financing of new school construction. She was also a member of the House National Security Committee, plus its Oversight and Investigations Subcommittee, Welfare and Recreation Subcommittee, and Special Oversight Panel on Morale.

Sanchez is a member of numerous unofficial caucuses and task forces: the Executive Committee of the Hispanic Caucus; the Hispanic Caucus Task Force on Education; the "Blue Dog Democrats" (a group of moderate Democrats trying to solve social and fiscal problems); the Democratic Caucus and its Education Task Force; and the bipartisan Woman's Caucus. Outside of Congress, her recent activities have included membership on boards of several organizations, past presidency of the National Society of Hispanic MBAs, and membership in Los Alamos of Orange County and the Anaheim Assistance League.

Current Address: House of Representatives, Congress of the United States, 1529 Longworth Bldg., Washington, DC 20515-0546.

Sources:

Alvarez, Lizette. "Freshman Democrat Is Dogged by Relentless Foe." *New York Times,* October 5, 1997, p. 12.

Berkman, Leslie. "Adviser Who Fell Into Muni Business Now Sits in Congress." *The Bond Buyer,* January 28, 1997, p. 6.

Congresswoman Loretta Sanchez' Home Page. Available at http://www.house.gov/sanchez.

Lee, Kenneth. "Hasta La Vista." *New Republic,* October 27, 1997, p. 13.

McCarthy, Sheryl. "Defeating the Status Quo." *Ms.,* March/April 1997, p. 23.

Rodriguez, Gregory. "Don't Count Me Out: Will Orange County's Changing Demographics Sink Bob Dornan?" *Los Angeles Magazine,* November, 1996, p. 22.

Stout, David. "Sanchez to Keep Seat Won from Nine-Term Congressman." *New York Times News Service,* February 4, 1998. Available at http://www.latinolink.com.

Zaret, Elliot. "Task Force Dismisses Fraud Allegation." *States News Service.* February 4, 1998. Available at http://www.latinolink.com.

Zaslow, Jeffrey. "Loretta Sanchez." *USA Weekend,* September 26-28, 1997, p. 23.

Esmeralda Santiago
(1948–)
Author

Selected writings:

When I Was Puerto Rican. New York: Vintage, 1994.
America's Dream. New York: HarperCollins Publishers, 1996.

Starts from Humble Background

Esmeralda Santiago's story begins in Spanish and ends in a bilingual flurry of literary acclaim. The eldest of 11 children, Santiago was born in 1948 in Puerto Rico and raised by a single mother. Her time in Puerto Rico was divided between a tiny village and Santurce, a suburb of San Juan. At the age of 13, she and her siblings were uprooted and moved to Brooklyn, New York. In her adult life, Santiago forged a writing career that focuses on the struggles of Puerto Rican women who are caught in the middle of Hispanic and Anglo-American cultures.

By the age of 15, Santiago had learned English well enough to gain admission to the Performing Arts High School. After graduation she spent eight years studying at community colleges and working full-time, until Harvard University granted her admission on a full scholarship. In 1976, Santiago graduated *magna cum laude* and later earned a M.F.A. degree in fiction writing from Sarah Lawrence College.

Develops Creatively

Santiago's memoir, *When I Was Puerto Rican,* debuted both in English and in Spanish in 1993. Her first novel, *America's Dream,* appeared in 1996. She has also written essays about Puerto Rican culture for magazines and newspapers. In partnership with her husband, Santiago founded a film and production company that has produced award-winning documentaries; she also helped establish a shelter for battered women.

Explores Cultural Identity

When Santiago began writing her memoir, she did not imagine that it would turn into a dialogue about cultural identity, according to a note by the author on the Internet. She reported that, during her travels, she has encountered many who can identify with her descriptions of cultural dissonance. Santiago found especially poignant the experiences of immigrants who return to their own countries and only then discover how much North American culture has changed them. They accept "the irony of the past tense in the title," she said—the notion that their "cultural purity" has been compromised by living in the United States and that they thus no longer feel totally comfortable either in their native countries or in their adopted one.

When Santiago returned to Puerto Rico after seven years of living in the United States, people told her she was no longer Puerto Rican. "My Spanish was rusty, my gaze too direct, my personality too assertive for a Puerto Rican woman, and I refused to eat some of the traditional foods like morcilla and tripe stew." Santiago still felt Puerto Rican, but natives now looked at her differently because of her "Americanisms"; conversely, in the U.S., she was marked as "foreign" because of her dark appearance, her accent, and her occasional lapses in translation from Spanish to English. She wrote *When I Was Puerto Rican*, partly to recapture the "Puertoricanness" she felt before she came to the U.S. The title reflects her former identity and also questions her current identity.

Sources:

Hispanic Heritage Month Internet site. Available at http://www.macontel.com/special/latina/html/latina8.html.
Reading Group Center, Vintage Books Internet site. Available at http://www.randomhouse.com/vintage/read/puerto/santiago.html.

Santos, Nancy A. de los
See de los Santos, Nancy A.

Schimmenti, Carmelita Vigil
See Vigil-Schimmenti, Carmelita

Ninfa Segarra
(1950–)
Municipal government official

As one of four deputy mayors of New York City, Ninfa Segarra oversees educational policy in all five boroughs - Manhattan, the Bronx, Brooklyn, Queens, and Staten Island - of the nation's largest urban community. As such, she is concerned with the intellectual growth of well over one million public schoolchildren. Appointed by Mayor Rudolph Giuliani when he took office on January 1, 1994, Segarra's areas of concern in the city's government are education and community affairs.

Grows Up in New York

Ninfa Segarra was born in New York City on June 4, 1950, to Pablo and Paola Velez. She graduated from New York University in 1973 and from New York Law School in 1982. Even before she earned a law degree, Segarra was involved in city services. During 1977-78, she was a technical assistant specialist with the Community Service Society. Her next job was as deputy assistant commissioner for the New York Department of Employment (1978-80), and, following that experience, she worked as a law intern with Advocate for Children (1981-82). For the next three years, Segarra was a legal counsel with the mayor's Office for the Handicapped. In addition to work as project manager for the New York Elections Project and executive director of the New York Voter Assistance Commission, Segarra became a member, from the Bronx, of the New York City Board of Education in 1990.

Enormous power rests with the members of the New York City Board of Education, if for no other reason than the number of students and schools in their control. More than one million youngsters move in and out of New York's classrooms each year. The majority are minority students, with African Americans and Hispanic Americans representing the two largest ethnic groups. The system employs about 65,000 teachers, and there are 124 public high schools in the system. It is an enormous social and fiscal responsibility and one often fraught with controversy.

Sparks Controversy in City Government

When Republican Rudolph Giuliani ran for the office of mayor of New York City in 1993, Segarra was one of his earliest Hispanic American supporters. But when Giuliani named her deputy mayor for education and community affairs, the appointment brought mixed reactions from other government workers. Segarra had for some time been the focal point of controversy for helping to oust Schools Chancellor Joseph A. Fernandez. A political conservative, Segarra disagreed with Fernandez's support for a school curriculum that discussed such topics as AIDS, condoms, and homosexuality. The reaction was even more mixed when Giuliani announced that he would broaden Segarra's powers as deputy mayor to include the city's vast array of health agencies and social services, which gave Segarra responsibility for some 50 percent of New York City's then-$32 billion budget. The symbolism of the mayor's first appointee being a Hispanic American woman was not lost on the New York press. It also underscored recognition of Segarra's long steady climb through the political establishment of the city.

Even before she took office as deputy mayor in January of 1994, Segarra was embroiled in another dispute, this time with Bronx Borough President Fernando Ferrer. He demanded that Segarra resign from her position as Bronx representative on the New York City Board of Education. He complained that she had remained silent in the face of school board corruption in the Bronx. At the time, then Mayor David Dinkins stepped in to calm the dispute between the two political figures. Segarra responded to the charges from Ferrer by saying that she intended to remain at her school board post until the term expired in 18 months.

Deputy Mayor Segarra has been highly visible since she took her new position. In late 1994, she accused the then-Schools Chancellor Ramon C. Cortines of refusing to give information on how the board spent money during the fiscal year. Also in 1994, Mayor Giuliani redefined the duties of Segarra's huge department, shifting the responsibility for health agencies away from her administration.

Ninfa Segarra is a dedicated political administrator who is not afraid of taking on controversy or following her own principles, no matter who disagrees. Whether they agree or disagree with her policies, colleagues do not deny that Segarra is a hard-working city official who goes after in what she believes.

Current Address: Office of the Mayor, City Hall, New York, NY 10007.

Sources:

Blue, Rose. Telephone interview with Segarra's assistant, Maria Santos, March 3, 1998.

Dubner, Stephen J. "The Education of Ninfa Segarra." *New York,* January 17, 1994, p. 26.

Lyons, Richard D. "Segarra Says She Will Stay on Board." *New York Times,* November 23, 1992, p. B3.

Mitchell, Alison. "Conservative on School Board is Chosen as Giuliani Deputy." *New York Times* December 2, 1993, p. A1.

Mitchell, Alison. "Fight Looms on Extending Cortine's Job." *New York Times,* December 13, 1994, p. B1.

Mitchell, Alison. "Giuliani Reshuffles Portfolios of Deputy Mayors." *New York Times,* February 5, 1994, p. A25.

Myers, Steven Lee. "At Center of a Sweeping Struggle: Ninfa Segarra." *New York Times,* December 2, 1993, p. B8.

Myers, Steven Lee. "Roles Shifted for Deputies by Giuliani." *New York Times,* December 17, 1993, p. B1.

Rosita Segovia
(1926–)
Dancer, choreographer, organization executive

As dancer, choreographer, and teacher on the exhilarating stage of the Spanish ballet, Rosita Segovia is its *estrella,* or star, on two continents. Native to Spain, she was the prima donna of Spanish ballet, flamenco, and classical Spanish dance there for 20 years from 1952 to 1972. She then became dance mistress at her own Escuela de Danza Rosita Segovia in Barcelona. However, at the invitation of the Hispanic community in Miami, FL, in 1973 she established the Ballet Español Rosita Segovia at the Conchita

Rosita Segovia

Espinosa Academy to share Spanish culture, especially dance, with the U.S. audience. As she told Valerie Gladstone of *Dance Magazine,* "I wanted to open doors to show the beauty of our dance," opening her arms wide to demonstrate.

Segovia was born in Barcelona, Spain, in 1926 to a theatrical family. Her father was a composer and her mother was an actress and singer, so she was introduced to the arts at a young age. She began by learning classical Spanish dance and ballet. In addition, young Segovia was taught the *escuela bolera,* a courtly Spanish dance by the noted teacher, Pauleta Pamies. "She was 84-years old" and ". . . she looked like a witch, with a kerchief on her head and a cane cut off from the end of a broom," recalled Segovia in her interview with Gladstone. Her flamenco teacher was equally colorful. She was the famous café dancer, called *La Tanguera,* or Madame Tango. Because her parents disapproved of flamenco, she practiced secretly. In the same article Segovia says, "She used to teach me in the kitchen, while cooking." Thus, she was able to learn Spanish dance in many different styles.

Becomes Primera Ballerina

Two years after making her professional dancing debut at the age of 12, Segovia became the primera ballerina of the Liceo de la Opera de Barcelona. She also danced with Alicia Alonso's Cuban dance company for a time. In 1953, she became the partner of Antonio, a world-famous flamenco dancer, and danced as the prima ballerina of his prestigious ballet company until 1972. The company performed around the world in Milan, Vienna, and New York, with Sol Hurok, the famous stage producer, managing theatrical successes for Segovia and Antonio, such as Léonide Massine's *Capriccio Español, The Three-Cornered Hat,* and *El Amor Brujo,* with Massine himself dancing the role of the ghost. She won the gold medal from the Beaux Arts Academy in Spain in 1958.

Segovia talked about her long dedication to dance in 1993. "That was my life," she explained to Gladstone. "Some people are born to dance. It is a very hard art. You have to live it totally with body and mind. Then, when you know everything, you must leave. Not the mind but the body gets old." Fortunately, Segovia's talents were not limited to performance. Her cultural gifts found a new outlet in her ability to teach and create Spanish dances for her students.

Goes Deep Inside the Movement

Since retiring from the stage in 1972, Segovia has become a renowned choreographer of Spanish dance, creating dances for her own company as well as for others. She established her own company and began giving classes at the Conchita Espinosa Academy in Miami in 1973. The girls at the Academy range from ages 8 to 15 and study classical dance techniques. Segovia integrates all the forms of old classical Spanish dance with flamenco styles and her own imagination to create entirely new dance forms. She elaborated in *Dance Magazine:* "Choreography is very easy for me. . . . I have a good sense of music and rhythm. I don't just make steps. I go deep inside the movement. That makes the dances look beautiful." The rounded port de bras, low arabesques, and small, quick footwork of Spanish dance form continuous swirls in space by the dancers whose arms end in a flourish. These movements blend with Segovia's own innovations which include lengthening the extension of a traditional Spanish dancer, adding folk and bolera steps to her dances, and using more movements of the popular dancing found at country fiestas. Another sign of Segovia's ingenuity is that she also uses music from non-Spanish composers such as Rachmaninoff, Paganini, and Scarlatti.

Demonstrates Genuine Originality in Classical Form

Segovia's distinguished adult company, Ballet Español Rosita Segovia, has developed into a world-class troupe. They performed at Seville's Expo '92, won a grant from the National Endowment for the Arts, and continue to receive glowing reviews in sold-out seasons in Miami. ". . . (Segovia's) company already shows fire, grace, professionalism, and signs of genuine originality within a classical form," wrote a *Dance Magazine* reviewer. Among the dances staged by Segovia for the 1992 season were *Suite of Basque Dances, Concierto de Aranjuez*—a powerful, sparsely elegant work— *Goyescas,* and *Danzas Fantásticas,* which was described as beautifully formed pictures.

Other dance companies benefit from Segovia's creative force. She frequently choreographs works for dancers in fellow Miami companies, such as the Maria Benitez Teatro Flamenco. Maria Benitez, a dancer and teacher at the Conchita Espinosa Academy, works with Segovia to design and stage productions for their own and other Florida groups, like the innovative New World School of the Arts. Thus, Segovia's vision of "opening doors" to Spanish dance in the New World continues to flourish. As teacher, choreographer, and cultural icon, Segovia enriches the Spanish community in Miami and the rest of the United States by generously sharing her gifts of dance and drama.

Current Address: Conchita Espinosa Academy, Miami, FL 33131.

Sources:

Gladstone, Valerie. "Rosita Segovia: America's Spanish Dance Estrella." *Dance Magazine,* June 1993, pp. 40-41.

Hering, Doris. "Marie Benitez Spanish Dance Company (Joyce Theater)." *Dance Magazine,* April 1990, pp. 83-84.

Koegler, Horst. *Concise Oxford Dictionary of Ballet.* London: Oxford University Press, 1977, p. 374.

Levin, Jordan. "Ballet Español Rosita Segovia (Gusman Center for the Performing Arts, Miami)." *Dance Magazine,* September 1992, p. 82.

Seijas Millán, Natacha
  See Millán, Natacha Seijas

Selena
(1971–1995)
Singer, actress

Selected discography:

Mis Primeras Grabaciones, 1984 (later reissued in 1995).
Selena y los Dinos, 1984
Alpha, 1986.
Meñequito de Trapo, 1986.
And the Winner is. . . , 1987.
Preciosa, 1988.
Dulce Amor, 1988.
Selena. EMI/Capitol, 1989.
Personal Best. CBS Records, 1990.
16 Super Exitos. EMI/Capitol, 1990.
Ven Conmigo. EMI/Capitol, 1990.
Entre a Mi Mundo. EMI/Capitol, 1992.
Baile Esta Cumbia. EMI, 1992.
Mis Mejores Canciones–17 Super Exitos. EMI, 1993.
Quiero. EMI, 1993.
Selena Live. EMI/Capitol, 1993.
12 Super Exitos. EMI/Capitol, 1994.
Amor Prohibido. EMI/Capitol, 1994.
Selena. Capitol/Cema Special Markets, 1994.
Dreaming of You. EMI Latin/EMI Records, 1995.
Siempre Selena. EMI Latin/Q Productions, 1996.
Selena: The Original Motion Picture Soundtrack. EMI Latin/
  Q Productions, 1997.
Selena Anthology. EMI Latin/Q Productions, 1998.

Selected filmography:

Don Juan DeMarco. 1995.

Overview

Selena was a popular Tejano singer who won a Grammy Award for her album *Selena Live* and recorded numerous albums during her brief career. By the age of 19, she was a millionaire; by the age of 21, she could draw crowds of 20,000 at the fairgrounds at Pasadena, TX. Music critics proclaimed she would be the next Madonna, i.e. a megastar of music and movies. Tragically, however, Selena's career was cut short when she was murdered by the president of her fan club at age 23.

Selena and her band performed *Tejano music-Mexican ranchera* style music mixed sounds owing influence to pop,

Selena

country and western, and Caribbean music. Tejano traditionally meant music by Texans of Mexican descent. But Selena, among others, modernized the traditional accordion-based Tejano or Tex-Mex music with country twangs, techno-pop beats, dance mixes, and international influences. More than 70 radio stations playing the uniquely Latino-styled tunes form a corridor from south Texas through California.

Selena Quintanilla was born April 16, 1971, in Lake Jackson, TX, a small industrial town near Houston. Her father Abraham Quintanilla, Jr. worked as a shipping clerk at the Dow Chemical plant. Abraham and his wife Marcela had three children: Abraham III, Suzette, and Selena, the youngest.

Seems Destined for Stardom

In his own youth, Quintanilla had performed as a vocalist with Los Dinos ("The Boys") a popular South Texas band. When Quintanilla heard his daughter sing at six years of age, he knew Selena was destined for a musical career and encouraged the musical talents that she revealed. In a 1995 *People* article, Quintanilla affirmed that Selena's "timing and [her] pitch were perfect. I could see it from day one."

Selena practiced with the music she enjoyed, from the soul music of Little Anthony and the Imperials to country and western music and even the stylized R&B of Michael

Jackson. Through her love of all different kinds of music and early jam sessions with her brother on bass and her sister on drums, Selena demonstrated her passion for the musical arts.

After years of working for others, Abraham Quintanilla opened his own Tex-Mex restaurant in Lake Jackson. There Selena first performed in public with her brother and sister as members of her band. But the economic recession of the early 1980s delivered a knockout blow that closed the family restaurant, forcing them to leave their home and sell all their belongings. Selena's talent would save them.

Takes Family Band on the Road

While the rest of the Quintanilla clan relocated in Corpus Christi, Selena and her siblings hit the road, performing throughout southern Texas as Selena y Los Dinos ("Selena and the Boys"). They played at weddings and in cantinas and honky-tonks to very small audiences—oftentimes less than ten people. In a dilapidated van with one foldout bed in the back, the troupe traveled and performed. In 1979, eight- year-old Selena recorded her first tune—a country song sung in Spanish; her Tex-Mex band was in full swing by 1980.

Selena left school in the eighth grade to spend more time travelling with the band and earning money for her family, but she eventually completed her high school equivalency requirements through a correspondence course. The band started playing larger venues, including ballrooms. They also recorded nearly one dozen albums for a small regional label.

In 1987, Selena—then 15-years-old—won Tejano Music Awards for best female vocalist and performer of the year. This was the big break that Selena and the band had worked for years to achieve. Two years later, the Latin division of the EMI Records Group signed the band to a record deal.

Though Selena was the rising star of Hispanic pop, she was still very much a Texan. She could not speak Spanish and learned the Spanish lyrics for her lively songs and romantic ballads phonetically, coached by her brother, who wrote the songs. At the advice of her father, turned manager, she began taking Spanish lessons in the early 1990s, so that she could project a more genuine Hispanic image during interviews on Spanish-language radio.

In 1992 Selena Quintanilla married the band's guitarist Chris Pérez. The union did not hamper Selena's sexy image. Rather, Selena became known as the "Tex-Mex Madonna" because of her sexy bustiers and provocative smiles on-stage, though off-stage she remained a wholesome, married woman who was devoted to her family.

Hires Fan Club President

Selena had repeatedly refused offers for fan clubs, keeping her career a family project, but a woman named Yolanda Saldivar expressed interest in founding and running Selena's fan club. She was an aunt of one of Selena's childhood friends, but beyond that she was a stranger to the singer. Saldivar lived near San Antonio, working as a registered nurse, and caring for three children abandoned by her brother. Despite Saldivar's remote connection to the Quintanillas, Selena and her family appointed Saldivar as the president of the Selena fan club, an unpaid position. In just four years, Selena's fan club attracted nine thousand members.

When speaking of her desire to work for Selena, Saldivar told the *Dallas Morning News* in 1994 that she became a devoted Selena fan after seeing a San Antonio concert in 1989. "Selena just inspired me—with her talent, her motivation. She gives her whole to you." The two developed a close friendship. Though Saldivar did not receive an official salary, Selena often bestowed the woman with gifts. Selena indulged Saldivar's penchant for spotted cows with cow- patterned rugs and phones; Saldivar reciprocated by transforming her apartment into a Selena shrine, laden with Selena photos and memorabilia, including a life-size cardboard pop-up of the singer.

Becomes Quick Success

Selena lost no time in the recording studio. She recorded among others, *Ven Conmigo, Entre a Mi Mundo,* and *Baile Esta Cumbia,* between 1990 and 1993. In 1993 *Selena Live* received a Grammy Award for best Mexican American album. Selena's 1994 album, *Amor Prohibido*—recipient of a Grammy nomination—sold six hundred thousand copies in the United States. The fourth single from the album, "Fotos y Recuerdos," reached the top ten on *Billboard* magazine's Latino charts.

By 1995, Selena's albums had sold a combined total of three million copies. Twice, she played to record crowds of sixty thousand at Houston's annual Livestock Show and Rodeo. Selena's "Bidi Bidi Bom Bom" won the singer a song of the year award at the Tejano Music Awards in early 1995. She also won five more of the fifteen awards presented at the 1995 Tejano Music Awards ceremonies, including best female entertainer; best female vocalist; album of the year; Tejano crossover song; and record of the year. An amazed Selena was quoted as saying in *Time* magazine, "Never in my dreams would I have thought I would become this big. I am still freaking out."

In 1994, Selena promoted Saldivar to a paid position as head of Selena Etc. Inc., a company devoted to overseeing two Selena boutiques/salons—one in Corpus Christi and one in San Antonio—and to marketing a line of Selena fashions to be sold in the boutiques as well as in other retail venues. But things began falling apart rapidly. First, fashion designer Martin Gomez quit, claiming that he could not work with Saldivar, who he accused of being "mean and manipulative." The problem escalated with reports of other lapses by Saldivar involving misuse of funds.

Meanwhile, fans were not receiving t-shirts and other Selena items that they had paid for, and money was disappearing from one of the salons. Selena and her father both confronted Saldivar about the reported abuses. Saldivar protested, claiming that she had documentation to prove her innocence and offered to show Selena the alleged papers.

Shooting Ends Life

•

Selena and Saldivar were supposed to meet alone at the Days Inn where Saldivar was staying. Instead Selena brought her husband; Saldivar proved not to have the papers she had claimed to possess. The next day Selena went to the Days Inn sometime before noon to talk with Saldivar. At 11:50 a.m., the Corpus Christi police received a 911 call of a shooting at the motel.

Police detailed that Saldivar met Selena at the door of her motel room with a .38-caliber revolver, shooting the singer in the back and shoulder. Selena staggered to the lobby before collapsing, though she remained conscious until paramedics arrived. Response teams rushed Selena to the hospital. Despite blood transfusions, Selena died a few hours after being shot, on March 31, 1995. Saldivar was charged with Selena's murder.

But the ordeal did not end with Selena's death. Saldivar holed up with the revolver in the cab of a pickup truck in the Days Inn parking lot. For hours she threatened to shoot herself while negotiating with police via a cellular car phone. As the news of Selena's murder spread, the singer's fans stood vigil at the Days Inn. Saldivar finally surrendered at 9:30 p.m.

Death Sparks Widespread Grief

In the wake of Selena's murder, grieving fans swamped the Quintanilla family with remembrances, including bouquets, rosaries, and votives. Condolences were sent to the Quintanillas by Julio Iglesias, Gloria Estefan, Madonna, and La Mafia, a well-known Hispanic singing group. Local radio stations devoted their programming to Selena's music, and more than one thousand Selena tapes and compact discs were sold at a frenzied pace during the next couple of weeks.

Fifteen hundred mourners attended a vigil for the singing star at the Bayfront Plaza and Convention Center prior to her funeral held at Corpus Christi's Memorial Coliseum, the arena where she had recorded her smash hit *Selena Live*. Ten thousand people flooded Corpus Christi to pass by Selena's coffin. In Los Angeles, four thousand people gathered at the Sports Arena Memorial to honor the slain singer. Mourners also gathered in San Antonio, the capital of Tejano music, at two separate sites.

Selena was killed just as her career was about to skyrocket in new directions. She had recorded six songs for an English-language album, her first with EMI's SBK division, making her only the third Hispanic performer to ever cross from the Latin division to the more mainstream part of the record company. The album was released as *Dreaming of You*. In addition, she had made her film debut as herself in *Dos Mujeres, Un Camino*, a Latino Television soap. In 1995, she continued to advance her film career as a mariachi singer in the film *Don Juan DeMarco*, and she had collaborated with former Talking Heads leader David Bryne on the song "God's Child" for the film *Blue in the Face*.

Cameron Randle, a recording industry executive specializing in Tex-Mex music, voiced his opinions of Selena in a retrospective of her career published in *Entertainment Weekly* in April of 1995. "Selena was not merely forging an exceptional career, she was defining a new genre as uniquely American as Delta blues or New Orleans jazz. There's every indication she would have been as enormously popular as [fellow Latinos] Jon Secada or Gloria Estefan. She was about to take center stage as the first Tejano performer to attempt a full-scale crossover, and she was robbed of that opportunity."

Selena's posthumous release *Dreaming of You* entered the *Billboard* 200 at the top of the chart—the second-highest chart debut after Michael Jackson's *HIStory*—and entered the *Billboard* Latin 50 at the same position. The jump into the top pop slot made Selena one the fastest selling female artists of all time, second only to Janet Jackson. An amazing 175,000 copies of the compact disc were sold on the first day of release. In addition to *Dreaming of You*, several other posthumous recordings of Selena's work have been released, including *Siempre Selena, Selena: The Original Motion Picture Soundtrack*, and *Selena Anthology*.

Life Story Depicted in Top-Grossing Film

Selena's life story was depicted in the movie *Selena*, which starred award-winning actors Jennifer Lopez, Edward James Olmos, Constance Marie, Jacob Vargas, and Jackie Guerra. Directed by Gregory Nava, who also directed such memorable films as *El Norte* and *Mi Familia/My Family*, the movie received rave reviews from critics and moviegoers alike and was one of the highest-grossing films of 1997.

Sources:

Burr, Ramiro. "Selena Reigns at Tejano Awards." *Billboard*, February 25, 1995, p. 39.
Gwynne, S.C. "Death of a Rising Star." *Time*, April 10, 1995, p. 91.
Hewitt, Bill. "Before Her Time." *People*, April 17, 1995, pp. 48-53.

Jebens, Harley. "Rhythm Revolution (Rising Popularity of New Latin Music.)"*Hispanic,* December 31, 1994, p. 36.

Katz, Jesse. "For Barrio, Selena's Death Strikes a Poignant Chord." *Los Angeles Times,* April 2, 1995, pp. A1-A9.

Katz, Jesse, and Stephanie Simon. "Latin Music Star Selena Shot, Killed in Texas Hotel." *Los Angeles Times,* April 1, 1995, pp. A1, A21-A22.

La Prensa de San Antonio, June 11, 1993, p. B1.

La Prensa de San Antonio, November 19, 1993, p. B1.

La Prensa de San Antonio, April 29, 1994, p. B2.

Milloy, Ross E. "For Slain Singer's Father, Memories and Questions." *New York Times,* April 3, 1995, p. A15.

Novas, Himilce, and Rosemary Silva. *Remembering Selena.* New York: St. Martin's Press, 1995.

Sanz, Cynthia, and Betty Cortina. "After Selena." *People,* July 10, 1995, pp. 36-41.

Seidenberg, Robert. "Requiem for a Latin Star." *Entertainment Weekly,* April 14, 1995, p. 20.

Verhovek, Sam Howe. "Woman is Arrested in Killing of Singer." *New York Times,* April 2, 1995, p. A18.

Williams, Frank, and Enrique Lopetegui. "Mourning Selena." *Los Angeles Times,* April 3, 1995, pp. B1-B3.

Nina Serrano

(1934–)

Poet, civil rights activist, teacher

Selected writings:

Heart Songs: The Collected Poems of Nina Serrano (1969-1979). San Francisco: Pocho-Che, 1980.

Overview

Nina Serrano is an important poet and leader in the Chicano movement. Having travelled extensively, she saw social injustices and revolutions firsthand, and those experiences heavily flavor her creative work. Throughout her life, she has been a strong voice for those who were too powerless to speak for themselves.

Grows Up in Love with the Arts

Serrano was born on September 1, 1934, in the Bronx to an immigrant from Santander, Colombia, and his wife, whose parents were from Eastern Europe. Since Nina's parents had to work in restaurants and cafeterias in Manhattan, her early years were under the tutelage of a man she called Uncle Paul—Augustín Polo Arroyo—who was born in Puerto Rico but lived in Cuba for many years. He loved the arts (performing, graphic, and visual) and was responsible for her love of them. Whether it was opera, ballet, theater, or vaudeville, he took young Serrano along. Her father also loved art—he was an artist—and so, like many working-class families in New York, they spent their Sundays in parks and museums where entry was free. Nina Serrano's interest in other peoples may have been spurred by the many languages heard as she passed through the city streets.

With regard to her formal education, Serrano recalls her early days at the San José day-care center where she was left in the morning on her parents' way to work and from which she was taken to attend classes in the New York public schools. Since Uncle Paul, with whom she spent a great deal of time, spoke mainly Spanish, the school authorities put her in speech-correction classes to eliminate her accent. As anything foreign was unpopular during World War II, she made an extreme effort to become proficient in English. When she was 14, a new public school called Performing Arts was opened; Serrano was in the first class. She continued improving her English and began training in theater. At 16 she began taking classes in a theater company and performing a classical repertoire.

Becomes Politically, Artistically Active

Serrano spent the year after her high-school graduation working in low-paying jobs, studying theater, and looking for work on Broadway. The following year, 1953, she married and accompanied her husband to the University of Wisconsin, where she suffered culture shock. She continued her interest in drama, became involved in children's theater, and gained her first political experience as a staff person for the "Joe-Must-Go Club," an anti-Joseph McCarthy group.

Studies Abroad

In 1955, after the birth of her son, Greg, she enrolled in the University of Wisconsin as a full-time speech-and-drama major. She became politically active in the peace and civil-rights movements and became president of the Student Peace Union. It was in this role that in 1957 she traveled by ship to England, where she left her infant son in the care of a babysitting service and continued on to Russia to attend the Moscow Youth Festival.

At the termination of the festival the young delegation was invited to go via the trans-Siberian railroad to China. Although the U.S. embassy warned the Americans of the consequences and required them to sign a document that they had been warned of the embargo being put on their trip, many of them, including Serrano, continued on. There were students from Indonesia, Australia, and Latin America, including future leaders of revolutions in Latin America. Serrano identified with that last group, who spoke Spanish and were fun-loving; this camaraderie helped her bear the separation from her husband and son.

While in China Serrano studied the roles of women and children in theater, especially the Shanghai theater. She also studied Peking opera and inquired about education during her two-month stay. When she returned to the University of Wisconsin, she encountered a cold reception, and was discouraged from continuing. When she became pregnant with her second child, she was told she was too old to continue her studies. Nevertheless, she took her first class shortly after her daughter, Valerie, was born in 1958. Serrano staged scenes from new British writers with a leftist orientation. She also became intensely interested in Bertolt Brecht's work.

Sees Poverty in Mexico

In 1959 Serrano went with her husband and sister-in-law to Morelia, Mexico, to visit a Mexican family that had lived next to them in Madison. On this, her first visit to Latin America, she was shocked by the poverty. All the stories of Mexico she had heard were picturesque; no one had mentioned the dust, mud, flies, and naked children. For her the country was a tremendous shock in its contrast to Russia and China, where poverty was greater but cleanliness was given a high priority. The poverty of Mexico was disheartening and demoralizing to Serrano.

Meets Revolutionaries in Cuba

Back in Madison in 1960 Serrano began working in an experimental school, team-teaching theater for children. She was excited about this educational principle, which she feels is still relevant. With the money she earned, she subscribed to magazines that brought culture from areas far from Madison. A summer (1960) issue of the *Monthly Review* featured Cuba, which had just gone through its revolution. This article, plus the fact that her husband was in Cuba, as well as her imaginings of Cuba based on Uncle Paul's reminiscences, prompted her to take her children and join her husband in Havana, where she met revolutionary artists who had returned from exile or emerged from underground. She was excited about the education and culture that were blossoming in Cuba, and she took the opportunity to visit state schools to enlarge her vision of education beyond that found in the United States.

Becomes Involved in Radio and Theater

Shortly after her return in 1961 Serrano headed for California, having been attracted to San Francisco by a book of photography showing life in North Beach. She settled, with her children, on Dolores Street in the Mission District and became involved in a community radio station, KPFA, where she produced children's programs—including plays about Gertrude Stein and Isadora Duncan—and a play by a New Left playwright. Because Serrano's children were of school age, she became active in the Alternative School and began teaching Spanish. The staff was complemented by people who were excited about teaching children, and was supported by parents with a strong sense of participation. She evolved a method of teaching Spanish through songs, games, and plays.

With her interest in the theater as strong as ever, Serrano became director of a San Francisco mime group and also got involved in European repertory drama. In 1967 she and her husband went to Uruguay, Guatemala, and Mexico at a time of great political ferment. They traveled deep into the countries and were in touch with the protest movements; what she saw affected Serrano greatly.

The following year, with her children, Serrano accompanied her husband to Cuba, where he was to make a film on Fidel Castro. She had to play a large part in the production. For four months she traveled all over the island by jeep—the first woman to accompany the army—and filmed everything. It was on this trip that she met the Salvadoran Roque Dalton, who was the person who had the greatest influence on her literary career. While there she did her first writing—a play in collaboration with Dalton for Cuban video. Dalton inspired her and made her laugh. It was an isolated time of extreme happiness for her.

Begins Writing Poetry

After working with Dalton, Serrano became interested in the works of the poet Pablo Armando Fernández. She began writing poetry, and all the themes from the theater that had been inside her came out in verse. Writing plays had been liberating, but through poetry she could reach an audience more easily.

A key year in Serrano's involvement with the Chicano movement was 1972. While working in bilingual radio back in the United States, she met two men who wanted her to help cover the Raza Unida Conference in El Paso, TX. There she met many active Hispanics, among them Reies López Tijerina of the Land Grant movement. She also met Lillian del Sol, a key community organizer in the Chicano moratoriums. Serrano built up an archive of television programs that are still used from time to time. She produced a Latin-American history program on KPSA in Berkeley, as well as a radio program called "Reflecciones de Raza" (Race Reflections) which was a model for bilingual radio programming.

In 1974 Serrano took a year off from her active participation in Chicano activities in the Mission District. Her marriage had just broken up, and her daughter wanted a change from the inner-city high school she attended. So the two of them returned to Cuba, where Serrano took a job, and Valerie repeated tenth grade, developed good study habits, became interested in learning, and polished her Spanish.

On their return Serrano, who was a contributing editor to *Tin-Tan* (a quarterly published by Editorial Pocho-Che that lasted six issues), wrote a report on "The Second Congress of Women," which had been held in Cuba in November of 1974. In the same publication she did a translation of Fernández's poem about Luis Talamántez and also commented on the latter's book *Life Within the*

Heart Imprisoned (1976), judging it to be "a useful tool in La Raza [Chicano], ethnic and prison studies classes." (Talamántez was one of the San Quentin Six, a group of prisoners accused of five murders.)

Publishes *Heart Songs*

In 1980 Serrano had her poems published in book form. The title, *Heart Songs*, aptly describes the contents. Fernando Alegría, in the introduction to the work, describes it as "poetry of hidden fire, [which] moves like a lens high and distant over the streets of San Francisco, the plains of Wisconsin, the toasted mesa of New Mexico and the battle of buildings against bridges, windows against glass, in the multiple loneliness of New York."

The sixty poems are divided into five parts: "Early Songs," "Songs of Struggle," "Single Woman Songs," "Tropi-Cuba," and "End of the California Drought." Although the majority of Serrano's poems deal with the social problems of the 1960s and 1970s, there are several short lyric poems. One, accompanied by a whimsical drawing, is titled "Daughter Haiku": "Bright butterfly! Bringing joy./ How good it is/ to watch your flight." Another one, "For My Son . . . So Far Away," is dedicated to her son, Greg: "As the tree feels the flight of the leaf/ and the rosebush the parting of her flower/ and the grass thirsts for the dew/ so I, my son, miss you."

There are poignant poems such as "In Memoriam," in which Serrano commemorates the death of Uncle Paul, and "Poetry in Action," in which she honors the Filipino worker, poet, and community organizer Serafin Syquia, also deceased. Many of Serrano's poems take up the cause of the underdogs, of those struggling for freedom. In the poems "San Francisco Chinatown Fair" and "New York City: March 9, 1970, to March 23, 1970," she focuses on explosive themes of the late 1960s and early 1970s: university uprisings and racial riots.

Having traveled extensively, Serrano was personally aware of conflicts in places such as Nicaragua, Cuba, Puerto Rico, Mexico, and Chile. The last lines of her "Elegy for Pablo Neruda" best sum up how she feels about innocent victims caught in the fray: "Because we're human/ we cannot allow ourselves to be oppressed./ Because we're human/ we cannot allow our sisters/ and brothers to be oppressed./ Because we're human/ we love./ Because we love,/ we struggle./ Because we love,/ because we're humans,/ we write poems./ We sing with our insides."

Eulogizes Women in Poetry

Serrano has also written poems that eulogize women. One of these is "Lolita Lebrón," in which Serrano goes back to the 1950s in New York, where Lebrón worked for the benefit of Puerto Rican immigrants. Serrano recalls "the times of hate / the times of fear." There were witch-hunters pursuing communists, "naming names." There was wholesale banning of books. She comments on the execution of the Rosenbergs, the Taft-Hartley Act, and Elvis Presley howling, "I'm [*sic*] nothing but a hound dog." But the main focus of the poem is the activist and garment-factory worker Lebrón, who "looked at the moon / on hot nights / from her tenement roof," while "Her mind was on cutting the chains / tying her green island [Puerto Rico] / to the greedy mainland."

A tragic ending is painted in a poem about another woman, "Stone Cold Dead on Market Street": "the crazy beautiful black Carmen / dancing . . . dancing, waving her delicate fan, / cooling the dancing bodies" is "murdered / by her junkie-lover with a gun." The poet condemns the remorseless killer to "loveless nights / because [he] killed / a life lover." The poems in Heart Songs run the gamut from lyrical, familial themes and love songs to works about witches, pirates, nightmares, and revolutions. The tone that unifies the whole is Serrano's deep feeling of maternal love, compassion, and outrage at oppression and injustice.

Begins Teaching

Education had been an integral part of Serrano's development, so her involvement in New College of California for the San Francisco youths of the barrio is consonant with her previous contributions. In 1983 she began teaching a course called "Third World Voices," the history and literature of African and Asian Americans, Hispanics, and Native Americans. Later she was hired to recruit Hispanic students for the developmental-studies program, and this job led to a position for her in the admissions office as community outreach coordinator. When the opportunity arose to teach oral communication, she accepted it; her theater background had prepared her for the job.

A poem by Serrano was published in August of 1985 in a new Oakland journal, *Cambio*. "Blessed Be" honors Ralph Madariaga, the founder and ongoing codirector of Galería de la Raza in San Francisco. The poem, which one might consider a modern beatitude, recalls this "Servant of art/ Magician of film" who is an example to his students and who has filled many corners with color. Serrano fittingly conjures up a personified triptych of creativity, community, and tranquillity in the man who has given many years to local arts.

Nina Serrano continues to write poetry that springs from her passionate views on social justice. She summed up much of her life's work in a recent letter: "I believe the Chicano movement embodies in it the need for world peace, cultural exchange and understanding, as well as the burning desire for a more just and democratic society." No doubt Serrano's future work will reflect her hopes and dreams for the world.

Sources:

Harvey, Nick, ed. *Mark in Time, Portraits and Poetry/San Francisco*. San Francisco: Glide, 1971, p. 107.

La Mujer Chicana: An Annotated Bibliography. Austin, TX: Chicana Research and Learning Center, 1976, p. 78.

Beverly Silva
(1930–)
Author, poet

Selected writings:

The Second St. Poems. Bilingual Press/Editorial Bilingüe, 1983.
The Cat and Other Stories. Bilingual Press/Editorial Bilingüe, 1986.

Overview

Beverly Silva's short stories and her confessional poetry give a touching and powerful vision of her struggle for self-expression and economic independence. Important themes of the Hispanic and feminist perspectives make Silva's work a personal reflection of significant social movements of the past 20 years. Her work reflects the life of one who survived hardship to become a stronger individual.

Silva was born in Los Angeles on May 12, 1930; her parents divorced when she was two. Because of the onslaught of the Depression, her maternal grandparents moved north to a ranch in Oregon, taking her with them. Her grandfather, a bricklayer with no formal education, spoke a smattering of six languages, and was a "born philosopher, storyteller and linguist." On weekends he would play the banjo and they would sing. In retrospect Silva finds her grandfather's gifts to her—his humor, courage, and ability to thrive in both North American and Mexican cultures—of the greatest importance in her own formation as an individual.

When Silva was six years old, she left her grandparents to live with her newly married mother and stepfather in Portland, OR, the first of many family moves, since Silva's stepfather was a highway worker. She estimates that she had attended some twelve different schools by the time she entered high school. Despite the continual disruption in her education, she was always at the head of the class. Silva's desire to be a writer was born early, and the first writing she did was poems and skits for a geography class in fifth grade. Silva had also become an avid reader; her childhood favorites included fairy tales by the Brothers Grimm, Batman comics, Judy Bolton mysteries, and *Cosmopolitan* magazine.

Experiences Troubled Childhood

Silva describes her teenage years as a nightmare. Her maternal grandparents had moved back to Mexico, and she sorely missed them. Her parents sent her back and forth between their homes in Southern California and Oregon, her stepfather was cruel, and she found herself in a home environment bereft of books and kindred spirits interested in intellectual pursuits. Although she made known her desire to attend college, study literature and languages, and become a writer, she was placed in a vocational-secretarial track and shut out of the kind of education she wanted. Unhappy at school, she frequently cut classes and read works by William Shakespeare; Lord Byron; John Keats; Alfred, Lord Tennyson; and the novels of John Galsworthy. From the age of 14 she wrote stories, but she had to hide them because of ridicule from both family and friends.

During her senior year in high school in Oregon, Silva found an English teacher who helped her turn her anger into creative pursuits. Silva wrote, directed, and acted in school plays, and edited and wrote stories for the school newspaper. In addition, she edited the yearbook, wrote the class prophecy, and gave the senior speech at graduation. Yet, after earning her diploma from the small high school, there was no way for her to continue her studies. There were then no community colleges in the state, and no financial assistance was available from her family.

Silva's choices after high school were severely restricted: work in the fields, a department store, or a restaurant. She did a little of all three and then got married. Her husband, a logger, was killed by a falling tree five weeks after their marriage. Silva's story "A Small Western Town," in *The Cat and Other Stories* (1986), records the initiation of a young high-school graduate into the tedium of small-town, adult life. The protagonist lives a silent existence in the home of her dour aunt and dreams of being a writer. She saves money to escape to New York or California. Without resources to attend the nearby university, she is confined to work during the day as a waitress; loneliness and inertia lead her to spend long evenings at the local bar. Soon she is married, and her savings furnish the home she briefly shares with her husband. After her husband's sudden death just weeks after their marriage, she leaves the place where she has been so unhappy. At the end of the story the young narrator gets on a bus headed for California.

Tragedy Strikes Again

After her first husband's death, Silva went to live with her maternal grandparents, who had moved back to California. Six months later she went to Las Vegas, where she married a man she had known only ten days. Together they hitchhiked around the western United States for six months. They then returned to Silva's grandparents' home in Los Gatos, where she gave birth to a son. Five happy years followed. During the day her husband worked with her grandfather as a hod carrier, and in the evenings after work she and her husband wrote stories and sent them—without luck—to magazines. A year after their second child was born, her husband had a mental breakdown and was committed to a state hospital. After nine months of treatment he was released, but he disappeared, and Silva has never seen him again. Her second husband was the first real friend to take an interest in her writing, and his illness and subsequent disappearance were terrible blows.

A year later Silva married a man considerably older. They had two children and spent thirteen years together, the first five in Yellow Springs, OH. During her years in Ohio, the only part of her life spent away from the West Coast, she enjoyed the contact she had with educated people who shared her interest in literature. When she returned with her husband and children to California, she found herself on a prune ranch amid in-laws who disapproved of women's suffrage and most other activities away from the ranch.

Silva's third husband, like her family, found her desire to write both foolish and threatening. After one particularly unpleasant episode with him in 1964, she burned all her writings. Despite this discouragement, in 1965, when her youngest child entered school, Silva began part-time classes at San Jose City College, transferring to San Jose State University four years later. She began her college career in her thirties, with all the advantages and liabilities of the self-taught. She had favorite authors—poets Robert Service and Edgar Allan Poe and novelists John Dos Passos and Ernest Hemingway—and higher education added new writers to her list. Silva discovered the intensity and directness of John Donne and Emily Dickinson and developed a special appreciation for the street language of Langston Hughes, the humor and narrative skill of Geoffrey Chaucer, the beauty of Shakespeare's language, and the intense drama of Eugene O'Neill's works. Silva's admiration for Maya Angelou also reveals much about the aesthetic that informs Silva's own writing.

Writings Comment on the 1960s

Silva started writing again in college, but she was timid about showing her work to anyone. When she did, she received mixed reactions. At this time Silva wrote mostly plays and short stories. In 1975, under the pressure of comprehensive examinations, she turned to writing poetry, which she found more satisfying because she could begin and end a piece quickly.

Although she did not participate in the student tumult of the late 1960s and early 1970s, Silva was a close observer and sympathizer. Her futuristic story "The Poster," included in *The Cat,* provides an ironic look at the student protesters fifty years after the uprisings in May of 1970. The former students have become a conservative bunch, and the bankers are now the revolutionaries attempting to overthrow the university. They carry banners demanding:

"Freedom, Equality, All Power for the People, Money for the People."

Another view of the 1960s is found in Silva's poem "Letter to an Old Friend," in *The Second St. Poems* (1983). A variation on the Dear John letter, the work gives a retrospective view of the bohemian style of that bygone era, pointing out its need for revision: "Now i haven't turned establishment/ John,/ but like i said/ the hippies are dead/ & your Goodwill clothes & love beads/ just don't make it now./ Sure, i miss you, John,/ but/ the cockroaches in your pad/ aren't funny anymore/ a girl gets tired of sharing the sofa/ with your dog/ & somehow two master's degrees/ don't make up for a night on the town." The poem contrasts Silva then and now, her changing tastes and values. The appeal of the work lies in its straightforward yet rhythmic language and the succinct statement of its intention. Like many of Silva's poems, it is most effective when read aloud. María Inés Lagos-Pope has commented on Silva's use of *i* in lower case for the poetic *I*, even to start a sentence. Lagos-Pope interprets this usage as an indication that Silva "considers herself an equal of those who surround her and that the emphasis is on communication, on sharing, and not on the self."

Life Changes Dramatically

Silva found her life greatly changed by the political events on campus of the late 1960s and early 1970s, and she was later unable to resume her unsatisfactory existence on the ranch. She subsequently divorced her third husband. Her story "Precious," also included in *The Cat,* records a woman's difficulties with a painful divorce in which every attempt she makes to support or improve herself is distorted into proof that she is crazy, unfit to be a mother, and unworthy of financial assistance. Society overwhelmingly favors the husband, who is able to deceive the judge about his financial situation. Ultimately the female narrator is alone, abandoned even by her children, with only her loyal cat, Precious, for company and solace.

The turbulence of Silva's personal life, however, did not deter her from achieving her goal, and she graduated from San Jose State in 1976 with an M.A. in English. She notes that at that time there were no classes in Hispanic literature, and women's writing was only just beginning to penetrate the canon. Only after her comprehensive exams and her studying of the seventeenth and eighteenth centuries was she able to "discover" women's writings. She did not learn about Hispanic writing until she was out of school.

The year after her graduation Silva published "This Is No Poem: This Is a Woman" (November 1977), in which she addresses Walt Whitman, a symbol of the confident and accepted Anglo-Saxon American male writer, and asks for her place on the stage of literature: "i am the other half / & i, too, want to sing America. / . . . i am the other sex & for too long i was told to be / patient & perfect, Walt

Whitman. While Ezra Pound / made a pact with you, my sisters had to wait." The speaker thinks she understands Hughes better than poets such as Whitman, Pound, and Allen Ginsberg because Hughes "dared to sing America even when he was sent to eat in / the kitchen when company came." He, too, was told to be "patient & perfect," but his response was to dream, boogie, and dare to sing "of the darker side of America." Silva's speaker invites Whitman to a reception of women poets and tells him that he can freely express his views on the "deliciousness of sex"—among Anne Sexton, Erica Jong, and Judy Grahn. He will be introduced to his female counterpart, "the common woman," who is no longer patient and perfect but who, with her sisters, welcomes Whitman and tells him in the poem's last line, "we, too, are America."

Endures Economic Hardship

Despite her college degree, Silva still found economic survival to be a struggle. She was flexible and resourceful, though, and she found work as an apartment manager, a tutor, an English teacher with Poets in the Schools, and a ghost-writer for the welfare department. The late 1970s and early 1980s were the difficult years during which most of *The Second St. Poems* were written. Many of the poems depict the pain, violence, and uncertainty of life in this neighborhood (Second Street in San Jose) as they also describe Silva's loves, family, disappointments, and struggles. "Always close to death on Second St." records the all-night sirens, barroom knifings, prostitutes, poverty, drugs, and alcohol that define this environment: "Who could ever forget their mortality / living this close to death? / Still, who is prepared for the stranger / who breaks in late at night / leather jacket and fist in the face / all that can be remembered?" In this collection "Jose Luis," "Mi negro amor malcontento" (My Unhappy Black Love), and "He's Gone" portray Silva's lovers and her difficulties with them. The brief, touching poem "Pain," conveys the psychological distress, which, coupled with the hazardous social conditions, made life on Second Street so difficult: "Pain/ is a box./ i'm in a box/ It is a house./ Walls and a roof/ & a solid floor,/ but no door."

Poetry Lends the Immediacy of Experience

An economic system that humiliates the recipient of its aid and implicitly doubts her honesty is the backdrop of several of Silva's poems. For example, "General Assistance Is as Low as You Can Get" enumerates in telling detail the poet's material poverty and spiritual yearnings: "my total worth consisting of crates of books / & a heart filled with dreams. / i returned to my $60 a month room / looked at my $109 monthly grant / & said General Assistance really is as low as you can get. / Someday i'll write a poem about that." Here and in other poems the reader senses the immediacy of the experience that gave rise to the work of art; yet the self-consciousness of making poems about individuals and experiences at times detracts from the poem. The events and feelings of Silva's experiences could

benefit from greater distillation. There is a tendency toward cliché, which detracts from the power of the experiences presented. With greater maturity, her vigor, vitality, and the point of view of an individual whose life refuses to be anonymous might be expressed with the forceful language it deserves.

Silva's dedication to her craft, despite the numerous and diverse hardships that she has encountered, evokes admiration. Aware of her difficult position outside the mainstream, she has persisted in writing. Although the work she does to earn her living leaves little time to pursue her writing, she has seized the little opportunities she has found. She has achieved a measure of recognition and critical attention, and she has completed her artistic apprenticeship. Her voice deserves to be heard, and one can only hope that she will continue to express the struggles she knows so well.

Sources:

Lagos-Pope, María Inés. "A Space of Her Own: *The Second St. Poems* by Beverly Silva," introduction to *The Second St. Poems.* Ypsilanti, MI: Bilingual Press/Editorial Bilingüe, 1983.

Laura Angelica Simón
(1965–)
Filmmaker

Selected filmography:

Fear and Learning at Hoover Elementary. Fear and Learning, Inc., 1997.

Overview

In a mere few months, Laura Angelica Simón went from a relatively unknown elementary school teacher to an award-winning filmmaker lauded by First Lady Hilary Rodham Clinton. Yet, she might be the first to admit that her first career is not only invaluable, but is the reason behind her new role in the film industry.

Lacking any previous filmmaking experience, Simón's *Fear and Learning at Hoover Elementary* was inspired by her frustration with the 1994 passage of California's Proposition 187, an act that would ban illegal immigrants from public schools. A second- and fourth-grade teacher at the school located in one of Los Angeles' most violent inner-city neighborhoods, Simón saw the proposition's emotional impact on her students—one that generated fear and low self-esteem. A Mexican immigrant herself, Simón knew that these children needed a voice of their own and decided to document her students' plight for the world to see. Not only did Simón film a documentary, but it won the Freedom of Expression Award at the 1997 Sundance Film Festival and aired nationally on PBS in July of the same year.

Simón was born in Mexico in the mid-1960s. Her family legally immigrated to the United States in 1971, first settling in San Francisco, then later moving to Los Angeles. She clearly remembers starting kindergarten in a U.S. school at age six, not yet having learned English. She told Michael Quintanilla in a *Los Angeles Times* article, "When we came to the United States, I didn't realize we had gone to another country until I went to school. Suddenly, everyone around me was dressing differently . . . and speaking a different language. I didn't fit into anything. The class would go left and I would go right. I went in the bathroom in my pants because I just simply didn't know how to ask, 'Where is the bathroom?'"

Simón went on to reveal that she often felt alienated and was mercilessly teased about her ethnicity by other children. Hurt by this discrimination and the damage it caused to her family's dignity, Simón became determined to defend herself through education. "I wanted to have a voice desperately in this country. [At an early age] it became very clear that I had to speak English. I made a contract with myself to not only learn it, but to become very devoted to school. . . ."

After arriving in California, Simón's father initially worked in the shipyards, and her mother worked in the garment industry. Her parents eventually started their own business selling fruit-flavored popsicles and were able to send Simón and her younger brother to good schools. Simón helped out in the family business from age 10 through high school graduation by selling popsicles from a pushcart. In the meantime, she did very well as a student. By the fourth grade, she was fluent in English. She graduated as valedictorian of her high school class.

Simón won a scholarship to Claremont McKenna College, located near Los Angeles, and majored in philosophy and economics. There, she was class president and a speaker at her commencement. Despite her love of education, her career as a teacher was unplanned. Her goal was to work as a substitute teacher to earn money to travel the globe. She quickly realized, however, that she did not want to leave the children that she taught.

Life as a dedicated teacher did not stop Simón from traveling. She has traveled Asia and Europe extensively and mastered Italian, her third language. Simón used her own love of education to inspire her students. She said to Quintanilla, "I'm almost romantic about the idea of education. It changed my life." Proud to be a tough-as-nails educator, she was known to have prepared her fourth graders for the SAT and motivated her students to complete their homework by showing up at the homes of all who had

not. There was reason for her strictness: Quintanilla quoted her to say, "I know that if my kids learn to read and write and get the math skills . . . they will grow up to be much more than what I have become. They will be the doctors, the professors, the teachers of tomorrow."

Passage of Proposition Leads to Film

Yet, it is was very difficult to encourage the benefits of a good education to young children that were threatened to be kicked out of school for reasons beyond their control. Even before Proposition 187, Hoover Elementary's young students faced many problems. The school—located in the city's Pico-Union section, regarded as the Ellis Island of L.A.—sits on the boundaries of two rival gang territories. The school building shares a block with a crack house. Most students' families live below the poverty line. But in 1994, California voters passed Proposition 187, and many of Hoover's students also faced denial of an education. Simón was shocked by the passage. She said to Stephanie Elizondo Griest in a *New York Times* article, "I didn't take it seriously at first because I never thought people would vote for something that would kick kids out of school." Her fellow teachers at Hoover were divided in the issue; but her students were fearful. When a Salvadoran student named Mayra raised her hand and asked, "Are you a cop now? Are you gonna kick me out of the classroom?", Simón likened the question to a physical blow, devastated by the child's anxiety. She tried to reassure her students that they were safe, knowing in her heart that it was not true.

Simón decided the best way to act against Proposition 187 was to make a film documenting its impact on her immigrant students, as well as the differences in opinion amongst her colleagues. Simón called for assistance from longtime friend Tracy Trench, a director of production at 20th Century Fox. Simón and Trench combined their money, found a crew willing to work for free, obtained tapes donated by Los Angeles's Museum of Tolerance, and produced 30 hours of tape, which Simón eventually edited to 53 minutes.

The taping of the film was an adventure in itself. To ensure their safety in Hoover Elementary's neighborhood, Simón warned the film's ground crew not to wear jewelry, heavy makeup, bandannas, or bright colors, and to conceal their equipment in canvas bags. For one taping in a neighoborhood park, a police escort was necessary. Before the film was completed, however, Simón and Trench ran out of funds. Trench suggested they submit the film to the festivals anyway and sent a rough version to Sundance, America's most prestigious festival for independent films. Within three weeks, the film was accepted. Suddenly, Simón was receiving phone calls from publicity agents and journalists. Still, she kept teaching her students as her top priority. When Trench informed her that the film had been accepted by Sundance, Simón made sure she heard correctly then immediately hung up to return to her waiting classroom full of students. *Fear and Learning at Hoover*

Elementary won the Freedom of Expression award at the 1997 Sundance Film Festival. That July, it was aired nationally on PBS's *Point-Of-View* series. Hilary Rodham Clinton saw the documentary and sent Simón a letter praising her efforts.

Despite her positive recognition for the film, not everyone was impressed or happy with Simón's portrayal of the proposition issue. To present a fair documentary, Simón did not impress her opinions on the film. Some complained that Simón did not oppose the measure strongly enough; on the other hand, there was hostility from those who supported the proposition. In the end, the documentary did not provide comfortable conclusions. "Some people get frustrated with me for not telling them what to think," Simón was quoted to have said in *U.S. News & World Report*. "This is not a black and white issue that can be resolved in a tidy way in an hour." She told the *New York Times*, "As a teacher, you're supposed to present the facts, but you never tell your students what to think. That's what I did in this film. That's my bible in teaching and my bible in filmmaking."

Career Switch to Filmmaking

During the hoopla over the film, Simón remained a teacher at Hoover Elementary. Amidst offers from television executives to produce a pilot, Simón at first seemed committed to remain a teacher. She soon realized, however, that remaining at the school was not in her best interests. "I got hate letters, hate calls. My peers treated me differently after they viewed the movie," she said to Quintanilla. "I knew if I had to go on teaching, I couldn't do it at Hoover. Maybe somewhere else, but there wasn't anywhere else to go. These days, when I walk into a room with educators, I trigger discussion and debate." Thus, Simón left Hoover Elementary at the end of the 1997 school term and turned her efforts to filmmaking. Her immediate projects included a film for HBO and another documentary called *The New Immigrants* for the producers of the acclaimed film, *Hoop Dreams*. Simón also hoped to begin work on an interracial love story.

Simón did not leave Hoover Elementary without making yet another lasting impact. She and actress Meg Ryan helped start the Children's Basic Needs Fund for the school and raised more than $20,000 for food, clothing, blankets, eyeglasses, and emergency medical care for Pico-Union's children.

Although she will undoubtedly continue to find success in the film industry, Simón may always remain an educator at heart. She told Quintanilla, "Education to me was the miracle of America. A miracle in that today I am a professional, fluent in three languages, and that I could make a movie and get the sort of national attention that I am now getting." She went on to say, "To come here and to have the point of view that I have from two worlds—to be able to easily go back and forth between languages, between cul-

tures, to have that sort of hybrid. I just love being Mexican. I love being an immigrant. I love being an American."

Sources:

Hardigg, Viva. "When Prop. 187 Comes to the Classroom." *U.S. News and World Report*, February 3, 1997, p. 50.

Griest, Stephanie Elizondo. "Immigrant, Teacher and Now Filmmaker." *The New York Times*, June 30, 1997, p. C10.

Quintanilla, Michael. "A Teacher's Dedication to Immigrant Kids." *Los Angeles Times*, May 7, 1997, p. E3.

———. "Out of the Mouths of Babes." *Los Angeles Times*, May 27, 1997, p.E1.

———. "Teacher/Documentarian Shifts Her Focus to Movies." *Los Angeles Times*, December 31, 1997, p. E1.

Sobek, María Herrera
See Herrera-Sobek, María

Madeleine Stowe
(1958–)
Actress

Selected filmography:

The Gangster Chronicles, 1981.
Blood and Orchids, 1986.
Stakeout, 1987.
Worth Winning, 1989.
Revenge, 1990.
The Two Jakes, 1990.
Closet Land, 1991.
China Moon, 1992.
The Last of the Mohicans, 1992.
Unlawful Entry, 1992.
Another Stakeout, 1993.
Short Cuts, 1993.
Blink, 1993.
Bad Girls, 1994.
Twelve Monkeys, 1995.
Tempting Fate, 1997.

Overview

Her brunette good looks and a lucky break got Madeleine Stowe her first acting job. But it was almost ten years before the statuesque actress gained star status in Hollywood's competitive movie industry. Finally, in 1992, after her critically praised performance in the historical

Madeleine Stowe

drama *Last of the Mohicans,* Stowe's name began appearing on cinema marquees, as well as on the lists of Hollywood directors. Despite her fragile beauty and her penchant for being cast as a vulnerable woman in a host of films, Stowe has a behind-the-scenes reputation for being down-to-earth and determined to do things on her own terms. "[She's] not push-aroundable," comments director Robert Altman of the actress, who turned in an award-winning performance in his 1993 film *Short Cuts.* Fellow director Jonathan Kaplan agrees. "Madeleine is so delicate and graceful, but she has a strong, iron will. It's unusual to have . . . her kind of fragile body language in a woman who is really tough and so utterly fearless when it comes to authority."

Born August 18, 1958, in Los Angeles, California, Stowe was one of three children born to Robert Stowe, a civil engineer, and his wife, Mireya Mora, the daughter of a well-to-do Costa Rican family. Her mother supported Stowe's early love of music by arranging piano lessons for her daughter; her father had other ideas. His possessiveness and violent outbursts of temper, which were soon diagnosed as symptoms of multiple sclerosis, kept her home life tense and, for a young girl, confusing. "Neighbors would come running, and here we were these three little kids trying to pretend that nothing was wrong," Stowe told the *Los Angeles Times,* recalling the many times her father lost control in public. "I kept wishing that my mother would stand up to him, but she was such a saint. I always felt a little bit evil compared to her." Stowe's father died in 1983.

Sidesteps College on Way to Hollywood

After graduating from high school, the quiet Stowe enrolled at the University of Southern California, inspired by a love of old movies, to major in film direction. However, fate intervened, in the form of an overriding urge to cut classes in favor of haunting the local theater as a stagehand. While passing out programs at a production starring actor Richard Dreyfuss, Stowe was noticed by Dreyfuss' agent, who got the 19-year-old college student a bit part on *Baretta,* a popular nighttime television series. Although she looks back on these early appearances and shudders, the actress seemed to have found her niche.

Other more challenging roles soon came the way of the strikingly beautiful Stowe. After several years of playing what she termed "ethereal" roles, however, the actress felt the need to take a break from the camera and get in touch with who she really was. "So I just stopped and traveled through Central America," she told Margy Rochlin in *Interview,* "where I have family, and I went to a couple of islands in the Caribbean. All I know is that a year and a half later, when I came back to acting, I had a different perspective on things." Stowe returned to work in projects like the miniseries *The Gangster Chronicles* and *Blood and Orchids.*

The 1987 comedy-thriller *Stakeout* was Stowe's first motion picture role; although the film received mixed reviews, her performance forced critics to give her a second look. Other films followed, including being cast next to costar Kevin Costner in the 1990 thriller *Revenge,* and playing girlfriend to actor/director Jack Nicholson in *The Two Jakes.* It was not until 1992, when she hit her stride as the high-spirited daughter of a doomed British general in *Last of the Mohicans* that Stowe proved to audiences that she was capable of taking a leading role. Cast opposite Daniel Day-Lewis' Hawkeye, Stowe stood her ground in this lushly filmed frontier epic, adapted from the classic American novel by James Fenimore Cooper.

Last of the Mohicans Marks Turning Point

Her role alongside Lewis in *Last of the Mohicans* marked a shift for Stowe for yet another reason. Up until this point, she had mainly been cast—by virtue of her fragile looks—in the role of the imperiled, helpless girlfriend, a part that usually involved on-camera nudity. "There was a certain amount of sniggering about the amount of nudity she engaged in in her films," explained Michael Apted (who directed Stowe in *Blink*) in the *Los Angeles Times,* but Madeleine sees that as part of her ammunition. She's like the great actresses in the '30s and '40s, very beautiful but with nothing cute about her looks, a woman who is not afraid of her own sexuality." To be sure, while the nudity itself never concerned Stowe, what it represented did. "You know, they want a woman to be pretty, to be sexy, and they want her to be desirable," the actress explained to Rochlin. "What they don't want is for her to speak, to aggressively pursue anything. They can project anything they want onto her and not have her talk back. I was really shocked by that [in filming *Revenge*]. I find these characters are remarkably silent." By the time she came under Apted's direction, Stowe was determined to have a hand in balancing the role between her and her costar, Aidan Quinn, building his character into more than just the "love interest" she had been relegated to playing for so long.

Under the direction of Robert Altman in his 1993 *Short Cuts,* Stowe broke away from her typical roles and gave a performance that earned her the nod as best supporting actress from the National Society of Film Critics. As the down-to-earth, no-nonsense wife of two-timing policeman Tim Robbins, Stowe proved that her acting talents ran much deeper than mere physical presence. She followed that success with several more films, including *China Moon,* shot in 1992 as a starring vehicle for actor Ed Harris, and Apted's *Blink,* a 1993 thriller in which she was cast in her first starring role as a semi-blind violinist who witnesses a murder.

More recent film appearances include 1994's *Bad Girls,* and *Twelve Monkeys,* a film directed by Terry Gilliam in 1995. In *Twelve Monkeys,* Stowe is cast as a psychiatrist alongside Bruce Willis and Brad Pitt; with former Monty-Pythoner Gilliam at the helm, the cast crosses the time barrier in this off-beat thriller-romance. The actress went back in time for the filming of *Bad Girls,* where Stowe and costars Mary Stuart Masterson, Andie MacDowell, and Drew Barrymore get the chance to let loose and have some fun as a pack of gun-toting, tobacco-spitting former prostitutes who head for the high country in the wild west of the 1890s. Despite the problems she had with the film's title—"It's totally politically incorrect," she announced in the *Los Angeles Times*—*Bad Girls* was especially fun for Stowe because of the amount of time she got to spend in the saddle. An avid horse rider, she owns a four-horse ranch near Luckenbach, Texas, with her husband, actor Brian Benben.

Enjoys Acting Career

Married since 1986, the couple had their first child in 1996. In addition to motherhood, Stowe plans to continue her acting career, seeing it as the ideal job. "I love the life of an actor," she told Hilary de Vries in the *Los Angeles Times,* "because you spend brief amounts of time with other people and then you just leave. I need to be alone a lot, and I need to be outdoors." She returned to the screen in 1997 for *Tempting Fate,* a film with actor Neil Patrick Harris (of television s *Doogie Howser, M.D.* fame). She plays a feminist writer who hires Harris to father a child because her husband (William Hurt) is sterile.

Sources:

Boston Globe, January 23, 1994, p. B35.

Giles, Jeff. "Stowe Says Goodbye To All That." *Newsweek,* February 14, 1994, p. 52.

McGough, Michael. "Looking For A Creative Life After 'Doogie Howser, M.D.'" *New York Times,* November 2, 1997, Section 2, p. 32.

Rochlin, Margy. "Madeleine Stowe." *Interview,* May 1990, pp. 92- 93.

Smith, Steven. "Movies: Rattling the 'Monkeys' Cage. . . ." *Los Angeles Times,* January 30, 1994, p. 7.

Suarez Rivero, Eliana
See Rivero, Eliana Suarez

Sutherland Martinez, Betita
See Martinez, Elizabeth Sutherland

Sweet, Maria Contreras
See Contreras-Sweet, Maria

T

Cristina Teuscher
(1978–)
Swimmer

At 18 years of age, Cristina Teuscher (pronounced *toy-skier*) set an Olympic record at the 1996 Atlanta Games, swimming the fastest 200-meter leg in the women's 800-meter freestyle relay and helping the U.S. relay team win a gold medal. She won numerous other competitions during her teens, including a junior national championship at age fourteen and an U.S. championship only two years later. In 1995 Teuscher brought home three gold medals from the Pan American Games in Argentina, her parents' native country. She is a powerful, versatile swimmer, competing in races from 100 meters to a mile in length. Both Teuscher's long, fluid stroke and her sense of competitive equilibrium often give her the edge over opponents.

Discovers Natural Athletic Talent

At 6 feet tall and 130 pounds, Teuscher is lean and strong, a natural athlete. She grew up in New Rochelle, NY, in an athletic family. Her father and mother, Enrique and Monica, met each other while performing aikido, a South American martial art, in their native country of Argentina. Her parents were not involved in swimming, however, and learned about it along with Cristina as she became more involved in the sport. Teuscher reported that her parents have never pushed her to compete, as do those of many young athletes, but that they support her goals and help her keep them in perspective. Wayne Coffey reported in *Scholastic Update* that Teuscher sometimes phones her father, a psychiatrist, from poolside before a race to ask for some last-minute advice on preparing herself mentally for the competition. She attributes much of her success to her close-knit family.

Teuscher admitted that when she first started swimming competitively at age six, she did not like it. "It was hard to get me into the pool. But I liked making friends and going to races, and it gave me a world outside of school," she told James O'Connor of the *New York Times*. By the time coach John Collins of the Badger Aqua Club noticed her at swim practice, she had become fully committed to swimming.

He began coaching her when she was 13, placing her on his senior team made up of his most promising swimmers aged 14 to 24. Collins was immediately impressed by Teuscher's powerful swimming style. "It was her stroke I noticed right away when I saw her," he told Chuck Slater of the *New York Times*. "She has a very good technique and bodywise is able to go very high in the water. And she has always had superior desire." Teuscher blossomed under Collins' coaching and took home a junior national championship only one year after starting with him. This was the beginning of Teuscher's promising athletic career.

Excels as High School Scholar-Athlete

During her high school years Teuscher took home two national championships, won three gold medals at the Pan American Games, and a gold at the Olympics. In order to keep in top shape for these competitions, Teuscher trained rigorously. "If you ultimately want to be a national champion it takes years of training," coach Collins said in an interview with O'Connor. Teuscher's regimen included being in the pool for 12 workouts a week, swimming both in the morning and evening 6 days a week. In addition to swimming workouts, Teuscher trained daily on an exercise machine designed especially for swimmers. From the time she started swimming competitively, the longest break Teuscher ever took from her training regimen was two weeks. She practiced year-round and traveled worldwide while trying to keep up with the social life of a normal teenager and to maintain her high academic record.

Teuscher told O'Connor that such intensive training for competition necessarily takes away from some of the things most high school students take for granted. "It's hard to spend time with friends when I'm training so much. Sometimes I'm out of touch with things that are going on." But she put things in perspective when talking to Wayne Coffey. "I think I've sacrificed like any other athlete who is in high school," she told him, "But I'm happy. I don't feel like I've missed out on anything. Because when you think about it, how many kids get to say, 'Gee, I'm going to the Olympics?'"

Swimming is not the only key to success in Teuscher's eyes. By staying focused and bringing a stack of textbooks to the pool, Teuscher made it through high school with an impressive grade point average. She graduated from New Rochelle High School ranked tenth out of a class of 500. With these stellar all-around qualifications she was accepted at both Stanford and Columbia Universities the same spring that she qualified for the Olympic team. After much thought, Teuscher opted for Columbia, which affords her the opportunity to be near her family.

Exhibits Competitive and Calm Persona

The pressure heated up for Teuscher with the approach of the 1996 Summer Olympics. Although she approached it with the same confidence and aplomb as her many other commitments, Teuscher admitted to being anxious before a big competition, going over the race again and again in her head. After the pre-race tension, swimming the race itself is a release and a relief. Teuscher told Chuck Slater of the *New York Times* that when she was a baby, her mother would put her in the bathtub to stop her from crying. "It was the only thing that calmed me down," she said. Just like when she was a baby, being in the water allays Teuscher's fears. "When you finally get in the blocks you relax. You know you're ready. There's no more time to dwell on it. You just let yourself go, and it's a great feeling." Competitive pressure gets the best of many young athletes, but in an interview for *Scholastic Update,* her coach observed that Teuscher "keeps cool, calm, and collected and that serves her well." Despite her easygoing demeanor, he reported, "she's a vicious competitor."

Sources:

Coffey, Wayne. "Cristina Teuscher: Making a Splash." *Scholastic Update,* April 12, 1996, p. 4.
O'Connor, James V. "New Rochelle Swimmer Steps Up Her Pace for Olympic Trials." *New York Times,* February 18, 1996, p. WC1.
Slater, Chuck. "Country's Olympic Hopes Rest on Four Athletes." *New York Times,* July 14, 1996, p. WC1.

Thompson, Linda Chavez
See **Chavez-Thompson, Linda**

Liz Torres
(1947–)
Actress, singer

Selected filmography:

Phyllis (TV series). 1975.
All in the Family (TV series). 1976.
Scavenger Hunt. 20th Century Fox, 1979.

Liz Torres

Checking In (TV series). 1981.
City (TV series). 1986.
The New Odd Couple (TV series). 1986.
America. 1986.
Hot to Trot. Warner Brothers, 1988.
Sunset. TriStar, 1988.
Thieves of Fortune. 1989.
Lena's Holiday. Crown International, 1990.
Bloodfist 4: Die Trying. Concorde Films, 1992.
The John Larroquette Show (TV series). 1993-1996.
Rescue Me. 1993.
Body Shot. 1993.
A Million to Juan. Samuel Goldwyn Co., 1994.
Just Cause. Warner Brothers, 1995.
Happily Ever After: Fairy Tales for Every Child. HBO, 1995.
Over the Top (TV series). 1997.
The Wonderful Ice Cream Suit. Buena Vista Films, 1998.
The Odd Couple II. Paramount, 1998.

Described as Triple-Threat Performer

A consummate professional, Liz Torres is that rare individual who can truly be described as a "triple-threat performer." Equally adept at acting, singing, and stand-up comedy, this talented Hispanic American broke into television with stand-up comedy performances on the *Tonight Show,* and has built a career that spans two decades. In television, movies, and theater, Torres has demonstrated that she is more than able to handle whatever acting challenge might come her way.

Gains Theater Experience

Born on September 27, 1947, to parents of Puerto Rican descent, Torres was raised in New York City's Hell's Kitchen on the west side of Manhattan. Torres got her start in show business singing in the city's small nightclubs where she and Bette Midler shared Barry Manilow as their musical conductor. She first cut her acting teeth in the theater, demonstrating her talent in a variety of roles. On the stage, Torres starred as Googie Gomez in the Broadway production of *The Ritz*. She starred as Bunny in the widely acclaimed *House of Blue Leaves* at the Coconut Grove Theatre in Miami, played Rosie opposite Tab Hunter in a touring production of *Bye Bye Birdie*, and Gittel Mosca opposite John Raitt in the national company of *See Saw*. Torres also has appeared in leading roles in productions of *Ladies, Murders of 1940, A Funny Thing Happened on the Way to the Forum, She That One He the Other, Beautiful Mariposa, Kiss Me Kate, Murder at the Howard Johnson,* and *A Girl Could Get Lucky*.

Moves to Television Industry

In the mid-1970s, Torres broke into the medium for which she became best known: television. She joined the cast of the television series, *Phyllis* in 1975, and followed that up with a year-long part in *All in the Family,* in 1976. Since then she been a series regular in a dozen television series, including *Checking In* (1981), *The New Odd Couple* (1982), and, more recently, in the series *City* (1990), *The John Larroquette Show* (1993-1996), and *Over the Top*. She also has numerous credits for guest appearances on shows such as *Murphy Brown, Nurses, Wonder Years, Almost Grown, Knots Landing, L.A. Law, Blue Thunder, Ally McBeal, The Nanny,* and *Murder, She Wrote*.

Amasses Impressive List of Movie Credits

In addition to her extensive work on stage, Torres has amassed a long list of film credits spanning two decades and multiple genres. In 1979, she played a small part in the film *Scavenger Hunt,* in which 15 potential heirs to a fortune must compete in a scavenger hunt to win it all. *America,* made in 1986, included Liz Torres in a story about a New York cable station that achieves worldwide fame when their signal bounces off the moon. The year 1988 saw Torres in the movie *Hot to Trot,* a comedy about a talking horse. That same year she appeared with Bruce Willis and James Garner in the Western farce *Sunset*. A small part in the 1989 movie *Thieves of Fortune,* was followed by another bit part in *Lena's Holiday* in 1991. She portrayed a cop in *Bloodfist IV: Die Trying* in 1992, and took on a role in the adventure film, *Rescue Me* the following year. She added a thriller to her list of credits when she appeared in *Body Shot* in 1993, and she made a cameo appearance in the 1994 rags-to-riches tale, *A Million to Juan*. In 1995 she played opposite Sean Connery in *Just Cause*. She then played the role of Ruby Escadrillo in *The Wonderful Ice Cream Suit* in 1998, and that same year appeared in a supporting role in

Odd Couple II, which starred Jack Lemmon and Walter Matthau. In addition to her feature films, Torres has several television movies on her resumé. Torres also participated in HBO's bold attempt in 1995 to bring some diversity to well-known fairy tales in the animated production *Happily Ever After: Fairy Tales for Every Child*. In a twist on the Cinderella folktale, HBO's version boasted images of a clearly Hispanic American Cinderella dancing to the strains of mariachi music. Jimmy Smits supplied the voice of Prince Felipe, while Torres played the Fairy Madrina.

At nightclubs across the country, Torres has brought her own brand of magic to a wide audience. She has taken her hit one-woman show to audiences in New York, Los Angeles, Las Vegas, Lake Tahoe, San Juan, and Chicago. Additionally, she has worked live with such performers as Liza Minnelli, Tony Bennett, Helen Reddy, Billy Eckstein, Lionel Hampton, and Errol Garner. She was the host for the twentieth anniversary celebration of the Improv comedy club in New York.

Earns Numerous Awards and Nominations

For her portrayal of Mahalia Sanchez on *The John Larroquette Show,* Torres was nominated for an Emmy in both 1994 and 1995. She also received a 1995 Golden Globe nomination for the same role. In 1995, she received an American Comedy Awards nomination for the outstanding individual performance in a comedy series. The following year she received an American Comedy Awards nomination as best female television performer. In 1997, she received the El Angel Award for her contributions to Hispanic art in America and a Bravo Award for the outstanding individual performance in a comedy series.

As if her work in television, film, theater, and nightclubs were not enough, Torres has achieved success as a recording artist for RCA Records, has given a command performance for Morocco's King Hassan II, and was invited to the White House by President Jimmy Carter for the country's first celebration of National Hispanic Week.

When she finds a little time away from show business, Torres devotes her energies to such worthwhile causes as the battle against AIDS, funding for public television, and expanded higher educational opportunities for minorities. In 1995, she was one of the headliners for "Divas: Simply Singing," a benefit concert in Los Angeles to help combat AIDS. Torres is also a member of the National Hispanic Foundation for the Arts.

Sources:

Amerman, Donald. Letter from Liz Torres, March 5, 1998.

"Bringing Diversity to Fairy Tales." *Michigan Chronicle,* May 9, 1995, p. 1C.

Dungee, Ron. "Singing Divas Invade Los Angeles." *Los Angeles Sentinel,* April 26, 1995.

Rivera, Miluka. "Hispanic Journal: Film and TV Perpetuate Invisibility." *Hispanic,* June 30, 1996, p. 12.

Treviño, Gloria Velásquez
See Velásquez-Treviño, Gloria

Gloria Tristani
(1953–)
Federal government official

In 1994, Gloria Tristani was named the first woman to the New Mexico State Corporation Commission. Within two years, she was elected chair of the Commission, and on November 3, 1997, she was sworn in as a commissioner on the Federal Communications Commission (FCC). Tristani has demonstrated her resolve in her fight to limit children's access to violence on television and has proven her abilities in dealing with the Telecommunications Act of 1996.

Gloria Tristani

Influenced by Family Ties

Tristani was born in Puerto Rico on December 20, 1953, but grew up with strong ties to New Mexico, where her grandfather was the late Senator Dennis Chavez. Even though she was only nine when he died, she was influenced by the reputation he built as a U.S. Senator, serving for over 30 years (1935-1962). In an interview in 1997 for *New Mexico Business Journal,* Tristani said that his memory was vibrant in both her own family but also throughout the state. "When I was running for office two years ago, I couldn't believe the stories I heard from older people about my grandfather. I thought I really got to know him during the campaign."

Tristani grew up in Puerto Rico, but moved to New Mexico in 1982. Between 1983 to 1987, she worked as an aide to Senator Jeff Bingaman of New Mexico. She graduated from Barnard College at Columbia University in 1987 with a degree in medieval studies and, the following year, married Gerard W. Thomson, who later became a district judge in New Mexico. The couple has two children, Vanessa and Jorge.

Tristani returned to school, receiving her law degree from the University of New Mexico School of Law in 1990. She soon became a member of the New Mexico and Colorado bars and was an attorney in private practice in Albuquerque. While working there, Tristani gained valuable knowledge working on legal tasks for the state's largest electric utility, one of the law firm's clients. She remained with the firm for four years, until she was appointed to the New Mexico State Corporation Commission (SCC).

Enters the Political Fray

In 1994, just four years out of law school, Tristani made her first foray into politics. She ran against incumbent Louis Gallego for the Democratic nomination of the SCC post and then went on to win in the general election, making her the first woman to obtain a position on the Commission. In an article in the FCC's *Communications Daily,* Tristani said that she had run for the office "on a consumer platform." She stressed that her goal was to make sure all the people in New Mexico would "benefit from the telecommunications revolution" by ensuring that rural areas in the state would not be forgotten.

While serving as a member of the SCC, she gained a reputation as an aggressive consumer advocate, focusing on issues such as health care and telecommunications.In an interview with the *New Mexico Business Journal* in January of 1997, Tristani explained her concern about health care. "Now that we're moving into the managed care/HMO environment, there are more and more complaints and concerns about how that's happening." Tristani's goal was to see New Mexico become proactive on the subject and, under her leadership, the SCC proposed several regulations for dealing with managed care, including a patient's rights and responsibilities clause. The regulations also required health care companies to provide expanded basic health care services and more choices for their clients.

In 1996, Tristani was elected to chair the SCC and, in that capacity, she was instrumental in helping implement the Telecommunications Act of 1996 in her state. She also worked actively with the National Association of Regulatory Utility Commissioners' committee, which dealt with telecommunication issues. That same year, Tristani was nominated to receive the Governor's Award for Outstanding New Mexico Women. Soon, however, Tristani began eyeing another position in the state government. The Republican governor of the state, Gary Johnson, elected in 1994, had been experiencing difficulties working with the legislature. When he did not publicly announce his plans to run for reelection, several key state Democrats put their names forward. In May of 1997, Tristani decided she, too, would run for the office of governor. Her chances of becoming the first woman governor of the state were not considered strong, but within two months that point was moot and her campaign was suddenly in limbo. Tristani's name had been raised as a possible nominee to the FCC.

Federal Communications Commission

On September 15, 1997, President Bill Clinton officially nominated Tristani for the post at the FCC. His announcement surprised many in the broadcast and cable industry, because most had not heard of her. Yet, she was confirmed by the Senate on October 28 and was sworn in on November 3 of the same year. In *Communications Daily* Tristani said that the reason she gave up her candidacy to pursue the FCC position was "because of the challenge of the job." She also jokingly admitted that convincing 100 senators to vote for her was easier than convincing a million voters.

As the FCC Commissioner, Tristani became vocal on violence in television and its effect on children. Addressing the Puerto Rican Congress in early 1998, Tristani said that there was not "much doubt that TV has an impact on children." Her biggest concern, however, was the amount of violence they were being exposed to while watching television programs. She stated that over 1,000 studies have indicated a link between this violence and children's anti-social behavior, and she emphasized that the time for studying the problem is over: what was needed was action. She stressed the need for parents, society, the entertainment industry, and the government to take responsibility for regulating what children view on television. In particular, she gave strong support for the V-chip legislation that Congress enacted in the 1996 Telecommunications Act.

By the end of the year, the chair of the FCC appointed Tristani to the Federal-State Joint Board on Universal Service, an issue close to Tristani. The 1996 Telecommunications Act required the FCC and states to provide the funding for telecommunication services to all people in the United States. Even in rural or low-income areas, schools,

libraries, and health care providers are to be connected to the telecommunications network. In particular, Tristani is concerned whether all states can pay their share and whether Internet providers should help share in the cost of providing universal service. Tristani's term at the FCC ends in 1998, and unless she is reelected, she will return to New Mexico. She has not ruled out another run for the governor or any other forays into politics, and she plans to be remain an active voice for consumers of all backgrounds and economic levels.

Current Address: Federal Communications Commission, 1919 M St., NW, Washington, DC 20554.

Sources:

"Children and TV Violence Speech." *FCC Home Page.* Available at http://www.fcc.gov/spgt803.html
"Gloria Tristani." *Communications Daily,* November 18, 1997, p. 1.
"Pro-consumer FCC Prospect." *Broadcasting & Cable,* September 1, 1997, p. 14.
"The Regulator." *New Mexico Business Journal,* January, 1997, p. 14.
"The Universal Service Fund: What Every Educator Should Know." *National Association of Secondary School Principals.* Available at http://www.nassp.org/service.htm.

Sara Martinez Tucker
Organization president

As president and CEO of the National Hispanic Scholarship Fund (NHSF), the United States' largest Hispanic scholarship program, Sara Martinez Tucker has an ambitious plan to double the rate of Hispanics earning college degrees by the year 2006. Since its existence, NHSF has awarded more than 31 million dollars in scholarships to more than 32,000 students. Appointed in 1997, Martinez Tucker brings a wealth of administrative and business experience to the NHSF. She said in a telephone interview, "My mission, stated very simply, is to dispel the myth that Hispanics do not value education."

Martinez Tucker was born and raised in Laredo, TX, one of three children in a middle-class working family. Her father was a civil servant; her mother, a bank clerk. Her parents never doubted their children would go to college, instilling in them the value of higher education. Martinez Tucker told *Hispanic* magazine in October of 1997: "My parents struggled to give us a college education because father always talked to us about having a choice in life, and he said an education would give us that choice." At the

Sara Martinez Tucker

University of Texas at Austin, Martinez Tucker put her parents' teachings into action. She became an honors student, earning a bachelor's degree in journalism in 1976 and a master's degree in business administration in 1979. In between her degrees, she worked as a general assignments reporter for the San Antonio *Express*.

Enters the Business World

Martinez Tucker spent 16 years at AT&T, where she held positions in customer service, sales, and human resources. Her promotion in 1990 to director of Human Resources and Quality for the Network Services Division made her the first Hispanic female to reach AT&T's executive level. She later served as national vice president for AT&T's Global Business Communications Systems. When Martinez Tucker was offered to head the NHSF in 1997, she was ready to seek new challenges. Already on NHSF's board of directors, she knew that heading the organization would give her the chance to make a difference in educating young Hispanics.

As president and CEO, Martinez Tucker has two main objectives: to oversee a plan to double the rate of Hispanics earning college degrees by the year 2006, and to create new partnerships with corporations that will initiate programs to attract Hispanic students to college. The organization, however, is faced with a challenge. According to the NHSF, the dropout rate for Hispanic students is 33 percent, the largest of any racial or ethnic group in the United States.

Martinez Tucker wants to change that statistic. She proposes a method to rally the Hispanic community by launching a nationwide public awareness campaign. She states in an NHSF brochure: "Hispanics are not an underclass—we strive to be economically healthy, we respect our families and our country. The potential exists to rally our community to destroy the myth that we don't care about education, to show, by our giving, that we support our youth." In a telephone interview, Martinez Tucker had a few simple words of advice to young Hispanic students: "Stay in school."

Martinez Tucker heads an organization that was ranked in 1994 by *Worth* magazine as the nation's most efficient charity, with 95 percent of the money raised going into efforts to send underprivileged Hispanic students to college. Despite these achievements, the new president wants to improve the organization. In a 1997 issue of *Latina Style* magazine, Martinez Tucker spoke of the new mission at NHSF: "We believe that the benefits of investing in Hispanic education are clear. Hispanics' access to better jobs and higher family incomes increases the spending power of the fastest growing segment of the American population. Hispanics with college degrees earn more. Over a lifetime, income increases $500,000 for men and $400,000 for women. More importantly, a higher family median income increases the likelihood that our children will go to college."

Current Address: National Hispanic Scholarship Fund, 1 Sansome St., Ste. 1000, San Francisco, CA 94104.

Sources:

Blue, Rose. Interview with Sara Martinez Tucker, April 16, 1998.
Hispanic, December 1997, p. 58.
Martinez Tucker, Sara. "Holiday Giving." *Latina Style*, 1997, p. 48.
"100 Most Influential Hispanics." *Hispanic Business*, October 1997, p. 81.
Segal, Troy. "The Best Charities for Your Money." *Worth*, November 1994, pp. 147-149.

Christy Turlington
(1969–)
Model, entrepreneur, community activist

Selected filmography:

Christy Turlington Backstage. Lifetime Channel (TV special), 1993.

Overview

With her refined good looks gracing the pages of the world's most prominent fashion magazines since 1986, model Christy Turlington has managed to translate her classic features into an annual income of upwards of $1.5 million—all before she reached her mid-twenties. Turlington is one of the latest crop of international supermodels, which include Claudia Schiffer, Linda Evangelista, and Paulina Porizkova, and her success confirms the advertising truth of the 1990s: ethnic sells. With an olive-skinned beauty that *New York* magazine calls "unspecified ethnic," Turlington does, indeed, sell. "There's a suggestion of an inner life and intelligence in those eyes," explained Linda Wells, editor-in-chief of *Allure* to the *New York Times*. "To advertisers, she's money in the bank."

The second of three daughters born to Dwaine and Elizabeth Turlington, Christy arrived on the scene January 2, 1969. Raised in Walnut Creek, California, a quiet suburb of San Francisco, she travelled frequently because of her father's background as a pilot for Pan-Am Airlines; her mother, a native of El Salvador, had met her husband while working as a stewardess on a flight to Hawaii. When Turlington was ten, the family moved to Coral Gables, Florida, where, like many girls her age, she caught horse fever and began to ride competitively. It was on one of her visits to the stables to ride that Turlington was discovered by a local photographer, Dennie Cody, who, as he told *New York*, "knew right away. You don't run across many girls you know can make it to the top."

From Riding Trail to Fashion Runway

With Cody's encouragement and her supportive mother never far from her side, Turlington began modeling for local businesses, working after school for upwards of $60 an hour. Cody cautioned both the young model and her mother that the only thing that would hold her back in the fashion business would be motivation, something that, along with beauty, Turlington had in abundance. In 1983, after her father suffered a heart attack and the family returned to the San Francisco area, she continued going to school and spending some of her afternoons in front of the camera. The following year 15-year-old Turlington and her mother visited fashion houses and photographers in Paris, but did not get an overly enthusiastic response. Undaunted, the high school junior arrived in New York City during the summer of 1985, determined to find a place in the field of modelling. After distributing her portfolio to photographers and magazine editors throughout Manhattan, she was a day away from boarding a plane back to the West Coast when *Vogue* cast a net for the brown-eyed beauty. Although she returned home in time for school in the fall, photo shoots for the magazine took Turlington to Paris and New York throughout the school year; during the following summer she modeled for Eileen Ford, staying in a townhouse on Manhattan's Upper East Side that Ford reserved as a dormitory for young, aspiring models.

By December 1986 the soon-to-be supermodel had moved to New York City, where, at age 18, she rented a Soho loft next door to Katie Ford, Eileen Ford's daughter. "I got a little kitten, I had a suitcase, and Katie put a bed in my room," Turlington recalled to *New York*. "That was all I had." But by the following year things had certainly changed: In addition to working for some of New York's best fashion photographers, including Herb Ritts, Irving Penn, and Steven Meisel, Turlington could count models like British-er Naomi Campbell among her best friends. New York City had, indeed, begun to feel like home for the West Coast native.

In 1988, as a result of her work on his notorious, sexually suggestive ad campaign for the perfume Obsession two years earlier, Turlington was hired by designer/merchandiser Calvin Klein to be the face attached to his new "Eternity" fragrance line. Although Ford herself attempted to dissuade her, the young and inexperienced model was quick to sign on the dotted line, both flattered by Klein's attention and excited by the high visibility the job would give her. By 1992 Turlington's classic profile had graced the pages of magazines worldwide in fronting the successful Eternity ad campaign, for which she would earn almost $3 million for the 80 days of work she did before the camera during each of the next four years. But she also learned an important lesson, not forgotten when, in 1992, she signed an equally lucrative five-year contract with Mabelline.

Receives Crash Course in Contract Negotiations

In her new contract with the cosmetics giant, Turlington would be earning almost $1 million a year for two week's work; not only was it more money than her contract with Klein had paid, but it was also a non-exclusive contract. When a model is contracted to a particular product line, his or her face becomes associated with those products; by that same contract he or she is not allowed to appear in magazine articles, cover shots, interviews, or any other form of advertising. By signing a non-exclusive contract with Mabelline, Turlington could supplement her contract salary with work for other companies on non-competitive ad campaigns, plus several other smaller jobs—including runway jobs, which can average between $7,000 and $25,000, depending on the client. Turlington finally quit accepting runway assignments because, as she was quoted as saying in the *New York Times,* they "encourage fashion people to become critical, mean, and vicious." Fortunately, in the case of her contract with Klein, the model renegotiated the terms and got herself back out in circulation on the pages of magazines nationwide.

Turlington's face continues to sell products; under the basic laws of supply and demand, she has been able to dictate her own terms. A four-time *Cosmopolitan* cover-girl by the time she was 23, as a supermodel she feels that the fees she can charge clients are fair, considering the business she's in. "There's a tremendous amount of money that's being made," she noted of the fashion and cosmetic business in *Forbes*. "So when you think of it as being your commission, it's not that ridiculous."

In addition, customers are more than happy to pay and not just because of Turlington's selling power. "She can be an Indian or a mulatto or Miss Debutante," explained photographer Arthur Elgort in *New York*. "Her eyes are not on the clock. She'll drive the Jeep. She'll help with the suitcases. She's never outside herself, looking at herself, saying, 'This'll be good for my career.' You never hear 'Christy got in late' or 'Christy's tired.' She is worth every nickel."

While consistantly referred to as one of the "nicest" models in the industry, Turlington senses a different reaction to her success from the general public. "People don't want to like you," she told *New York* in a discussion of the way she, Campbell, and fellow model Linda Evangelista had been portrayed by the media during the late 1980s. "You're young and beautiful and successful. They think you don't have a skill. So when things go well for you, they aren't happy. That's just human nature." But she hasn't let her success spoil her upbeat nature; when she did the inevitable bathing-suit calendar on the heels of her success in modeling for Klein, Turlington donated her entire share of the proceeds to a relief fund to aid the inhabitants of El Salvador.

Features in Television Special

The months she spent as a contract model for Calvin Klein's Eternity campaign left Turlington with a lot of free time between shoots; to fill up the space she enrolled in literature and writing classes at the University of California at Los Angeles. She was also featured in the Lifetime Channel's cable-TV special *Christy Turlington Backstage,* a portrait of the daily grind of a high-fashion model that aired in February 1993. In 1994 she could be seen in a television commercial for Kellogg's cereal. Turlington joined fellow supermodels Campbell, Schiffer, and Elle Macpherson as a figurehead for the Fashion Cafe in 1995, a theme restaurant located in New York City's Rockefeller Center that caters to a tourist clientele.

Where does she plan to spend her time after her grueling modeling days are through? Attending college full-time, where Turlington would like to accelerate her part-time studies in literature and architecture. And after that? Writing. While heads may turn now at the mention of her name, she would like to translate her millions into gaining the ability to turn pages as a professional writer. Meanwhile, between modeling assignments the successful supermodel alternates between her New York apartment and California's Bay Area, where she has been a co-partner in an acid blues club called the Up & Down Club since 1993. Her hobbies include collecting arts and crafts-era furniture and photographs.

Joins Activist Movements

In 1995, Turlington joined actress Kim Basinger and model Naomi Campbell to pose nude for a People for the Ethical Treatment of Animals (PETA) advertising campaign, "I'd rather go naked than wear fur." Turlington also serves as the chairwoman for a newly formed nonprofit organization, International Committee for Intercambios Culturales of El Salvador. It is a cultural exchange center that opened in San Salvador in the fall of 1995 with the purpose of rebuilding the post-civil war country. It offers educational programs and has a public library, community technology center, and gallery. In addition, at the invitation of U.S. Vice President Al Gore, Christy Turlington joined entertainment industry leaders at the White House on December 3, 1997, in issuing a statement to protect children from the dangers of tobacco.

Sources:

Chun, Rene. "What's A Nice Supermodel Doing Here?" *New York Times,* July 2, 1995, p. 33.
Gross, Michael. "Model model." *New York,* March 9, 1992, pp. 38- 46.
Grunbaum, Rami. "PETA Moving to Seattle Area." *Puget Sound Business Journal,* July 21, 1995, Section 1, p. 1.
Moscosco, Eugene. "Classic Christy." *Hispanic.* Available at http://www.hisp.com/apr95/christy.html.
Wechschler, Linden et al. "Put Them At Risk!: Corporate America's Most Powerful People." *Forbes,* May 25, 1992, p. 164.

María-Luisa Urdaneta
(1931–)
Professor, anthropologist, lecturer, women's rights activist

Selected writings:

Deleites de la Cocina Mexicana. Austin, TX: University of Texas Press, 1996.

Overview

So much of María-Luisa Urdaneta's success is a result of her late mother's work ethic and strong faith in God. Urdaneta said, "'I have the strength to face all conditions

María-Luisa Urdaneta

by the power that Christ gives me.' This verse was our mother's motto, from which came the values she taught us."

A Mother's Determination

María-Luisa Urdaneta was born in Cali, Colombia, on October 2, 1931, the youngest child of Rafael and Doña Agripina Urdaneta. At the age of 30, Doña Agripina was left to raise and support María-Luisa, brothers Antonio and Alvaro, and sisters Ines and Cecilia. Early on, Doña Agripina worked as a housekeeper and cook for Presbyterian missionaries, who were in the process of opening Colegio Americano, the first private coeducational school in Colombia. As an employee, Doña Agripina's children were able to attend one of the country's elite schools at a fraction of the cost. This advantage was important to her because the government-run schools offered a poorly structured curriculum and, although she had only six months of formal schooling, she always believed in the necessity of a quality education for her children. A loving and demanding mother, Doña Agripina was protective of her children. She did not approve of others criticizing her children—even schoolteachers. Urdaneta remembers, "She knew well who her children were and, if they needed correcting, it was she and no one else who would mete out the punishment." Even close friends "had to undergo a screening worthy of the Central Intelligence Agency."

Urdaneta's mother continued to stress the importance of education. "She knew she could do what many other parents in similar financial situations did—allow the children to work as helpers without a secure future," said Urdaneta. "But for her, these alternatives were not acceptable." So in the 1940s, one by one, the Urdaneta children came to the United States in search of better prospects. "My mother always wanted us to come here to better ourselves through education so that we could taste the honey of our accomplishments," said Urdaneta.

Children Emigrate

Eldest brother Antonio was the first to leave when he moved to Charlotte, North Carolina, to work as a mechanic at Delta Air Lines. He later pursued his aeronautical engineering degree at the University of California. (He went on to become a prominent engineer in his native country and also served as Colombia's ambassador to Uruguay.) With each success came an increasingly stable financial situation for Doña Agripina and her children.

By the late 1940s, all the children except Cecilia had left Colombia for North Carolina. María-Luisa stayed with a minister and his family in Greensboro, and, in May of 1949, graduated from Curry High School after just two-and-a-half years. Interested in a nursing career, she applied to the Duke University School of Nursing. In September of that year, while waiting to be accepted, she took classes for one semester at the Women's College of the University of North Carolina at Greensboro. Accepted at Duke, she began there the following semester but left shortly thereafter when she was told that the language barrier would prove too difficult to overcome.

Meanwhile, her Greensboro roommate, Greta Waldas, had transferred to the University of Miami and invited Urdaneta to come to Florida. Urdaneta welcomed the change—as well as a move to a climate more similar to the one she had left behind in Colombia. Though not a student, Urdaneta "bunked" with her friend in her dormitory room for ten days. "There were bed checks every night, so each of us alternated—one slept on top of the bed, the other under the bed," she recalled. Over the next several months, she worked as a housekeeper and nanny, elevator attendant, waitress, and department store clerk. In 1951, she had earned enough money to take stewardess courses at the University of Miami. Urdaneta planned to work as stewardess and save her earnings for future education.

In May of 1952, Urdaneta became a naturalized citizen of the United States. "Our family had always looked at the U.S. as a mecca—a place to fulfull your dreams," said Urdaneta. "Becoming a naturalized citizen was second nature. It was an unbelievable gift."

Becomes a New Texan

After learning that Braniff Airlines was seeking bilingual attendants for its Dallas, Texas, to Lima, Peru, routes, she considered moving. Coincidentally, Urdaneta learned that the minister at her church in Miami was being transferred to a church in Dallas. She accompanied the minister and his family to their new home, and they split expenses. There, she met Maria Moreno, the social worker who was helping the minister's family. Moreno happened to be a friend of Dr. Bolton Boone, a prominent administrator at nearby Methodist Hospital. Learning of Urdaneta's interest in nursing and of the problems she had encountered at Duke, Moreno and Boone helped arrange a three-year nursing scholarship for her, and she began a nursing diploma program at Methodist Hospital.

Urdaneta earned her nursing diploma from Methodist in 1956. Two years later, she received a nurse anesthetist degree from Baylor University Hospital in Dallas. She then began studying at the University of Texas at Austin, where she received her bachelor of arts degree in psychology in 1963. Friends helped her land a full-time position as a staff anesthetist at nearby Brackenridge City/County Hospital, and she worked there from 1961 to 1968.

Deciding that she preferred work with human beings to lab work with rats, Urdaneta switched her educational focus to sociology, which led to a master's degree at the University of Texas at Austin in 1968. Along with her Brackenridge job, she had also become the anesthetist and director of nurses at Mount Carmel Hospital and Clinic in Austin. It was a busy time for Urdaneta, but she remembers the lesson her mother had taught her: "Seize the opportunity and make the most of it."

She shifted her academic interest to anthropology and attended Southern Methodist University (SMU) in Dallas, where she completed her master's degree in 1972. "I decided I wanted to look at resource management, sustainable development, and the history of humanity," said Urdaneta.

Finds New Life in San Antonio

Late in 1973, while on a plane returning to Austin from an anthropology conference in Tucson, Arizona, Urdaneta started a conversation with the passenger next to her. The man, Dr. Douglas Foley, was a friend of Dr. Peter Flawn, the president of the University of Texas. He told her of the university's plans for a new campus in San Antonio, which would emphasize an educational experience in a bilingual and bicultural atmosphere. With Foley's help, Urdaneta interviewed with Flawn and was offered the position of assistant professor of anthropology. The only drawback was that the job did not start until the fall of 1975 and she needed a job right away. Flawn helped find a position for her at the University of Texas Health Science Center in San Antonio where, from 1974 until 1975, Urdaneta worked as a clinical instructor and research associate in the Department of Family Planning. Urdaneta completed her doctoral dissertation in anthropology in 1977. In 1980, she became an associate professor of anthropology.

A firm believer in giving back to country and community, Urdaneta has frequently lectured on such subjects as health in Mexican Americans, folk medicine, cardiopulmonary resuscitation, and nutrition. In 1993, she was program co-chair and co-organizer of the annual meeting of the Society for Applied Anthropology. In 1994, she was one of three keynote speakers at the Annual Hispanic Consumer Health Information Conference. She volunteered for one week in 1997 with a team of U.S. medical missionaries at a clinic in Mexico. "To empower the people is to empower the community," says Urdaneta.

A self-proclaimed feminist, Urdaneta shares her mother's belief in education—especially for women. In 1984, she was among sixty Texas women selected as participants in a Texas Foundation for Women's Resources program that identifies and develops women leaders in Texas. She has also been a member of the Executive Board of the Association for Feminist Anthropology and of the Mexican American Business and Professional Women of San Antonio.

Takes Interest in Diabetes

Urdaneta's work as a member of the Texas Diabetes Council (1983-86) and the San Antonio Chapter of the American Diabetes Association advisory board (1984-87) made her aware of the high rate of adult-onset diabetes and obesity among Mexican Americans. "I was appalled at the fact that Mexican Americans are at a much higher risk than Anglo Americans," said Urdaneta. Researchers have identified Mexican Americans as five times more susceptible to developing diabetes. She went on to do research in this area and co-authored articles entitled "Dietary Fat Intake Behavior of Mexican Americans from Different Socioeconomic Status" and "The Prevalence of Obesity in Mexican Americans of South Texas."

In 1996, she co-authored *Delights of the Mexican Kitchen* (*Deleites de la Cocina Mexicana*), a bilingual cookbook whose two hundred nutritious recipes focus on grains, fruits, vegetables, and other healthy ingredients. Urdaneta says Mexican food would be "a very healthy diet" if people used more traditional ingredients and cooked "like our grandmothers." Urdaneta has donated her portion of the royalties to the Mexican American Business and Professional Women's Club of San Antonio for college scholarships.

Continues Important Work

Currently, Urdaneta is an associate professor of anthropology in the division of Behavioral and Cultural Sciences at the University of Texas at San Antonio. She is a member of the Society for Applied Anthropology, the Council of Nursing and Anthropology, the Society for Medical Anthropology, and the Mexican American Business and Professional Women's Club of San Antonio, who named her "Woman of the Year" in 1980. She was also inducted into the San Antonio Women's Hall of Fame in 1985. She is working on a book on organ donations between Mexican Americans and Anglo Americans and the corresponding values and attitudinal differences.

In 1996, Urdaneta's mother, Doña Agripina, died at the age of 94. Two doctoral scholarships were set up in her memory for Presbyterian students from Cali, Colombia, to attend the University of Arizona at Tucson, home of one of the country's foremost applied anthropology programs. It was the final, grand gesture—"a superb inheritance"—of a woman whose influence on María-Luisa Urdaneta is unquestioned.

Current Address: Div. of Behavioral and Cultural Sciences, Univ. of Texas at San Antonio, 6900 N. Loop 1604 W., San Antonio, TX 78249-0652.

Sources:

Baker, Beth. Telephone interviews with María-Luisa Urdaneta, March 25, 26, and 29, 1998.

Shannon, Kelley. "Nutritionists, Restaurateurs Embrace Healthier Mexican Cooking." Associated Press. June 1, 1997. Available at http://www.lubbockonline.com/news.

Urdaneta, María-Luisa. Curriculum vitae, 1998.

Urdaneta, María-Luisa. "The Enduring Legacy of a Great Lady" (unpublished eulogy for funeral of Mrs. Agripina Urdaneta.), May 12, 1996.

Patssi Valdez
(1951–)
Painter

Patssi Valdez's paintings bridge the gap between folk art and fine art. A founding member in 1971 of the multimedia group *Asco* meaning "nausea" or "disgust," Valdez's work as a visual artist in Los Angeles combines the imagery of her ancestral Mexico with the modern sophistication of artists such as Pablo Picasso and Henri Matisse. Although she has moved further away from the avant-garde work she did with Asco, Valdez remains on the cutting edge of the art world.

Patssi Valdez

Valdez was born in Los Angeles on December 31, 1951, to Jovita Zamora, a hairdresser, and Albert Valdez, a butcher. Originally named Patsy, Valdez changed the spelling of her first name after someone misspelled it when she was 18. "I thought, 'That looks cool,'" she said in a telephone interview. Valdez knew from an early age that she wanted to be a great painter. As a child, she copied a painting from a magazine that she later realized was Picasso's *Ladies of Avignon.* Art teachers in school encouraged her. One told her she had great "potential," a word Valdez had to look up in the dictionary to learn its meaning.

During her senior year in high school, Valdez became friendly with fellow artists Harry Gamboa, Jr., Glugio Glonk Nicandro, known as "Gronk," and Willie Herron. The four shared a free-spirited outlook and an irreverent sense of humor. They worked together on the magazine *Regeneración,* and decided in 1971 to have an art exhibit even though they were less than pleased with their own work. "Oh my God, this work gives us *asco,*"Valdez remembered them saying. Thus, the group's name was born.

Launches Asco

Asco was avant-garde for its time. Members related to neither the mainstream culture, with its negative stereotypes of Hispanic Americans, nor to the more conservative or militant stances of fellow Mexican Americans. Asco made art out of its own sense of displacement, using the glamour industries of cinema, television, and fashion as its reference points. In 1972, Valdez dressed up as the Virgin of Guadalupe for a walking mural presented by Asco. "The costumes were pretty wild," she recalled. "I remember an older lady, a grandmotherly type, gasped. People didn't know what to think."

Although Asco's work defied easy categorization, some critics pigeonholed them as ethnic, Mexican American artists. "I thought, 'It's so limiting,'" Valdez said. "'Why are you putting me in a box? Why are you labeling me?'" She wanted to debunk stereotypes and change the world. As a member of Asco, Valdez shied away from visual art and took refuge in photography and acting. She felt frustrated because drawing and painting seemed to come more easily to other members of the group.

During the mid-1970s, Asco became increasingly multimedia. The group acted out scenes in front of the camera to present as slide shows called *No Movies.* They wore colorful costumes and were so broke they made their own free soup out of the ketchup and hot water at the International House of Pancakes.

Valdez left Asco in the late 1970s to study photography at Otis/Parsons College in Los Angeles. As graduation approached in 1985, Valdez's sister, Karen, became seriously ill and required brain surgery. The experience had a profound impact on Valdez. "I learned not to be complaining about silly, little, petty things," she said.

In 1986 Valdez presented the multimedia piece *Resurrection* as an homage to friends who had died within the past year. She applied spray paint, acrylics and dyed photographs directly to gallery walls. "I'm putting down a lot of baggage I've been carrying for a long time," she told *High Performance* in 1986. "I want to start in a new, positive direction."

Becomes a Painter

Valdez began to see her hopes of changing the world as naive. "I was an angry young woman," she said in retrospect. With age came the belief that the only person she could change was herself. She left photography and began teaching art to children. "Children freed me up," Valdez recalled. "I could be free to make mistakes." Away from the pressure of the art world, she experimented with mixing colors and learned how to maintain the vibrancy of the pigment.

Suddenly Valdez felt like a new artist. In 1988, she had her first exhibition as a painter. Using vivid colors and quirky angles, she made household scenes vibrate with energy. Her interiors reflected what was going on inside her own mind. Objects in her paintings took on lives of their own. Clothes flew out of bureau drawers. Tables looked like they had been swept up in a storm. In *Brown Huevos,* two sunny-side up eggs emerged from a field of red to issue what appeared to be a silent cry for help. "Patssi Valdez's chili-hot, topsy-turvy domestic visions capture the turmoil of a Latina assessing an East L.A. culture animated by dualities: family loyalty and violence, pride and self doubt," wrote a writer for *Art News* in 1991. "Although Valdez refers to ethnic roots through her exuberant colors and accessories, she reaches beyond the confines of their Hispanic American reference to an all-inclusive human dimension." Valdez's artwork attracted the attention of such Hollywood celebrities such as Jimmy Smits and Cheech Marin. She designed the statue for the Bravo award and its successor, the American Latino Media Arts Awards (ALMA).

Critics compared Valdez's distortion of space to that of Picasso and her use of color to that of Matisse. Her *Blue Room* appeared to pay tribute to Matisse's *Red Room* of 1908-1909, although Valdez focused on the room itself rather than the landscape outside the open window. "It is as if Valdez is slyly demonstrating that the world inside her mind is infinitely more compelling than the rather ordinary world outside, where the rest of us live," wrote art reviewer Susan Kandel in the *Los Angeles Times* in 1992.

Continues to Evolve

The artist's painting continued to evolve in the 1990s. She shifted to softer colors and made her windows larger. Finally, she got all the way outside of her rooms and painted her first landscapes. No longer did she see being part of an ethnic group as a limitation. "Chicana art has all these faces, all these styles," she observed. "You can create any kind of art you want to be. You don't need to limit yourself. You can open up the umbrella."

Sources:

Axelrod-Contrada, Joan. Telephone conversation with Patssi Valdez, April 1998.

Durland, Steven. "Art with a Chicano Accent." *High Performance,* Issue 35, 1986, pp. 40-45, 48-57.

Hammond, Pamela. "Daniel Saxon Gallery, Los Angeles: Exhibit." *Art News,* Summer, p. 140.

Kandel, Susan. "Valdez's Morbid Vision of Domesticity." *Los Angeles Times,* March 20, 1992, p. F18.

Kapitanoff, Nancy. "Artist Patssi Valdez Finds Answers on a Painted Canvas." *Los Angeles Times,* March 21, 1992, p. F2.

Pagel, David. "A Look at Latino Diversity." *Los Angeles Times,* October 28, 1991, p. F9.

Sorell, Victor Alejandro. "Citings from a Brave New World: The Art of the Other Mexico." *New Art Examiner,* May 1994, pp. 28-32.

Torres, Anthony. "Patssi Valdez at the San Jose Museum of Art." *Artweek,* October 1995, pp. 20-21.

Wilson, William. "Trio of California Artists Mix it up in 'The Mythic Present." *Los Angeles Times,* December 9, 1995, p. F1.

Diana L. Vargas

Vallbona, Rima de
See de Vallbona, Rima

Diana L. Vargas
(1961–)
Media executive

In January of 1997, Diana L. Vargas became vice president and general manager of the second-largest television market in the nation, KTTV/FOX 11 in Los Angeles. When Vargas began her career at the station, KTTV was known primarily as the station that broadcast the Los Angeles Dodgers games; nine years later, the station dominates prime-time, and *Fox News at 10* has won the local Emmy and Golden Mike awards for the best daily 60-minute newscast. Vargas, who says "the KTTV team" is largely responsible for this success, came to her career by chance. Vargas said in a telephone interview with the author, "I fell into my profession," she said. "But when I did, I knew it was what I wanted to do. And I love what I do."

Enjoys Reading and Writing at Early Age

Vargas, whose parents were born in Puerto Rico, was born on August 26, 1961, in the Bronx. She was raised by her mother who worked primarily in counseling. "I wouldn't change anything about my childhood," Vargas said. "My exposure [to life] was huge. We lived in a very rough neighborhood, but somehow I was sheltered from all that, even though I grew up in the middle of it." As a child, Vargas was a voracious reader, and was an equally avid writer. Vargas commented, "Even when I was very little I read volumes and volumes of books. I also loved to write because writing allowed my imagination to take me anywhere. It was a form of expression and escape." School was another refuge from the crime and poverty surrounding her early years, and Vargas loved it so much that she did not miss a single day. "Being an only child, school was my social life," she said. Learning came easily to Vargas, and she was placed in advanced programs. She even skipped grades and entered college at the age of 17. Vargas credits much of her academic success to the devotion of her teachers who went out of their way to counsel young Vargas. "Even at an early age, I appreciated my teachers. They were phenomenal, going above and beyond what they were expected to do. There were special counselors who spent extra time with me, talking about life. And they did it for free." Vargas was known for her willingness to ask questions and was encouraged by her mother and her teachers to pursue journalism as a career. In spite of their support, Vargas did not consider journalism as a career option. "Growing up, the focus was to either be a teacher, a social worker, a doctor, or a lawyer," Vargas said. "Communications was just being introduced as a major but, to me, it was simply a way of getting information."

CNN Internship Serves as Turning Point

When Vargas entered Hunter College in 1978, she had no definite career goals and decided on a double major in psychology and English. The turning point of her college career happened during an internship at CNN. The political situation between Iran and Iraq was at a crisis point, and the station needed more reporters to cover the story. Even though Vargas was only an intern, they sent her to the United Nations building to ask questions. Vargas found the experience invigorating and toyed with the idea of becoming a broadcast journalist. She decided to drop her psychology major in order to major in communications.

Rises Through the Ranks

During her last year in college, Vargas worked full-time for a small company that sold programming to television stations. When the company closed its doors, Vargas had such a good reputation that former clients began calling her with suggestions of possible employers. She was hired by Group W Productions in New York as a sales assistant, later becoming their first sales trainee. The company transferred her to Los Angeles in 1986 as an account executive specializing in syndication research. Vargas thrived in Los Angeles and received a series of quick promotions. That same year, she was hired by KCOP-TV as a sales trainee and was then promoted to account executive. Two years later, she joined KTTV/FOX 11 as their local account executive. In 1990, she became their national sales manager and was promoted to local sales manager in 1991. Three years later, she became vice president, general sales manager. By 1997, she had risen through the ranks to her present position as vice president and general manager of the station.

Of Fox's twenty-two stations, only seven are managed by women, and Vargas is the first Hispanic American woman to manage a major English-language Los Angeles station. In an interview with the *Los Angeles Business Journal*, Vargas said she never really thought about the significance of being a woman in her role until people began asking her about it. "I'm not looking at myself as just a representative of women, or this age group, or this ethnicity," she said. "The one thing I can say about Fox is that the moves I have managed to make have been earned. . . I was as accountable as the next person."

Credits Personal Philosophies for Success

When speaking of her personal success and the heights she has helped KTTV/FOX 11 to attain, Vargas notes several important philosophies that have laid the foundation of her career. Drawing on her own love of learning and

her appreciation for teachers, Vargas stresses the importance of training programs in the workforce. She fosters a healthy working environment by making herself available to employees at all levels in the company and respecting their opinions. "I hope I inspire people," Vargas said in a telephone interview. "I came up through the ranks, and I always want to maintain a sense of humility and a sense of where I came from."

Vargas credits her childhood for giving her courage and confidence. "Through reading, I put myself into other situations outside my environment," she said. "Also, although my family was very small, they believed in me, loved me unconditionally, and encouraged and supported me without pressure. No matter what career I would have chosen, they would have supported my decision." Passionate about life, Vargas said, "I make the most of every day. I try not to look back with regret. We may not always be where we want to be, either in our profession, or city, or in our personal lives. But wherever I am or whatever I'm doing, I want the place I go to work to in the morning to be where I want to be. It's not always easy, but I have staying power." As for the future, Vargas claims "I may slow down a little. I don't need to be king of the world."

Current Address: KTTV–Los Angeles, 1999 S. Bundy Dr., Los Angeles, CA 90025–5235.

Sources:

Hispanic Business, October, 1997, p. 81.

Medina, Hildy. "Leading KTTV to the Top." *Los Angeles Business Journal*, July 21, 1997, p. 14.

Thompson, Märie L. Biographical material from and telephone conversation with Diana L. Vargas, April, 1998.

Elizabeth Vargas

News correspondent, television anchor/host

Elizabeth Vargas has cut out her own niche in the world of broadcast journalism as a news correspondent for such top-rated shows as *20/20* and *PrimeTime Live*. Alongside of such news veterans as Barbara Walters and Diane Sawyer, Vargas earned a reputation as a dynamic journalist who is more than able to handle the stress of a live news broadcast. As a woman at the top of her field, she has faithfully reported the news to millions of Americans.

Spends Teenage Years in Belgium and Germany

The first of three children, Elizabeth Vargas has made quite a name for herself in television news for someone

Elizabeth Vargas

who admits she "grew up without TV." Vargas, who has one sister and one brother, spent her teenage years in Belgium and Germany, countries in which her father, retired U.S. Army Colonel Ralf Vargas, was then stationed. Attending Heidelberg High School, she was bitten by the journalism bug, but it was the print media that first captured her heart. "My strength was writing," she recalled in an interview. "I was editor-in-chief of my Heidelberg High School newspaper."

After spending much of her high school years abroad, Vargas returned to the United States for college, working toward a bachelor's degree in journalism at the University of Missouri in Columbia, Missouri, where she began to learn the trade on the job as well as in the classroom. While attending classes, she worked part-time first as a news reporter and later as an anchor at the college-owned NBC affiliate KOMU-TV. Although the newscast on which she worked was top-rated, she was paid only $3.35 an hour. "I had to waitress to make ends meet," she recalled. When restaurant customers recognized her from television and asked if she was a newscaster, "I'd say, 'Yes, I am, would you like rice pilaf or a baked potato with your entree?'"

An interest in broadcast journalism was not awakened until a college professor at the University of Missouri's prestigious School of Journalism suggested that she consider making a career in the field. An internship with National Public Radio helped to whet her appetite for more exposure to the broadcast side of journalism, but it was a

broadcast journalism course she needed in order to graduate that really set her on the career path she has since followed. "I only took the course after I was told I couldn't graduate without it," Vargas recalled. "But it was in this class that I learned where the real power lies. Nothing compares to the impact of television on the lives of the public. After this, I was hooked."

After receiving her journalism degree in 1984, Vargas left Columbia, Missouri, moving first to KTVN-TV, the CBS affiliate in Reno, Nevada, where she worked as a reporter/anchor. After Reno she worked from 1986 until 1989 as the lead reporter at KTVK-TV, the ABC affiliate in Phoenix, before breaking into the big-time at WBBM-TV in Chicago, one of the nation's top television markets. She spent four years as a reporter and anchor for WBBM. Looking back on her time in Chicago, she recalled, "I really loved Chicago and hoped that I would never move." The feeling was apparently mutual, according to Joe Kolina, who was executive producer for news when Vargas worked there. Of her abilities as a journalist, Kolina said, "She was very careful and aggressive as a reporter. I would have loved to have Elizabeth stay with WBBM."

Receives Overture from the Network

It was an offer from the NBC network that lured Vargas from Chicago and WBBM. She had caught the eye of network executives who offered her a spot on their news magazine show *Dateline NBC*. It was an offer that no ambitious newscaster could refuse. When Vargas moved to New York in 1993 to take the job on *Dateline*, she managed to keep busy, filling in occasionally as the news anchor for NBC's *Today* and as a substitute anchor for the weekend editions of *NBC Nightly News*. Of Vargas's work ethic, Sharon Isaak, an associate producer for *Dateline NBC*, recalled, "She never got to see her apartment because she was always working. It's important to her that people respect the work she does." During her time as a correspondent for *Dateline NBC*, Vargas reported on a wide variety of issues, including breast cancer research and the war against wearing fur waged by People for Ethical Treatment of Animals. Another report that drew wide attention was her investigation into a controversial drunk-driving case in New Mexico.

Moves to ABC

Impressed by the work she was doing for NBC, news executives at ABC in 1996 began negotiations to lure Vargas to their network, specifically as news anchor for their morning show *Good Morning America*. Of the decision she faced, Vargas recalled, "I really hated leaving NBC; it was such a great network to work for. But ABC lured me away. They basically made me an offer I couldn't refuse." However, while the negotiations were under way in the early spring of 1996, she said she was overwhelmed by the offers and counteroffers coming her way as ABC and NBC both campaigned for her services. She feared that she might spend the rest of her life regretting her decision if she made the wrong one. Vargas has credited Diane Sawyer, co-host of ABC's *PrimeTime Live,* with helping her to get through this difficult period. Sawyer, who some years earlier made a well-publicized jump from CBS to ABC, "called me up one day and asked me to come over. She invited me over to her home on Saturday afternoon for lunch, and we spent several hours hashing things out. She was just enormously helpful."

Once the decision had been made and Vargas joined *Good Morning America* as its news anchor, she said she found Barbara Walters, another ABC News veteran, to be "incredibly warm and helpful. She has given me some great advice." Of both Sawyer and Walters, Vargas said "their best advice and leadership is by example. They are phenomenal journalists, and quite frankly, in a business where it is kind of cutthroat and competitive, they are women who aren't looking at me as competition. They have treated me as an equal and yet someone to whom they would lend their expertise."

Equally warm in her welcome was *Good Morning America* former co-host Joan Lunden, though some members of the press did their best to invent a feud between the two. At the time Vargas joined the morning show, there were rumors in the press that she had been hired to replace Lunden, a scenario somewhat reminiscent of the brouhaha that surrounded Jane Pauley's replacement by Deborah Norville as co-host of *Today* several years earlier. The press also suggested that there was considerable tension between Vargas and Lunden on the set. Nothing could have been further from the truth, Vargas said. Looking back on the rumors, she said the whole episode "was so sexist. Joan was very welcoming and warm to me from day one. I was so puzzled by all of that publicity and so happy to see it finally, after several months, fade away. Everybody thinks that women must be competing and clawing each other's eyes out, and that's so ridiculous."

Conducts Several Exclusive Interviews and Profiles

While holding down the post of news anchor at *Good Morning America,* Vargas managed to do a good deal more than just report the news. She conducted the first exclusive live morning interview with Israeli Prime Minister Benjamin Netanyahu, and she also spoke with actor Bill Cosby about how his family was coping with the murder of his son. She did a number of profiles, including independent presidential hopeful Ross Perot; Lewis Jordan, chief executive of embattled Valujet Airlines; New York Lieutenant Governor Betsy McCaughey; and Tony Award-winning Savion Glover from the hit Broadway musical *Bring in da Noise, Bring in da Funk.*

One of the bonuses of working in the national news business has been the opportunity to meet a number of celebrities and other people "you don't normally meet," Vargas said. However, not nearly as appealing has been the increased media scrutiny of her own life. "It's strange, really strange," she observed, shortly after joining *Good Morning America.* "It's very unusual to have people interested in where I'm going or who I'm seeing. I'm still adjusting to it, to be honest. I can't think why anybody's interested."

Becomes Television News Magazine Correspondent

In the spring of 1997, Joan Lunden's announcement of her decision to leave *Good Morning America* reignited press speculation that Vargas was almost certain to succeed her as co-host. However, ABC News executives tapped Lisa McRee, a news anchor from the Los Angeles ABC affiliate KABC-TV, to join Charles Gibson in hosting the morning show. Three months before McRee joined *Good Morning America* in September of 1997, ABC News announced its plans to reassign Vargas to the post of correspondent for its news magazine showcases *20/20* and *PrimeTime Live.* She continued her work on *Good Morning America* until the Friday before Labor Day of 1997.

In addition to her work on *Good Morning America, 20/20,* and *PrimeTime Live,* Vargas has filled in as anchor on *World News Tonight Saturday.* She also hosted two *Turning Point* special reports: "Same Sex Marriages" and "Surrogacy." Vargas is involved in the network's Children First Program, having taken part in a Children First Safety Special and its March Against Drugs.

Though her busy work schedule leaves her little time for anything else, Vargas does manage to find some time for those things important to her. These include the theater, exercise, and sampling the international flavor of New York City. Of her exercise routine, Vargas recently said, "I'm a huge workout buff. I work out about five days a week. It's just a great way to relieve stress. It's really important when you have a 14-hour day at work. I have to make time every day, because if I don't, I'll go out of my mind."

Few Hispanic Americans in Television News Ranks

The daughter of a father of Puerto Rican ancestry and a mother of Irish descent, Vargas said in an interview she has faced few real career obstacles because of her gender or ethnicity. "I've adopted a philosophy in my career: I'm a journalist first and foremost. I strive to do the best job I can as a journalist, period, not as a woman or a Latina."

Recent statistics from the National Association of Hispanic Journalists indicate that Hispanic Americans represent only one percent of television evening news personalities. Vargas is one of the exceptions to this rule, and she feels fortunate to have avoided any significant prejudice on her upward climb in the television news business. However, she conceded in an interview that she has not completely avoided the specter of discrimination in her work, though it came from a viewer and not an employer. "I remember getting a letter once from some person who demanded that I get out of television and go back to Mexico. I was appalled that there are people out there who still think this way."

Vargas acknowledges the contributions of women who have preceded her in television news, a business that traditionally has been dominated by white males. "I'm very fortunate that people forged a path ahead of me," she said in an interview. "Barbara Walters and Diane Sawyer broke the barriers and shattered stereotypes. While this is still predominately a white-male-dominated industry, you're seeing more women and minorities being hired. I've been very fortunate."

Sources:

ABC News Online. Available at http://www.abcnews.com/onair/wkn_news/html_files/vargase.html

Johnson, Peter. "Lunden, Vargas Say All Is Sunny at 'GMA.'" *USA Today,* July 11, 1996, p. 1D.

Lipton, Michael A., and Anne Longley. "In New York City, On the Move: Making News Elizabeth Vargas Stirs Up GMA-and Lyle Lovett's Heart." *People,* September 9, 1996, pp. 113-114.

Menard, Valerie. "Viva Vargas! Good Morning America's Elizabeth Vargas Clears Up the Controversy." *Moderna,* Spring 1997.

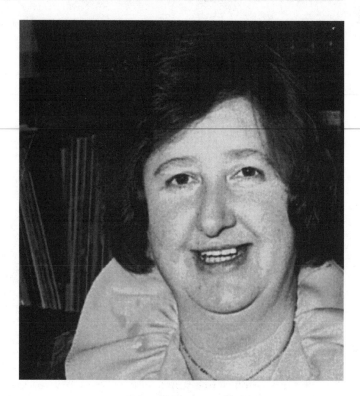

Norma Varisco de García

Norma Varisco de García
(1931–)
Poet, author, women's rights activist

Selected writings:

Ideas que explotan en el infinito y Lejos, hace tiempo. Sobral de Elia Editores, 1995.
Hispanic Women: Portraits of Leadership. Doctoral dissertation, 1990. Publication forthcoming.

Overview

When Norma Varisco de García retired in 1995, she ended a career of over 25 years, advancing the cause of Spanish-speaking people and of Hispanic American women in particular. As early as 1979, Fordham University honored her with a Special Award for Contributions to Bilingual Education, Women's Rights and Spanish Literacy. Since that time she has continued to serve the needs of those with limited English proficiency, with a particular focus on both the needs and the contributions of Hispanic American women.

Born in La Paz, Argentina, on May 29, 1931, Norma Varisco was one of seven children. Her father, Juan Maria Varisco, was a medical doctor, and one of her brothers eventually also became a doctor. Like many Argentines, Varisco's father was the son of Italian immigrants, while her mother was of Spanish and Indian descent. Norma Varisco had some health problems as a child and so was sent to live with her aunt on a ranch. The pleasures of this early life, the wide-open spaces, the horses and sheep, and the beauty of the landscape are revealed in some of the poetry she published later in life. She went to school in La Paz and Buenos Aires, and eventually earned a B.S. and teaching certificate in 1951.

Heads to the United States

As a young adult, Varisco became active in Acción Católica (Catholic Action), a movement that encouraged Catholic laity to be active in political and social life. She fell into disfavor with the government of Juan Perón as a result of this activity and went to Rio de Janeiro, Brazil, where she lived for seven years. During this time she learned to speak Portuguese. She already spoke Italian and English as well as Spanish. On her return to Argentina she worked toward a degree in psychology.

One of her brothers was named the Argentine Air Force attaché in Washington, DC, and an older sister also moved to the United States. Norma Varisco had longed to travel to the United States, and so she moved to New York City in

1961. She went back to school and earned a M.A. in Romance languages and literature from the City College of New York in 1965. She also completed most of the work for a Ph.D. in Romance languages at New York University. In 1966 she became a U.S. citizen.

Begins Work in Government

After doing postgraduate work in Buenos Aires, she returned to the United States and worked at several colleges in the New York City area. From 1968 to 1971 she was director of the Foreign Students Program at Mercy College in Dobbs Ferry, NY. In 1972 she became deputy director of the National Spanish Speaking Management Association, which took her to Washington, DC. In 1974 she went to work for the White House as senior education and manpower specialist for the Cabinet Committee on Opportunities for Spanish Speaking People. From there she went to work for the what was then called the Office for Education of the U.S. Department of Health, Education, and Welfare.

For 20 years she worked at the U.S. Department of Education in the Office of Bilingual Education and Minority Languages Affairs (OBEMLA). For ten years, starting in 1976, she was branch chief of the Eastern region, responsible for all bilingual education programs at the elementary and secondary level, multicultural resource centers, state education agencies, refugee and immigrant programs, and teacher training programs across a large part of the country. More recently she was a senior program officer, advising the director of OBEMLA, and the director of the Division of State and Local Programs. She was also a team leader for an area that included New York and a number of other states and U.S. territories. She coordinated training activities for all OBEMLA headquarters staff, as well as for grantees and contractors providing bilingual education and training programs for teachers and others involved in the education of children with limited proficiency in English.

Acts as Advocate for Women

Varisco de García has also engaged in issues of importance to Hispanic American women. She has been active on the local, national, and international levels in a variety of Hispanic American women's organizations, including the Puerto Rican Society of Elizabeth, NJ, the National Association of Cuban American Women, and the National Council of Hispanic Women. She also served as a special assistant to the president of the Interamerican Commission of Women of the Organization of American States. She has published articles and presented papers about the education of Hispanic women and their roles in society. In 1990 she completed her Ph.D. in education with a dissertation entitled *Hispanic Women: Portraits of Leadership,* which is soon to be published. She was honored with an award for contributions to women and bilingual education by the National Association of Cuban American Women and a special award from Fordham University.

Since her retirement, Varisco de García spends several months out of the year in Argentina. She is married to Felipe García-Carrión and has a stepson, Joseph García-Luftig. In 1995 she published a book of poems, *Ideas que explotan en el infinito y Lejos, hace tiempo.*

Current Address: 117 Love Creek Park A1A, Lewes, DE 19958-9268.

Sources:

Distelzweig, Howard. Letter to Felipe García-Carrión, March 25, 1998.
Varisco de García, Norma. Curriculum vitae, 1998.
Who's Who of American Women, 10th edition, 1977-1978. New Providence, NJ: Marquis Who's Who, 1978.

Enedina Casárez Vásquez
(1945–)
Artist, author, poet

Selected writings:

Recuerdos de Una Niña. Centro de Comunicación, Misioneros Oblatos de María Inmaculada, 1980.

Overview

The workshop of Enedina and Arturo Vásquez in San Antonio, TX, displays picture cards of St. Jude, St. Anthony, and many other religious figures. They hang in plastic bags waiting to be pasted into *nichos,* or miniature box altars. Arturo makes the boxes, and Enedina paints the cards. In their efforts, the Vásquezes are keeping alive a religious folk art form that has nearly disappeared from southern Texas. When Enedina, a painter, poet, and writer, discovered her late mother's collection of *nichos*—a disappearing part of the Mexican-American culture—she and her husband decided to dedicate themselves to reviving the art.

Enedina Casárez Vásquez was born in San Antonio, TX, on December 20, 1945, one of seven children born to Policarpo and Paula Casárez. The family was poor and at times lived as migrant workers, which Vásquez says profoundly influenced her adult years. She graduated from San Antonio's Fox Tech High School in 1964, married Arturo Vásquez in 1968, and had one son. In 1984 she graduated from Our Lady of the Lake University in San Antonio. In addition to being an art teacher, Vásquez has also taught high school English and Spanish. She is a poet-in-residence on the Texas Commission on the Arts and poet-in-residence, San Antonio Independent School District. She has won many awards for her artwork and is a published author of short stories, poems, and plays.

Rediscovers Nichos Folk Art

Vásquez knew her mother to be a very religious woman and, when Paula Casárez died in 1986, Vásquez discovered her substantial collection of *nichos*, or small box altars made of recycled wood, religious calendar art, and brightly colored symbolic patterns. The practice of building these small altars in the home had nearly disappeared from the south Texas area, spurring Vásquez to do some research. She traced the roots of the *nichos* to the historic period when the Spanish brought statues to Mexico and commanded the native Indians to worship them. The Indians in Mexico, however, worshipped nature instead of saints, so, rather than bringing them into their homes, they built small huts outside the towns to hold the statues. As the years passed, however, the *nichos* became part of the religious culture and were brought indoors.

Further research on the small altars took Vásquez and her husband to Mexico, where they became reacquainted with this art form of pasting holy cards onto boxes and other surfaces. The research eventually led to the start of a business. Arturo quit his job as a refrigeration service man to work full-time on building boxes for his wife's art.

Creates a Career

In creating *nichos*, Arturo searches for wood that he can recycle, usually from wine crates, and then builds a basic *nicho* form for his wife to paint. It is part of the tradition that the wood must have been used for something else before it is turned into an altar box. The cards, which are mass-produced, depict nearly every saint in the Roman Catholic Church. The size of the cards varies, from a magazine page to baseball-card size.

When the Guadalupe Cultural Arts Center included the Vásquezes' *nichos* in their folk art and crafts sale, the business really blossomed. Their popularity received a bigger boost in the early 1990s when the Smithsonian Institute in Washington, DC, began displaying the *nichos* in its gift shop, which is known to show leading examples of American folk art. Today, the Vásquezes' *nichos* can be found nationwide, from New York to Florida to California, and are featured in more than 30 galleries. Although their altar boxes provide income for the Vásquez family, they also provide emotional satisfaction. Vásquez, who travels the country for her business, is gratified by the reaction of many Hispanics when they see this old art form, which often conjures childhood memories. More often than not, buyers deliver a hug with their payment. Yet, many of the buyers are neither Hispanic nor Catholic. Said Vásquez in the San Antonio *Express*, "The *nichos* perpetuate a need to reach out and share dreams and hopes with people. Just about everyone can connect with that regardless of their background."

Since recovering from cancer some years ago, Vásquez has become a strong believer in persistence triumphing over adversity. She has expanded the *nichos* theme to include figures other than saints, including people who have overcome a handicap or great misfortune. One of the people honored in a Vásquez *nicho* is a 17th-century Mexican nun, Sister Juana Inez de la Cruz, a leading Spanish-language poet strongly opposed by church officials for her feminist poems.

Vásquez finds time for her artwork while still teaching in a parochial school. When school is out, she and her husband travel to arts and crafts markets across the Southwest. She says that she has no plans to retire from teaching or art. Vásquez told the *Express*, "Making artwork is the most relaxing thing you can do. Everyone should take care of their creative side. I never get tired of making the *nichos* because everyone is different." For young people interested in art, she advises, "Create art that is yours, you and your culture and experience." She says that the inspiration for her own work comes from the belief of Mexico's Huichol Indians that "everything you do is an extension of yourself."

Current Address: 2216 Monterey St., San Antonio, TX 78207.

Sources:

Bennett, Steve. "Altared State." *San Antonio Express*, August 24, 1997, p. 15.
Blue, Rose. Interview with Enedina Casárez Vásquez, April 10, 1998.
King, I. Tavera. "Buenos Nichos." *San Antonio Express*, January 6, 1991, p. 1G.

Enriqueta Longeaux Vásquez
(1930–)
Author, civil rights activist

Selected writings:

Viva La Raza! The Struggle of the Mexican-American People. Garden City: Doubleday, 1974.

Overview

It is not easy to define Enriqueta Vásquez, and attempts to fit her into some neat, precise description would do her an injustice. She is a world traveler, writer, artist, and educator, as well as a political and spiritual activist. But those are merely roles, avenues for achieving her goal. Simply put, Vásquez is a unwavering warrior in the ongoing battle for human and civil rights.

Enriqueta Longeaux Vásquez

Studies Across The Globe

Vásquez was born and raised in Cheraw, CO, of Mexican Purepecha and Tarascan parentage. While Vásquez received her formal training at the University of New Mexico, she considers herself to be a lifelong student of the world. Her travels have taken her through China, Cuba, Europe, Canada, and Mexico. She holds a B.A. from the University of New Mexico for fine arts and philosophy. Beginning with clerical office work and later in the legal profession, she moved into the civil service as an executive secretary at Hughes Aircraft in California, the U.S. Attorney's office in Denver, and finally, in 1966, as the skills bank director for Operation SER. This was the first Hispanic agency funded by the Department of Labor. Vásquez also worked as a substitute teacher for the Taos School District. Her artistic talents as a muralist are on display in a variety of cities, including Taos, AZ. She also plays an active role in her community. On one occasion, she constructed a calendar targeted at Arizona farm workers. This particular project was a fundraiser for the community. She was also the organizer and founder of Las Hembras de Colores, (a women's group) in Taos. Moreover, May 5th became designated as Women's International Day thanks to the efforts of Vásquez.

Experiences Discrimination Early in Life

As a young child in school, Vásquez was not allowed to speak Spanish in the classroom or on the playground.

There was a separate swing for the Hispanic children, and they were not permitted to use the other swings at any time, even if they sat empty and unused. These discriminatory practices continued even after she graduated from high school and moved to Denver in 1950. She painfully recalls being denied employment "because people were not quite ready to hire a Spanish-American girl in their office." After that incident, Vásquez silently vowed to prevent such discriminatory job practices. This experience, combined with the experiences of raising two children alone, motivated her to become a top notch professional who, at that same time, would be an avid political activist. The lifetime of experiences piqued in the 1960s when the Civil Rights Movement swung into full force. She marched with her children, Ruben and Ramona, in Denver as a protest against the murders in Selma, AL.

Shortly thereafter, Vásquez remarried. Vásquez, along with her husband, became completely committed to social change, working closely with their good friend Rodolpho "Corky" Gonzales, founder of the Crusade for Justice in Denver. A friend offered the three activists the use of his ranch in San Cristobal, NM, so Enriqueta and her family moved there to help activate the ranch. The purpose for the ranch was to create a place for Chicano youth to appreciate the land and their culture, while also studying and learning survival skills. As it turned out, this was exactly what was needed, as it attracted activists from all over the country. When the Crusade for Justice opened, Escuela Tlatelolco students came to San Cristobal for block studies. This school remains active today.

Begins Writing

Vásquez was part of the founding editorial staff of *El Grito Del Norte* which became one of twenty-nine Chicano newspapers of the Chicano Press Association. During this time she traveled to many conferences and became well-known for her column, "Despierten Hermanos," and her trip to Cuba to celebrate the tenth anniversary of the Cuban revolution. Most important was her groundbreaking article, "The Woman of La Raza," written in 1969. The article, the first of its kind, marked a beginning for Raza women's articles all over the country. In fact, this had been the first article written in the Southwest on the Mexican American woman since 1910. These first writers, including Vásquez, gave voice to Hispanic women's issues and activism. As Vásquez noted in correspondence with the author: "Women began to look at themselves, understand and define their history and culture for a greater appreciation of who they were." After this there were many productive conferences for Vásquez who grew to articulate and speak for herself and her community. Today, "The Woman of La Raza" is incorporated in numerous anthologies and books, such as *Chicano Voices* in 1975 and *Options in Rhetoric* in 1981, among others. Her book, *Viva La Raza,* co-authored with Elizabeth "Betita" Sutherland Martinez also gained recognition. *Viva La Raza* is about the struggle of the Mexican American people and can be found in many libraries and part of the curriculum in classrooms in many parts of the country, especially in Colorado and California. Vásquez and Martinez received an award from the Jane Adams Peace Association in 1975.

Continues to Participate in Chicano Studies

Since 1970, Vásquez has been involved in workshop presentations and lectures, and remains so today. Topics have included La Chicana and the movement, women in the 1980s, and a presentation on behalf of the Tonantizin Land Institute, an agency which focuses on the problems of Chicanos and Native Americans. She continues to encourage youth to study their language, their ancient history, and their indigenous heritage. To this end, Vásquez has researched and written a women's history book, *The Women of La Raza*, which she hopes will be published shortly. This literary work is the result of years of travel and research from many sources. It is as much historical as it is contemporary. She strengthens her own indigenous beliefs through sundance, ritual, and ceremony, all learned as child.

Vásquez serves on the Elders Council for the Kanto de la Tierra, Council of Indians of North America (CINA), and attends its yearly earth purification "healing" ceremony in Texas. (Kanto de la Tierra went to Europe and met with Queen Sophia of Spain in 1992, delivering a message centered on world peace and justice. The Council then traveled to Germany with the same message.) Vásquez remains close to the Crusade for Justice and the Escuela Tlatelolco in Denver.

Current Address: PO Box 43, San Cristobal, NM 87564.

Sources:

Kubiac, Brenda. Factsheet from and telephone conversation with Enriqueta Vásquez, March 11-14, 1998.

Matlock, Stacy. "Taoseños have a dream too." *The Taos News,* January 16, 1997, p. A1.

Martha Vásquez
(1953–)
Judge

Martha Vásquez has made a career of fighting discriminatory practices aimed at any invidual, regardless of race,

economic or social standing. Vásquez has chosen to take her fight into the arena of the U.S. judicial system. Whether as a lawyer arguing a point of view or as a federal judge presiding over cases, Vásquez has emerged as a committed protector of rights who stands by her legal convictions no matter the consequence.

Experiences Discrimination

Vásquez's road to success was not easy, as she had to overcome many challenges at an early age. Her parents, seeking a different way of life, left Mexico as young adults, choosing to relocate to sunny California. As is the case with many immigrant families, her parents did not know anyone in the sunshine state and, even more intimidating, they did not know English. This hard-working couple was determined to make a life for themselves in the United States, and they succeeded. Working as many as three jobs apiece, her parents supported the family, which had grown to five children. In return, their parents demanded much from their children. The Vásquez children were encouraged to speak English fluently to ensure their success in school. But while adapting to the new, the family never lost touch with their cultural roots. Spanish was always spoken in the home.

Vásquez's parents were proud of their roots and required their children to maintain the utmost respect for their own ethnic and cultural identity. Even though they sometimes encountered racist and xenophobic attitudes throughout their childhood, they were taught to take pride in their rich heritage. None of this escaped young Vásquez. She witnessed the manner in which many impoverished Mexican American families were treated, and it stirred her to action. She knew that one way to bring about change is to make the change from within the legal system, so she decided to become a lawyer. In this arena she could help those in need and, perhaps in doing so, affect some measure of change on a larger scale.

Breaks Through Barriers

Upon graduating from high school, Vásquez embarked on a number of "firsts." She was among the first group of women allowed to enter Notre Dame University in 1972, the first year that this historic institution ever opened its doors to women. She received her law degree from the University in 1978. Following graduation, Vásquez worked for three years as a public defender for the state of New Mexico. She accepted a position with the law firm of Jones, Snead, Wertheim, Wentworth, and Jaramillo in 1981. As a member of the firm, Vásquez practiced criminal defense, personal injury, and general civil law. She specialized in civil litigation, including divorce, employment, and commercial cases. Vásquez became a partner with the firm in 1984, and the focus of her practice shifted to personal injury, wrongful death, criminal defense, employment, and insurance litigation.

While engaged in private legal practice, one of Vásquez's most notable cases involved her representation in 1985 of a man who had been exposed to high levels of formaldehyde while working for a chemical manufacturer. Environmental medicine was in its infancy at that time, and the defense of such cases was a relatively new field. It required thorough understanding of a medical issue as well as the legal skills to successfully defend a case. Moreover, proving cause was extremely difficult—so much so, that no other lawyers were willing to take the case. The challenges did not deter Vásquez. Ultimately, she was forced to serve as sole counsel, directing every aspect of her client's case, including all related investigations, preparation of witnesses, and medical research. Vásquez's diligence and perseverance paid off handsomely: her client was awarded full benefits and legal fees at the conclusion of the trial in 1993. It was this type of effective and ethical practice that made Vásquez a prime candidate for judicial service. That same year, she was called to serve on the bench of the United States District Court, marking another first for her. Her appointment distinguished Vásquez as the first woman to serve as a judge in the 142-year history of the federal judiciary in New Mexico.

Takes The Judicial Oath

Vásquez was sworn in as a federal judge on October 6, 1993. She remains in that position today, and continues to build on her reputation as a steadfast defender of individual rights. During her tenure, Vásquez has decided a number of noteworthy cases. One such case involved the admissibility of evidence in criminal trials, an issue that has been the subject of intense debate across the U.S. legal system. In this 1995 ruling, Vásquez stated that polygraph tests could be used as evidence in a trial if the reliability of the polygraphist could be positively established. During the same year, she granted a defendant's motion to suppress certain evidence. A police dog detected 32.6 kilograms of cocaine in the defendant's luggage. The defendant raised doubts as to the reliability of the dog in the establishment of probable cause to search the luggage and, thus, the dog's ability could not be guaranteed by its trainers and handlers.

Moreover, Vásquez has not lessened her commitment to environmental protection. In 1996 she dealt a legal blow to the U.S. Army when she ruled that a permit allowing the U.S. Army to hunt bison at the Fort Wingate Army Depot was invalid. Vásquez noted that the Army failed to submit the project to an environmental impact assessment as mandated by the National Environmental Policy Act. That same year, Vásquez presided over another interesting case that gave insight into her dedication to fostering a law-abiding community. This case addressed Native American-owned gambling establishments in New Mexico. Vásquez found that the casinos, whose operation had been permitted by a compact involving the governor of New Mexico and the federal Department of the Interior, needed the approval of the state legislature before their operation could continue.

Standing by her convictions earned Vásquez the Charlie Driscoll Award, recognizing compassion in the discharge of a public office, and the Las Primeras Award in 1996. In 1997, she was awarded the Camino Real Award from the New Mexico Hispano Chamber of Commerce del Norte, presented annually to New Mexicans who have made a lasting and significant contribution in their fields of endeavor. Vásquez received the Graciela Olivarez Award, named in honor of the first female graduate of Notre Dame Law School and recognizing outstanding Hispanic American attorneys or judges in April of 1998.

Despite the rigorous demands of her career, Vásquez, like her parents, is devoted to her family. She resides in New Mexico with her four children, ranging in age from eight to sixteen.

Current Address: U.S. District Court, PO Box 2170, Albuquerque, NM 87504.

Sources:

Eldridge, Grant. Biographical material sent from Martha Vásquez, April, 1998.
"We Don't Intend to Close." *Albuquerque Journal*, July 23, 1996, p. A1.

Vasquez Villalpando, Catalina
See **Villalpando, Cathi**

Gloria Velásquez-Treviño
(1949–)
Poet, author

Gloria Velásquez-Treviño consciously began her career with the knowledge that her audience was chiefly Hispanic as she publishes mainly in Spanish-language journals. She has developed a wide range of discourse, including images from pre-Columbian times to those of modern farm and urban workers, a discourse that features a clear, Chicana feminist voice. Her literary language exhibits influences from Mexican and Latin American literatures—specifically, in her latest productions, magical realism. She has been published widely in journals.

Rootless Childhood Gives Way to Education

Born in the small town of Loveland, CO, on December 21, 1949, Velásquez-Treviño claims heritage from a long-standing New Mexican family, with Navajo blood from her paternal grandfather. Her parents, Francisca Molinar-Velásquez and Juan Velásquez, earned a living until 1963 as migrant workers, traveling between Colorado and Texas, until finally settling as factory and hospital workers in Johnstown, CO. Velásquez-Treviño experienced the migrant cycle of constant change as a child; she received her early education in Loveland, attended one school in Texas, and finished in Johnstown.

After graduating from Roosevelt High School in Johnstown, Velásquez-Treviño worked as a secretary at the local Hewlett-Packard plant, attending college classes at night. After serving as a teacher's aide at local primary and secondary schools, she received a full-time fellowship to study at the University of Northern Colorado. Thus Velásquez-Treviño earned her B.A. in 1978, with a double major in Spanish and Chicano studies.

Velásquez-Treviño participated in various "Canto al Pueblo" (Song of the People) festivals in Milwaukee, WI; Albuquerque, NM; and Corpus Christi, TX, between 1977 and 1979. These popular events had a profound effect on her writing, thus motivating her to pursue graduate studies in Latin-American literature at Stanford University. In her second year she won a literary prize from the department of French and Italian. She later delved into the subject of women in Chicano literature, concentrating on Chicana narrative production from the early 1900s to the 1970s. With the completion of her dissertation, "Cultural Ambivalence in Early Chicana Prose Fiction," Velásquez-Treviño received her Ph.D. in Spanish literature in 1985.

Writing Themes Focus on Chicana History and Identity

According to Arnold C. Vento in his *Contemporary Chicana Poetry: 1969-1977* (1978), Velásquez-Treviño's main themes include Chicana history and identity, the plight of the farmworker, antiwar protests, male dominance, incest, the desertion of single mothers, the lack of medical care, and the problems of old age and alcoholism. To disseminate her message of resistance against marginality, economic denial, and male dominance, she relies on such techniques as satire, irony, and symbolism. Furthermore, one finds in her work magical realism, raw images of oppression, the narrator's direct link with the ill and abused, and her open repugnance for a sordid environment. She writes eulogies (to farmworkers, motherhood, and educational achievement), uses the image of the river as a symbol of regeneration, and makes use of historical similes grounded in poetic images of pre-Columbian society.

Velásquez-Treviño's main concerns are the female experience and the plight of the farmworker. The poem "Chicana" (1978), a eulogy to the speaker's mother, is a synthesis of both concerns: "As I struggle to understand, / to seek answers to / fill the voids, / the needs / in my life, / I feel the strength of my mama / when she went to the field / and returned tired / at night / to some more work." Two of her other poems on the Chicana experience reveal her voice in its best form: "¿Quién soy?" (Who Am I?, 1977) and "Superwoman" (1978). "¿Quién soy?" establishes for Chicanas a feminist identity grounded in myth and history; "Superwoman," with its irony, demystifies all current female roles, such as the suffering mother, the dedicated wife, and the liberated woman. The second stanza in "Superwoman" presents self-criticism: "I am the super-liberated chicana / attending classes, / writing papers, / discussing psychology, / yet always silent."

In Velásquez-Treviño's story "La Carta" (The Letter), published in the Mexican newspaper *El Día*, the action unfolds as follows: the narrator/protagonist, Esperanza, fulfills her dead brother Antonio's last request, to deliver his letter from Vietnam to his fiancée, Alegría, but, due to her own mourning, Esperanza does not deliver the letter until a year after its arrival. During this time she suffers depression, drinks heavily, and consults unproductively with doctors. The hard fact of Antonio's death recalls the close bond she shared with her brother, as does the obligation to deliver his letter, especially since Esperanza originally saw Alegría as an intruder and edited all her brother's love letters to his fiancée. In memorable detail "La Carta" shows the pain of families whose relatives were killed in the Vietnam War. Very few Hispanic writings of the 1970s examined this important issue.

Portrays the Plight of Women

The plight of women in a male-dominated society, as seen in Alegría's marriage of convenience—after hearing of Antonio's death—receives further development in "Fragment: 'Mercedes'" (1982) from the unpublished novel *Soldaditos y muñecas*. The work first presents the protagonist as a victim of incest and then of desertion by the father of her children. "Mercedes" includes vivid, raw images of female oppression: "How many times had she climbed those moldy stairs, breathed the smell of dirty diapers and recently cooked tortillas that turned her stomach, forcing her to cover her mouth and pause for a moment? . . . —Let me tell you [Mercedes says] last night a woman jumped from the sixth floor. Many onlookers showed up, firetrucks came and then Channel 7, you know, they always like to sensationalize things because we live in welfare housing. . . ."

On a positive note, the same short story introduces the image of the river as a symbol of regeneration. Beyond her own death wish, Mercedes sees in the river a form of escape from witnessing the oppressive situation faced by women: "How many times had she thought of committing suicide? Two, three, twenty. At age six she had wished to jump into the river, taste its water, allowing it to purify her, but something held her back." The narrator/protagonist directly links herself with the abused.

The short story "El Doctor Merry" (1985; also from the unpublished novel) exposes the poor quality of medical care for Hispanics. The cause lies in insensitivity on the part of some Anglo doctors, such as the ironically named title character, who primarily pursue pleasure and wealth: "At nine o'clock he arrived and very sophisticatedly climbed off his Porsche, eaglelike nose, wearing his perfectly pressed shirt, holding his black briefcase with his long and cold fingers known by the whole town. Whistling a tune, he walked forward to the large doors on his office and disappeared."

Inversion, satire, irony, and humor, according to Gloria Velásquez-Treviño, serve to expose the passive image and subordinate position of Chicanas in a patriarchal society, which itself lives under domination. She continues to produce literary discourse with the specific intent of providing resistance to cultural domination.

Sources:

Vento, Arnold C. *El Hijo Prodijo: A Critical Index of Twentieth Century Mexican Thought*. Albuquerque, NM: Pajarito Publications, 1978.

Vélez, Deborah Aguiar
See **Aguiar-Vélez, Deborah**

Lauren Velez

Actress

Selected filmography:

I Like It Like That. Columbia, 1994.
New York Undercover. Fox-TV, 1994-present.
City Hall. Columbia Pictures, 1996.
OZ, (cable television series). 1997.
Stand-Up Tragedy. Turner Network Television (TNT), 1998.

Plays Tough Detective Moreno

Lauren Velez is best known as the actress who plays a tough-minded detective, Nina Moreno, on Fox Television's hit show *New York Undercover*. Television, however, was never her goal. Her first love was the theater, and she spent ten hard years on stage before even landing her first film role. That role, playing a spunky Puerto Rican house-

wife in the critically acclaimed, urban hip film *I Like it Like That*, won her instant respect in Hollywood. Whether on stage or screen, she garners praise for her acting, and provides a much-needed Hispanic American female voice and face in the world of popular culture.

Leads Normal Nuyorican Childhood

The daughter of Puerto Rican parents, Lauren Velez was born in Brooklyn, NY. Her father, Jose, was a police officer, and Lauren was one of eight children. Raised in Rockaway Beach, she attended public schools and led a normal Nuyorican childhood. Her acting career is sometimes said to have begun in the second grade, when she was cast in the lead role of a groundhog in a school play for Groundhog's Day.

After graduating from school, Velez spent ten years as a theater actress, landing some good roles in successful shows. Like so many actresses of color, though, she struggled to find quality parts that were not demoralizing or degrading for a Hispanic American actress. Appearing on and off Broadway, she took part in such plays as *Into the Woods, Dreamgirls,* and *Much Ado About Nothing.* Meanwhile, like many aspiring actors, she continued a series of "day jobs" to support her artistic career, working as a receptionist and restaurant hostess to pay the rent.

Breaks Into Film

In 1994, Velez got her big break when she landed the main role in *I Like it Like That*, a coming-of-age tale set in the Bronx. The film, by writer-director Darnell Martin, was the first feature film for a major studio made by an African American woman. Full of realistic characters and vibrant language, it was a perfect movie for Velez's film debut, as it allowed Velez to show a range of acting skills. The film tells the story of Lisette, a young Puerto Rican wife and mother whose life changes when her husband goes to jail for stealing a stereo and she gets a job for the first time. Her boss brings her home from work in an expensive car, and everyone in her neighborhood assumes the worst. Velez identified with her character, a strong, focused Puerto Rican from an urban background. Her performance received rave reviews from critics. "Velez," wrote a reviewer in *Cosmopolitan,* "creates a marvelously rounded individual—fiery, proud, vulnerable, and resilient."

Immediately after the filming of *I Like it Like That,* Velez married Mark Gordon, a personal trainer. With the critical approval of her work in her first film, her professional career looked as if it would take off. Even though she lived in New York City, she had high hopes for a successful career in Hollywood.

Joins Cast of *New York Undercover*

Velez's plans for a film career took a detour, however, when she decided to accept the part of undercover detective Nina Moreno on Fox-TV's hip and hard-boiled cop show *New York Undercover.* For Velez, television was more of an afterthought, something she did not actively pursue because the theater was her first love. But the role of an intelligent, street-smart, strong woman was too good to pass up. "If I were a cop I'd be just like Nina," Velez told a reporter for *Essence.* "She's tough and smart, and she has a very strong work ethic."

Velez was immediately noticed for the depth she brought to her character on the high-rated drama. The critical acclaim Velez earned on *Undercover* led to her part in the feature film *City Hall,* alongside film great Al Pacino. Velez was cast as the grieving widow of a dead police officer in the political thriller about corruption in city government. The accolades continued following her film performance when the *Atlanta Constitution* singled her out as among television's best bets for stardom in 1997. Not surprisingly, more television work followed. In addition to guest-starring roles on *True Blue* and *The Cosby Mysteries,* she got the part of Dr. Gloria Nathan, a prison doctor, on the cable series *OZ.* Most recently, Velez starred in *Stand-Up Tragedy,* a film based on the award-winning play by Bill Cain and his actual experiences as a teacher in a New York City mission school. According to *Hispanic* magazine, the film ". . . takes an unwavering look at the brutal and often deadly world of drugs and violence."

Receives Awards for Television Role

Velez has received the most acclaim, however, for her work with *New York Undercover.* Her fellow actors, as well as critics, remark that she has added an important voice to the show. She received the NAACP Image Award and the NCLR Bravo Award for best actress in a television series for her work on the drama.

Perhaps more satisfying for Velez is the assurance that her work is important to an audience of Hispanic American women and girls. Female police officers have congratulated her on the street for her realistic portrayal of a female officer as smart and savvy. And for young Hispanic American women, she has become an important role model. "I get a lot of young Latino girls," she told *People Weekly,* "who say to me 'It's so nice to finally see a person on TV who looks like me'."

Sources:

"Arresting Officer: A Cop's Daughter Stands Out on Fox's Undercover." *People,* January 20, 1997, p. 78.

Flatley, Guy. "I Like It Like That." *Cosmopolitan,* November 1994, p. 24.

Gregory, Deborah. "Working girls: 'Mamas' no more, these actresses are playing career women!" *Essence,* March 1996, p. 60.

"Hispanic Calendar: Arts." *Hispanic,* May 1998, p. 90.

Lupe Vélez
(1908–1944)
Actress

Selected filmography:

What Women Did For Me. 1927.
Sailors Beware, 1927.
The Gaucho. United Artists, 1927.
Wolf Song, 1929.
Tiger Rose, 1929.
The Storm. Universal Pictures, 1930.
East Is West, 1930.
The Squaw Man. MGM, 1931.
Men in Her Life, 1932.
The Girl From Mexico. RKO, 1939.
Mexican Spitfire Series, RKO, 1939–1943.
Playmates. RKO, 1941.
Six Lessons from Madame La Zonga, 1941.
Nana. 1944.

Overview

Lupe Vélez was a Hollywood star from the late 1920s to the early 1940s. Initially considered a dramatic actress, her flamboyant personality, her petite physique, striking good

Lupe Vélez

looks, and her comedic gifts led her to the role of "Mexican Spitfire," in a series of popular low-budget comedies. "Lupe Vélez was a favorite of producers and moviegoers for more than 15 years—a long time for someone regarded as a personality rather than as an actress. One explanation for such audience fidelity may lie in the fact that moviegoers found her ebullience and emotional excesses quite genuine. . . . Lupe shared religious faith, feminine whims, and blatant sexuality in equal parts. There is no doubt that she was a real show business personality," wrote Alfonso Pinto in *Films in Review.*

Born in San Luis de Potosi, Mexico

Throughout her career, Vélez courted the attention of the press by telling exaggerated stories of her private life and family background. Details of her early years are uncertain. She was born Maria Guadalupe Vélez Villalobos in San Luis de Potosi, near Mexico City in 1908 or 1909. Some sources say Vélez's father, Jacob, was a pharmacist. Other sources, including Vélez herself, indicated he was a colonel in the Mexican army, who was called El Gallo (The Rooster) by his troops, and was killed in a governmental uprising when Vélez was in her teens. Vélez's mother, Josefina, had been an opera singer. The family included Vélez's two sisters, Mercedes and Josefina, and a brother, Emigdio. At about age 13, Vélez was sent to the convent school of Our Lady of the Lake in San Antonio, TX, where she was an undisciplined, inattentive student learning little except how to speak English. Years later in Hollywood Vélez would often exaggerate her Mexican accent for dramatic or comic effect.

In her mid-teens Vélez left school and returned to Mexico City where she worked as a sales clerk in a department store. In her spare time she took singing and dancing lessons which led to a part in a local musical revue *Rataplan.* Receiving a vague offer to appear in a U.S. stage production, Vélez moved to Los Angeles around 1926. Though the offer came to nothing, the vivacious and darkly beautiful Vélez was soon hired as a dancer in a musical revue at Hollywood's Music Box Theatre. Film producer Hal Roach saw Vélez in the Music Box show and signed her to a short term contract at a minimum salary. Vélez made her first screen appearance as a bit player in Roach's *What Women Did for Me* in 1927, a short film or "two reeler," starring comedian Charley Chase. Later in 1927, she worked for Roach in the Laurel and Hardy comedy short *Sailors Beware.*

Appears with Prominent Leading Men

Douglas Fairbanks, the silent screen's leading swashbuckler, was looking for a spirited dark-haired beauty to appear in his adventure film *The Gaucho* and hired Vélez after Delores Del Rio, an established star, turned down the part. A silent movie with a sequence in Technicolor, *The Gaucho* opened in November of 1927. A reviewer for *Variety* called Vélez "a feminine Fairbanks" adding that

"when it comes to acting she does not have to step aside for anyone. . . this kid has a great sense of comedy value to go with her athletic prowess."

It was the outdoor adventure drama *Wolf Song* (1929), a part silent/part sound picture directed by Victor Fleming, that established Vélez as a star. Her leading man in the film was Gary Cooper and their highly publicized off-screen affair did much to increase audience interest in the picture. Vélez and Cooper's romance lasted for about three years. Rumor had it that the couple planned to marry but Cooper's mother, to whom Cooper was strongly attached, disapproved of the impetuous and Hispanic Vélez.

Vélez's first all-talking film was *Tiger Rose* (1929), an outdoor drama similar to *Wolf Song,* in which she played a hot-tempered French Canadian in love with a young railroad engineer played by Grant Withers. Vélez's striking dark features led to her being cast in a variety of "ethnic" or "exotic" roles. In *The Storm* (1930) she was again French Canadian, this time on the lam with her smuggler father from the Northwest Mounted Police. In *East is West* (1930) she was a Eurasian immigrant in San Francisco. A Cecil B. DeMille-directed screen adaptation of the turn-of-the-century stage melodrama *The Squaw Man* (1931), saw Vélez as a Native American woman who saves the life of a British aristocrat.

Gains Popularity with Spanish-Language Films

Vélez was especially popular with Latin American audiences. To capitalize on this, Universal Pictures, to which Vélez was under contract in the early 1930s, had her appear in Spanish-language versions of some of her films. For example *East is West* was redone as *Oriente Es Occidente,* and *Resurrection* (1931), in which Vélez co-starred with John Boles, was refilmed as *Resurrección* (1931) with Vélez and Gilbert Roland, another Mexican-born performer who had achieved success in Hollywood. Vélez also appeared in *Hombres en mi Vida* (1932), a Spanish-language version of *Men in Her Life,* which had starred Lois Moran.

Vélez's busy private life drew almost as much attention as her films. After finally breaking up with Gary Cooper in the early 1930s she had a high profile romance with John Gilbert, a major film star and a leading Hollywood man about town. While on a publicity tour in New York City, Vélez met Olympic swimming champion Johnny Weissmuller, who had just completed the first in his series of films as Tarzan. The diminutive Vélez and the brawny Weissmuller were married in 1933 and their stormy relationship made good copy for gossip columnists for several years. They were divorced in 1938.

Moves to the Stage

Like many stars of the late silent and early talking film era, Vélez, by the mid-1930s, began to be overshadowed by a new crop of East Coast stage-trained performers who had come to Hollywood after the advent of sound. In an attempt to bolster her sagging career, Vélez appeared on Broadway, where she exhibited her talents as a singer, dancer, and mimic. Vélez co-starred with Bert Lahr in the 1932 musical comedy *Hot-Cha!*, produced by the aging impresario Florenz Ziegfeld, and in 1933 appeared with Jimmy Durante in the revue *Strike Me Pink*. In his review of *Strike Me Pink*, Brooks Atkinson of the *New York Times* wrote that "Lupe Vélez comes off rather better than ever. Her flares of temperament provide good comedy in more than one sketch, and she has an incendiary abandon for her song numbers." Traveling even further afield, Vélez spent most of 1935 and 1936 in England where she made three mediocre films and participated in the musical revue, *Transatlantic Rhythm*, at London's Adelphi Theatre.

In 1937, Vélez returned to Mexico to star in a Mexican-produced feature film *La Zandunga*, a romance set in the Isthmus of Tehuantepec. Arturo de Cordova was her leading man. Vélez was greeted by thousands of fans when she arrived in Mexico City to make the film, which turned out to be a great box office draw in Latin America. When *La Zandunga* played at the Teatro Hispano in New York City, the New York Times wrote that Vélez's acting was "first-rate. In her happier and snappier moods she seems rather calmer than in her English stage and film work." In the autumn of 1938, Vélez made her final Broadway appearance in *You Never Know*, a musical revue starring Clifton Webb with music by Cole Porter. Vélez sung several duets with Webb, including "From Alpha to Omega" and offered imitations of film stars such as Katherine Hepburn and Shirley Temple.

Returns to Hollywood

Back in Hollywood in 1939, Vélez starred in *The Girl from Mexico*, a low-budget comedy for Radio-Keith-Orpheum (RKO) Pictures. The unexpectedly popular film established her "Mexican Spitfire" character, an irrepressible young lady from "South of the Border" whose unreserved antics shock and amuse her U.S. associates. Apparently accepting that her days as a dramatic star in Hollywood were over, Vélez gamely appeared in a series of "Mexican Spitfire" sequels. These are *Mexican Spitfire* (1939), *Mexican Spitfire's Baby* (1941), *Mexican Spitfire at Sea* (1942), *Mexican Spitfire Sees a Ghost* (1942), *Mexican Spitfire's Elephant* (1942), and *Mexican Spitfire's Blessed Event* (1943). James Robert Parish in *The RKO Gals* called the Mexican Spitfire films "mindless entertainment of high satisfaction for audiences of the day." Vélez played variations on the "Spitfire" character in other low-budget comedies, including *Playmates* with John Barrymore, and *Six Lessons from Madame La Zonga* (1941), based on a popular novelty song. Vélez made one last try at more dignified film by starring in a Mexican-produced screen adaptation of Emile Zola's novel *Nana* in 1944. Directed by Celestino Gorostiza, the film was criticized for turning Zola's naturalistic novel into a conventional melodrama, but Vélez was credited with giving the best performance of her career.

Meanwhile Vélez's always turbulent personal affairs took several turns for the worse. Her relationships with men, including those with actors Bruce Cabot and Guinn "Big Boy" Williams, had come to nothing. Her affair with Harald Ramond, a Hollywood drifter said to have been an actor in Europe, resulted in an unwanted pregnancy. Despite her frequent displays of bravura, Vélez was said to have a low opinion of her herself and her hectic private life was seen by some as an attempt to ward off loneliness. In December of 1944, a four-months pregnant Vélez deliberately overdosed on sleeping pills at her Beverly Hills home and was found dead the following morning. Her suicide note asked God to forgive her and gave instructions to a housekeeper to look after her dogs. Somewhat fittingly, considering Vélez's love of embroidering the facts, lurid stories developed in regard to Vélez's death, including a rumor that she carefully planned her demise in conjunction with a hairdresser, a make-up artist, and florist so as to leave behind a beautiful corpse surrounded by flowers.

Sources:

Atkinson, Brooks. "Strike Me Pink Revue." *New York Times*, March 6, 1933, p. 16.
"At the Teatro Hispano." *New York Times*, May 14, 1938, p. 18.
"The Gaucho." *Variety*, November 9, 1927.
Parish, James Robert. *The RKO Gals*. New Rochelle, NY: Arlington House, 1974.
Pinto, Alfonso. "Lupe Vélez: 1909-1944." *Films in Review*, November 1977, p. 513-524.
Wayne, Jane Ellen. *Cooper's Women*. New York: Prentice Hall, 1988.

Vélez Villalobos, Maria Guadalupe
See **Vélez, Lupe**

Vendrell, Armida
See **Armida**

Carmelita Vigil-Schimmenti
(1936–)
Military officer

On October 1, 1985, Brigadier General Carmelita Vigil-Schimmenti, U.S. Air Force, became the first Hispanic woman in military service to attain the rank of general.

Her exemplary military service resulted in her rise through the Air Force ranks, working in the area of nursing in her various positions. Now retired, Vigil-Schimmenti stands out as military figure who overcame prejudice to earn honor in service to her country.

Born in Albuquerque, NM, in 1936, Vigil-Schimmenti can trace her family's origins in that area back to 1695. These deep roots lend to her feeling that her life has been shaped by a strong sense of family and community ties. The first ten years of Vigil-Schimmenti's life were spent on the family ranch in Torrance County, NM. She told Rose Diaz in the book, *Nuestras Mujeres: Hispanas of New Mexico,* that farm life was a struggle for survival, and it tended to make leaders of people who might not otherwise be leaders. She credited her father, Francisco, with instilling in her a sense of family values; and her mother, Piedad, a schoolteacher, with giving her a love of reading and studying. After several years of drought and hardship on the ranch, the family moved to the Albuquerque area in 1946. Her father went to work for the Santa Fe Railroad, which afforded the family a degree of financial security they had previously never experienced. Vigil-Schimmenti remembers Albuquerque as an attractive city. She told Diaz, however, "I also remember the good old days not being such good old days and my first experiences with the kind of bias that was part and parcel of Albuquerque. Instinctively, one knew which restaurants, shops, and public places were open to Hispanics. Every day one could read job advertisements in the newspapers or in storefront windows that clearly stated, 'Spanish-speaking people, Negroes, and Indians need not apply.'"

Vigil-Schimmenti graduated from Albuquerque's St. Mary's High School in 1954. Three years later, she earned a nursing diploma from the Regina School of Nursing in Albuquerque. Kirtland Hospital was located on Sandia military base in the city, and Vigil-Schimmenti was familiar with military life by the time she graduated from nursing school. She felt that as a whole, military personnel seemed not to have a prejudice about one's ethnic background and decided that the military would be a good place to begin a career.

Makes the Military Life Her Career

Following in the footsteps of an aunt who had been an army nurse, Vigil-Schimmenti joined the U.S. Air Force in 1958. She began her military career at Wright-Patterson Air Force Base in Ohio as a hospital nurse. She earned a bachelor's degree in nursing in 1966 and a master's degree in public health in 1974. She continued her education at the prestigious Air Force Flight Nurse School, the Air War College, and the Inter-Agency Institute.

The military opened up many avenues for responsibilities, travel, and achievement. After duty in Ohio, Vigil-

Schimmenti's next assignment took her to Hickam Air Force Base in Hawaii. From there, she was transferred to the 9th Aeromedical Evacuation Squadron in Japan. The next stop was the University of Pittsburgh and then School of Health Care Sciences in Texas, where she was an instructor. She returned to Japan with a transfer to Okinawa and later to Travis Air Force Base in California. She held positions on the Air Force Inspection Team, the Command Surgeons Staff, and became chief of nursing services at Lackland Air Force Base in Texas, the Air Force's largest facility. Vigil-Schimmenti's final assignment before retirement was chief nurse of the U.S. Air Force, Washington, DC. In 1985, she made history when she attained the rank of brigadier general, becoming the first Hispanic woman in military service to do so.

After 30 years of military service, Vigil-Schimmenti left the service and returned to Albuquerque with her husband, retired Marine Lieutenant Colonel Joseph A. Vigil-Schimmenti. Early in her retirement, she devoted herself to volunteer services in her community, including serving on the board of trustees of University Hospital Mental Health Center and volunteering for the local Meals on Wheels program. At the same time, she attended the University of New Mexico, studying for a degree in the Spanish language. She and her husband eventually moved to California.

Vigil-Schimmenti is a member of the American Nurses Association, the Texas Nurses Association, the Association of Military Surgeons of the United States, the National League for Nursing, the Air Force Association, and the Aerospace Medical Association. Her military decorations include the Legion of Merit, Meritorious Service Medal with one oak leaf cluster, the Air Force Commendation Medal with one oak leaf cluster, the Air Force Outstanding Unit Award, the Air Force Organizational Excellence Award, the National Defense Service Medal, the Armed Forces Expeditionary Medal, and the Air Force Longevity Service Award Ribbon with five oak leaf clusters.

Vigil-Schimmenti attributes her success to her family life and training. She told Diaz: "I worked very hard. I had the advantage of having grown up with parents who taught me that when committing yourself to an employer, you give them your best. And so, I went into the military with a good philosophy and work ethic that I thank my parents for."

Current Address: 2905 El Toboso Dr., Albuquerque, NM 87104.

Sources:

Blue, Rose. Interview with Carlos Vasquez, April 13, 1998.
Diaz, Rose. "Carmelita Vigil-Schimmenti." *Nuestras Mujeres: Hispanas of New Mexico.* Academia/El Norte, 1992.

Lydia Villa-Komaroff
(1947–)
Educational administrator, molecular biologist

For molecular biologist Lydia Villa-Komaroff, the secret to success was in the genes. In a 1995 interview for the book *Journeys of Women in Science and Engineering: No Universal Constraints* (*JWSE*), Villa-Komaroff said, "I am interested in the question of development: how you get from a single cell the fertilized egg to a person, where all of the tissues are in the right place and each organ knows what to do and when to do it." Villa-Komaroff spent more than 20 years studying genes, mainly concentrating on protein synthesis, cell development, and growth mutations. She gained international recognition in 1978 as one of the pioneers in the emerging field of cloning. From 1985 to 1995, the award-winning scientist was on the faculty at Harvard University Medical School.

Villa-Komaroff now serves as the vice president for research and graduate studies at Northwestern University in Evanston, IL. "I haven't left science," she said of her new job in a 1998 telephone interview, "I've just left the bench." In a school publication from that same year, she summed up her office's primary function: "Research occurs in every

Lydia Villa-Komaroff

corner of the university, and we're here to expedite all of it."

Credits Strong Family History for Success

Villa-Komaroff partially credits her own genetic makeup for her personal development and professional success, both as a manager and a scientist. Her family history includes many tales of victory over adversity. *Invisible Frontiers: The Race to Synthesize a Human Gene* recounts one such family legend: While trying to escape the Mexican Revolution, her grandfather, Encarnación Villa, came face-to-face with the revolutionaries. The rebels had captured his northbound getaway train and ordered all passengers to disembark. They were given three choices: join the fight, donate valuables to the cause, or be shot. The young Encarnación stood firm, refusing to abandon his family yet holding nothing of value. Just then the revolutionary leader Pancho Villa rode up. When he heard the prisoner's surname, the general freed Encarnación and ordered him: "Have many sons with that name."

Villa-Komaroff was born on August 7, 1947, and grew up in Sante Fe, NM. As the eldest of six children, she developed teamwork- and consensus-building skills out of necessity; these skills would later serve her well in the lab and the workplace. Taking cues from those above her, Villa-Komaroff had many relatives who served as strong role models. Her mother worked as a teacher and social worker. Villa-Komaroff's paternal grandmother had been a *curandera,* or a healer, and her maternal grandmother, a lone breadwinner with three children, had sold chemical toilets on horseback up in the mountains. Villa-Komaroff's parents encouraged their offspring to follow their dreams. In *JWSE,* Villa-Komaroff spoke at length of her father, a schoolteacher and musician: "I remember when I was five he brought home the *World Book Encyclopedia,* and he said that everything I wanted to know was in those books. I was very excited by that notion. He bought the books and my mother read to us—that's one of my earliest and warmest childhood memories."

Discovers Career Path at Early Age

Villa-Komaroff knew by age nine that she wanted to be a scientist. While still in high school, she won a minority scholarship from the National Science Foundation to attend a summer lab program at a college in Texas. "There is not a child in the world, I don't think, who doesn't begin as a scientist," said Villa-Komaroff in a 1995 speech for a National Science Foundation conference. In 1965, she enrolled as a chemistry major at the University of Washington in Seattle. After an advisor told Villa-Komaroff that women did not belong in chemistry, she switched majors, finally settling on biology. Commenting on her parents' whole-hearted backing of her budding resolve, Villa-Komaroff noted in *JWSE,* "In the Mexican American family, what papa says goes, so it's clear that his support made a difference in my life. What's also amazing is that my parents fully accepted and supported my decision to go far away to college. . . . In the southwestern Chicano culture that I came from, many parents, consciously or unconsciously, discourage children from pursuing higher education because they are afraid that education will change their children or that the children will be lost to them. I think it's incumbent on people like me to convince parents that they won't lose their child to education, but that it will enrich the child and thus the family."

When her boyfriend, a 26-year old medical student named Anthony Komaroff, moved to Washington, D.C., for his internship in 1967, Villa-Komaroff followed. She was eager to get her degree, but since her first choice, Johns Hopkins University, was not accepting female students, Villa-Komaroff applied to its sister school, Goucher College in Maryland, and was admitted as a junior. In 1970, she married Komaroff and moved with him to Boston.

In Boston, Villa-Komaroff went to the Massachusetts Institute of Technology (MIT) for graduate work under Nobel Laureate David Baltimore. She recalled her mindset in *JSWE*: "I wanted to do research in developmental biology, but the people who were doing it were not the people with whom I wanted to work. So I decided I should learn more about the field of molecular biology, and I found that the best work in molecular biology was being done using viruses." In the spring of 1972, Villa-Komaroff started her dissertation on the polio virus.

While she seemingly faced little discrimination as an Hispanic, Villa-Komaroff did encounter gender inequality in the pursuit of higher education. Women made up only one-third of her small graduate class at MIT. In *JWSE*, Villa-Komaroff said of her MIT experience, "There were some people who didn't think women belonged, but the other women graduate students and I simply avoided them. I must say that I was pretty oblivious to the attitudes of others about my being a woman in science. I guess that was a blessing because I never felt I didn't belong or shouldn't be pursuing something that I loved. I learned early on that it's a very good ploy to act confident even when you're not because then people perceive you as confident, and that makes a big difference." Villa-Komaroff earned her Ph.D. in cell biology from MIT in 1975, only the third Mexican American woman in the United States to receive a doctorate in the sciences.

Conducts Groundbreaking Research

As part of a prestigious fellowship, she spent three years of postdoctoral training at Harvard, focusing on recombinant DNA technology. Unfortunately, Cambridge banned such experiments in 1976, citing concerns about public safety. Villa-Komaroff explained in *JWSE*, "The fear some people

had was that if we took genes from one organism (a human) and put them into bacteria, we might somehow create a supergerm, a new disease." So Villa-Komaroff temporarily moved to a Long Island lab run by DNA discoverer James Watson. At the Cold Harbor Springs Lab, she tried to isolate, study, and clone the genes that form a silkworm's eggshell. She described that year as a frustrating and lonely time, packed with scientific failure.

In 1977, Cambridge lifted its ban but placed strict controls on gene splicers. That year Villa-Komaroff returned to join an insulin cloning team headed by Nobel Laureate Walter Gilbert. In compliance with the new rules, MIT sequestered the team in an isolated wing, hanging a Day-Glo-orange biohazard symbol outside the antechamber to offer warning of the potentially dangerous experiments. Before entering the lab, Villa-Komaroff had to slip on blue plastic shoe covers, milky translucent gloves, and a yellow gown. Nothing was permitted to leave the lab alive, save the researchers. Every scrap of refuse produced in the lab was put in bags which were then decontaminated and put in cans; the cans were put in autoclaves; and after the refuse had been pressure-cooked at high temperature, the garbage was tossed out. The irrepressible Villa-Komaroff steadfastly continued her work with a rat gene. "I was much more comfortable working with this recombinant DNA stuff than I would have been working in, say, a microbiology lab, where they're taking cultures from people who are sick," she said. Villa-Komaroff played a key role in the team's speedy success. In early 1978, she generated great excitement by showing that bacteria could be persuaded to make insulin, the first time a human hormone had been synthesized in bacteria.

Teaching and Managing Workload Consumes Time

Late in 1978, the rising young star landed at the University of Massachusetts Medical School (UMMS). For six years, a heavy teaching and committee workload consumed Villa-Komaroff, leaving her little time to write scientific papers based on her current research, which was funded largely through grants from the National Institutes of Health, the American Diabetes Association, the American Cancer Society, and the March of Dimes Birth Defects Foundation. She cites her reluctance to submit a paper until it was "just right" as another factor that curbed her output, according to a 1995 article in *The Scientist*. In the "publish or perish" world of academia, the lapse threatened the assistant professor's nomination for tenure. She fought hard and won tenure in 1984 despite her acknowledged "mistake."

The following year Villa-Komaroff left UMMS for Harvard, taking a non-tenured position that carried a lighter teaching load and greater research and managerial responsibilities. Working twelve-hour days for ten years, the neurology professor accumulated more than sixty publishing credits. Her interest, expanding to many areas of molecular biology, finally focused on growth factors in brain development. Villa-Komaroff served on numerous high-profile committees and chaired reviews for the first studies to transplant cells into human brains. Furthering her notoriety, public television highlighted Villa-Komaroff and her work on mapping mouse genes in a television documentary called "DNA Detective," which first aired in 1995. The segment ran as part of a six-part series on women in science, under the umbrella title *Discovering Women*.

Leads A Satisfying Life

In 1996, Northwestern University appointed Villa-Komaroff to a top administrative position, as well as making her professor of neurology in its medical school. After two promotions, she is now in charge of the university's entire research budget ($181 million in 1997). Villa-Komaroff has herself become a strong role model. As a founding member of the Society for the Advancement of Chicanos and Native Americans in Science (established in 1973), she has opened up opportunities for minority youths in her lab and spoken to diverse groups about the challenges they face and the achievements others have made. In *JWSE*, Villa-Komaroff said, "I've been lucky to have had options in my life. That, combined with hard work, has paid off enormously for me and resulted in an exciting and completely satisfying life."

Current Address: Office of the Vice President for Research and Graduate Studies, Northwestern Univ., Evanston, IL 60208.

Sources:

Ambrose, Susan A, et al. *Journeys of Women in Science and Engineering: No Universal Constraints.* Philadelphia, PA: Temple University Press, 1997.

Finn, Robert. "Study Finds Gender Disparity Even Among High Achievers in Science." *The Scientist,* November 13, 1995, p. 3.

Hall, Stephen S. *Invisible Frontiers: The Race to Synthesize a Human Gene.* New York: Atlantic Monthly Press, 1987.

Holden, Constance. "Public TV to Air Series on Women Scientists." *Science,* October 15, 1993, p. 336.

"New Leadership for Research and Graduate Studies." *The Catalyst,* Winter 1998, pp. 1-3.

Villa-Komaroff, Lydia. "Opening Night Celebration: Reaching into the Future." National Science Foundation Women & Science Conference, December 13, 1995.

Worhach, Denise. Telephone conversation with Lydia Villa-Komaroff, April 16, 1998.

Villalobos, Maria Guadalupe Vélez
See Vélez, Lupe

Cathi Villalpando
(1940–)
Former federal government official

As a Republican Party organizer and special assistant to the president during the Reagan Administration, Cathi Villalpando opened the ranks of government to Hispanic Americans. Later, as one of the few Hispanic women to achieve such high governmental office, Villalpando served as U.S. Treasurer to President Bush during his administration. Although her conviction on tax evasion and obstruction charges threaten to overshadow her achievements, she was honored with special achievement awards from various government agencies and was also asked to serve on the U.S. Commission on Civil Rights.

Born in Texas

The father of Catalina Vasquez Villalpando was born in Mexico, while her mother was a Texan of Mexican descent. Augustin, who had six children with his wife Guadalupe, was a hardware store salesman. Catalina or Cathi was born on April 1, 1940 in San Marcos, a little town between Austin and San Antonio. Cathi was their eldest child and one of three girls. Augustin would often take her and the

Cathi Villalpando

others on trips to local fields in order to show them what it was like to pick crops, always the most likely job for a new immigrant. The family was religiously conservative and financially challenged. Though the Villalpandos were staunch Democrats, their eldest child was destined to make a name for herself among the rival Republicans.

After attending local public schools and graduating from the high school in San Marcos, Villalpando enrolled as a part-time student at Southwest Texas State University. Although she never completed a degree, she did take courses at various institutions including Southern Methodist University and the Austin College of Business. It was while taking a business course that Villalpando encountered Republican Party recruiters. As she recalled for the magazine *Nuestro* in 1985, Republican headquarters just happened to be in the same building and, coincidentally, in need of part-time clerical help. Although she felt politically jaded at the time, she confessed that she became slowly impressed by the openness of the party. Villalpando formally became a Republican Party member in 1969.

Works for Federal Government

Villalpando began immediately to work in certain federal positions, which required her to work in Texas, especially in the Austin and Dallas regions. Her specialties became economic development, particularly regarding minority businesses, and public relations. Villalpando worked for the Department of Commerce, the Office of Economic Opportunity, and the Minority Business Development Administration during the 1970s. After two and one-half years as Hispanic liaison for the party, the Republicans trusted her with campaign assignments during 1980. Villalpando coordinated the Hispanic outreach effort during George Bush's primary bid, then later filled in as assistant director at the state level during Reagan's presidential run.

Move from DC to Dallas and Back

After the Reagan victory, Villalpando was brought to the White House as personnel staff assistant for the transition team. When her work was done there, she returned to Texas and entered the private sector. Two businesses offered her high offices. First, Mid-South Oil Company of Dallas made her vice-president; then Communications International, Inc. (CII) of Atlanta, Georgia, elected her senior vice-president. In 1983, however, Sen. John Tower of Texas recommended her for a post in the Reagan administration. Villalpando worked from the Public Liaison Office as special assistant to the president regarding Hispanic affairs.

Villalpando was proud of her success in bringing together groups that may not have otherwise interacted on issues crucial to Hispanics. She was also instrumental in coordinating the efforts of the Department of Education and a congressional representative who had been working on a bill regarding bilingual education.A controversial immigration bill was studied by Villalpando and the Public Liaison Office, in order to help offer an alternative to deportation by fostering the reform of employment practices.

Appointed U. S. Treasurer

While still involved with Communications International, Inc., Villalpando was appointed U.S. Treasurer by President Bush in the late 1980s. Although Villalpando had apparently cleared the company's payment of a $250,000 bonus after she accepted the government post, she was still reprimanded during 1990 over how the payments had been handled. As the controversy over the CII fee and other suspected dealings increased, members of the National Council of La Raza and the Congressional Hispanic Caucus Institute came to her personal defense. However, the FBI increased their surveillance, eventually searching company offices and Villalpando's apartment.

Although Villalpando herself was never accused directly of influence peddling, the charges brought against her after she was forced to take administrative leave included obstruction. She eventually admitted, while pleading guilty to three felonies, to obstructing an investigation of a housing scandal dating back to the Reagan Administration. Villalpando was also charged with evading income taxes and deliberately under reporting income to the government. Although the maximum possible sentence for each of these charges might have been five years, Villalpando was instead sentenced in 1994 to a four-month term in federal prison. Following that term, she was additionally required by the court to be allowed only supervised release for another three years, and to perform 200 hours of community service.

Villalpando's short-lived marriage to a high-school sweetheart produced no children.

Sources:

New York Times, February 18, 1994, pp. A11, A17; September 14, 1994, p. A12.
Nuestro, January-February, 1985, 9:1.
Time, February 28, 1994, p. 19.
Washington Post, September 15, 1983; October 30, 1992, p. A1; October 31, 1992, p. A8; January 10, 1993, p. A1; September 14, 1994, p. A5.

Helena Maria Viramontes
(1954–)
Professor, author

Selected writings:

The Moths and Other Stories. Arte Publico Press, 1985.
Chicana Creativity and Criticism: Charting New Frontiers in American Literature. Edited with María Herrera-Sobek, Arte Publico Press, 1987.
Under the Feet of Jesus. Dutton, 1995.
Chicana (W)rites: On Word and Film. Edited with María Herrera-Sobek, Third Woman Press, 1995.

Overview

Helena Maria Viramontes is one of a new generation of Hispanic American women fiction writers. She is known for her striking use of language and her realistic portrayal of women—for creating characters that are far from the idealized versions of feminists successfully battling patriarchy, as the critic Yvonne Yarbro-Bejarano has observed.

Helena Maria Viramontes

Condemns Oppression Through Writings

Viramontes's fiction centers on women of different ages, mainly Chicanas from the Southwest, struggling against all economic obstacles to raise their children. One of her themes is the violence women endure as a result of being dominated by men. Her writing, she believes, is a way of condemning oppression, whether it involves racism or sexism. Her work has been influenced by such African American writers as Toni Morrison, Alice Walker, and Ntozake Shange, as well as by contemporary Latin American writers, especially Gabriel Garcia Marquez. Chicana feminist writers Ana Castillo and Sandra Cisneros have also had a great impact upon Viramontes, who considers herself a feminist. "If we are going to improve as a society, we have to re-teach ourselves as well as the men to develop the feminine side of our natures, something that has been lost. It is the feminine aspect that will strive to save the environment, making the world safe for all creatures," she remarked in her interview.

Viramontes was born February 26, 1954, in East Los Angeles, California, where she attended primary and secondary schools. She began writing in college while studying English literature at Immaculate Heart College, where she received he BA in 1975. Her first attempts were in poetry, but she soon determined she was better suited for fiction writing, particularly short stories. Her tales initially revolved around those close to her. "Whenever I finished a story, I would read it to my friends, and they would tell me how these things had also happened to them. It made me realize that I was not just writing about myself but about a whole community of women," Viramontes explained in a telephone interview with Silvia Novo Pena. As a result, the author began to record in her short fiction some of the stories other women were telling her about their own lives.

Achieves Recognition

Before long Viramontes entered her work in contests and achieved recognition. Her stories began to appear in several national and regional publications, and in 1977 she won first prize for fiction from *Statement Magazine,* a publication of California State University in Los Angeles, for her short story "Requiem for the Poor." The following year she again won first prize in the *Statement* contest for her short story "The Broken Web." In 1979 her short story "Birthday" was recognized as the best fiction entry in the University of California at Irvine Chicano Literary contest. In 1983 her stories "Snapshots" and "Growing" appeared in the anthology *Cuentos: Stories by Latinas,* published by Kitchen Table/Women of Color Press. Her award-winning story "The Broken Word" appeared in the 1984 Arte Publico Press anthology of Hispanic women writers, *Woman of Her Word,* edited by the poet Evangelina Vigil. Viramontes's first collection of short stores, *The Moths and Other Stories,* was published by Arte Publico Press in Houston, Texas in 1985. As of May 1998 it had sold over 25,000 copies.

Viramontes has collaborated on two non-fiction projects. In 1983 she edited with María Herrera-Sobek the anthology *Chicana Writers: Word and Film,* published by Third Woman. With the same author in 1988 she produced another non-fiction anthology, *Chicana Creativity and Criticism: Charting New Frontiers in American Literature,* published by Arte Publico Press.

Adapts Story for Film

In 1989 Viramontes received a National Endowment for the Arts fellowship to attend a workshop on storytelling by Nobel Laureate Gabriel Garcia Marquez offered at the Sundance Institute. She was one of six writers nominated from a nation pool for this honor. Two years later, Viramontes adapted one of her stories, "Paris Rats In East L.A.," for film. Picked up by director Ana Maria Garcia and produced by the American Film Institute, as of May of 1998 this half-hour film was in post production.

Viramontes has organized a number of readings and panels aimed at attracting attention to her work and that of her fellow professional writers. Her engagements have included those at high schools, middle schools, universities, public libraries, and community cultural events. She has also been instrumental in the creation of the Southern California Latino Writers and Filmmakers group, the first attempt to organize Latino writers in the Los Angeles area

Gains Critical Acclaim for *Under the Feet of Jesus*

A 1989 National Endowment for the Arts in Fiction grant resulted in the 1995 publication of her first novel, *Under the Feet of Jesus.* This critically acclaimed work went on to be nominated for the 1995 "New Voices," Quality Paperback Book of the Month Club. It also placed as a "Discover Great New Writers" finalist for Barnes and Nobles in 1996. Translated into Hindi, Spanish, and German, *Under the Feet of Jesus* has been included as required reading for university humanities classes across the country and around the world.

While completing her graduate studies, Viramontes served as a visiting professor in the English Department at California State University. In 1994 Viramontes graduated with a master of fine arts degree from University of California at Irvine in creative writing. In January of 1995 she was appointed assistant professor in the creative writing program at Cornell University where she continues to write and teach. As of May of 1998 she was working on her second novel, *Their Dogs Came with Them,* and a collection of short stories titled *Paris Rats in East L.A.* With Viramontes, "[l]ove and anger of family and community" continue to inspire her work, and Los Angeles remains "the city of imagery" she visits every day.

Current Address: Creative Writing Program, Dept. of English, Cornell University, Ithaca, NY 14853.

Sources:

Archives, Arte Publico Press, Houston Texas.

Viramontes, Helena Maria. Curriculum vitae and brief narrative, 1998.

Yarbro-Bejarano, Yvonne. "Introduction." *The Moths and Other Stories.* Arte Publico Press, 1985.

Carmen Delgado Votaw
(1935–)
Organization executive, author, human rights activist, women's rights activist

Selected writings:

Puerto Rican Women. Lisboa Associates, 1996.

Overview

"**E**mpowerment comes through education," said civil rights leader and activist Carmen Delgado Votaw, who was born on September 29, 1935, in Humaco, Puerto Rico. Votaw, director of government relations for United Way of

Carmen Delgado Votaw

America, earned her B.A. in international studies at The American University in Washington, D.C. Deeply concerned about human rights, Votaw has devoted her life to empowering the oppressed—particularly women and especially Latin American women. Votaw's career includes serving as director of government relations for Girl Scouts of the U.S.A.; vice president of Information and Services for Latin America, Inc.; U.S. representative to the Inter American Commission of Women and its executive committee; president of Inter American Commission of Women of the Organization of American States; co-chair of the National Advisory Committee on Women; and national president of the National Conference of Puerto Rican Women. Travelling to 69 countries, often as a United States representative on human rights issues, she has participated in more than 40 meetings with the United Nations and Organization of American States (OAS), and lectured at innumerable universities and institutions world-wide.

Inspires Others to Act

"My passion is activism—getting people to get off their duffs to do something," said Votaw during a telephone interview. "Everyone is busy, but we must all do something to positively impact others. I love Gloria Steinem's quote: 'Do an outrageous act every day.' I'm not sure where children (today) get that," said Votaw. "Growing up, we were expected to do something for others. An old lady in our town who lived alone was simply expected at our house every lunch time, and we children were expected to have lunch out for her. We had to be kind to all old folk and talk to lonely people. My father would ask: 'Did you stop and talk to Mama Lola today?' And the whole town was my keeper. If I was where I shouldn't be, people would go to my home and say: 'Do you know where Carmencita is. . .?' Growing up like that you know who you are—know you are important," she said.

Votaw's parents, Cándida Paz Ruiz and Luis Oscar Delgado, were both educators. Her mother was her third and fifth grade teacher. "I didn't think it wonderful at the time," Votaw said, "and I was glad to escape having my father as a teacher when I was sent to school in San Juan in seventh grade." Today, however, Votaw appreciates her parents' emphasis on education. "My father coached me on many things. He owned the only bookstore in town, and he guided me through those books."

Chooses Career of Commitment

Votaw's career spans more than 30 years. Marriage to Gregory B. Votaw, economist and historian, in Puerto Rico in 1960 brought her to the United States in 1962. She began tutoring inner-city African American children and international students in her suburban county. "Puerto Ricans in the United States have the lowest educational attainment of all immigrants. There is still much to be done," she said. This experience led her to volunteer with the League of Women Voters where ". . . our thrust was to help empower women in Latin America—Bolivia, Colombia, Peru—by helping them organize. It was a time when people opposing authority were being shot," Votaw recalled. As president of the Conference of Puerto Rican Women, she helped identify differences with other aspects of the women's movement, encouraging and facilitating collaboration between groups while educating participants on how the women's movement could benefit them.

When President Carter appointed the National Advisory Committee on Women, Votaw, selected as co-chair, was instrumental in the implementation of the National Plan of Action for Women adopted in 1977. As co-founder and board member of the Inter American Institute on Human Rights, Costa Rica, she worked diligently in Latin America, "convincing presidents to sign conventions to improve the situation of women." Fluent in English, Spanish, and French, Votaw was president from 1978 to 1980 of the Inter American Commission on Women of the Organization of American States—the oldest organization in the world established to defend women's rights. Votaw's commitment to her cause also includes participation in many civic and professional organizations, such as the Society for International Development; United Nations Association; Inter American Institute of Human Rights in Costa Rica; National Women's Conference Committee; and the advisory committee of the National Women's Political Caucus.

Works for the Future

Votaw is encouraged by the development of women's and labor movements in recent years. Votaw sees an increasing societal awareness that women's rights are an integral part of human rights. She also sees labor unions becoming more cognizant of women's issues in the workplace, and women themselves realizing the need to network and build coalitions between small groups with similar goals. Recalling her participation at the United Nations' Fourth World Conference on Women in Beijing, China, in 1995, Votaw said, "Groups representing Latin American domestic workers participated for the first time on the international scene. And it was exciting to see women from so many countries knowledgeable about the agenda—learning how to lobby and be advocates for themselves and others." However, she said there is still much improvement needed on basic issues, such as education, health, employment, and empowerment.

Votaw also realizes the importance of the past. "Puerto Rican women do not appear in history. They need to be recognized for their contributions," she said. The author of the bilingual book *Puerto Rican Women* (1996), and numerous articles, Votaw also authored profiles of two Puerto Rican women which she strongly recommended for inclusion in the second volume of *Notable American Women* (1980). "Until then, not one Puerto Rican woman was included," she said.

Reaps the Rewards

Among the many awards bestowed upon Votaw are induction into the Maryland Women's Hall of Fame; honorary Ph.D. of humanities from Hood College; National Institute for Women of Color Award as outstanding woman in international affairs; and the prestigious National Hispanic Heritage Award for Education. She is profiled in the *Maryland Women's History Resource Packet,* a collection of biographies designed to expose students to positive role models and mentors. "It's exciting to visit schools and have a student recognize me," she said. "It tells me the packets are having some impact."

Votaw is also recognized in *Who's Who of American Women; Women's International Register, Who's Who Among American Women in the Caribbean, Washington Who's Who Among Latin Americans, World Who's Who of Women, World Personalities,* and *International Who's Who of Professional and Business Women.*

Current Address: United Way of America, 701 N. Fairfax St., Alexandria, VA 22314-2045.

Sources:

Thompson, Märie L. Telephone conversation with and information material from Carmen Delgado Votaw, March, 1998.

Diana Dominguez Weir
Legislative chief of staff, civil rights activist

Diana Dominguez Weir has been a faithful representative of the Hispanic community in New York, working behind-the-scenes in the Republican Party to ensure that the Hispanic voice is heard in the rough-and-tumble world of politics. Once a successful banker, she made the switch to politics in the early 1990s. She now devotes most of her time to political activism, serving in 1996 as campaign manager in Republican Congressman Michael P. Forbes's successful bid for re-election and as his chief of staff. She also has served as national secretary for the Republican National Hispanic Assembly, which is headquartered in Washington, DC

Weir was born and raised in New York City. Her father, Angel Maria, had emigrated from Colombia to study engineering in the United States, while her mother, Rosario Aviles, had moved to New York from her native Puerto Rico. Educated in New York City schools, Weir attended New York University in 1962 and 1963. Between 1972 and 1974, she attended classes at the American Institute of Banking. She studied data processing system design, systems analysis, and programming at the IBM and Burroughs (UNISYS) education centers between 1976 and 1978. From 1984 to 1988, she studied business at St. Joseph's College in Patchogue, NY, earning a place on the dean's list for most of that period.

Launches Banking Career

Weir first became involved with banking at the Bank of Smithtown on New York's Long Island. She went to work there in 1972 and left 16 years later as senior vice president and cashier. During her first 11 years at the Bank of Smithtown, she established the bank's in-house computer system, supervising and coordinating the implementation and maintenance of all systems, applications software, and hardware. She also developed the institution's internal audit program and its disaster recovery plan. In 1983, Weir was named senior vice president. In that position, she administered the bank's stock transfer department as vice president and corporate secretary for Smithtown Bancorp, the bank's holding company. As the bank's second highest ranking officer, she coordinated and administered all operations and data processing activities.

After leaving the Bank of Smithtown in 1988, Weir joined the Bank of the Hamptons in 1989 as senior vice president and branch administrator. While at the bank, also on Long Island, she implemented its annuity sales program, licensing 15 branch representatives. In a period of 6 months, she sold more than $250,000 in annuities to existing customers. Among her other responsibilities at the Bank of the Hamptons, she supervised the operations and administration of the bank's network of branch offices and directed the Human Resources Department's operations.

Enters Politics

In 1994, Weir struck out on her own as an investment and data processing consultant, setting up Diana Weir Consulting, of which she was both president and owner. From April to November of 1994, she served as finance director for Congressman-elect Michael Forbes. In that position, she coordinated all fund-raising events for Forbes in New York's First Congressional District. She also developed and maintained relations with campaign contributors. The same year, she served as chairperson of the Suffolk County Executive Robert Gaffney's Hispanic advisory board, a volunteer position. During that period, she told a reporter, she was "the eyes and ears of the county executive within the Latino community. I try to help convey the concerns they have with language assimilation, immigration problems, education, and services. I try to help bridge the lines of communication between government and the community. I try to work with both groups to develop better understanding."

Hispanics Gather in Albany

In 1994, Weir attended "Somos El Futuro" (We Are the Future), a statewide conference in New York's capital of Albany to educate public officials about the needs of the state's growing Hispanic community. The conference, which drew hundreds of Hispanics of all political leanings from throughout the state, was described by Weir as "the major networking opportunity of all time." A strong supporter of Republican politics, she noted at the time that her fellow Republican Hispanics were trying to distance themselves from "the social services perspective—that everybody Hispanic is looking for a handout, because we're not." However, regardless of ideology, she welcomed increased Hispanic participation across the political spectrum, noting that it was vital for Hispanics to have clout in both major parties. "You can't fix the system from the outside," she said.

Beginning in 1995, Weir became the chief of staff for Representative Forbes, directing the overall operation of his congressional offices, both in Washington, DC, and back home on Long Island. Her responsibilities as chief of staff include the budget for the congressional offices, the management of all congressional office staff, and the development and implementation of the congressional plan. She represents the congressman at local meeting and events when he is unable to attend and coordinates local town meetings and forums.

Weir, who maintains homes in both Washington, DC, and Wainscott, NY, has a son and daughter and two grandchildren. Her community involvement spans 30 years of service on various boards and committees working to promote equity for Hispanics. A founding member of the East Hampton Town Hispanic Advisory Committee, she also served on the Suffolk County Human Rights Commission and on the executive board of the Long Island Housing Partnership. La Union Hispanica named her "Outstanding Hispanic in Banking/Business" in 1993. In 1994, she was honored by the Suffolk County Executive and the Suffolk County Police Hispanic Society during Hispanic Heritage Month.

Current Address: 5 Clyden Rd., PO Box 1152, Wainscott, NY 11975-1152.

Sources:

Amerman, Donald. Letter to Diana Dominguez Weir, April 14, 1998.

Vestal, Joy. "Newsmaker Diana Dominguez Weir." *Newsday,* April 12, 1994, p. A30.

Whitehouse, Beth. "Empowerment Fest for Hispanics." *Newsday,* March 29, 1994, p. A29.

Vanna White
(1957–)
Television host

Selected filmography:

Graduation Day. 1981.
Looker. 1981.
Goddess of Love (TV movie). 1988.

Selected writings:

Vanna Speaks. New York: Warner Books, 1987.
Vanna's Afghans A to Z: 52 Crochet Favorites. Birmingham, Ala.: Oxmoor House, 1994.
Vanna's Afghans All Through the House. Birmingham, Ala.: Oxmoor House, 1997.

Overview

Vanna White and *The Wheel of Fortune* have proved to be a winning combination. The long-running, syndicated television game show has made White something of a household name in homes across the nation and abroad. Revamped shortly after she joined the show in 1982, *The Wheel of Fortune* skyrocketed in popularity as viewers watched

Vanna White

the very attractive hostess turn letters while contestants tried to solve word puzzles. She more recently was named a cohost of the show. While some have difficulty pinpointing the reasons for her popularity, perhaps her fans admire her genuine down-to-earth personality, her style, and her all-American good looks.

Spends Early Years with Grandparents

Born Vanna Marie Rosich in Conway, SC, on February 18, 1957, she was the daughter of Miguel Angel Rosich and Joan Marie Rosich. For a brief period her parents had lived in New York City, but they moved back to South Carolina when Joan Marie became pregnant with Vanna. Her parents separated when she was only a few months old. White went to live with her maternal grandparents in the small resort town of Myrtle Beach, SC, while her parents went their separate ways: her father back to New York and her mother to Miami, where she took a job as a waitress.

In her autobiography, *Vanna Speaks,* White said that she never thought of herself as coming from a broken home, and she wrote respectfully of both of her birth parents. Her mother married again, to Herbert Stackley White Jr., the owner of the Miami cafe where she worked, and they returned in 1959 to care for Vanna in North Myrtle Beach. Vanna's brother, Herbert III ("Chip"), was born the next year. A stable life began to take shape for the family as her mother opened a home-based stationery supply store and her stepfather went to work for the post office. Of her mother, White wrote in her book, "She had the brains and drive to do anything she wanted. In different times maybe she would have become a professional of some sort."

Seeks Glamorous Television Job

As a child, Vanna became enamored with television and all the associated glamour. Once, while visiting with her birth father in New York City, she had the opportunity to view a taping of the NBC game show *Concentration.* By that time, she had set her sights on becoming a television star. During her teen years she had a number of boyfriends and was a high school cheerleader. Her mother, although deeply religious, took a fairly liberal approach to raising her daughter. She encouraged White to follow her dreams and said she would back her in whatever she decided. White, still star-struck, had no desire to go to college. Nor did she have any desire to get married—at least not yet. Her mother nudged her toward acting or modeling, careers for which she herself had once had ambitions.

Deciding to try her hand first at modeling, White moved to Atlanta, where she enrolled in the Atlanta School for Fashion and Design. She attended the school for about a year and then looked for practical experience. She got several jobs during 1978 and 1979 with the help of her agent, Kathy Hardegree, of Atlanta Models and Talent. Some of her jobs won her advertising spots in *Harper's Bazaar, Vogue,* and *Cosmopolitan* magazines. She also worked

as a model for department store catalogs. It was during this time that she met and moved in with a boyfriend, Gordon Watson. The relationship proved to be troublesome and was short-lived. Meanwhile, she competed in the Miss Georgia Universe pageant and was the fourth runner-up in the beauty contest.

Her ambitions for Hollywood were growing stronger around this time, and she was looking forward to exploring the possibilities there. Unfortunately, her quest was not an easy one. After breaking up with her boyfriend, she rented a truck and made the trip to Hollywood in January of 1980. She soon found out that breaking into the modeling business out West was more difficult than on the East Coast since the West Coast modeling standards were much more stringent. At five feet, six inches, she was considered too short by West Coast modeling agents, and she had to accept lesser modeling jobs. To help pay the bills, she worked as a waitress at a restaurant called Luigi's, where Hollywood's aspiring actors and celebrities often gathered. At one point she was so desperate for money to pay the rent that she posed for lingerie pictures, something she would later regret when the pictures turned up in *Playboy* magazine. During this time she binged on food and gained about 25 pounds. "I was out of work, struggling," she explained in an interview with *People* magazine. "I'd eat whole pies, cakes, meatloaves." But she lost the weight when she cared for her mother who was dying from cancer. White's career took a backseat as she stayed with her mother and took care of her every need until her mother's death in the summer of 1980.

White's career got a boost when she won minor roles in a handful of movies, two of which were *Graduation Day* and *Looker.* Her personal life also improved when in 1982 she met John Gibson, an actor and Chippendale dancer; they eventually moved in together. The couple had something in common: both were trying to get their careers off the ground. Gibson, who acted in the soap opera *The Young and the Restless,* died in May of 1986 when a plane he was piloting crashed. "His death was devastating to me. We were very much in love and had spent many years together," White said in an interview with *Good Housekeeping.*

Receives Game Show Break

In 1982 White got her big break when she was called to audition for *The Wheel of Fortune,* a game show created by Merv Griffin. In the *Good Housekeeping* article, Pat Sajak, the host of what was then a daytime show, recalled, "I wasn't sure that Vanna was going to get through her audition. She was so nervous, she could hardly turn the letters. I've never seen anyone so shy and frightened. But Merv saw the potential, and so did I." Merv Griffin picked White to replace the departing Susan Stafford.

The popularity of the show increased markedly after White joined, so much so that Griffin and King World Enterprises introduced a syndicated show less than two years later. The new show had grander prizes and more glitz, becoming one of the highest rated syndicated shows ever. At one time, White manually turned the hidden letters on the giant board, but now with advances in technology, she touches a corner of the letter and it lights up. Of her job and her cohost, she told *Good Housekeeping,* "I've learned everything from Pat. I am the first to make fun of my job. It doesn't take much training to turn letters. They could replace me with a computer, but they haven't." White's genuine enthusiasm for the contestants, which she displays by clapping as they seek to solve word games, is very obvious. In 1992 the *Guinness Book of World Records* named White television's most frequent clapper, averaging 720 claps a show.

White's popularity continued to grow, despite some negative press. An article by newspaperman Bob Greene in late 1985 that poked some playful fun at White's abilities served as a springboard for the show to promote her with advertisers. She has become something of a cottage industry, with television, personal appearances, and product endorsements. She has marketed products on the *Home Shopping Club* and has her own fragrance, "Vanna." In 1987 Warner paid her a $250,000 advance for her autobiography, *Vanna Speaks,* in which she discusses her childhood, her career, and the death of John Gibson. She also writes about her sudden success in Hollywood.

Achieves Personal Happiness

White married on New Year's Eve of 1990. Her husband, George SantoPietro, has a grown son from a previous marriage. The two now own a house in Beverly Hills and have two young children, Nicholas and Giovanna. "Motherhood has changed my whole attitude about a career," she said. "Being a mother is the most important thing." She has said that if she ever had to get another job, it would involve children. "I have a wonderful life," White said in an interview before her second child was born. "I'm very grateful for my job. I'm healthy. I have a wonderful husband who's a great cook and who loves me. And I have a perfect baby son."

White has a true appreciation for all the work done by the *Wheel* behind-the-scene staffers to make the show such a success. "All you see on the TV screen are our contestants, Pat, and me," she explained in an online interview. "But it's the scores of other people who put the show on that really make *Wheel of Fortune* spin like it does."

Wins Court Case

In 1994, White won damages of $403,000 against Samsung Electronics Co. and its advertising agency for violating "her right of publicity." She proved to a jury that the company had used her identity in a 1988 advertisement for its VCRs. The ad depicted a robot with a blond wig turning letters on a giant board. This battle was a victory not only for White but also for other celebrities who want to safeguard their identities. Previous court rulings have upheld the right of celebrities to sue for outright theft of a name or a face, but this was the first victory involving a "likeness."

Sources:

Moritz, Charles, ed. "White, Vanna." *Current Biography Yearbook.* New York: H.W. Wilson Co, 1988.

Scott, Vernon. "Vanna White's New Baby, New Home, New Life." *Good Housekeeping,* January 1, 1995, p. 82.

Sony Pictures Entertainment Home Page. Available at http://www.spe.sony.com/tv/shows/wheel/.

"TV's Hall of Flukey Fame: Who'd'a Thunk It? A Letter Turner, a Professional Liar, and an Electric Talk Show Host Lead a Pack of Long Shots Who Prove That Off-Beat is On-Target When It Comes to Success." *People,* August 25, 1986, p. 62.

"Vanna White Lighter Than Air, TV's Letter-Perfect Hostess Rose to the Pinnacle of Fortune." *People,* December 22, 1986, p. 80.

Graciela Zayas
(1925–)
Interpreter, professor

Graciela Zayas is a former professor at the Defense Language Institute in Monterey, CA, and an interpreter for International Telephone and Telegraph (ITT), also based in California. As a professor, Zayas was responsible for training linguists who would then use those language skills in the service of the United States abroad. Now, as an interpreter, her language skills continue to benefit her country as Zayas provides translating and interpreting services for the U.S. government.

Zayas was born in Havana, Cuba, in 1925, the daughter of Enrique and Angelica Fernandez De Castro Zayas. She attended the University of Havana, graduating in 1956. In 1961, she moved to the United States with her 11-year-old daughter, Maria, having separated from her husband, Dr. Eduardo Valdes Santo Thomas, whom she married in 1949. She first settled in Miami and later moved to New York City, working as a teacher. The move was very difficult for Zayas. She admitted in a telephone interview, "New York was a shock. Cuba was much different. Far more conservative in its values. [In Cuba,] a teacher did not have to discipline the students." For a time, Zayas taught Spanish in Saugerties, NY. She then attended State University of New York in New Paltz, earning a master's degree in education in 1970.

In 1973 Zayas moved to Washington, DC, to join the Defense Language Institute Foreign Language Center (DLIFLC), the largest foreign language institute in the world, and was eventually transferred to the Institute's headquarters in Monterey, CA. The DLIFLC was founded to train linguists who would protect the interests of the United States worldwide. It is the largest and finest foreign language institute in the world, and the heart of its mission is its quality foreign language instructional programs. Zayas was among the 680 instructors at the Institute who trained people for work in foreign nations, the FBI, the border patrol, and the military services. Zayas retired from the Institute in 1987. Wanting to remain active, however, she did not stay retired for long. She became an interpreter for ITT language line services, which provides translating and interpreting services for the government.

Zayas's proudest accomplishment is her daughter, who graduated from American University in Washington, DC, and now lives in Greece, the mother of four children. When asked in a telephone conversation for advice to young people, Zayas remarked, "In order to have success in life, you need self-discipline and respect for yourself, your roots, and the family you must be part of."

Sources:

Blue, Rose. Interview with Graciela Zayas, April 17, 1998.
Catalog Defense Language Institute Foreign Language Center.

Daphne E. Zuñiga
(1963–)
Actress, model, community activist

Selected filmography:

The Dorm That Dripped Blood. 1981.
The Initiation. 1983.
The Sure Thing. Embassy Pictures, 1985.
Vision Quest. 1985.
Modern Girls. 1986.
Spaceballs. MGM, 1987.
Last Rites. MGM, 1988.
The Fly II. Brooksfilm, 1989.
Gross Anatomy. Touchstone, 1989.
Staying Together. 1989.
Mad At The Moon. Republic Pictures, 1992.
Melrose Place. FOX-TV, 1992-1996.
Eight Hundred Leagues Down The Amazon. 1993.
Degree of Guilt. NBC-TV, 1995.
Pandora's Clock. NBC-TV, 1996.

Daphne E. Zuñiga

Overview

Actress and model Daphne Zuñiga was born on October 28, 1963. Zuñiga gained notoriety as a rising young star in numerous popular films of the 1980s, including 1985's *The Sure Thing, Vision Quest,* and Mel Brooks's 1987 farce *Spaceballs.* After some forgettable films, Zuñiga turned her talents to television, starring in the popular nighttime soap opera *Melrose Place* as the troubled photographer Jo Reynolds. Zuñiga and the series were hugely successful. Nevertheless, Zuñiga left *Melrose Place* after four seasons, feeling her career was stagnating. Since then, Zuñiga has continued to appear in television miniseries and in films, as well as devoting her time to various charitable causes.

Remembers Life's Early Lessons

Zuñiga, who is of Guatemalan descent, spent her childhood in Berkeley, CA, and Vermont. Her parents divorced when she was only six. Zuñiga's mother was just twenty-one when she gave birth to her daughter. Zuñiga remembers the difficulty her young mother had supporting a family. Zuñiga recalled in an interview with the *Daily News,* "[My mother] did everything to support us, from being an elevator operator to a phone operator to a gift wrapper. It gave me a sense of value of money. I don't have the illusion it will buy you happiness." The lesson stayed with Zuñiga, who continued to live in a house with five friends and share a bedroom, even after she had completed three feature films. Zuñiga has also remained deeply devoted to her Latin roots. Despite early recommendations from agents to change her name to something easier for English speakers to pronounce, Zuñiga refused to turn her back on her heritage and retained her name.

Works in Both Film and Television

Zuñiga made her screen debut in the 1981 horror film *The Dorm That Dripped Blood.* Her mainstream film debut came in director Rob Reiner's 1985 film *The Sure Thing,* where she played the object of John Cusack's affections and shared the screen with future stars Anthony Edwards and Tim Robbins. Film critic Roger Ebert praised her performance in that film, calling her a "gifted young actor." In 1987, she appeared in director Mel Brooks' science fiction spoof *Spaceballs.* Following that role, Zuñiga appeared in a number of less successful films, including the 1989 sequel, *The Fly II,* and the low-budget Roger Corman film *Eight Hundred Leagues Down The Amazon* in 1993.

Lands Role on *Melrose Place*

Feeling movie work was becoming too risky and seeking greater financial security, Zuñiga turned to television in 1992. There she landed her popular role on the Fox soap opera *Melrose Place.* Zuñiga played troubled photographer Jo Reynolds. Zuñiga herself did not take the role or the show too seriously, understanding that *Melrose Place* appeals to a certain audience. In an interview with *The Irish Times,* she described the show as "equal opportunity beefcake and cheesecake." The success of *Melrose Place* caught Zuñiga off guard. She admitted to *USA Today* that "It's pretty surprising how many people around the country watch my show. . . All this hype on *Melrose Place* scares me, 'cause what goes up fast goes down fast."

Despite believing she was too old to take chances, Zuñiga left *Melrose Place* after four seasons. She recalled in an interview with *Time* magazine, "When I took *Melrose,* I wondered, 'Will, Martin Scorsese want to meet me if I am on this show?'" Still, Zuñiga found her decision to leave *Melrose Place* a difficult one. As she told Roger Anderson, she ". . . spent a week on Martha's Vineyard going through withdrawal." She found the recognition that accompanies television popularity reassuring. Zuñiga said in the same interview, "When I was on the show, people came up and said, 'Oh, you're great.' Once I left, I wondered, 'Am I still great?'" She describes the period as "a mini-identity crisis."

After leaving *Melrose Place,* Zuñiga appeared in numerous television mini-series, including 1995's *Degree of Guilt* and 1996's *Pandora's Clock.* Zuñiga also modeled in a series of print ads for Sasson sportswear, which appeared in major magazines like *Rolling Stone* and *Vogue.* The art director for the ads described Zuñiga as "young, hip, intelligent, and quite loving."

Zuñiga recently purchased a home in the hills of Southern California, which she shares with her younger sister, Jennifer, also an actress. She enjoys hiking in the California hills with her dog, Lou, and exercising; she built a personal gym in her new home. She also enjoys riding motorcycles, the music of Shawn Colvin, and watching the food channel.

The slender 5' 8" actress tries not to be overly concerned about her eating habits or appearance. At one point, she became obsessed with her weight after a bad experience with a modeling photographer in the early 1980s. After that experience, Zuñiga stopped placing so much emphasis on the scale. Zuñiga told the *Daily News,* "I don't even weigh myself anymore. It's torture, and it's horrible that women in this country have to be so worried about it. . . It's not easy, being in this business, and on *Melrose,* where everybody is a size 2." Zuñiga admits to a sweet tooth, but tries to avoid eating the junk food prevalent on film sets.

Enjoys Charity Work

Zuñiga has worked to raise money for the Multiple Sclerosis Foundation and AIDS Project Los Angeles, as well as donating time to the Southwest Voter Registration Education Project, which aims to encourage Latin American women to vote. She is devoted to Central American political causes and has lent her support to the American Civil Liberties Union's support for free artistic expression. "It's so easy for people to become insulated, close-minded, fearful and contracted. . . The more different people are allowed to express themselves, the easier it is for the rest of us to look and learn and feel something," Zuñiga told the *The Los Angeles Times.*

In 1995, Zuñiga was nominated for a Desi Award for Best Television Actress for her work on *Melrose Place.* The awards, named for actor Desi Arnaz, honor Hispanic entertainers.

Daphne Zuñiga has made her mark in film and television, compiling an impressive body of work at young age. The affinity viewers felt towards her *Melrose Place* character is a testament to her talent and personality. Her devotion to her Latin roots and to charitable causes make her much more than the average soap star.

Sources:

Anderson, Roger. "Actress Suffers 'Melrose' Withdrawal." *The Stuart News,* November 11, 1996, p. B6.

Archerd, Army. "Just for Variety." *Daily Variety,* July 27, 1994.

Carol, Troy. "Daphne Zuñiga: No More Ms. Nice Girl." *Mademoiselle,* April, 1989, p. 100.

"Celeb Picks." *People,* December 26, 1994, p. 10.

Cunningham, Kim. "What's A Zuñiga?" *People,* November 27, 1995, p. 158.

Ebert, Roger. *Roger Ebert's Video Companion.* Andrews & McMeel, 1994.

Ehrman, Mark. "Into The Night: You've Got A Right To Party, Too." *Los Angeles Times,* March 3, 1994, p. E2.

Facter, Sue. "Love Finds A Home At 'Melrose Place'." *USA Today,* September 20, 1995, p. 2D.

Gliatto, Tom, et al. "Hot Property!; With Heather Locklear running the joint, Fox's juicy Melrose Place has become prime time's unsung guilty pleasure." *News Tribune,* February 21, 1994, p. 64.

Guthrie, Marisa. "Plugged In." *The Boston Herald,* October 22, 1995, p. 2.

Kim, Jae-Ha. "Superman, After Hours; Dean Cain Tells Celeb Hobbies." *Chicago Sun-Times,* July 31, 1995, p. 33.

Kornblut, Anne E. "Man Trouble? Not Me, Says Daphne: 'Melrose Place' Star's Life is Very Different From Troubled Roles." *New York Daily News,* October 29, 1995, p. 13.

Kuklenski, Valerie. "People." *UPI,* June 9, 1995.

Kuramoto, Yoko. "People: Koppel Gets Into His Story—No Holds Barred." *News Tribune,* November 11, 1994, p. A16.

Maxwell, Bea. "Charity Scorecard: $25,000 Raised For Travelers Aid Group." *Los Angeles Times,* May 7, 1993, p. E8.

Monaco, James, ed. *Baseline's Encyclopedia of Film.* New York: Perigee, 1991.

Morris, Melanie. "New soap takes to the catwalk. . ." *The Irish Times,* September 3, 1994, p. 5.

Parker, Donna. "Desi Noms for 'Juan,' Estevez." *The Hollywood Reporter,* April 12, 1995.

Sloan, Robin Adams. "Personality Mailbag." *The Houston Chronicle,* March 5, 1995, p. 7.

"Star Tracks." *People,* February 27, 1995, p. 6.

Wedlan, Candace A. "Guest Workout; Body Watch; Her Gym Is At Daphne's Place." *Los Angeles Times,* May 15, 1996, p. E3.

"What's Up." *The Charleston Gazette,* January 24, 1996, p. 4D.

Yancy, Kitty Bean. "D.C. Dinner a stage for stars." *The Baltimore Sun,* April 25, 1994, p. 2D.

Zurawik, David. "'Melrose Place' is a steamy hit for the twentysomethings." *The Baltimore Sun,* January 17, 1994, p. 1D.

Occupation Index

Ethnicity Index

Ethnicity Index

Subject Index

Personal names, place names, events, institutions, and other subject areas or keywords contained in *Notable Hispanic American Women, Book II* entries are listed in this index with corresponding volume and page numbers indicating text references. Also cited are the names of individuals with main entries in *Notable Hispanic American Women, Book I,* as indicated by their corresponding volume and page numbers.

Subject Index

Subject Index